Macroeconomics
A European Text

FIFTH EDITION

Michael Burda
and
Charles Wyplosz

OXFORD
UNIVERSITY PRESS

OXFORD
UNIVERSITY PRESS

Great Clarendon Street, Oxford OX2 6DP

Oxford University Press is a department of the University of Oxford.
It furthers the University's objective of excellence in research, scholarship,
and education by publishing worldwide in

Oxford New York

Auckland Cape Town Dar es Salaam Hong Kong Karachi
Kuala Lumpur Madrid Melbourne Mexico City Nairobi
New Delhi Shanghai Taipei Toronto

With offices in

Argentina Austria Brazil Chile Czech Republic France Greece
Guatemala Hungary Italy Japan Poland Portugal Singapore
South Korea Switzerland Thailand Turkey Ukraine Vietnam

Oxford is a registered trade mark of Oxford University Press
in the UK and in certain other countries

Published in the United States
by Oxford University Press Inc., New York

British Library Cataloguing in Publication Data

Data available

Library of Congress Cataloging in Publication Data

Data available

Typeset in 9/12.5pt OUP Swift by Graphicraft Limited, Hong Kong
Printed in Great Britain on acid-free paper by Ashford Colour Press Ltd, Gosport, Hampshire

ISBN 978-0-19-923682-4

1 3 5 7 9 10 8 6 4 2

Macroeconomics by Burda and Wyplosz has all the best ingredients of a modern macroeconomics text: it focuses throughout on the open economy; it puts the long-run analysis first and it steps away from traditional short-run analysis to be consistent with the modern practice of monetary policy. The book has become easier to read, but, unlike some rivals, it does not hide the necessary mathematics.

This book is one of the best. It is truly international, modern, well-written, and rigorous where necessary.

Andrew Newell, Head of the Department of Economics, University of Sussex.

This new edition is a major accomplishment. It has two unique and invaluable features: it explains the modern approach to macroeconomics with simplicity and rigour, while retaining the focus on the special aspects of the European economy.

Professor Guido Tabellini, Bocconi University.

This well-known book by Michael Burda and Charles Wyplosz has justifiably established itself as a leading textbook for economics students interested in the European economy. It is well-written, well-illustrated, and achieves a good balance between theory and practice. Although a 'European text', it is not about Europe. It is a mainstream intermediate economics textbook that has examples and discussion of issues that are of more interest to European scholars than a North American textbook would have. But there is also discussion of many examples from economies outside Europe, ranging from China to sub-Saharan Africa. The book is a good educational tool for anyone with a serious interest in economics, wherever located.

The fifth edition is more compact and better-written than the fourth edition. An important innovation is that monetary policy is now shown by the Taylor rule instead of the money supply rule of the conventional model. The ease with which the authors have built the '*TR*' curve into the conventional framework for short-run equilibrium is admirable. The conventional *IS–LM* model has guided our intuition about policy for many decades but current practice requires different thinking, and the fifth edition of Burda and Wyplosz is an excellent place to learn about it.

Professor Christopher Pissarides, Norman Sosnow Chair in Economics, LSE.

What sets *Macroeconomics* 5e by Burda and Wyplosz apart from the rest of the field is its wide-ranging treatment of macroeconomic theory, policy, and institutions within a European as well as an international context. This is an ideal intermediate text for economics and business students across Europe and the world.

Professor Thorvaldur Gylfason, University of Iceland.

Preface to the Fifth Edition

For us, the fifth edition of *Macroeconomics: A European Text* represents something of a milestone—written fifteen years after the first edition was published in the Spring of 1993. Beyond the usual pedagogical improvements and updating of boxes, tables, and figures, this edition incorporates several significant substantive revisions that reflect the changing field of macroeconomics.

The main innovation is the introduction of the Taylor rule as an alternative to the *LM*. We long thought that the key assumption behind the *LM* curve, that central banks determine the money supply, was no longer consistent with actual practice, and explaining this to students was becoming increasingly tedious. Yet frankly, we were reluctant to abandon such an iconic construction, which represents a six-decade-old legacy of Sir John Hicks. A survey of teachers who use the book, kindly organized by our Editor, sent a clear signal: given that most central banks around the world—and especially in Europe—have long abandoned monetary targeting, it was time to move on. While several central banks have not yet officially adopted the inflation targeting strategy, nearly all of them now set and announce an interest rate target, allowing the money supply to respond endogenously. In addition, a substantial body of literature has worked out the theory that describes this new world, providing us with a widely agreed-upon framework; moreover, central banks empirically appear to behave this way. We had feared that teachers would resent giving up a time-tested framework, but the survey results showed that most are now well-acquainted with the new theory and actually eager to teach the new stuff. So it is goodbye *IS–LM*, hello *IS–TR*! (or for the traditionalists: hello *IS–LM–TR*!).[1]

Introducing the Taylor rule has led to a number of important changes in the book's structure and focus. In earlier editions, we devoted an entire chapter to the money supply. We have now simplified this material and condensed the treatment into a single chapter—Chapter 9—that presents monetary policy and the Taylor rule. In the next chapter, we still present the *IS–LM* framework as a bridge to the *IS–TR* framework, which allows students to easily grasp the difference between the two strategies when we present the Mundell–Fleming open economy version (Chapter 11). The Taylor rule makes the derivation of the aggregate demand schedule in Chapter 13 particularly user-friendly. We also thoroughly revised the chapter on aggregate supply and the Phillips curve (Chapter 12), to make it more accessible. In this sense, the heart of the book, consisting of Chapters 9 to 13 that derive the basic macroeconomic model, is completely new. It now closely corresponds to the modern New Keynesian synthesis that is arguably the consensus in the profession and is being used in central banks and international institutions around the world.

The second important change concerns growth. In previous editions, we presented the Solow growth model early on, concluding with a primer on endogenous growth, and towards the end of the text we offered a discussion of policies that emphasized endogenous growth. We believe that

---

1 In doing so, we don't give up the *LM* curve but we certainly put it on the back burner!

half-a-quarter century of theoretical and empirical research has vindicated the Solow growth model but also taught us a lot about the 'Solow residual'. This has led us to regroup two chapters early on. Chapter 3 presents the Solow growth model and Chapter 4, while mentioning endogenous growth theory, focuses on the role of externalities, knowledge, and innovation.

The third significant innovation in the fifth edition is our treatment of the exchange rate. Following the logic of presenting first the flexible-price long run—the real economy—and next the Keynesian short run—the monetary aspects—we had devoted an early chapter to the real exchange rate and dealt with the nominal exchange rate within a late chapter dedicated to asset markets. Following suggestions from teachers, we now present the exchange rate in a single chapter. Chapter 15 offers an integrated treatment of short-term exchange rate determination with a simplified analysis of the long-run equilibrium real exchange rate. It follows a chapter on financial markets and asset prices, which has been simplified and emphasizes the role of expectations.

Finally, many teachers thought that the chapter on business cycles was too long and too detailed. In the fifth edition, we retain the highly intuitive Burns–Mitchell diagrams in the introductory chapter to motivate the notion of business cycles, and transfer other material to Chapter 16, which is wholly devoted to the ongoing debate on demand management and macroeconomic policy-making.

In addition to rewriting almost all chapters for substance, style, or both, we have updated our examples, prepared new Boxes to illustrate recent events, and, with the help of a professional editor, undertaken a thorough rewriting to make our text as clear and pleasant to read as possible.

In a way, therefore, this is a new text which, we hope, teachers and students will find more congenial and in many ways simpler than previous editions. Yet, we have retained the characteristics that have made our text popular: respect for theory, emphasis on relevance, abundance of real-world examples, and prominence to issues of importance to Europe.

The book is shorter than the previous editions, intentionally so. It can be used in second- or third-year BA courses, as well as courses offered in business schools, and public policy and political science programs. While it is designed for a full semester course, it can be used for shorter courses as well. Here are three possible tracks.

Full course	Medium-length track	Short track
All 20 chapters		10 chapters
General introduction	15 chapters	General introduction
Chapters 1 and 2	General introduction	
The long run and the real economy	Chapter 2	Chapter 2
Chapters 3 to 6	The long run and the real economy	The long run and the real economy
The short run	Chapters 3, 4, and 5	Chapters 3 and 5
Chapters 7 to 13	The short run	The short run
Financial markets and the exchange rate	Chapters 8 to 13	Chapters 8 to 13
Chapters 14 and 15	The exchange rate	The exchange rate
Policies and debates	Chapter 15	Chapter 15
Chapters 16 to 19	Policies and debates	
History of macroeconomics	Chapters 16 to 18	
Chapter 20		

We are indebted to our Commissioning Editor, Kirsty Reade, whose trust in the value of this book has been a great source of encouragement. Kirsty organized several surveys of teachers throughout Europe, which led to the deep changes introduced in this edition. Development Editor Monika Faltejskova carried out the polling and thoroughly interpreted the results, all the way to suggesting most of the changes that we then implemented. We are also grateful to Helen Cook for her tireless care and precision in handling the manuscript and to Julie Harris for highly professional proof-reading. A number of anonymous reviewers provided outstanding comments on the first draft; we owe them many ideas, fewer mistakes, and a much improved text. We are also indebted to Stan Standaert, our translator into the French edition, who has relentlessly tracked errors and all potential sources of confusion, and Sarah Bury who went through the manuscript and superbly improved on our prose.

We are grateful to Katja Hanewald, Verena Proske, and especially Patrick Bunk and Daniel Neuhoff for diligent research assistance.

Brief Contents

Detailed Contents

List of Tables

List of Figures

List of Boxes

PART I

Introduction to Macroeconomics

Part I of this textbook sets the stage for macroeconomics as a subject. Chapter 1 explains the objectives and methods of macroeconomics, its history and usefulness, as well as its controversies and open questions. It provides a number of essential definitions and offers a preview of what will follow.

Macroeconomics is about measurement as well as analysis. Chapter 2 introduces the methods of measurement used in macroeconomics. In particular, we will explore the national income accounts, the language economists use to describe and communicate the economic activities of a region or a nation, and the balance of payments, which summarizes its transactions with the rest of the world.

What is Macroeconomics? 1

The Theory of Economics does not furnish a body of settled conclusions immediately applicable to policy. It is a method rather than a doctrine, an apparatus of the mind, a technique of thinking, which helps its possessor to draw correct conclusions.

J. M. Keynes

1.1 Overview of Macroeconomics

Whether we like it or not, economic themes tend to dominate the news. A day seldom passes when we do not hear about unemployment, inflation, economic growth, stock markets, interest rates, or foreign exchange rates—either at home or somewhere else in the world. We hear and read so much about these phenomena because, directly or indirectly, they affect our well-being. It is perhaps mostly for this reason that **macroeconomics**, the study of these economy-wide phenomena, is so exciting. Macroeconomics is more than just headlines, however: it is a fascinating intellectual adventure. The breadth of issues it covers is evidence enough of its inherent complexity. All the same, we will see that simple economic reasoning can take us a long way. And it is often surprising how well a few simple ideas can explain complex situations.

Macroeconomics can also be useful. The economic well-being of all consumers, rich or poor, is affected by movements in interest rates, exchange rates, the rate of inflation, and other macroeconomic variables. Businesses can gain or lose large amounts of money when their environment changes, regardless of how well they are managed. Being prepared for such changes in macroeconomic fortunes can have considerable value. More generally, it makes us all better citizens who are able to grasp the complex challenges that our societies face. Macroeconomics is relevant to voters who wonder what their governments are up to, but also can help governments avoid severe economic crises that have afflicted modern industrial societies over the past century—depressions, when overall economic activity is very far below average, and hyperinflations, when prices are increasing at monthly rates of 50% or more. These extreme situations can tear at a society's social fabric, yet can be prevented when policymakers apply sound economic principles.

1.1.1 Income and Output

The most important indicator of a nation's economic well-being is a measure of its output and income, the **gross domestic product (GDP)**. At this point, it is enough to think of the GDP simply as an indicator of the goods and services which an economy produces in a year for final uses; the concept will be discussed in greater detail in the next chapter. For example, in 2006, the GDP in the UK amounted to about 1.30 trillion pounds. In Germany, GDP was 2.32 trillion euros; in France 1.79 trillion euros; in Italy 1.48 trillion euros; in the Netherlands 534 billion euros; and in Denmark 1.64 trillion kroner. These are very large numbers.[1] Yet on a per-head basis in a common currency, they are much closer, ranging from 25,000 to 40,000 euros per capita. Comparing these data over time is difficult because, as we will learn in Chapter 2, changes in prices can also affect the nominal value of goods and services an economy produces. Table 1.1, which corrects for this effect, displays the development of GDP over the past century.

Macroeconomics is concerned with many aspects of the GDP, which simultaneously signal income and production. The two most salient features are that (1) most countries are characterized by the steady growth of GDP over time, but that (2) there are significant and recurring fluctuations of GDP

---

[1] It is always useful to state for the record that one (American) billion is one thousand millions, or 1,000,000,000; an American trillion (English billion) is one million millions, or 1,000,000,000,000. Keeping with international practice, we shall use the US American convention throughout the textbook.

Table 1.1 Real Income per Capita (GDP in euros, 2000 prices)

	1900	1913	1929	1950	1987	1992	1999	2002	2007	Av. growth rate
Austria	2,462	2,961	3,160	3,167	13,085	14,937	17,145	17,920	20,064	2.0
Belgium	3,188	3,606	4,319	4,667	13,280	15,078	17,010	17,987	19,842	1.7
Denmark	2,578	3,343	4,337	5,933	15,401	16,192	19,017	19,717	21,627	2.0
Finland	1,426	1,804	2,322	3,634	13,144	12,837	15,931	17,152	20,680	2.5
France	2,457	2,978	4,025	4,504	14,144	15,774	17,549	18,610	19,347	1.9
Germany	2,550	3,117	3,462	3,316	13,417	14,433	15,737	16,399	17,580	1.8
Italy	1,526	2,191	2,643	2,992	12,771	14,216	15,612	16,339	17,089	2.3
Netherlands	2,925	3,459	4,861	5,124	13,447	15,165	17,966	18,493	20,491	1.8
Norway	1,604	2,091	2,895	4,639	15,521	16,715	21,019	22,093	24,512	2.6
Sweden	2,188	2.646	3,306	5,759	14,483	14,509	16,962	18,144	21,019	2.1
Switzerland	3,275	3,645	5,410	7,745	16,912	17,800	18,590	· 19,179	20,629	1.7
United Kingdom	3,838	4,205	4,703	5,930	13,154	13,785	16,650	17,817	20,176	1.6
Canada	2,488	3,800	4,328	6,231	15,678	15,511	18,347	19,654	21,400	2.0
USA	3,496	4,529	5,895	8,170	18,618	19,908	23,669	24,383	26,841	1.9
Argentina	2,355	3,245	3,732	4,261	6,237	6,406	7,443	6,083	8,189[a]	1.2
Bangladesh	417	443	445	461	515	574	708	778	906[a]	0.7
China	466	472	481	383	1,484	1,822	2,702	3,586	6,016	2.4
India	512	575	622	529	961	1,146	1,568	1,719	2,388	1.4
Japan	1,008	1,185	1,731	1,641	13,887	16,648	17,597	17,918	19,568	2.8

[a] 2006 data

Source: The Conference Board and Groningen Growth and Development Centre, Total Economy Database, January 2008, available at <www.conference-board.org/economics/database.cfm> and <www.eco.rug.nl>.

around its trend, or average tendency over time. We return to these themes in separate sections below. In addition, one might be concerned whether GDP or GDP per capita is a good indicator of individual well-being. In any case, it says little about the distribution of income in the economy, which may also matter to its citizens. Many researchers are now examining issues related to happiness and quality of life to economic output. One of the robust findings on research in this area is that while GDP is not everything, it is certainly an important factor, if not a necessary condition, for economic and social well-being.

1.1.2 Unemployment

One important phenomenon associated with cyclical fluctuations is **unemployment**, the fact that people seeking paid work cannot or do not find it, sometimes even when the economy is growing rapidly. The **unemployment rate** is the ratio of the number of unemployed workers to the size of the **labour force**. The labour force consists of those who are either working or are actively looking for a job. In comparison with the total population, it leaves out young people who are not yet working, the old who are retired, and those who do not wish to work—or have given up hope of working.

There are many reasons why we are concerned about unemployment. It is natural to associate idle workers with a loss of output and income to the economy. At the same time, we need to ask whether the unemployed are receiving offers of work, whether they are turning down job offers, and if so, for what reason. Are the jobs that workers are searching for available at all, or are workers truly available for the jobs on offer, perhaps because their expectations are unreasonable? The answers to these questions will help us better understand this complex phenomenon.

Unemployment is generally not a pleasant affair. Even with well-developed and efficient unemployment assistance programmes, long-term jobless workers can experience emotional stress and their skills may deteriorate. Even if they are not measurable, the social and psychological costs of unemployment are high for the affected individuals and for society as a whole. By that criterion, Europe has not done well over the last decades, as Figure 1.1 shows. The average rate of unemployment has grown inexorably to reach double-digit numbers. In the USA, in contrast, unemployment has closely followed the business cycle, rising in periods of slowdown, declining when growth returned. At the

same time, not all European countries have shared this misery, as the case of Switzerland shows. Chapters 5 and 18 will present explanations for these different experiences.

1.1.3 Factors of Production and Income Distribution

The output of an economy, its GDP, is by and large the result of work effort by men and women combined with equipment—'machines', but also buildings and other structures. **Labour** and **capital** are the technical names given to the two main **factors of production**, or inputs.[2] The distribution of total income between these two factors of production is often a political matter, even if it is largely determined by economic forces. Understandably, wage-earners wish to enlarge their share of the pie. In stock markets, ownership of companies, or shares, is traded in open markets and valued on the basis of the firms' profitability, or what is left after wages and other costs are paid. Figure 1.2 shows the share of income in manufacturing that goes to labour, the **labour share**. It also plots the evolution of the stock market **index** over the same period, which tracks the value of shares in companies traded on the stock exchange or bourse. An index is an indicator of the evolution of some phenomenon over time, designed to take a standardized value (e.g. 1 or 100) on a particular date to highlight relative changes. The figure reveals a clear, but not perfect, inverse relationship between the labour share and average stock prices. When the share of income going to labour is high, less is available for the firms' owners, and stock prices tend to be lower. While it would be premature to assert that one causes the other, it is certainly plausible that both are driven by common economic phenomena. In Chapter 8, we will see that depressed stock prices may adversely affect the accumulation of productive equipment and, ultimately, the growth and size of the economic pie itself.

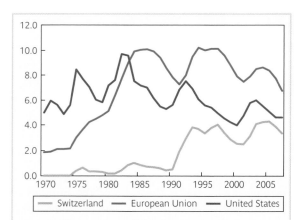

Fig. 1.1 Unemployment Rates in the European Union, Switzerland, and the USA, 1970–2007

The unemployment rate, measured as the proportion of workers who do not have a job but are looking for one, varies considerably across countries. In the USA, the unemployment rate moves tightly with the business cycle. In contrast, the European Union rose markedly in the 1970s and 1980s and stayed there for a long time. In contrast, Switzerland avoided high unemployment for the entire period, but has also suffered a significant increase over the past two decades.

Source: OECD.

---

[2] Land, energy, intellectual property, and many other inputs also matter, but are quantitatively less important in macroeconomics and will be ignored to make matters simpler.

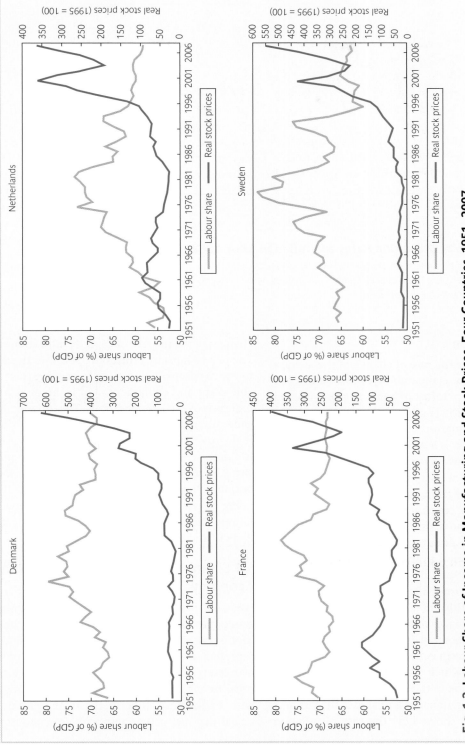

Fig. 1.2 Labour Share of Income in Manufacturing and Stock Prices, Four Countries, 1951–2007

Labour and capital share the fruits of the economic activity. The labour share is the fraction of economic output which accrues to workers in wages and other forms of compensation. The valuation of firm assets reflected in stock prices is negatively associated with the labour share.

Sources: OECD; IMF; US Department of Labor.

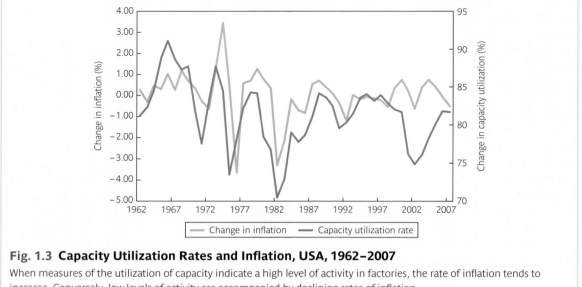

Fig. 1.3 Capacity Utilization Rates and Inflation, USA, 1962–2007
When measures of the utilization of capacity indicate a high level of activity in factories, the rate of inflation tends to increase. Conversely, low levels of activity are accompanied by declining rates of inflation.
Sources: IMF; OECD, *Main Economic Indicators*.

1.1.4 Inflation

Inflation refers to the rate of change of the average level of prices. For comparability, the inflation rate is usually stated in terms of percentage change per year, even when it is measured more frequently, such as every quarter or every month. Most of the time, inflation is low or moderate at rates ranging from just above 0% to 4%. In the 1970s, many European countries experienced double-digit inflation, with rates rising to 10%, 20%, or even more. In a number of countries, for example in Latin America or in the transition countries of Eastern Europe, inflation rates of several hundred per cent were quite common in the 1980s. When inflation is very high it is usually measured on a monthly basis; the term **hyperinflation** describes situations when this monthly inflation rate exceeds 50%. A sign of exceptional economic distress, hyperinflation has been observed in Central Europe in the early 1920s, in Latin America in the 1980s, and in many countries which emerged from the collapse of the Soviet Union in the early 1990s.

In normal times, inflation is related to the business cycle. Figure 1.3 shows how the rate of inflation

changes when the rate of **capacity utilization** varies. The rate of capacity utilization measures the degree to which companies are truly employing their available plant and equipment, and it serves as a good indicator of cyclical conditions. The inflation rate is generally **procyclical**: it tends to rise in periods of high growth and declines in periods of slow growth. In contrast, the unemployment rate is **countercyclical**: it moves against the cyclical behaviour of output, falling when output is growing rapidly and rising when output is growing more slowly or falling. The behaviour of inflation is investigated in Parts IV and V of this book.

1.1.5 Financial Markets and the Real Economy

Financial markets play a central role in modern economies. Either literally or with the help of sophisticated communications technologies, they represent arenas where buyers and sellers of financial assets such as bonds, stocks, currencies, and other financial instruments meet to trade. Together with banks and other financial institutions, financial markets gather resources from households in the form of savings and lend them out to others who will spend them. One specific feature of these markets is the extreme day-to-day variability of prices at which financial instruments are traded.

Physical investment, the accumulation of productive capital by firms, is intimately related to financial conditions. It is one channel through which financial markets affect the **real economy**. The other channel is consumption spending by households. Stocks—shares in corporations—represent one form of private wealth. When share prices rise, people feel richer and consume more. The real economy is contrasted with the financial or **monetary economy**: the former concerns the production and consumption of goods and services, and the incomes associated with productive activities; the latter deals with trade in assets, i.e. monetary and financial instruments. Chapter 10 brings the real and the monetary spheres of the economy together to understand how output and interest rates are determined from year to year. Chapter 11 explores these short-run linkages in more detail when the economy is open to trade in financial assets. Chapters 12 and 13 bring together the issues of inflation, output, and exchange rate determination.

1.1.6 Openness

In the modern world, all countries engage in international trade by exporting and importing goods and services to and from each other. In addition, an increasing number of countries are also connected through trade in financial assets. One measure of a country's **openness**, or exposure to the various economic influences coming from the rest of the world, is the ratio of the average of its exports and imports to its GDP. Table 1.2 shows that openness has considerably increased over the past decades. This process of increasing trade and trade integration in goods, services, and financial assets over time is frequently called **globalization**. Smaller countries tend to be more open than larger countries, and indeed the USA and Japan are fairly closed by international standards. This is also the case of the European Union *vis-à-vis* the rest of the world, even though considerable trade integration has taken place among its member countries and with the

Table 1.2 Openness (ratio of average of exports and imports to GDP, %)

	1960	2007
European Union	6.1	16.7
United States	5.2	14.6
Japan	10.7	13.3
China	—	5.1[a]
Belgium	38.3	87.1
Denmark	32.7	54.8
Germany	19.0	46.8
Hungary	—	114.0
Ireland	30.6	75.5
Netherlands	46.3	80.5
Poland	—	41.2
Portugal	16.0	40.2
Russian Federation	—	27.5[b]
Spain	8.9	34.7
Sweden	22.7	49.2
Switzerland	27.7	51.6
Ukraine	—	48.6[b]
United Kingdom	20.9	29.2

[a] 2005 data
[b] 2006 data
Sources: Eurostat; IMF; OECD.

rest of the world. Since mid-2004, the European Union has expanded to 27 nations to become an economic region of more than 490 million inhabitants. These substantial enlargements have further accentuated the importance of international trade, financial, and policy links between EU member countries.

As a consequence, no country's fate is truly independent of events that occur elsewhere, sometimes very far away. A good example is the financial crisis that began in the summer of 2007 in the USA but has since spread not only to Europe and Asia but to remote parts of Africa and South America. Chapter 19 looks more closely at these problems and potential solutions.

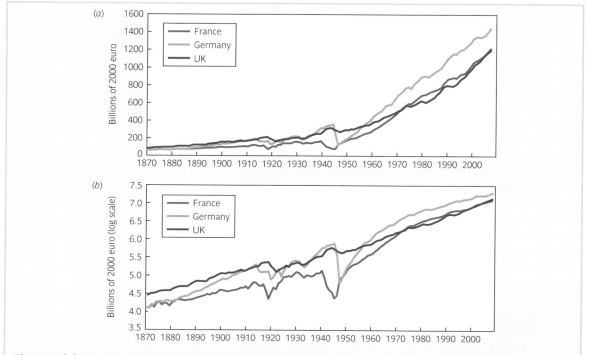

Fig. 1.4 (a) Gross Domestic Product (GDP), Germany, France, and the UK, 1870–2007 (b) Gross Domestic Product (GDP), logarithmic scale, Germany, France, and the UK, 1870–2007

National output and income, as captured by the gross domestic product, exhibits a robust growth trend. Growth tends to be exponential; that is, annual percentage increases are reasonably stable in the long run. This does not preclude significant year-to-year variations. When the data are displayed on a logarithmic scale instead (panel *b*), the slope of the curve measures the annual rate of growth.

Source: The Conference Board and Groningen Growth and Development Centre, Total Economy Database, January 2008, available at <www.conference-board.org/economics/database.cfm> and <www.eco.rug.nl>.

1.2 Macroeconomics in the Long Run: Economic Growth

Figure 1.4(a) displays the evolution of GDP for France, Germany, and the UK since 1870. A positive long-run general tendency, or **trend,** clearly dominates shorter-run fluctuations. The trend rate of growth has been fairly stable, perhaps with a slight increase after the Second World War. Another way of seeing this is to plot the natural logarithm of GDP against time, as in panel (*b*) of Figure 1.4. With this so-called **logarithmic scale** the slope of the curve is a direct measure of the annual growth rate: a constant growth rate would yield a straight line.[3] In the

---

[3] For mathematically-inclined readers, if $x(t)$ grows at constant rate g, which is defined as $(1/x)dx/dt$, then $x(t) = Ae^{gt}$ and $\ln x(t) = \ln A + gt$, where A is a constant and t stands for time.

long run, on average, we seem very close to a rather robust and steady trend.

This trend growth in total output implies remarkable increases in living standards. Let's take another look at Table 1.1. Note that per capita, or average, income increased to more than sixfold in Belgium since 1900, ninefold in Sweden, and 18-fold in Japan. Yet the growth phenomenon is not shared by all countries at all times. In Bangladesh, real income per capita rose by only 120% over the same period. Some countries have faced serious setbacks, such as wars and famines, while others have expanded rapidly. Some, like China and India, stagnated for many decades before suddenly entering a period of rapid increase in living standards. China poses a particularly interesting case because its explosive takeoff was so recent, and because it was the world's most advanced economy 700 years ago.

Because of the diverse nature of experience when studying the wealth of nations, **economic growth** is one of the most exciting issues in macroeconomics. Chapter 3 explores in detail the reasons why economies grow. One reason is an increase in population, since more people can work and produce more output. Another is the accumulation of means of production: plant and equipment, roads, communication networks, and other forms of infrastructure make workers more productive. Most important is the development and harnessing of knowledge and technology to economic ends. The sharp acceleration of scientific discoveries towards the end of the eighteenth century is thought to have triggered the industrial revolution, and some believe we are now witnessing the onset of a new wave of advances related to information and telecommunications technology.

1.3 Macroeconomics in the Short Run: Business Cycles

While output and income have increased by staggering amounts over many decades, this growth is not constant or even steady. A second important message contained in Figure 1.4 is that real output tends to fluctuate around its trend. This is even more apparent in Figure 1.5, which plots the quarterly rate of change in GDP for the UK. Quarterly data tend to accentuate the relative importance of short-run fluctuations. These sustained periods of ups and downs are called **business cycles**. One important challenge of macroeconomics is to explain such deviations of GDP from its underlying trend. Why do these fluctuations occur and persist over periods ranging from three to ten years, and what can be done, if anything, to avoid the disruptions that are associated with them? This is the common theme of Parts III, IV, and V of this book.

Macroeconomics has come to recognize that while business cycles are hardly identical across countries and across time, they have a number of common features. These features can be summarized statisti-

cally, but they can also be represented in diagrams. The **Burns–Mitchell diagram** can help us organize our thoughts about these common features of the business cycle. The idea is simple. Imagine cutting up a series like those depicted in Figures 1.4 or 1.5 into a set of cycles. To do this, it is necessary to identify calendar dates for cyclical turning points of output (GDP)—here we will be concerned with peaks, but the procedure can be used for troughs as well. Having identified those cyclical peaks, simple numerical averages of other macroeconomic variables of interest can be calculated around the calendar date of the output's peak. The behaviour of those variables around the turning points of output tells us something about whether the variables are leading— meaning that they can help forecast future turning points in output. More importantly, they can help inform the formulation of theories which will help us better understand how business cycles arise and develop over time. Box 1.1 provides more details on the Burns–Mitchell methodology.

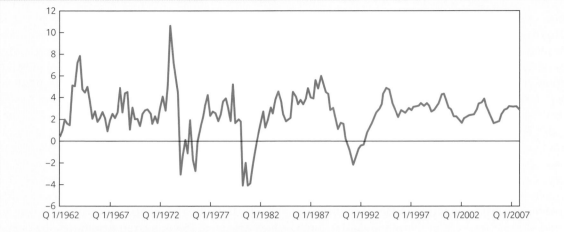

Fig. 1.5 Quarterly Gross Domestic Product, UK, 1962: 1–2007: 4

With quarterly data, fluctuations of economic activity become more apparent.

Sources: IMF; OECD.

 Box 1.1 **Burns–Mitchell Diagrams, Now and Then**

The sharp fluctuations of economic activity in the rapidly industrializing economies of Europe and the USA attracted the professional interest of many economists in the early part of the twentieth century. In the 1920s and 1930s, the National Bureau of Economic Research (NBER) in New York was a centre of such research, associated with Gottfried Haberler, Simon Kuznets, Wassily Leontief, Allyn Young, and many other economic luminaries of the day. A common view of these researchers was that the emergence of powerful statistical methods made it possible to study economic phenomena in general, and the trade cycle in particular, in a more scientific fashion.

Two NBER researchers, Arthur Burns and Wesley Mitchell, were somewhat sceptical of the statistical approach but committed to a data-driven, descriptive assessment of business cycle regularities. Mitchell had already written a book in 1927 that more or less laid out the research programme, but together with Burns the project ultimately came to fruition after the Second World War. The idea was to reduce the time series of data to a sequence of cycles and then study the *average* behaviour of other important variables a number of periods before and after the peak of the average cycle. This highly data-intensive empirical approach was considered modern and useful, even if it was criticized in some quarters as 'measurement without theory'.

The identification of business cycles is always a tricky procedure with some element of arbitrariness. We employ a particular method which has gained acceptance in recent years and apply it to eight advanced economies over about 35 years of quarterly data.[4] The result is a reference cycle which appears in the first panel of Figure 1.6. The cycles identified by procedure are used to produce the other panels of Figure 1.6, which give the behaviour of variables 10 quarters before and 10 quarters after the cyclical peak, usually stated in proportion to the average value over that period. In Figure 1.7, we present the original findings of Burns and Mitchell, who worked on primarily monthly US data from the late nineteenth and especially the early twentieth century.

---

[4] The method is due to Harding and Pagan (2001) and can be summarized as follows. For a 4-quarter moving average of the original series, define a peak as the quarter for which GDP is higher than the two preceding and the two successive quarters. In case two or more consecutive peaks are found, only the highest is retained. Next examine the highest and lowest points in a neighbourhood of the peaks. Now repeat the procedure using an unweighted short-term moving average of the original series. In the neighbourhood of these intermediate turning points, troughs and peaks are determined in the unsmoothed time series. If these pass a set of additional restrictions on the magnitude of the fluctuation, they are selected as the final cyclical turning points.

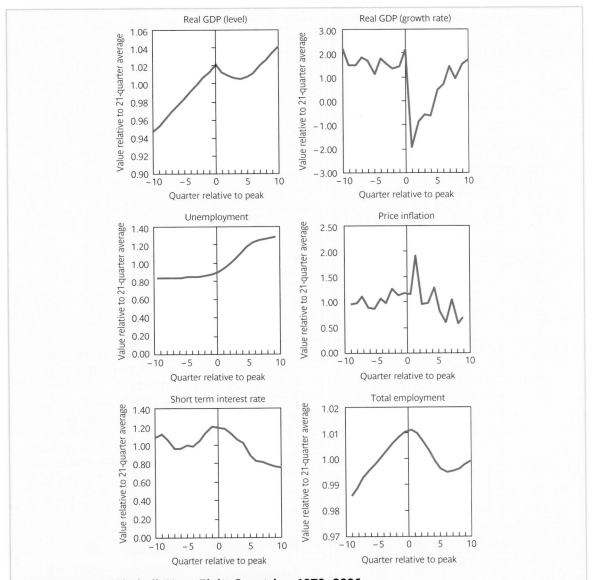

Fig. 1.6 Burns–Mitchell, Now: Eight Countries, 1970–2006

These figure show the average behaviour of variables around cyclical peaks, where the cycle is measured using a procedure described in the text. The vertical line around zero shows the quarter in which real GDP hits its peak (upper left panel). The peak is followed on average by a sharp drop in the growth rate of output (upper right panel). Unemployment is countercyclical, rising most after the peak in GDP has been passed, but is rising across cycles, indicating that unemployment rates in the sample were increasing on average. The inflation rate is procyclical but lagging, peaking in the quarter after output. Short term interest rates and employment are strongly procyclical.

Sources: OECD; authors' calculations.

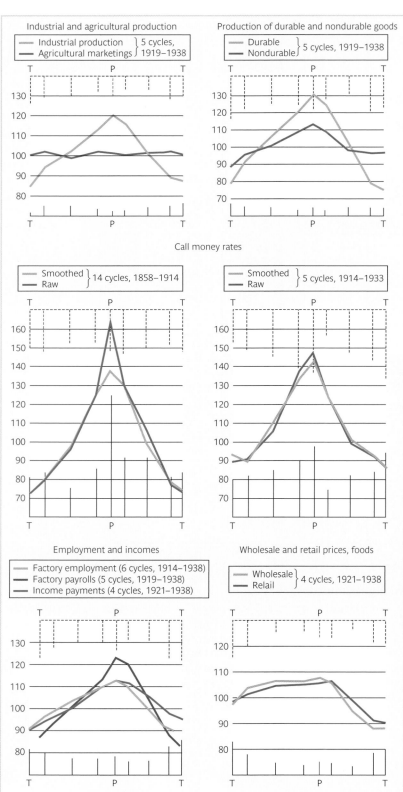

Fig. 1.7 Burns–Mitchell, Then: US Monthly Data, 1914–1938

These original figures document the work of Burns and Mitchell on monthly US pre-Second World War data for industrial and agricultural production as well as durable and non-durable goods, interest rates, employment, payrolls, and food prices (GDP data did not exist at the time these diagrams were constructed). As in Figure 1.6, the cyclical peak is identified using a well-defined procedure, and averages of the cycles around that peak (denoted 'P') to trough (denoted 'T'). Production, employment, wages, wholesale prices, and interest rates are procyclical and coincident, while retail prices seem to lag slightly. The procyclical behaviour of interest rates became significantly less pronounced after 1914, which was the year after the US central bank, the Federal Reserve System, was founded.

Source: Mitchell (1951).

1.4 Macroeconomics as a Science

1.4.1 The Genesis of Macroeconomics

Why do we observe cyclical fluctuations—ups and downs—in the level of GDP around its trend? Why is unemployment generally countercyclical, while changes in inflation appear procyclical? For a long time, economists paid little attention to such phenomena. In fact, it was believed that properly functioning markets would deliver the best possible outcome, to a good approximation at least, and that there was no point in looking into their aggregate behaviour. This principle was called '**laissez-faire**'. Laissez-faire was opposed by proponents of **interventionism**, who advocated government support for particular markets and industries, including subsidies and protection from foreign competition.

This does not mean that business cycles were ignored completely. In fact, cycles of varying lengths were identified and studied, ranging from inventory cycles of one or two years' duration to long-wave cycles lasting half a century. Box 1.2 provides details on these cyclical movements. Such cycles were seen as the cumulative outcomes of disturbances such as discoveries, inventions, exceptionally good or bad crops, wrong bets by firms on goods that customers want to buy, or even changing tastes of consumers at home and abroad. Inflation was seen as the consequence of rapidly growing money stocks, first because of gold discoveries in the nineteenth century, afterwards because of reckless paper money creation by central banks. As will be seen in Chapter 16, much of this wisdom remains valid today. Yet the Great Depression of the 1930s, which spread worldwide and sent millions into unemployment and misery, seemed too severe to be simply bad luck. Reflecting upon the Great Depression in 1936, British economist John Maynard Keynes published *The General Theory of Employment, Interest and Money*, a book that is often said to have started the field of macroeconomics. Keynes stressed the role of aggregate demand in macroeconomic fluctuations. His followers later persuaded policy-makers to engage in **aggregate demand management**, that is, to manipulate government demand in order to smooth out fluctuations, mainly to avoid protracted recessions.

 Box 1.2 All Kinds of Cycles

Business cycles, like comets, bear the names of their discoverers. Simon Kuznets (1901–1985) was a Russian-born US economist who received a Nobel Prize for his work on growth. Russian economist Nikolai Kondratieff (1892–1938) developed his theory of long-wave cycles in the 1920s before he was arrested and disappeared; the official Soviet Encyclopaedia then wrote about his work: 'this theory is wrong and reactionary'. It was also in the 1920s that Joseph Kitchin (1861–1932), a South African statistician and gold trader, uncovered his own more rapid cycles of 2–4 years periodicity, which are associated with inventory movements, bank clearings, and wholesale prices. Clement Juglar (1819–1905), a nineteenth-century French physician, first studied cycles in human births, deaths, and marriages before turning his skills to interest rates and credit conditions. These Juglar cycles—which involve fluctuations of investment spending, GNP, inflation, and unemployment—are perhaps the closest thing to the business cycle that we will study in this book.

Interestingly, one of the most robust and regular cycles in economic activity is the seasonal cycle, which coincides with the seasons of the year. Movements of output in agriculture, manufacturing, construction, and tourism have obvious seasonal components which sometimes swamp business cycle fluctuations in magnitude, as do patterns in overall output associated with bank holidays, summer and winter weather, and harvests.

An evaluation of the success of demand management policies—which is the subject of Chapters 16 and 17—is not conclusive. There have been both benefits and costs. Since the Second World War, the amplitude of the business cycle appears to have diminished considerably, as can be seen in Figure 1.4. While earlier generations assumed that favourable periods of growth were inevitably followed by periods of declining activity, today we worry mostly about slowdowns of growth. At the same time, economists have also begun to think hard about the supply side—meaning the productive capacity of an economy—and more efficient utilization of labour and capital resources. This applies especially to unemployment, which remains a big problem in Europe. These topics are the subject of Chapter 18.

Another remarkable change in the behaviour of the post-war economy concerns the general **price level**, or the cost of goods in terms of money. Until the First World War, prices were as likely to rise as they were to fall, as can be seen from Figure 1.8. Apart from war periods, the price level was trendless; over long periods of 20 to 50 years, the cost of living—a measure of the average price level—was remarkably stable. One interpretation of the post-war era—a controversial one, as we shall see—is that macroeconomics has led to more steady output growth at the cost of inflation. In the mid-1980s, concern with high inflation triggered a change of heart. In particular, most central banks have given up Keynesian policies and refocused their energy on keeping inflation low.

1.4.2 Macroeconomics and Microeconomics

The macroeconomy is just the sum of hundreds or thousands of markets, each of which is explained by microeconomic principles. Microeconomics is devoted to the study of prices of individual goods and of the markets where these goods are produced and sold. Why do we need two separate disciplines? To a great extent they are linked. Microeconomics is dedicated to the analysis of market behaviour of individuals. Macroeconomics is concerned with collective behaviour, the outcome of individual decisions taken without full knowledge of what others do. Keynes stressed the notion of **coordination failures**, which arise in decentralized markets as illustrated in the following example.

A consumer wants to purchase a car, but his income is insufficient for him to do so. A car manufacturer could actually hire him to build cars, and with his salary he would then be able to buy one. That one sale, however, would not suffice to pay his salary, so other buyers would need to be found. In order to generate sufficient demand for his employment, several other individuals would need to be hired, perhaps in different industries. For this scheme to work, a considerable amount of coordination among producers and consumers would be required. The laissez-faire principle is that prices and markets automatically and perfectly perform this coordinating role.

Keynes' critique of markets was that sometimes they fail to produce the desired result as quickly as we would like to see. There may be many consumers wishing to buy goods and willing to work to produce them, and many firms that would benefit from hiring them if only they could be persuaded that their sales would increase. But this potential may not be realized and we have both recession (fewer sales) and unemployment (fewer jobs). Even if market forces tend to correct this imbalance —which they eventually do—the period of time necessary may be long enough to involve significant social costs.

Macroeconomics started with the idea that prices and markets do not continuously resolve all the coordination requirements of a modern economy. As microeconomics has moved in this direction too, the sharp distinction between the two fields has faded. Modern macroeconomics starts from sound microeconomic principles, and we follow this approach in the early chapters. We then focus on market failures to study business cycles and what can be done about them.

1.4.3 Macroeconomics and Economic Policy

Early macroeconomists argued that governments have the means and the duty to correct market failures. The experiences of the past decades have shown that governments too may fail. Indeed, one

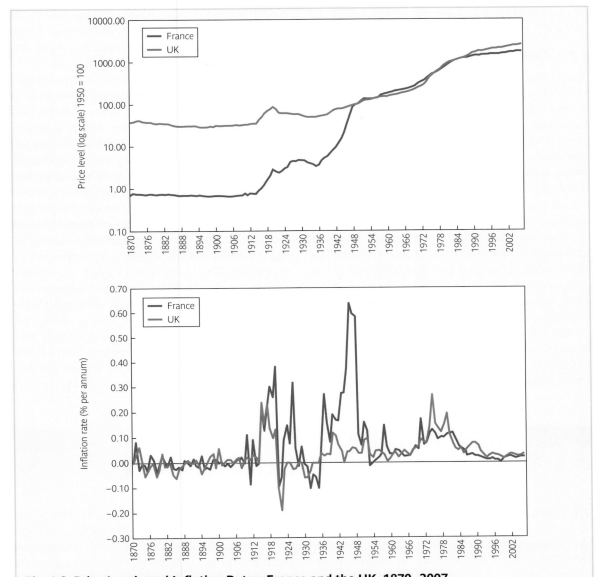

Fig. 1.8 Price Levels and Inflation Rates, France and the UK, 1870–2007

Until the outbreak of the First World War, the price level was stable, and inflation was close to zero on average. Since the Second World War, the price level has risen secularly, average inflation has been positive, high in the late 1970s and much of the 1980s, declining over the 1990s.

Sources: Maddison (1991); OECD.

major dividing line among macroeconomists is between those who primarily fear market failures on the one side, and those who primarily fear government failures on the other. Yet, in nearly every country, governments are held responsible for the good health of the economy. At election times incumbent governments are judged, first among many other issues, on their economic performance. This is largely a consequence of the **Keynesian revolution**. It explains why the study of macroeconomics is so intertwined with policy and politics.

1.4.4 Demand and Supply

In its most concentrated form, macroeconomics boils down to separating events into two categories: (1) those that affect the demand for goods and services, and (2) those that affect the supply of those goods and services. The **demand side** relates to spending decisions by **economic agents**—households, firms, and government agencies—both at home and abroad. The principle of aggregate demand management policies is that the government can take actions to offset or smooth out those of private agents—firms and households—in order to dampen or eliminate fluctuations in total spending. The idea is to take the edge off recessions as well as booms. Two traditional demand management instruments are fiscal and monetary policy. **Fiscal policy** manipulates government expenditures or taxes in an attempt to affect the volume of national spending. This subject is studied in detail in Chapter 17. **Monetary policy** is directed at influencing interest and exchange rates, and more generally conditions in financial markets. This in turn affects spending on goods and services. Chapter 9 provides an in-depth analysis of money and monetary policy.

The **supply side** relates to the productive potential of the economy. The choice of hours worked by households, the productivity of their labour, and in general the efficiency with which resources are allocated in generating a nation's output, all affect an economy's aggregate supply. Accordingly, supply-side policies represent government's effort to increase an economy's long-run capacity as well as its overall efficiency. Frequently, this effort is about reducing or eliminating government-induced inefficiencies, which were introduced before the importance of the supply side was understood, or as the result of successful lobbying by interest groups. It is also about bringing idle or underutilized resources into productive uses. Unemployment policy—designed to fight the scourge of market economies—occupies a key role in the supply side. Chapter 18 explores these issues and shows how the government can improve or worsen the economic climate.

1.5 The Methodology of Macroeconomics

1.5.1 What is to be Explained?

Macroeconomics is concerned with aggregate activity, the level of unemployment, interest rates, inflation, wages, the exchange rate, and the balance of payments with other countries. As a scientific undertaking, macroeconomics deals with phenomena which have highly complex channels of causation. Let's consider a relatively simple example. In this book you will learn that inflation affects the determination of the rate at which foreign money is traded for domestic money, the **exchange rate**. You will also learn that the inflation rate is also affected *by* the exchange rate.

Before beginning to think about these questions, it is essential to be clear about what we want to explain and what we take as given, or outside the realm of analysis. The variables to be explained using economic principles are called **endogenous** variables. The other variables—those we do not try to explain—are called **exogenous** variables. This distinction is represented in Figure 1.9. Examples of variables considered exogenous are policy instruments (the tools of fiscal and monetary policies), economic conditions abroad (foreign levels of activity and interest rates), the price of oil, and sometimes even domestic social conditions such as business optimism or trade union militancy.

The distinction between endogenous and exogenous variables is necessarily arbitrary. Many exogenous variables are not strictly independent of the endogenous variables. Because the analysis occurs

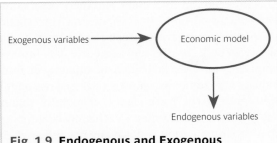

Fig. 1.9 Endogenous and Exogenous Variables

Endogenous variables are the object of analysis in an economic model. Exogenous variables are determined outside the economic model. The weather, political decisions, and the onset of time are examples of variables usually considered exogenous.

in steps, many variables considered exogenous or given initially are later made endogenous, or endogenized. For example, fiscal and monetary policy decisions are often responses to the course of inflation or unemployment. While it is convenient to take policy variables as exogenous, it is sometimes useful to understand how they themselves are determined. Chapters 16 and 17 take some steps in this direction.

1.5.2 Theory and Realism

Macroeconomics proceeds by making simplifying assumptions. We never literally believe in our assumptions, but we need them in order to see through the vast complexity of an economy. This is why the distinction between endogenous and exogenous variables is artificial. Truly exogenous variables are rare. Two examples are climatic conditions (and even these may be affected by economic events, such as the greenhouse effect) and scientific discoveries and inventions (which also may result from economic decisions). The task of systematically linking the behaviour of endogenous variables to changes in exogenous variables is accomplished by specifying relationships between all the variables of interest. You might say that economics —and in particular macroeconomics—is in the business of establishing relationships involving causality.

All these relationships, when brought together, constitute a theory. Almost by definition, theory is an abstraction, an intentional departure from realism. If the real world could be understood without simplifying assumptions, theories would be unnecessary. The problem is not with economics, but rather with the world's inherent complexity. Karl Marx, who was no friend of conventional political economy, seemed to hit it on the head:

The body in its entirety is easier to study than are the cells of that body. In the analysis of economic forms, moreover, neither microscopes nor chemical reagents are of use. The force of abstraction must replace both. ((1867) Foreword to Volume I.)

Progress is made by weeding out those assumptions and theories that lead us to false conclusions. As time passes, some theories prove to be unfounded, while others gain acceptability. This process is long and complex, and far from complete. Because macroeconomics is a young discipline, a number of controversies continue to dominate, and this aspect is discussed in Section 1.6 below.

1.5.3 Positive and Normative Analysis

Macroeconomic analysis and policy are closely linked. Because a number of exogenous variables are under the control of government, it makes sense to ask what is good and what is bad policy. At its best, macroeconomics can explain the economy. For example, it can link particular events to exogenous events or policy decisions. This is **positive economics**: it refrains from value judgements. **Normative economics** takes a further step and passes judgement or makes policy recommendations. In so doing, it must specify what criteria are used in arriving at particular conclusions. This inevitably implies a value judgement. Economists generally like to make policy recommendations. As long as they are truthful about their own preferences and reveal their criteria, this is part of their professional activity. In this textbook, we will generally refrain from normative economic analysis.[5] At the

---

[5] Many are motivated by 'social conscience' to study economics. Much like medical doctors who want to cure the sick, economists are often eager to provide relief to the disadvantaged and suffering.

same time, we believe and hope that many readers will make use of their newly acquired knowledge to indulge in the normative side of macroeconomics: this is what makes it fun.

1.5.4 Testing Theories: The Role of Data

The generally accepted way of evaluating theories is to subject them to scientific testing. In macroeconomics, this means looking at the facts, i.e. at data.

This is easier said than done, and there are a number of unusual difficulties. First, data correspond to sometimes elusive concepts, as Chapter 2 will show. Second, constructing aggregate data implies enquiring into the behaviour of millions of individuals, who sometimes have good or bad reasons to misrepresent the truth. Third, economics shares the predicament common to other social sciences that experimentation is not really possible—when observed, people often change their behaviour. Not

---

Box 1.3 Forecasting the Year 2006

Economic forecasts can be wrong, and often spectacularly so. Table 1.3 presents forecasts of GDP growth and inflation published every six months by the Organization for Economic Cooperation and Development (OECD), an organization of industrialized countries. In France, Japan, and Korea, the OECD was remarkably on target. Output in the USA was overpredicted by 0.7%, while in Germany output was significantly underpredicted by about the same margin. Inflation in 2006 turned out to be considerably higher in the USA and France than first expected from the perspective at year end 2004, while it was significantly lower in Japan and Korea and some-

what lower in Germany. For the most part, the forecasting performance was relatively good, since there is little systematic tendency to make mistakes across countries. Table 1.3 also shows how being wrong can change over time. This is because forecasters gather information over time and must decide whether to modify their predictions as new evidence arrives or stay put. Sometimes, however—as in the case of French and Korean inflation or UK growth—the OECD clung stubbornly to its forecast, showing either that useful information was not available, or that it was not considered important enough to lead to a revision.

Table 1.3 Forecasting the Year 2006

	France	Germany	Japan	Korea	UK	USA
Growth in real GDP (% per annum)						
Forecast (December 2004)	2.3	2.3	2.3	5.0	2.4	3.6
Forecast (June 2005)	2.0	1.8	1.7	5.0	2.4	3.3
Forecast (December 2005)	2.1	1.8	2.0	5.1	2.4	3.5
Actual outcome	2.2	3.1	2.2	5.0	2.8	2.9
Inflation rate (% per annum)						
Forecast (December 2004)	1.7	0.9	−0.3	1.0	2.3	1.7
Forecast (June 2005)	1.7	0.9	0.0	1.0	2.2	2.2
Forecast (December 2005)	1.7	0.7	−0.1	1.0	1.7	2.5
Actual outcome	2.3	0.6	−0.9	−0.4	2.6	3.2

Source: OECD, *Economic Outlook*.

only is it possibly immoral—no macroeconomist would wish to start a hyperinflation just to test a theory—but more crucially, many important variables simply are not observable. This is the case of people's expectations of the future, for example. Macroeconomists are forced to conduct empirical tests with the data that they have. They develop statistical techniques, often sophisticated ones, to deal with observation and measurement errors. They refine their techniques for gathering and analysing data. This allows the elimination of inadequate theories and the modification of others. The surviving theories will be those that withstand the test of time in this scientific process.

1.5.5 Macroeconomic Modelling and Forecasting

Economists are frequently asked to make forecasts. Governments, international organizations, and large financial institutions frequently employ large teams of economists to prepare forecasts. If macroeconomics were to be judged by the performance of forecasts, the verdict would not be unkind. However, the respectable track record of forecasters has been sullied by some large historical errors. Box 1.3 illustrates this fact by examining the accuracy of forecasts, after the fact, for the year 2006.

There are several reasons why economic forecasting is inherently difficult. First, even an excellent understanding of an economy's structure—how its endogenous variables interact—can fall victim to unexpected changes in exogenous variables. Good examples of this are the oil price increases of 1973 and 2000, the Gulf War of 1991, or the global financial difficulties starting in 2007. Second, expectations—which are volatile in nature—wield an important influence over the economy. Governments sometimes react to their own forecasts by implementing policies designed to prevent those forecasts from happening. Political changes occur quickly and can disrupt the economic environment. Finally, it takes time—often several months—to know what has really happened at any given point, so forecasts are always based on provisional information which becomes more precise only with time.

Most forecasts are generated by computer-based models. These models resemble those that we present in this book. They are made of hundreds, sometimes thousands, of equations. Constructing these equations is a long and difficult task. The exogenous variables must be guessed by forecasters before they can ask their computers for an answer. This introduces many margins of error. The models can never be fully reliable, and the exogenous variables may be difficult to pinpoint. For these reasons, the forecasters themselves take their results with a grain of salt, and often, when the outcome is not completely satisfactory, 'drop in' their own subjective factor to the results.

1.6 Preview of the Book

1.6.1 Structure

The book proceeds in steps. Parts I–III build up an understanding of the measurement and the behaviour of the underlying economy. Part I is concerned mostly with defining terms and constructing a macroeconomic vocabulary. Part II studies the behaviour of the economy in the long run: growth and output, labour markets, and prices and exchange rates. Part III develops our understanding of macroeconomy in the short run, that is, from quarter to quarter or from year to year. This part spans many subjects, ranging from the demand of households and firms for goods and services, the financial system, the short run determination of output, interest rates, and the exchange rate. It also extends the analysis to include the analysis of inflation, output, asset prices, and exchange rates over a longer horizon. It introduces a framework for thinking about inflation and the business cycle. Part IV then uses this framework to explore policy issues facing governments: demand management, fiscal policy, and macroeconomic policies designed to enhance long-run performance. The book concludes with an extensive look at the world international financial system, and the state of economic thought late the first decade of the twenty-first century.

1.6.2 Controversies and Consensus

Economists often make a bad name for themselves by quarrelling in public. Visible disagreements among economists frequently have to do with finer points, if not outright hair-splitting. This discourse is intellectually healthy, but misleading to outside observers, whose opinions are often based on accounts in the popular press and more apt to recall sensational talk-show appearances rather than sober analysis of theory and data. It is unfortunate that many disagreements have important policy implications. Perhaps as a result, politicians often see economics as a sort of debating event, with economists acting as advocates for one particular ideology or another, and may even abuse economists' opinions to get a stamp of approval for a particular policy.

In this textbook we do not shy away from presenting some of the most important disagreements among economists, leaving the reader free to judge. Yet we do not dwell upon these controversies either, choosing to focus rather on the common ground. Because there is so much that is not controversial, it is best first to understand the broad areas of consensus. Box 1.4 provides more details.

1.6.3 Rigour and Intuition

The only possible scientific approach to the complexities of the real world is the rigour of reasoning. However, to be useful, macroeconomics must be versatile and easily put to work when we want to understand particular events. This is why a great deal of macroeconomics amounts to the organized accumulation of intuition about particular phenomena. Our objective is, therefore, to leave readers

with an natural understanding of how the economy functions. We do this by trying to draw robust yet simple conclusions from the various and often intricate principles presented. Such intuition is never completely rigorous, but can be useful in practice. Rigour plays its crucial role in reminding us when intuition is correct, and when it should be used with caution.

1.6.4 Data and Institutions

Macroeconomics is fascinating because it tells us a great deal about the world in which we live. It is not merely a set of abstract principles with interesting logical properties. Many theories will look odd at first sight, yet they capture key aspects of the real world. This is why at each important step we pause to look at facts. Facts can be data or particular episodes. Studying them carefully shows how theories work and shape our understanding of macroeconomic phenomena. It broadens our knowledge of important events that have shaped the lives of millions of people.

On the other hand, a graph or a table is no substitute for more rigorous analysis of the data. Merely demonstrating that two economic variables move closely together is a far cry from proving that one causes the other. Our motive in using data to illustrate economic phenomena is to give readers a feel for economics itself. On our website we offer a list of suggested reading for each chapter—which is by no means meant to be exhaustive—for those who want to learn more about the theory and practice of macroeconomics.

Finally, good economic theories must be valid under different conditions. At the same time, the response of different countries to economic shocks is often shaped by their particular economic and political institutions. These include their form of government, the existence of labour unions and employers' associations, and regulations. The interplay of macroeconomic principles and institutions is an essential part of a proper understanding of the field, and this is why we spend a lot of time reviewing them. The economics of these institutions is, however, far beyond the level of this textbook.

Box 1.4   Macroeconomic Schools of Thought: A Primer

Almost from the beginning, macroeconomics has been divided into two main schools of thought. Keynesians (and their neo-Keynesian heirs) and monetarists (and neo-monetarists) continue to pursue the old debate about the role of the marketplace and government in society. Keynesians are more likely to believe that markets function imperfectly and that governments can and should use economic policy actively to combat recessions. Monetarists[6] tend to reject this view, seeing politics and the power of bureaucracies as barriers to government efforts to steer the economy away from business cycles and more generally market failures, which they see as either unavoidable or of lesser importance. Given these premises, each school uses theories and data to build and support its case.

These labels are not exclusive. In the USA, where much of the debate takes place, reference is sometimes made to salt-water versus freshwater macroeconomists. Salt-water economists come from universities located on the two US seaboards (Harvard, MIT, Yale, Stanford, Berkeley) and tend to defend the Keynesian legacy. Freshwater economists are more frequently associated with monetarism and laissez-faire; they hail from universities located near the Great Lakes, e.g. Chicago, Rochester, or Minnesota. In Europe, similar controversies characterize national, and increasingly European, debates. National traditions tend to make British and French economists more Keynesian, while German or Swedish economists are more monetarist. Dutch, Italian, and Spanish economists are hard to classify, having as many exceptions as examples for any rule. In recent years, older Keynesian ideas have enjoyed a renaissance among politicians in France and Germany, primarily, who endorse more active fiscal and monetary policy. Later on in this book, we will see how this new emphasis on activist policy is a consequence of the common European currency, the euro, which was introduced in 1999.

1.6.5 Europe

Our textbook bears the subtitle 'A European Text'. Does this mean that we think that macroeconomics in Europe is fundamentally different from macroeconomics in the USA, Asia, or Latin America? Most certainly not! To the contrary, we take the view that macroeconomics is sufficiently global in scope to apply to economies around the world. This includes the transforming economies of Central and Eastern Europe as well as the newly emerging economies of Southern and Eastern Asia. On the other hand, we do wish to send a more subtle signal: we believe strongly that European economies have important distinguishing features that make them hard to study through the lens of, say, the leading textbooks from North America.

There is much in Europe that warrants such a European emphasis. Rather than a collection of states under a federal government, Europe is a mosaic of nation-states, each with a sovereign macroeconomic policy-maker, but also with distinct preferences and endowments. Surely, the completion of the Single European Market, the creation of a monetary union, and the significant enlargement of the European Union will increase the pressure towards integration, raising specific new challenges along the way. In addition, to varying degrees, European countries share a common view of the relationship between market forces and social justice. The attachment to fairness and economic solidarity is deeply ingrained in Europe's traditions and history, which explain why her labour markets differ so much from those in the USA. This observation alone warrants a markedly different perspective, even if the underlying theory is the same.

---

6   The term 'monetarist' derives from the Latin 'moneta' signalling their original emphasis on excess money growth as the sole cause of inflation. Now the term is sometimes applied to those who advocate unregulated markets and criticize government intervention at both the microeconomic and the macroeconomic level.

⊙ Key Concepts

- macroeconomics
- gross domestic product (GDP)
- trend
- logarithmic scale
- economic growth
- business cycle
- Burns–Mitchell diagram
- unemployment rate
- labour force
- labour
- capital
- factors of production
- labour share
- index, index number
- inflation
- hyperinflation
- capacity utilization

- procyclical and countercyclical
- real economy, monetary economy
- laissez-faire versus interventionism
- aggregate demand management
- price level
- coordination failures
- Keynesian revolution
- demand side
- economic agents
- fiscal policy
- monetary policy
- supply side
- exchange rate
- endogenous
- exogenous
- positive and normative economics

➔ Media

Students can greatly benefit from reading daily the economic section of their newspaper. Some publications with high-quality analyses (but not free of prejudices) are (in English): the *Financial Times* and *The Economist*. There is also a wealth of information on the internet. See our website for further hints.

Data are produced by national statistical institutes and central banks. Some international institutions produce comparable data and are of easy access: the IMF's *International Financial Statistics* and its biannual survey *World Economic Outlook*, the OECD's biannual *Economic Outlook*, the World Bank's *World Development Report* and *Global Economic Prospects*, the European Commission's *European Economy*, and the European Bank for Reconstruction and Development's annual *Transition Report*. All maintain websites, more or less generous in allowing access to their publications.

Macroeconomic Accounts 2

Facts and theories meet in analysis. The combination of the two is essential if economics is to progress, since it is neither a pure subject, like mathematics, of which one does not ask that the theories should be applicable to actual phenomena, nor is it a collection of facts, like the objects on a junk heap, of which one does not ask how they are related.

Richard Stone[1]

2.1 Overview

Every science has its own special language; not necessarily to exclude non-experts, but to make discussion more meaningful and precise. In this chapter we will start learning to speak the language of macroeconomics. We first provide a quantitative description of the economy and definitions of more frequently used concepts. As a natural point of departure, the chapter begins with a discussion of the national income accounts and **accounting identities**—how magnitudes we are interested in relate to each other, by construction. The national income accounts play a central role throughout the study of macroeconomics.

Chapter 2 will be limited to a description of what happens in an economy. Knowing the facts and how these facts are measured are essential for understanding the underlying behaviour of aggregate magnitudes. The distinction between description (this chapter) and analysis (the rest of the book) is similar to that found in biology. As was already noted in the last chapter, it is important to know that living organisms consist of a collection of different cells; yet this biological description is only a first step. Analyzing and understanding how cells function and affect each other is vastly more important. In a similar way, decomposing the gross domestic product into its components and examining the external accounts describe interactions and relationships without explaining how or why. That is the job of subsequent analytic chapters. It is thus unavoidable to spend time with these definitions. As we shall frequently see, there is much more to them than first meets the eye.

2.2 Gross Domestic Product

2.2.1 Three Definitions of Gross Domestic Product

The **gross domestic product** (GDP) is defined for a particular geographic area—usually a country, but possibly a region or a city, or a group of countries such as the European Union (EU) or the euro area. It is also defined over a time interval, usually a year or a quarter. This is because the GDP is a **flow variable**, much like the amount of water flowing down a river. Flow variables differ from **stock variables**, which are always defined with reference to a particular point in time, such as the quantity of water held back by a dam.[2]

---

[1] Sir Richard Stone (1913–1991) of Cambridge University received the Nobel Prize in Economics in 1984 and is generally regarded as the father of national income accounting.

[2] Another example of a stock variable is a company's balance sheet, which measures its financial state at a single point in time, say 31 December; in contrast, an income statement records the profit or loss attributed to the firm over a time period, say 1 January to 31 December, and is a flow variable.

A country's GDP is a measure of its productive activity. It turns out that there are three ways to measure it, and there are thus three definitions. Our first definition is the sum of all final sales of goods and services sold during the measurement period.

Definition 1:
GDP = the sum of final sales within a geographic location during a period of time, usually a year.

This definition refers specifically to **final sales**, i.e. goods and services sold to the consumer or firm that will ultimately use them. For example, the purchase of a loaf of bread or a motor car by a household is a final sale. In contrast, a car sold to a dealer which is subsequently resold during the measurement period, or a loaf of bread purchased by a grocery store which is later sold to a household are not final but **intermediate sales**. Intermediate sales are excluded from GDP to avoid double counting. For this reason, GDP should never be confused with total sales, or turnover. Consistent with this approach, exports are always counted as final sales regardless of how the foreigners use them, because they leave the geographic borders of the national economy.

Our second definition of GDP recognizes that each final sale of a good or service represents the ultimate step that validates all the efforts that have gone into producing and making it available to the buyer. It encapsulates a chain of economic activities which are each seen as **value added**.

Definition 2:
GDP = the sum of value added occurring within a given geographic location during a period of time.

A firm creates value added by transforming raw materials and unfinished goods into products it can sell in the market place. The firm's value added is the difference between its sales (turnover) and the costs of raw materials, unfinished goods, and imports from abroad. If the firm produces intermediate goods, its sales are costs to its customers, who themselves are producers. This value added should not be counted twice, and it is deducted from those customers' own sales in computing its own value added. When the final consumer purchases a good or a service in the market, the price includes all the value added created at each stage in the production process; hence the consistency between Definitions 1 and 2. Box 2.1 uses a concrete example to show how various productive activities contribute to a country's total value added.

GDP includes all incomes earned within a country's borders—by residents and non-residents alike. Because one person's final spending must be someone else's income, the third definition of GDP is also consistent with the first.

Definition 3:
GDP = the sum of factor incomes earned from economic activities within a geographic location during a period of time.

GDP statistics are quoted daily in the financial and political press. The GDP, and in particular, its rate of growth, are generally considered to be the most important indicators of an economy's health, and their evolution is closely watched by managers, economists, and politicians. They allow us to study the performance of a single economy over time as well as to compare different countries.

(1) For comparison over time, we want to distinguish two reasons why GDP can increase: (1) more real economic activity and (2) higher prices for the same economic activity. This aspect is taken up in Section 2.2.2.

(2) For comparison across countries, we need to convert all GDP measures into a common currency. But, as we will see later, exchange rates are quite volatile and may give a faulty picture. For that reason, we usually use the concept of purchasing power parity, which is presented in Chapter 6.

(3) Small countries tend to have small GDPs, and yet they may be well off. This is why we often look at **GDP per capita**, dividing the GDP measures by the size of the population.

The definition of GDP contains a fair amount of arbitrariness, and it is open to debate whether every positive movement in GDP constitutes an improvement in national well-being. All the same, it

Box 2.1   Value Added and Value Subtracted: Two Examples

Consider the following example of value added. A keg of beer is produced and sold for final use by consumers at the price of €100. It is useful to break up this final sale into the steps of value added which were involved in its production. First, a brewery bought barley from a farmer, paying €10, used and paid for energy in the brewing process with a value of €20, and bought a keg from a keg manufacturer at a cost of €5. (For simplicity, the intermediate inputs of the farmer, energy producer, and keg manufacturer are assumed to be zero.) The beer is sold to a wholesaler for €80, so the brewery's own contribution to value added per keg is €45, given by his sale price (€80) less costs of inputs (€10 + €20 + €5 = €35). Next, the wholesaler sells the filled keg for €90 to a retailer, contributing value added of €10. The retailer sells the keg for €100, generating €10 of value added on his own. Summing up, the final price can be broken down into value added at each stage of production and delivery of the final good:

Value added contributed by the:

Farmer	€10
Energy producer	20
Keg manufacturer	5
Brewery	45
Wholesaler	10
Retailer	10
Sum	**€100**

Each step in the value added chain represents a source of income for factors of production involved. Suppose for example that the brewer had labour costs of €35 (wages and salaries as well as social security contributions) and €5 in beer taxes. Then the brewery's activity led to profits of €5, which are the income to the owners—assuming there were no further costs such as interest on loans, royalties for brands or trademarks, or rent. Similarly, if the wholesaler had no costs (employees, rent, or interest), the €10 of value added would represent his income, which can also be thought of as the profit which he receives as owner of the business. The example shows how the division of the value added is arbitrary and potentially separable from the issue of whether value added is generated at all.

Because value added is essential for generating income, it is reasonable to think that few economic activities could survive very long if they *subtracted* value, i.e. if sales did not even cover material input costs. Not only would labour and capital receive no income for their efforts, but also someone would have to pay for the operating loss on each unit of output sold. Yet there are many examples of value subtraction. One is automobile production in Eastern Germany immediately following the fall of the Iron Curtain in 1989. Under communism, many citizens of the German Democratic Republic had to wait years to pay up to 15,000 marks for the mediocre Trabant car produced by the 'people's combine' *VEB Sachsenring*. After the wall came down, demand evaporated and the price of Trabants dropped so sharply that production represented value subtraction at world prices for inputs. Production continued for some time afterwards, with workers' wages paid by Western German taxpayers. It became clear that this was not a sensible option, and Trabant production was stopped in 1991.

is the best indicator we have. More details on this controversial issue are provided in Box 2.2.

2.2.2 Real versus Nominal Quantities, Deflators versus Price Indices

Real and nominal GDP

Now that we know what GDP is and how GDP data are constructed, we can immediately see how the national income statisticians have solved the problem of adding up apples and oranges: the solution is to use *prices* to convert volumes (the numbers of apples and oranges) into values (sales of apples and oranges). Suppose an economy produces these two goods and requires no imports. Final sales of apples and oranges are obtained by multiplying the quantities of apples and oranges sold, Q^a and Q^o, by their respective prices, P^a and P^o, yielding **nominal GDP**, or GDP at current prices:

$$\text{(2.1)} \qquad \text{nominal GDP} = P^a Q^a + P^o Q^o.$$

Yet there is always a catch. If the price of oranges increases from one year to the next, nominal GDP rises even while the volume of final sales has not changed at all! An increase in nominal GDP can result from either higher prices *or* more output. To separate the effects of output and price movements, national income accountants distinguish between nominal and **real GDP**. Increases in real GDP correspond to increases in physical output, the number of apples and oranges produced and sold. Whereas nominal GDP is computed, as in (2.1), using the actual selling prices, real GDP is computed by using prices observed in some agreed base year.[3] In our example, if prices of apples and oranges were P_0^a and P_0^o in the base year, the real GDP in year t, when net final sales of apples and oranges are Q_t^a and Q_t^o, is:

(2.2)   real GDP$_t = P_0^a Q_t^a + P_0^o Q_t^o$.

This distinction is very general and applies to all macroeconomic variables: nominal variables represent values at current prices; real variables represent volumes at constant prices. As an example, Table 2.1 reports growth rates of nominal and real GDP for the euro area.[4]

Price deflators and indices

The distinction between nominal and real GDP can be used as a measure of the general price level, or the price of goods in terms of money. The **GDP deflator**, one way of measuring the price level at some particular time, is simply the ratio of nominal to real GDP:

(2.3) GDP deflator = nominal GDP/real GDP.

In the base year, nominal and real GDP coincide and the GDP deflator equals 1.0. (Sometimes it is multiplied by 100 for ease of comparison over the years.) It can be thought of as an average of all prices of

Table 2.1 Growth Rates of Nominal GDP, Real GDP, and GDP Deflator: Euro Area 1997–2006 (% per annum)

	Nominal GDP	Real GDP	GDP deflator
1997	2.2	2.6	−0.4
1998	3.9	2.9	1.0
1999	4.6	3.1	1.5
2000	5.2	4.0	1.3
2001	4.3	2.0	2.4
2002	3.5	0.9	2.6
2003	2.9	0.8	2.1
2004	4.0	2.1	1.9
2005	3.4	1.5	1.9
2006	4.6	2.8	1.8

Source: Eurostat.

final goods in terms of money, where each price is implicitly weighted by the proportion of the corresponding good in the GDP. As these proportions change over the years, so do the weights.

The inflation rate can be measured by the rate of increase in the GDP deflator, which in turn can be approximated by the following formula:[5]

(2.4) $$\frac{\text{GDP deflator}}{\text{inflation}} = \frac{\text{nominal GDP}}{\text{growth rate}} - \frac{\text{real GDP}}{\text{growth rate}}.$$

For example, Table 2.1 shows that in 2005 the nominal GDP of the euro area rose by 3.4% while the real GDP increased only by 1.5%. On average, therefore, prices rose by roughly 1.9%.[6]

An alternative measure of inflation is based on an average of prices with fixed weights, called a

---

[3] Problems arise when new goods are introduced (MP3 players), or existing goods improve in quality (personal computers). National income accountants have devised procedures to deal with such effects.

[4] In previous decades, it was common to update the base year for prices used every five or more years. Rapidly changing product mixes and globalization have increased the value of redefining base years more frequently. It is now EU national income accounting practice to redefine the base year *every* year, effectively rendering real GDP a so-called chain standard index. With this change, growth rates in real GDP are more reliably measured. As a result, some national statistically authorities have even stopped publishing real GDP levels.

[5] Box 6.3 in Chapter 6 provides the arithmetical background for this formula. If we denote nominal GDP as Y, real GDP as Q and the GDP deflator as P, we have $Y = PQ$, which means $P = Y/Q$. Then, using the results from Box 6.3, we have $\Delta P/P = \Delta Y/Y - \Delta Q/Q$.

[6] To see why this formula is an approximation, suppose real GDP increased at rate g and inflation at rate π. The rate of nominal growth must be $(1+g)(1+\pi) - 1 = g + \pi + g\pi$. For g and π small, $g\pi \approx 0$, so the rate of growth of nominal GDP is approximately equal to $g + \pi$.

Box 2.2 **What GDP Measures**

The GDP is a measure of recorded market transactions. This leaves out many activities which are not carried out through legal channels or which do not reach the market place, like growing vegetables in the garden. Furthermore, since the value of goods and services are measured using their transaction prices, two identical goods may enter the GDP differently if one of them is sold at a discount. Finally, it is not a measure of happiness: painful expenses (having a tooth removed, for example) enter the GDP in the same way as pleasurable ones. When someone dies, GDP rises: the funeral service, the hospital expenses, and the execution of the will by lawyers and bankers all represent additional final sales of goods and services. Pollution and other forms of environmental damage are ignored in the GDP, since they are not traded in markets.

Services enter the GDP exactly like goods. Services include medical doctors' fees or an estate agent's commission when an existing house is sold. The GDP also excludes many forms of income. In the case of real estate, if the house's value has increased since it was purchased, the previous owner enjoys a capital gain, but capital gains do not enter the GDP. Used-goods sales, such as cars or antique furniture, do not enter the GDP either. Such transactions represent a transfer of ownership rather than production. These goods entered GDP when first sold, but the fees of the dealers represent a service which is accounted for. Sales by retailers from inventory accumulated in earlier periods actually reduce GDP, as they represent a depletion of stocks.

Public services are part of GDP, even if they are not really sold. Their price is simply measured by their cost of production. For example, public education enters GDP as the sum of teachers' salaries, operating costs such as electricity or heating costs, and equipment including rents. Similarly, the national defence enters the GDP as total expenditure on armed forces.

A related measure is **gross national income** (GNI).[7] Unlike the location-based GDP, the GNI is *ownership based*. It is the value added attributable to all factors of production owned by a country's residents, regardless of where those factors are actually employed. It thus includes value added or income earned abroad and repatriated by residents. For example, an Italian living in Como and commuting to work in Lugano in Switzerland contributes to the Italian GNI and to the Swiss GDP, but not to the Italian GDP or Swiss GNI. Because GNI is harder to measure, economists tend to follow GDP more closely. We will do the same.

To see how important the distinction between GDP and GNI can be, consider the case of Ireland. After several years of high economic growth, Ireland's GDP per capita rose above that of the UK in the late 1990s. Nevertheless, many of Ireland's factories are owned by foreigners—Britons, Germans, or Americans—or were purchased with money borrowed abroad. Investment income and interest paid to those foreigners was significant enough that until 2005, Irish per capita GNI remained lower than the UK's. Since then, however, Irish residents even have a higher GNI per capita than those of the UK, a remarkable turn of the economic tables!

price index. A basket of goods is selected and the amount of each good, or category of goods, in the basket is used to weight the corresponding prices. An example is the **consumer price index (CPI)**. This is based on a basket of goods consumed by a representative or average individual.

Figure 2.1 shows the growth rates of the GDP deflator and of the CPI in Italy. Differences between the two measures of inflation are usually not very large, but they can become significant when the price of imports changes relative to output pro-

duced domestically. In the early 1990s and in 1999–2000, for example, the price of crude oil increased faster than prices of goods and services produced in Italy, as measured by the GDP deflator. Since Italians consume many goods which involve petroleum products (gasoline, diesel fuel, heating oil, plastics, paints, etc), the CPI increased at a faster rate

---

7   This measure was known previously as the gross national product (GNP).

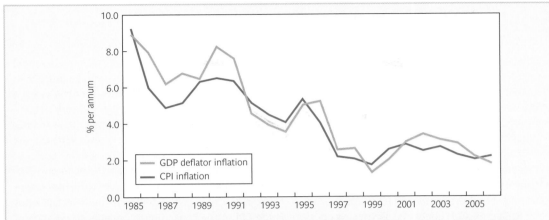

Fig. 2.1 GDP Deflator and the Consumer Price Index Inflation Rates: Italy, 1985–2006
Both the GDP deflator and the consumer price index (CPI) measure the price level, or the price of goods in terms of money. The inflation rate is simply the rate of growth of one of these price level measures. The figure shows that both GDP deflator and CPI measures of inflation tend to move together over time, with occasional exceptions when the difference in the underlying 'baskets' matters. In the late 1980s, world oil prices declined sharply. Since gas and heating oil are part of household consumption, inflation measured by the CPI declined. Since oil is imported, it does not contribute value added directly in Italy, and has only a small impact on the GDP deflator.
Source: International Financial Statistics.

than the GDP deflator. In contrast, when oil prices fell in the 1980s and late 1990s, imports became cheaper and CPI inflation fell behind, as can be seen from Figure 2.1.

Price indexes can be tailored to describe the prices of certain types of goods, of certain types of consumer, or for certain sectors of the economy. Along with price deflators, there is a large menu to choose from, each price index or deflator having its own special emphasis. Box 2.3 presents some frequently used deflators and indexes.

2.2.3 Measuring and Interpreting GDP

The GDP, which represents the economic performance of an entire economy, is not easy to measure. The task is generally carried out by official statistical offices which draw on various sources of information. One natural source is the tax authorities. Firms report sales (first definition of GDP), individuals report incomes (third definition), and in most countries (all EU countries, but not the USA) value added taxes (VAT) are collected by intermediate and final sellers who then report

their value added when they pay the tax (second definition).

The fact that GDP figures are collected through tax returns immediately raises the suspicion that individuals and firms may misrepresent their finances to the fiscal authorities. Such unreported income and output is frequently referred to as the **underground economy**. Box 2.4 presents estimates of how large it could be. It also alerts us to the importance of work that is not paid for in the marketplace.

Another shortcoming associated with the magnitude of the task is the time it takes to get reasonably accurate numbers. Data from tax returns are usually processed with delay. Usually at the end of the first month of each quarter, figures for the preceding quarter are released. Box 2.5 explains how such flash estimates are produced and updated several times over the following years. The inaccuracy of these estimates is unsettling because they are frequently used by governments when deciding on economic policies, by investors when valuing their assets, and by firms deciding on hiring or

Box 2.3 Price Deflators and Price Indexes

The price index closest to the GDP deflator is the producer price index (PPI), with fixed weights corresponding to a basket representative of national production. Similarly, the CPI is closely tracked by the consumption deflator, the ratio of nominal and real aggregate consumption expenditures by households. A price index like the CPI or the PPI is an example of a fixed-weight, or *Laspeyres index*. The consumption deflator, which is based on the actual share of goods in the corresponding year's consumption, is called a variable weight or *Paasche index*. The CPI and the consumption deflator include goods and services produced abroad and imported, while the PPI and the GDP deflator do not, but these latter measures include goods and services locally produced and exported. Figure 2.1 suggests a growing divergence between the PPI and the CPI in Italy in the late 1980s. The reason is that imported goods prices increased by less than those of domestically produced goods.

Other frequently used deflators are related to exports, imports, investment goods, and government purchases. The wholesale price index (WPI) measures the average price of goods at the wholesale stage, and various commodity price indexes track the evolution of raw materials prices. The dizzying diversity of indexes and deflators simply reflects the fact that there is no absolute 'average' price. Different price levels are used for different purposes. For example, wage-earners wish to tie their wages to their cost of living; in this case, the relevant index is the CPI or the consumption deflator. In the case of Italy, linking wages to the CPI rather than to the PPI resulted in higher profits for firms whose sales are better tracked by the PPI. Because the CPI and other Laspeyres indexes are easier to compute, they tend to be used most often in practice.

 Box 2.4 The Underground Economy and Unpaid Work

Who hasn't had an offer from a carpenter, a car mechanic, or painter to do some work 'without a receipt'? Agents engage in the underground, or informal economy for straightforward reasons. First, they want to avoid taxes (the value added tax, employment and social security charges, profit taxes). Second, while significant, criminal activities, such as drug-dealing, prostitution, or racketeering, are intentionally concealed and kept underground by market participants. By definition, the size of the underground economy is unknown, but national income statisticians often attempt to guess its importance. They use various approaches such as monitoring household electricity use, which tends to be higher in economies where unreported market activity is more significant, or looking at the amount of large-denomination currency in circulation, since underground transactions do not use bank accounts and profits are conveniently held in large bills. The sale of intermediate inputs related to final production often

indicates underground economy activities. For example, a large discrepancy exists between the purchase of construction materials and reported construction activity. Table 2.2 shows the extent of the underground economy in a number of countries.

Another serious drawback of GDP as a measure of economic activity is unpaid work. Minor repairs around the house, caring for children, cooking for the family and cleaning up take up much time and effort. Wealthier people hire help for these chores, in which case it becomes part of GDP (if reported to the tax authorities). Most people do it themselves, and it is unrecorded. Table 2.3 presents estimates for the Netherlands of the size of this 'lost output'. The first part shows that women perform much unpaid work. The second part shows that unpaid work represents a sizeable part of official GDP. The estimates depend on which salary we impute to this activity, the lowest figure corresponds to the minimum wage, the highest to the average wage.

Table 2.2 Estimates of the Size of the Underground Economy (% of GDP)

Africa		Central Europe	
Nigeria, Egypt	68–76	Hungary, Bulgaria, Poland	20–28
Tunisia, Morocco	39–45	Czech Republic, Romania, Slovakia	9–16
Latin America		**Former Soviet Union**	
Mexico, Peru	40–60	Belarus, Georgia, Ukraine	28–43
Chile, Brazil, Venezuela	25–35	Baltic States, Russia	20–27
Asia		**OECD**	
Thailand	70	Belgium, Greece, Italy, Spain, Portugal	24–30
Philippines, Malaysia, Korea	38–50	All others	13–23
Hong Kong, Singapore	13	Austria, Japan, USA, Switzerland	8–10

Source: Schneider and Enste (2000).

Box 2.5 How National Accounts Estimates Vary over Time

Because governments, firms, and investors require timely information about the economy, national statistical institutes in advanced economies have devised ways of quickly producing preliminary estimates of GDP. The procedure is based on the knowledge that the value added of, for example, the 100 largest corporations represents a given proportion of GDP. If the proportion were 10%, as these firms fill in VAT tax reports or respond to specially designed questionnaires, multiplying by 10 their combined value added provides a rough early estimate of GDP. A few months later, revised estimates can be based on data provided by a larger sample of firms. Waiting still longer will allow the incorporation of estimates based on an early and partial analysis of tax returns. Detailed analysis of all tax returns data—using procedures to reconcile differences between measures based on the three definitions—leads to a final figure. Table 2.4 shows successive estimates of German GDP in 2004. The first estimate, published in January 2005, fell short of the final figure by €29 billion, or by about 1.3% of the initial estimate. This represents the GDP of the German state *Saarland* and more than all real growth recorded in Germany in the period 2003–2004 (1.2%).

Table 2.3 Unpaid Work: The Netherlands in 1990

Hours per week	Average paid work	Average per week unpaid work
Men	32.6	17.5
Women	9.4	39.8
% of GDP		36–58

Source: Bruyn-Hundt (1996).

firing workers and on acquiring new plant and equipment. This is why other indicators are often used to supplement the GDP figures.[8] It is also why analysts tend to concentrate on growth rates rather than levels. As long as the distortions do not change much over time, measured GDP growth rates offer a good picture of average economy performance.

---

[8] Chapter 16 discusses some of the most frequently used indicators.

Table 2.4 **Estimates of 2004 German Nominal GDP**

Date of estimate	GDP in 2004 (billions of euros)	% change from previous estimate	% deviation from Jan 2005 estimate
Jan 2005	2178.2	—	—
Feb 2005	2177.0	−0.06	−0.06
May 2005	2207.2	1.39	1.33
Nov 2005	2215.7	0.39	1.72
May 2006	2215.7	0.00	1.72
Nov 2006	2207.2	−0.38	1.33
Feb 2007	2207.2	0.00	1.33

Source: Estimates as published in the monthly bulletin of the Deutsche Bundesbank, various issues.

It is tempting to compare GDPs across countries. Because countries have different populations, it is natural to look at GDP per capita, or the average income earned within a country's boundaries. Such data must be regarded with caution, however. First, GDP is a measure of income, not wealth. Income is a flow, while wealth is the stock of assets accumulated over longer periods of time. For example, the average income earned in the UK is lower than that of Abu Dhabi. Yet average British wealth is likely to be much higher because Britain has been accumulating wealth for centuries, in the form of private assets (e.g. houses, factories, jewels, stocks) and national assets (e.g. the London Bridge, paintings in the British Museum, railroads, highways and telecommunication networks, and much more).

Second, a large number of transactions are not recorded, especially in developing countries. They belong to what is sometimes called the informal economy. For example, much food can be produced within the extended family (a non-market activity), or exchanged for other food (a non-reported market activity). Very low reported per capita income levels in developing economies underestimate true value added and income. Finally, GDPs are measured in the country's local monetary unit, or currency, and are then converted into a common currency using the exchange rate. But local costs are often much lower in poor countries, for reasons presented in Chapter 7. To correct for this effect, economists often use GDP figures which have been adjusted for differences in purchasing power.

2.3 Flows of Incomes and Expenditures

2.3.1 The Circular Flow Diagram

From final expenditures to net taxes and factor income

Each individual's expenditure necessarily contributes to some other individual's income. The simplified **circular flow** diagram represented in Figure 2.2 is based on this simple truth and goes a long way in tracking the functioning of an economy. Based on

the first and third definitions of GDP, it shows how GDP arises as final sales, and how it is paid out to households, the owners of the factors of production. In addition, it shows how firms—around which market activity is organized—households, and the government interact to make GDP possible.

The GDP appears in the left part of the figure. It represents the final net sales of firms. Since firms are owned by households, the GDP represents the gross

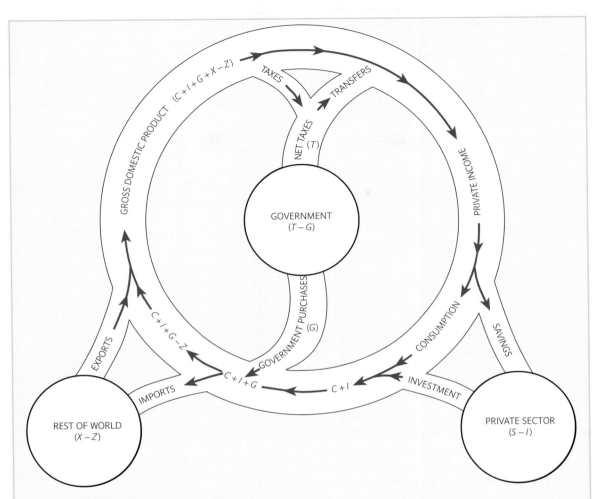

Fig. 2.2 The Circular Flow Diagram

The lower left part of the wheel represents final sales of goods and services which are domestically produced. It is the sum of consumption spending (C), investment spending (I), government purchases (G), and exports (X) less imports (Z). In the upper left part of the wheel this is interpreted as income to residents. This income is taxed by the government, but is also supplemented by transfers to households and firms (T). The remainder is private income, which may be saved (S) or spent (C). The private sector invests in productive equipment (I), which it finances in part by savings (S); the balance $S - I$ is the private sector's net saving behaviour. Similarly, the public sector's budget surplus is $T - G$. The balance $X - Z$ represents at the same time net exports of goods and services as well as the net import of financial assets (claims against the rest of the world).

income of factors of production employed in the geographic region under consideration.[9] To see

9   Technically, GDP also includes 'sales' of labour services by the self-employed. It also excludes sales of households' labour and capital services abroad. In order to keep things simple, we will ignore these latter components of GDP in what follows, so that all value added in the economy represents income to residents.

what firms do with revenues coming from their final sales, we move clockwise. The government, shown as the circle inside the flow diagram, takes (in the form of taxes) and gives (in the form of various transfers). It also purchases goods and services. Because it needs to pay for them, the government will almost always take in more than it gives away in transfers. The difference between taxes and transfers is called **net taxes** and is represented by T. These taxes are taken in at several points of the value added chain—as indirect taxes such as value-added taxes, or as direct taxes on different types of income. Here we consolidate them for simplicity. What is left of GDP after these taxes and transfers are subtracted is called **private income**, $Y - T$.

From private income to absorption plus net exports—GDP

Private income is ultimately earned by those households which own the factors of production involved in creating the value added. The largest part of private income is wages and salaries paid to workers plus payments for rent and royalties, as well as net interest on loans from banks. The residual which remains after firms pay all these other factors is known as gross profit. This profit can either be saved by the firm or redistributed back to firm owners as income.[10] Since all factors of production are ultimately owned by some households, households receive income as employees, as bondholders, as shareholders, as owners of land, and as holders of patents. Households can either save this income, or spend it on **consumption**.

The private sector represents the consolidation of households with the firms that they own. The flow diagram shows how the aggregate savings of the private sector (S) are deposited with the financial sector. The financial sector includes banks, financial institutions, and stock markets whose function is to collect savings and channel them to firms seeking to invest, that is, to purchase productive equipment. This activity, called **financial intermediation**, is represented by the lower-right circle. In the aggregate, the private sector uses its **savings**—the income that it does not consume—to finance, or pay for, the acquisition of new productive equipment by firms. The stock of existing productive equipment, including structures, is referred to as **physical capital**, while the purchase of new equipment is called **investment**. The excess of private saving over investment ($S - I$) is called net private saving. Net

private saving can be positive or negative. Firms and households spend their income—part of it borrowed—to consume (C) and to invest (I).[11]

To private sector expenditures on goods and services ($C + I$) the government adds its own demand (G). Governments purchase goods (roads, military equipment, newly built buildings, and stationery for the bureaucracy) and services (of civil servants and other employees). In addition, governments transfer income, distributing various subsidies to firms and households, and pay interest on the public debt. Total national spending, sometimes called **absorption**, is the sum ($C + I + G$) of private and public spending on all goods and services. Part of absorption includes the purchase of imported goods and services (Z). This is shown as the branch going into the leftmost circle, which represents the rest of the world. It should not be thought of merely as merchandise purchases, but as covering all kinds of services, including labour and capital services, as long as they are rendered within the boundaries of the nation. Similarly, while some domestic income thus leaks abroad, foreigners buy domestically produced goods and services, the country's exports (X). Netting these two flows with the rest of the world gives net exports ($X - Z$). When positive, net exports increase demand for domestic production above that originating with domestic residents; when negative, demand for domestic production is less than total domestic demand.

The sum of absorption and net exports represents the total final sales that occur within the geographic area, i.e. the GDP. The circular flow of income is closed. This circularity is the essence of economic activity: we (collectively) earn to (collectively) spend.

2.3.2 Summary of the Flow Diagram

The flow diagram can be summarized using the first and third definitions of GDP, which is represented

---

[10] The other production costs are mainly land and buildings, financial costs (borrowing from banks and bondholders), and raw materials and intermediate goods which, for the country as a whole, are frequently imported.

[11] There is an important difference between this terminology and that used in the business or popular press, in which 'investment' includes the acquisition of existing assets or financial instruments. Although stocks and bonds are often issued by firms to finance purchases of productive equipment, their simple acquisition or sale does not necessarily imply 'investment' in economics, i.e. the creation of new productive capacity.

by the symbol Y. As net final sales, the GDP is broken down into four main categories: (1) final sales of consumption goods and services (C), (2) final sales of investment goods and additions to inventory stocks (I), (3) final sales to the government (G), and (4) sales to the rest of the world (X). Since part of domestic income leaks abroad to pay for imported goods, imports (Z) must be subtracted, which gives the first decomposition of GDP by final expenditures:

$$(2.5) \qquad Y = C + I + G + X - Z.$$

The flow diagram also shows that GDP can be viewed as net incomes earned by factors of production. What do they do with this income? The three possibilities are given on the right-hand side of the flow diagram: they pay taxes net of transfers (T), they save (S), and they consume (C). Hence the second decomposition by uses of income:

$$(2.6) \qquad Y = C + S + T.$$

Table 2.5 displays the components of the first decomposition as a percentage of GDP for a few countries. Consumption typically represents about 60% of GDP. The investment rate—the ratio of investment expenditures to GDP—ranges from 16 to 30%. Because investment corresponds to the accumulation of productive equipment, it matters for future economic growth. Since governments also invest in infrastructure equipment (roads, bridges, public utilities), what is considered investment in some countries may be undertaken by the government in others. The 'size of government' is considerably greater than the share of government expenditures (14-23%) since transfers must also be included. It varies considerably, even among advanced economies. When total spending is considered, adding transfers to expenditures, the government often 'handles' more than half of GDP: many goods and services that are privately produced elsewhere are delivered freely as public goods in many countries of Europe; these include medical services, schools, child care, and public transport.

The flows of incomes and spending captured by Figure 2.2 constitute the real, as opposed to financial, side of an economy. Parts of these flows leak out to the financial side in the form of corporate and household savings; others leak out to the government in the form of tax payments or social security contributions; others to foreigners through imports. To the extent that withdrawals of resources from the circular flow due to a particular sector is not matched exactly by inflows in the form of spending, then that sector's net asset position must

Table 2.5 Components of GDP by Expenditure, 1999–2006 (% of GDP)

	Consumption (C)	Investment (I)	Government purchases (G)
Australia	58.3	25.2	18.1
Germany	58.9	18.6	19.0
France	56.3	19.8	23.4
UK	64.7	17.7	20.5
Italy	59.2	20.7	19.5
Japan	57.0	24.0	17.6
Canada	56.0	20.6	19.2
Switzerland	60.3	22.0	11.5
USA	69.7	19.5	15.4
Euro area	57.1	20.9	20.3

Source: IMF.

Table 2.6 **GDP and Household Disposable Income, 2006**

	GDP (billions of €)	Household disposable income	
		Level (billions of €)	% of GDP
France	1,779.1	1,124.0	63.2
Germany	2,310.2	1,486.4	64.3
Sweden	306.7	149.1	48.6
Switzerland	301.7	180.8	59.9
United Kingdom	1,892.2	1,223.7	64.7
United States	10,550.0	7,584.3	71.9

Sources: OECD, *Economic Outlook*; ECB.

be changing, by definition.[12] If savings of the private sector exceed investment spending, for example, this means that net accumulation of assets in the private sector is positive. The same holds for the consolidated government if net taxes exceed government purchases of goods and services, or for the nation if net export of goods and services, broadly defined, is positive. Asset accumulation or de-cumulation has economic consequences. How the financial side of the economy functions, and how the real and financial sides are linked, is studied in Part III of this book.

2.3.3 More Detail

While GDP represents the collective income earned within a nation's boundaries, not all of it ends up in the hands of private individuals. What households actually receive to spend or save is called **personal disposable income**. Table 2.6 shows that some 25–55% of GDP does not reach individual households. It either goes to the government (net taxes) or is saved by firms (retained earnings).

Figure 2.3 starts with GDP and, moving right, decomposes it by its ultimate recipient. The first

[12] If the net outflow is positive, net assets owned by the sector must be increasing; if the net outflow is negative, net assets are decreasing. Technically, increasing net assets can occur either by increases in gross financial assets (claims on other sectors), or by reducing gross liabilities (i.e. paying off existing debt to other sectors).

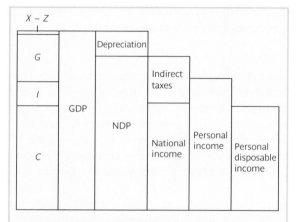

Fig. 2.3 From Expenditure to Income to Personal Disposable Income

Depreciation is stripped away from GDP to obtain net domestic product (NDP). When net factor income from abroad is zero, we can subtract indirect taxes from, and add subsidies of firms to, NDP to obtain national income (NI). (If net factor income from abroad is not zero, it must then be added at this stage.) National income can be distributed in a number of ways: firms' savings (retained earnings), taxes on businesses, and contributions to social security are subtracted from national income, leaving various forms of income paid in the end to households. The government also transfers income to households (social security, unemployment insurance, etc.). This results in personal income (PI). After income taxes and some miscellaneous fees, we are left with personal disposable income (PDI), that is, resources available to households for spending or saving.

item is **depreciation**: in the process of producing GDP, productive equipment is subjected to wear and tear and obsolescence. Properly measured, this depreciation should be subtracted from GDP to give a clearer picture of the output that is actually available as income. Subtracting depreciation from GDP gives us the **net domestic product (NDP)**.[13] Moving further to the right, national income is what is left for firms once indirect taxes are paid out. Indirect taxes vary from country to country, and include the value added tax (VAT) and excise taxes (on petrol, tobacco, alcohol). They are collected by sellers on behalf of the government.

After indirect taxes, firms dispose of the value added they generate in four ways. First, they pay wages and salaries and other compensation to their employees. This includes contributions to social insurance. Second, they pay interest to bondholders and banks. Third, they pay corporate or business income taxes. What remains is profits to the firms' owners, or shareholders. These profits are either distributed as dividends or held back as retained earnings, sometimes called net corporate saving.[14]

To summarize, what is not paid as corporate taxes or saved by firms is ultimately paid out to households as the firms' employees, their owners, or indirectly as their creditors. When government transfers (e.g. unemployment benefits, disability payments, health care reimbursements, family allowances) are added to labour incomes and distributed profits, the result is personal income. Households cannot freely dispose of their personal income: they must first pay personal income taxes, as well as non-tax payments like parking fines and other governmental fees. The result is personal disposable income, which can either be consumed or saved.

2.3.4 A Key Accounting Identity

The two decompositions of GDP, (2.5) and (2.6), are accounting identities: they hold by definition. Therefore it is always the case that:

$$C + S + T = C + I + G + X - Z.$$

Consumption C appears on both sides of this equality and can be eliminated. When this is done and terms are rearranged, the two accounting identities yield a third one:

(2.7) $$(S - I) + (T - G) = (X - Z).$$

The last term, $X - Z$, is the balance of exports over imports of goods and services, now extended to include the services of facors of production employed outside the national borders (see footnote 9). Parentheses highlight the fact that the corresponding expressions appear in Figure 2.2 as net flows of the private sector (household and business), government, and the rest of the world, respectively. Each of the three net flows can be thought of as a form of saving, a leakage out of (if positive), or an injection into (if negative) the circular flow of income and expenditure. If $S > I$, the private sector as a whole is a net saver. If $S < I$, the private sector is a net borrower. Similarly, if $T > G$ the government is saving, and if $G > T$ it is borrowing by issuing public debt to domestic or foreign residents. The identity (2.7) shows how these leakages are linked, by definition.

Table 2.7 presents the accounting identity (2.7) for several countries in 2006. In the USA, both private and public sectors are spending much more than they take in; the country as a whole is running a large external deficit of 6.1% of GDP. In Japan, the private sector's massive surplus swamps the public sector's deficit, leaving the country with an external surplus of almost 4% of GDP. The euro area shows net balance with the rest of the world, with total private and public sector imbalances cancelling each other almost exactly. At the same time, individual member countries display widely different external balances, for different reasons.

2.3.5 Identities versus Economics

In a manner of speaking, identity (2.7) implies that all goods and services produced must be purchased. The total demand for goods and services must equal

---

[13] In practice, financial accounting of depreciation is determined by tax regulations. Firms are allowed to subtract from their revenues a given proportion of the book value of equipment for computing taxable profits. It may under- or overstate actual economic depreciation by a wide margin.

[14] Adding depreciation to net corporate savings gives gross corporate savings. It represents the resources that firms set aside to replace used equipment and generally to strengthen their financial position.

Table 2.7 **The Accounting Identity in 2006 (% of GDP)**

	$S-I$	$T-G$	$X-Z$
USA	−3.6	−2.5	−6.1
Japan	6.1	−2.2	3.9
Belgium	1.2	0.8	2.0
Denmark	−1.3	3.7	2.4
France	0.5	−1.7	−1.2
Germany	6.2	−1.1	5.1
Italy	1.0	−3.4	−2.4
Netherlands	7.2	1.8	9.0
Spain	−10.6	1.9	−8.7
Sweden	4.7	2.0	6.7
UK	−0.6	−2.8	−3.4
Euro area	1.1	−1.0	0.1

Source: OECD.

supply. For example, if private savings in a country exceed private investment ($S > I$), either net exports must be positive or the government budget must be in deficit, or both. At the same time, identities tell us little or nothing about causation. Without more information, it is impossible to know whether (1) the government deficit is at the origin of positive net private savings, (2) high exports are generating income that is simply saved by residents, or (3) low domestic investment spending is coinciding with a domestic recession, in which both imports and tax revenues are low and putting current account surplus and/or government budget into deficit. This is the difference between simply collecting data and interpreting them. This is also the difference between accounting and economics. The identity (2.7) is not only a requirement that accounts be correctly measured; we will see later that it can also be seen as a market equilibrium condition which implies that adjustment mechanisms are at work.

2.4 Balance of Payments

The **balance of payments** accounts record all economic transactions between a country and the rest of the world. Most countries have adopted the same classification, which has been designed by the International Monetary Fund. We also follow this classification. The presentation in Table 2.8 separates out international transactions in goods and services in the broadest sense (the upper part I) from financial transactions (the lower part II). Financial transactions imply the purchase and sale of assets such as stocks and bonds, loans and credit, bank deposits and currency, as well as real estate and other forms of wealth.

A simple rule to help understand the meaning of entries is the following: transactions involving *outflows of our money* are recorded as *deficit* (−) items, while those involving inflows of domestic money are considered as surplus (+) items. Box 2.6 (see p. 43) offers a number of examples, which will become clear as we move along.

2.4.1 The Current Account and its Components

The first account to consider in Table 2.8 records exports and imports of goods and services. Imports are entered with a minus sign (deficit item), while exports contribute positively to the balance (surplus item). The net result is line IA, the **balance of goods and services**. The balance of trade in goods (line IA1) includes merchandise trade as well as trade in intermediate inputs, goods repair, goods held in ports, and non-monetary gold. The balance of trade in services (line IA2) incorporates a wide and growing variety of invisibles such as transport and travel, communication, insurance, financial, and other services. It also includes royalties and license fees.

A second account to consider is the **balance of international income** (line IB). This account summarizes the net income of a nation which originates

Table 2.8 The Balance of Payments

I. Current account
A. Goods and services
1. Goods
2. Services
B. International income
1. Wages and compensation
2. Investment income
C. Current transfers
II. Capital and financial account
A. Capital account
B. Financial account
1. Direct investment
2. Portfolio investment
3. Other investment
4. Reserve assets
C. Errors and omissions

abroad. Two important components of international income are worth mentioning.

- Wages and salaries paid for work by individuals in countries different from their place of residence (line IB1).
- Profits or interest income received by residents *less* profits and interest paid to foreign residents (line IB2).

The third important item of the current account is the **balance of current transfers** (line C). These are payments which are not associated with commercial or financial transactions. An example is the remittance of guest workers to their home countries. When a Polish plumber living in London sends money to relatives living in Warsaw, this counts as a surplus to the Polish balance of transfers and as a deficit to the UK's. Another example is development or emergency aid offered by one country to another one.

The sum of the balances of trade in goods and services, international income, and current transfers is called the **current account balance**. A current account surplus may be interpreted as the net sales of goods and services, broadly defined to include the services of capital and labour services, know-how, and goodwill ('purchased' with remittances or foreign aid).

The importance of the current account is best seen by returning to the definition of decomposition (2.5). If we define Y this time more broadly as gross national income (GNI), we can rewrite this decomposition as follows:

$$(2.8) \qquad CA = Y - (C + I + G) = Y - A,$$

where $A = C + I + G$ is referred to as absorption, or total domestic spending on goods and services, both domestic and foreign, by households, firms, and government agencies. By definition, the current account is the excess of income over spending. It signals whether the country is a net borrower or a net lender. When a country earns more than it spends (i.e. $CA = Y - A > 0$), it is a net lender *vis-à-vis* the rest of the world. Conversely, a country running a current account deficit spends more than it earns ($CA < 0$ and $A > Y$) and must match the difference by borrowing abroad.

Table 2.9 illustrates the balance of payments accounts for a number of different countries with widely different experiences. The enormous current account deficit in the USA is due to a deficit in goods and services trade. Turkey, Mexico, and China are three countries which receive significant transfers from abroad. In the case of Turkey and Mexico, many citizens work as guest workers abroad and remit their income regularly. Sweden and the UK find themselves in the opposite situation; many foreign workers live there and remit money to their home countries. This is also the case for the EU overall, as well as the USA.

2.4.2 The Capital and Financial Accounts

Part II of Table 2.8 describes financial transactions. As the balance of payments is an accounting exercise, the sum of all entries in the balance of payments must equal zero. This is also a consequence of (2.8): if the current account is in surplus, a country is exporting more to the rest of the world than it is importing. Earning more than it spends, that country

Table 2.9 **Balance of Payments, Various Countries, 2005 (US$ billion)**

	Euro area	USA	Sweden	Turkey	Mexico	China	UK
Trade balance	59.01	−778.94	19.70	−33.53	−7.59	134.19	−125.08
Balance on goods and services	101.68	−716.73	27.71	−18.26	−12.89	124.80	−80.23
Balance on goods, services, and income	88.38	−705.44	28.26	−24.06	−25.39	135.43	−33.07
Unilateral transfers	−87.69	−86.07	−4.62	1.46	20.47	25.38	−21.93
Current account	**0.69**	**−791.51**	**23.64**	**−22.60**	**−4.92**	**160.82**	**−55.00**
Capital account	**14.98**	**−4.35**	**0.31**	**NA**	**NA**	**4.10**	**2.80**
Financial account	**9.87**	**771.35**	**−22.23**	**38.79**	**12.79**	**58.86**	**73.80**
Direct investment abroad	−372.03	−9.07	−27.56	−1.08	−6.47	−11.31	−91.71
Direct investment inward	113.01	109.75	10.68	9.80	19.74	79.13	195.55
Portfolio investment: assets	−512.00	−180.13	−13.02	−1.23	NA	−26.16	−291.52
Portfolio investment: liabilities	697.72	908.55	17.10	14.67	10.19	21.22	240.34
Financial derivatives: assets	278.50	NA	30.46	NA	NA	NA	NA
Financial derivatives: liabilities	295.49	NA	−31.27	NA	NA	NA	16.53
Other investment assets	−715.58	−251.70	−18.30	0.26	−7.72	−48.95	−931.59
Other investment liabilities	816.22	193.95	9.68	16.37	−2.95	44.92	936.20
Net errors and omissions (balancing item)	**−48.45**	**10.41**	**−1.48**	**6.99**	**−0.90**	**−16.44**	**−19.88**
Overall balance	**−22.91**	**−14.10**	**0.25**	**17.85**	**6.96**	**207.34**	**1.73**
Reserves and related items	**22.91**	**14.10**	**−0.25**	**−17.85**	**−6.98**	**−207.34**	**−1.73**

Source: IMF.

must be experiencing a net financial outflow; it is either lending to the rest of the world by acquiring assets abroad, or it is paying down its debts. Conversely, a current account deficit implies borrowing from abroad, so financial capital is flowing into the country. Accordingly, the remainder of the balance of payments, representing financial transactions, must be equal to, and of opposite sign to, the current account. The remaining question is: Who actually performs the balancing act, and how?

The answer is to be found in the **capital and financial account**, which consists of two components. The capital account (line IIA) registers unusual and sporadic financial transfers such as debt forgiveness of public or private debts. The more important component of the capital and financial account is the financial account balance (line IIB). The IMF defines four categories of financial transactions which affect this account.

(1) Direct investment (line IIB1)—purchases and sales of shares (equity investment) in business enterprises in excess of 10% of the total value; reinvested profits; real estate purchases.

(2) Portfolio investment (line IIB2)—purchases and sales of shares (equity investment) in business enterprises of less than 10% of total value; purchases and issues of bonds, money market instruments, and financial derivatives.

(3) Other investments (line IIB3)—trade credits; loans by banks; deposits held at banks; currency.

(4) Reserve asset transactions (line IIB4)—transactions involving monetary gold, special drawing rights and reserve positions with the IMF, and foreign exchange reserves.

While the first three types of financial account transactions can be conducted by the private or public sector, the fourth item is performed exclus-

Box 2.6 Examples of Balance of Payments Accounts

In the main text we noted that international transactions give rise to deficit items when they involve an outflow of our *money*, and are surplus entries when they imply *receipt* of our money. This includes both 'above-line' or current account as well as 'below-line' capital account transactions. Example: a Swedish company which exports a car to France and receives Kroner for it gives rise to a surplus in the current account (export of goods), while if it sells stock to a French resident it causes a surplus entry in the capital account (capital and financial account, portfolio investment). In Table 2.10 we give some examples of transactions and how they are recorded, using the simple rule. Note that the transactions are always symmetric in their effect, when properly recorded.

ively by the monetary authorities, usually the central bank. This balance is also called the **official account**. The official account captures the fact that the monetary authorities may act as the residual agent in the balancing process. When the official account is in deficit, it means that residents have sent more money abroad than they received, through either commercial transactions—the current account—or financial transactions—the financial account—or any combination of both. This was the case of the euro area in 2005, as can be seen in Table 2.9. In that case the monetary authorities make up the difference, bringing domestic money back home; hence the positive surplus entry in the table. Put differently, the monetary authorities have sold some of their **foreign exchange reserves** (foreign currencies that they own) and received domestic currency for it in return.[15] Such actions are called **foreign exchange market interventions**. When a monetary authority buys back its own currency, it necessarily spends some of the foreign currencies that it holds. The distinction between private and official financing is further taken up in Section 2.4.4.

2.4.3 Errors and Omissions

There is a final item in Table 2.8, 'Errors and omissions' (line IIC), which requires some explanation. By definition, the total of the balance of payments should be zero:

$$(2.9) \quad \underset{\substack{\text{current} \\ \text{account}}}{CA} + \underset{\substack{\text{capital and} \\ \text{financial} \\ \text{account}}}{FA} + \underset{\substack{\text{official} \\ \text{intervention}}}{OFF} = 0.$$

While accounting guarantees the consistency of current and financial accounts in theory, the nature of data gathering for payments statistics virtually guarantees discrepancies. Trade data originate with customs authorities. Financial data come from the banking system, since international transactions are mediated by financial institutions. Official interventions are known by the monetary authorities, which are often responsible for collecting the data and producing the balance of payments accounts. Because these data come from different sources, relationship (2.9) will never hold in practice. This is why an additional account called 'Errors and omissions' is needed. This is necessary to obtain zero at the bottom of the table. While there are genuine mistakes—the sheer volume of data to be treated is an invitation for errors—there may also be omissions which are less than innocent.[16] Table 2.9 shows that errors and omissions can at times be embarrassingly large.

2.4.4 The Meaning of the Accounts

A current account imbalance must be matched, or financed, one-for-one by either the private financial account or official interventions by the monetary authorities. What is the difference between the

---

[15] Note that this follows the rule of thumb mentioned above for thinking about the sign of an entry in the balance of payments: ask yourself whether it means that domestic money comes in (a plus) or goes out (a minus).

[16] By definition, the sum of the current accounts of all countries in the world should equal zero. In fact, it is systematically negative, as receipts are 'omitted' more often than expenditures.

Table 2.10 **Balance of Payments: Some Examples**

Transaction	Surplus (+) or deficit (−)	Country	Account
UK exports chemicals to France to the amount of £1 million	+£1 m	UK	Goods and services
	−£1 m	France	Goods and services
French school trains German cyclists for €500,000	+€500,000	France	Goods and services
	−€500,000	Germany	Goods and services
German construction company is paid SF 5 million to build a Swiss bridge	+SF5 m	Germany	Goods and services
	−SF5 m	Switzerland	Goods and services
Swiss ski instructor is paid salary of €80,000 for work performed in Austria	+€80,000	Switzerland	International income
	−€80,000	Austria	International income
UK fast food franchises remit £1 million in profits to headquarters in the USA	+£1 m	USA	International income
	−£1 m	UK	International income
Austrian government gives €3 million in relief aid to tsunami victims in Thailand	+€3 m	Thailand	Current transfers
	−€3 m	Austria	Current transfers
Estonian worker in Denmark sends DK 100,000 to family in Tallinn	+DK100,000	Estonia	Current transfers
	−DK100,000	Denmark	Current transfers
Spanish government forgives debt of €10 million owed by Peru	+€10 m	Peru	Capital account
	−€10 m	Spain	Capital account
Swedish investor purchases a factory in Germany for €100 million	+€100 m	Germany	Financial account / direct investment
	−€100 m	Sweden	Financial account / direct investment
Portuguese bank buys €20 million of stock in German company from French bank based in France	+€20 m	France	Financial account / portfolio investment
	−€20 m	Portugal	Financial account / portfolio investment
UK bank based in London lends £50 million to subsidiary in Ireland	+£50 m	Ireland	Other investment
	−£50 m	UK	Other investment
Slovenian resident transfers €100,000 from home account to a bank account in Italy	+€100,000	Italy	Financial account / portfolio investment
	−€100,000	Slovenia	Financial account / portfolio investment
Bank of England purchases €5 billion from the European Central Bank (ECB) paying with pound sterling	−€5 b	UK	Reserve assets account
	+€5 b	European Monetary Union	Reserve assets account

two mechanisms? A country with a current account deficit makes more payments abroad than it receives. More domestic money must be flowing out than is entering the country. If the private financial account is in balance, the imbalance between inflows and outflows must translate into excess supply of the domestic currency on exchange markets worldwide. This excess of sellers over buyers —or excess supply—will depreciate, or reduce the value of, the domestic currency.[17]

Now two things are possible. First, the monetary authorities may wish to prevent the depreciation. They must then step in immediately and buy up the excess supply of the domestic currency—using their own holdings of foreign currency. This transaction represents a positive entry in the official financial account (OFF) in (2.9). The country's current account deficit is financed by sales of foreign exchange reserves.[18]

The second possibility is that the central bank may refuse to intervene (OFF = 0). In this case the domestic currency would be in excess supply on world markets. With an excess of sellers, it would tend to depreciate, or lose value. This exchange rate depreciation works towards reducing the current account deficit, as foreign goods become more expensive and domestic goods become cheaper. It will also prompt capital inflows as foreigners take advantage of the low exchange rate to acquire domestic assets. In the accounting identity (2.9), either the current account deficit disappears or the private financial account is positive, or both. Similarly, a current account surplus can be financed privately (a negative financial account), publicly (purchases of foreign exchange reserves), or both.

The monetary authorities determine if, and to what extent, a current account imbalance translates into a change in the exchange rate. At one extreme, the monetary authorities may be committed to maintaining a fixed exchange rate. If so, they must intervene in the market, purchasing or selling foreign exchange in whatever amount necessary to keep the exchange rate constant. At the other extreme, the monetary authorities never intervene and the exchange rate is determined solely by market forces. This is the **overall balance**—sometimes called the balance of payments (BoP).[19] It is the sum of the current and financial accounts (including errors and omissions). The overall balance attracts special attention because it is the mirror image of interventions by the monetary authorities during the period under study and reveals their behaviour. Ignoring errors and omissions,

$$(2.10) \qquad BoP = CA + FA = -OFF.$$

A balance of payments surplus means that the authorities have acquired foreign exchange reserves. Put differently, they have sold the domestic currency to match an excess demand for the domestic currency, thus preventing or reducing pressure for an exchange rate appreciation (OFF < O). Accordingly, the official account is in deficit. A balance of payments deficit corresponds to a loss of reserves as the monetary authorities buy back the domestic currency to prevent a depreciation (OFF > O). The official account would then be in surplus.

---

[17] Later chapters will explore this process in much greater detail. A currency appreciates when its value in terms of other currencies increases. Conversely, if its value decreases, we speak of a depreciation.

[18] Technically, this can be thought of as an official credit from foreign monetary authorities, or the calling in of loans made to them in previous periods.

[19] It is misleading to use this term because, strictly speaking, the term 'balance of payments' refers to the whole set of accounts. The official balance is its bottom line and the one that attracts the most attention. We defer to tradition and use the symbol 'BoP' for the official balance.

❶ Summary

1 The gross domestic product (GDP) can be defined in three equivalent ways: (1) as the sum of final sales, (2) the sum of factor incomes, or (3) the sum of value added. GDP is a flow variable measured over a well-defined time interval, usually a year.

2 Because nominal GDP measures final sales at market prices, an increase in the price level leads to an increase in GDP even if quantities sold are constant. Real GDP is computed by pricing current output with constant prices, corresponding to a chosen base year.

3 The GDP deflator is the ratio of nominal to real GDP. It is one measure of the price level. Inflation is approximately equal to the difference between the nominal and real GDP growth rates. Price indexes, also used to compute inflation rates, use constant-weights baskets of goods and services.

4 Measurement of GDP is imperfect, costly, and time-consuming. A large amount of economic activity is unmeasured, such as household services and the underground economy. Yet year-on-year comparisons, such as annual growth rates, are less affected by measurement problems.

5 GDP is equal to the sum of consumption, investment, government spending, and the current account ($Y = C + I + G + CA$). At the same time, GDP is equal to consumption, plus private sector savings, plus net taxes (gross taxes less public transfers received by the private sector) ($Y = C + S + T$). It follows as an identity that the current account surplus is equal to the surplus of the government plus the surplus of the private sector ($CA = (T - G) + (S - I)$).

6 The balance of payments is a record of current account transactions and their financial counterparts, the capital and financial (or simply financial) account. The current account is the sum of the merchandise, invisibles, and transfer accounts. Any surplus or deficit must be matched by an equal and opposite sum of private long-term capital, short-term financial errors and omissions, and official accounts.

7 When the monetary authorities undertake to maintain the value of their country's exchange rate, they must intervene on exchange rate markets to match any possible balance of payments imbalance. Conversely, the exchange rate floats freely when the monetary authorities refrain from intervening; then all adjustment for balance of payments equilibrium occurs within the private sector, as a result of changes in the market-determined exchange rate.

☻ Key Concepts

- accounting identities
- gross domestic product (GDP)
- flow versus stock variables
- final versus intermediate sales
- value added
- gross national income (GNI)
- nominal and real GDP
- GDP deflator
- price index, consumer price index (CPI)
- underground economy
- circular flow
- net taxes

- private income
- consumption
- financial intermediation
- savings, net private saving
- physical capital
- investment
- absorption
- personal disposable income
- depreciation
- net domestic product (NDP)

- balance of payments
- balance of goods and services, of international income and current transfers
- current account
- capital and financial account
- official account
- foreign exchange rate reserves
- foreign exchange market intervention, official account
- overall balance

❷ Exercises

1 You are given the following data:

GDP	2,500
Depreciation	250
Before-tax corporate profits	500
Social security contributions	350
Transfers to households and firms	500
Net interest to foreigners	100
Proprietary income	35
Net corporate saving	300
Indirect taxes	500
Subsidies to enterprises	200
Fines and fees	50
Net remittances to rest of world	250
Corporate taxes	50
Consolidated government deficit	50
Personal taxes	750
Household savings	100
Investment expenditure	600

Compute: NDP, national income, personal income, personal disposable income, consumption, government purchases, GDP, the current account balance. State your assumptions clearly.

2 What happens to GDP when a music teacher marries his student whom he was tutoring previous to the marriage, but stops billing her for her private lessons? What happens when a housewife becomes self-employed as her own day-care centre?

3 'Services do not contribute to GDP as much as industry because industry produces *things*—tangible goods.' Comment on this using what you have learned about the national income accounts.

4 I bought my house for €100,000. I have just sold it for €200,000, and the estate agent received a 10% commission from the buyer. What is the effect on GDP?

5 Suppose you have the following data on prices and quantities transacted:

Prices (€)

	Apples	Pears	Petrol
2006	1.0	2.0	5.0
2007	1.0	3.0	6.0

Quantities

	Apples	Pears	Petrol
2006	300	100	50
2007	400	150	40

(a) If the economy produced all three (and only these three) goods, compute the nominal GDP in both periods, and real GDP at 2006 prices. What is the rate of inflation in 2007, as measured by the change in the GDP deflator?

(b) Suppose a CPI is constructed using weights corresponding to quantities produced in 2006. What is the rate of inflation measured by the CPI?

6 Give the three definitions of GDP. Explain whether the following transactions contribute to UK GDP, and, if so, explain how all three definitions apply.

(a) A resident of York purchases a bag of sweets produced in Manchester.

(b) A tourist visiting York purchases a bag of sweets produced in Manchester.

(c) An operator of a Slovakian food chain purchases a large order of sweets produced in Manchester which are sent in the measurement period to Bratislava.

(d) A Manchester businessman purchases a machine to mould the sweets, which is manufactured in the Czech Republic.

(e) A store manager purchases several boxes of sweets from the Manchester sweet company, but stores them in the stock room, where they sit until the beginning of next year.

(f) The city government of York purchases several boxes of sweets from the Manchester sweet company for its reception for the Lord Mayor.

7 Over the past five years taxes were about 60% of GDP in Sweden. Yet disposable income over the past five years also amounted to 60% of GDP. How can these numbers be reconciled?

8 'Commuters increase GDP because they send home a large fraction of their earnings.' Comment.

9 How would the following transactions be recorded in the *French* balance of payments?

  ◆ A French resident buys an Austin Mini produced in the United Kingdom.
  ◆ A French resident purchases stocks in a German corporation from a German bank based in Germany.
  ◆ A French national living in Switzerland buys stock in a French company from a bank based in Switzerland.
  ◆ A French resident builds a house in Italy, paying Italian residents to do the job.
  ◆ A French resident gives money to Greenpeace located in Hamburg, Germany.
  ◆ A French banker sends a wire transfer of euros to his daughter at the Humboldt University of Berlin.
  ◆ The same French banker wires euros from his bank account in Berlin to his account in Paris.
  ◆ A Tunisian worker in Marseilles sends money to his family in Tunis.
  ◆ Peugeot SA, a French concern, pays dividends to a resident of Finland.
  ◆ Profits of Owen Corning, a US company, are reinvested in capacity expansion of a factory in Fontainebleau, France.
  ◆ The Banque de France (a part of the European Central Bank) purchases Danish kroner to prevent the exchange rate (in euro) from falling in Copenhagen.
  ◆ A French resident of Colmar, a town in Alsace near the German border, smuggles home a stereo purchased in Freiburg (Germany).

10 In Table 2.9, China has a very large surplus in the *overall balance*—many times greater than other countries shown. What does this mean for the official transactions balance? What does this imply for the behaviour of the People's National Bank of China?

→ Essay Questions

1 Evaluate the following statement: 'Bringing the underground economy above ground would increase the GDP, but worsen tax receipts and the balance of payments.'

2 In recent years firms in Europe as well as in the USA have begun to 'outsource' or divest themselves of many traditional service functions, purchasing them on the market instead. Companies are increasingly obtaining computer, catering, legal, consulting, and other business services by ordering them from outside, independent companies. What is the effect of outsourcing on GDP? (Think of the example of a firm which turns its cafeteria into an independent contractor.) How does your answer depend on what the new firm does with its independence?

3 GDP mixes up everything. It includes 'goods' such as apples we eat and theatre shows we enjoy, but also 'bads' such as petrol burnt in traffic congestion and burial costs. It ignores many 'goods' as well: the value of a good neighbour or the free time that we can spend watching a sunset. Comment and explore how you would compute gross domestic happiness?

4 Countries which generate most economic activity from the exploitation of natural resources often experience large fluctuations in their national income and product account results. Explain why this might be the case, carefully defining the terms value added and costs of production. Why might the national income and product accounts lose their relevance for these countries? How might the problem be solved?

5 'The EU member states don't need balance of payments statistics. The individual states of the USA get along fine without them.' Discuss.

PART II
The Macroeconomy in the Long Run

Part II studies the long run. The long run is what economists mean when they talk about the behaviour of an economy over a period of decades, rather than over short time spans of quarters or a few years. It describes attainable and sustainable aspects of the national economy, and goes far beyond the short-term perspective of the business cycle fluctuations described in Chapter 1. Most important, it represents the basis of sustainable evolution of standards of living.

We begin with economic growth, the most fundamental of all long-run macroeconomic phenomena. Economic growth is the rate at which the real output of a nation or a region increases over time. As the ultimate determinant of the poverty or wealth of nations, sustained economic growth is a central aspect of the long run. Because this is such an important topic, two chapters are dedicated to studying it.

Next, we look at the labour market, one of the most important markets in modern economies. In the labour market, households trade time at work for the ability to purchase goods and services in the goods market. We will see how labour is allocated: where it comes from, who demands it, and how to think about unemployment.

The last chapter in Part II introduces the long-run role of monetary and financial variables: money, interest rates, and the nominal exchange rate, which are generally denoted in nominal terms—in pounds or euros or dollars. Nominal variables determine the real terms of exchange between goods within a country, between countries, or over time—the command of resources represented by one type of goods and services over others.

The Fundamentals of Economic Growth

3

The consequences for human welfare involved in questions like these are simply staggering: Once one starts to think about them, it is hard to think about anything else.

R. E. Lucas, Jr[1]

3.1 Overview

The output of economies, as measured by the gross domestic product at constant prices, tends to grow in most countries over time. Is economic growth a universal phenomenon? Why are national growth rates of the richest economies so similar? Why do some countries exhibit periods of spectacular growth, such as Japan in 1950–1973, the USA in 1820–1870, Europe after the Second World War, or China and India more recently? Why do others sometimes experience long periods of stagnation, as China did until the last two decades of the twentieth century? Do growth rates tend to converge, so that periods of above-average growth compensate for periods of below-average growth? What does this imply for levels of GDP per capita? These questions are among the most important ones in economics, for sustained growth determines the wealth and poverty of nations.

This chapter will teach us how to think systematically about growth and its determinants. The production function is the tool that will help us identify the most important regularities of economic growth among nations around the world. These stylized facts serve to point economic theory in a sensible direction. First, investment can add to the capital stock, and a greater capital stock enables workers to produce more. Second, the working population or labour force can grow, which means that more workers are potentially available for market production. This growth can arise for many reasons—increases in births two or three decades ago, immigration now, or increased labour force participation by people of all ages, especially by women. The third reason is **technological progress**. As knowledge accumulates and techniques improve, workers and the machines they work with become more productive. For both theoretical and empirical reasons, technological progress turns out to be the ultimate driver of economic growth. Because it is such an important topic, a detailed discussion of technological progress will be postponed to Chapter 4.

3.2 Thinking about Economic Growth: Facts and Stylized Facts

3.2.1 The Economic Growth Phenomenon

Despite setbacks arising from wars, natural disasters, or epidemics, economic growth seems like an immutable economic law of nature. Over the centuries, it has been responsible for significant, long-run material improvements in the way the world lives. Table 3.1 displays the annual rate of increase in real GDP—the standard measure of economic

---

[1]   Robert E. Lucas, Jr (1937–), Chicago economist and Nobel Prize Laureate in 1995, is generally regarded as one of the most influential contemporary macroeconomists. Among his many fundamental contributions to the field, he has researched extensively the determinants of economic growth.

Table 3.1 The Growth Phenomenon

	Average rates of growth in GDP (% per annum)							Av. growth GDP per capita 1820–2006 (% per annum)
	1820–2006	1820–1870	1870–1913	1913–1950	1950–1973	1973–2001	1973–2006	
Austria	2.1	1.4	2.4	0.2	5.2	2.5	2.4	1.6
Belgium	2.1	2.2	2.0	1.0	4.0	2.1	2.1	1.5
Denmark	2.4	1.9	2.6	2.5	3.7	2.0	2.0	1.6
Finland	2.6	1.6	2.7	2.7	4.8	2.4	2.6	1.8
France	2.0	1.4	1.6	1.1	4.9	2.3	2.1	1.6
Germany	2.2	2.0	2.8	0.3	5.5	1.8	1.7	1.6
Italy	2.1	1.2	1.9	1.5	5.5	2.3	2.0	1.5
Netherlands	2.4	1.7	2.1	2.4	4.6	2.4	2.3	1.4
Norway	2.7	2.2	2.2	2.9	4.0	3.4	3.2	1.9
Sweden	2.3	1.6	2.1	2.7	3.7	1.9	2.0	1.6
Switzerland	2.4	1.9	2.5	2.6	4.4	1.2	1.3	1.7
United Kingdom	2.0	2.0	1.9	1.2	2.9	2.1	2.2	1.4
Japan	2.7	0.1	2.4	2.2	8.9	2.7	2.6	1.9
United States	3.6	4.1	3.9	2.8	3.9	3.0	2.9	1.7

Source: Maddison (2007).

output of a geographic entity—for various periods in a number of currently wealthy countries since 1820. (The early data are clearly rough estimates.) Over almost two centuries, GDP has increased by 60- to 100-fold or more, while per capita GDP has increased by 12- to 30-fold. Our grandparents are right when they say that we are much better off than they were.

The table also reveals that the growth process is not very smooth. We will see that this variation reflects the effect of wars, colonial expansion and annexation, and dramatic changes in population as well as political, cultural, and scientific revolutions. Despite these swings, it is striking that the overall average growth of GDP per capita is remarkably similar across these countries, regardless of where they come from.

Small average annual changes displayed in Table 3.1 cumulate surprisingly fast. The advanced economies of the world grow by roughly 2–4% per year. A growth rate difference of 2% per annum compounds into 49% after 20 years, and 170% after half a century. The recent phenomenal growth successes

of China and India and the troubling slowdowns in Germany and Japan show that growth is by no means an automatic birthright. Moreover, fortunes can change: as Box 3.1 shows, China was a leading world economy in the fourteenth century, only to fall into a half-millenium of decline and stagnation. For this reason, politicians and policy-makers are concerned about persistent differences in growth rates between countries.

3.2.2 The Sources of Growth: The Aggregate Production Function

It is common and useful for economists to reason abstractly about economic growth. To do so, they usually think of an economy producing a single output—real GDP—using various inputs, or ingredients. We discussed these inputs, the factors of production, in Chapter 2. To recap, these are:

(1) labour;

(2) physical capital, which is equipment and structures;

(3) land and other measurable factors of production.

Box 3.1   China and the Chinese Puzzle of Economic Growth

Most scholars agree that, at the end of the fourteenth century, China was the world's most advanced economy. While Europe was just beginning to recover from centuries of inward-looking backwardness and relative decline, Chinese society had reached a high degree of administrative, scientific, and economic sophistication. Innovations such as accounting, gunpowder, the maritime compass, moveable type, and porcelain manufacture are just a few attributable to the Middle Empire. Marco Polo was one of many famous European traders who tried to break into the Chinese market. According to crude estimates by economic historian Angus Maddison, fourteenth-century Western Europe and China were on roughly equal footing in terms of market output—and many experts claim the Chinese were technically more advanced.[2] Yet over the next six centuries, standards of living increased 25-fold in Western Europe compared with only sevenfold in China.

Most of that sevenfold increase in GDP per capita has occurred in China over the last 25 years. This makes the Chinese story a growth phenomenon without comparison. After adopting far-reaching market economy reforms in the 1980s, economic growth has averaged a phenomenal 10.2% per annum since 1990. At this rate, the economy will double in size every seven years.

If this growth continues, China will easily reach the standard of living of poorer EU countries by 2025.

The Chinese growth phenomenon raises a host of intriguing questions. Why did China stagnate for centuries, while Europe flourished? Why did China literally explode in the 1990s? While there are many theories, it is widely agreed that the Chinese success story would have been impossible without China's recent policy of openness to international trade and foreign direct investment. Almost as a converse proposition, some historians associate the economic stagnation of China after the fifteenth century with the grounding of 3,500 great sailing ships of the Ming dynasty in 1433, the world's largest naval expeditionary fleet under the command of Admiral Zheng He. A policy of 'inward perfection', fear of Mongol threats, lack of government funding, and a deep mistrust of merchant classes which benefited most from the international excursions of the Imperial 'Treasure Fleet', all led China to close itself off from foreign influences, with disastrous consequences. For many economists, this is a warning shot about potential risks of unbridled anti-globalization. In Chapter 4, we revisit the theme of international trade and economic growth in more detail.

Growth theory asks how sustained economic growth across nations and over time is possible. Do we produce more because we employ more inputs, or because the inputs themselves become more productive over time, or both? What is the contribution of each factor? To think abstractly about growth, we will need a number of tools. The most important tool we will use is the **production function**. The production function relates the output of an economy—its GDP—to productive inputs. The two most important productive inputs are the physical **capital stock**, represented by K, and labour employed, represented by L. The capital stock includes factories, buildings, and machinery as well as roads and railroads, electricity, and telephone

networks. Employment or labour is the total number of hours worked in a given period of time. The labour measure L is the product of the average number of workers employed (N) during a period (usually a year) and the average hours (h) that they work during that period ($L = Nh$). We speak of person-hours of labour input.[3] Symbolically, the production function is written:

(3.1) $$Y = F(K, L).$$
$$+ \quad +$$

---

[2]   Maddison (1991: 10).

[3]   Since output and labour inputs are flows, they could also be measured per quarter or per month, but should be measured over the same time interval. Note that capital is a stock, usually measured at the beginning of the current or end of the last period. We discussed the important distinction between stocks and flows in Chapter 1.

Box 3.2 For the Mathematically Minded: The Cobb–Douglas Production Function

The use of mathematics in economics can bring clarity and precision to the discussion of economic relationships. An illustration of this is the notion of a production function, which formalizes the relationship between inputs (capital and labour) and output (GDP). One particularly well-known and widely-used example is the Cobb–Douglas production function:

(3.2) $Y = K^{\alpha} L^{1-\alpha}$,

where α is a parameter which lies between 0 and 1, and is called the elasticity of output with respect to capital: a 1% increase in the capital input results in an α increase in output.[4] Similarly $1 - \alpha$ is the elasticity of output with respect to labour input. It is easy to see that the Cobb–Douglas production function possesses all the properties described in the text.

Diminishing marginal productivity

The marginal productivity of capital is given by the derivative of output with respect to capital K: $\partial Y / \partial K = \alpha K^{\alpha-1} L^{1-\alpha} = \alpha (L/K)^{1-\alpha}$. Since $\alpha < 1$, the marginal product of capital is a decreasing function of K and an increasing function of L. Similarly, the marginal productivity of labour is given by $\partial Y / \partial L = (1 - \alpha)(K/L)^{\alpha}$, which is increasing in K and decreasing in L.

Constant returns to scale

The Cobb–Douglas function has constant returns to scale: for a positive number t, which can be thought of as a scaling factor,

(3.3) $(tK)^{\alpha}(tL)^{1-\alpha} = t^{\alpha} t^{1-\alpha} K^{\alpha} L^{1-\alpha} = t K^{\alpha} L^{1-\alpha} = tY$.

Intensive form

The intensive form of the Cobb–Douglas production function is obtained by dividing both sides of (3.2) by L, which is the same as setting $t = 1/L$ in equation (3.3), to obtain:

(3.4) $Y/L = y = (K^{\alpha} L^{1-\alpha})/L = K^{\alpha} L^{-\alpha} = (K/L)^{\alpha} = k^{\alpha}$,

where $k = K/L$ and $y = Y/L$ are the intensive form measures of input and output defined in the text. Since $\alpha < 1$, the intensive form production is indeed well represented by Figure 3.2.

The plus ('+') signs beneath the two inputs signify that output rises with either more capital or more labour.[5]

The production function is a useful, powerful, and widely-used short-cut. It reduces many and complex types of physical capital and labour input to two. In microeconomics, the production function helps economists study the output of individual firms. In macroeconomics, it is used to think about the output of an entire economy. Box 3.2 presents and discusses the characteristics of a widely-used production function, the Cobb–Douglas production function.

The production function is a *technological relationship*. It does not reflect the profitability of production, and it has nothing to do with the quality of life or the desirability of work. It is meant to capture the fact that goods and services are produced using factors of production: here, equipment and hours of labour. In the following, we describe some basic properties that are typically assumed for production functions.

Marginal productivity

One central property of the production function describes how output reacts to a small increase in one of its inputs, holding other inputs constant. Consider an economy producing output with workers and a stock of capital equipment. Then imagine that a new unit of capital—a new machine—is added to the capital stock, raising it by the amount ΔK, while holding labour input constant.[6] Output will also rise, by ΔY. The ratio $\Delta Y / \Delta K$, the amount of new output per unit of incremental capital, is called the economy's **marginal productivity**. Now imagine

---

[4] To see this, note that the elasticity of output with respect to capital is defined as $(dY/dK)(K/Y)$ and is given by $(\alpha K^{\alpha-1} L^{1-\alpha})(K^{1-\alpha} L^{\alpha-1}) = \alpha$. Similarly, $1 - \alpha$ is the elasticity of output with respect to the labour input.

[5] Formally, this means that the two first partial derivatives $F_K(K, L) \equiv \partial F / \partial K$ and $F_L(K, L) \equiv \partial F / \partial L$ are positive.

[6] Throughout this book, the symbol 'Δ' is used to denote a step change in a variable over some period of time.

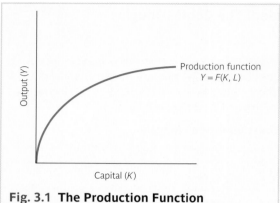

Fig. 3.1 The Production Function

Holding labour input L (the number of hours worked) unchanged, adding to the capital stock K (available productive equipment) allows an economy to produce more, but in smaller and smaller increments.

repeating the experiment, adding capital again and again to the production process, always holding labour input constant. Should we expect output to increase by the same amount for each additional increment of capital?

Generally, the answer is no. As more and more capital is brought into the production process, it works with less and less of the given labour input, and the increases in output become smaller and smaller. This is the principle of **diminishing marginal productivity**. It is represented in Figure 3.1, which shows how output rises with capital, holding labour unchanged. The flattening of the curve illustrates the assumption. In fact, the slope of the curve is equal to the economy's marginal productivity.

It turns out that the principle of diminishing marginal productivity also applies to the labour input. Increasing the employment of person-hours will raise output; but output from additional person-hours declines as more and more labour is being applied to a fixed stock of capital.

Returns to scale

Output increases when either inputs of capital or labour increases. But what happens if both capital and labour increase in the same proportion? Suppose, for example, that the inputs of capital and labour were both doubled—increased by 100%. If output doubles as a result, the production function is said

to have **constant returns to scale**. If a doubling of inputs leads to more than a doubling of output, we observe **increasing returns to scale**. **Decreasing returns** is the case when output increases by less than 100%. It is believed that decreasing returns to scale are unlikely. Increasing returns, in contrast, cannot be ruled out, but we will ignore this possibility until Chapter 4. In fact, the bulk of the evidence points in the direction of constant returns to scale.

With constant returns we can think of the link between inputs and output—the production function—as a zoom lens: as long as we scale up the inputs, so does the output. In this case, an attractive property of constant returns production functions emerges: output per hour of work—the **output–labour ratio** (Y/L)—depends only on capital per hour of work—the **capital–labour ratio** (K/L). This simplification allows us to write the production function in the following intensive form:[7]

(3.5) $y = f(k),$

where $y = Y/L$ and $k = K/L$. The output–labour ratio Y/L is also called the average productivity of labour: it says how much, on average, is being produced with one unit (one hour) of work.[8] The capital–labour ratio K/L measures the capital intensity of production.

The intensive-form production function is depicted in Figure 3.2. Because of diminishing marginal productivity, the curve becomes flatter as the capital–labour ratio increases. The intensive-form representation of the production function is convenient because it expresses the average productivity of labour in an economy as a function of the average stock of capital with which that labour is employed. If average hours worked per capita are held constant, the intensive form production function is a good indicator of standards of living (Y/N).

---

[7] The constant returns property implies that if we scale up K and L by a factor t, Y is scaled up by the exactly same factor—for all positive numbers t, it is true that $tY = F(tK, tL)$. In the text we use the case $t = 2$; we double all inputs and produce twice as much. If we choose $t = 1/L$, we have $y = Y/L = F(k, 1)$. Rename this $f(k)$ because $F(k, 1)$ depends on k only. The intensive production function $f(k)$ expresses output produced per unit of labour (y) as a function of the capital intensity of production (k).

[8] It is important to recall the distinction between average productivity (Y/L) and marginal productivity ($\Delta Y/\Delta L$).

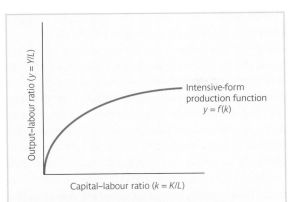

Fig. 3.2 The Production Function in Intensive Form

The production function shows that the output–labour ratio y grows with the capital–labour ratio k. Its slope is the marginal productivity of labour since with constant returns to scale $\Delta Y/\Delta K = \Delta y/\Delta k$. The principle of declining marginal productivity implies that the curve becomes flatter as k increases.

It follows from (3.5) that in a world of constant returns, the absolute size of an economy does not matter for its economic performance. Indeed, Ireland, Singapore, and Switzerland have matched or exceeded the per capita GDP of the USA, the UK, or Germany.

3.2.3 Kaldor's Five Stylized Facts of Economic Growth

At this point it will prove helpful to look at the data: How have inputs and outputs in real-world economies changed over time? In 1961, the British economist Nicholas Kaldor (1908–1986) studied economic growth in many countries over long periods of time and isolated several **stylized facts** about economic growth which remain valid to this day. Stylized facts are empirical regularities found in the data. Kaldor's stylized facts will organize our discussion of economic growth and restrict our attention to theories which help us to think about it, just as a police detective uses clues to limit the number of possible suspects in a criminal investigation.

The first of Kaldor's stylized facts concerns the behaviour of output per person-hour and capital per person-hour.

Stylized Fact No. 1: output per capita and capital intensity keep increasing

The most remarkable aspect of the growth phenomenon is that real GDP seems to grow without bound. Yet labour input, measured in person-hours of work (L), grows much more slowly than both capital (K) and output (Y). Put differently, average productivity (Y/L) and capital intensity (K/L) keep rising. Because income per capita is closely related to average productivity or output per hour of work, economic growth implies a continuing increase in material standards of living. Figure 3.3 presents the evolution of the output–labour and capital–labour ratios in three important industrial economies.

Stylized Fact No. 2: the capital–output ratio exhibits little or no trend

As they grow in a seemingly unbounded fashion, the capital stock and output tend to track each other. As a consequence, the ratio of capital to output (K/Y) shows little or no systematic trend. This is apparent from Figure 3.3, but Table 3.2 shows that it is only approximately true. For example, while output per hour in the USA has increased by roughly 600% since 1913, the ratio of capital to output actually fell slightly over the same period. At any rate, the capital–output ratio may not be exactly constant, but it is far from exhibiting the steady, unrelenting increases in average productivity and capital intensity described in Stylized Fact No. 1.

Stylized Fact No. 3: hourly wages keep rising

The long-run increases in the ratios of output and capital to labour (Y/L and K/L) mean that, over time, an

Table 3.2 **Capital–Output Ratios (K/Y), 1913–2008**					
	1913	**1950**	**1973**	**1992**	**2008***
France	n.a.	1.6	1.6	2.3	2.7
Germany	n.a.	1.8	1.9	2.3	2.5
Japan	0.9	1.8	1.7	3.0	3.7
UK	0.8	0.8	1.3	1.8	2.1
USA	3.3	2.5	2.1	2.4	3.0

* Estimates
Sources: Maddison (1995); OECD; authors' calculations.

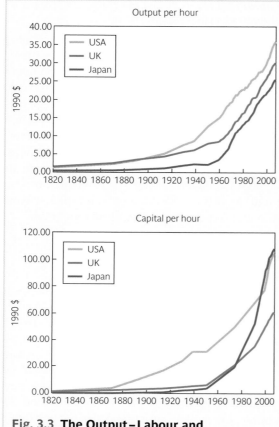

Fig. 3.3 The Output–Labour and Capital–Labour Ratios in Three Countries

Output–labour and capital–labour ratios are continuously increasing. Growth accelerated in the USA in the early twentieth century, and after 1950 in Japan and the UK.

Sources: Maddison (1995); Groningen Total Economy Database, available at <www.ggdc.net>, OECD, *Economic Outlook*, chained.

hour of work produces ever more output. Simply put, workers become more productive. It stands to reason, then, that their wages per hour also rise (this link will be shown more formally in Chapter 5). Growth delivers ever-increasing living standards for workers.

Stylized Fact No. 4: the rate of profit is trendless

Note that the capital–output ratio (K/Y) is just the inverse of the average productivity of capital (Y/K).

The absence of a clear trend for the capital–output ratio (K/Y) implies that average productivity too is trendless: over time, the same amount of equipment delivers about the same amount of output. It is to be expected therefore that the rate of profit does not exhibit a trend either. This stands in sharp contrast with labour productivity, whose secular increase allows a continuing rise in real wages. Yet income flowing to owners of capital has increased, but only because the stock of capital itself has increased. Indeed, with a stable rate of profit, income from capital increases proportionately to the capital stock.

Stylized Fact No. 5: the relative income shares of GDP paid to labour and capital are trendless

We just saw that incomes from labour and capital increase secularly. Surprisingly perhaps, it turns out that they also tend to increase at about the same rate, so that the distribution of total income (GDP) between capital and labour has been relatively stable. In other words, the labour and capital shares have no long-run trend. We will have to explain this remarkable fact.

3.2.4 The Steady State

Stylized facts are not meant to be literally true at all times, certainly not from one year to the other. Instead, they highlight central tendencies in the data. As we study growth, we are tracking moving targets, variables that keep increasing all the time, apparently without any upper limits. Thinking about moving targets is easier if we can identify stable relationships among them. This is why Kaldor's stylized facts will prove helpful. Another example of this approach is given by the evolution of GDP: it seems to be growing without bounds, but could its growth rate be roughly constant? The answer is yes, but only on average, over five or ten years or more. In Chapter 1, we noted the important phenomenon of business cycles, periods of fast growth followed by periods of slow growth or even declining output. As we look at secular economic growth, we are not interested in business cycles. We ignore shorter-term fluctuations—compare Figures 1.4 and 1.5 in Chapter 1—and focus on the long run.

This is why it is convenient to imagine how things would look if there were no business cycles at all. Such a situation is called a **steady state**. Its characteristic is that some variables, like the GDP growth ratios, or the ratios described in the stylized facts—the capital–output ratio or the labour income share—are constant. Just as the stylized facts are not to be taken literally, think of the steady state as the long-run average behaviour that we never reach, but move around in real time. From the perspective of 10 years ago, we thought of today as the long run, but now we can see all the details that were unknown back then. Given that modern GDPs double every 10–30 years, a temporary boom or recession which shifts today's GDP by one or two percentage points amounts to little in the greater order of things, the powerful phenomenon of continuous long-run growth. Steady states—and stylized facts—are not just convenient ways of making our lives simpler; they are essential tools for distinguishing the forest from the trees.

3.3 Capital Accumulation and Economic Growth[9]

3.3.1 Savings, Investment, and Capital Accumulation

Kaldor's first stylized fact highlights a relationship between output per hour and capital per hour. This link is in fact predicted by the production function in its intensive form. It suggests that a good place to start if we want to explain economic growth is to understand why and how the capital stock rises over time. We will thus study how the savings of households—foregone consumption—is transformed in an economy into investment in capital goods, which causes the capital stock to grow.

The central insight is delivered by the familiar circular flow diagram in Figure 2.2. GDP represents income to households, either directly to workers or to the owners of firms. Households and firms save part of their income. These savings flow into the financial system—banks, stock markets, pension funds, etc. The financial system channels these resources to borrowers: firms, households, and the government. In particular, firms borrow—including from their own savings—to purchase capital goods used in production. This expansion of productive capacity, in turn, raises output, which then raises future savings and investment, and so on.

We now examine this process in more detail. To keep things simple, we first assume that the size of the population, the labour force, and the numbers of hours worked are all constant. At this stage, we ask some fundamental questions: can **capital accumulation** proceed without bound? Does more saving mean faster growth? And since saving means postponing consumption, is it always a good idea to save more?

3.3.2 Capital Accumulation and Depreciation

Let us start from the national accounts of Chapter 2. Identity (2.7) shows that investment (I) can be financed either by private savings by firms or households (S), by government savings (the consolidated budget surplus, or $T - G$), or the net savings of foreigners (the current account deficit, $Z - X$):

$$(3.6) \qquad I = S + (T - G) + (Z - X).$$

As a description of the long-run or a steady state, suppose that the government budget is in balance ($T = G$), and the current account surplus equals zero ($Z = X$). In this case, the economy's capital stock is ultimately financed by savings of resident

---

[9] This section presents the Solow growth model, in reference to Nobel Prize Laureate Robert Solow of the Massachusetts Institute of Technology.

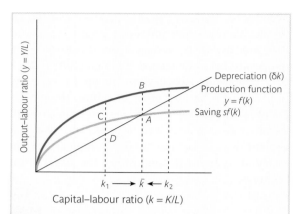

Fig. 3.4 The Steady State

The capital–labour ratio stops changing when investment is equal to depreciation. This occurs at point A, the intersection between the saving schedule $sf(k)$ and the depreciation line δk. The corresponding output–labour ratio is determined by the production function $f(k)$ at point B. When away from point A, the economy moves towards its steady state. Starting below the steady state at k_1, investment (point C) exceeds depreciation (point D) and the capital–output ratio will increase until it reaches its steady-state level Q.

households.[10] More precisely, we reach the conclusion that, in the steady state, $I = S$. Investment expenditures are financed entirely by domestic savings. This is a first explanation of the growth phenomenon: we save, we invest, we grow. As a first approximation, let s be the fraction of GDP which households save to finance investment. That investment equals saving implies:

(3.7) $I = sY$ and therefore $I/L = sY/L = sy = sf(k)$.

This relationship is shown in Figure 3.4 as the **saving schedule**. It expresses national savings as a function of national output and income. The saving schedule lies below the production function because we assume that national saving is a constant fraction of GDP.

---

[10] This need not be true for a region within a nation: the capital stock of southern Italy, eastern Germany, or Northern Ireland may well be financed by residents of other parts of their countries. Yet even these financing imbalances are unlikely to be sustainable for the indefinite future.

We next distinguish between **gross investment**, the amount of money spent on new capital, and **net investment**, the increase in the capital stock. Gross investment represents new additions to the physical capital stock, but it does not represent the net change of the capital stock because, over time, previously installed equipment **depreciates**—it wears out, loses some of its economic value, or becomes obsolescent. Some fraction of the capital stock is routinely lost. It is called **depreciation** and the proportion lost each period δ is called the **depreciation rate**. The depreciation rate for the overall economy is fairly stable and will be taken as constant: the more capital is in place, the more depreciation will occur. Depreciation is represented in Figure 3.4 by a ray from the origin, the **depreciation line**, with a slope δ.

If gross investment exceeds depreciation, net investment is positive and the capital stock rises. If gross investment is less than depreciation, the capital stock falls. While it may seem odd to imagine a shrinking capital stock, it is a phenomenon not uncommon in declining industries or regions. Net investment is therefore:

(3.8) $$\Delta K = sY - \delta K$$

or equivalently, written in intensive form:

$$\Delta k = sy - \delta k.$$

We see that the net accumulation of capital per unit of labour is positively related to the savings rate s and negatively related to the depreciation rate δ. The role of capital intensity k is ambiguous: on the one hand, it increases income ($y = f(k)$) and therefore savings and investment but, on the other hand, it increases the amount of depreciation. This ambiguity is a central issue in the study of economic growth and will be addressed in the following sections.

3.3.3 Characterizing the Steady State

Let us summarize what we have done up to now. The production function (3.5) relates an economy's output to inputs of capital and labour. Its intensive form, presented in Figure 3.3 and Figure 3.4, relates the output–labour ratio to the capital–labour ratio. According to equation (3.8), capital accumulation is also driven by the output–labour ratio. Putting all these pieces together, we find that capital accumulation (Δk) is determined by previously accumulated stock of capital (k):

(3.9) $\Delta k = sf(k) - \delta k$.

In Figure 3.4, Δk is the vertical distance between the savings schedule $sf(k)$ and the depreciation line δk. It represents the net change in the capital stock per unit of labour input in the economy. The sign of Δk tells us where the economy is heading. When $\Delta k > 0$, the capital stock per capita is rising and the economy is growing, since more output can be produced. When $\Delta k < 0$, the capital stock per capita and output per capita are both declining. At the intersection (point A) of the saving schedule and the depreciation line, gross investment and depreciation are equal, so the capital–labour ratio (point B) no longer changes. The capital stock is thus similar to the level of water in a bathtub when the drain is slightly open: gross investment is like the water running through the tap, while depreciation represents the loss of water through the drain. The newly accumulated capital exactly compensates that lost to depreciation—the water flows into the bathtub at the same speed as it leaks out. This is the steady state.

Capital formation process is not a perpetual motion machine. Wherever it starts, the economy will gravitate to the steady state and stay there. Suppose, for instance, that the economy is to the left of the steady-state capital–output ratio $\bar{k}$, say at the level k_1.[11] Figure 3.4 shows that gross investment $sf(k_1)$ at point C exceeds depreciation δk_1 at point D. According to (3.9), the distance CD represents net investment, the increase in the capital–labour ratio k, which rises towards its steady-state level $\bar{k}$.

Can the capital stock proceed beyond $\bar{k}$, going all way to say, k_2? It turns out that it cannot. As the economy gets closer to point A, net investment becomes smaller and smaller and nil precisely when the steady state is reached. To see how the economy behaves when capital is above its steady state, consider $k_2 > \bar{k}$. Gross investment $sf(k_2)$ is less

than depreciation δk_2, the capital–labour ratio declines, and we move leftward towards $\bar{k}$, the economy's stable resting point. Later we shall see that the stability of capital and output per capita carries over when we account for population growth.

3.3.4 The Role of Savings for Growth

We now show that the more a country saves, the more it invests; the more it invests, the higher is its steady–state capital–output ratio; and the larger its capital–output ratio, the higher its output–labour ratio in the steady state. Thus, as a long-run proposition, we should expect to find that countries with high savings and investment rates have high per capita incomes. Is this true? Figure 3.5(a) looks at the whole world and indeed detects such a link. The poor countries of Africa typically invest little, in contrast to richer countries of Europe and Asia.

Yet, the link is not strong. In addition, Figure 3.5(b) shows that the investment rate fails to account for differences in economic growth between countries. Obviously, our story is too simple and we will soon put more flesh on the bare bones that we have just assembled. Still, at this stage, we can explain why savings and investment only affect the steady-state *level* of output, and *not* its growth rate. This means that nations which save more should have higher standards of living in the steady state, not that they will not indefinitely grow faster. This is an important and slightly counter-intuitive result.

To see this, consider Figure 3.6, which illustrates the effect of an increase in the savings rate from s to s'. The savings–investment schedule shifts upwards while the production function schedule remains unchanged. As announced, the new steady-state output–labour and capital–labour ratios are both higher at point B than they were at point A beforehand. It will take time for the economy to reach the new steady state. Now that the saving state has increased, at point A, the initial steady-state position, gross investment has risen, depreciation is the same, so net investment is positive. The capital–labour ratio starts rising, which raises the output–labour ratio. This will go on until the new steady state is reached at point B. During this interim period, therefore, growth is higher, which can

---

[11] In general, steady-state values of variables will be indicated here with an upper bar, e.g. $\bar{k}$, $\bar{y}$, etc.

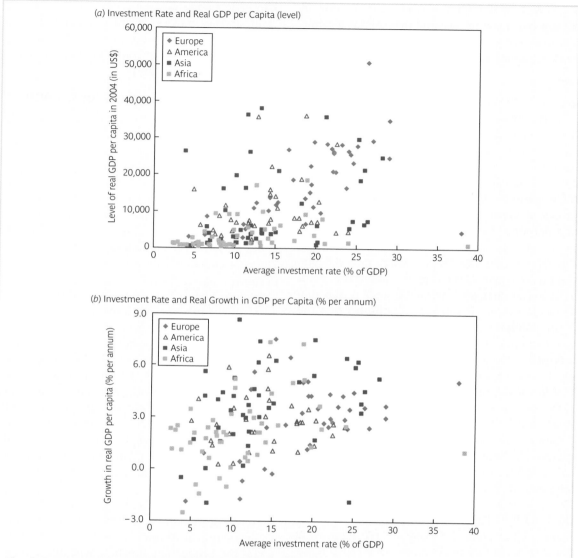

Fig. 3.5 **Investment, GDP per Capita, and Real GDP Growth**

For a sample of 174 countries over the period of 1950–2004, the correlation coefficient between the investment rate (the ratio of investment to GDP) and the average per capita GDP over the period is high and positive (0.51). The correlation of the investment rate in the countries with real GDP growth is also positive but less striking (0.31).

Source: Penn World Table Version 6.2 September 2006.

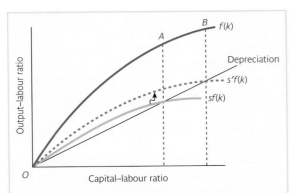

Fig. 3.6 An Increase in the Savings Rate

An increase in the savings rate raises capital intensity (k) and the output–labour ratio (y).

give the impression that higher investment rates cause higher economic growth. The boost is only temporary: once the steady state has been reached, no further growth effect can be expected from a higher savings rate. We still need a story to explain growth in output per capita. This is the story told in Sections 3.4 and 3.5.

It may be surprising that increased savings does not affect long-run growth. The reason that higher savings cannot cause capital and output to grow forever is the assumption of diminishing returns. An increase in savings causes the capital stock to rise, but as more capital is put into place, more capital depreciates and thus needs to be replaced. Increasing amounts of gross investment are needed just to keep the capital stock constant at its higher level. Yet the resources for that increased investment are not forthcoming, because the marginal productivity of capital decreases. Further additions to the capital–labour ratio yield smaller and smaller increases in income, and therefore in savings. Depreciation, however, rises with the capital stock proportionately. Put simply, the decreasing marginal productivity principle implies that, at some point, saving more is simply not worth it.[12]

3.3.5 The Golden Rule

Figure 3.6 contains an important message: to become richer, you need to save and invest more. But is being richer—in the narrow sense of accumulating capital goods—always necessarily better? Saving requires the sacrifice of giving up some consumption today against the promise of higher income tomorrow, but does saving more today always mean more consumption tomorrow? The answer is not necessarily positive. To see why, note that in the steady state, when the capital stock per capita is $\bar{k}$, savings equal depreciation and the steady-state level of consumption $\bar{c}$ (the part of income that is not saved) is given by:

(3.10) $$\bar{c} = \bar{y} - s\bar{y} = f(\bar{k}) - \delta\bar{k}.$$

In Figure 3.7, consumption per capita is given by the vertical distance between the production function and the depreciation line.[13] If we could choose the saving rate, we could effectively pick any point of intersection of the savings schedule with the depreciation line, and therefore any level of consumption we so desired. Figure 3.7 shows that consumption is highest at the capital stock for which the slope of the production function is parallel to the depreciation line.[14] The corresponding optimal steady-state capital–labour ratio is indicated as $\bar{k}'$. Now remember that the slope of the production function is the marginal productivity of capital (MPK) while the slope of the depreciation schedule is the rate of depreciation δ. We have just shown that the maximal level of consumption is achieved when

(3.11) $$\text{MPK} = \delta.$$

This condition is called the **golden rule**, and can be thought of as a recipe for achieving the best use of existing technological capabilities. In this case, with no population growth and no technical progress,

---

[12] In Chapter 4, we will see that the outcome is very different when the marginal productivity of capital is not declining.

[13] Note that everything, including consumption and saving, is measured as a ratio to the labour input, person-hours. As already noted, if the number of hours worked does not change, the ratios move exactly as per capita consumption, saving, output, etc.

[14] An exercise asks you to prove this assertion.

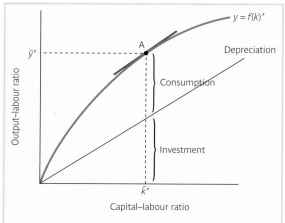

Fig. 3.7 The Golden Rule

Steady-state consumption $\bar{c}$ (as a ratio to labour) is the vertical distance between the production function and the depreciation line $\bar{k}$. It is at a maximum at point A corresponding to $\bar{k}$, where the slope of the production function, the marginal productivity of capital, is equal to d, the slope of the depreciation line.

the golden rule states that the economy maximizes steady-state consumption when the marginal gain from an additional unit of GDP saved and invested in capital (MPK) equals the depreciation rate.

What are the consequences of 'disobeying' the golden rule? If the capital–labour ratio exceeds $\bar{k}'$,

too much capital has been accumulated, and the MPK is lower than the depreciation rate δ. By reducing savings today, an economy can actually *increase* per capita consumption, both today and in the future. This looks like a free lunch, and indeed, it is one. We say that the economy suffers from **dynamic inefficiency**. Dynamically inefficient economies simply save and invest too much and consume too little.

A different situation arises if the economy is to the left of $\bar{k}'$. Here, steady-state income and consumption per capita may be raised by saving more, but not immediately; consumption only can be increased in the long run after the adjustment has occurred. No free lunch is immediately available, but must be 'earned' by increased saving and reduced consumption at the outset. Moving towards $\bar{k}'$ from a position on the left requires current generations to sacrifice so future generations can enjoy more consumption which will result from more capital and income in the steady state. An economy in such a situation is called **dynamically efficient** because it is not possible to do better without paying the price for it. The difference between dynamically efficient and inefficient savings rates is illustrated in Figure 3.8, which shows how we move from one steady state to another one with higher consumption.

In the dynamically inefficient case (*a*), it is possible to permanently raise consumption by consuming

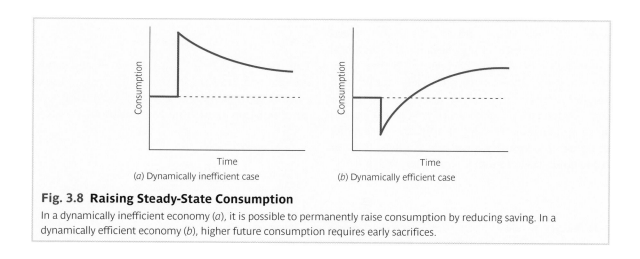

Fig. 3.8 Raising Steady-State Consumption

In a dynamically inefficient economy (*a*), it is possible to permanently raise consumption by reducing saving. In a dynamically efficient economy (*b*), higher future consumption requires early sacrifices.

more now and during the transition to the new steady state. In the dynamically efficient case (b), a higher steady-state level consumption is not free and implies a transitory period of sacrifice.

Dynamic inefficiency arises when excessive savings have led to too high a stock of capital. Saving must remain forever high merely to replace depreciating capital. Dynamic inefficiency may have characterized some of the centrally planned economies of Central and Eastern Europe. We say 'may' because the proof that an economy is inefficient lies in showing that its marginal productivity of capital is lower than the depreciation rate, and neither of these is easily measurable. What we do know is that Communist leaders often boasted about their economies' high investment rates, which were in fact considerably higher than in the capitalist West. Yet overall standards of living were considerably lower than in market economies, and consumer goods were in notori-

ously short supply. Box 3.3 presents the case of Poland.

In dynamically efficient economies, future generations would benefit from raising saving today, but those currently alive would lose. Should governments do something about it? Since it would represent a transfer of revenues from current to future generations, there is no simple answer. It is truly a deep political choice with no solution since future generations don't vote today. A number of factors influence savings, such as taxation, health and retirement systems, cultural norms, and social custom. Importantly, too, saving and investment are influenced by political conditions. Political instability and especially wars, civil or otherwise, can lead to destruction and theft of capital, and hardly encourage thrifty behaviour. As we discuss in Chapter 4, in many of the world's poorest countries, property rights are under constant threat or non-existent.

 Box 3.3 Dynamic Inefficiency in Poland?

From the period following the Second World War until the early 1990s, Poland was a centrally planned economy. Savings and investment decisions for the Polish economy were taken by the ruling Communist party. The panels of Figure 3.9 compare Poland with Italy, a country with one of the highest saving rates in Europe. The first graph shows the increase in GDP per capita between 1980 and 1990 (the GDP measure is adjusted for purchasing power to take into account different price systems). While Italy's income grew by 25%, Poland's actually shrank by about 5%. The second graph shows the average proportion of GDP dedicated to saving over the same period. Clearly, Poland saved a lot, but received nothing for it in terms of income growth.

As the third and fourth panels of Figure 3.9 show, the situation was reversed after 1991, when Poland introduced free markets and abandoned central planning. From 1991 to 2004, per capita GDP increased by 68%, with a lower investment rate than Italy's (which grew by 17%). However, our theory predicts that savings affect the

steady-state level of GDP per capita, not its growth rate. In 1980, Poland invested 21.6% of its GDP. By 1990 this rate had fallen to 18.3%. In the period 1990–2004 per capita consumption rose in Poland from $2,908 to $7,037, an increase of 142%, compared with 61% in Italy over the same period. Is this proof of dynamic inefficiency, i.e. that a significant part of savings was used merely to keep up an excessively large stock of capital? Anecdotal evidence would suggest so. Stories of wasted resources were common in centrally planned economies: uninstalled equipment rusting in backyards, new machinery prematurely discarded for lack of spare parts, tools ill-adapted to factory needs, etc. One important cause of wastage was a reward system for factory managers. These were often based on spending *plans*, and not on actual output. An alternative interpretation is that the investment was in poor quality equipment, which could not match western technology. No matter how we look at it, savings were not put to their best use in centrally planned Poland.

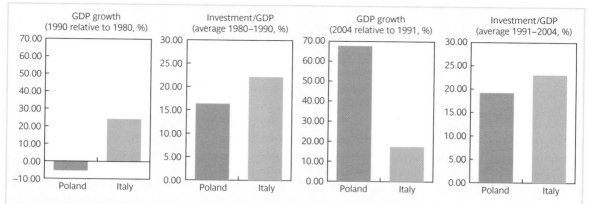

Fig. 3.9 Was Centrally Planned Poland Dynamically Inefficient?

Despite a high investment and savings rate, Polish per capita GDP shrank during the period 1980–1990 while Italy's grew. During the transition period, Poland grew much faster, with a lower investment rate than in Italy.

Source: Heston, Summers, and Aten (2006).

3.4 Population Growth and Economic Growth

A major shortcoming of the previous section is that it does not explain permanent, sustained growth, our first stylized fact. Capital accumulation, we saw, can explain high living standards and growth during the transition to the steady state but the law of diminishing returns ultimately kicks in. Clearly, some crucial ingredients are missing. One of them is population growth, more precisely, growth in the employed labour force. This section shows that sustainable long-run growth of both output and the capital stock is possible once we introduce population growth.

Recall that labour input (person-hours) grows either if the number of people at work increases, or if workers work more hours on average. Later on in this chapter and Chapter 5, we will see that the number of hours worked per person has declined steadily over the past century and a half. Figure 3.10 shows that, despite this fact, employment has been rising, either because of natural demographic forces (the balance between births and deaths) or

immigration. Overall, more people are at work but they work shorter hours, so the balance of effects is ambiguous. Because the number of hours worked per person cannot and does not rise without bound, we will treat it as constant. Then any change in person-hours is due to exogenous changes in the population and employment, and output per person-hour changes at the same rate as output per capita.

Even though population and employment are growing, the fundamental reasoning of Section 3.3 remains valid: the economy gravitates to a steady state at which the capital–labour and output–labour ratios ($k = K/L$ and $y = Y/L$) stabilize. With L growing at the exogenous rate n, output Y and capital K will also grow at rate n. The relentless increase in the labour input is the driver of growth in this case. Quite simply, if income per capita is to remain unchanged in the steady state, income must grow at the same rate as the number of people.

The role of saving and capital accumulation remains the same as in the previous section, with only

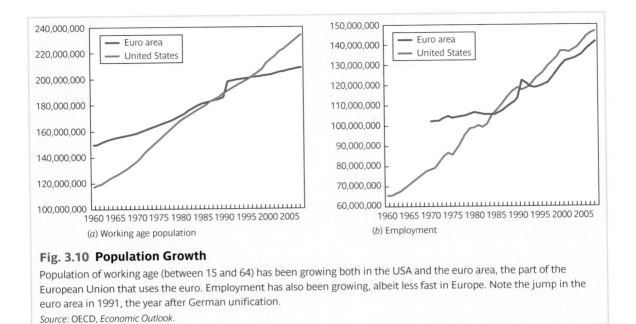

Fig. 3.10 Population Growth

Population of working age (between 15 and 64) has been growing both in the USA and the euro area, the part of the European Union that uses the euro. Employment has also been growing, albeit less fast in Europe. Note the jump in the euro area in 1991, the year after German unification.

Source: OECD, *Economic Outlook*.

a small change of detail. The capital accumulation condition (3.9) now becomes:[15]

(3.12) $\Delta k = sf(k) - (\delta + n)k.$

The difference is that, for the capital–labour ratio to increase, gross investment must not just compensate for depreciation, it must also provide new workers with the same equipment as those already employed. This process is called **capital-widening** and it explains the last term (n).

The situation is presented in Figure 3.11. The only difference with Figure 3.4 is that the depreciation line δk has been replaced by the steeper **capital-widening line** $(\delta + n)k$. The fact that the capital-widening line is steeper than the depreciation line captures the greater need to save when more workers are being equipped with productive capital. The steady state occurs at point A_1, the intersection

of the saving schedule and the capital-widening line. At this intersection $\bar{k}_1$, savings are just enough to cover the depreciation and the needs of new workers, so $\Delta k = 0$.

The role of population growth can be seen by studying the effect of an increase in the rate of population growth, from n_1 to n_2. In Figure 3.11 the capital-widening line becomes steeper and the new steady state at point A_2 is characterized by a lower capital–labour ratio $\bar{k}_2$. This makes sense. We assume that the savings behaviour has not changed and yet we need more gross investment to equip new workers. The solution is to provide each worker with less capital. Of course, a lower $\bar{k}$ implies a lower output–labour ratio $f(\bar{k})$. Thus we find that, all other things being equal, countries with a rapidly growing population will tend to be poorer than countries with lower population growth. Box 3.4 examines whether it is indeed the case that high population growth lowers GDP per capita.

At what level of investment does an economy with population growth maximize consumption per capita? Because the number of people who are able to consume is growing continuously, the

---

[15] The proof requires some calculus based on the principles presented in Box 6.3. The change in capital per capita is $\Delta k/k = (\Delta K/K) - (\Delta L/L)$. After substituting $\Delta K = I - \delta K$ and $\Delta L/L = n$ and setting $I = sY$, the equation can be rearranged to yield $\Delta k = sy - \delta k - nk = sf(k) - \delta k - nk$.

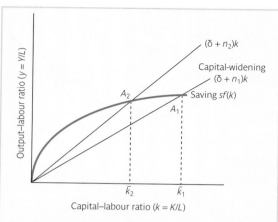

Fig. 3.11 The Steady State with Population Growth

The capital–labour ratio remains unchanged when investment is equal to $(\delta + n_1)k$.

This occurs at point A_1, the intersection between the saving schedule $sf(k)$ and the capital-widening line $(\delta + n_1)k$. An increase in the rate of growth of the population from n_1 to n_2 is shown as a counter-clockwise rotation of the capital-widening line. The new steady-state capital–labour ratio declines from $\bar{k}_1$ to $\bar{k}_2$.

golden rule must be modified accordingly. Following the same reasoning as in Section 3.3, we note that steady-state investment per person-hour is $(\delta + n)\bar{k}$, so consumption per person-hour $\bar{c}$ is given by $f(\bar{k}) - (\delta + n)\bar{k}$. Proceeding as before, it is easy to see that consumption is at a maximum when

(3.13) $\text{MPK} = \delta + n.$

The 'modified' golden rule equates the marginal productivity of capital with the sum of the depreciation rate δ and the population growth rate n. The intuition developed above continues to apply: the marginal product of an additional unit of capital (per capita) is set to its marginal cost, which now includes not only depreciation, but also the capital-widening investment necessary to equip future generations with the same capital per head as the current generation. A growing population will necessitate a higher marginal product of capital at the steady state. The principle of diminishing marginal productivity implies that the capital–labour ratio must be lower. Consequently, output per head will also be lower.

 Box 3.4 Population Growth and GDP per Capita

Figure 3.12 plots GDP per capita in 2003 and the average rate of population growth over the period 1960–2004. The figure could be seen as confirming the negative relationship predicted by the Solow growth model. Taken at face value, this result might be interpreted as support for the hypothesis that population growth impoverishes nations. Thomas Malthus, a famous nineteenth-century English economist and philosopher, also claimed that population growth causes poverty. He argued that a fixed supply of arable land could not feed a constantly increasing population and that population growth would ultimately result in starvation. He ignored technological change, in this case the green revolution which significantly raised agricultural output in the last half of the twentieth century. As we confirm in Section 3.5,

technological change can radically alter the outlook for growth and prosperity.

Yet the pseudo-Malthusian view has been taken seriously in a number of less-developed countries, which have attempted to limit demographic growth. The most spectacular example is China, which has pursued a one-child-only policy for decades. At the same time, we need to be careful with simple diagrams depicting relationships between two variables. Not only do other factors besides population growth influence economic growth, but it may well be that population growth is not exogenous. Figure 3.12 could also be read as saying that as people become richer, they have fewer children. There exists a great deal of evidence in favour of this alternative interpretation.

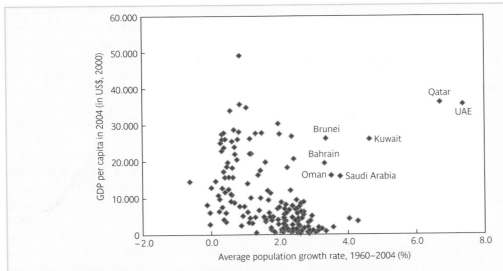

Fig. 3.12 Population Growth and GDP per Capita, 1960–2000
The figure reports data on real GDP per capita and average population growth for 182 countries over almost a half century. The plot indicates a discernible negative association between GDP per capita and population growth, especially when the rich oil-producing countries (United Arab Emirates, Qatar, Kuwait, Bahrain, Oman, Brunei, and Saudi Arabia) are excluded. The sharp population growth observed in these countries is largely to due to immigration.
Source: Heston, Summers, and Aten (2006).

3.5 Technological Progress and Economic Growth

Taking population growth into account gives one good reason why output and the capital stock can grow permanently, and at the same rate. While this satisfies Kaldor's second stylized fact, the picture remains incomplete: in our growth model, capital–labour and output–labour ratios were *constant*. Standards of living are not rising in this economy, and this is still grossly inconsistent with Kaldor's first stylized fact and the data reported in Table 3.1. Under what conditions can per capita income and capital stock grow, and grow at the same rate?

So far, we have ignored **technological or technical progress**. It stands to reason that, over time, increased knowledge and better, more sophisticated techniques make workers and the equipment

they work with more productive. With a slight alteration, our framework readily shows how technological progress works. To do so, once more, we reformulate the aggregate production function introduced in (3.1). Technological progress means that more output can be produced with the same quantity of equipment and labour. The most convenient way to do this is to introduce a measure of the state of technology, A, that raises output at given levels of capital stock and employment:

$$(3.14) \qquad Y = F(A, K, L).$$
$$\qquad\qquad\qquad\quad +\ +\ +$$

When A increases, Y rises, even if K and L remain unchanged. For this reason, A is frequently called

total factor productivity. It should be emphasized that A is *not* a factor of production. No firm pays for it, and each firm just benefits from it. It is best thought of as 'best practice' and is assumed to be available freely to all. At this point, it will be convenient to assume that A increases at a constant rate a, without trying to explain how and why. Technological progress, which is the increase in A, is therefore considered as exogenous.

It turns out that it is possible to relate our analysis to previous results in this chapter in a straightforward way. First, we modify (3.14) to incorporate technical progress in the following particular way:

(3.15) $Y = F(K, AL)$.

In this formulation, technological progress acts directly on the effectiveness of labour. (For this reason it is sometimes called *labour-augmenting technical progress*). An increase in A of, say, 10% has the same impact as a 10% increase in employment, even though the number of hours worked hasn't changed. The term AL is known as **effective labour** to capture the idea that, with the same equipment, one hour of work today produces more output than before because A is higher. Effective labour AL grows for two reasons: (1) more labour L, and (2) greater effectiveness A. For this reason, the rate of growth of AL is now given by $a + n$.

Now we change the notation a little bit. We redefine y and k as ratios of output and capital *relative to effective labour*: $y = Y/AL$, $k = K/AL$. Once this is done, it is possible to recover the now-familiar production function in intensive form, $y = f(k)$.[16] Not surprisingly, the ratio of capital to effective labour evolves as before, with a slight modification:

(3.16) $\Delta k = sf(k) - (\delta + a + n)k$.

The reasoning is the same as when we introduced population growth. There we noted that, to keep the capital–labour ratio K/L constant, the capital stock K must rise to make up for depreciation (δ) and population growth (n). Now we find that, to keep the capital–effective labour ratio $k = K/AL$ constant, the capital stock K must also rise to keep up with

workers' enhanced effectiveness (a). So k will increase if saving $sf(k)$, and hence gross investment, exceeds the capital accumulation needed to make up for depreciation δ, population growth n, and increased effectiveness a. From there on, it is a simple matter to modify Figure 3.11 to Figure 3.13. The steady state is now characterized by constant ratios of capital and output to effective labour ($y = Y/AL$ and $k = K/AL$).

Constancy of these ratios in the steady state is a very important result. Indeed, if Y/AL is constant, it means that Y/L grows at the same rate as A. If the average number of hours remains unchanged, then income per capita must grow at the rate of technological progress, a. In other words, we have finally uncovered the explanation of Kaldor's first stylized fact: the continuous increase in standards of living is due to technological progress. Since K/AL is also constant, we know that the capital stock per

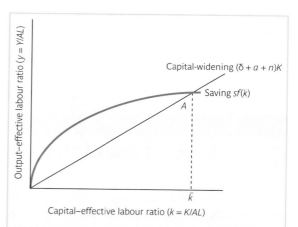

Fig. 3.13 The Steady State with Population Growth and Technological Progress

In an economy with both population growth and technological progress, inputs and output are measured in units per effective labour input. The intensive form production function inherits this property. The slope of the capital accumulation line is now $\delta + a + n$, where a is the rate of technological progress. The steady state occurs when investment is equal to $(\delta + a + n)k$ (point A), which is the intersection of the saving schedule $sf(k)$ with the capital-widening line $(\delta + a + n)k$. At the steady-state Q, output and capital increase at the rate $a + n$, while GDP per capita increases at the rate a.

---

[16] Constant returns to scale implies that $y = F(K, AL)/AL$
= F(K/AL, 1).

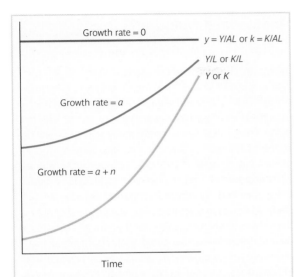

Fig. 3.14 Growth Rates along the Steady State

While output and capital measured in effective labour units (*Y/AL* and *K/AL*) are constant in the steady state, output–labour and capital–labour ratios (*Y/L* and *K/L*) grow at the rate of technological progress *a*, and output and the capital stock (*Y* and *K*) grow at the rate *a + n*, the sum of the rates of population growth and technological progress.

over the centuries. Technological progress is essential for explaining economic growth in the long run. Rather than creating misery in the world, it turns out to be central to improvements in standards of living.

Note that an increase in the rate of technological progress, *a*, makes the capital-widening line steeper than before. In Figure 3.13 this would imply lower steady-state ratios of capital and output to effective labour. This does not mean that more rapid technological progress is a bad thing. On the contrary, in fact, when *Y/AL* is lower, *Y/L* grows faster so that standards of living are secularly rising at higher speed.

The discussion can be extended in a natural way to address the issue of the golden rule. Redefining *c* as the ratio of aggregate consumption (*C*) to effective labour (*AL*), the following modified version of (3.10) will hold in the steady state:

$$\bar{c} = f(\bar{k}) - (\delta + a + n)\bar{k}.$$

The modified golden rule now requires that the marginal productivity of capital be the sum of the rates of depreciation, of population growth, and of technological change:

(3.17) $$MPK = \delta + a + n.$$

Maximizing consumption per capita is equivalent to making consumption per unit of effective labour as large as possible. To do this, an economy now needs to invest capital per effective unit of labour to the point at which its marginal product 'covers' the investment requirements given by technical progress (*a*), population growth (*n*), and capital depreciation (δ).

capita also grows secularly at the same rate, i.e. Kaldor's second stylized fact. Figure 3.14 illustrates these results. Because of diminishing marginal productivity, capital accumulation alone cannot sustain growth. Population growth explains GDP growth, but not the sustained increase of standards of living

3.6 Growth Accounting

3.6.1 Solow's Decomposition

As shown in Figure 3.14, we have now identified three sources of GDP growth: (1) capital accumulation, (2) population growth, and (3) technological progress. It is natural to ask how large the contributions of

these factors are to the total growth of a nation or a region. Unfortunately, it is difficult to measure technological progress. Computers, for instance, probably raise standards of living and growth, but by how much? Some people believe that the 'new economy', brought on by the information technology

Box 3.5 The New Economy: Another Industrial Revolution?

The striking changes brought about by the ICT (information and communications technologies) revolution, which include the internet, wireless telecommunications, MP3 players, and the conspicuous use of electronic equipment, have led many observers to conclude that a new industrial revolution is upon us. Figure 3.15 reports estimates of overall increases in multifactor productivity in the USA, computed as annual averages over four periods. A difference of 1% per year cumulates to 28% after 25 years. The figure shows a formidable acceleration in the period 1913–1972, and again over 1995–1999; hence the case for a second industrial revolution.

While initially there was much scepticism about the true impact of the ICT revolution—Robert Solow himself said early on that 'computers can be found everywhere except in the productivity statistics'—there is compelling evidence that ICT have indeed deeply impacted the way we work and produce goods and services, and have ultimately increased our standards of living significantly. These total factor productivity gains, according to recent research by Kevin Stiroh, Dale Jorgenson, and others, can be found both in ICT-*producing* as well as ICT-using sectors.[17] Strong gains in total factor productivity have been observed in the organization of retail trade, as well as in manufacturing and business services. Even more interesting is the fact that not all economies around the world have benefited equally from productivity improvements measured in the USA. In particular, some EU countries continue to lag behind in ICT adoption as well as innovation.

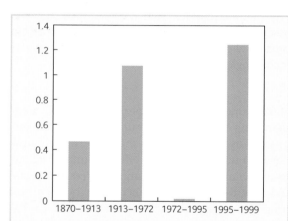

Fig. 3.15 Multifactor Productivity in the USA (average annual growth, %)

The average annual increase in A (multifactor productivity) accelerated sharply after 1913, came to a near stop over 1972–1995, and seems to have vigorously bounced back at the end of the 1990s.
Source: Gordon (2000).

Robert Solow, who developed the theory presented in the previous sections, devised an ingenious method of quantifying the extent to which technological progress accounts for growth. His idea was to start with the things we can measure: GDP growth, capital accumulation, and man-hours worked. Going back to the general form of the production function (3.14), we can measure output Y and two inputs, capital K and labour L. Once we know how much GDP has increased, and how much of this increase is explained by capital and hours worked, we can interpret what is left, called the **Solow residual**, as due to the increase in A, i.e. $a = \Delta A/A$:

$$\text{Solow residual} = \frac{\Delta Y}{Y} - \text{output growth due to growth in capital and hours worked.[18]}$$

We now track down the **Solow decomposition**.

---

[17] See the references at the end of the book.

[18] Formally, the Solow residual is $\dfrac{\Delta A}{A} = \dfrac{\Delta Y}{Y} - \left[(1 - s_L)\dfrac{\Delta K}{K} + s_L\dfrac{\Delta L}{L}\right]$, where s_L is the labour share, defined as the share of national income paid to labour in the form of wages and non-wage compensation, and $1 - s_L$ is the income share of capital. The WebAppendix shows how this formula can be derived from the production function.

revolution, will push standards of living faster than ever. Others are less optimistic that the effect is any larger than other great discoveries which mark economic history. Box 3.5 provides some details on this exciting debate.

Table 3.3 Growth of Real Gross Fixed Capital Stock, 1890–2008 (% per annum)

	1890–1913	1913–1950	1950–1973	1973–1987	1987–2008
France	n.a.	1.2	5.1	4.5	3.2
Germany	3.1	1.1	6.6	3.5	2.2*
Netherlands	n.a.	2.4	5.8	3.3	2.8
UK	2.0	1.5	5.1	2.9	3.9
USA	5.4	2.1	3.2	3.3	4.2
Japan	3.0	3.9	9.1	7.6	3.2

* 1991–2008
Sources: Maddison (1991); OECD, *Economic Outlook*.

3.6.2 Capital Accumulation

Table 3.3 shows that, typically, capital has been growing at about 3–5% per year over most of the twentieth century in the developed countries. Capital accumulation accelerated sharply in the 1950s and 1960s as part of the post-war reconstruction. Many European countries accumulated capital considerably faster than the USA and the UK up until the mid-1970s, the reason being that continental Europe was poorer at the end of the Second World War. These sustained periods of rapid capital accumulation fit well the description of catch-up, when the capital stock is below its steady-state level.

3.6.3 Employment Growth

The most appropriate measure of labour input is total number of hours worked. For several reasons, however, growth in population or the number of employees does not necessarily translate into increased person-hours. To understand this, we can rewrite the total number of hours in the following way:

total hours worked = (hours/employee) × (employee/population) × population.

The total number of hours worked can increase for three reasons:

Table 3.4 Population, Employment, and Hours Worked, 1870–2006

	Population growth (% per annum)	Employment growth (% per annum)	Growth in hours worked per person (% per annum)	Hours worked per person in 1913	Hours worked per person in 2006
France	0.3	0.3	−0.5	2,588	1,529
Germany	0.5	0.6	−0.5	2,584	1,437
Netherlands	1.1	1.3	−0.5	2,605	1,413
United Kingdom	0.5	0.6	−0.4	2,624	1,624
United States	1.5	1.7	−0.4	2,605	1,791
Japan	1.0	0.9	−0.4	2,588	1,775

Sources: Maddison (2006); Groningen Growth and Development Centre and the Conference Board, Total Economy Database, January 2007.

- Obviously, population growth. Everything else unchanged, more people provide more working hours. But many things change.

- The proportion of people who work. Some working-age people are unemployed and others voluntarily stay out of work for various reasons. In addition, people live longer, study longer, and retire earlier. Furthermore, women have increased their labour force participation over the past 30 years.[19]

- Hours worked per person. Over time, those who work tend to work fewer hours per day and fewer days per year.

Table 3.4 shows that these effects have roughly cancelled each other out so that, in the end, employment and population size have increased by similar amounts in our sample of developed countries.

Table 3.4 also documents the sharp secular decline in the number of hours worked per person in the developed world. The long-run trend is a consequence of shorter days, shorter workweeks, fewer weeks per year, and fewer years worked per person. This is why the number of person-hours has declined across the industrial world. Overall, European labour input has increased between nil and 0.3%, while immigration lifted it well above 1% in the USA and Australia. The dramatic decline in hours worked per person is a central feature of the growth process; an average annual reduction of 0.5% per year means a total decline of 40% over a century. As societies become richer, demand for leisure increases. The last two columns of the table reveal a massive jump in leisure time available, which is as important a source of improvement of human welfare as increases in material wealth.

3.6.4 The Contribution of Technological Change

Table 3.5 presents the Solow decomposition in two different contexts. The first employs historical data for the period 1913–1987. The second examines the same countries over the last two decades. We see that growth in inputs of labour and capital account

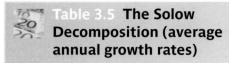

Table 3.5 The Solow Decomposition (average annual growth rates)

(a) **1913–1987***

Country	GDP	Contribution of inputs	Residual
France	2.6	1.1	1.0
Germany	2.8	1.4	0.8
Netherlands	3.0	2.0	0.4
UK	1.9	1.2	0.5
USA	3.0	2.0	0.7
Japan	4.7	3.0	0.5

* An adjustment is made to account for the modernization of productive capital
Source: Maddison (1991: 158).

(b) **1987–1997**

	GDP	Contribution of inputs	Residual
France	2.0	1.1	1.0
Germany*	1.4	0.2	1.2
Netherlands	2.9	1.8	1.1
United Kingdom	2.2	1.4	0.7
United States	3.0	2.5	0.5
Japan	2.7	1.4	1.3

* 1991–1997

(c) **1997–2006**

	GDP	Contribution of inputs	Residual
France	2.2	1.3	1.0
Germany	1.4	0.6	0.8
Netherlands	2.3	1.4	0.9
United Kingdom	2.7	1.7	1.0
United States	3.0	1.9	1.1
Japan	1.2	0.1	1.1

Sources: Maddison (1991); authors' calculation based on Groningen Growth and Development Centre and the Conference Board, Total Economy Database, January 2007, available at <www.ggdc.net>; OECD, *Economic Outlook*.

---

[19] Chapter 4 explores these and related issues in more detail.

for only one-half to two-thirds of total economic growth in these economies. The rest is the Solow residual, and confirms the importance of technological progress. A puzzling observation is the apparent slowdown in technological change during the 1970s and the 1980s, which contrasts with reports of an acceleration since the late 1990s. In the table, only the USA and Germany exhibit higher growth in technical progress (the Solow residual) in the second decade, which is generally thought to be a period associated with technological acceleration.

❗ Summary

1 Economic growth refers to the steady expansion of GDP over a period of a decade or longer. Growth theory is concerned with the study of economic growth in the steady state, a situation in which output and capital grow at the same pace and remain in constant proportion to labour in effective terms. This approach reflects key stylized facts.

2 The aggregate production function shows that output grows when more inputs (capital and labour) are used, and when technology improves the effectiveness of those inputs.

3 The capital stock, the sum of productive equipment and structures, is accumulated through investment, and investment is financed by savings. When savings are a stable proportion of output, the steady-state capital stock is determined by savings and capital depreciation.

4 The assumption that the marginal productivity of capital is declining implies that output, and therefore savings, grow less proportionately to the stock of capital, in contrast to depreciation, which is proportional to capital. This implies that capital accumulation eventually exhausts the potential of savings and comes to an end. At this point, the steady state is reached.

5 In the absence of population growth and technological change, the steady state is characterized by zero output and capital growth. Adding population growth provides a first explanation of secular output growth, but standards of living—measured as output per capita—still do not increase. It is only when we allow for technological progress that permanent growth in per capita output and capital is possible.

6 The golden rule describes a steady state in which consumption is as high as possible. It occurs where the marginal productivity of capital equals the rate of depreciation (so as to replace worn-out capital) plus the rate of population growth (to provide new workers with adequate equipment) plus the rate of technological change (adjusting capital to enhanced labour effectiveness): $MPK = \delta + n + a$.

7 An economy is dynamically efficient when steady-state consumption can be raised tomorrow only at the expense of lower consumption today. An economy is dynamically inefficient when both current and future steady-state consumption can be increased. In the former case, the capital stock is lower than the golden-rule level. In the latter case, the capital stock is above the golden-rule level.

8 Saving does not affect the steady-state growth rate, but only the level of output per capita.

9 The Solow decomposition is a method of accounting for the sources of economic growth. It breaks down growth in GDP into the sum of growth attributable to changes in the factors of production and growth due to improved production. The latter is called the Solow residual, and is usually interpreted as technological change.

☺ Key Concepts

- economic growth
- technological progress
- Solow growth model
- stylized facts
- steady state
- capital accumulation
- aggregate production function
- diminishing marginal productivity
- returns to scale (constant, increasing, decreasing)
- output–labour ratio
- capital–labour ratio

- saving schedule
- gross investment
- depreciate, depreciation rate
- depreciation line
- capital-widening line
- golden rule
- dynamic inefficiency, dynamically efficient
- effective labour
- Solow decomposition
- Solow residual
- total factor or multifactor productivity

❓ Exercises

1 Draw intensive-form production functions $f(k)$ with decreasing, constant, and increasing returns to scale.

2 Use graph paper (or a computer spreadsheet) to plot the following intensive-form production functions (expressing y as a function of k) from the interval [0, 100]:

(a) $f(k) = 2k$;
(b) $f(k) = 10 + k^{0.5}$;
(c) $f(k) = k^{1.1}$;
(d) $f(k) = 10 + 2k - 0.5k^2$;
(e) $f(k) = \max(0, -10 + 2k)$.

Which of these functions has constant returns? Decreasing or increasing returns? Are your answers always unambiguous, i.e. do they hold for all $k \in [0, 100]$?

3 Define the steady state. How is a steady state important in the context of the Solow growth model? Explain why stylized facts are necessary to organize the discussion of economic growth.

4 Suppose K/Y is constant at 2. (a) Assume first that there is no population growth and no technological progress. What is the steady-state saving–output ratio consistent with a rate of depreciation of 5%? (b) Now allow for positive economic growth, due to either population growth or technological progress. What is the steady-state saving–output ratio consistent with a rate of depreciation of 5% and 3% real growth?

5 Consider a country with zero technological progress and $K/L = 3$. Its population grows at the rate of 2% per year. What is the steady-state rate of growth of GDP per capita if the saving rate is 20%? If it is 30%? How do your answers change if depreciation occurs at a rate of 6% per year?

6 Suppose the aggregate production function is given by $Y = \sqrt{KL}$. Does it have increasing, decreasing, or constant returns to scale? Show that the marginal products of capital and labour are declining. Show that they are increasing in the input of the other factor.

7 Define the concept of a golden rule. Explain why it is achieved at $\bar{k}'$ in Figure 3.7. To establish this result, imagine that you start to the left of $\bar{k}'$ and explain why moving to the right increases consumption. Similarly show that consumption decreases when moving rightwards from a position to the right of $\bar{k}'$.

8 The golden rule (3.17) is MPK = $\delta + a + n$. In comparison with the no-technological change case, we now require a higher marginal productivity of capital. With diminishing marginal productivity, this means a lower capital stock per effective unit of labour. Is that not surprising? How can you explain this apparent paradox?

9 Draw a graph showing the evolution of Y/L in the catch-up phase and then in the ensuing steady state when the economy starts from a capital–effective labour ratio below its steady-state level. Draw a picture showing investment (not the capital stock).

10 Explain, formally or informally, the difference between average labour productivity and output per capita.

11 In the steady state, output per effective labour Y/AL is constant. What happens to output per capita when the average number of hours worked declines, holding all else constant?

→ Essay Questions

1 Japan in the 1960s, Korea in the 1980s, China in the 1990s, and India in the current decade have experienced periods of rapid growth, in effect catching up on the richer and more developed countries. How can you explain this phenomenon, and why did it not happen earlier?

2 In earlier centuries, colonial expeditions were launched to increase a country's land and population. How might such activities make a country richer?

3 'Globalization is bad for growth since it means that countries invest abroad and expand the capital stocks of other countries instead of their own. The Solow model would consider this a decrease in the savings rate, thus leading to lower GDP per capita.' Comment.

4 Examining the panels of Figure 3.5, one immediately notices that African countries are bunched in the lower left-hand part of the diagram, while the European countries are clustered in the upper right-hand region. What explanation of this fact is offered by the Solow growth model? Do you think this is a sufficient explanation? Explain.

5 It is often claimed that the defeated nations after the Second World War grew faster than the victor nations. Is this hypothesis consistent with the Solow growth model?

Explaining Economic Growth in the Long Run

4

No one could have ever intended to deny that technological change is at least partially endogenous to the economy. Valuable resources are used in the pursuit of innovation, presumably with some rational hope of financial success.

Robert M. Solow

4.1 Overview

In Chapter 3, we identified three sources of economic growth: (1) increases in the working population, (2) capital accumulation, and (3) technological progress. Its message was that two countries with identical economic characteristics should have equal output and income per capita in the long run, regardless of their initial conditions. In effect, the Solow model predicts that countries as diverse as Algeria, Bangladesh, Paraguay, or Zambia can all hope to reach living standards of the wealthiest nations of the world in reasonable time. Yet reality is not as clear-cut or encouraging. Rather than converging to a common growth path, we observe very different outcomes around the world—wealthy, middling, and poor—and they don't seem to be pulling together in the way theory predicts. While the Organisation for Economic Cooperation and Development (OECD) countries continue to converge to a common (high) standard of living, other countries have diverged or congregated around common, stagnating regional averages.

To begin to understand the diverse growth experiences across the world, we need to recall that another conclusion of Chapter 3 was that technological progress—as measured by the Solow residual—is the only true engine of growth. The most convincing explanation of divergence of economic development in the modern world must therefore lie in explaining differences in levels and growth of total factor productivity. But what is total factor productivity? Can anything be done to better understand, harness, or even accelerate this formidable source of economic prosperity?

Chapter 4 delves into these fascinating and important questions. First, by extending our description of the aggregate production function to account for labour quality, we can explain a great deal of the differences in per capita income levels across countries. Labour is not homogeneous: some workers are highly skilled, others much less so. Human capital (skills acquired on the job or through investment in education, and kept in use through good health care) contributes a great deal to explaining why workers in wealthy countries are so productive. Second, countries have different levels of public capital or physical infrastructure—streets and highways, bridges, hospitals, airports, to name just a few examples. Third, intangible aspects such as law and order, efficient court systems, and transparent governmental administration also contribute to income differences around the world and cannot be ignored. Here it is sensible to speak of social as well as physical infrastructure.

Yet to explain economic growth over many decades, we must return to technological progress. In Chapter 3, technological progress was the engine of growth because it never runs out of fuel. Productivity was assumed to increase exogenously, irrespective of economic and social circumstances. This is unsatisfactory for both intellectual and practical reasons. Technological progress is the result of costly efforts at research and development (R&D). R&D consists not only of pure production of knowledge (research), but also making that knowledge work for us (development). R&D represents an economic activity in its own right. Yet why doesn't R&D fall victim to decreasing returns, as is the case with other factors of production? The question of whether the evolution of technological progress itself could be endogenous is an open area of macroeconomics. It also raises the question of whether government policies can improve the long-run growth performance of nations.

4.2 The Convergence Hypothesis

4.2.1 The Boundless Optimism of the Solow Model

In Chapter 3, output per capita in the long run was explained by (1) the savings rate and (2) the state of technology as summarized by the 'height' of the production function. All other things being equal, countries with higher savings rates and more productive technologies will have higher output per capita than those with lower saving rates and less productive technologies. Countries with similar savings rates and comparable technological sophistication should have the same income per capita in the long run. Moreover, even if countries have different savings rates, they should grow at the same rate, if they have access to the same technology as the leading economies—either by copying international best practice or by allowing in foreign corporations that transfer their know-how.

The Solow growth model thus contains a fundamentally optimistic view of economic development. Given the similar underlying conditions, GDP or income per capita should converge in level and growth rate across countries. Furthermore, the farther a country's GDP is from its steady state, the faster it will grow in subsequent years. These predictions are known as the **convergence hypothesis**.

Panel (*a*) of Figure 4.1 plots the average growth rate of 25 advanced countries over the period 1960–2003 against their real per capita GDP in 1960. The convergence hypothesis would predict that countries with low initial per capita GDP will grow faster than those that started up richer, which are presumably closer to their steady state. We would therefore expect to see a negative relationship between initial conditions (per capita GDP in 1960) and the growth which followed. This does indeed appear to be the case. As Box 4.1 explains, among

---

 Box 4.1   A Snail's Pace: The 2% Convergence Rule

The convergence hypothesis can be expressed in the following way:[1]

$$\text{(4.1)} \qquad \frac{\Delta Y_t}{Y_t} - a = \beta \frac{\bar{Y}_t - Y_t}{\bar{Y}_t},$$

which asserts that the *growth rate* of an economy in period t, $\frac{\Delta Y_t}{Y_t}$, will be higher than its steady-state growth rate (a) when current GDP (Y_t) is less than the steady-state *level* ($\bar{Y}_t$) predicted by savings and technology. The parameter β captures the speed of convergence. The greater the distance is between the current GDP and its steady-state value, the faster the rate of growth. For the countries shown in Figure 4.1, Robert Barro of Harvard and Xavier Sala-i-Martin of Pompeu Fabra University[2] conclude that β is about 0.02, which means that about 2% of the gap in per capita income is closed per year, on aver-

age. This implies that it takes roughly 35 years to eliminate 50% of the difference between a given region and the leading one.[3] As an example, consider the convergence of regions within the USA. In 1880, the US South had a GDP per capita of about one-third of the richer, north-eastern New England region. This very low initial condition reflected the destruction of capital and infrastructure during the Civil War. It has taken more than a century of convergence for GDP per capita of the two regions to move to within roughly 10% of each other. Similarly, the hopes and expectations that southern Italy, eastern Germany, or western Spain will converge quickly to the leading regions of their respective countries have not been entirely fulfilled. We will look at some reasons why convergence may be held in check, an issue of burning relevance to some countries of Eastern and Central Europe.

---

[3] This is the useful rule-of-thumb for computing doubling time or half-lives. Suppose a variable x grows at a constant positive rate of g% per annum, then it will double in roughly $70/g$ years. If it is shrinking at rate g, it will shrink to half its size in $70/g$ years. See the WebAppendix for a derivation of this rule.

[1] Interested readers can see in the WebAppendix how this formulation is derived.
[2] See Barro and Sala-i-Martin (1991).

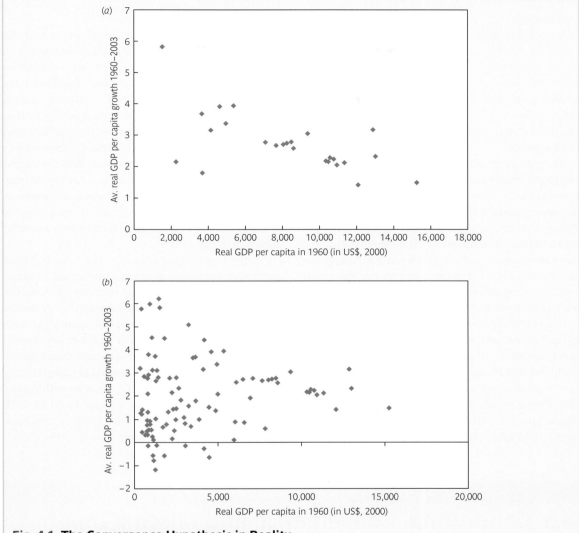

Fig. 4.1 The Convergence Hypothesis in Reality

All things equal, growth theory predicts that poorer countries should grow faster than richer ones. Panel (*a*), which plots the average growth rate for 25 advanced OECD countries over 1960–2003 against initial GDP per capita in 1960, lends strong support to the convergence hypothesis. Panel (*b*), which displays the experience of 102 countries over the same period, does not.

Sources: Heston, Summers, and Aten (2006); authors' calculations.

these countries, it takes about 35 years to eliminate half of the gap between any nation and the richest ones. While the optimistic message of the convergence hypothesis is that poorer countries should grow faster than average, practical experience teaches us that the process is slow, even under the best of circumstances.

4.2.2 Reality: Growth Clubs and Growth Traps

While panel (*a*) shows that the convergence hypothesis does remarkably well among the club of richer nations, panel (*b*) of Figure 4.1 shows that, for the world as a whole, there is little or no evidence of convergence. Evidently, per capita incomes differ considerably and that, for many poor countries, income differences persist or have even widened. While standards of living among the wealthier countries seem to be organized around **convergence clubs**, many poorer countries seem to be 'stuck' in **growth traps** with low per capita GDP and low or even negative growth. How can we explain this apparent contradiction with the principles laid out in Chapter 3?

One possibility is that countries with low income per capita suffer from insufficient capital accumulation because of inadequate saving or destruction by war or natural disaster. Yet low or inadequate domestic savings alone cannot explain the situation. While we stressed in Chapter 3 that investment must equal savings, this need not be true out of the steady state. It is very possible for foreigners —either individuals or corporations—to invest in poor countries. In this case, investment could be financed through foreign borrowing. In fact, if capital is free to move, we should expect multinational firms, investors, and financiers to move capital to countries where capital–labour ratios are low and, therefore, returns on investment ought to be high. Over time, capital–labour ratios (k) should be equalized across countries. This process may take some time, of course, but a process of convergence towards similar capital–labour ratios, and therefore per capita GDPs should occur.

A second possibility is that chronically poor countries suffer from technological backwardness or a lack of a properly functioning economy. It must be that, for some reason, the poorest countries have not yet been able to reach a steady-state level attainable by rich countries—point B in Figure 3.4. In that case, when and if they eliminate the barriers that prevent them from moving towards their steady states, they should catch up and therefore grow faster than the wealthy economies, which can only grow at the speed of technological progress. A prominent example is China, which has grown by some 10% per year ever since it abandoned central planning in the 1980s.

Plainly, this process may have occurred in China and India recently, but it hasn't occurred in many countries.[4] Poorer countries' inability to close the income gap represents a massive challenge to the international community and to economics as well. It calls into question the basic assumption that all benefit from free markets. It also casts doubt on the validity of the principles presented in Chapter 3. At the very least, it suggests that there is something systematic at work that we have not taken into account. Could our story just be too simple? Let us try to review what could be changed to better explain the facts.

4.3 Conditional Convergence and Missing Inputs

So far, we have implicitly assumed that all countries have access to the same technology, represented by the production function. What if they were to differ? Figure 4.2 shows an example of dissimilar production functions in two otherwise identical economies, in which households save the same fraction of their income and with the same capital-widening lines in both. The figure shows that two countries with dissimilar production functions will converge to different steady states. The notion that convergence occurs, but to steady states which depend on the individual attributes of an economy, nation, or region, is called **conditional convergence**.

---

[4] Nobel Laureate Robert E. Lucas, Jr of Chicago estimated that if India and the United States had the same production function, the marginal product of capital in the former would have to be about 58 times the marginal product in the latter! In his words, 'If this model were anywhere close to being accurate, and if world capital markets were anywhere close to being free and complete, it is clear that, in the face of return differentials of this magnitude, investment goods would flow rapidly from the United States and other wealthy countries to India and other poor countries. Indeed, one would expect *no* investment to occur in the wealthy countries in the face of return differentials of this magnitude.' (Lucas 1990: 92.)

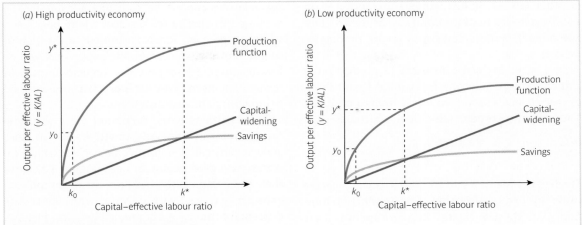

Fig. 4.2 Conditional Convergence

The economies depicted in the two panels are identical in all respects except that the available production technology is more productive at all levels of capital per capita in (*a*) compared with (*b*). In the steady state, the more productive economy is richer because it has a higher capital–effective labour ratio. For two countries with identical initial capital stock per effective labour (k_0), conditional convergence will occur to fundamentally different steady states. The richer economy at the outset will also grow faster along its path to the steady state, as predicted by equation (4.1). Conditional convergence means taking not only an economy's initial condition into account, but also its steady state.

But why should production functions differ across countries? International differences are unlikely due to technology in the strict sense. It is hard to see why knowledge or the mere availability of state-of-the-art methods can differ across countries for any period of time. Information is freely available, so producing clothing or electronic chips in an internationally competitive market will necessarily involve the same production techniques whether in Taiwan, Germany, India, or Zimbabwe. Yet, most experts would agree that productivity per head in these countries would be significantly different even if they had the same amount of capital per head to work with.

The most important reason why production functions are different is the existence of other observable inputs to the production function which make capital and labour more productive, just as technological progress does. Research has identified a long list of such influences. While they can be thought of as 'technology' in the broader sense, they are observable and often are quite evident features distinguishing rich, fast-growing countries from poor and stagnant ones. Which factors are they,

exactly? We now examine a number of possible explanations.

4.3.1 Human Capital

Education and training

Just as firms acquire physical capital for producing goods and services, individuals expend time, energy, and money to acquire knowledge and learning how to use that knowledge. These activities range from going to school, learning a skill, or taking a training course. Acquisition of knowledge is an investment. It represents a sacrifice today—foregoing a paid job, or the costs of education—for gains in the future. Such sacrifices are generally made because future gains exceed the initial costs.[5] It is for this reason that one speaks of investment in **human capital**. Better-trained and educated workers are more productive, and more productive workers can earn higher wages. Beyond this, more educated workers tend to enhance the productivity

---

[5] In Chapters 7 and 8 the notion of an investment and the assessment of the desirability of investment will be made much more precise.

of other factors. Skilled workers are better at operating complex machines, and may be used to manage other labourers and organize the production process.

Thus, it makes sense to think of production as combining not only physical capital K and hours of work L, but also a third input, human capital H. The economy's production function becomes

(4.2) $$Y = A\,F(K, L, H).$$
$$+ \quad + \quad +$$

Much of the reasoning in Chapter 3 can be repeated using this extended version of the production function. Like physical capital, human capital is accumulated over time and is subject to depreciation as knowledge progresses and people age. This implies that countries that invest more in education and training tend to be better off in the long run—they would tend to have a production function in panel (*a*) of Figure 4.2 rather than in panel (*b*).

Yet, this does not quite explain away all the puzzles. If the production function (4.2) exhibits constant returns to scale in all three factors—capital, pure labour, and human capital—then the marginal product of human capital must be decreasing, just as it was for capital in Chapter 3.[6] Then, again, it follows that, in the steady state, long-run growth rates in economies with low and high 'savings' rates in human capital will still be the same, determined by the rate of technological progress. Of course, the country that invests more in human capital will be richer and more productive.

Health

Human capital is not just education. It includes anything that raises labour productivity for a given capital stock. In particular, human capital also includes the state of health of workers. Freedom from disease and chronic illness as well as access to adequate medical care are considered by many to be fundamental human rights, but they also represent a critically important determinant of economic prosperity. Workers who are ill or must care

for relatives cannot be available for productive activities. Furthermore, in places where health services are poor or access is limited to the richest segment of the population, life expectancy will be low. Reduced life expectancy reduces incentives for individuals to invest in education, and can lead to emigration of wealthy elites.

Poor health services, therefore, are a plausible further interpretation of growth traps. But does good health cause high income, or does high income cause good health, or both? Figure 4.3 shows that the relationship between income and life expectancy is positive, but by no means linear. Life expectancy increases dramatically with income. Not only is life expectancy shamefully low in the very poorest countries, but the growth benefits from improved human condition in these countries are likely to be shamefully high. In large parts of the world, existing medicines could cure endemic sicknesses, but people cannot afford them. The AIDS disaster in Africa is a tragic example of a vicious circle in which poverty shortens life expectancy, which further cripples incentives to invest in human capital and future growth.

4.3.2 Public Infrastructure

A second important factor which is missing from the production function is **public infrastructure**. This includes streets, public transport, telecommunication, postal services, airports, systems of water distribution, electricity provision, and sewage treatment, etc. Like the private capital stock, public infrastructure are goods which contribute to general productivity and are widely available, often at low or no cost, and are most often provided by the government. Firms use roads and telephone lines as much as they use their own computers, machines, and lorries. At the aggregate level, the production function can be further augmented to include the stock of public capital, which we will call K^G:

(4.3) $$Y = A\,F(K, L, H, K^G).$$
$$+ \quad + \quad + \quad +$$

The importance of public infrastructure raises a number of questions. Public infrastructure is often free to use, but it is definitely not costless. Like private physical capital, it must be financed. Gov-

---

6 In general, if the production function is subject to constant returns to scale in all inputs, it must be the case that the marginal productivity of each input taken individually is decreasing.

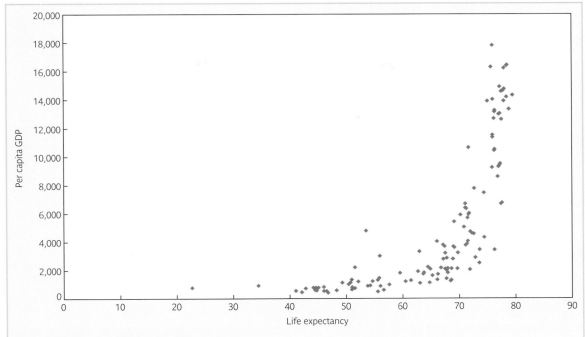

Fig. 4.3 Life Expectancy and Income

In a cross-section of nations, life expectancy declines dramatically at low to moderate income levels. It is difficult to believe that general health conditions do not influence investment decisions, especially in skills and education. At the same time, the demand for health depends on income.

Source: Bloom, Canning, Graham, and Sevilla (2000).

ernments are generally in charge of infrastructure spending, and use taxation or user fees to finance these expenditures. While private firms are under constant pressure from their owners to evaluate the balance of costs and benefits from acquiring more equipment, it is difficult, if not impossible, for the government to evaluate the benefits that accrue in millions of ways to millions of users. Furthermore, politicians rarely reap the benefits of infrastructure spending directly. At best, infrastructure enhances tax revenues in the future, and politicians may not be in power to claim credit for those future growth effects. Figure 4.4 shows the average amounts that European governments spent on capital accumulation over the period 1995–2005. The wide variation across countries signals both needs to modernize their infrastructures (Ireland, Portugal, and Spain) and constraints of fiscal policy (Germany and the UK).

A number of difficulties arise in getting the level of spending on public infrastructure right. Some governments tend to underinvest because other uses of taxpayers' money are more politically rewarding, or because pressures to cut the budget force spending cuts. On the other hand, some other governments might spend too much on infrastructure because political lobbies for public works defend this budgetary item. Growth may be held back for lack of adequate infrastructure in the first case and because of excessive taxation in the second case. In order to reduce the risk of such slippage, a number of governments have increasingly decided to privatize these areas. Indeed, over the last decade, the production of electricity, telephone, water, railways, etc has been turned over to the private sector. Yet, we must remember that there is no guarantee that public infrastructure will be adequately provided, an issue to which we return in Chapter 18.

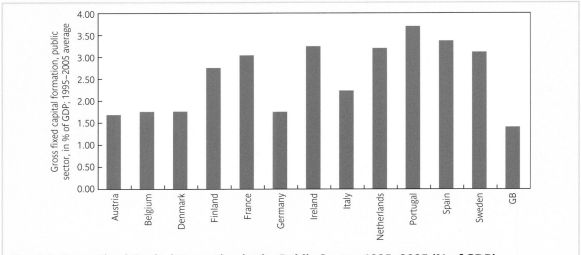

Fig. 4.4 Gross Fixed Capital Formation in the Public Sector, 1995–2005 (% of GDP)

On average, European countries spend 2–3% of GDP on public infrastructure. Yet the variation across countries is high.

4.3.3 Social Infrastructure

Even accounting for 'hard factors' like education, health, and infrastructure, it remains difficult to account for the enormous differences in total factor productivity between the richest and the poorest nations of the world. Researchers Robert Hall and Charles Jones have pointed out that the level of GDP per capita in the USA is roughly 35 times as high as in Niger in Africa.[7] This means that an average US worker works 10 days to produce the *annual* output of a worker in Niger. Naturally, part of this difference is linked to the fact that US workers have better capital equipment, education and skills, and public infrastructure to work with. Yet even if these differences are taken into account, US workers are still almost eight times more productive in per capita terms. Economists attribute this wide gap to 'soft' factors which improve both directly and indirectly the effectiveness of workers.

The first of these is **property rights**. A recurrent theme of Chapters 3 and 4 is that growth is driven by investment. In Chapter 3, emphasis was placed on physical capital, while in this chapter we have seen that the concept of investment is flexible enough to include public infrastructure, health, and human

capital. The common feature of an investment, which will be spelled out in more detail in Chapters 7 and 8, is that it means spending now for uncertain benefits in the future. It is often taken for granted that ownership of capital will be unquestioned both today and in the future, and that individuals will be able to use the skills that they acquire. In both cases, we can speak of clearly defined rights of ownership, or property rights, which are respected by others and systematically enforced by the state. While property rights are well established in the richest countries of the world, they cannot be taken for granted universally.

Property rights require clear, credible, and enforceable legislation or constitutional provisions which guarantee that individuals and firms cannot be dispossessed of their belongings, except if they violate the law and even then, only after due process. The concept of property rights is not restricted to merely retaining one's belongings. In the extreme case, it would guarantee that one's possessions can always be used as intended and disposed of, under all circumstances. Such absolute property rights are rarely observed: landowners are seldom allowed to build 'the house of their dreams' without the implicit or explicit permission of their residential area. More relevant for economic growth, property

---

[7]   Hall and Jones (1999).

rights are denied if a firm is taken over by the state, say, to produce weaponry against the will of its owners. Nationalizations, which occurred in France as recently as the early 1980s, similarly violate property rights, even if the owners are compensated, because they break the link between investment and its intended use. Nationalizations are an example of retroactive legislation, enacted after the original investment was carried out. They damage the fabric of trust between capital owners and the government, which depends on productive economic activity to finance its activities.

At the individual level, property rights should be extended to **human rights**. Being arbitrarily sent to jail, being barred from jobs, or being prevented from performing (non-harmful) economic activities prevents people from using their human capital. Mere threats of imprisonment or assassination also deny property and human rights. As long as individuals do not have basic freedoms of association, expression, and protection from violence—and these irrespective of sex, race, political opinions, or religious beliefs—their property rights are not established.

It is easy to see why property rights are a precondition for long-run economic growth. If investors cannot be sure that they will own their investments tomorrow, why bother to invest today? This would also explain why capital does not always seem to flow from rich to poor countries. Even if the rate of return on capital in poor countries is much higher, the risk of expropriation or arbitrary restriction of property rights may convince investors to keep their money in richer, more stable places. And if investment is held back, future growth will be too. This elementary proposition is far from being universally accepted. Box 4.2 examines communism, a doctrine which explicitly rejected private ownership of means of production. More

Box 4.2 Communism and Economic Growth in Communist Countries

In its unrecanted form, communism holds that private ownership of capital leads to the never-ending concentration of wealth in a few hands, while workers are subordinated and kept at the subsistence level of existence. A revolution would ultimately collectivize ownership of the capital stock ('the means of production' in Marxian terminology), by nationalizing large private firms, and in some countries even by banning small ones as well. In several countries, collective ownership was extended to land and housing. While communism or state socialism has been in decline since the mid-1980s, there are still a number of countries which adhere to its tenets (Cuba, Venezuela, North Korea). While undoubtedly one of the most dynamic market economies of the world today, China still claims to be a 'people's republic' and still shows the baggage of decades of socialism in the thousands of state enterprises still in government ownership.

While driven by lofty aims of creating a better society, communism suffers from fundamental flaws. Most economists agree that incentives to work, invest, and innovate are severely attenuated in societies of collectivized ownership and centralized economic planning. To counteract this, communist regimes offered a combination of centrally organized carrots (rewards) and sticks (penalties). Firm managers negotiated production plans with the central planning office, and were provided with the necessary means, equipment, and salaries. Both managers and workers were also offered various incentives to produce more: more money, medals, better housing, and other benefits. Under-performance was punished, sometimes harshly so.

How did it work? Figure 4.5 shows that, up until the early 1970s, the growth performance was good, certainly on a par with Western Europe. Part of the reason was catch-up after the destruction of the Second World War, which affected both East and West. But then things turned sour, much worse than in Western Europe. Most centrally-planned countries experienced two decades of negative growth rates, an extraordinary failure. Central planning simply did not work, and brought the collapse of the communist regimes. The odd man out is China: a poor performance over the first period, followed by fast growth. Certainly, the explanation of the Chinese success story is the gradual relaxation of central planning, accompanied by the introduction of private ownership. But another part of the story seems to be the strict discipline imposed by the regime, a puzzling observation.

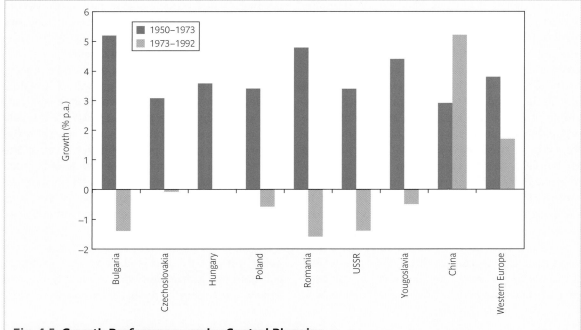

Fig. 4.5 Growth Performance under Central Planning

The good performance over the first 25 years has been followed by a catastrophic decline over the following two decades. China stands out as a different and puzzling story.

Source: Maddison (1995).

generally, property rights are routinely denied by arbitrary, undemocratic regimes and by wars, both civil and international.

The relationship between property rights, broadly defined, and growth is more complicated than meets the eye. There is powerful evidence that rich and fast-growing countries tend to be democratic, law-abiding, and peaceful, but it is not clear what comes first—economic well-being or property rights. One view is that property rights are a prerequisite for sustained economic growth. Another view is that affluence makes basic freedoms and property rights more desirable. It could well be that each aspect strengthens the other, generating either virtuous circles of growth and better-established rights, or vicious circles leading to poverty traps which combine economic stagnation and the absence of property (and human) rights.

Indeed, there are cases of countries which embarked on a stable, often fast growth path while enjoying limited property and human rights: the

communist countries, Chile under Pinochet, or some countries of South-East Asia. Conversely, it can be argued that some countries visibly fail to grow because property rights are non-existent. A sobering example is Sub-Saharan Africa, which has grown by a mere 1.5% (GNI per capita) over the years 1965–1997, while the world's overall growth over the same period stood at 50.9%. As Figure 4.6 shows, this average performance conceals a wide disparity, depending on the policy regime.

Another main threat against property rights is armed conflict, which destroys both physical and human capital. If wars are occasional, a catch-up process sets in once they are over. This was the experience of Europe after 1945, which enjoyed rapid growth while building supra-national institutions (the common market, the European Court of Justice, monetary union) and peace-enhancing mechanisms (NATO, the Organization for Security and Cooperation in Europe) to reduce the risk of renewed conflict.

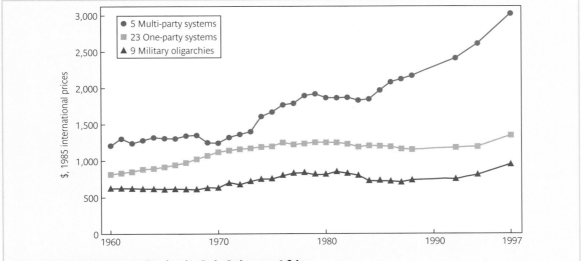

Fig. 4.6 Real GDP per Capita in Sub-Saharan Africa

Over the period 1960–1999, the five countries with democratic political regimes (Botswana, Gambia, Mauritius, Senegal, and Zimbabwe) display a much better growth performance than countries with one-party systems. Countries with military regimes have stagnated.

Source: Ndulu and O'Connell (1999).

Civil wars can also pose an enormous hindrance to economic development. Africa has been devastated by civil conflict as states inherited from colonial times have tried to come to grips with ethnic diversity. For example, the index of ethnic fractionalization stands at 67.6% in Sub-Saharan Africa, and at 32.7% on average in other developing countries.[8] Besides the obvious material destruction, investment is held back and human capital declines through the emigration of wealthy and powerful elites. Figure 4.7 establishes an unmistakable link between growth and property rights, where the latter is measured by a legal index of the rule of law prevailing in the country.

4.3.4 Contributions of Missing Inputs

Alongside capital and labour, human capital, public and private infrastructure should be taken as inputs of the production function. Although precision is obviously limited, most of the missing inputs can be quantified, or expressed in a readily comparable form. Do they account for average growth over a period of several decades, in a type of statistical 'horse race'? Table 4.1 presents estimates of their effects on average annual growth rates.

1 Catch-up (convergence). Starting far below its steady state, a country should be accumulating capital, both physical and human, more rapidly, as well as adopting new technologies. The table indicates that the economic backwardness is closed at a rate of about 2.5% per year (the higher is initial GDP, the less it subsequently grows).

2 Human capital. People's knowledge, ranging from basic literacy to sophisticated skills, represents an additional factor of production. One common measure of investment in education is the average number of years spent in secondary or higher education by males.[9] Raising the population's

---

[8] This index reports the probability that two people randomly chosen in a country belong to two different ethnic groups; Collier and Gunning (1999).

[9] This does not mean that female schooling is unimportant, even if the study reported here does not detect any clear *direct* effect. Female schooling is usually found to be more socially productive than male schooling, but this effect is more complex, and mostly *indirect*. In many developing countries, female school attendance is much lower than for males, so a little effort produces large effects. Also better-educated females make better mothers, with considerable impacts on children's education, health, and, more widely, approach to life. Female education also affects fertility.

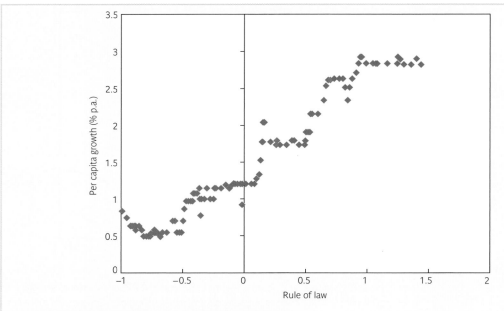

Fig. 4.7 Rule of Law and Growth, 1960–1998
Based on a large sample of countries, the figure relates average economic growth over nearly four decades with an index measuring how well the rule of law applies. The index ranges from −2.5 (complete breakdown) to +2.5 (perfect legal protection). It includes political corruption, likelihood of government repudiation of contracts, risk of government expropriation, quality of bureaucracy, and overall maintenance of law. The figure sends a very strong message: the better is the rule of law enforced, the faster a country grows. Note the beneficial effect only sets in after some minimal threshold.
Source: Easterly (1999).

Table 4.1 What Drives Growth? Some Estimates

Factor	Effect on annual growth rate
Initial per capita GDP (effect of 1% higher level)	−2.5
Education (effect of 1 more year)	0.4
Life expectancy (effect of 10% increase)	0.8
Fertility rate (effect of a 50% increase)	−0.6
Government consumption (effect of a 10% higher ratio)	−0.6
Rule of law (effect of an increase of 0.1)	0.2
Investment (effect of a 10% ratio)	0.8

Source: Barro and Sala-i-Martin (2004).

average schooling by one year is found to speed up growth by 0.4% per year.

3 Health. A ten-year increase in life expectancy at birth raises average growth by 0.8%—a very large effect indeed. As stated already, the effect is likely to come through investment in human capital and, more generally, more effective labour input and greater work effort. This effect is unlikely to be important in rich countries where it is retirement that limits the length of active lifetime. It may be crucial in the poorest countries where few people ever reach retirement age.

4 Fertility. The negative effect of the rate of fertility (the average number of children per woman) seems related to two main effects: capital-widening and time spent by mothers in child rearing instead of economic activity.

5 Public consumption. Reducing public consumption by 10% of GDP raises growth by 0.6%. This measure excludes spending on public infrastructure. The negative effect probably reflects the fact that high public employment tends to be inefficient and invites corruption, as well as high tax collection, which acts as a disincentive to savings, investment, and innovative activity.

6 Rule of law. Lasting, credible property rights are a precondition for investment in both physical and human capital. Going the full way from the worst to the top ranking raises growth by a whopping 2% annually.

4.4 Possibility of Endogenous Growth[10]

The analysis of Chapter 3 showed that technological change is the ultimate engine that pushes the output–labour ratio—and GDP per capita—ever higher. While differences in human capital, public investments, and social infrastructure can explain differences in long-run levels of national prosperity, they do not change the bottom line. Per capita growth in the long run settles down to the rate of technological change, which is exogenous at rate *a*. Technological progress is the engine of growth because it is assumed never to run out of fuel; it increases exogenously, irrespective of what happens.

Can the growth process be as simple as that? Might not technological progress itself—or at least part of it—be driven by man-made decisions? Technological progress is related to investment in education and science, to efforts in research and development (R&D), and to millions of discoveries, small and large. Might not those discoveries be affected by what others do?

We will find that growth can only perpetuate itself when the marginal product of capital stops falling. As we explore the nature of technological progress, we open up the hunt for possible sources of non-decreasing marginal productivities. **Endogenous growth theory** attempts to explain how growth in the leading economies can vary in the long run—meaning over several decades at a time. Because it represents the boundary of economic research, it is not accepted by all, for reasons we discuss below.

4.4.1 A Sufficient Condition for Endogenous Growth

A hallmark of the analysis of Chapter 3 is that the capital–labour ratio will converge to a steady-state value which is predetermined by the economy's individual characteristics. Declining marginal productivity is responsible for this result. Graphically, this feature is captured by the gradual flattening out of the aggregate production function shown in Figure 3.13. As the capital stock in an economy increases, the marginal product of additional investments and additions to the capital stock declines, as do their contribution to generating new income. As the marginal income from investment falls, savings and investment decline and the economy grows more slowly.

But suppose that marginal productivity did not decline enough, and that the slope of the production function schedule always exceeded the slope of the capital-widening line. This would mean that, for sufficiently high levels of the capital–effective labour ratio, the production function schedule would become a straight line. This would remain consistent with output increasing at the same rate as new capital is being accumulated, one of the stylized facts discussed in Chapter 3.

Figure 4.8 shows how things change radically. If the capital–labour ratio is initially at k_1, savings and investment correspond to point A and lie above the

---

[10] The material in this section is somewhat more advanced.

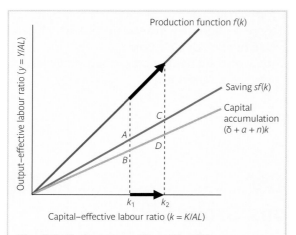

Fig. 4.8 Endogenous Growth with Non-Declining Marginal Productivity

When the marginal productivity of capital is constant, the production function is a straight line. If saving is large enough to exceed depreciation and the need for capital-widening, the capital stock will increase without bound. For example, starting from per capita capital stock k_1, AB represents new capital being installed, which takes the economy to k_2. There CD corresponds to a further increase in the capital stock, and so on.

capital-widening line (point B). The ratio of capital to effective labour ratio $k = K/AL$ will thus increase by the distance AB. As this ratio grows to reach the level k_2, saving is determined by point C and the capital–effective labour ratio keeps rising even faster as indicated by the distance CD.

Because the marginal productivity of capital does not decline, more of it produces more income and therefore more saving. The striking consequence is that the output–labour and capital–labour ratios never stop growing.[11] This contrasts sharply with the case of declining marginal productivity in Figure 3.13, in which a unique steady state is always reached with $y = Y/AL$ constant, and GDP per capita Y/L growing at the constant rate a. Now y itself is

rising secularly, while Y/L is rising even faster.[12] Another implication of non-declining marginal productivity of capital is that an increase in the saving rate makes the saving schedule rotate upwards, leading to faster accumulation of the capital stock and permanent growth in GDP per capita.

We have thus found a sufficient condition for endogenous growth: the marginal product of capital must stop declining. The question is whether this condition is reasonable and whether it occurs in reality. The next two sections outline some possible economic mechanisms which could give rise to endogenous growth.

4.4.2 Externalities and Constant Returns in Accumulated Factors

One important reason that the marginal product of capital ceases to decline is because the law of diminishing returns no longer holds. For some reason, the accumulation of capital—physical as well as human or infrastructural capital—no longer diminishes its marginal product *from the perspective of the aggregate economy*. The English economist Alfred Marshall hypothesized that the perceived effect of an individual's actions can differ substantially from the factual outcome if others act in the same way. In particular, while each individual perceives diminishing marginal returns to investment, it could well be that, when *everyone* engages in the same activity, effective marginal productivity does not fall, but remains constant. Marshall, in fact, was introducing a new concept—economic externality.

An externality occurs when the actions of individuals affect the welfare or productivity of others in ways which are not mediated by the market. For example, someone listening to loud music on an MP3-player may disturb those around him; he imposes a cost on others but one for which there is no market. There is no market because a property right is not assigned: it is not clear whether one owns the 'right' to quiet surroundings or to listen

---

[11] A simple example: suppose the production function in intensive form is simply $y = Ak$ where A is a positive constant. Then the capital accumulation equation is $\Delta k = sAk - (\delta + a + n)k$, which implies a growth rate of k given by $\Delta k/k = sA - (\delta + a + n)$. Furthermore, $\Delta y/y = \Delta k/k$, so a higher growth rate of capital per capita (k) forever implies a higher growth rate of output per capita (y) forever.

[12] Note that, in this case, the saving line must lie above the capital accumulation line ($sA > \delta + a + n$). If this were not the case, the capital–effective labour ratio would instead shrink to zero over time, because savings would never be sufficient to make up for depreciation and capital-widening.

Box 4.3 **Constant Returns in Accumulated Factors: Some Mathematical Examples**

Using the Cobb–Douglas production function,[13] it is easy to see how constant returns in accumulated factors could arise and lead to the production function shown in Figure 4.8.

The simplest example involves human capital. Suppose that aggregate output of an economy is given by the function $Y = K^{\alpha}(AL)^{1-\alpha}$, and that $A = H$, that is, human capital is the same thing as labour augmenting technical progress. A doubling of human and physical capital will lead to a doubling of output, holding labour input constant. If agents save constant fractions s_K and s_H of their income in physical and human capital, respectively, then K and H will grow along a steady-state growth path at the same rate as Y. In addition, this rate will depend on the savings rates s_K and s_H.

A second example of constant returns in the accumulated factors involves infrastructure. Let K^G be the stock of infrastructure capital described in Section 4.2.2, and is financed by taxation on output at the rate τ: $\Delta K^G = \tau Y$. Let the production function be $Y = AK^{\alpha}L^{1-\alpha}$. Finally, let $A = (K^G)^{\gamma}$, meaning that total factor productivity is increasing in infrastructure, but at a decreasing rate ($\gamma < 1$). Under these conditions, the economy's production function is given by $Y = (K^G)^{\gamma}K^{\alpha}L^{1-\alpha}$. If $\gamma = 1 - \alpha$, the economy has constant returns in K and K^G, the two factors which can be accumulated by saving out of current income, and will behave exactly as in Figure 4.8. Here the

tax rate τ acts like the savings rate. Note that a similar argument could be made for human capital, substituting H for K^G throughout the example. This would support the case for government-financed education.

A third example is a Marshallian externality. Suppose an economy consists of a very large number of identical firms, each producing with the same production function $Y_i = AK_i^{\alpha}L_i^{1-\alpha}$. But now suppose that A depends on the sum of what all the producers are doing, but no single producer can perceive her individual effect on A. To make the point, let $A = Z^{\gamma}$ where Z is an indicator of the sum of all the outputs of the individual firms: $Z = \Sigma_i K_i^{\alpha}L_i^{1-\alpha}$ and assume that $\gamma < 1$. Again, if $\gamma = 1 - \alpha$, this economy will have constant returns in capital alone, even though no individual producer perceives this to be the case.

All these examples require restrictive assumptions on the parameters of the model. In the first, human capital acts as labour-augmenting technical progress without any slippage (loss of marginal productivity). The second two cases require the 'knife-edge' condition $\gamma = 1 - \alpha$. These assumptions led Robert Solow, the intellectual father of growth theory, to criticize models of endogenous growth precisely because they lack robustness, i.e. they are sensitive to such assumptions. If there is little reason to believe that these conditions hold exactly, the overall plausibility of the conclusions is easy to challenge.

to music in an unrestricted way. This is an example of a negative externality, because one's action imposes a cost on others. Externalities can also be positive. For instance, working alongside skilled and educated people may increase your own productivity as they give you tips and provide advice.

That individual activities could increase aggregate productivity, even if the individual does not perceive any effect of his own actions, is called a **Marshallian externality**. If the Marshallian externality creates conditions of constant returns to scale with respect to accumulated factors *only*—physical

capital, human capital, or infrastructure—then the marginal product of capital need not decline with growth, and endogenous growth is possible. In Box 4.3, the mathematics of such conditions is spelled out in more detail.

4.4.3 Knowledge

The term A has been defined as 'the state of technology', but what is it exactly? A very particular feature of knowledge is that it is a **public good**. Two features characterize public goods. First, they are non-excludable, meaning that the consumer of a good cannot legally or physically prevent others from consuming it at the same time. Second, they are non-rivalrous to the extent that the consumption of

---

[13] The Cobb–Douglas production function was introduced in Box 3.2.

Table 4.2 Non-rivalrousness and Excludability: A Taxonomy of Goods

	Rivalrous	Non-rivalrous
Excludable	Most conventionally marketed private goods	Police protection, patented inventions, copyrighted material, subscription cable television programming
Non-excludable	Parking spaces, public tennis courts, beaches, park benches, congested highways	National defence, good weather, radio/television programming, internet, knowledge

Box 4.4 The Origins of Icons

Because it is easy to borrow, copy, or steal new ideas or basic research results, innovative activity frequently yields far greater gains to society than to the clever individuals who first came up with them. A striking new example is the 'technology' of icons, cursors/pointers, double-clicking, and windows. This paradigm for working with information was developed by the Xerox Corporation in their Palo Alto research facility in the 1970s, before personal computers and the mouse were even invented. Apple was able to convert the technology into a usable system and Microsoft, Intel, and other companies were able to make enormous amounts of money on what was essentially a free technology. Describing the invention, Professor DeLong of Berkeley writes:

The net result? Large benefits to the economy and the society in terms of expanded productivity growth from the work carried on at Xerox's Palo Alto Research Center in the 1970s. But barely a cent returned in revenues to Xerox from this particular drain on its cash flow. Companies that are in business to make money will not long spend a great time and effort on such research projects that do not boost productivity and revenues, even if they boost industry productivity and revenues manifold. Thus there is every reason to believe that the private sector tends to underinvest in research and development.[14]

a good by one person does not affect others' ability to enjoy it. Table 4.2 shows how goods and services we encounter in our economic life can be classified according to their excludability or the rival nature of their use. Knowledge turns out to be both non-excludable and non-rival. It is non-excludable because, once produced, it tends to be freely available. In the form of education or TV and radio programmes, knowledge is also non-rival; the consumption by one person does not preclude someone else from consuming (or using) it at the same time.

Because knowledge can be used over and over again, it cannot be characterized by diminishing returns. Some mathematical formulae from ancient times (e.g. the area of a circle) have been put to such extensive use since their discovery that they could well be among the most productive investments ever made! Yet, as Box 4.4 shows, the ultimate discoverers are frequently underpaid for their efforts. This crucial observation implies that, under intuitive and plausible conditions, knowledge can be the secret to endless growth.

Innovation and knowledge creation represent a clear case of a positive externality. Social gains resulting from the activities of creative, inventive thinkers generally exceed their private return. But the creation of new knowledge does not come free. Innovators work hard and invest lots of their own money in their ideas, blueprints, and inventions—as well as money of investors. It is hard to know whether these contributions to economic activity will be remunerated sufficiently. Will the inventors

[14] DeLong (1997).

of the next wonder drug or telecommunication device reap rewards for their hard work, or will copycats or 'intellectual pirates' steal the idea? And because they do, will the inventors and investors expend less effort than they should to achieve their goals? Later we discuss how societies encourage this engine of growth by establishing property rights over ideas for some limited time, enforcing them with judicial systems, and thereby seeking to encourage entrepreneurial activity essential to research and development.

4.4.4 Evidence for Endogenous Growth: Long Waves

Innovations add to our stock of knowledge but they come in many forms and shapes: new ideas (e.g. Newton's discovery of gravity), new techniques (electricity, the steam and combustion engines, computers), new processes (float glass, household appliances, the internet), or new consumer brands, designs, and products. How do these major discoveries really occur?

One view is that discoveries appear more or less randomly. R&D produces innovations, some big, some small, continuously restarting growth by boosting the existing technology. Another view, initially proposed by Harvard economist Joseph Schumpeter, is that big discoveries tend to be associated with long-term waves in economic activity, because they are followed by a number of subsequent, related secondary innovations. Figure 4.9 shows the average annual rate of increase in total factor productivity. We see a sharp acceleration in the UK and the USA early on in the twentieth century, which continues until the early 1970s. This wave is often associated with a succession of great inventions in the latter part of the nineteenth century: electricity, engines, petro-chemistry, pharmaceuticals, telephone, radio, etc. According to Schumpeter's vision of innovations, major innovations were bunched in their occurrence but required decades to diffuse across the economy.

To explain why innovation came in long waves, Schumpeter puts the entrepreneur at centre stage. When growth slows, some enterprising managers react by investing more in risky R&D projects. More research effort eventually pays off, producing

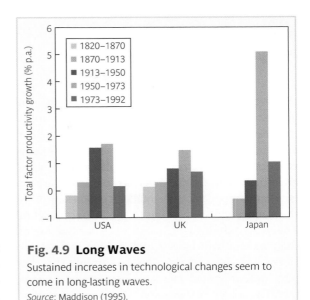

Fig. 4.9 Long Waves
Sustained increases in technological changes seem to come in long-lasting waves.
Source: Maddison (1995).

a number of innovations that emerge more or less simultaneously, all within a decade or two. As profits rise spectacularly, fierce competition sets in. Competition takes two forms: improvements and imitation. Both erode monopoly power of the original innovators, eating into their profits and reducing their ability and desire to pursue vigorous R&D. Technological progress slows down, ending the big wave of accelerated growth. As profits gradually decline, a new generation of entrepreneurs emerge and prepare the next long wave.

The **Schumpeterian theory of innovation** represents one of the most compelling accounts of the evolution of growth of advanced economies over the past two centuries. Although we still lack sufficient data to firmly establish its validity, the Schumpeter account is supported by the fact that long waves in growth occur across countries together, and that leading nations do tend to grow in a synchronous way. This supports the notion that innovations involve ideas and knowledge which travel rather well across national boundaries, even if they require some time. The leading nations tend to be those which innovate frequently, pushing out the frontiers of technological possibilities, while follower nations adopt later and adapt or perfect the technologies.

4.5 Growth Policy

What can governments do to increase long-run economic growth? When the issue of policy arises it is usually a good idea to follow the rule 'if it ain't broke, don't fix it'. In properly functioning economies, it is best to let the interplay of households and firms run its course, unless a convincing case for government policy can be made. A good example is the savings rate. According to the Solow model of Chapter 3, nations which save a greater fraction of their income will have a higher level of GDP per capita, but this certainly does not imply that the government should increase the national savings rate. The golden rule (Section 3.3) made it clear that a higher savings rate does not necessarily mean more consumption per capita, or more welfare for that matter.

Much of the discussion of Sections 4.3 and 4.4 centred around missing and possibly non-marketed factors in the production function and externalities. Here it is possible to make a convincing case for government intervention. Among other things, it may pay off to subsidize education, research and development, other innovative activities, and even certain types of investment spending. It may be worth improving the rewards to entrepreneurial activity, but it may also make sense to increase protection of innovators from copycat activity. It is generally a good idea to encourage trade and a stable economic environment. In the following sections we briefly discuss these policy options.

4.5.1 Education and Research

It is well established that education is a key factor for economic growth. Although education is frequently a private investment, it is difficult to borrow to pay for it. Unlike many investments, human capital does not involve collateral, an asset which can be pledged in case repayment of the loan does not occur. While firms can raise money from banks, stock markets, or their owners to buy equipment, many people cannot pay for their own education, especially in poor countries. The usual response is that

governments provide public education, along with scholarships for poorer students. Yet if the returns from education are better salaries, should the state provide public money for private benefit? The answer may still be yes, if human capital creates a Marshallian externality. Being the only one in a country who knows how to read and write is less useful, both privately and collectively, if most others cannot read and write. As noted in Box 4.3, human capital may not face diminishing marginal productivity at the collective level.

Human capital is a linchpin for any theory of growth which is based on inventions and innovation. It raises current productivity and helps speed the **diffusion** of innovations. Figure 4.10 shows that countries that began the growth journey in 1960 with more average schooling generally grew at a faster pace over the next four to five decades, but the correlation is not perfect. One interpretation is the message of conditional convergence in Section 4.2 of this chapter: a low stock of human capital hampers growth, *ceteris paribus*, for reasons expressed by equation (4.2) and Figure 4.2.

As an example, compare the Republic of Korea and Honduras. In 1960, the GDPs per capita of the two countries were roughly equal. By 2005, Korea's GDP per capita exceeded that of Honduras *by a factor of 667%*. The most striking difference between the two countries appears to be education. In 1960, the average Korean had almost twice as much completed years of schooling than the average Honduran.

Naturally, causality could and probably does also run the other way as well. Poor countries simply cannot afford accumulating much human capital, given the costs of education systems. We need not choose between these two interpretations, because *both* can be correct at the same time. Taken together, they suggest the existence of poverty traps: poor countries cannot invest enough in human capital, which in turn hinders growth. For the same reasons, individuals too can be trapped

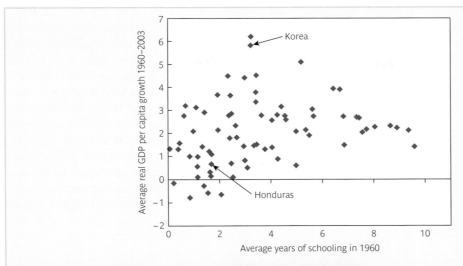

Fig. 4.10 Human Capital and Economic Growth, 1960–2003

The initial endowment of human capital—expressed crudely as average years of schooling in 1960—is strongly positively correlated with real growth over the following 4–5 decades. The cases of Honduras and Korea are striking examples of the correlation between education and growth.

in poverty, even in developed countries, which provides a justification for means-tested scholarships.

Externalities can also justify state subsidies for research laboratories. Indeed, a great deal of research—especially basic research—must be funded by government or non-profit institutions. But then, the problem encountered with public infrastructure also arises with knowledge: it is difficult if not impossible to determine the proper level of public financing of research. To make things even more complicated, research is inherently uncertain and often entails very long gestation periods, it is a risky undertaking. This all makes it very possible that not enough is spent on an activity that is obviously not politically attractive and yet, over the long haul, may be an essential source of increases in standards of living.

4.5.2 Intellectual Property, Patents, and Competition Policy

Because knowledge is unlikely to face diminishing returns, it is a potential source of endless growth. To encourage the private production of knowledge, governments should protect its excludability for

some period. Policies have been designed over the centuries to do precisely this. One is the **patent**. A patent confers on its owner the exclusive legal right to exploit an invention commercially, usually for a limited period of time. While not generally granted to ideas *per se*, patent protection is reserved for inventions which are sufficiently novel and wide-reaching. Similarly, **copyrights** safeguard artistic expression from plagiarism or outright duplication, and **trademarks** recognize exclusive use of a name or symbol to distinguish a firm's product in the market place. Like patents, copyrights and trademarks establish **intellectual property rights** on certain forms of knowledge.

With the possibility of obtaining intellectual property rights, investing in innovation—R&D, artistic expression, and brand development—can pay off. For some period, the holder of the patent can charge prices which are at least high enough to cover the costs of the research and development of the product. But there is a side-effect: patents confer monopoly power on their owners and thus allow them to charge much more than development costs. In one sense, monopoly is bad, since it allows the seller to set monopoly prices. Because demand is discouraged, patents limit the full exploitation of useful knowledge. At the same time, patents offer powerful incentives to researchers. Without them, knowledge creation and its contribution to economic growth would probably proceed at a much slower pace. As Box 4.5 shows, the border between fair remuneration and exploitation of monopoly power is arbitrary and subject to considerable legal wrangling.

This is why, even if patent protection confers monopoly power on their inventors, it may be a necessary evil for promoting the production of knowledge and thus for economic growth. If the widely-shared benefits of knowledge production are not reflected in their compensation, researchers will not deliver as much innovation as is socially desirable, if only because too few bright students will choose this career. Viewed this way, it is perhaps less objectionable that successful innovators derive extra profits from their temporary monopoly power. Naturally, after an invention is patented, the owner of the patent will charge a high price, possibly even higher than normal costs would warrant. Given that the invention has become public knowledge, governments have a strong *ex post* in-

 Box 4.5 Protecting and Punishing Monopolists

To many people, Bill Gates is a bad, mean monopolist. Monopoly rights belonging to the Microsoft Corporation have made him into one of the richest men in the world, since virtually every computer in the world is equipped with its software products. Perhaps this is why many cheered when the US Department of Justice and the European Commission initiated lawsuits against Microsoft. The lawsuits, however, were not about monopoly power derived from legal patents and copyrights. They were aimed at Microsoft's alleged stifling or even elimination of new competitor products and services. While Microsoft has made it possible for hundreds of millions of people to use computers for work and pleasure, history and innovations must continue. New innovators will continue to improve computers' software, and should be encouraged to do so.

Microsoft's encounter with justice is reminiscent of an equally famous trial pitting the US Justice Department against International Business Machines (IBM) in the late 1970s. At the time, IBM dominated the computer hardware industry: PCs didn't exist, and there was hardly a competitor which could produce powerful mainframe computers the way IBM did. The charge was very similar. IBM was accused of using its dominant position to eliminate new competitors. In the end, IBM argued that it retained its lead only thanks to its ability to innovate, and was hard-pressed to do so because of pressure from the competition. IBM won twice. The case against it was dismissed and its argument was soon proved correct as it lost ground to competition, especially with respect to small portable computers and networking machines. In relative terms, IBM is now a shadow of its former self. Microsoft was punished severely by the European Commission for not revealing details about its operating system software to firms which use it. Whether it will soon become a minor player remains to be seen.

An altogether different story involves the pharmaceutical industry. Most wonder drugs are indeed patented, and their inventors reap massive profits. What makes the case different is that drugs are paid for by health insurance, private or public. Insurance agencies agree with the pharmaceutical industry on 'fair' prices, which exceed the marginal cost of producing the drugs by a factor commonly believed to be ten or more. Pharmaceutical firms claim that this is the only way for them to recoup the huge costs of R&D. Critics call the industry's profits excessive, but find it difficult to find solid evidence to back their claim. They correctly note that a significant part of humanity cannot afford these drugs and die or are permanently incapacitated as a result, a fact most recently underlined by the global AIDS epidemic. Even more troubling is the absence of priority in the pharmaceutical research community to develop drugs which could eliminate tropical diseases, such as malaria, which kill or cripple hundreds of thousands. These diseases are ignored because they affect primarily poor people in poor countries with no ability to pay for the R&D costs.

centive to abrogate the original patent agreement. This would clearly make everyone better off in the short run, but would probably bring research and development to a standstill, since the promise of a patent would no longer be credible. For this reason, governments generally avoid breaking their promises.

4.5.3 Openness to Trade and Competition

International trade is an engine of growth. First, openness to trade and the resulting competition from foreign firms serves to spread knowledge and technology across national boundaries. Competition encourages domestic firms to adopt leading-edge production techniques and become more efficient. Multinational corporations, which operate in several countries at once, serve as an important channel in the diffusion of innovations. This view is based on the phenomenon of **learning by doing**, whereby people and firms improve their knowledge on the job. When a multinational establishes a production unit in a developing country, it usually brings with it a technology invented in its home country. Individuals who work in such firms acquire the technology and can subsequently create their own firms based on the new technology, or migrate to other firms which can then tool up. This possibility should be kept in mind when considering controversies that surround multinational corporations. From a *social* perspective, they contribute to convergence by accelerating the diffusion of innovations and thus the transfer of knowledge.

Growth and openness to international commerce are known to be positively related. Countries which have large trade exposure—measured as the ratio of exports plus imports to GDP—tend to grow faster. The experience of more open Western European countries, and especially the Asian Tigers of the last two decades, suggest that open economies grow faster, all things considered. This faster growth can be attributed to a number of possible effects. First, closed economic systems impede the transfer of knowledge, effectively excluding some individuals from what should be a non-excludable good. Openness allows for ideas to flow more easily across national boundaries. Second, openness means

increased competition from abroad. Domestic producers cannot rely on protection to shield their market positions from the threat of imports. They must constantly remain at the 'cutting edge' of new areas of innovation and development. To use the terminology of Section 4.4.3, this requires either innovation or imitation; either will have positive effects on productivity and growth.

4.5.4 Politics: Democracy, Equality, and Stability

We saw in Section 4.3 that credible property rights and peace are important elements of social infrastructure and are essential for economic development. Beyond property rights, the legitimate scope of government and its behaviour should be directed towards establishing stability and continuity, rather than interrupting it. The system of government can therefore do much for economic growth in a passive way: it can work towards the establishment of stable conditions that improve the business climate. Since it is most likely to represent the wishes of its citizens, democracy should be the ideal means of translating the common will into policy. Democracy should be conducive to a better growth performance, for all the reasons reviewed so far: property rights, economic and political stability, health, and institutions which have broad public acceptance.

Democracies are not perfect institutions, and the relationship between democracy and economic growth is a controversial one. Democratically elected governments may change frequently—with shifting coalitions of smaller parties, for example—and this may lead to constantly changing tax and expenditure policy. This type of uncertainty, especially if it applies to the taxation of physical or human capital, may deter longer-term projects from being undertaken. The rule of majority does not preclude actions against minorities, including some that violate property and human rights. Such actions may include legal pressure on 'the rich', ranging from nationalizations to heavy taxation, both of which discourage investment. At the same time, well-organized lobbies in many democracies enable wealthy minorities to exert disproportionate influence on decision-making. Democracies often find it difficult to organize the sacrifices necessary for sustained economic growth. Some salient examples are: (1) increasing the savings rate to accumulate capital for future generations; (2) the restructuring of economic activity which implies the painful decline of some sectors (agriculture, mining, or heavy industries, for example); (3) reform of the social safety net and labour market regulations, and (4) migration towards cities, which is accompanied by some degree of social and family dislocation. In facing up to such painful changes, democracies can encounter political difficulties. Some have concluded that only dictatorships are capable of suppressing opposition to changing conditions long enough for economic growth to take hold. In their view, democracy is a luxury that only rich societies can afford.

At the same time, only democracies have the legitimacy to guarantee the property rights needed for investment in human and physical capital (see Section 4.3). Inequality is harmful to growth if the poorest citizens are denied access to health, education, and a functioning infrastructure. Inequality is better tolerated when the political regime receives legitimacy from a majority of citizens. It is even argued that such legitimacy is necessary to carry out the deep reforms that accompany sustained growth. Dictatorships can impose changes, for a while; but eventually the changes themselves, which may be desirable from an economic viewpoint, become as unacceptable as the dictatorship itself, and may be swept away in painful revolutions. Finally, democracies rarely go to war with each other.

❗ Summary

1 The Solow model predicts that countries with identical production functions, savings rates, depreciation rates, and population growth will achieve the same level of production and income per capita, and they will grow at the same rate in the steady state. According to the convergence hypothesis, poorer countries should grow faster than wealthier ones.

2 Empirically, the convergence hypothesis fails in its unconditional form. While rich countries and wealthy regions of the world seem to converge in both level and growth rate of GDP per capita, a large part of the world does not. Many poorer countries appear to be locked in a poverty trap of economic stagnation.

3 The most compelling explanation of the lack of convergence in the data is that production functions are different across countries. Yet these differences are not likely to be due to different technologies in the narrow sense, since blueprints, information, and techniques are readily transferred across national boundaries. International differences in production functions are mostly due to missing inputs which enhance the productivity of capital and labour.

4 The conditional convergence hypothesis states that nations converge to levels implied by these missing inputs. When they are accounted for, nations do seem to converge to their individual steady states. An important conclusion is that nations can improve their economic condition by increasing their endowments of these missing, complementary inputs: human capital, public infrastructure, and social infrastructure.

5 Human capital is a central missing input in the production function. It ranges from education and training to the health of individuals. Countries with better educated, trained, and healthier workers are more productive, all else constant.

6 Public infrastructure, defined as those public goods which are accessible to all and often provided by the government, include roads and bridges, highways, airports, railways, and hos-

pitals. Public infrastructure is also an important determinant of the position of the production function, all other things being equal.

7 One of the most important missing factors for explaining the poor performance of many nations empirically is social infrastructure. Social infrastructure refers to those 'soft' factors which facilitate economic relations and thereby make all factors of production more effective. These factors include property rights and human rights, but extend to the rule of law and the sustainable absence of armed conflict.

8 Even if missing factors can explain a great deal of growth internationally, explaining the overall evolution of transferable technology in the leading nations remains a central goal of economics. This opens up the possibility of endogenous growth.

9 Endogenous growth is possible when the marginal product of capital or other accumulated factors is bounded from below by a value which exceeds the slope of the capital deepening line. An increase in the savings rate can then lead to permanently higher growth.

10 One of the most promising explanations of endogenous growth lies in seeing research and development as the outcome of economic decisions. This requires understanding the nature of blueprints, ideas, and knowledge in general. The social return from innovation exceeds the private return on this activity, so the incentives to innovate could affect long-run growth.

11 Growth policy should not second-guess the decisions of firms and households. It should aim to improve the quality of missing inputs in the production function, and to provide conditions which improve innovation. Most important, providing limited intellectual property rights for innovations without stifling competition is an important challenge of growth policy.

🔑 Key Concepts

- **convergence hypothesis**
- **convergence clubs**
- **growth traps**
- **conditional convergence**
- **human capital**
- **public infrastructure**
- **public good**
- **property rights**
- **human rights**

- **endogenous growth theory**
- **Marshallian externality**
- **non-excludable and non-rival**
- **intellectual property rights**
- **Schumpeterian theory of innovation**
- **diffusion and imitation**
- **patent, copyright, trademark**
- **learning by doing**

❓ Exercises

1 Explain, using a diagram, why the Solow model with exogenous technical progress implies convergence of both levels and growth rates of GDP per capita.

2 Give a definition of the convergence hypothesis. Explain why the convergence hypothesis in its *unconditional* form is unlikely to hold across countries of the world.

3 Suppose two regions in the same country have identical production functions, savings rates, population growth rates, and depreciation rates. Suppose that per capita GDP differs by 20% between them, but that this gap is closed by 2% per annum. How many years will it take to close the gap to 5%?

4 Define the notion of conditional convergence. Give some examples of factors upon which the convergence hypothesis should be conditioned (i.e. take account of).

5 Suppose output Y is produced with physical capital K, human capital H, and labour L using the production function $Y = K^\alpha H^\beta L^{1-\alpha-\beta}$. Assume that households save a fraction s_H of their income in human capital and s_K in physical capital and that $s_H = s_K = s$ and that both forms of capital depreciate at the rate $\tilde{\delta}$. Solve for the steady-state level of output and output per capita. Why isn't this economy growing?

6 Define a Marshallian externality. Give at least two examples.

7 Why must knowledge not be subjected to diminishing returns if it is to be a permanent source of growth?

8 Use the example from Problem 5, but this time assume that production is given by the function $Y = K^\alpha H^\beta L^\gamma$ and $\alpha + \beta = 1$ and $\gamma < 1$. Explain why growth in this economy will now depend positively on the savings rate s, even if total factor productivity is constant.

9 Define non-excludable and non-rival goods and give examples of both. Can you name some that have both traits?

10 Name concrete ways which governments can use to promote innovation and explain how they work. Why are these measures enacted for only a limited period of time?

➲ Essay Questions

1 Why is the acquisition of human capital called an investment, like the acquisition of physical capital? Explain why knowledge and human capital depreciate, like physical capital. What is the link between property rights and investment in both physical and human capital?

2 Explain, with reference to elements of social infrastructure, why much of Africa seems unable to grow and eradicate poverty. What measures are most likely to improve the economic fate of African nations?

3 What aspect of public goods is more likely to inhibit the private production of goods: non-rivalry or non-excludability?

4 'Corruption stunts growth.' Comment.

5 Give arguments for and against democracy as a factor promoting economic growth.

Labour Markets and Unemployment 5

In our present day complicated economic life we are likely to be confused by the many industrial operations and money transactions. But net income remains exactly what it was to primitive Robinson Crusoe on his island—the enjoyment from eating the berries we pick, so to speak, less the discomfort or the labour of picking them.

Irving Fisher[1]

Labour is the source of all value.

Karl Marx[2]

5.1 Overview

In the last two chapters, we showed how output is a function of the **endowment** of factors of production—capital and labour—as well as technical sophistication. We examined the evolution of the capital stock and of technology in some detail, but we took the supply of labour as given, regardless of the wage or other variables. Even in storybooks, life is not so simple. In the famous novel by Daniel Defoe, the shipwrecked castaway Robinson Crusoe was endowed with a stock of capital (coconut trees) to produce output (coconuts), but needed to expend time and effort to gather and transport the fruits that he would eventually consume. Like most people, Crusoe had to choose whether to work or not, and how much effort he would put into it. Presumably, the rewards to work played a role in his decision. And the decision of how much to work determined how many coconuts would be harvested. This chapter is all about the labour market, which determines how much people work and earn.

To introduce the labour market, we need to think hard about the decisions of households, which supply hours of work to the market, and of firms, which demand them. Households work so that they can consume, but they also want to spend some of their time not working and enjoying **leisure** or free time. The supply of labour is seen as a trade-off between consumption and leisure. At the same time, someone must be willing to employ and pay for the hours of work that workers want to supply. If firms demand labour, it must have some value to them in production. As we study the interaction of the demand and supply of labour, we will learn how **unemployment** emerges.

We begin by looking at a household that supplies hours of work to the labour market. Then we turn to the demand for labour by firms. This leads naturally to the standard confrontation of demand and supply, which is sorted out by the wage, the price of labour. Yet we will see that labour is not a standard 'commodity'. Workers are not identical, and the quality of labour services is difficult to ascertain and harder to monitor. Unlike machines or raw materials, workers can decide whether they would like to work for a particular employer and under which conditions to sell their labour services. Frequently, the employment relationship involves explicit and implicit arrangements specific to both firm and employee. The functioning of labour markets is also influenced by country-specific institutions, such as labour law or collective bargaining, and is subject to

---

[1] Irving Fisher (1867–1947) was an American economist who is often described as one of the greatest mathematical economists of all time. Among other subjects, he contributed to the theory of investment, capital, and interest rates; monetary economics and the theory of inflation; and most notably to the theory and practice of price index numbers. He was founder and first president of the Econometric Society.

[2] Karl Marx (1818–1883) was a German economist and political philosopher whose theories predicted the immiseration of the working class and the ultimate crisis and collapse of market (capitalist) economies. Although he clearly got all that wrong, his empirical observations on the plight of the working class and his focus on issues relating to product and labour markets—and his influence on the lives of millions of people who lived and worked under communism and socialism—earn him a central place in the history of economic thought.

complex legal rules and customs. Finally, the labour market is dynamic, with suppliers and demanders of labour entering into and exiting employment relationships at a remarkable rate. We show how these interactions help us to understand the concept of equilibrium unemployment, which may differ from actual unemployment observed at a particular point in time.

5.2 Demand and Supply in the Labour Market

While Karl Marx may be out of favour these days, he was certainly right to see labour as the most important factor of production. Virtually everything stems directly or indirectly from labour. Raw materials are brought forth from the earth by human hands. Equipment used in this and other forms of economic activity is made using labour and previously manufactured equipment, itself the output of labourers and capital in a more distant past. Even the knowledge embodied in people—human capital—comes from our own efforts at mastering skills and techniques, as well as the time our teachers spent trying to educate us.

5.2.1 Labour Supply and the Consumption–Leisure Trade-off

In modern societies, consuming goods and services requires income. Earning income most often means working for firms for a wage or salary.[3] But labour has a cost, too: every hour of work means an hour less of free time. Because households value both consumption and leisure, they balance the two the best they can, given the possibilities available to them. This trade-off is known as the **consumption–leisure trade-off**. The consumption–leisure trade-off is best illustrated by the choices faced by Robinson Crusoe.[4]

The Crusoe we consider consumes all the fruits of his labour, which are the coconuts that he picks up on the beach, shucks, and cracks open—hard work by anyone's measure. (We postpone issues related to saving and investment to Chapters 7 and 8.) Crusoe values both the consumption (coconuts) and the free time he can enjoy *not* working to obtain them (resting, contemplating, watching the stars at night). His preferences or tastes with respect to consumption and leisure can be summarized with **indifference curves**. Each indifference curve presented in Figure 5.1 shows combinations of consumption and leisure which make Crusoe equally happy, or to have the same **utility**—the word economists use for a consumer's state of satisfaction.

Indifference curves are designed to tell us something about the preferences of households. Higher

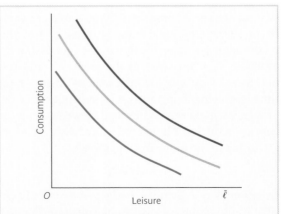

Fig. 5.1 Household Preferences

An indifference curve shows how readily a household is willing to substitute consumption C for leisure, ℓ holding its level of satisfaction or utility constant. Curves further out from the origin correspond to higher levels of utility.

---

[3] 'Firms' are understood to include public as well as private enterprises, national, regional, and local governments. It can even mean working for oneself, in the case of self-employment. In what follows we will focus on firms which strive to maximize profits.

[4] The use of this character, based on the classic novel by Daniel Defoe (1660–1731), is traditional in economics and will be seen again in Chapters 7 and 8, in which goods are distinguished by the point in time that they are consumed.

indifference curves correspond to higher levels of utility or happiness. The negative slope of the curve shows that a trade-off is involved: taking a unit of consumption from Crusoe requires compensation in the form of more leisure. The (absolute) slope or steepness of each curve at a given point shows how readily Crusoe substitutes consumption for leisure, holding his level of satisfaction constant. The bowed shape of Crusoe's indifference curves tells us that the greater his consumption relative to its leisure, the more of that consumption he is willing to give up for an additional unit of relatively scarcer leisure. The rate at which a household is willing to give up consumption for leisure, holding satisfaction constant, is called the **marginal rate of substitution** of consumption for leisure. An important principle is that as a good becomes increasingly scarce, the marginal rate of substitution of other goods for that particular good increases.

On Crusoe's island there is no money, but there is time, in fact, lots of it. Yet even Crusoe's time is in limited supply over a certain period (a day, a month, or year), after sleep and other important functions are accounted for. All scarce resources have a price, and time is no exception. The price of an hour of leisure is its opportunity cost: how much could one otherwise earn in that hour by working in the market? For the representative household with access to a labour market, the price of leisure is the **real (consumption) wage**. In practice, it is measured as a ratio of an average nominal (money) wage (W) to the consumer price index (P), the price of goods. If total available time for work is denoted as $\bar{\ell}$ and the hourly real wage is $w = W/P$, the value of Crusoe's total time endowment in terms of consumption is $\bar{\ell}w$. This endowment can be allocated between C units of consumption and ℓ hours of leisure, with value ℓw, according to the following equation:[5]

(5.1) $$\bar{\ell}w = \ell w + C.$$

Equation (5.1) is Crusoe's budget; it states all possible combinations of leisure and consumption that he can afford. It is depicted in Figure 5.2 as the

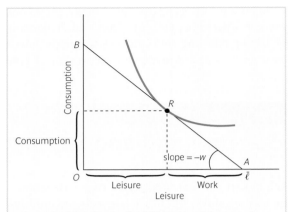

Fig. 5.2 The Household Budget Line and Optimal Choice

The household has a total of $\bar{\ell}$ hours at its disposal (measured by the distance OA) for either leisure or work. For every unit of leisure that it gives up, it can earn w consumption goods. The real wage w determines the slope of the budget line AB. Given the budget line, the highest possible utility is achieved at point R, where an indifference curve is tangent to the budget line.

negatively sloped line AB. The horizontal distance OA is equal to $\bar{\ell}$, the number of hours at his disposal. The distance OB measures the value of that endowment in terms of consumption goods. It is the total amount of consumption attainable when leisure is zero—i.e. if Crusoe were to work all the time.[6]

The negative slope of the budget line ($-w$) measures the trade-off of consumption for leisure ℓ offered by the market: how much consumption must be given up to get an additional unit of leisure, or how much consumption can be 'purchased' with an additional hour of foregone leisure. It explains why the real wage w is often referred to as the **relative price** of leisure in terms of consumption. If the real wage changes, the budget line rotates around point A, which is the fixed time endowment $\bar{\ell}$. It represents the amount of leisure possible when consumption is zero.

---

[5] The nominal budget constraint is $\bar{\ell}W = \ell W + PC$. To write it in real terms of consumption goods in (5.1), we simply divide by P, the price of consumption goods.

[6] If Crusoe possessed some initial wealth to begin with, the budget line would be shifted upwards (vertically) by that amount. This would then represent consumption attainable without having to work at all.

Optimal choice and the individual labour supply schedule

Crusoe maximizes his utility by choosing the highest possible indifference curve without moving to the right or above his budget line. This is achieved at point R in Figure 5.2, where the indifference curve is tangent to the budget line. At this point, the marginal rate of substitution of consumption for leisure is equal to the real wage w. Given the terms of trade offered by the market, he cannot make himself any better off (reach a higher indifference curve) by choosing any other point on the budget line, i.e. by trading leisure against consumption.

An important issue is the influence of the real wage on household behaviour. How does the household react to an increase in the real wage depicted in the first panel of Figure 5.3? Graphically, OB increases and the budget line rotates clockwise. Crusoe's optimal choice is now represented by point R'. This point is above R—Crusoe's consumption increases—but it is not clear whether it is to the left—Crusoe works less—or to the right—he works more. This ambiguity is a consequence of two different effects. First, the relative attractiveness of leisure *declines* because its relative price has *risen*. Taken alone, this would encourage Crusoe to take less leisure, work harder, and consume more. This is called the **substitution effect**. Second, and at the same time, each hour of Crusoe's labour is paid better. Holding leisure constant means earning more income overall. A normal reaction to an increase in income should be to enjoy both more consumption and more leisure, which means working less. This incentive to work less in response to a wage increase is called the **income effect**.

So, if the wage rises, will Crusoe work more or less? This question cannot be answered unambiguously without knowing more about preferences. In Figure 5.3, the substitution effect dominates, so the net effect is positive: an increase in the wage leads to a decline in leisure and an increase in labour supply. This is depicted in the second panel of Figure 5.3 as an upward-sloping **household labour supply curve**.

In practice, the response to rising wages varies widely across individuals, depending on tastes, family circumstances, age, etc. It also depends on the

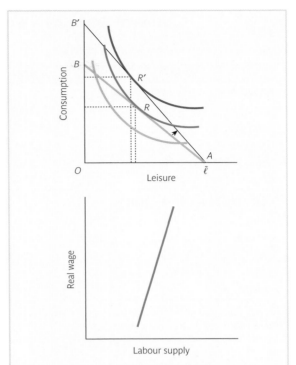

Fig. 5.3 Reaction of the Household to a Wage Increase: Labour Supply

When the real wage increases, the budget line rotates around point A (the endowment of time remains unchanged) and becomes steeper, because a unit of leisure is exchanged for more units of consumption. This allows both consumption and leisure to increase at the same time (income effect). Because leisure is more expensive, however, some is given up (substitution effect). In the case depicted here, the substitution effect dominates.

time horizon under consideration.[7] In the short run, most individuals do not seem to react much to changes in the real wage. Over the very long run, increasing real wages have led to decreasing labour supply as the income effect dominates. Table 5.1 shows that, over the last 100 years, real wages have increased by five- to fifteen-fold, while working hours have declined by one-half. Labour supply behaviour also varies according to sex. For men, the average work-week, the retirement age, and the

---

[7] For details, the reader is invited to look at the WebAppendix.

Table 5.1 Annual Total Hours Worked and Average Wages, 1870–2007

	1870	1913	1938	1973	1992	2000	2007
Annual hours worked per person							
France	2945	2588	1848	2020	1695	1591	1559
Germany	2941	2584	2316	1870	1566	1473	1432
UK	2984	2624	2267	1919	1653	1653	1607
USA	2964	2605	2062	1887	1786	1855	1785
Sweden	2945	2588	2204	1642	1565	1685	1601
Real wage (index: 1870 = 100)							
France	100	205	335	1048	1565	1701	1884
Germany	100	185	285	944	1226	1372	1408
UK	100	157	256	439	689	774	919
USA	100	189	325	596	697	807	931
Sweden	100	270	521	1228	1639	2102	2545

Sources: Hours worked are from Maddison (1991) for years 1870–1938 and from Groningen Growth and Development Centre and The Conference Board, Total Economy Database for the years 1973 to 2007; wages are from Mitchell (1978, 1983), and OECD, *Economic Outlook*, German wage data from 1913–1938 are approximated using average labour productivity growth.

labour force participation rate have fallen secularly since 1900.[8] In contrast, labour force participation and hours per week of women have risen in the past half-century. One possible interpretation is that the income effect of higher wages dominates for men, whereas the substitution effect dominates for women. Another interpretation is that customs and sociological factors change. Services such as child care and schooling have made it possible for more women to take up paid jobs.

The aggregate labour supply curve

We have studied a representative household's decision to work. The next step economists take is to add up the supplies of individual households across the economy, while noting the special aspects of labour and labour markets. In many instances, individuals cannot vary the hours of work that they supply. At best, they can choose between working or not working at all. Most labour contracts specify a

standard working time (length of the work-week, days of holiday leave per year). Workers frequently receive and accept 'take it or leave it' job offers. Sometimes workers are better off not working at all. In cases such as these, small wage increases may not be sufficient to motivate households to take up jobs, although large ones might.[9] In any case, the aggregate labour supply remains the sum of many individual decisions (to work or not work, and how many hours to work). While individual labour supply is measured in hours during some period of time (e.g. per year as in Table 5.1), aggregate supply is measured in **person-hours**, the total amount of hours supplied by all workers during that same period.[10] As in Chapter 3, total hours are the product

---

[9] These important cases are taken up in detail in Chapters 16 and 18.

[10] Aggregate employment is sometimes measured as the number of people who have a job. Generally, we will use the first definition (person-hours), and make explicit mention when referring to the number of employed workers. Under any definition, when more workers enter the labour force, the labour supply curve shifts to the right independently of the wage level.

---

[8] The labour force participation rate is defined as the proportion of working-age people which is either working or registered as unemployed.

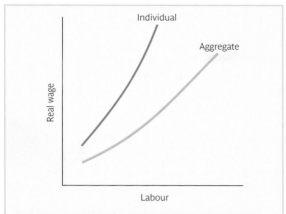

Fig. 5.4 Individual and Aggregate Labour Supply

The aggregate labour supply curve is less steep than that of individual households for two important reasons. First it represents the summation of a great number of upwardly sloped individual supply curves. Second, new workers choose to enter the labour force as wages rise.

of the number of persons in work times the hours worked per person. When wages rise, even if those who already work do not modify their supply of labour (the benchmark case), others who had preferred not to work may now decide to join the

labour force. Figure 5.4 shows how it is then possible for a steep or even near-vertical (inelastic) labour supply curve at the individual level to be consistent with a flatter aggregate supply curve.

5.2.2 Labour Demand, Productivity, and Real Wages

The labour demand curve and its slope

Firms use both capital and labour to produce goods and services. As discussed in Chapter 3, the capital stock at any particular point in time is best thought of as given; from month to month firms vary their output by adjusting employment of labour (man-hours). Holding capital constant, we can express the link between output Y and employment L using the production function, as shown in Figure 5.5. The slope of the production function measures the **marginal productivity of labour** (MPL), the quantity of additional output which results from one more unit of labour input (an hour). The shape of the curve reflects the principle of decreasing marginal productivity. With all else held constant, the MPL in a representative firm declines as the amount of labour employed increases.

In deciding how much labour to employ, the representative firm seeks the highest possible profit

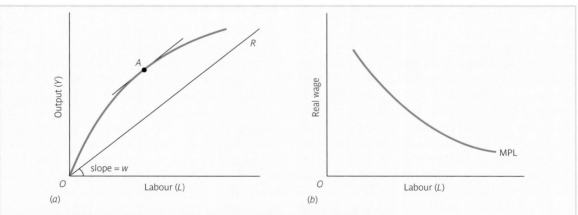

Fig. 5.5 The Production Function and the Labour Demand Curve

When labour input increases, output increases, but at a declining rate. This additional output is the marginal productivity of labour (MPL). In panel (*a*), the ray *OR* represents the labour cost of producing when the hourly real wage is *w*. The vertical distance between the production function and the cost line represents the firm's profit. The firm maximizes its profit at point *A*, where the curve is parallel to *OR*, i.e. where MPL = *w*. Its demand for labour is given in panel (*b*) by the declining marginal product of labour (MPL) curve.

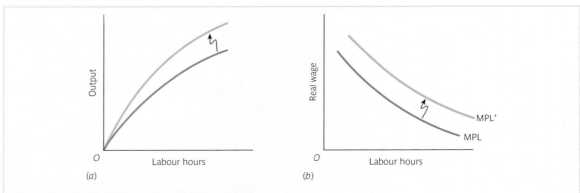

Fig. 5.6 An Increase in Labour Productivity

Labour can become more productive either because more capital is put in place, or because technological progress makes labour more productive using the existing stock of equipment. In panel (*a*), at any level of labour input, more output is produced and the production function is everywhere steeper. The MPL increases and the demand for labour schedule shifts up in panel (*b*).

given the cost of labour, the real hourly wage *w*. The line *OR* represents the total cost of labour to the firm at different levels of employment. Because *L* hours of work cost *wL*, its slope is *w*. For each level of employment, profit is measured as the vertical distance between the curve depicting the production function and the labour cost line *OR*. Profit is at a maximum at point *A*, where the production function is parallel to *OR*. At this point, the MPL, the slope of the production function, is equal to the real wage, the slope of *OR*. If the MPL exceeds the real wage, hiring one more hour of work raises revenues by the amount MPL, while raising costs by only *w*. This implies an increase in profits. A firm interested in maximizing profits would hire the extra hour, and continue to do so as long as the MPL exceeds the wage. But the MPL will decline as more employment is utilized, so the expansion of employment has a natural end: the point at which MPL equals the real wage. Suppose, taking the opposite case, that the real wage exceeds the MPL. Now the firm can increase its profit by *reducing* its demand for labour. Because it is optimal to set labour such that MPL = *w*, the MPL schedule in panel (*b*) of Figure 5.5 is also the firm's **labour demand curve**.

The slope of the labour demand curve depends on the rate at which the MPL falls. If MPL is relatively insensitive to labour and falls only slightly as labour

inputs are increased, then the demand curve will be relatively flat. Small changes in the wage will lead to large responses in the demand for labour. The labour demand curve is **elastic**. In contrast, if the MPL drops sharply as labour inputs are increased, the labour demand curve is steep and the demand for labour is unresponsive to changes in the wage. We say that the demand for labour is **inelastic**.

Shifts in the demand for labour

After studying the slope of the labour demand curve, we consider reasons for the labour demand curve to shift—to change its position. One possible reason is an increase in the capital stock *K*, which is taken here to be exogenous. At the aggregate level, an increase in the capital stock tends to make additional labour more productive. In panel (*a*) of Figure 5.6 this is shown as an increase in MPL—the production function becomes steeper at every level of production. In panel (*b*), this implies that the labour demand curve shifts out. A technological improvement that makes labour more productive at any given level of capital and labour input will have a similar effect on the MPL. This is identical to an increase in total factor productivity discussed in Chapter 3. Increasing total factor productivity can help account for the fact that wages have grown secularly over time.

Conversely, it is also possible for labour demand to shift back, i.e. to decline holding the wage constant. A decline in the capital stock brought about by war, natural disaster, or technical obsolescence causes the labour demand curve to shift inwards, i.e. down and to the left. In the case of labour-saving technical change, it is possible for labour demand to decline, even as total output is increasing. Box 5.1 explains the important phenomenon of technical change in more detail.

5.2.3 Labour Market Equilibrium

We now have the building blocks for understanding the labour market: a supply curve derived from household behaviour, and a demand curve derived from firm behaviour. The interaction of supply and demand for labour is depicted in Figure 5.7. Equilibrium occurs at the intersection of the two curves (point A). At wage w the market clears (there is no excess demand or supply): L is the number of

---

 ### Box 5.1   Technical Change and Unemployment

What is the effect of technological progress on jobs? A common perception is that technology destroys jobs by making people redundant, i.e. unnecessary for the production of goods and services. Aren't cars mostly produced by robots? Don't computers reduce the need for secretaries? Isn't the internet replacing mail and jobs in the post office? It would be hard to deny that technological advances destroy some jobs, occupations, or even whole sectors of economic activity. At the dawning of the industrial revolution in the early nineteenth century, the Luddites in Britain or the *soyeux* in France agitated against mechanized weaving machines and mobilized mobs to destroy them in large numbers. And indeed, weaving cloth by hand has disappeared as a trade, as have many other technically backward activities. Nevertheless, overall productivity of labour has increased roughly tenfold in the nations of Western Europe in the past 120 years, and if anything, unemployment is somewhat lower now than it was a century and a half ago, so the story must be more complicated than simply technology killing jobs.

Indeed, the story is more complicated. Technological progress does mean that the same output can be produced with fewer man-hours, but this does not mean that overall employment must fall. It depends on how output Y behaves over the same period. In fact, if output rises at least as fast as output per hour (Y/L) does, employment L *must increase*. (To see this mathematically, write employment L as $Y/(Y/L)$.) The key question is: How are increases in labour productivity split between growth in output and employment? Because both employment and output are endogenous, a correct answer requires much more knowledge in order to follow all the mech-

anisms that influence the final outcome. Sorting this out is the task of macroeconomics. The facts definitely imply that wages keep up with productivity—this is the consequence of a stable long-term wage share, which was Kaldor's fourth stylized fact discussed in Chapter 3. The wage share is WL/PY, which can be rewritten as $w/(Y/L)$. Wages must have kept up with productivity on average, over the decades. Over the same period, hours worked per worker fell, but the number of workers employed in the US and Europe has increased dramatically—a consequence of increasing labour force participation. A more reasonable interpretation is that technological progress has made us wealthier and able to work fewer hours per person, even while the number of jobs increased.

It is hard to avoid concluding that the Luddites and their modern-day equivalents are guilty of the 'fallacy of composition': the disappearance of some jobs or the decline of some regions need not apply to the economy as a whole. The demand for secretaries may have fallen, but who builds, programs, and maintains the computers that make secretaries redundant? Who designs, markets, and services the cars built by robots? New jobs replace old jobs. Of course, these are not the same people. At the aggregate level, old skills are replaced by new skills, but some individuals must be retrained, which takes time, and some are sidelined. That some people become unemployed does not mean that total employment declines. Economic progress may be painful for some, but it is by no means a systematic job-killer. And from Chapter 3 we have learned that it is the most important engine of sustainable increases in the standards of living.

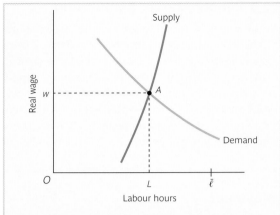

Fig. 5.7 Equilibrium in the Labour Market

Labour market equilibrium occurs at point A where demand and supply are equal. The real wage w clears the market at employment level L. Since total labour endowment is given by $\bar{\ell}$, the distance $\bar{\ell} - L$ is voluntary unemployment.

usefulness. Panel (a) shows the outcome of an increase in labour productivity resulting from capital accumulation or technological advances, already examined in Box 5.1. The labour demand curve shifts outwards; the supply curve remains unaffected. The result is an unambiguous increase in real wages. In the figure, employment increases, but if the labour supply curve is vertical, employment remains unchanged and labour income wL rises proportionally with the real wage. It turns out that if the income effects of wage increases dominate the substitution effect, the supply curve can even be backward-bending: employment (man-hours) would even decline. Table 5.1 suggests that this has been the case over the past century.

The second panel of Figure 5.8 shows that an exogenous increase in the supply of labour leads to an increase in employment, but also to a reduction in real wages. Yet, this is a short-run effect. One of the growth stylized facts presented in Chapter 3 states that, in the long run, real wages grow with productivity. Indeed, the increase in labour supply initially lowers the capital–labour ratio K/L. Another stylized fact mentioned in Chapter 3 is that this ratio tends to remain constant in the long run. Indeed, a lower capital–labour ratio means that the productivity of capital has risen, which should lead to more capital accumulation. As the capital–labour

hours firms want to hire and households want to work. Both the real wage rate and employment are endogenously determined in the labour market.

This basic characterization of the labour market is an important part of an economist's toolkit, and its predictions serve as the benchmark for the rest of the chapter. Figure 5.8 provides two examples of its

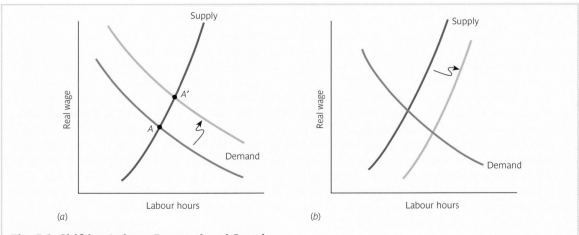

(a)   (b)

Fig. 5.8 Shifting Labour Demand and Supply

When labour demand increases (panel (a)), for example because of additional capital or technological progress, the real wage and the employment level both increase. When labour supply increases instead (panel (b))—because of new entries into the labour force, for example—employment rises but the real wage declines.

Box 5.2 Market Hours at Work: Europe Versus the USA

International comparisons should always be taken with a pinch of salt, because data from different countries—especially labour market data—are frequently difficult to compare. Yet often differences are just too large to attribute to measurement error. Table 5.2 compares hours worked per week, on average, per adult of working age (in general, aged 15–65). Evidently, most Europeans spend less time in market work than US Americans or Britons do, 20–25% less in some cases. Yet there are clearly different trends in the data, reflecting the outcome of changing labour supply at two different margins: a decrease in average hours worked by those already in work as documented in Table 5.1 (the so-called intensive margin), versus a trend of increasing labour supply at the extensive margin (labour force participation). In Denmark and the Netherlands, weekly hours per capita actually rose over the past decade, reflecting the successful reactivation of the long-term unemployed and the rising entry of women in the labour force. In Italy, efforts to increase part-time and marginal employment have begun to bear some fruit. In other countries, such as France and Germany, hours per capita continue to decline, as the negative trend in hours worked per employee dominate the upward trend in participation.

Does this mean that continental Europeans are lazy? Despite such striking international differences, underlying economic behaviour is remarkably similar. Research on time use has given economists important insights into the way people use their time, and it turns out that market work is not the only type of work that people perform. For example, we know that in 2000–2003, when US Americans were working about 45% more in the market on average than Germans, they only worked about 8% more overall. How can this be? The answer is that Germans—both men and women—work much more at home, performing services that many Americans would purchase in the market.

ratio returns to its previous level, the demand curve shifts outward (not shown). In the long run, an increase in the supply of labour is eventually matched by an increase in the stock of productive capital, and unchanged capital–labour ratio and therefore no reduction in real wages.

5.2.4 The Interpretation of Unemployment

While the supply-and-demand apparatus allows us to evaluate the effect of various changes on equilibrium employment and real wages, it is disappointing in one crucial respect. At point A in Figure 5.7, labour supplied is equal to labour demanded and denoted by L. Any unemployed labour—literally, labour not employed—reflects the voluntary decisions of households and firms. If total potential labour supply is $\bar{\ell}$, unemployment (measured as hours of work not employed) is simply $\bar{\ell} - L$. Since point A is on the labour supply curve, it reflects the optimal behaviour of households. The standard interpretation of unemployment in Figure 5.7 is that the real wage w in equilibrium is simply too low to persuade all workers to give up all

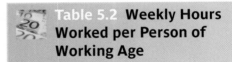

Table 5.2 Weekly Hours Worked per Person of Working Age

	1995	2006
Austria	17.9	17.5
Canada	19.9	20.8
Denmark	17.5	18.5
France	15.2	14.8
Germany	15.7	14.2
Italy	15.0	15.8
Netherlands	14.7	16.3
Sweden	18.1	18.0
United Kingdom	18.9	19.0
United States	22.3	21.9

Source: International Labour Office.

their leisure: some may wish to work only part-time, others may not want to work at all. In Figure 5.7, no hours are unemployed involuntarily at the wage w.

It might be disturbing to think that unemploy-ment could be chosen freely. Yet **voluntary unem-ployment**—or, more precisely, the decision not to work—is an important phenomenon in modern economies. It is not only the very wealthy who can afford not to work. Those who receive an income from other sources (from a spouse or from the state, for example) may also find that the net wage they can earn does not compensate for foregone leisure or non-market activities, including working at home or raising children. Voluntary unemployment is likely among low-skilled people who cannot earn much, or in countries where taxes are so high that working yields little net gain. The most obvious costs to working are faced by families with chil-dren. The high cost of child care—or simply the unavailability of such services—explains why two-earner families are not as common in some countries as in others. Box 5.2 presents more general evid-ence on how very different patterns of household labour supply can emerge, suggesting that labour

market institutions may have a more important role for explaining differences across countries than preferences themselves.

The decision for women to enter and remain in the labour force is of central importance for an economy's productive potential. Table 5.3 displays the labour force participation rate (the proportion of women of working age in the labour force, whether em-ployed or not), the female unemployment rate, and the proportion of women of working age actually employed. The variation of these indicators across countries is significant, and points to differences in both cultures and institutions. For example, female participation in the labour force is very high in countries like Denmark and Sweden, which have a highly developed and subsidized child care system. It is lower in societies in which women have tradi-tionally played a greater role at home, but also where taxation may discourage a second earner in the family.

Table 5.3 **Female Labour Force Participation Rates, Unemployment Rates, and Employment Ratios**

	Labour force participation rate	Unemployment rate	Employment/ population ratio
Belgium	58.9	9.0	53.6
Canada	73.5	6.1	69.0
Denmark	76.7	4.6	73.2
Finland	73.2	8.1	67.3
France	63.9	10.7	57.1
Germany	68.5	10.3	61.5
Ireland	61.3	4.1	58.8
Japan	61.3	4.1	58.8
Netherlands	69.4	4.8	66.0
Norway	74.8	3.4	72.3
Portugal	68.4	9.5	62.0
Spain	61.1	11.6	54.0
Sweden	77.7	7.2	72.1
United Kingdom	70.3	5.0	66.8
United States	69.3	4.7	66.1

Source: OECD, *Employment Outlook* 2007.

5.3 A Static Interpretation of Unemployment

Our first attempt at defining unemployment in the last section is somewhat unsatisfactory. Surely, unemployment is more than simply labour with-held voluntarily from the market. The International Labour Organization (ILO) and the Organization for Economic Cooperation and Development (OECD) define an individual as unemployed if he or she does not have a job during the reference period, is actively looking for one, and is ready to work. Let us start by defining the labour force as those members of the adult population who are either working (L) or unemployed (U). The labour force mainly excludes young people in school, the retired, and those who are not looking for work. It corresponds closely to the amount of labour supplied to the market, given current conditions, including the level of real wages. Denoting the labour force as L^S, we can write:

(5.2) $$L^S = L + U.$$
labour force = employment + unemployment

The unemployment rate u is then given by the fraction of the labour force which is out of work, or $u = U/L^S$. Perhaps it is now clear why the picture of unemployment in Figure 5.7 is incomplete: according to the ILO definition, it would have to be zero! In the rest of this chapter, we examine alternative reasons for unemployment.

5.3.1 Involuntary Unemployment and Real Wage Adjustment

One interpretation of unemployment in the ILO definition is the excess of labour supply over labour demand. In equilibrium depicted in Figure 5.7 this outcome was ruled out by assumption, because the labour market was assumed to clear. Figure 5.9 considers the important case where the real wage is fixed at $\bar{w}$, which is higher than the level which equates supply and demand, w. At $\bar{w}$, firms are willing to hire $\bar{L}$ labour, while workers supply L^S. Since firms cannot be forced to hire more than they wish, actual employment is $\bar{L}$, and $L^S - \bar{L}$ is labour

supplied but not demanded by the market. The labour market does not clear and there is **involuntary unemployment**. Involuntary unemployment occurs when labour is willing and able to work at the wage $\bar{w}$ but cannot find employment. At point B, the marginal product of labour (MPL) exceeds the valuation of leisure time by households which are out of work. Put differently, at point B, firms are not willing to hire all labour that workers are willing to supply at wage $\bar{w}$.

The solution to the problem in Figure 5.9 appears rather straightforward. If the real wage were to fall to w at point A, demand would increase, supply would decrease, and unemployment would be eliminated. It is the failure of the wage to decline that perpetuates unemployment. This is a key result: the existence of involuntary unemployment must be explained by **real wage rigidity**, which we examine next.

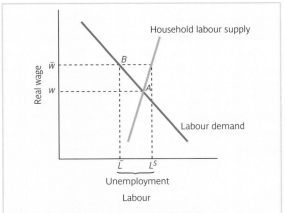

Fig. 5.9 Involuntary Unemployment
At the real wage rate $\bar{w}$ workers supply L^S of labour but firms demand, and hire, only $\bar{L}$. The quantity $L^S - \bar{L}$, which is supplied by households but not demanded by firms, represents involuntary unemployment. If the real wage were to adjust to the level w, the market would clear at point A.

5.3.2 Collective Bargaining and Real Wage Rigidity

For sustained real wage rigidity to occur, involuntarily unemployed workers must be unable, on average, to supply their labour services at wages below $\tilde{w}$, or firms must be unwilling to take up such offers, or be unable to make their own.[11] There are many reasons why wages may not adjust, or do so only slowly. The most important features of labour markets which have been neglected until now are **labour market institutions**. Labour market institutions are distinguishing national features of labour markets based on legal, cultural, operational, or organizational characteristics, which are designed to interfere with or modify the functioning of labour markets.

Labour (or trade) unions are one of the most fundamental and universal institutions that operate in modern labour markets today. Unions are organizations of employees which advocate interests of labour in a number of dimensions, including workers' rights, working conditions, and most importantly, wages. They exist because workers have considerably less ability to influence these conditions individually than collectively. Labour unions are often matched by equally powerful **employers' associations**. Bargaining between employers and unions contrasts sharply with the perfect-competition description of labour markets described in Section 5.2. In what follows, we need to study the motives of negotiators, and how they impact on wage determination. In doing so, we discover how unemployment can be voluntary from the perspective of trade unions, and nevertheless be involuntary from the viewpoint of the individual household.[12] We will also see that unions try to smooth out the ultimate fundamentals of the labour market as determined by supply and demand in Figure 5.7. At the same time, it is impossible to ignore them.

The rationale for labour unions

The employer–employee relationship has inherently conflictual aspects. One is the distribution of income. While economic principles assert that income should be split according to marginal productivity, marginal productivity in practice is difficult, if not impossible, to measure. Another more subtle reason is that firms cannot observe the work effort, a key element of productivity, which is under the control of each individual employee. Individual workers facing a large employer are in a poor bargaining position. They have little influence over their own wage rate and may not even feel safe discussing working conditions, fearing reprisals in the form of a salary cut or dismissal. They may even feel pressure to accept conditions that would not be acceptable under competitive conditions.

Historically, workers have organized themselves into unions to help resist such pressures, in particular, to achieve higher pay levels and a voice in the day-to-day operation of the workplace. Table 5.4 gives some details on union organizations and their organizational strength (membership) and impact on workers' contracts (coverage). Clearly, this labour market institution varies considerably from country to country. Scandinavian countries have a tradition of centralized unionization. German workers are organized by industry; workers in Britain according to craft or occupation. In France, Italy, and Spain, unions are frequently tied to political parties. In the Nordic economies, union membership is generally greater than three-quarters of the workforce and coverage is often as high as 90%, while in the USA unions have more or less disappeared from the private (non-governmental) workplace.

These vast differences reflect social history as well as the costs and benefits associated with union membership. The costs are dues (fees) that members must pay. The benefits vary, ranging from higher wages and protection from arbitrary employer decisions to more specific advantages, including priority for certain jobs and income supplements when

---

[11] It is important to stress 'on average', since workers are different, varying by occupation, skill level, and industrial affiliation. Thus, real wage rigidity may affect workers with low productivity more than those with high skill levels.

[12] It should be stressed that we limit ourselves strictly to the economic significance of trade unions. As the history of the labour movement amply demonstrates, unions have had an enormous influence on modern society beyond their economic impact.

Table 5.4 European Trade Unions: Membership and Coverage, 1950–2004

Country	Structure	Union membership (%)					Union coverage (%) (2001–2004)
		1950	1970	1990	1997	2004	
Sweden	Umbrella (ILO, TCO, SACO)	67	67	82	86	77	92
Finland	Umbrella (SAK, STTK, AKAVA)	30	51	73	78	70	90
Denmark	Umbrella (LO, HK, FTF)	56	63	75	76	80	83
Norway	Umbrella (LO, AF, YS)	45	50	56	55	n.a.	n.a.
Belgium	Party, religious (ACV/CSC, ABVV/FGTB, ACLVB/CGSLB)	43	42	50	532	50	96
Ireland	Mostly crafts in ICTU, fragmented	42	59	59	522	43	40
Austria	Umbrella/industrial (ÖGB)	62	57	47	39	33	98
Italy	Party, religious (CGIL, CISL, UIL)	45	37	39	37	34	70
United Kingdom	Mostly crafts (TUC)	45	50	43	362	29	35
Germany[1]	Umbrella/industrial (DGB, IG Metall, Ver.di)	38	32	36	27	18	68 (West)/ 53 (East)
Portugal	Party, relgious/Umbrella (CGTP, UGT)	—	—	40	302	25	71
Netherlands	Party, religious (FNV, CNV, MHP)	43	37	24	24	20–25	81
Greece	occupational/sectoral (GSEE, ADEDY)	—	—	34	—	20	65
Spain	Industrial, company level (CC.OO, UGT, ELA, CIGA)	—	—	12	17	16	81
France	Party, religious (CGT, CFDT, CGT-FO, CFTC, CFE-CGC)	30	20	14	10	8	95
Memo: US	Mostly local plant-level (AFL-CIO)	—	—	—	16	7.40	14

[1] West Germany until 1990

Source: EIRO, country profiles
<http://www.eurofound.europa.eu/eiro/country_index.htm>.

unions are on strike. In some countries, many advantages accrue to all workers, so there is little point in paying union dues. This is the case in France, for example.[13] In other countries, such as Belgium and in Scandinavia, unions help manage

some social benefits systems, including unemployment insurance. In the USA, some unions even issue credit cards and provide other financial services to their members. In the end, the influence of unions is usually much stronger than simple membership statistics would suggest, and is partly related to labour laws which institutionalize their role. This is evident from the coverage statistics in Table 5.4, which shows the fraction of all workers working under contracts negotiated by unions, whether or not they are union members.

[13] This is an illustration of the so-called free-rider problem. If no workers pay dues, the union disappears and no one is protected. So some workers must pay the dues for all to have a union. Often workers tend to join unions for reasons related to peer pressure, social norms, or ideology.

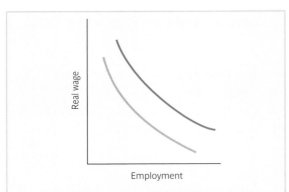

Fig. 5.10 **Trade Unions' Indifference Curves**

When a trade union values both higher wages and more employment, its preferences are described by indifference curves. A 'hard-line' union is not willing to give up much in lower wages to raise employment. A union mainly preoccupied with employment is represented by steep indifference curves.

The economics of labour unions

Simplifying somewhat, we can think of two primary economic objectives which motivate unions: higher real wages, and more jobs.[14] It is helpful to think of union preferences in terms of indifference curves shown in Figure 5.10. The slope of the indifference curve represents the willingness of the union leadership to trade-off employment for wages. It is flat for 'hard-line' unions which are unwilling to trade wages against employment, steeper for unions which care relatively more about jobs than wages.

In contrast to Section 5.2, we now describe a labour market in which union indifference curves replace those of the representative individual as the relevant preferences. This captures the fact that the active agent in the labour market is not the individual, but the labour union, or the collective bargaining process more generally. The 'budget line' faced by the union is simply the labour demand curve. From Section 5.2.2 we know that labour demand is given by the MPL (either a firm's MPL, or that of an industry or the entire economy:

if firms are all alike, their individual demand does not differ from the collective one represented by an employers' association).[15]

Given the demand for labour that it faces, the optimal choice for the union is the tangency point of the highest indifference curve with the current demand for labour. This outcome is the best the union can do, given the economic environment it faces, which is the behaviour of firms. Should the demand for labour shift, the union's menu of options will change too. Capital accumulation or technological progress which shifts out the labour demand curve, for example, will increase the wage that firms are willing to pay at a given employment level, or increase the sustainable employment that can be hired on, holding the wage constant. Inward shifts of labour demand are also possible. These are attributable to destruction or obsolescence of the capital stock (e.g. due to wars, earthquakes, the lack of new investment), or new inventions which make some labour obsolete in their current use. They have the opposite effect, shrinking available options to the union. As the labour demand schedules shifts, the set of tangency points map out the **collective labour supply curve** shown in Figure 5.11. The curve describes the most desired joint evolution of real wages and employment from the union's perspective.

The slope of the collective labour supply curve thus reflects the preferences of the union for employment and wages as well as its economic environment. It will also reflect whether demand is shifting outward or inward.[16] Union members who are currently employed, or who enjoy seniority or job protection, tend to fight for a hard-line union.

---

[14] As noted already, unions care about many other aspects of labour markets, such as safety at work, working time, employees' rights and influence over working conditions and organization. To simplify the analysis, these aspects are not considered here.

[15] Here we assume that firms are behaving competitively—each firm on its own. More likely than not, associations of employers will arise in response and exert their own power in the bargaining process, presuming they can organize and discipline enough firms. A more general treatment of bargaining when employers are non-competitive is possible but beyond the level of this textbook.

[16] Note that the collective labour supply curve depends on the successive shifts in the demand for labour that we imagine. Different shifts can change both the position and the slope of the labour demand curve. A number of outcomes are possible. These are described in more detail graphically in the WebAppendix to Chapter 5.

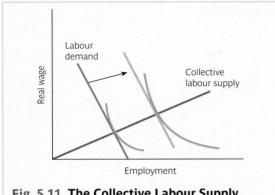

Fig. 5.11 The Collective Labour Supply Curve
The collective labour supply curve is obtained by connecting the points of tangency between the indifference curves and a shifting labour demand schedule.

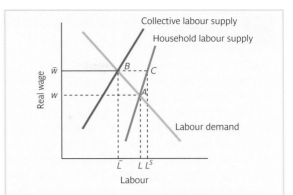

Fig. 5.12 Labour Market Equilibrium with a Trade Union
When a labour union represents workers at wage negotiations, labour market equilibrium occurs at point B. If the union collective labour supply curve is above the individual labour supply curve, the real wage $\bar{w}$ is higher and employment $\bar{L}$ (hours or number of workers) lower than at point A, which would be the outcome if individuals were negotiating individually. The result is the existence of union-voluntary, individual-involuntary unemployment ($L^S - \bar{L}$): it is the difference between actual employment $\bar{L}$ and the amount of work L^S that workers are willing to supply individually at the real wage rate $\bar{w}$ (point C).

If their influence is high, the slope of the collective labour supply curve will be steep. In contrast, a 'jobs-first' union accepts moderate real wage increases and supplies more labour. It will tend to exhibit a flat collective labour supply curve. (More details on different possible shapes of the collective labour supply curve are discussed in the WebAppendix.)

Employment effects of collective bargaining

The collective labour supply curve resembles the individual supply curve of Figure 5.3, but has different origins. Collectively, through their unions, workers increase their bargaining power and, accordingly, aim at better outcomes. In particular, for a given amount of labour supplied, they ask for higher real wages: the union-driven collective labour supply curve can only lie above the individual labour supply curves. Without the union's influence on wage setting, equilibrium would occur in Figure 5.12 at point A: individuals would be willing to work up to L at wage w. They cannot, however, because the wage is set in negotiations between the firms and the trade union, and individuals cannot simply underbid their employed colleagues. The outcome is $\bar{w}$, and the resulting unemployment ($L^S - \bar{L}$) is involuntary for affected individuals, but voluntary from the union's point of view.

How can unions enforce wage rigidity, apparently against the will of unemployed workers? One reason is that the leadership is typically elected by the employed, sometimes called the **insiders**. The employed are always a dominant majority of the membership, even at record high unemployment rates of 10% or 20%. Unemployed workers often give up their membership or lose interest in union affairs. They are called the **outsiders**. Unions end up representing the insiders, who have jobs, rather than the outsiders, who are an unemployed minority. Employed workers lobby for high real wages (for themselves) at the cost of some unemployment (for others). Box 5.3 illustrates how the relentless rise of unemployment in Europe after the two oil shocks can be explained by this effect.

The split between unions and unemployed workers cannot go too far, though. After unemployment increased to high levels in Europe in the 1970s and

Box 5.3 **The European Unemployment Problem**

Two major negative shifts to the demand for labour occurred during the past 30 years. Both were associated with the sudden oil price increases of the mid-1970s and early 1980s, and are called the oil shocks. By all accounts, they corresponded to a significant inward shift of the aggregate labour demand curve. If trade unions react to a smaller membership by demanding higher wages, the collective labour supply curve shifts upwards. Owing to the behaviour of the 'insiders' who have jobs, employment prospects for 'outsiders' are reduced. After the oil shocks are absorbed, the employment level

is permanently reduced. That such an effect—dubbed the 'hysteresis effect'—has been observed in several European countries is suggested by the step-wise increase in the unemployment rate following each oil shock (Table 5.5). In contrast, unemployment rates in the USA increased at the time of each oil shock, but then reverted towards earlier levels. As unemployment rises, pressure to do something does as well. In a number of countries, measures have been taken to help these countries turn the corner on the European unemployment problem.

Table 5.5 **Standardized Unemployment Rates (% of labour force)**

	1960–1969	1970–1979	1980–1989	1990–1999	2000–2006
France	2.0	3.8	8.6	10.6	9.2
Germany	0.8	2.4	5.8	7.6	8.4
Italy	3.8	4.7	7.8	10.3	8.4
Spain	2.5	4.4	14.7	15.9	10.3
Sweden	1.7	2.0	2.6	7.2	6.0
United Kingdom	1.8	4.2	9.5	8.0	5.0
USA	4.8	6.2	7.3	5.8	5.1

Source: OECD.

1980s, unions became more employment-conscious and real wage growth moderated significantly. There are several reasons for this wage moderation. First, members became worried that they too might become unemployed. Second, there was criticism from the non-unionized workers. Third, the loss in membership revealed in Table 5.4 has meant lower income from union dues as well as less overall influence.

It would be unfair to assert that unions are solely responsible for real wage rigidity. Employers' associations can also contribute to real wages rigidity. The employers' associations represent the collective interests of firms. They represent an additional mechanism for policing collective bargaining agreements reached with unions. In the end, employers'

associations do not control the demand for labour: this is the prerogative of the individual companies. So, while it is in firms' interest to keep wages low, it is also in their interest to 'take the wage out of competition'. This means keeping the wages of their competitors high, or at least preventing them from hiring cheap labour.

5.3.3 Social Minima and Real Wage Rigidity

Beyond trade unions and employers' associations, several other institutional and economic factors can contribute to wage rigidity, and therefore involuntary unemployment. Frequently mentioned in the European context are social minima, or minimum standards for income and earnings mandated by the government for reasons of social equity or protection. Social minima may stem from social or unemployment benefits, since few will work for a net wage which falls below the level available for no work at all. They can also be set at a higher level by **minimum wages**, which are legal limits on how low wages can be.

Minimum wages have been enacted for a variety of reasons. One was to prevent employers with excessive market power from abusing it by depressing wages. Another reason was to protect young people from exploitation. With schooling rudimentary and poverty endemic, for many youngsters on-the-job training was the only way to get started. Unscrupulous employers would offer very low wages, sometimes below minimal survival needs. Social protection was and often still is justified. Even in countries without statutory or legal minimum wages, it is frequently the case that collective agreements are extended to uncovered workers, and contract wages assume the characteristics of a legal minimum wage. With occasional exceptions, this is generally the case in continental Europe.

The primary economic effect of minimum wages is to discourage firms from hiring workers with low MPL, which tend to be the young, the unskilled, those with little training, or those with the wrong skills. Figure 5.13 illustrates the effect of minimum wages. To serve any purpose at all, the minimum

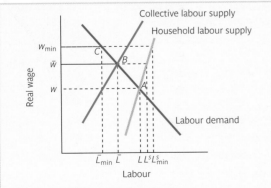

Fig. 5.13 Minimum Wages
Minimum wages reduce the demand for labour below the level that would result with either union-negotiated wages or individual-supplied labour.

wage $w_{\min}$ must be higher than the wage that would be obtained otherwise ($\bar{w}$), and which is itself higher than what individuals would accept with market clearing (w). The result is unemployment ($L^S_{\min} - \bar{L}_{\min}$), even higher than the level implied by the wage set in collective bargaining ($L^S - \bar{L}$).

Some evidence on the effect of minimum wages is discussed in Box 5.4. Those most likely to be hurt by the existence of minimum wage legislation are poorly educated young people with no job experience and older workers with obsolete skills. The minimum wage can affect jobs paying more than the floor, because once in place, it tends to push up into the higher echelons of the wage pyramid, just like a spring which is compressed. This is because natural forces tend to re-establish wage premia between different skill and productivity levels.

5.3.4 Efficiency Wages and Real Wage Rigidity

Another reason why real wages may not decline in the presence of involuntary unemployment is that firms themselves may not wish to lower them for various reasons. The phenomenon is often called **efficiency wages**, and it is related to another special aspect of labour. In contrast with other factors of production, work effort is not easily observed by firms, and yet it matters a lot. By paying higher wages, firms may attempt to elicit more work of better quality. A worker who is dismissed for lack of effort is unlikely to obtain such a good deal elsewhere, especially if dismissals are interpreted as a sign of poor work effort. Firms may also pay higher wages to obtain a better selection of applicants and to keep workers from quitting too often. If all firms behave this way, the outcome will be wages which exceed the market-clearing value.

In capital-intensive industries, where shirking could seriously disrupt the production process and where a high-quality workforce is of primary importance, firms may have a strong incentive to pay efficiency wages. In this case, the function of real wages goes beyond simply equilibrating demand and supply in labour markets. Generally, wages will not be able to satisfy both functions. They will tend to be rigid and lie above the market-clearing level, as in Figure 5.12.

Box 5.4 Minimum Wages and Youth Unemployment

It is striking that teenagers in the USA often work during the summer when their European counterparts go on vacation. One reason might be that wages that must be paid for young, unskilled labour are too high in Europe. The US minimum wage amounts to about one-third of the average manufacturing wage, while in many European countries it well exceeds 50%. This is one reason why filling station attendants and grocery shop assistants have all but disappeared in most European countries. Table 5.6 shows non-employment and unemployment rates for young people in a number of countries, as well as the average minimum wage, as a fraction of the average overall wage. In interpreting the table, it is important to note that Danish youth under 18 years receive a deep discount from a collectively bargained minimum wage, as they do in the USA, while in France, Belgium, and the Netherlands, the minimum wage as a fraction of the median wage is high, meaning that a great many jobs are paid the minimum wage.

In France, the minimum wage, called the SMIC (Salaire Minimum Interpersonel de Croissance), is an important element of the collective bargaining system. It is set by a council on which both the government and

unions are represented. Many government employees receive the SMIC. In recent years, 10–15% of workers in industry, commerce, and services earned the SMIC or near it, a much higher proportion than in the USA (about 3–4%). While the minimum wage in general has a negative effect on youth employment, it may lead to a substitution of adults for youths, even increasing the employment of the former. Recent evidence from Portugal's experience with the minimum wage supports this hypothesis.

We have emphasized the economic effects of minimum wages. The public debate, in contrast, is frequently guided by considerations such as social equity and social norms. A minimum wage is supposed to help the fight against 'working poverty'. Yet it is rarely mentioned that the minimum wage destroys jobs as long as the labour demand curve is elastic. Thus, those who might have held those jobs are 'financing' the minimum wage—those whose productivity is just below the level necessary to justify the job's existence. It may be worth asking if the public purse might not be a better approach to solving the problem of the working poor.

Table 5.6 Minimum Wages and Youth Labour Market Experience, 2003

	Minimum wage as % of median wage	% affected (at or near minimum)	Youth minimum as % of adult level (relevant age)	Non-employment ratio for youth age 15–24. 2005 (%)	Unemployment rate for youth aged 15–24. 2005 (%)
Belgium	47	4	Slightly less	74.8	19.9
Denmark	Collective agreements	6	40 (<18)	31.8	7.9
France	61	11	80 (16); 90 (17); 30–75 for trainees	79.9	22.8
Germany	Collective agreements	—	Industry agreements	55.6	15.2
Italy	Collective agreements	—	Industry agreements	74.8	24
Netherlands	51	3	34.5 (16); rising to 84 (22)	38.9	9.6
Spain	29	7	66 (<18)	71.1	19.7
UK	44	—	None	39	11.8
USA	32	4	None	42	11.3

Source: OECD.

5.4 A Dynamic Interpretation of Unemployment

5.4.1 Labour Market States and Transitions

Any person in the working-age population is either employed, unemployed, or out of the labour force. Figure 5.14 displays these three states and how flows occur between them. A striking aspect of labour markets in developed economies is the sheer size of these flows. Table 5.7 shows that the flow of individuals moving into and out of unemployment over a year represents several times the stock of unemployment at any given point in time. In contrast to the static impression conveyed by Section 5.3, labour markets are remarkably dynamic, even when unemployment seems stuck at high levels.

There are three ways of becoming unemployed.

- First, new entrants to the labour market may join the labour force before they have found work, but are unsuccessful, at least initially.
- Second, **separations** of workers from jobs may lead to unemployment. Quits represent voluntary separations from the employee's viewpoint. They account for roughly 50% to 66% of all separations from employment in the UK, and up to 70% in the USA. Yet quits rarely lead to unemployment, and

most workers who quit one job take up another immediately—a transition from employment to employment. Of those who quit but do not start a new job, most leave the labour force, usually for family reasons (e.g. maternity leave), return to school, or retire.

- Finally, job losers—those who are involuntarily separated—tend to flow into unemployment (some may just decide not to look for work). Job loss may result from expiration of short-term contracts (common in France and Spain), unanticipated redundancies or layoffs (more common in Denmark, the UK, and the USA), and closure or relocation of factories (which occurs everywhere).

5.4.2 Stocks, Flows, and Frictional Unemployment

No two positions and no two persons are the same. Pairing a worker and an unfilled job opening or vacancy is not always easy and may take time. The matching of skills, occupation, industry, and geographical location requires a large amount of information. The more efficient the labour markets are, the faster the match is achieved. In the meantime,

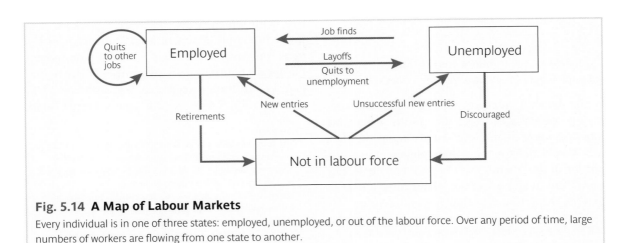

Fig. 5.14 A Map of Labour Markets
Every individual is in one of three states: employed, unemployed, or out of the labour force. Over any period of time, large numbers of workers are flowing from one state to another.

Table 5.7 **Unemployment Stocks and Flows, 2006**

	Average unemployment stock, millions	Unemployment Flows (millions of cases per year):	
		Inflows	Outflows
Austria	0.24	0.92	1.07
Germany	4.49	6.88	7.38
UK	0.92	2.52	2.47
USA	6.99	31.34	31.83

Sources: AMS (Austria); Bundesagentur für Arbeit (Germany); Department of Employment (UK); Bureau of Labor Statistics (USA).

frictional unemployment occurs. This is an unavoidable result of the dynamics of labour force movements, and the normal process of job creation and destruction.

In addition to the efficiency of the job matching process, frictional unemployment depends on the number of job separations and the number of vacancies. If we ignore the flows from and to 'Not in the labour force' in Figure 5.14, the number of workers who become unemployed (per month or per year) represents a fraction s, called the **separation rate**, of existing employment relationships (L). While sL workers flow into unemployment each period, a number of unemployed workers find jobs and flow out of unemployment. If we use f to denote the job **finding rate**, i.e. the fraction of the unemployed (U) who find employment during the period, the change in unemployment in a given period is given by

(5.3) $$\Delta U = sL - fU.$$

$$\frac{\text{change in}}{\text{unemployment}} = \frac{\text{inflows into}}{\text{unemployment}} - \frac{\text{outflows out of}}{\text{unemployment}}$$

In the dynamic interpretation of labour markets, unemployment is the stock that results when flows into and out of unemployment are equal, or when $\Delta U = 0$ in (5.3). Expressing unemployment as a proportion of the labour force $L^S = L + U$ and neglecting transitions in and out of the labour force allows us to write the **frictional unemployment rate** u^f as[17]

(5.4) $$u^f = \frac{s}{s+f}.$$

We can think of the proportion s of workers separated from their jobs as the probability of losing a job if currently employed and, similarly, the proportion f of unemployed workers represents the probability of finding a job if unemployed.[18] Frictional unemployment is higher, the higher the job separation rate and the lower the job finding rate. The next two sections will examine more closely the determinants of these two indicators—the job separation rate s and the job finding rate f.

5.4.3 Job Separation and the Incidence of Unemployment

The separation rate s is a measure of the incidence of unemployment. It has structural and cyclical components. The structural aspect is linked to the ease with which firms can dismiss workers. It is lower in countries where legal and social restrictions on layoffs exist (as in most continental European countries) than in countries where redundancies are more acceptable (e.g. Denmark, UK, and the USA).[19] The cyclical aspect simply refers

---

[17] If $\Delta U = 0$, it follows that $sL = fU$. Substituting $L^S - U$ for L and dividing by L^S yields (5.4).

[18] These figures hide a large degree of heterogeneity in the labour market: some individuals find a job readily after becoming unemployed, whereas others may have very low probabilities of exiting unemployment.

[19] It is, however, usually the case that outflow rates in countries with employment protection are also lower because firms are more reluctant to hire new workers. For that reason, the effect of employment protection on unemployment is ambiguous.

Table 5.8 Inflows into Unemployment and Unemployment Rates in the UK, March 2004

	Inflow rate into unemployment (monthly, as % of employment)	Unemployment rate (% of relevant labour force)
By region: Britain		
East Midlands	0.7	2.9
Eastern	0.5	2.3
London	0.8	3.6
North-East	1.0	4.6
North-West	0.8	3.3
Northern Ireland	0.7	4.0
Scotland	0.9	3.9
South-East	0.5	1.8
South-West	0.5	1.9
Wales	0.8	3.5
West Midlands	0.8	3.6
Yorkshire and the Humber	0.8	3.4
Total	0.7	3.1
By demographic group: UK		
Aged 16–17	1.0	21.1[a]
Aged 18–24	2.2	9.9[a]
Aged 25–49	0.6	3.9[a]
Aged 50 and over	0.4	2.5[a]
Male	0.9	4.3
Female	0.4	1.7

[a] Average from Dec 2003 to Feb 2004.
Source: UK Labour Market Trends, March 2004.

exhibit higher separation rates of inflow into unemployment tend to have higher unemployment rates.

5.4.4 Job Finding and the Duration of Unemployment

Like the separation rate, the job finding rate f has cyclical and structural components. It is highly procyclical, increasing when output and employment are rising and declining when the economy is contracting. On the structural side, the job finding rate depends on a number of long-run factors, including labour market institutions, the effectiveness of the worker–job matching process, and the suitability of the unemployed for work in the vacancies which firms are posting. It depends on how hard the unemployed look for jobs, how many job openings are available, and how easy it is to spot an opportunity (and how many opportunities are available). It depends on incentives to remain unemployed, and unemployment insurance may therefore slow down the exit rate out of unemployment. Many of these aspects will be discussed in Chapter 18.

Unemployment benefits are intended to assist the jobless while they search for work. Table 5.9 shows that unemployment benefit systems vary considerably from country to country, with respect to eligibility criteria, income replacement, and the period over which they are paid. While **unemployment benefits** reflect a widely perceived need for income insurance, solidarity, and social conscience, they may encourage unemployed workers in declining industries to wait for an unlikely recovery rather than to retrain and change sectors, possibly at a lower wage. They also act as a disincentive for looking for a job, or as an incentive for being 'choosier'.[20] If the benefits are generous, and particularly if they are long-lasting, unemployed workers may take more time to find an acceptable job, a time in which their skills and re-employability

to the fact that during recessions the probability of losing a job rises and so, therefore, does frictional unemployment.

Table 5.8 shows that in one particular country (the UK) in a given year (2004), job separation rates vary considerably across various characteristics of labour market participants. Just as equation (5.4) implies, those specific labour force groups that

[20] Strictly speaking, this applies only to those who already qualify for benefits. Prior work experience is often required before one can draw unemployment insurance benefits. In this case, individuals will be more willing to accept the first job. This is called the 'entitlement effect'.

Table 5.9 Unemployment Compensation: Conditions for Eligibility and Benefit Levels, 2007

| Country | Eligibility conditions: | | Maximum benefit duration (in weeks) | Replacement rate of net earnings/ benefit level[c] | Conditions and restrictions | Long term unemployment (>12 months) as % of all unemployed, 2006 |
	Employment	Period				
Austria	28 weeks	12 month	52	55%	According to wage class	27.3
Belgium	312 days	18 month	Indefinite	60%	Of max earnings	55.6
Canada						8.7
Denmark	52 weeks	3 years	208	90%	Of average earnings	20.4
Finland	43 weeks	24 month	24	€23.50	Per day	24.8
France	Registered employment		116	57.4–75%	Of average daily wage	44.0
Germany	12 months	2 years	77	60%	Of net earnings	57.2
Greece	200 days	2 years	52	40% (50%)	Daily wages (monthly salary)	55.6
Ireland	39 weeks	Last 1 year	64	€165.80	Per week	34.3
Italy	52 weeks	2 years	30	40%	Of gross average daily wage	52.9
Japan	6 month	12 month	47	50–80%	Of average daily wages	33.0
Netherlands	26 weeks	39 weeks	26	70%	Of minimum wage	45.2
New Zealand	Resident for 24 months		Indefinite	NZ$173.92	Per week	7.1
Norway	Registered employment		104	0.2%	Of annual income per day	14.1
Spain	12 month	Last 6 years	26	70%	Of average earnings	29.5
Sweden	450 hours	6 month	43	320 kr	Per day	14.2
Switzerland	12 months[a]	2 years	74	80%	Of last earnings	39.1
UK			26	£57.45	Per week	22.1
USA	15–20 weeks[b]	1 year	26	50%	Of last earnings, taxable	10.0

[a] Contributions must have been paid on earnings equal to at least 25 times weekly lower earnings limit (£84 from April 2006) in one of two tax years

[b] Different across US states

[c] Single household without children

Sources: Social Security Programs Throughout the World: for Europe, United States, New Zealand, Japan for 2006, OECD <http://www.ssa.gov/policy/docs/progdesc/ssptw/2006-2007/europe/index.html>.

may deteriorate. This 'unemployment trap' often applies to unemployed low wage-earners who face loss of benefit upon taking on a new job. The last column of Table 5.9 shows a tendency for people to remain unemployed longer in countries where unemployment benefits are more generous, paying more income over longer periods. As the finding rate declines, frictional unemployment rises. This confirms an uncomfortable trade-off between social concern and economic efficiency.

5.5 The Equilibrium Rate of Unemployment

5.5.1 The Concept

If all unemployment were voluntary, it would hardly attract any attention. The existence of high and evidently involuntary unemployment means that labour markets do not function like other markets. The existence of market imperfections, arising from both economic and institutional factors, makes it necessary to qualify the market-clearing paradigm of Section 5.2. We should also consider alternative perspectives of equilibrium to the equality of demand for labour by firms and the supply of labour by households.

The unemployment rates shown in Figure 1.3 clearly fluctuate in the short run over 2–3 year intervals, but also move slowly over a longer horizon. It is these longer-run movements in unemployment which are of interest to us now. Long-run labour market equilibrium can be summarized by an unemployment rate that would occur in the absence of cyclical disturbances. Because of imperfections, labour markets may be in equilibrium and yet unemployment may not be limited to voluntary unemployment. **Equilibrium unemployment** can be thought of as the sum of frictional and structural unemployment:

(5.5)   equilibrium unemployment =
frictional unemployment +
structural unemployment.

Frictional unemployment occurs because it takes time for a match to occur between a worker seeking a job and a vacancy needing to be filled. It depends on the efficiency of the labour market, including the eagerness of both parties to find a match quickly. The frictional unemployment rate may well vary over time, not just because the market's efficiency changes, but because economic conditions make it more or less likely for people to find jobs or to become unemployed. Is frictional unemployment voluntary or involuntary? Probably a bit of both. Some laid-off workers do find it genuinely difficult to quickly find a new job. Others may be choosy.

Structural unemployment describes unemployment caused by inappropriate wage levels that are not allowed to reach their market-clearing levels. It has many causes. The common theme is that the demand and supply of labour are influenced by a number of institutions and regulations. Collective labour supply, which is brought into balance with labour demand in equilibrium, does not quite match individual supply behaviour. Some workers are involuntarily unemployed even when real wages equate the collective supply of labour with the demand of firms.

Estimates of equilibrium rates of unemployment are provided in Table 5.10. The contrast between Europe and North America is striking. The equilibrium unemployment rate was generally very low in Europe in the 1960s. Since then it rose considerably while remaining stable in the USA. A comparison of Table 5.10 with Table 5.4 shows that actual unemployment has followed the same pattern. To begin to understand this dramatic evolution, we return to the two components of the equilibrium rate of unemployment—demand for labour and the supply of labour.

Table 5.10 Estimates of the Equilibrium Unemployment Rate (in %)

	1970–9	1980–9	1990–9	2000–9
Germany	N/A	N/A	6.4	7.2
Italy	4.5	7.1	9.4	7.7
Japan	1.9	2.3	3.0	3.9
Spain	5.6	11.0	14.0	10.1
United Kingdom	2.5	7.0	7.1	5.4
United States	6.1	6.2	5.4	4.8

Source: OECD Stat; Economic Outlook Database.

5.5.2 The European Experience

The evidence suggests that European unemployment rose when large numbers of workers lost their jobs at the time of the oil shocks. The expected subsequent return to pre-oil-shock levels was thwarted in many European countries by a fall in the finding rate, so exit from unemployment became increasingly harder. Is the development of the social safety net to be blamed for having provided workers with the incentive to wait out their unemployment? Simple comparisons between Europe and the USA, such as the one in Figure 5.15, seem to confirm the suspicion

that an extensive social safety net has become a barrier to more employment.

Yet there is also some striking counter-evidence. The social safety net is even more developed in Denmark, Sweden, and Norway, where long-term unemployment has remained lower. This implies that what really matters is not the safety net itself, but the disincentives that it can generate. Unemployment benefits, for example, provide an alternative to finding a new job, and help transform temporary unemployment into permanent—structural—unemployment. Long-term unemployment has become increasingly widespread, and as workers

---

 Box 5.5 **'Eurosclerosis' and 'Euro-Recovery'**

Most European countries—especially France, Germany, and Italy—have experienced chronically high rates of unemployment since the mid-1970s. For many, high and rising unemployment was an accepted fact of life, with average unemployment rising after every economic downturn (see Figure 1.1). Yet it may be surprising that in the 1960s and early 1970s, Europe had lower unemployment rates than in the USA. A number of things happened in the 1970s which were not particularly favourable for countries with an important role for collective wage setting. First, two severe oil price increases—in 1973–1974 and 1979–1980—acted like large negative productivity shocks and shifted labour demand to the left. These 'oil price shocks' were reinforced by a slowdown in investment by firms in response to bad times. Second, a slowdown in the rate of total factor productivity growth shrank the pie over which unions could bargain. Third, the late 1960s and early 1970s were a particularly militant period for European trade unions, with a number of general strikes and labour unrest across the continent and the UK. 'Hard-line' unions pushed real wages higher and increased their downward rigidity. The term 'Eurosclerosis' was coined by German economist Herbert Giersch of the Kiel Institute of World Economics to characterize this period of gloom and doom. Facing this rising tide of unemployment, many leaders simply accepted unemployment as inevitable and as beyond the influence of policy.

Figure 5.15 compares the experience of the euro area (calculated back to include the time before the euro was actually introduced) with that of the USA. Evidently, the USA and Europe had different experiences. European wages shot up in the early part of the period, and employment growth was sluggish. In contrast, the USA showed wage moderation in the 1970s and 1980s, which created the conditions for more job creation. It is tempting to conclude that US labour markets are closer to the market-clearing and took their medicine when it was time to do so. Because the US population and labour supply has increased faster, a direct comparison is not quite fair. Yet the experience of a number of EU countries since the 1990s—Spain, Ireland, Denmark, and the Netherlands for example—teaches us that it is possible to have high rates of employment growth and lower unemployment rates.

What brought about the partial recovery in the EU? After many years, reforms have begun to bear fruit. In many smaller countries, such as the Netherlands, cooperative solutions brought unions and employers together to agree on wage moderation in return for other concessions. It is believed that the introduction of the euro has increased the elasticity of the demand for labour and forced collective bargaining—especially in smaller open economies—to avoid wage policies which price workers out of international markets. The lesson is that Euro-pessimism is unfounded. Unemployment can be brought down, but it takes time, and political will.

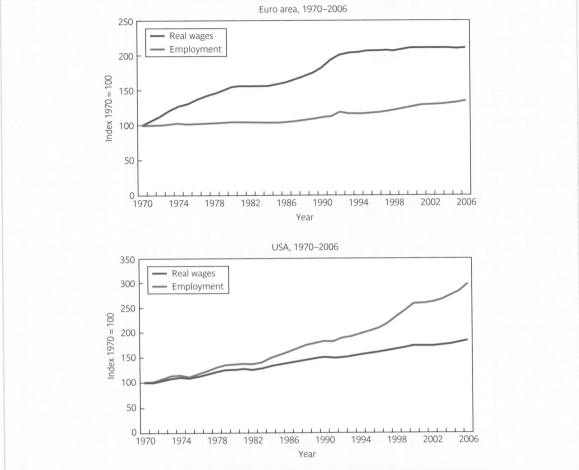

Fig. 5.15 Employment and Real Wages in the Euro Area and the USA, 1970–2006

Over the period 1970–1990, real wages doubled in the euro area, while employment rose by about 10%. During the same period, real wages in the USA increased by only about 50%, while employment rose more than 70%. (Real wages = total compensation per employee deflated by the GDP deflator.) Since 1990, real wage growth in the euro area has moderated sharply, and growth of employment has increased. The distribution of this growth across Europe is not even, however. *Source*: OECD.

gradually lose their human capital and contact with the active labour force, they become unsuitable for any vacancy.

The strikingly different evolution of the equilibrium unemployment rate across countries also points to the importance of wage-setting institutions. The comparison between Europe and the USA in Box 5.5 shows that high unemployment in the EC appears to be related to steep real wage increases, amounting to what has been dubbed the European 'wage shock'. Labour costs consist not only of wages received by workers. In many European countries, labour taxes and contributions to the social security system have also been allowed to rise steeply. Of importance, too, is the regulation of the use of labour (length of the work-week, dismissal procedures, part-time work, etc). We return to these issues in Chapter 18.

5.5.3 Actual and Equilibrium Unemployment

It can take many years before real wages adjust to their long-run values in Figures 5.7 and 5.12. In the meantime, actual unemployment can deviate from equilibrium unemployment. Actual employment is below, and actual unemployment above, equilibrium when the real wage is above the equilibrium level, as at point A_1 in Figure 5.16. When the real wage is low, firms may be able temporarily to move away from the union-set collective labour supply curve towards the individual labour supply curve (point A_2), for example by using agencies specializing in temporary jobs or overtime work. Workers may have overestimated the real wage by underestimating the rise in the price level. Firms may be willing to hire more workers at the going wage. In such situations employment is above, and unemployment below, the equilibrium level. These deviations, while short-term in nature, tend to be associated with fluctuations of the economy that we know as the business cycle. We revisit this important topic in Chapter 12.

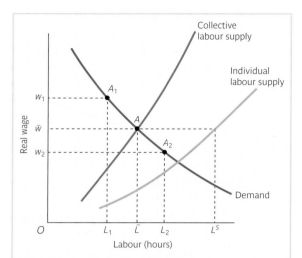

Fig. 5.16 Actual and Equilibrium Employment

When unions negotiate on behalf of workers, market equilibrium occurs at point A, and equilibrium unemployment is $L^S - \bar{L}$. Actual employment and unemployment may differ if the real wage is slow to move to its equilibrium level $\bar{w}$. If it is above the market equilibrium level ($w_1 > \bar{w}$), firms reduce employment to L_1 and actual unemployment exceeds equilibrium unemployment. Conversely, below-equilibrium real wages ($w_2 < \bar{w}$) enable firms to connect with structurally unemployed workers willing to work at lower wages than the union-set level. The resulting unemployment rate is lower than the equilibrium level.

ⓘ Summary

1 Households trade off leisure against consumption. An increase in wages can induce more labour supply if the substitution effect dominates, i.e. labour supply is relatively elastic. It will supply less labour if the income effect dominates. There will be no change at all if the labour supply is inelastic and the two effects offset each other.

2 Individual labour supply seems to be inelastic in the short run. But in the long run it is more

likely to be backward-bending, as the higher incomes afforded by higher real wages allow households to enjoy both more leisure and more consumption. Aggregate labour supply is more responsive to real wage changes than that of households in the short run, as real wage increases draw new individuals into the labour force.

3 The demand for labour by firms depends on its (marginal) productivity, which is determined

by the available technology and the capital stock. Firms hire labour to the point where the marginal productivity of labour is equal to the real wage. The labour demand schedule is shifted outwards by an improvement in technology or an increase in the capital stock.

4 Equilibrium employment and the wage level are given by the intersection of labour demand and labour supply. Improvements in technology or increases in capital will be reflected in higher wages if labour supply is inelastic, and in higher employment if labour supply is elastic.

5 Involuntary unemployment arises when real wages do not decline to clear the market so that not all labour supplied by households is hired.

6 Labour unions care about real wages and employment. In determining their target wage, given the demand for labour by firms, they ask for higher real wages than if the labour market were perfectly competitive. While the resulting unemployment rate is (optimal and) voluntary for unions, it may be involuntary for individuals.

7 Because firms cannot easily monitor work effort or wish to elicit lower turnover or improve worker quality, they may pay efficiency wages. This is yet another reason why real wages may be set above market-clearing levels.

8 Labour markets are also characterized by widespread government interventions. Minimum wages, designed to protect workers, can actually cause unemployment. Despite this, governments may see minimum wages as an effective means of guaranteeing a socially acceptable minimum income for those who want to work.

9 The labour market is characterized by large flows between states of employment, unemployment, and being out of the labour force. Job search is an important aspect and results in frictional unemployment. Alongside structural unemployment, it is a source of equilibrium unemployment.

10 The efficiency of job search can vary across individuals and countries, and is affected by government labour market policies. Unemployment benefits, designed to make unemployment more bearable, provide disincentives to finding a new job quickly, thereby increasing frictional unemployment. Other programmes, such as training and relocation subsidies, can reduce frictional unemployment.

11 Because there are labour market institutions as well as natural market imperfections, equilibrium unemployment is never zero or entirely voluntary. Individuals may be willing to work at lower wages than those prevailing in equilibrium, but may not be able to underbid in the market. This is the sense in which real wages are downwardly rigid.

12 Real wages are slow to adjust to disequilibria, if only because they fulfil many other roles. This speed of adjustment will depend on labour market institutions, among other things. As a result, actual and equilibrium unemployment may differ for some time.

🔑 Key Concepts

- endowment
- leisure
- unemployment
- consumption–leisure trade-off
- indifference curves

- utility
- marginal rate of substitution
- real (consumption) wage
- relative price
- substitution effect

- ◆ income effect
- ◆ household labour supply curve
- ◆ labour force, labour force participation rate
- ◆ person-hours
- ◆ marginal productivity of labour
- ◆ labour demand curve
- ◆ elastic, inelastic
- ◆ voluntary unemployment
- ◆ involuntary unemployment
- ◆ real wage rigidity
- ◆ labour market institutions
- ◆ labour (or trade) unions

- ◆ employers' associations
- ◆ collective labour supply curve
- ◆ insiders and outsiders
- ◆ minimum wages
- ◆ efficiency wages
- ◆ frictional unemployment
- ◆ separations, separation rate
- ◆ finding rate
- ◆ unemployment benefits
- ◆ equilibrium unemployment
- ◆ structural unemployment

❷ Exercises

1 Suppose that the household in Figure 5.2 receives an inheritance. Show the effect on its decision to work and to consume. According to this result, do rich people work more or less than poor people? Explain your answer.

2 Suppose Robinson Crusoe is paid a higher wage ('overtime pay') if he works more than 8 hours a day, but only has 16 hours at his disposal.

   (a) Draw his budget line in this case.

   (b) Does the existence of overtime necessarily make him better off?

   (c) Show Crusoe's optimal behaviour for 'normal' indifference curves.

   Under which conditions will he choose to work overtime? Under which conditions will he refuse?

3 Suppose Crusoe must pay for his work tools (coconut husks?) and must spend an hour a day to climb the trees to get to the coconuts. Think of these as fixed costs which must be paid as long as he is working at all in the labour market.

   (a) Draw his budget constraint in this case.

   (b) Show Crusoe's optimal choice for the case that he goes to work, grumbling about the

fixed costs, but voluntarily. What do you conclude about his utility level compared with staying home?

   (c) Now sketch the case in which Crusoe decides to stay home. What can you say about his utility level and preferences in this case? Show that if the wage rises enough, Crusoe can be enticed to leave his tree house.

   (d) Now apply this to a modern-day worker who faces commuting cost as well as a monetary/resource cost of working, regardless of how high the wage is or how many hours are worked. Show both cases—the worker who works and the worker who stays home. How could an 'in-work' grant to those who work any positive amount of time entice the worker to accept a job? Could it fail?

4 It is frequently claimed that Europe's unemployment problem is due to high labour taxes in the form of employer and employee contributions to social security, which are proportional to wages for some range. Assume that individuals care about after-tax wages.

(a) Using the machinery of Figure 5.3, show the effect of a high tax versus low tax environment. What is the effect on labour supply and equilibrium wages? State your assumptions carefully.

(b) What is the effect on equilibrium employment levels resulting from the increased tax for the case of the utility function $U = c^\alpha \ell^{1-\alpha}$ (ignore labour demand).

(c) What changes in your answer to (b) if the tax revenues are rebated to the households as a lump-sum payment, i.e. unrelated to their income tax payments? Given that high labour taxation (social security charges and income taxes) in France, Germany, and Italy coincides with high rates of transfers to households (as opposed to Denmark and Sweden) how could you explain the observed pattern of market labour supply in Table 5.2?

5 Derive the collective labour supply curve graphically. Show how different union preferences can interact with the same shift of labour demand and lead to: (a) rigid wages around some 'target level' with flexible employment; (b) flexible wages around some target level of employment; (c) flexible wages when employment is rising, but rigid when employment is declining.

6 In the 1980s, many European countries tried to tackle the unemployment problem by encouraging early retirement, with arguments that only a fixed amount of jobs are available for job-seekers. Use the supply and demand framework to show how the advocates of such a policy might have argued. Why do you think that most policy-makers have now given up on early retirement as a way of fighting unemployment?

7 It is well-known in Europe that the unemployment rate among well-educated workers is considerably lower than for those who left school early or without training. Why might this be the case? How might an 'education offensive' help solve the unemployment problem, even if wages for the low-skilled are rigid?

8 In Japan the bonus system is widespread. Workers often receive 30% of their pay in the form of a profit-contingent payment, which can go up or down depending on the fortunes of the enterprise in which they work. What are the implications of such a system for real wage rigidity and equilibrium employment?

9 It is sometimes claimed that the influx of foreign migrants into the labour force is a cause of unemployment. Show the effect of immigration on the labour market as described by Figure 5.12. What does it mean for real wages and employment?

10 Show the effect of a technological innovation which raises the MPL in a market with an upward-sloping supply curve for labour when: (a) wages are flexible; (b) wages are rigid. Now show the effect of technical change which *reduces* the MPL. Given these differences, evaluate how unions might regard technical change differently, depending on their preferences. Given your answer, assess why unions are frequently in disagreement about the merits of a minimum wage.

→ Essay Questions

1 How would you determine whether unemployment is voluntary or involuntary? How do you respond to the criticism that it is virtually impossible to distinguish the two?

2 Critically evaluate the statement that labour unions should assume responsibility for the administration, financing, and disbursement of unemployment benefits.

3 Severance regulations—government interference with the separation of workers from firms which frequently occurs in modern economies—are universally thought to influence labour markets,

but it is hotly disputed whether they increase or decrease unemployment. Discuss. Do you think there are other costs involved in the regulation of redundancies?

4 Discuss both sides of the minimum wage debate. What kind of hard facts might help resolve the argument?

5 From equation (5.4) it follows that all policies which reduce unemployment can be boiled down to two types of measures: reducing the inflow rate s and increasing the outflow rate f. Discuss policies which could affect these two rates. Are they necessarily good for the economy—in the sense of increasing output of the economy or utility of members of society?

Money, Prices, and Exchange Rates in the Long Run 6

It is indeed evident that money is nothing but the representation of labour and commodities, and serves only as a method of rating or estimating them. Where coin is in greater plenty, as a greater quantity of it is required to represent the same quantity of goods, it can have no effect, either good or bad . . . any more than it would make an alteration on a merchant's books, if, instead of the Arabian method of notation, which requires few characters, he should make use of the Roman, which requires a great many.

David Hume[1]

Money frees you from doing things you dislike. Since I dislike doing nearly everything, money is handy.

Groucho Marx

6.1 Overview

In this chapter we introduce a new actor on the macroeconomic stage: money. Money is a central theme in macroeconomics—in fact, so central that macroeconomics is sometimes even called monetary economics. It may be surprising that we waited until now to introduce this concept! But there is a good reason to do so. The key message from this chapter is the **principle of monetary neutrality**. In the long run, the supply of money does not matter for the real aspects of the economy considered up to now: long-run economic growth, standards of living, employment, and unemployment. Until now, we did not need to bring money into the picture because we were focused on the long run. This chapter therefore represents a critical junction: it is the last one dealing with the long run and it is the first one dealing with money.

In addition to money, this chapter introduces another innovation that will remain with us for the rest of the book: we now open up the economy. To do this we need to introduce the **exchange rate**. This will give us a glimpse into the concept of external competitiveness. It will also provide another implication of money neutrality: in the long run there is not much that monetary policy can do about competitiveness. Short-run changes in the price of one money in terms of another cannot increase our long-term welfare.

We start by presenting the logic behind the neutrality principle. This leads us to derive its central implication—that inflation is a monetary phenomenon. The evidence is compelling. If you wonder why a country undergoes persistently high inflation, you have nowhere else to look but to the central bank, which has let money grow too fast. In addition, the overwhelming evidence also shows that high-inflation countries see their currency depreciate at about the same rate.

In order to understand this second result, we will need to define two exchange rates: a nominal and real one. The **nominal exchange rate** is familiar; it is the price of one money in terms of another that is quoted in newspapers and by banks. The **real exchange rate** is a more subtle concept which tries to address the notion of what money can actually buy in the two countries being compared. It involves price levels at home and abroad to provide a measure of external competitiveness. The neutrality of money implies that the real exchange rate is constant in the long run, and independent of monetary factors.

One difficulty with quoted exchange rates is that they always link two monies, very often the home currency and the US dollar. But what about other bilateral exchange rates that relate the home currency to important neighbours and trading partners? In order to tackle this issue, we present effective exchange rates, both nominal and real, which are averages of bilateral nominal and real rates.

---

[1]   David Hume (1711–1776) was arguably Scotland's greatest moral philosopher and economist (although Adam Smith is pretty strong competition). Hume's most noteworthy contribution to economics was his essay *Of Money* (1752), from which this quotation is taken.

In the end, this chapter serves two purposes. First, it presents the fundamental neutrality result and some of its implications. This will serve as a bridge between the long run discussed up to now and the short-run evolution of the economy that is the subject of the next seven chapters. Second, it introduces key variables—money and the exchange rate—which are the bread and butter of macroeconomics.

6.2 Money and the Neutrality Principle

6.2.1 Money

We all think we know what money is, don't we? After all, it is rare to spend a day not having to deal with money in some form or another. Well, it is considerably trickier than it looks and Chapter 9 will provide a detailed definition, or rather several definitions, of money. To make things even more confusing, people tend to use the term 'money' when they mean income (wages, interest, or retirement benefits) or wealth. For economists, money is what you use when you go shopping: cash, your bank accounts, and possibly other forms of purchasing power.

A related question is where that money comes from in the end. Again, a full explanation will have to wait until Chapter 9. It is sufficient here to assert that, in the end, the ultimate control of the supply of money is exerted by the monetary authority, the central bank.

A fundamental principle of economics is that money only affects the price level, leaving the real side of economy untouched. This is what David Hume meant in the epigram to this chapter. Think of money as a numbering system that allows us to express prices of all the goods and services we buy and sell in common terms. This implies that prices and the nominal exchange rate should grow at the same rate as money, in the long run at least. This common-sense idea is called the **neutrality principle**. It is readily illustrated in the left-hand side chart of Figure 6.1, which shows average annual inflation and money growth over about 30 years, a suitably long time period. Later chapters (Chapters 9 and 12) will provide more precision about what we mean by 'the long run'. The chart shows that, indeed, those countries where money has been growing fast have had high inflation rates. But the figure also shows that the neutrality principle suffers from many exceptions. We will look first at why the principle makes sense and then at why it is only an approximation of reality.

6.2.2 Money and Prices

Money is held by households and firms to carry out transactions. For this reason, money is often called a medium of exchange. As a first approximation, we will simply suppose that people want to hold enough cash to cover a proportion k of their spending. In Chapter 9, we will refine this analysis. For a country as a whole, total spending is measured by GDP, so the total demand for money, denoted M, is simply proportional to GDP:

(6.1) $$M = kPY.$$

This equation is known as the **Cambridge equation**, and is the simplest and most readily understood formulation of the demand for money.[2] Note that it relates the demand for money to *nominal* GDP (PY), not to *real* GDP (Y). This is because money is the most fundamental nominal variable of all, as

---

[2] This relationship is called the Cambridge equation because it was first elaborated formally by Cambridge (UK) economist Arthur Cecil Pigou (1877–1959). A variant is the quantity theory of money, which defines the velocity of money as $V = 1/k$ to obtain $MV = PY$. It is called velocity because it measures how often, on average, one unit of money—say one pound—is used during the year to support spending (indeed $V = PY/M$ relates the total value of all final transactions to the money stock). The quantity theory of money is due to the American economist Irving Fisher (1867–1947).

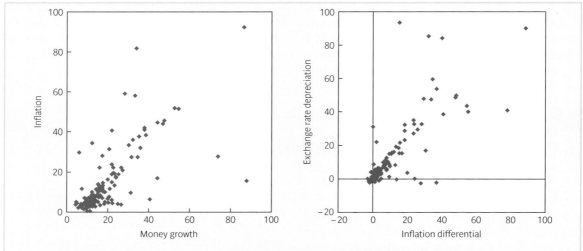

Fig. 6.1 Money Growth, Inflation, and Exchange Rate Depreciation, 1975–2006

The left-hand side chart shows the average annual rates of inflation rate and money growth in 155 countries. The average annual depreciation *vis-à-vis* the US dollar is related to the average annual difference of inflation in the same countries (excluding the USA) and in the USA is displayed in the right-hand side chart. We have excluded the pathological countries where inflation rates have been in excess of 100% per year on average during this period. For most countries, the annual averages are computed over the period 1975–2006. For some, the period is shorter, because data are not available for the whole period (this concerns the formerly planned economies until about 1995 and the euro area countries after 1999 since the latter have abandoned their own monies).

Source: International Financial Statistics, IMF.

defined in Chapters 1 and 2. To see why, it might be helpful to consider the following thought experiment.

Imagine that prices of all goods and services in the economy in terms of money were to double overnight. As a result, a €20 banknote today only buys today what a €10 banknote could buy yesterday. In contrast to relative prices, whose values are independent of the level of prices by construction, the value of money—the purchasing power of money—has fallen by 50%. In fact, its value is inversely proportional to the price level. Because money is the ultimate nominal variable, all other nominal variables are measured in monetary values: euros, pounds, dollars, roubles, kronas, etc. We will even sometimes use the word 'monetary' as a substitute for 'nominal'. Box 6.1 uses the introduction of the euro in continental European countries as a plausible illustration of monetary neutrality.

Since the purchasing power of money is inversely proportional to the price level, it can be written as the ratio M/P. This is also called real value of money, or real money for short. M/P measures the purchasing power of the money stock M. Dividing both sides of the equation by P, we can rewrite (6.1) in real terms as

(6.2)
$$\frac{M}{P} = kY.$$

This expression relates real money demand to the real GDP Y. This is logical; real variables ought to be associated with each other, but not to nominal variables. Now let us go a step further. Money, we noted, is created by the central bank. What happens if the central bank doubles the stock of money overnight and distributes the new banknotes to everyone? People will be happy at first! They will want to buy more goods and services. The question

Box 6.1 Evidence for Monetary Neutrality: The Introduction of the Euro

An excellent example of monetary neutrality was the introduction of the euro, the money currently used by over 320 million Europeans. On 1 January 1999, 11 members of the European Union gave up their national currencies 'irrevocably' and adopted the euro as their new money. On 1 January 2002, euro banknotes became legal tender for transactions in Austria, Belgium, Finland, France, Germany, Ireland, Italy, Luxembourg, the Netherlands, Portugal, and Spain. The adoption of irrevocable exchange rates three years earlier had already rendered these national currencies 'non-decimal units' of the euro. Greece joined in 2001, Slovenia in 2007, and Malta and Cyprus in 2008. As monetary neutrality would predict, the introduction of the euro and the abandonment of national moneys represented nothing but a mere rescal-

ing of prices, an excellent example of a purely monetary event, with no consequences for the real economy. The short-term impact of the event on the inflation rate has been estimated at 0.2–0.5% and this was a one-off effect, well within the margin of measurement error.

What has followed the introduction of the euro is a different story, however. It lies at the heart of the distinction between and the interaction between real and nominal variables. The introduction of a new money means new institutions and agencies—the European Central Bank—as well as new responsibilities for the creation of money. In addition, the introduction of the euro has affected the behaviour of many economic agents in the euro area. This is the exciting subject of the rest of the textbook.

is how producers and sellers will respond. In the short run, they might well supply more goods and services to their customers, a process that we will examine in great detail in Chapters 10 and 11. But this is unlikely to last very long; otherwise, it would mean that growth could be increased simply by printing more and more money! Most would think that this is too good to be true, and indeed it is. Every few years, another country tries the recipe and fails. Box 6.2 tells the story of Zimbabwe. The unfortunate fact is that, for reasons to be fully spelled out in Chapter 12, faster money growth will result in higher inflation. More precisely, the neutrality principle asserts that money has no long-run effect on output and, more generally, it has no long-run effect on any real variable.

Let us try to make this reasoning more formal. If the nominal money stock M doubles, the left-hand side of (6.2) also doubles, all other things equal. The monetary neutrality principle says that, in the long run, real GDP is unaffected. This implies that the right-hand side remains unchanged. From a purely logical standpoint, this can only work in equation (6.2) if k or P changes. If k is constant, as we assumed thus far, P must perform the balancing act. Indeed, if P also doubles, then the real money stock M/P remains

constant and nothing has changed. Thus the long-run neutrality principle implies that money and prices must remain proportional to each other in the long run. Formally, the neutrality principle implies that inflation π, the growth rate of the price level, is equal to the growth rate of money:

(6.3)
$$\pi = \frac{\Delta M}{M}$$

inflation = money growth.

We have reached this conclusion by logical means, but there is an important economic story lurking in the background. When we say that the central bank prints more money, we are really talking about an increase in the *supply* of money. When we say that households and firms collectively want to hold cash in a proportion k of their purchases, we mean the *demand* for money. Then, we can interpret (6.1) or (6.2) as a money market equilibrium condition: demand (on the right-hand side) must equal supply (on the left-hand side). Equilibrium in the money market requires that demand and supply be kept equal. How does money market equilibrium come about? With k constant, M exogenously set by the central bank, and Y unaffected by M as a consequence of

Box 6.2 Zimbabwe: The Top of the Inflation Heap

The country with the highest inflation rate in the world is the African nation Zimbabwe. Over past years, Zimbabwe's inflation was so high that it qualified as a hyperinflation, an episode in which the price level increases by 50% per month or more. The latest figure available for this economy indicates that during the month September 2007, prices rose by an impressive 39%. Figure 6.2 presents quarterly measurements of the inflation rate, expressed at an annualized rate of change. Over the 12 months prior to September 2007, prices had risen cumulatively by almost 8,000%. According to an article in the *New York Times* in April 2006, the price of a single roll of toilet paper was given as 145,750 Zimbabwean dollars—about 50 euro cents.

Inflation in September looks quite good in comparison with April, when prices only doubled in just one month. Has President Mugabe found the solution to the hyperinflation? Hardly. The reason why inflation appears to be slowing is illusory. In June 2007, the government ordered firms and stores to cut prices by half. Rather than eliminating inflation, this measure forced firms to sell their goods in the illegal underground market, where prices have since exploded. The shops have become so bare that, as of October 2007, the Central Statistical Office stopped producing the consumer price index. Its chief statistician, who refused to sample prices in the informal markets, candidly explained that 'there are too many data gaps'.

The root cause of the hyperinflation is the fact that the central bank is creating money at full throttle, and has been doing so for some time. It does so because the government is broke and cannot pay for essential services, like the police or the army. To pay for them, the government simply borrows money from the central bank, the Reserve Bank of Zimbabwe, which gladly accommodates and prints the banknotes in the amount of the loan. (President Mugabe actually announced that he would follow this policy several years ago, so this is no surprise to anyone.) Yet the Reserve Bank blames the underground economy, threatening to 'take stern and unprecedented punitive measures against the dark forces of parallel market trading and financial disintermediation'. According to the bank, 'the blossoming cash barons, smugglers and other illicit dealers will threaten the stability of our national payment systems.'

the neutrality principle, it is the price level P that brings supply back in line with demand.

This reasoning is represented in Figure 6.3, which depicts the supply of money by the central bank (S) and the demand for money by the private sector (D). Equilibrium occurs at the intersection of the two schedules and determines the price level. An increase in the nominal money supply is met by a proportional increase in the price level.

6.2.3 Money, Prices, and Output

Let us now be a little more sophisticated. The left-hand side chart in Figure 6.1 provides only limited support for the neutrality principle as stated so far. The various observations tend to line up along the diagonal, but there are many deviations from the general pattern. For example, so far we reasoned as if output is constant but, in the long run, we expect real GDP to grow along the principles developed in Chapter 3. Importantly, money was never mentioned in that chapter. This is in line with the neutrality principle. The view that nominal variables do not affect real variables in the long run, also called the **dichotomy principle**, implies that money is not among the factors that determine long-run growth. On the other hand, growth proceeds at its own path and affects real money demand; this may explain some of the apparent departures from neutrality in Figure 6.1.

To see why, note that as the economy grows, more transactions will occur, and more money is needed to conduct those transactions. Indeed, the logic of (6.1) is that nominal money demand increases proportionately to GDP as long as k remains constant. Nominal money demand also increases proportionately to the price level. Using the arithmetic presented in Box 6.3, we can be even more precise and amend equation (6.3), which was derived by assuming zero output growth—Y was assumed to be constant—to take into account GDP growth. Then we

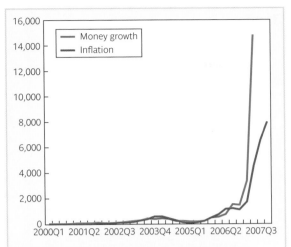

Fig. 6.2 Annual Inflation in Zimbabwe, 2000–2007

The figure displays the rate of increase of the consumer price index and of the money stock over the previous four quarters. Surprisingly, the price level seems to be growing less rapidly than money since 2006. This is when the government started to impose price controls. Observers report that inflation is much higher than recognized by the official numbers. The figure suggests that the observers are probably right.

Sources: Reserve Bank of Zimbabwe and IMF.

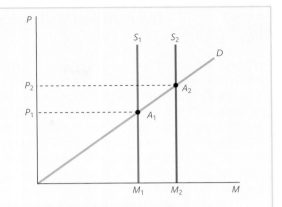

Fig. 6.3 Money Market Equilibrium

Nominal supply, the right-hand side of (6.1), is represented by the vertical schedules S_1 for M_1 and S_2 for M_2. According to the left-hand side of (6.1), demand is proportional to P (for given k and Y), which is represented by the line D. Money market equilibrium occurs at A_1 when the supply is M_1 and at A_2 when the money supply is M_2.

find that the growth rate of money demand is equal to the sum of GDP growth and inflation:

$$(6.4) \qquad \frac{\Delta M}{M} = \pi + \frac{\Delta Y}{Y}$$
$$\text{money} = \text{inflation} + \text{GDP} \atop \text{growth} \qquad\qquad \text{growth.}$$

Now, we can reason as before. If the central bank determines the money supply and if GDP growth is driven by other, non-monetary factors, as explained in Chapter 3, this relationship in fact explains inflation. To see this formally, we can rearrange (6.4) to find

$$(6.5) \qquad \pi = \frac{\Delta M}{M} - \frac{\Delta Y}{Y}$$
$$\text{inflation} = \text{money} - \text{GDP} \atop \text{growth} \qquad\qquad \text{growth.}$$

This result can be interpreted as follows. Money demand is driven by GDP growth. Money supply is

set by the central bank. If, for instance, the central bank lets the money supply grow faster than GDP, there is too much money around. People, i.e. household and firms, have more money than they wish to hold. Of course, no one throws money away. People spend it. There is now too much money chasing too few goods and services (the GDP) and inflation plays the balancing act. Rising prices reduce the purchasing power of money, i.e. the real value M/P of money, until (6.1)—or (6.2)—is satisfied. Conversely, if money grows more slowly than GDP, inflation is negative. Put differently, the only possibility of reconciling discrepancies between real money demand (M/P) and nominal supply (M) growth is for inflation to be an endogenous variable which can help ultimately restore long-run money market equilibrium. Note that (6.3) is a special case of (6.5), corresponding to the situation where GDP is constant.

How does this analysis help explain the left-hand side chart in Figure 6.1? Consider two countries: one grows fast and the other grows more slowly, say not at all. In the second country, in the long run, inflation is equal to the money growth rate, as in (6.3), while it is the excess of money growth

Box 6.3 The Arithmetic of Rates of Change

In several parts of this book, we use two arithmetic principles concerning rates of changes. If we look at a variable x, we may be interested in its rate of change $\Delta x/x$, where Δx represents the change over a given period (a day, a month, a year, etc.). Rates of change are most often expressed in percent per annum (per year). For example, if x increases from 10 to 12, $\Delta x = 12 - 10 = 2$, so $\Delta x/x = 2/10 = 0.2$, which is also 20%. The two principles concern the rates of changes of products and ratios. With two variables, say x and y, we can ask what is the rate of change of their product xy. The intriguing answer is that it is the *sum* of the rates of change of the individual variables x and y: $\frac{\Delta(xy)}{xy} = \frac{\Delta x}{x} + \frac{\Delta y}{y}$. (This is an approximation, which is acceptable when the rates of changes are not too big.) Similarly, the rate of change of a ratio is the difference of the rates of change of the individual variables:

$$\frac{\Delta\left(\frac{x}{Y}\right)}{\frac{x}{Y}} = \frac{\Delta x}{x} - \frac{\Delta y}{y}.$$

As an example, consider the real money stock M/P. Its rate of growth is the difference with the nominal growth rate and inflation, the rate of growth of the price level P:

$$\frac{\Delta(M/P)}{M/P} = \frac{\Delta M}{M} - \frac{\Delta P}{P} = \frac{\Delta M}{M} - \pi.$$

If the real money stock M/P is constant, $\Delta(M/P) = 0$ and it must be the case that $\Delta M/M = \pi$.

over GDP growth that determines inflation in the first country, as in (6.5). Now imagine that money growth rates are equal in both countries. Obviously, inflation will be lower in the first country, by an amount equal to its GDP growth rate. Graphically, it means that the point representing the first country in the left-hand side chart in Figure 6.1 will lie below the point representing the second country. If all countries were growing at the same rate, we would expect to see all the points neatly set along a straight line, parallel to the first diagonal, but below it. If growth rates differ among countries, we expect deviations from this line. These deviations should seem small if the growth rates are not too different. This observation explains many, but not all, of what we see in the chart. To explain the rest, we need to understand why k is not necessarily constant, which will be shown in Chapters 9 and 16. For the time being, we accept the rule of thumb given by (6.5) and the money neutrality principle.

This rule of thumb is illustrated in Table 6.1, where we assume that real GDP grows in the long run, on average, at a rate of 3%. This means that the real demand for money also grows by 3% per year. If the central bank allows the nominal money stock to grow at the same 3% per year, demand and

Table 6.1 Inflation and Money Growth in the Long Run: A Rule of Thumb (assuming that real money demand grows at 3% per annum)

Nominal money supply (%)	Inflation rate (%)
0	−3
3	0
8	5
50	47
103	100

supply coincide when the average inflation rate is 0%. Were the nominal money stock to grow at an average annual rate of 8%, inflation would have to be 5%. Only then would the real money stock grow at the same 3% rate as real money demand (8% nominal money growth less 5% inflation). This shows that, in the long run, inflation is a monetary phenomenon. It occurs when the nominal money supply grows faster than real money demanded by the public.

6.3 Nominal and Real Exchange Rates

The neutrality principle is very general. It applies in particular to the exchange rate, which is an important variable that we have not yet encountered. This section will give a few definitions and then show an implication of money neutrality.

6.3.1 Nominal Exchange Rates

Everyone who ever travelled to a foreign country has encountered nominal exchange rates. These rates are posted in foreign exchange rate booths at airports and border posts and they tell us how much it costs to swap one currency for another. These exchange rates are an annoying aspect of tourism for most of us, yet as the relative price of money, they are an essential part of our lives and we need to know how they work. Nominal exchange rates are set in foreign exchange markets. These markets are studied in detail in Chapter 15, which also explains how markets determine nominal exchange rates.

Exchange rates can be quoted in either of two ways. The first, as the number of foreign currency units per domestic unit, is called **British terms**, e.g. $2 per £1 from the perspective of UK residents, or $1.5 per €1 from the point of view of European Monetary Union. A second way of quoting the foreign exchange rate is sometimes called **European terms** because, before the euro, most European countries used it to quote the US dollar or British pound sterling. It is the inverse of British terms and is the number of domestic currency units needed to buy one unit of foreign currency. For example, we have CHF1.6 per €1 for Switzerland, or DKR8 per 1€ for Denmark.

We will adopt the convention of British terms since it is commonly used for quoting the euro and the pound. With this convention, an **appreciation** of a currency conveniently corresponds to an increase in its value in terms of foreign currencies, so the exchange rate rises (e.g. from $1.1 to $1.3 for €1). Conversely, a loss of value, or **depreciation**, implies a decline in the exchange rate.

6.3.2 Real Exchange Rates

Nominal exchange rates compare the relative prices of different monies. They don't say anything about how much one can buy with each money. The higher is the price level, the less one can buy with, say, one unit of money. However, because domestic prices are measured in the domestic currency and foreign prices in the foreign currency, price levels cannot be directly compared. Before we do any comparison, we must convert prices into the same currency, and this is where the real exchange rate comes in.

Consider the following simple example. In Berlin, a haircut costs €20. In New York, you have to pay $36 for the same service. To decide where you will go next time, you must take the exchange rate into account. Assume that it is 1.5 dollars per euro. This tells us that in dollars, the Berlin haircut costs $30, less than in New York. What happens if we compute the price in euros? The New York haircut costs ($36)/(1.5$/€) = €24, still more expensive than in Berlin. Obviously, it does not matter which currency we use. The relative price of haircuts in Berlin relative to New York is the ratio of these two prices expressed in the same currency. It is 0.833, the ratio of €20 to €24 or, equivalently, the ratio of $30 to $36.

Real exchange rates normally compare broad price level indices such as the CPI of the GDP deflator.[3] Let the price index in the euro area be denoted P, and P^* in the US. The price index represents the cost of a basket of goods; a European basket that is worth €100 in the euro area and another US basket worth $200 (the baskets need not be the same). Denote the nominal exchange as S. In our example, $S = 1.5$, so the dollar value of the European basket is $SP = \$150$. The real exchange rate is the ratio of these two baskets expressed in the same currency. In dollars this works out to be $SP/P^* = 1.5 \times 100/200 = 0.75$. For this comparison, we used the dollar but we could have looked at the

---

[3] Price indices are presented in Chapter 2.

euro values of these baskets. The euro value of the dollar basket is $P^*/S = 200/1.5 = 133.33$. The relative price is therefore €100 (P) divided by €133.33 × (P^*/S) which is again 0.75.

Note that in the first example we compared the same thing, a haircut, and could decide where it is cheapest. Now the real exchange rate is the ratio of two index numbers, or average prices for different baskets of goods in two different places. Thus the value of the real exchange rate does not mean much. The European basket collects goods and services in proportions that represent European tastes and habits. It may be at 100 for a particular reference year. The US basket includes goods and services in different quantities (more baseball equipment, less soccer balls) and it may be at 100 on a different year. In the next section, we see that what matters are movements in the real exchange rate.

In the end, the real exchange rate is

(6.6) $$\sigma = \frac{SP}{P^*} = \frac{P}{P^*/S}.$$

$$\underset{\substack{\text{both prices} \\ \text{in foreign} \\ \text{currency}}}{} \qquad \underset{\substack{\text{both prices} \\ \text{in domestic} \\ \text{currency}}}{}$$

The real exchange rate can be thought of as the nominal exchange rate 'doubly deflated' by foreign and domestic goods prices. Like their nominal counterparts, real exchange rates appreciate when σ increases, and depreciate when σ declines.

6.3.3 Movements in Nominal and Real Exchange Rates

We already noted that nominal and real exchange rates move in tandem, as long as inflation is the same at home and abroad, so that P/P^* remains unchanged. Now let us look at the case when the nominal exchange rate S is constant. If inflation at home is higher than it is abroad, domestic prices are rising faster than foreign prices and the ratio P/P^* must be increasing. The real exchange rate σ appreciates. Conversely, a lower inflation at home results in a real depreciation.

Thus we find that the real exchange rate can appreciate for two different reasons: (1) when the nominal exchange rate appreciates and inflation rates at home and abroad are equal; and (2) when the nominal exchange rate is stable but inflation is higher at home. More generally, using the arithmetic presented in Box 6.3, we can compute the rate of change of the real exchange rate:

(6.7) $$\frac{\Delta\sigma}{\sigma} = \frac{\Delta S}{S} + \frac{\Delta P}{P} - \frac{\Delta P^*}{P^*} = \frac{\Delta S}{S} + \pi - \pi^*.$$

$$\underset{\substack{\text{rate of} \\ \text{change} \\ \text{of the} \\ \text{real} \\ \text{exchange} \\ \text{rate}}}{} \qquad \underset{\substack{\text{rate of} \\ \text{change} \\ \text{of the} \\ \text{nominal} \\ \text{exchange} \\ \text{rate}}}{} + \underset{\substack{\text{domestic} \\ \text{inflation} \\ \text{rate}}}{} - \underset{\substack{\text{foreign} \\ \text{inflation} \\ \text{rate}}}{}$$
$$\underset{\text{inflation differential}}{}$$

This decomposition shows that the real exchange rate σ is driven by two factors: (1) the nominal exchange rate S, and (2) the **inflation differential**, the difference between domestic (π) and foreign (π^*) inflation. The logic is simple. A real appreciation is a loss of competitiveness, as our goods become expensive relative to foreign goods. This happens when the nominal exchange rate appreciates, or when domestic inflation exceeds foreign inflation. In the first case, the foreign price of domestic goods (SP) rises even if the domestic price is unchanged, or the domestic price of foreign goods (P^*/S) declines even if the foreign price is unchanged. In the second case, even if the nominal exchange rate is unchanged, domestic goods become relatively more expensive since $\pi > \pi^*$ implies that P/P^* increases. These various possibilities are illustrated in Figure 6.4, which presents effective exchange rates—effective rates are explained in the next section—for the Dutch guilder.

6.3.4 Measuring the Real Exchange Rate in Practice

In practice, measuring real exchange rates poses two problems. The first concerns the definition of 'foreign'. 'Foreign' stands for the rest of the world, the various countries with which our country has significant trade and financial relationships. Exchange rates tend to be quoted in terms of the US dollar. This practice reflects both the size of the US economy and the role of the dollar as an international currency. Yet, the USA cannot really stand for the rest of the world. It is convenient because the rest of the world comprises a large number of countries, with which each home country has a bilateral exchange rate. How should one go about aggregating these individual rates? The same question can also be applied to *the* foreign price level P^*: *Which* foreign price level?

The solution to this problem consists of computing an 'average exchange rate' and an 'average foreign price level' using weights that reflect the relative importance of the partner country (ideally, all of them), and 'an average nominal exchange rate' S as a weighted average of our nominal exchange rate *vis-à-vis* each of them. The weights assigned to each country are chosen to represent its importance to us, e.g. in trade or in financial flows. Box 6.4 explains how this is done. The corresponding values of S and σ are called nominal and real **effective exchange rates**, respectively. These are indices—we can no longer express the nominal exchange rate in value terms, e.g. dollars per euro—which are normalized to take a simple value, such as 1 or 100, in some base year. Figure 6.4 presents an example.

A second problem arises when deciding which prices to compare. In fact, a real exchange rate is simply the price ratio of two baskets of goods and services, one of which represents domestic goods and services and the other foreign goods and services. Since 'domestic' and 'foreign' are rather vague, many baskets, and many definitions of 'the' real exchange rate, are possible. So far, we have looked at the ratio of consumer price indices, but there are a number of alternatives.

◆ One frequently used real exchange rate is the ratio of domestically produced exports to foreign-produced import prices. It is called the **external terms of trade** because it indicates how many imports we get in return for our exports.

◆ Another definition considers the ratio of non-traded to traded goods prices, sometimes called the **internal terms of trade**. This recognizes that many goods are not traded internationally and measures the price of those goods relative to goods that are.

◆ Still another possibility is to measure the real exchange rate on the basis of the price of labour, using wages, total earnings, or total labour costs, including employer contributions to social insurance.

In the end, there is no uniformly appropriate measure. Different questions are best answered with different indices.

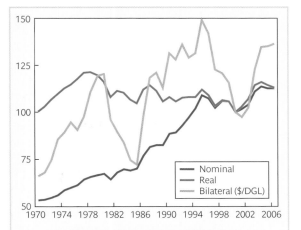

Fig. 6.4 The Dutch Guilder's Nominal and Real Exchange Rates, 1970–2007

Three exchange rates are displayed: (1) the nominal bilateral rate between the Dutch guilder and the US dollar (after the adoption of the euro in 1999, the figure converts the euro exchange rate using the rate at which guilders were then converted into euros); (2) the nominal effective exchange rate; and (3) the real effective exchange rate. These rates are all computed as indices that take the value 100 in 2000. From year to year, inflation differentials are relatively small, so the nominal and real effective exchange rates tend to move together. Over the longer run, however, inflation differentials accumulate to sizeable magnitudes and the effective nominal and real exchange rates move differently. This is what happened until the late 1990s. The nominal exchange rate appreciates sharply while the real rate remains trendless. From equation (6.7), we can deduce that inflation in the Netherlands was lower than abroad. In fact, the negative inflation differential and the nominal exchange appreciation offset each other. Since the late 1990s, inflation differentials have vanished and the nominal and effective rates move closely together. Notice that the dollar bilateral rate is much more volatile than the effective rate. This is normal since the latter is a weighted average of many bilateral rates, one of which, not the most important, is the US dollar. Yet, dollar exchange rates receive considerable attention, which may give an exaggerated impression of volatility.

Sources: OECD, *Economic Outlook* and International Financial Statistics, IMF.

Box 6.4 **Computing and Comparing Effective Exchange Rates**[4]

Effective exchange rates are computed using a number of partner-countries. Each partner-country receives a weight typically representing its importance in trade for the country in question. For example, its share of our exports or our imports, or the average of both. Geometric averaging is applied to price indices in these countries and to our bilateral exchange rates *vis-à-vis* their currencies. If n countries are selected and S_i is the bilateral nominal exchange rate *vis-à-vis* country i with trade weight w_i, our effective nominal exchange rate is

$$S = (S_1)^{w_1} (S_2)^{w_2} (S_3)^{w_3} \dots (S_n)^{w_n},$$

where the weights sum up to 1 ($\Sigma w_i = 1$). The effective foreign price level P^* is computed by applying the same weights to each partner-country's price index P_i:

$$P^* = (P_1)^{w_1} (P_2)^{w_2} (P_3)^{w_3} \dots (P_n)^{w_n}.$$

Then the effective real exchange rate is simply the average of our real exchange rates *vis-à-vis* each partner-country:

$$\sigma = \left(\frac{S_1 P}{P_1}\right)^{w_1} \left(\frac{S_2 P}{P_2}\right)^{w_2} \left(\frac{S_3 P}{P_3}\right)^{w_3} \dots \left(\frac{S_n P}{P_n}\right)^{w_n} = \frac{SP}{P^*}.$$

The effective real exchange rate is thus a weighted geometric average[5] of the individual bilateral exchange rates which characterize a country's international trade.

This approach can be applied to other classes of goods. A frequently-used measure of the real exchange rate is the ratio of export to import prices. It differs from the ratio of non-traded to traded good prices in two ways: (1) it suppresses non-traded goods, and (2) it compares the price of traded goods which are produced domestically and exported with imported goods produced abroad. In this view, the 'home' goods are exports instead of non-traded, and the 'foreign' goods are imports instead of all traded goods lumped together. The choice between this or that measure really depends on the characteristics of the country at hand and on the question of interest.

6.4 The Exchange Rate in the Long Run: Purchasing Power Parity

We now present a second implication of money neutrality, which is displayed in the right-hand side chart in Figure 6.1. For each of the 155 countries, it plots the average annual rate of nominal exchange rate *depreciation vis-à-vis* the US dollar (i.e. $-\Delta S/S$, or the *negative* of the rate of appreciation) against the inflation differential *vis-à-vis* the US, the difference between the country's inflation rate and the US inflation rate ($\pi - \pi^*$). The chart suggests that, in the long run, countries which have a high rate of inflation see their currencies depreciate in proportion. Conversely, the currencies of countries with a low rate of inflation appreciate in the long run.

This result can be written formally as $-\frac{\Delta S}{S} = \pi - \pi^*$. Changing signs on both sides of the equality, we find that the rate of exchange rate appreciation is equal to the difference between foreign and domestic inflation:

(6.8) $$\frac{\Delta S}{S} = \pi^* - \pi.$$

This property is expected to hold in the long run. It carries a pretty striking implication, which can be seen by noting that together (6.7) and (6.8) imply

$$\frac{\Delta \sigma}{\sigma} = \frac{\Delta S}{S} + \pi - \pi^* = 0.$$

---

[4] Nominal and real effective exchange rates are computed and published by various sources. Among them, *International Financial Statistics*, a monthly publication of the International Monetary Fund, presents a variety of real exchange rates (using GDP deflators, export prices, CPIs, labour costs) computed using a sample of 18 advanced economies.

[5] There are two ways of computing weighted averages. The most common approach is arithmetic averaging, which sums up values of the variables of interest $x_1, x_2, \dots$, etc., with their respective weights w_1, w_2, etc.: $w_1 x_1 + w_2 x_2 + \dots$. Geometric averaging uses products: $x_1^{w_1} \cdot x_2^{w_2} \dots$.

In other words, the real exchange rate is constant over the long run. This conclusion should not surprise those who looked carefully at Figure 6.4. Over the 36 years, the effective real exchange rate of the Dutch guilder has fluctuated, but in a narrow margin, and most importantly, the absence of any trend is suggestive of long-term constancy. The conclusion that the real exchange rate is constant in the long run is sometimes presented as the principle of **purchasing power parity** (PPP), which comes in two versions.

The version presented here is called **relative PPP**. It is a natural implication of monetary neutrality. As they are nominal variables, the nominal exchange rate and the price level are not expected to durably affect real variables, including the real exchange rate. This is a manifestation of the dichotomy principle. In the long run, the domestic money supply proportionally affects domestic prices. The same holds abroad, but not the real exchange rate.

The logic behind PPP is quite simple. Suppose that monetary policy is more expansionary at home than abroad. With money growing faster, we expect inflation eventually to be higher at home. If the nominal exchange rate remains unchanged, the real exchange rate appreciates. This means that domestic goods and services become expensive relative to foreign goods and services. As a result, domestic producers gradually lose competitiveness. This obviously cannot go on forever, and indeed it will not. The nominal exchange rate will depreciate, and this will work towards restoring competitiveness. If it depreciates by the full amount of the accumulated inflation differential, the loss in competitiveness is entirely erased. Thus PPP can be seen as simply asserting that, in the long run, a country must retain its competitiveness.

The second version of purchasing power parity, **absolute PPP**, is a stronger proposition. It starts with the **Law of One Price**. This posits that the same good should trade everywhere at the same price, when prices are expressed in the same currency. If prices were to differ significantly, it is asserted, traders would buy the goods where they are cheapest, sell them where they fetch a higher price and make a profit. Demand would rise where the prices are low, and so would supply where they are high. **Arbitrage**, as this process is called, should continue until profit opportunities have disappeared. This occurs only when prices have been equalized. That prices of the same goods are the same in different countries leads to the absolute PPP principle, and is a stronger assertion than relative PPP. Absolute PPP requires not only that the real exchange rate σ be constant, as stated by relative PPP, but that it be equal to unity. Indeed, according to the Law of One Price, $P^* = SP$, which implies $\sigma = SP/P^* = 1$. In practice, the Law of One Price is known to be grossly violated, not just across countries but within the same country, on a month-to-month or even year-by-year basis. Yet, all the same, in regions and countries of similar development, price levels in the same currency do not drift away from each other for very long.

All in all, relative PPP is a pretty good rule of thumb. It is backed by considerable empirical evidence, as Figure 6.1 shows. It is indeed a good guess that a continuously depreciating currency reflects persistently high inflation. Yet, the figure also indicates that relative PPP is not entirely robust, certainly not from quarter to quarter. There are interesting cases where the nominal exchange rate is not solely driven by inflation differentials. Chapter 15 will explain the conditions under which real exchange rates are constant in the long run.

! Summary

1 We hold money because we need it to carry out day-to-day transactions.

2 The Cambridge equation asserts that the demand for money is a constant fraction of nominal GDP.

3 The monetary neutrality principle asserts that money does not affect real variables. This is a manifestation of the dichotomy principle. The principle is understood to hold in the long run. It

implies that, in the long run, prices, nominal exchange rates, and all nominal variables change at the same rate as money is growing.

4 The nominal exchange rate defines the price of a currency in terms of another one.

5 Real exchange rates measure the price of domestic goods in terms of foreign goods.

6 Effective nominal and real exchange rates are weighted averages of a country's exchange rates *vis-à-vis* the rest of the world—in practice, its main trading partners.

7 Relative purchasing power parity is obtained when the equilibrium real exchange rate is constant. In that case, the rate of change of the nominal exchange rate is equal to the inflation differential, the difference between foreign and domestic inflation. The inflation differential is a fundamental determinant of the long-run evolution of the nominal exchange rate.

8 Absolute purchasing power parity states that the equilibrium real exchange rate is not just constant but equal to unity. The Law of One Price asserts that prices for the same good are the same in different countries. If that were true, absolute purchasing power parity would tend to be verified. The evidence tends to reject purchasing power parity for most countries.

🔑 Key Concepts

◆ **demand for money**

◆ **Cambridge equation**

◆ **nominal and real exchange rates**

◆ **external competitiveness**

◆ **inflation differentials**

◆ **British/European terms**

◆ **appreciation/depreciation**

◆ **neutrality principle and dichotomy**

◆ **effective exchange rates**

◆ **absolute and relative purchasing power parity (PPP)**

◆ **arbitrage**

❓ Exercises

1 Table 6.1 implies a relationship between money growth and the inflation rate when the GDP trend growth rate is 3% per annum. Represent graphically this relationship. Show graphically how this relationship would change if the GDP trend growth rate would be instead 8%. What conclusions can you draw?

2 What happens to the real exchange rate between two countries if the price level at home doubles, all other things given? If the price of foreign goods doubles? If the nominal exchange rate doubles?

3 The following figure displays the evolution of the nominal and real effective exchange rates of Portugal since 1970. What can you conclude about the rate of inflation in this country?

4 Money is neutral in the long run, but is it neutral in the short run? Looking at the Cambridge equation (6.2), how could money increase without the price level increasing proportionately?

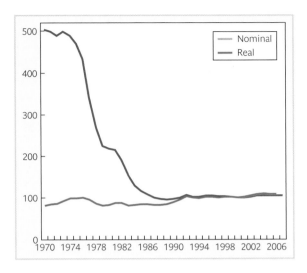

5 Consider an economy where the stock of money is growing by 5% per year while GDP expands by 2.5% annually. Assume that inflation abroad is 3.5%. What will be the rate of change of the exchange rate in the long run?

6 Use equations (6.5)—written for both the home and foreign countries—and (6.8) to find an expression that describes the long-run evolution of the nominal exchange rates as driven by the domestic and foreign money and GDP growth rates. Denote domestic and foreign money supply as M and M^*, respectively, and domestic and foreign GDP as Y and Y^*.

→ Essay Questions

1 Most governments regard a depreciation as a sign of weakness. Does it make sense to resist a depreciation when inflation is high?

2 'Money neutrality simply says that there is no way to cheat with money'. Comment.

3 A strong currency is a currency that tends to appreciate. In what sense is this a desirable objective?

4 The Law of One Price does not hold. Can you imagine reasons why?

5 Box 6.2 tells the story of Zimbabwe. It also notes that hyperinflations often occur after a war. In your view, why do the authorities allow this to happen?

PART III

The Macroeconomy in the Short Run

With its emphasis on long-run and sustainable trends, Part II sets a natural stage for the study of what happens in the meantime: in the short run. In Part III, the object of interest is not the development over the next decade, but rather over the next few months or quarters. To do this, we study the short-run behaviour of aggregate demand—the sum of spending decisions by households, firms, and governments. We start by laying out their budget constraints and then examine what shapes their spending decisions.

In the long run, the real and nominal sides of the economy can be studied separately; in the short run, they are tightly intertwined. This interaction gives rise to the phenomenon of business cycles, the succession of periods of rapid economic growth and recession. The central role of interest rates and the financial system leads us to look at money, how it is created, what role it plays in a modern, open economy, and how central banks conduct monetary policy.

Next, we take the most important step: the integration of all these different decisions in a way that ensures their consistency. This type of economic reasoning, which is called general equilibrium, analyses the simultaneous determination of output, employment, the interest rate, and finally the price level and the rate of inflation. The concept of macroeconomic equilibrium is first developed for the case of a country that only trades goods and services with the rest of the world, with capital flows playing a passive role. The next step is to examine how financial openness changes the situation. Next, we turn to inflation, the rate of growth in the general level of prices. After the origins of inflation are explored in Chapter 12, Chapter 13 presents the aggregate demand–aggregate supply (*AD–AS*) framework as a powerful tool for explaining the behaviour of both output and inflation over short-run horizons. Finally, the understanding of the short-run is rounded out by looking at asset markets and the exchange rate. Asset markets are places where financial and real claims are traded. Financial markets, and the market for foreign exchange in particular, look forward to the future when determining the prices at which assets are traded. The exchange rate turns out to be a special and important example of an asset price, one which ultimately connects the short and long run.

Borrowing, Lending, and Budget Constraints

7

Many people despise wealth, but few know how to give it away.

Francois de La Rochefoucauld

What's the quickest way to become a millionaire? Borrow fivers off everyone you meet.

Richard Branson

7.1 Overview

Borrowing and lending is a fundamental fact of economic life. Each of the main economic players named in the circular flow diagram of Chapter 2—households and firms of the private sector, the government, and the rest of the world—have their own reasons to borrow and lend. In doing so, they shift income and spending between the present and the future. Borrowing brings future income forward to be spent today. Lending or, more generally, saving defers the use of current income to some later date. This link between the present and the future takes the form of **intertemporal budget constraints**: the liabilities of each sector must be repaid someday, while accumulated assets will eventually be spent. Decisions which are dependent on time are a central fact of macroeconomics, and in this chapter we will learn more about intertemporal trade—how households, firms, government, and a nation as a whole can transfer resources through time.

Borrowing is not a free lunch: what is borrowed must be repaid, usually with interest. Otherwise lenders wouldn't lend. Borrowing and lending decisions are thus motivated by expectations about the future. The importance of expectations for current behaviour cannot be overemphasized. Those who reasonably expect their incomes to grow rapidly will want to borrow now and raise their current standards of living instead of waiting. In contrast, the lucky winner of a lottery will probably save a large fraction of the prize, because it is unlikely to occur again. Firms' investment decisions, too, are a gamble on future demand. Not the present, not the past, but expectations of the future exert the greatest influence on firms' investment decisions.

The shifting of spending over time involves trade. One could think of a lender as a seller of money today, and the borrower as a buyer. Because people are impatient, time has a price. This price is determined by the interest rate. The intertemporal budget constraint provides the rules of the game and provides a powerful framework for understanding fundamental aspects of macroeconomics. Because the future is unbounded, it can be rather overwhelming to think about it in simple terms. This chapter adopts two simplifications. First, we reduce the course of time to just two periods, called today and tomorrow, the present and the indefinite future. Second, we will continue to employ Robinson Crusoe, introduced in Chapter 5, as a parable for consumer, producer, and his own government, all at once. These steps will make abstract and complex considerations a bit easier to handle.

7.2 Thinking About the Future

7.2.1 The Future Has a Price

It is a basic economic principle that anything of value must have a price. This includes money and goods delivered at future dates. In fact, markets exist for the sole purpose of pricing deliveries of commodities at some future date. The Euronext Liffe and the New York Mercantile Exchange (NYMEX) are markets where such futures contracts are traded. Markets for financial claims are everywhere. In most countries, markets for loans determine the interest rate—the price for borrowing and the return from lending. More advanced countries have stock markets which constantly place a value on companies, primarily on the basis of expected future earnings (profits).

Microeconomic principles can be readily used to understand how the future is priced. There is a parallel between *intertemporal* consumption choices (between present and future goods) and *intratemporal* consumption choices (among goods at a particular point in time). When we choose between consuming now or in the future, we effectively decide whether to save or to borrow. As rational households plan spending over time, they take into account their future incomes and needs, and balance these against the interest rate at which they can borrow or save. Similarly, firms need to forecast the profitability of plant and equipment in which they invest. They compare the return from lending their money at some available interest rate, which represents either the cost of funds or, if funds are available, the best alternative use for them.

7.2.2 The Rational Expectations Hypothesis

Expectations about the future are crucial to all this. But how exactly do firms and households form their expectations? Do they get it right or wrong? In this book, we will generally take the view that economic agents' forecasts are right *on average*. This is the **rational expectations hypothesis**.

The rational expectations hypothesis does not mean that economists think that households and firms cannot make mistakes, or that they always forecast the future perfectly. It is simply a way to think consistently about the way economic agents think—we assume that they do not make *systematic* errors. Clearly, alternative assumptions about expectations are possible. These alternatives are logically weak, either because they rule out forward-looking behaviour, or because they assume that agents do not use all the available information about the future in a rational manner.[1] The rational

expectations hypothesis takes the opposite position by assuming that agents use all available information in a way that reflects its costs, and use it in a skilled enough way to be right, on average.

We adopt the rational expectations hypothesis for two reasons.

- First, economics itself is based on the hypothesis that agents behave rationally—that they take decisions in a logically consistent way. If agents are rational in planning their consumption, work, and production, then they should be rational when thinking about the future.

- Second, even if most people are not fully rational all the time, alternatives are no closer to realism because they assert that people are repeatedly and systematically wrong. If they are, they must suffer losses. Isn't it natural to expect them to take steps to avoid such errors in the future? In the end, there are no good alternatives to assuming that economic agents are at least as clever as economists are.

There is an even better justification for rational expectations. We are ultimately interested in how prices, interest rates, incomes, and spending interact on the market place. It is enough that a few well-informed agents behave rationally to drive the markets. If unions act on behalf of their members, it suffices that their expectations will be correct on average. In financial markets, all that is required is that a number of professional traders are well informed and have sufficient resources at their disposal. If they perceive that prices are too low compared with their valuation, they will buy, forcing prices upwards. If prices are too high, they will sell. Less well-informed customers end up accepting the market prices because they are, on average, right, even if never quite right.

As a short cut, we will adopt in this book a simple version of rational expectations known as perfect foresight. Perfect foresight assumes that people know everything that will happen in the future. The difference with rational expectations is that there is now no uncertainty at all. Perfect foresight can be thought of as an exploration of what the world would be like if the future were in fact perfectly known. Of course, no one thinks that this is

---

[1] Some alternatives to rational expectations are presented formally in the WebAppendix to this chapter.

realistic but, as with rational expectations, if surprises are sometimes good and sometimes bad, perfect foresight is a reasonable starting point.

7.2.3 The Parable of Robinson Crusoe

This chapter sets up the intertemporal budget constraint facing households, firms, the government, and the nation as a whole. We return to Robinson Crusoe as our representative household, already familiar from Chapter 5. As already mentioned, it is convenient to collapse time into two periods, 'today' and 'tomorrow', where tomorrow is a metaphor for the future. After tomorrow, Crusoe is rescued and will no longer need to concern himself with the economics of his island.

7.3 The Household's Intertemporal Budget Constraint

7.3.1 Consumption and Intertemporal Trade

Let's start by imagining that Crusoe's island does not even have coconut trees. Rather, the coconuts simply wash up on the beach. The number of coconuts that he (rationally) expects to have today and tomorrow is his exogenous **endowment**.[2] Until Robinson learns how to plant coconuts, he has no choice but to consume what nature gives him. Using subscripts to denote the relevant period in which they become available, we can represent his endowment of Y_1 coconuts today and Y_2 coconuts tomorrow by point A in Figure 7.1. Since coconuts cannot be carried over to the next period, Crusoe's consumption is also given by point A. This is the **autarky** point. A household or a country operates in autarky when it does not trade and consumes its endowment.

If we bend the story a little and allow for neighbouring islands inhabited by other economic agents, trade is possible. Because Crusoe's coconuts are just as good as his neighbours', we might not expect to observe any trade between them. Yet Crusoe may well be interested in **intertemporal trade**, or exchanging resources across time. He might lend his neighbours some coconuts today, if he expects to find only a few tomorrow, or if he prefers to consume more tomorrow. On the contrary, if today's 'harvest' is abnormally low or if Crusoe is impatient, he

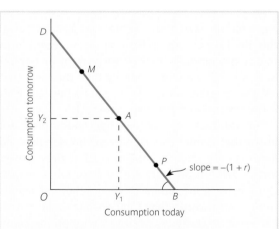

Fig. 7.1 Endowment, Wealth, and Consumption

Resources available today and tomorrow—the endowment—determine wealth and available consumption choices along the budget line *BD*. In the figure, the same level of wealth (*OB*) is attainable by a professional athlete (point *P*) or a university student (point *M*).

---

[2] For now, we will ignore uncertainty and assume that Crusoe has perfect foresight with respect to the future. Perfect foresight is the equivalent of rational expectations when there is no uncertainty. Second, we will neglect issues of labour supply in this chapter to focus on other issues. Effectively, we will assume that Crusoe's labour supply is perfectly inelastic (constant). Chapter 5 has already considered the important case when Crusoe enjoys leisure and puts a price on working (picking up coconuts) in an intratemporal setting.

could borrow coconuts now and repay later when times are better. Generally, borrowing and lending are associated with a price, the interest rate, which we will describe below in more detail.

The rest of the chapter will explore, in very simple terms, borrowing and lending. The activity of credit markets is of great importance in the real world and in macroeconomics. Seen as a way of moving away from autarky, it would seem obvious that borrowing and lending—and credit and capital markets more generally—are natural events in economic life, just as obvious as the trade of goods and services. Yet banking and credit markets have long suffered reputation problems, and the recent financial and credit crisis hasn't made matters better. Box 7.1 explores these reservations and possible reasons for them.

7.3.2 The Real Interest Rate

Crusoe and his neighbours must agree on the terms of repayment: how much should he pay (or receive) tomorrow for one coconut borrowed (lent) today? These terms are the **real interest rate**, which we denote by r and will treat as given (exogenous). This means that borrowing 100 coconuts will require paying back $100(1 + r)$ tomorrow—the principal of 100 plus interest payments of $100r$. Another, equivalent way of thinking of this transaction is that Crusoe agrees to sell $100(1 + r)$ coconuts tomorrow for the price of 100 today. Similarly, if Crusoe takes the other role and lends 100 coconuts today, he will receive $100(1 + r)$ coconuts tomorrow; to buy $100(1 + r)$ coconuts tomorrow he must save 100 coconuts today. The relevant intertemporal trade

---

 Box 7.1 Neither a Borrower nor a Lender Be: The Economics and the Sociology of Credit

In a well-known scene from Shakespeare's *Hamlet*, Polonius gives his son Laertes some parting advice: 'Neither a borrower, nor a lender be: For loan oft loses both itself and friend, and borrowing dulls the edge of husbandry.' In other famous plays, such as *The Merchant of Venice*, Shakespeare gives lenders a pretty tough time. Is it morally wrong to borrow (or to lend)? And what is wrong with charging interest, if borrower and lender freely agree to it? Although the economic arguments against autarky are convincing, many great religions of the world—including Islam, Christianity, and Judaism—have banned lending at a positive interest rate at one time or another in their histories. Why the ambivalence?

Perhaps it is because lenders have an unconditional claim on the resources of individual borrowers in a risky world. If the fortunes of a borrower go south, those of the lender do not—that is, unless the borrower declares bankruptcy. Perhaps it is because borrowers appear to be in a poor bargaining position, often seeking credit when all else has failed. Perhaps it is because individuals are frustrated when their bank won't give them the loan they think they deserve, because the credit officer deems us 'too risky'. And the market has ways of dealing with individual risks which are distasteful to many.

One is charging higher interest rates, which appears opportunistic since the poorest risks pay the highest premiums. Yet loan-sharking, with its illegal enforcement mechanisms, as well as 'payday loans' which amount to selling one's own wage packet in advance, at effective annual interest rates sometimes in excess of 600%, are accepted by many economic agents as a legitimate means of improving their well-being.

Even when lending at interest is prohibited as in many Islamic countries, the market finds ways around the ban, for example declaring loans to be 'equity stakes' which participate in profits and losses of the enterprise. Irving Fisher wrote in 1930 that:

Interest taking cannot be prevented by prohibiting loan contracts. To forbid the particular form of sale called a loan contract would leave possible other forms of sale, and the mere act of valuation of every property right involves an implicit rate of interest. . . . Indeed, as long as buying and selling of any kind were permitted, the virtual effect of lending and borrowing would be retained. (Fisher 1930: 116.)

In the end, the fundamental truth is that the market for loans exists because there are gains from trade: different degrees of patience, different wants, different opportunities, and different information.

involves swapping $1/(1 + r)$ coconuts today for each coconut tomorrow. We say that a coconut tomorrow is worth $1/(1 + r)$ coconuts today.[3]

The price of tomorrow's consumption in terms of today's, $1/(1 + r)$, is called an **intertemporal price**. As the real interest rate r is positive, goods tomorrow are less valuable than goods today. The real interest rate measures the cost of waiting. Valuing future goods in terms of goods today (here, dividing by the interest factor, 1 plus the real interest rate) is called **discounting**. Box 7.2 presents the important concept of discounting more generally. It can be used, for example, to explain the inverse relationship between bond prices and interest rates, among other things.

Intertemporal trade allows Crusoe to choose consumption combinations represented by the line BD in Figure 7.1. This line must go through his endowment point A, since he can always choose not to trade at all. At point B Crusoe could forgo consumption tomorrow completely. In that case he would borrow fully against his future endowment Y_2, receives $Y_2/(1 + r)$ coconuts, and consumes $Y_1 + Y_2/(1 + r)$ coconuts today. At point D he would fast today and lend all his current endowment Y_1 in order to consume $Y_1(1 + r) + Y_2$ coconuts tomorrow. The line BD represents all the possibilities open to Crusoe, in between the extremes just described. It is called the **budget line**. Its slope[4] is given by $-(1 + r)$. If the rate of interest increases, the budget line becomes steeper. For a given amount of saving today, more will be available tomorrow.

7.3.3 Wealth and Present Discounted Values

If Crusoe's income 'from nature' in the first period is Y_1 and he consumes C_1 in the same period, his saving is $Y_1 - C_1$. If $Y_1 - C_1$ is positive, he is lending; if $Y_1 - C_1$ is negative, he is borrowing. In the second period, his maximal consumption C_2 will equal the sum of income Y_2 and $(1 + r)(Y_1 - C_1)$, i.e. the interest and principal on his savings from period 1. If saving was negative in the first period, this means paying back principal plus interest. Formally, we have

$$(7.1) \qquad C_2 = Y_2 + (Y_1 - C_1)(1 + r).$$

This fully describes Crusoe's intertemporal budget constraint. Dividing both sides by $(1 + r)$ and rearranging,

$$(7.2) \qquad \underbrace{C_1 + \frac{C_2}{1 + r}}_{\substack{\text{present} \\ \text{value of} \\ \text{consumption}}} = \underbrace{Y_1 + \frac{Y_2}{1 + r}}_{\substack{\text{present} \\ \text{value of} \\ \text{income}}} = \underbrace{\Omega.}_{\substack{\text{wealth} \\ \text{derived from} \\ \text{income}}}$$

The left-hand side is the **present discounted value** of consumption. It is the sum of today's and tomorrow's consumption valued in terms of goods today. The right-hand side is equal to the present discounted value of income (his endowment). It is the maximum consumption that Crusoe could enjoy today, given his resources today and tomorrow, and is represented by point B in Figure 7.1. Put differently, OB is the present discounted value of Crusoe's total endowment. In fact, it represents his wealth, which we denote by the symbol Ω.

Lending and borrowing enable individuals with the same total wealth but with very different income profiles to enjoy the same menu of possible consumption over both periods. It doesn't matter whether Crusoe is a university student with low current and high future income, as represented by point M in Figure 7.1, or a professional athlete with high current and low future income (point P). As long as these points are on the same budget constraint, the present discounted value of income is the same and intertemporal trade allows income to be shifted across time by borrowing and lending.

Now suppose Crusoe had initial tradeable wealth B_1 (an initial cache of coconuts). His wealth will increase by this amount and the budget constraint will be modified as follows:[5]

$$(7.3) \qquad \underbrace{C_1 + \frac{C_2}{1 + r}}_{\substack{\text{present value} \\ \text{of consumption}}} = \underbrace{Y_1 + \frac{Y_2}{1 + r} + B_1.}_{\text{total wealth}}$$

---

[3] As a simplifying assumption, we have assumed that the interest rate is the same, whether one is borrowing or lending. The world is more complicated, but the logic is unchanged, when we consider different rates of interest for borrowers and lenders. Section 7.5 provides more details.

[4] The slope of the budget constraint is negative and is given by -1 times the ratio OD/OB. From the text we know that $OD/OB = [Y_1(1 + r) + Y_2]/[Y_1 + Y_2/(1 + r)] = 1 + r$.

[5] This is obtained by noting that today's available resources are $Y_1 + B_1$ so that (5.2) is changed to $C_2 = Y_2 + (B_1 + Y_1 - C_1)(1 + r)$.

Box 7.2 **Discounting and Bond Prices**

Discounting is used in economics and finance to value future incomes or expenditures in terms of income today. It is frequently used to put a value on financial assets and debts. It asks: What is the amount of money required today, given an interest rate, to generate some payment or payments in the future? By valuing a coconut tomorrow only as worth $1/(1 + r)$ coconuts today, Robinson Crusoe has successfully applied discounting to a practical problem.

Let us apply discounting to a financial problem, and consider a simple bond which pays €100 in one year's time. (This type of bond is called a *pure discount* bond.) If the interest rate given by the market is 5%, what is the value of this bond today? It is the amount which, if invested now, yields €100 next year. If that amount is B, then it must be true that $B(1 + 0.05) = 100$, so $B = 1/(1.05) = €97.24$. Similarly, the value of a two-year discount bond is given by $B = 100/(1 + 0.05)^2 = €90.70$. The further into the future the payout is, the more heavily any amount is discounted, and the lower the discount bond price is.

Conversely, given discount rate r, the present value of a stream of payments a_t over n years, $t = 1, \ldots, n$ has present value given by

$$\frac{a_1}{1+r} + \frac{a_2}{(1+r)^2} + \frac{a_3}{(1+r)^3} + \ldots + \frac{a_n}{(1+r)^n}.$$

Now consider the case of a consol, a bond that promises to pay a fixed amount a forever. Is it possible to put a price on that income stream, even though the payments are infinite? As long as the interest rate is strictly positive, the answer is yes! The price of a consol p which pays a each period is simply the present discounted value of its payments:

$$p = \frac{a}{1+r} + \frac{a}{(1+r)^2} + \frac{a}{(1+r)^3} + \ldots + \frac{a}{(1+r)^n} + \ldots$$

$$= \frac{a}{1+r}\left[1 + \frac{1}{(1+r)} + \frac{1}{(1+r)^2} + \ldots\right]$$

$$= \frac{a}{1+r}\left[\frac{1}{1 - \dfrac{1}{1+r}}\right] = \frac{a}{r},$$

where we have applied the formula for a sum of a geometric series to the term in brackets. The price of a consol is inversely related to the interest rate. Other bonds have a finite maturity so the formula is more complicated, but the general principle survives that higher real interest rates imply lower bond prices.[6]

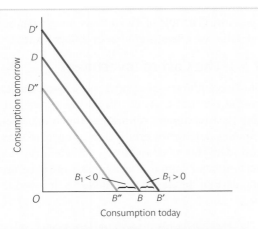

Fig. 7.2 Inheriting Wealth or Indebtedness
When wealth $B_1 > 0$ is inherited, the budget line shifts from BD to $B'D'$. Debt $B_1 < 0$ shifts the budget line to $B''D''$. The lines are parallel because the real interest rate is assumed unchanged.

If $B_1 > 0$, Crusoe can consume more in both periods. But B_1 could be negative, if Crusoe began his existence with debt. In that case, he will have to consume less (in present value terms) in order to repay the debt and interest. In general, total wealth Ω is the sum of inherited wealth or indebtedness B_1 and of the present value of income: $\Omega = Y_1 + \dfrac{Y_2}{1 + r} + B_1$. This is shown in Figure 7.2, where the inherited wealth or indebtedness is added to the present value of income. At a given real interest rate, it implies shifting the budget line BD to $B'D'$ (if wealth increases) or $B''D''$ (if it decreases).

---

[6]   In fact, the interest rate, or yield, is *determined* or implied by the bond price, which is set in the course of bond market trades. More details on bond valuation and interest rates can be found in Chapter 14.

7.4 The Firm and the Private Sector's Intertemporal Budget Constraint

7.4.1 Firms and the Investment Decision

Crusoe's income has been exogenous until now. In reality, income mostly comes from planned activities. As we saw in Chapter 3, production requires that resources are diverted from consumption and used to acquire productive capital. Crusoe could plant coconuts today which would grow into trees bearing coconuts tomorrow. Naturally, once planted, a coconut cannot be consumed: it is useful only for its future production. The use of valuable resources to produce more goods later is called **investment** or **fixed capital formation**. Indeed, many goods produced in modern economies are designed solely to make future production possible, and have no consumption value at all.

The investment decision also has a fundamentally intertemporal aspect. Firms decide to accumulate capital when it is sensible, i.e. profitable, to do so, and profitability depends on expected future outcomes. In order to finance their investments, firms can either obtain resources in the capital market (stock exchanges, bond markets, or banks) or use their own funds (retained earnings).

The discussion of this and the next chapter thus deviates from the growth model in Chapters 3 and 4. In those chapters, the supply of capital was the cumulated supply of available savings, and was an exogenous fraction of national income. In what follows, investment and savings will represent conscious choices of firms and households.

7.4.2 The Production Function

The investment decision depends upon the amount of output that can be produced with the available equipment (the number of coconuts to be obtained from a tree). The **production function** $F(K)$ captures this relationship between capital input and output and is depicted in Figure 7.3. It can be thought of as a special case of the production function of Chapter

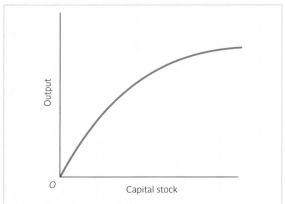

Fig. 7.3 The Production Function
As more input is added, output increases, but at a decreasing rate. This is the principle of declining marginal productivity.

3, in which labour input is exogenous.[7] The shape of the curve implies that, as more capital is accumulated, the additional or marginal yield declines. That marginal output decreases when input increases is the same principle of **diminishing marginal productivity** that we encountered in Chapters 3 and 5.[8]

7.4.3 The Cost of Investment

Starting with no capital stock (we assume that there are no coconut trees on the island at the outset), today's investment represents the total stock of capital available for production tomorrow. (Box 7.3 considers the more realistic case when previously accumulated capital already exists.) Crusoe understands that he can either invest K in productive

---

[7] In Chapter 3, the labour supply was exogenous. If we set $L = 1$, and $Y = F(K, L)$, as in Chapter 3, then $Y = F(K, 1)$.

[8] The reason behind this principle is that, given the existing amount of labour used to man the equipment (here, Crusoe's time), adding new equipment is less and less effective in raising output.

Box 7.3 **Gross Investment, Depreciation, and the Capital Stock**

When previously accumulated capital already exists in the amount K_1, the situation in the next period is more complicated. The stock of capital may differ in the future from the previously accumulated stock in two ways. First, new capital I_1 may be invested. Second, depreciation—wear, tear, and obsolescence—may remove some of the value of the old capital stock. It is a proportion δ of the capital stock. The new capital stock is

$$K_2 = K_1 + I_1 - \delta K_1$$

new capital = old capital + gross − depreciation
stock   investment

$$= (1 - \delta)K_1 + I_1.$$

The realized change in the capital stock, $\Delta K = K_2 - K_1$, is therefore equal to $I_1 - \delta K_1$, the difference between gross investment and depreciation of previously accumulated capital. For the capital stock to grow, new investment spending must exceed depreciation.

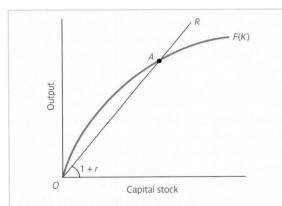

Fig. 7.4 Productive Technology

The cost of borrowing to finance investment is given by OR. As long as output exceeds the cost of borrowing, the technology is productive and the producer makes profit. Beyond A, she makes losses.

equipment, or lend K in the capital market. In the first case, he will receive output $F(K)$ tomorrow. In the second case, he will receive $(1 + r)K$ tomorrow. The real interest rate measures the **opportunity cost** of the resources used in investment. Because of the option of lending at rate r, the investment in this case must yield at least $1 + r$ to be worth undertaking.[9]

Figure 7.4 shows the opportunity cost of invested capital K as the ray OR from the origin, which is given by $(1 + r)K$. As long as the resulting output exceeds the cost, the technology is sufficiently pro-

ductive and investment is worthwhile. At point A, investment just covers its cost. There is no economic profit possible. To the right of A, investment uses up more resources than it produces. Positive economic profits occur only to the left of A.

The interest rate r is therefore a central determinant of the profitability of investment. Changes in the interest rate will change the set of investment levels that are productive. If the rate of interest were to increase, the OR line would rotate upwards to the left, moving point A to the left and shrinking the range of productive investment levels. Another angle on the problem is to compute the net return V from investing K. It is the difference between the present value of output tomorrow and investment today:[10]

(7.4) $$V = \frac{F(K)}{1 + r} - K.$$

An investment project is economically justifiable only if it has a positive present value. In terms of (7.4), that means $V > 0$ or if $F(K) > K(1 + r)$. Figure 7.5 illustrates a case when the technology is not productive enough given the real interest rate. In that case it does not pay to invest: it is more profitable simply to lend at the rate r. It would require either an improvement in technology (the production

[9] Alternatively, Crusoe could borrow coconuts for investment purposes. The interest rate then is the cost of investment. This is discussed in Box 7.5 and in the WebAppendix.

[10] By assumption the trees are assumed not to have resale value; they die after the second period. If they didn't, one would need to add back the resale value of the depreciated trees in the second period, which would increase the value of the investment activity. This modification is described in detail in Chapter 8.

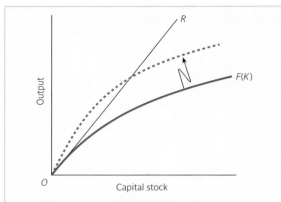

Fig. 7.5 Unproductive Technology

Given the interest rate, no firm will operate with the production function shown in the figure. A technological innovation which shifts the production function upwards can make an unproductive technology productive again.

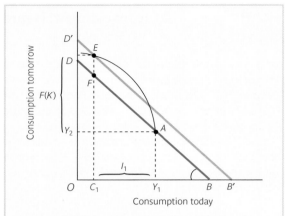

Fig. 7.6 Investment Increases Wealth

Investing I_1 (which becomes K_2) in a productive technology allows a household to increase its wealth over and above that corresponding to the initial endowment A. Here wealth increases by BB' as FE additional goods become available in the second period.

function schedule shifts upwards as in Figure 7.5) or a decline in the interest rate (the ray OR rotates downwards) for investment to be worthwhile. Box 7.4 gives a discussion of what productive and unproductive investments can mean in practice.

7.4.4 The Intertemporal Budget Constraint of the Consolidated Private Sector

The budget constraint of Section 7.3 took endowments as given. Once investment and production are taken into account, income tomorrow is no longer simply given by nature. The budget constraint now depends on the amount that is invested and on its profitability. As long as the investment project has positive present value, investment increases wealth. Figure 7.6 shows how this happens. Starting from point A, Crusoe can save either by lending, or by investing an amount I_1 up to a maximum of his endowment Y_1. Crusoe's savings is equal to investment, which is equal to the capital stock for tomorrow's output production. This is the difference between today's endowment Y_1 and consumption C_1:

(7.5) $$K_2 = I_1 = Y_1 - C_1.$$

The more he invests—the more we move to the left in Figure 7.6—the larger will be tomorrow's pro-

duction. This is why the production function AE is now the mirror image of the one shown in Figure 7.4: as we move leftwards from the endowment point A, investment increases and tomorrow's output becomes larger. Tomorrow's income is the sum of the endowment Y_2 (the coconuts lying on the beach) plus produced output $F(K_2)$:

(7.6) $$C_2 = Y_2 + F(K_2).$$

The intertemporal budget constraint determines the present value of consumption $C_1 + C_2/(1 + r)$ as equal to total wealth Ω. Recognizing that $C_1 = Y_1 - I_1$ is given by (7.5) and C_2 given by (7.6), the intertemporal budget constraint is now

(7.7) $\underset{\substack{\text{present} \\ \text{value of} \\ \text{consumption}}}{C_1 + \dfrac{C_2}{1+r}} = \underset{\substack{\text{total} \\ \text{wealth}}}{\Omega} = \underset{\substack{\text{wealth} \\ \text{from} \\ \text{income}}}{\left[Y_1 + \dfrac{Y_2}{1+r}\right]} + \underset{\substack{\text{value} \\ \text{of the} \\ \text{firm}}}{V.}$

Wealth now consists of two parts.[11] The first part is the present discounted value of the endowment as

---

[11] To see this, write wealth as the present discounted value of net income and rearrange using $V = \dfrac{F(K_2)}{1+r} - I_1$, which yields $\Omega = \left[Y_1 + \dfrac{Y_2}{1+r}\right] + \left[\dfrac{F(K_2)}{1+r} - I_1\right] = \left[Y_1 + \dfrac{Y_2}{1+r}\right] + V.$

Box 7.4 **Productive and Unproductive Investments**

In 2006 more than £250 billion was spent in the UK on capital goods. Those billions can be thought of as the sum of thousands, if not millions, of efforts to create more resources tomorrow by giving up resources today. While the aggregate effort will look like the project in Figure 7.4, individual projects do not have certain outcomes. Most projects are risky. While they are likely to look like Figure 7.4, there is always a positive probability that they will turn out unproductive and look like Figure 7.5.

Many projects look promising on the drawing board but don't pay off. One example is the famous Channel Tunnel connecting England and France, which had been discussed as a way of improving transport infrastructure between the two countries since the days of Napoleon. The project was not undertaken until the 1980s. UK Prime Minister Thatcher insisted that the 38 km tunnel, which was then projected to cost £7.4 billion, be financed by a private stock issue; 300,000 British and

French investors paid about €5.30 per share in 1987 for a piece of the 'Chunnel'. In the end, the project cost £15 billion and, despite its technological success, met stiff economic competition from improved ferry services and cheap air travel. The investment has not yielded the profits that its investors expected, and the company was reorganized under protection from its creditors in 2007.

And of course there are good investments. An investor who purchased a *single share* in Microsoft Corporation at a price of $21 when it was first offered on 13 March 1986 and held it for the next 18 years would have done quite well, ending up in mid-2008 (after stock splits) with 288 shares valued at roughly $25 each—a total value of $7,200! This represents a compounded annual rate of return of 32%. Had the investor sold at the peak of the high-tech market in 2000 at a price of 60, she would have done even better. Now *that* was a good investment.

---

before in (7.2). The second part is the increase in wealth represented by V, the net value of the investment activity, as in (7.4). In Figure 7.6 the outcome of investment I_1 is shown as point E. Note that E lies above the initial budget line. This is because the production technology is productive at the rate of interest r. The distance OB still represents the present value of the endowment. But now, for a choice of investment I_1 which brings Crusoe to point E, new total wealth is the distance OB. Since the value of future output is discounted at the same rate r, the new budget line is parallel to BD. The distance BB' represents the net present value of the investment project.[12]

In the parable, Crusoe stands for the private sector as a whole, which consists of individuals and the firms they own. Firms ultimately belong to their shareholders, and the net return from investment raises their wealth. In effect, the firm is simply a veil. It should be valued as the present value of net

income from all its activities. If shareholders anticipate that a firm will become more profitable in the future—because of a technological advance, as represented by the shift in Figure 7.5—then net expected returns rise and they are richer. This wealth gain takes the form of an increase in the value of the firm. In the real world, this would be reflected as an increase in the firm's value in the stock market.

While firms are the source of new wealth, does it matter whether firms borrow to finance the investment or use their own savings—in the language of business, their retained earnings? In Crusoe's world the answer is simple: it doesn't. This is easy to see from Figure 7.6. By borrowing the present value of his second period endowment, Crusoe can dispose of his total wealth and reach point B, and invest these resources. Yet if he invests the same amount $(Y_1 - C_1)$ as in Figure 7.6, the value of his wealth is unchanged! It does not matter whether a firm uses debt (borrowing) or equity (own saved funds) to finance the investment. This result, known as the **Modigliani–Miller Theorem**, is discussed in more detail in Box 7.5.

---

[12] Note that the production function cuts the new budget line $B'D'$, suggesting that this result might be improved by investing a little bit less than I_1. Chapter 8 shows that, when Crusoe behaves optimally, he will invest to push out his new budget line as far as possible.

Box 7.5 The Modigliani–Miller Theorem

Because firms are ultimately held by households, it is sensible in macroeconomics to consolidate the two. The activities of firms affect household wealth. In practice, firms are either owned directly by households (we speak of stocks or shares in the firm, or equity ownership), or firms borrow (by issuing debt or getting credit from banks). Shareholders are often called **residual claimants**, since they have a claim to whatever remains after firms have paid their workers, serviced their debt (outstanding bonds and borrowing from banks), and paid taxes. If a firm is declared bankrupt, those who have lent to the firm (bondholders, banks, and other creditors) have priority over equity holders. Under ideal conditions, it does not matter whether a firm uses debt or equity to finance an investment project. This result is known as the Modigliani–Miller Theorem.[13]

In the same vein, there is no difference between firms' savings and household savings lent to firms, at least to first approximation. Firms save when they retain earnings instead of distributing them to shareholders. In that case, shareholders are entitled to the future earnings generated by non-distributed profits. The number of shares does not change, but each share is worth more. In the second

case, the shareholders provide the firm with additional resources in return for future earnings associated with the new investment: they now hold more shares but the value of each share remains approximately unchanged. In both cases, for a given investment project, the shareholders' wealth is the same. In the first case, they implicitly lend to the firm the equivalent of undistributed earnings.

The firm is an agent which acts on behalf of its owners (the shareholders). It is irrelevant whether the firm itself or the shareholders do the saving. In practice, there is some evidence to support this view. While relative shares of saving by firms and households vary from one country to another, the sum of the two sources of saving appears more similar. For example, as seen in Figure 7.7, the bulk of saving is done by households in firms in Italy and Germany. In contrast, corporations account for a larger share of total savings in Japan, the Netherlands, and the UK. One reason for this variation is the difference in the tax treatment of dividends, retained earnings, and capital gains. When the capital gains associated with retained earnings are taxed less heavily than dividend income, for example, shareholders are better off when firms save on their behalf.

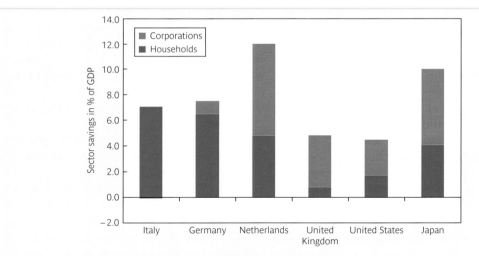

Fig. 7.7 Corporate and Household Net Saving, 1997–2005

Total private net saving rates differ across countries, but not as much as the share of saving of the corporate and household sectors. Tax treatment of income from saving probably explains the lion's share of country differences. In Germany and Italy, households contribute most to private savings while firms perform this function in the UK and the USA. In the Netherlands and Japan, both sectors are important contributors to net savings.

[13] It is named after the two Nobel Prize laureates, Franco Modigliani of MIT (1918–2003) and Merton Miller (1923–2000) of the University of Chicago.

7.5 Public and Private Budget Constraints

7.5.1 The Public Budget Constraint

There was no government on Robinson Crusoe's island. In the real world, there is a public sector which collects taxes, purchases goods and services, and makes transfers to households. Yet the government is little different from other economic agents. It can borrow and lend, but must be expected to repay its debt with interest or be repaid by its debtors. Consider a government which spends G_1 today and G_2 tomorrow, and raises net taxes T_1 and T_2.[14] The government has debt outstanding at the beginning of the period in the amount D_1. This debt must be serviced (interest must be paid) at interest rate r_G, and must be repaid in the last period.

Suppose Crusoe's government spends $(G_1 + r_G D_1)$ and has net tax revenue (T_1) today. It is running a deficit in the amount $G_1 - T_1 + r_G D_1 > 0$, and must borrow to finance that deficit. Following a convention of the OECD, the government's total borrowing requirement can be broken down into two parts: (1) the **primary deficit** $(G_1 - T_1)$, the amount by which non-interest expenditures exceed revenues, and (2) interest payments $(r_G D_1)$.

In the second and last period, the government obeys its intertemporal budget constraint when it repays its obligations in full. This means that its primary surplus $(T_2 - G_2)$ must be sufficient to repay today's deficit $(G_1 - T_1)$ plus interest on that deficit $r_G(G_1 - T_1)$, but also the inherited debt from the past D_1, *plus* interest $r_G D_1$:

$$(7.8) \quad T_2 - G_2 = (1 + r_G)(G_1 - T_1) + D_1 + r_G D_1$$
$$= (1 + r_G)(D_1 + G_1 - T_1).$$

The government budget constraint can be rearranged as

$$(7.9) \quad D_1 = (T_1 - G_1) + \frac{T_2 - G_2}{1 + r_G}$$
$$= \left[T_1 + \frac{T_2}{1 + r_G} \right] - \left[G_1 + \frac{G_2}{1 + r_G} \right]$$

public debt = present value of budget surpluses.

For the government to obey its intertemporal budget constraint, the sum of the present value of primary budget surpluses is equal to initial outstanding debt. This also means that the present value of government income must be sufficient to cover the present value of purchases plus the initial debt.

The government budget constraint is illustrated in Figure 7.8 for the case of no initial debt or assets $(D_1 = 0)$. The budget line has slope $-(1 + r_G)$ and passes through the origin.

Do governments really obey their budget constraints? At first glance, one is likely to be sceptical. Many countries have chronic budget problems and in modern history there have been spectacular examples of government defaults, or repudiation of past debts. Most were associated with sharp political

[14] It should be stressed that G represents government purchases of goods and services. It is not the same as total government outlays, which include transfer payments. In our notation, transfer payments are deducted from taxes to give net taxes T. Although interest payments are treated like transfers in the national income and product accounts, they are such a central component of the intertemporal budget constraint that we will always distinguish them from other transfers throughout this book.

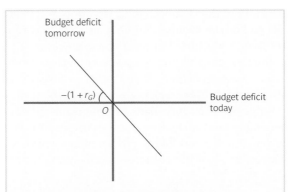

Fig. 7.8 The Government Budget Line

A deficit today must be matched by a budget surplus tomorrow, or vice versa, if the government is to obey its intertemporal budget constraint.

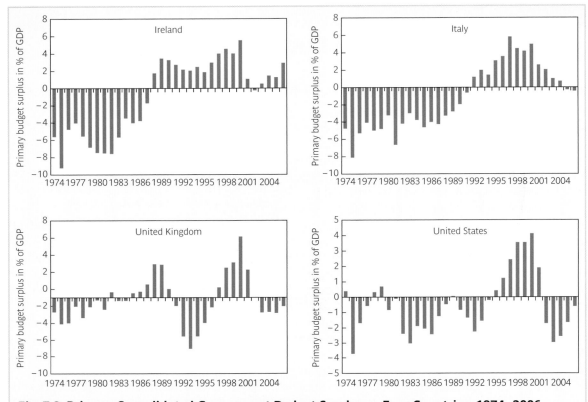

Fig. 7.9 Primary Consolidated Government Budget Surpluses, Four Countries, 1974–2006

Over time, primary budget balances must add up, in present-value terms, to initial public debt. Some governments, like the UK, have maintained primary budget balances on average over many years. Those that have allowed deficits to cumulate into large indebtedness will eventually have to run surpluses, as has been the case in Ireland, Italy, and the USA.

Source: OECD, National Accounts.

upheavals: the turbulent years of the French Revolution, the October 1917 revolution in Russia, the end of the Weimar Republic in 1933, Castro's revolution in Cuba.[15] In most cases, however, it is politically difficult for a government to default. Latin American defaults in the 1980s, or Russia's in 1998, were traumatic events.

An error commonly made by politicians and the general public is to look only at the current absolute deficit as a measure of the government's solvency. Especially when the economy is growing robustly,

tax revenues can be expected to grow over time as well, thus easing some of the burden.[16] For that reason, it is always a good idea to measure expenditures and tax revenues relative to GDP. Still, in order to avoid defaults, today's primary deficits require primary surpluses later, and conversely. Given spending plans, lower taxes today are followed by higher taxes tomorrow. Alternatively, for a given path of taxes, more spending today requires spending cuts tomorrow. How long does 'today' last before a government is hit 'tomorrow' by the budget constraint? Figure 7.9 presents examples of primary budget balances relative to the size of the economy

---

[15] The public debt should be distinguished from the external debt, although in some instances the public debt is held by foreigners and represents the bulk of the external debt. This chapter assumes that the public debt is held by domestic residents.

[16] The implications of economic growth for government budget constraints and stabilization policy will be explored in detail in Chapter 17.

(GDP). Some countries (the UK) show a succession of primary deficits and surpluses. In other cases (Ireland, Italy, the USA) deficits have been sustained over many years, yet eventually the budget constraint has prevailed and the primary budgets were corrected, sometimes moving into spectacular surpluses.

7.5.2 The Consolidated Public and Private Budget Constraint

In Section 7.4, households' net wealth took into account the underlying value of the firms they own. Yet since the households and firms—which are owned by households—ultimately have to pay the taxes, could this logic be extended to public sector budget constraints as well? Could households see through the public sector financing veil, just as the corporate veil was pierced when we consolidated budget constraints of the household and firm? In this section we pursue this line of thought.

For simplicity, we ignore the existence of firms and set initial government debt to zero. The private and public intertemporal constraints are, side-by-side as follows:

(7.10) $\quad C_1 + \dfrac{C_2}{1+r} = Y_1 - T_1 + \dfrac{Y_2 - T_2}{1+r},$

(7.11) $\quad G_1 + \dfrac{G_2}{1+r_G} = T_1 + \dfrac{T_2}{1+r_G}.$

In the first budget constraint, the private citizens pay the taxes, while in the second, the government receives them. The government and the private sector do not necessarily face the same interest rates when they engage in borrowing or lending activities. The government sector borrows and lends at rate r_G, while the private sector borrows and lends at rate r. Combining the private and public budget constraints yields[17]

(7.12)

$$C_1 + \frac{C_2}{1+r} = (Y_1 - G_1) + \frac{Y_2 - G_2}{1+r} + \left[\frac{r-r_G}{1+r}\right](G_1 - T_1)$$

present = present value of + present value of
value of private resources the government's
consumption net of government financing
spending advantage.

This consolidated budget constraint points out that the household can only consume the output that the government has not taken for itself. In the first instance, it is government spending which reduces private wealth. Yet taxes are not irrelevant. An increase in today's taxes will reduce private wealth as long as the government can finance its activities at a better interest rate.[18] Conversely, a tax cut will expand the present consumption possibilities available to households! Of course, it is also true that if the government borrows on *worse* terms than its citizens, it can *reduce* net wealth of its citizens. The central question, which we address below, is: Is r greater than or less than r_G?

7.5.3 The Ricardian Equivalence Proposition

Yet the plot gets even more interesting. Suppose for the moment, that the interest rates of the private sector and the government are exactly equal, so $r = r_G$. Now the last equation reduces to

(7.13) $\quad C_1 + \dfrac{C_2}{1+r} = (Y_1 - G_1) + \dfrac{Y_2 - G_2}{1+r}.$

This looks very much like the private sector budget constraint (7.10), except that taxes have completely disappeared. In fact, the private sector has fully internalized the public sector's budget constraint. The hypothesis that the private sector fully internalizes the public sector's budget constraint is known as the **Ricardian equivalence proposition**.[19]

---

[17] To derive this result, multiply both sides of (7.11) by $(1+r_G)/(1+r)$, and rewrite as

$$G_1 + \frac{G_2}{1+r} + \frac{r_G - r}{1+r}G_1 = T_1 + \frac{T_2}{1+r} + \frac{r_G - r}{1+r}T_1$$

or

$$T_1 + \frac{T_2}{1+r} = G_1 + \frac{G_2}{1+r} + \frac{r_G - r}{1+r}(G_1 - T_1).$$

Substitution of this last expression into (7.10) yields (7.12).

[18] Contrary to appearances, there is no 'free lunch' here. The government is simply borrowing more cheaply than the private sector can. In doing so, it effects a transfer from lenders to the beneficiaries of the tax cut, who experience an increase in the present value of their resources. In reality, lenders could be foreigners, but are more likely to be wealthier domestic residents.

[19] Named after English economist David Ricardo (1772–1823), who first formulated this idea, only to dismiss it as unlikely. The idea has been revived and championed by Harvard economist Robert Barro.

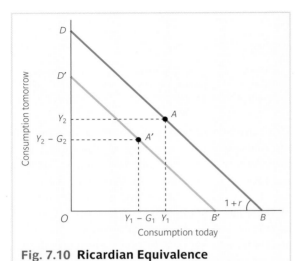

Fig. 7.10 Ricardian Equivalence

The government's spending and taxing activities reduce private wealth. Given government purchases, the precise scheduling of taxes does not matter.

budget constraint.[20] The second is that private sector wealth—which can be spent on private consumption—is the difference between the present value of production or income on the one hand and public purchases of goods and services on the other. The intriguing implication is that, for a given pattern of public spending decisions, taxes can be levied today or tomorrow. The pattern of taxation over time has no effect on private wealth. What matters in the end is public spending, which represents resources taken away from the private sector. Finally, Ricardian equivalence means that government debt is not treated as net wealth by its citizens. Government's indebtedness does not appear as part of private wealth on the right-hand side of (7.13). The private sector does pierce the veil of government. It recognizes that the government's promises to pay—the principal and interest on public debt—are matched by taxes levied to service the debt, today or tomorrow. Public bonds are an asset to households which is exactly offset by the value of their tax liabilities.

7.5.4 When Ricardian Equivalence Fails

For obvious reasons, the Ricardian equivalence result is highly controversial. It means that the path of taxes is irrelevant for the behaviour of the private sector. It implies that the stock of government debt does not, on net, contribute to the wealth position of households. Holding constant the path of government purchases of goods and services, budget deficits do not matter! This section reviews the many assumptions required to reach the Ricardian equivalence result. In the end, the result of this discussion is that budget deficits probably do matter, and that at least some fraction of public debt is regarded by the private sector as wealth.[21]

Different interest rates

A central assumption behind the Ricardian equivalence result is that the government and the private

In Figure 7.10, point A represents Crusoe's endowment measured before taxes. Once public spending is taken into account as in (7.12), the private endowment is represented by point A'. The government reduces Crusoe's private wealth by an amount represented by the distance BB', which is either the present value of taxes or the present value of public spending—the two are equal because of the government budget constraint. Public spending can be financed either by current taxes or by borrowing. If the government reduces taxes today without changing its expenditures, it borrows today and will raise taxes tomorrow. For the private sector, this means more net-of-tax income today and less tomorrow. As long as the public and private sectors borrow and lend at the same rate ($r = r_G$), these intertemporal shifts are equivalent and the public borrowing can be matched one for one by private saving along the same private budget line.

The Ricardian equivalence proposition can be stated in a number of different ways. The first is that total national spending—the sum of private and public spending on goods and services—cannot exceed the country's wealth. The country can borrow or lend abroad, but it must respect its (national)

---

[20] This can be readily shown by rewriting (7.13) as

$$(C_1 + G_1) + \frac{C_2 + G_2}{1 + r} = Y_1 + \frac{Y_2}{1 + r}.$$

[21] Other potential failures of the Ricardian equivalence proposition are related to the behaviour of agents under uncertainty, and go beyond the scope of this book.

Table 7.1 Interest Rates for Government and Corporate Bonds, May 7th 2008 (% per annum)

	10-year government bond	Corporate bonds
Australia	6.36	8.80
Britain	4.71	7.45
Canada	3.81	N/A
Denmark	4.39	5.61
Japan	1.64	1.84
Sweden	4.06	4.71
Switzerland	3.07	3.10
United States	3.86	5.97
Euro area	4.18	5.32

Source: *Economist*.

sector face the same interest rate. Is that realistic? Table 7.1 displays interest rates for two categories of borrowing. Interest rates on Treasury bonds represent the cost of borrowing faced by the public sector. The corporate bond rate is the interest rate charged by the bond market for firms with the best reputation; most private borrowers face significantly higher rates (by some 1–2% more for businesses, and much more for households). In many but not all cases, private borrowing rates exceed the comparable public borrowing rate. This is probably because the government is considered a less risky borrower than most private businesses or individuals.

Mortal or new citizens

You might object that Ricardian equivalence must fail because citizens are not all alike when they face the taxman: some pay a lot more taxes than others. So the burden of public debt service is not equally borne by all citizens. Similarly, some hold government debt, and some don't. Yet, this does not imply that the aggregate household sector can escape the implications of equations (7.11) and (7.13). In the *aggregate* future tax burdens are the same. Some simply pay more than average, others pay less.

On the other hand, citizens are certainly mortal. If they are not alive in period 2, they may not fully incorporate the intertemporal budget constraint of the government into their own budget constraints. If the current private sector fails to factor in *all* future tax liabilities, it is possible that government debt represents private wealth to some agents, and bond-financed deficits increase their wealth. In a similar vein, new agents—immigrants, perhaps— who enter at some future date will pay taxes and thus break the link between the budget constraint of the presently living generations and future government revenues.

Restrictions on borrowing

Many households cannot borrow as much as future expected income would justify. They may be unable to convince lenders—typically banks—of their creditworthiness. For their part, lenders cannot comprehensively investigate the creditworthiness of borrowers when they apply for credit. In addition, future incomes are never really certain, so lending to households is risky. Borrowing rates exceed lending rates to compensate for this risk. In the worst case, no lending is extended and individuals are said to be credit rationed. The case of credit rationing is represented in Figure 7.11. With a net private endowment represented by point A, the agent can only move along her budget line on the segment AD. The segment AB is not attainable through private borrowing. If the government runs a deficit today, the agent may reach point A' as she consumes $Y_1 - T_1$, which is larger than $Y_1 - G_1$ since $T_1 < G_1$.

Most often, individuals face higher and rising costs of borrowing. Lending institutions frequently demand higher interest rates from individuals to compensate for additional risk. The situation is similar to the case studied in the previous section and is also illustrated in Figure 7.11. When lending, the constrained agent can move along AD, but for borrowing she moves along AB'. The budget line is now kinked at the endowment point. In this case, public debt contributes to citizens' wealth, and the time profile of taxes affects the private sector budget constraint. At point A' the constrained citizen is better off than anywhere along AB'. As in the previous section, the government borrows on behalf of its citizens, increasing the wealth of those who cannot borrow on those terms.

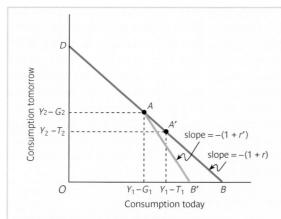

Fig. 7.11 Borrowing Constraints

When the household cannot borrow at all, its budget line is restricted to the segment AD, because it cannot consume today more than what is left of the endowment after public spending $(Y_1 - G_1)$. If the government reduces taxes and borrows instead (abroad), the household's borrowing line extends to the segment $A'D$. When borrowing constraints take the form of a higher private borrowing rate r', the budget line is the kinked line $B'AD$. A budget deficit at A' relaxes the private household's budget constraint.

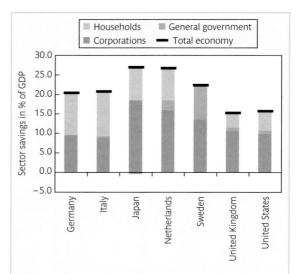

Fig. 7.12 Average Gross Sectoral Savings, 1997–2005 (% of GDP)

The level of the black bar shows the total gross savings of the consolidated household, firms, and general government, including that needed to cover depreciation. Variation in the red component—which represents gross savings of the government, does not appear highly correlated with total gross savings—which is a general implication of the Ricardian equivalence hypothesis.

Sources: OECD; author's own calculations.

Distortionary taxation and unemployed resources

Ricardian equivalence can fail because people change their behaviour in response to taxes. Most taxes are said to be distortionary. For example, taxation on labour income or wages may lead some to work less, and this will reduce output. In the parable of Crusoe, the endowments of coconuts are exogenous, so increasing taxes on them does not affect their supply. In the real world, taxes can reduce wealth because they reduce output. This is especially important in the presence of under-utilized resources, like unemployment. If a tax cut increases the level of economic activity and generates additional income, then the associated fiscal deficit will be associated with higher wealth.

Evidence

Given the long list of qualifications, it would seem quite unlikely that Ricardian equivalence could ever hold in practice. Yet, it receives some empirical backing, especially when the public budget moves

by large amounts that are clearly perceptible to the private sector, possibly signalling fundamental policy shifts.

At a very fundamental level, it is unlikely that the private sector would completely disregard what the government is up to. One general piece of evidence that supports this weak implication of Ricardian equivalence is presented in Figure 7.12. Simply put, the movements in gross savings by governments do not appear systematically correlated with the savings of the nation—the gross savings of the consolidated household, corporate and general government sectors.

A case that is difficult to explain using Ricardian equivalence is the Netherlands in the last quarter-century. The government deficit as a fraction of GDP declined from an average of 4.4% in the period 1975–1987 to 1.9% in the period 1988–2000. More impressively, the share of all government spending (including transfers) in GDP fell over the period from 58.3% to 51.7%, while government purchases of goods and services declined from 16.4% to 13.8%. According to the theory, this spectacular rollback of government borrowing should have been associated with a sharp decrease in private sector savings. Yet the private sector balance hardly budged over

the two periods, declining from 6.6% to 6.5% of GDP. To explain this outcome, we need to move beyond the simple Ricardian approach. One clue might be the movement of the Netherlands towards a pension system which is backed by private savings rather than paid for by the contributions of present workers.

7.6 The Current Account and the Budget Constraint of the Nation

7.6.1 The Primary Current Account

The consolidation of the budget constraints of the private and public sectors can be thought of as the intertemporal budget constraint of the nation. In Chapter 2 we saw that national net saving *vis-à-vis* the rest of the world occurs through the current account. Like the public sector budget surplus, it can be decomposed into a **primary current account** and net investment income:

$$(7.14) \quad \begin{matrix} \text{current} \\ \text{account} \\ \text{surplus} \\ (CA) \end{matrix} = \begin{matrix} \text{primary} \\ \text{current} \\ \text{account} \\ \text{surplus } (PCA) \end{matrix} + \begin{matrix} \text{net} \\ \text{investment,} \\ \text{income } (rF) \end{matrix}$$

where F represents the country's net asset position *vis-à-vis* the rest of the world, and r, as before, is the real interest rate paid on F. Net investment income is positive when the country holds more assets than liabilities ($F > 0$), or negative in the case of an indebted country ($F < 0$).[22]

It was a lesson from Chapter 2 that the consolidation of the public and private intertemporal budget constraints can be expressed in terms of primary current accounts. In the two-period framework,

the budget constraint of the nation requires that the present value of a country's primary current account surpluses be no less than the value of international assets in the first period:

$$(7.15) \quad PCA_1 + \frac{PCA_2}{1+r} \quad \geq \quad -F_1.$$

present value of   at least as   existing net
current and future   large as   external debt
primary accounts

If a country has net wealth at the beginning of period 1 (F_1 is positive), it can draw on it to run future current account deficits. If there is external debt (F_1 is negative), the present value of current accounts must be positive, by an amount sufficient to repay the external debt plus interest.

The implication for the country as a whole is the same as for the private and public sector. A primary current account deficit in the first period ($PCA_1 < 0$) must be repaid by primary current surpluses (in present value) in the second. Symmetrically, surpluses in the first period enable a nation to spend more than it produces in the future. It would seem wasteful for a country not to do this; otherwise it is literally giving away resources for claims on the rest of the world which it will never use. For that reason, it seems likely that the large surplus countries of the world today will eventually get wise and start using these surpluses to improve the standards of living of its citizens.

---

[22] In Chapter 2, it was noted that when writing (2.8) as $Y - A = CA$, Y is properly measured by the GNI. Equation (7.14) shows that if Y is the GDP, we have $Y - A = PCA$.

Box 7.6 Pyramids: Is it Possible to Beat the Budget Constraint?

Failure to understand the budget constraint can be costly to ordinary citizens and governments alike. The view that debts must be repaid is frequently lost on gullible gamblers who invest in 'pyramids'. A dubious financier offers depositors huge returns. When the time comes to pay out, he uses newly invested money from others to pay principal and interest to the earliest investors. For this to work, he must attract ever more depositors. And it often works. Word of mouth spreads news of the wonderful opportunity and when the first depositors get their money back the sceptics are silenced by the 'evidence'. More and more people want their share of the pie. So the scheme grows and grows, and grow it must to simply pay back maturing deposits. But it cannot grow indefinitely, simply because there is not an infinity of people in a country, or even in the world. Pyramids must eventually collapse and the people who set up such schemes know it. So they wait until they think that they have enough deposits at hand, and they suddenly disappear with the money, and thousands of investors discover that they have just lost their lifetime savings.

Pyramids are often called Ponzi-schemes, after Charles Ponzi, an Italian immigrant to the USA who operated a grand-scale scheme in the early twentieth century. Poor Ponzi did not run away fast enough; he went to jail, was later released, deported, and died a pauper in a Rio de Janeiro hospital.[23] Most countries ban pyramid schemes, but they flourished in the early years of transition in several former communist countries (with huge ones in Bulgaria, Romania, and Russia). Apparently, most ordinary citizens didn't grasp the mathematics of intertemporal trade and budget constraints, or were convinced by smooth-talking salesmen that they could pass the potato off to others in time. The collapse of the Albanian funds in late 1996 wiped out the savings of tens of thousands of already poor people, many of whom had sold their cattle and houses in response to promises of 300% return and more. Massive street demonstrations and social unrest subsequently brought down the government, which had failed to close down the pyramids after they had collected an estimated €1.1 billion in a country with a GDP of €2.3 billion.

Modern pyramid schemes are not the exclusive property of Eastern European countries. The recent 'subprime' crisis in the USA, in which low-quality, long-term loans for housing, or mortgages, were traded between banks and investors, has many aspects of a Ponzi scheme. Fundamentally bad mortgages loans were made, then pooled together and repackaged as investments, and then sold off to other investors, who rationalized the investments with expectations of ever-increasing rising house prices. As long as there is greed and the inevitable overestimation of one's own chances, there will be attempts to beat the intertemporal budget constraint. They are successful only for the few brilliant and greedy criminals who originated the scheme in the first place. Assuming they get away with it.

7.6.2 Enforcement of International Credit Contracts and Sovereign Borrowing

If a country fails to satisfy its budget constraint, eventually it will face a tough situation. Many of the crises of the 1990s can be traced back to growing fears that some countries were not going to meet their budget constraints. But ultimately international borrowers have more or less honoured their obligations. Research shows that despite spectacular exceptions, international borrowers in the twentieth century more often than not actually repaid their debts in present value terms.

Governments, just like private households and firms, face an intertemporal budget constraint which limits their ability to borrow at any point in time to the present value of lifetime resources. 'Lifetime' has a clear definition for individuals; for firms and governments less so, since the existence of firms and governments is never guaranteed. Nevertheless, within a legal jurisdiction, private borrowers and lenders will generally be able to rely on special institutions to enforce the budget constraint. Firms or individuals who simply walk away

---

[23] For more details on Charles Ponzi's life see
<http://en.wikipedia.org/wiki/Charles_Ponzi>.

from debts face bankruptcy and possibly jail. Of course, there are always exceptions, but they generally involve fraud, either via outright default ('take the money and run') or more complicated schemes such as pyramids described in Box 7.6. These tricks are usually declared illegal as soon as they are detected. In principle, these rules should also apply to governments, regardless of whether they borrow at home or abroad. As soon as they try to violate their budget constraint, the source of credit should dry up rapidly.

All the same, it is important to distinguish between international borrowing by private entities and **sovereign borrowing**, or borrowing by national governments from foreigners. A country cannot be bankrupted or jailed. Unlike private lending within a country, enforcement of sovereign loan contracts is legally difficult. What happens when a country's government is unable to serve its debt? The first reaction is that foreign lending immediately stops, and this often affects would-be private borrowers. The country must at least balance its current account, since it cannot borrow, which forces painful adjustments in private and public budgets. Thereafter negotiations start with the creditors to try to arrange a rescheduling of debt service. Rescheduling means that the terms of repayment are changed from the original loan agreement, but without changing the present value of those repayments. Debt forgiveness, in contrast, involves a reduction in the present value of the loan burden to the borrowing country, and a loss to the creditor.

ⓘ Summary

1 Because households may borrow or lend, their budget constraint is fundamentally intertemporal. It incorporates all current and future spending on the one hand, and all current and future income on the other. Future spending and incomes are discounted using the interest rate at which households can borrow or lend.

2 Wealth is the sum of the present value of current and future income and inherited assets less debts. The intertemporal budget constraint requires that the present value of spending be less than, or equal to, wealth. It applies to all economic agents, households, firms, the public sector, and the nation as a whole.

3 When firms invest, they forgo—on behalf of their shareholders—current consumption for future output. The profitability of investment depends both on the technology and on the rate of interest. The rate of interest is the opportunity cost of capital that investors apply to investment projects because it is available on other assets.

4 Budget constraints can be added together, or consolidated. Consolidating the households' and the firms' budget constraints gives the budget constraint of the private sector. To a first approximation, corporations are a veil: they provide their owners or shareholders with a means of increasing their wealth.

5 The public sector intertemporal budget constraint implies that, for a given time profile of government purchases, tax reductions today imply tax increases later on, and conversely. Alternatively, given a tax profile, more government spending today implies less spending later on, and conversely.

6 The Ricardian equivalence proposition asserts that the private sector internalizes the public sector budget constraint. Public debt does not represent private wealth, and the path of taxes over time does not affect the private sector budget constraint. If the private sector can freely borrow at the same rate as the government, additional public dissaving is matched one for one by private saving.

7 Ricardian equivalence is unlikely to hold for several reasons. Interest rates are fundamentally different and usually lower for governments than

private agents. Individuals may rightly expect that some current public debt will be repaid after they die. Many households face borrowing constraints. Yet there is some evidence that the private sector internalizes part of government debt.

8 The national budget constraint is the consolidation of the private and public sector budget constraints. It states that the present value of primary current account deficits cannot exceed the nation's net external wealth. It also implies that,

all things being equal, higher primary current account deficits today will require primary current account surpluses in the future.

9 Although it must also obey an intertemporal budget constraint, sovereign borrowing by a nation may differ from private international borrowing by its individual residents. One difference is that governments and countries cannot be bankrupted, and the assets of defaulting governments are hard to seize.

☯ Key Concepts

- intertemporal budget constraints
- rational expectations hypothesis
- endowment
- autarky
- intertemporal trade
- real interest rate
- intertemporal price
- discounting
- budget line
- present discounted value
- investment

- fixed capital formation
- production function
- diminishing marginal productivity
- opportunity cost
- residual claimants
- Modigliani–Miller Theorem
- primary deficit
- Ricardian equivalence proposition
- primary current account
- sovereign borrowing

❓ Exercises

1 Draw a budget line for Crusoe in a two-period world, assuming an interest rate r of 5% and an income of 100 in the first period (Y_1) and 200 in the second (Y_2). What is the value of total wealth Ω? Why are your answers different when instead $Y_1 = 200$ and $Y_2 = 100$?

2 Using the example above to consider the case of a higher interest rate $r = 10\%$. In terms of wealth,

which version of Crusoe has more to lose from an increase in the interest rate? Compare your answer to an individual with $Y_1 = 300$ and $Y_2 = 0$. Explain.

3 Suppose that Crusoe cannot trade intertemporally with his native neighbours, but coconuts no longer spoil completely, so he can store them for consumption tomorrow. Consider the case

$Y_1 = 200$ and $Y_2 = 100$, and suppose that 10% of the stored coconuts are lost because of spoilage. Represent this budget constraint graphically. Why does opening the market for loans always make him better off?

4 In the text, Robinson Crusoe does not want to leave any wealth beyond tomorrow because he will be rescued. The situation would be different if he wanted to leave his friend Friday a gift of a fixed amount B_3 in the second period (B_3 might also be thought of as a bequest). Write down Crusoe's budget constraint and represent it graphically.

5 The real interest rate is 5%. What is the value of a new firm which invests €200,000 initially and expects to have profits (sales minus costs) of €100,000 next year, €70,000 the year after, €40,000 the third year, and then to close down with equipment valued at zero? How does your answer change if the equipment bought initially is instead sold for €50,000? How does your answer change if the interest rate rises to 10%?

6 Sometimes when a firm announces a plan to take over another firm using its cash and not to distribute dividends to its shareholders, its share price decreases; and when the plans are cancelled, the share price rises again. Other times, the opposite pattern is observed. Can you explain why? Under what conditions would you expect such an action to have no effect at all?

7 Suppose the production function has the Cobb–Douglas form: $Y = AK^\alpha L^{1-\alpha}$, and assume labour input is fixed at $L = 1$. Let $\alpha = 0.5$ and $A = 1$. At an interest rate of 5% and no depreciation, what is the level of the capital stock K for which the project is just profitable? How does your answer change when the interest rate is 10%? When the depreciation rate is 5% per annum? When $A = 2$?

8 Write down the value of the firm when the production function is $Y_2 = F(K_2, L)$ with $L = 1$, and the capital stock in the second period is given by $K_2 = I_1 + (1 - \delta K_1)$. How does the initial and given stock of capital in the first period affect the firm's value? The depreciation rate? The rate of investment?

9 Consider a government in a two-period world starting with €1,000 in debt. $G_1 = G_2 = 500$ and $T_1 = 400$. If the interest rate $r_G = 0.05$, what do taxes in the second period need to be to guarantee the solvency of this government? How does your answer change when $r_G = 0.10$?

10 Starting from your answer to the previous problem, show how a tax cut in period 1 can increase wealth if $r_G = 0.05$ and $r = 0.10$? What happens if $r_G = 0.15$? If $r_G = 0.10$?

→ Essay Questions

1 Why do you think the interest rate is positive? What would be the consequence of a negative (real) interest rate?

2 For the government to honour its budget constraint, it is sufficient but not necessary that its budget be balanced every year. Why? Why might a balanced budget law not be a good idea? What conclusions do you draw?

3 Some contend that the 'pay as you go' system of social security in many European countries, in which the pension contributions of the currently employed are used to pay the pension benefits of older workers already in retirement, is a pyramid scheme. Do you agree or disagree? Explain.

4 When a country defaults on its external debt, a frequent controversy concerns whether the

country is unable or unwilling to honour its debt. Discuss this distinction and why it is difficult to resolve the controversy.

5 In recent years many newly emerging economies —China, Indonesia, and Russia to name a few— have accumulated large net asset positions in the form of foreign government bonds, but have begun to convert these into foreign direct investment positions via 'sovereign wealth funds'. Explain this phenomenon using the intertemporal budget constraint. Are these funds a good or bad thing? From the point of view of these countries, are high interest rates a good or a bad thing?

Private Sector Demand: Consumption and Investment

8

There is often misconception in reasoning about spending and investing. For example, Henry Ford's remark has been widely reported: 'No successful boy ever saved any money. They spent it as fast as they got it for things to *improve themselves*.' In this remark Mr. Ford drew no hard and fast line between spending for personal enjoyment and invest-ment for improvement. And there is no hard and fast line . . . Spending merely means expending money primarily for more or less *immediate* enjoyment. Saving or investing is spending money for more less *deferred* enjoyment.

Irving Fisher (1930)

8.1 Overview

We learned in Chapter 2 that GDP is income paid to production factors, and it also represents value added. Another equally important interpretation is that GDP represents the sum of all final goods expenditures. More precisely, it is the sum of consumption, investment, government purchases, plus exports minus imports in a year's time. These components of total spending represent demand for goods and services by various sectors—households, firms, the government, and foreigners. The sum of these components is often called aggregate spending, or aggregate demand.[1] In this chapter, we focus on explaining the behaviour of the most important private elements of aggregate spending: consumption and investment.

As the epigram to this chapter suggests, consumption and investment are driven by different motives. Private consumption spending, about two-thirds of GDP, is a much more stable component over time than investment, which is volatile and is often thought to be a major reason for business cycle fluctuations. We will see that while consumption represents the ultimate source of worldly existence and satisfaction, investment is only a means to an end, enabling the economy to produce more goods and services in the future. This pattern can be seen in the USA and the euro area as well as in Japan and in the poorer regions of the world. Among other things, this chapter will contribute towards explaining the strikingly different behaviour of consumption and investment. Moving from our long-run model of economic growth to the short-run view of business cycle fluctuations is all about understanding these differences.

As in previous chapters, we will continue to study the decisions of a representative consumer and a representative firm. Both are taken to be rational: they strive to do the best they can, given their available resources and opportunities. We often say that they take decisions to optimize, or achieve the best possible outcome. Although optimizing behaviour is sometimes understood as implying extraordinary intelligence or the ability to perform elaborate calculations, in fact it simply means that agents are rational and, possibly through trial and error, behave in a logically consistent fashion.[2] The final product of the chapter will be a **consumption function** and an **investment function**, two key building blocks of macroeconomic analysis.

---

[1]   Naturally, these goods and services are also *supplied* (i.e. sold) by domestic firms, so they also represent aggregate *supply*. In the chapters which follow, we will see how the role of demand is more important for the determination of short-run macroeconomic developments.

[2]   Introspection often makes us sceptical about such assumptions. Who hasn't given in to the temptation of buying a pastry when not really hungry or a stereo system when short of cash? Such departures from rationality are infrequent enough to be outweighed by a majority of reasoned decisions. This is why rationality in economics is the right way to think about reality—at least to a first approximation!

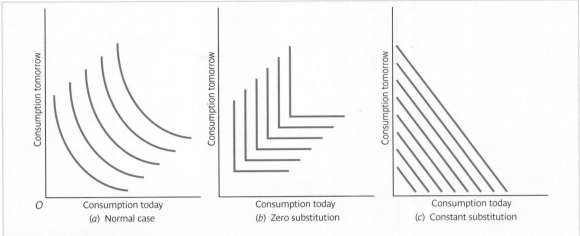

Fig. 8.1 Indifference Curves

Along any indifference curve, utility is constant. In panel (*a*), consumption tomorrow can be substituted smoothly for consumption today, but, as consumption today increases, at a decreasing rate. In (*b*), the consumer can be made better off only by increasing consumption today and tomorrow in fixed proportions. In (*c*), consumption today and consumption tomorrow are always substituted at the same rate. In all cases, indifference curves further up in the north-east direction correspond to higher utility levels.

8.2 Consumption

Households receive income from their labour or their asset holdings and have to decide what to do with it. The decision to consume is a decision not to save, and saving is a decision to postpone consumption. It is fundamentally intertemporal: now or later, which is better? *Micro*economics focuses on how households decide *what* to consume, e.g. apples or oranges. For *macro*economics, the emphasis is on *when* to consume. For this reason, we make the simplifying assumption that there is only one good to consume (Robinson Crusoe's coconuts) and the focus is the choice between now and later.

8.2.1 Optimal Consumption

Contemplating what do to with the coconuts that he finds on the beach, Crusoe realizes that he need not consume them on the spot. With access to a capital market, he can borrow or lend in intertemporal trade. In Chapter 7, we saw that the intertemporal

budget constraint allows him to choose from many different combinations of consumption today and consumption tomorrow (Fig. 7.1), but were silent about the choice he ultimately made. His optimal choice will depend on his **preferences**, which are summarized in Figure 8.1 using **indifference curves**.[3] Each curve corresponds to a given level of **utility**, or well-being. A particular indifference curve represents combinations of consumption today and consumption tomorrow that leave Crusoe indifferent. Higher indifference curves correspond to higher levels of utility.

Two central aspects of indifference curves are their slope and their curvature. For a particular choice of consumption, the slope of an indifference

---

3 Indifference curves were introduced in Chapter 5 to study the labour supply decision of households in an *intra*temporal setting.

curve shows Crusoe's willingness to swap consumption tomorrow for consumption today, holding utility constant. Where the curve is steep, for example, he is willing to give up a lot of future consumption to increase today's consumption. A horizontal curve indicates reluctance to give up consumption tomorrow for consumption today.

The second aspect of indifference curves, curvature, shows how the willingness to substitute depends on the relative abundance of consumption in the two periods. The more abundant consumption tomorrow is relative to consumption today, so the greater the willingness to swap tomorrow's for today's. Moving along an indifference curve upwards and to the left, Crusoe is less and less willing to give up coconuts today as the consumption of coconuts tomorrow relative to today grows larger and larger. Box 8.1 provides more details on the phenomenon of intertemporal substitution.

Naturally, Crusoe wants to consume as much as possible in both periods, but he is limited by that intertemporal budget, which is the straight line in Figure 8.2. The best that he can do is point R, where

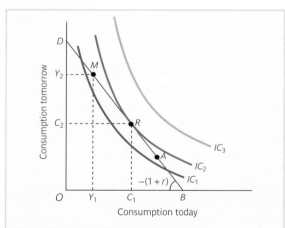

Fig. 8.2 Optimal Consumption

The budget line shows how much can be consumed today and tomorrow for given endowment (represented by point M) and real interest rate (the slope). Optimal consumption is achieved at point R. In this case the consumer borrows today $C_1 - Y_1$ and repays $Y_2 - C_2$ tomorrow. Consumption at R is also possible for an individual with endowment A, who lends today and dissaves tomorrow.

the highest possible indifference curve just touches the budget line. A more desirable indifference curve, such as IC_3, is beyond his means as it lies above his budget line. He can afford the utility level corresponding to IC_1 because this curve cuts the budget line, but can attain the higher utility level associated with IC_2, which is tangent to his budget line. Box 8.1 provides a more detailed interpretation.

When Crusoe is on his budget line, he spends his total wealth (OB) in the course of the two periods:

$$(8.1) \qquad C_1 + \frac{C_2}{1+r} = Y_1 + \frac{Y_2}{1+r} = \Omega.$$

If he can borrow or lend as much as he wants at the going interest rate, his consumption pattern over time depends only on the present value of his income—his budget constraint—and not on the particular timing of his income. In Figure 8.2, a 'student Crusoe' (with endowment M) borrows because his current income Y_1 is low relative to his future income Y_2, while a 'professional athlete Crusoe' (endowment point A) with high current and low future income will save. Since both individuals lie on the same budget line, they have the same wealth OB. If both have identical tastes, as described by their indifference curves, saving and borrowing allows them to have identical consumption patterns.

8.2.2 Implications

The principles developed above have wide-ranging and important implications both at the individual level and for a country as a whole. We examine some these implications.

Permanent versus temporary changes in income

A first implication is that we can understand how people react to changing economic circumstances. We take up three examples.

Case 1: a temporary increase in income

Imagine that, today, Crusoe's harvest is unusually plentiful, rising to Y_1' in Figure 8.3, while next period's harvest Y_2 is expected to remain unchanged. For simplicity, the figure represents the case where, initially, consumption was exactly matching income in both periods so that there was no need to borrow or lend (points A and R overlap).

Box 8.1 Indifference Curves and Intertemporal Substitution

Each indifference curve represents combinations of consumption today and tomorrow for which utility or satisfaction is held constant. Moving to the right along a given indifference curve, today's consumption increases while tomorrow's declines. At any particular point, the slope of the indifference curve shows how many units of goods tomorrow we are willing to give up for an additional unit of goods today. The technical term for this willingness to trade goods tomorrow for goods today is the **marginal rate of intertemporal substitution**.

In most cases, this willingness to substitute consumption across time reacts to moving along a given indifference curve. As we move left to right, the average curve becomes flatter and more horizontal, because we are willing to give up increasingly less consumption tomorrow for consumption today. The opposite occurs as we move from right to left. The curvature of the indifference curve captures the sensitivity of the marginal rate of intertemporal substitution to relative consumption. In Figure 8.1, panel (a) describes the normal situation, but it is worth thinking about two opposite extremes. At one end of the spectrum, there can be no substitutability at all. The consumer is better off only if consumption is increased in fixed proportion in both periods. The indifference curves would look like a series of right angles in panel (b) of Figure 8.1. At the other extreme, the marginal rate of substitution is constant. The consumer is always willing to substitute the same amount of consumption today for consumption tomorrow, regardless of how much is consumed. The indifference curves are straight downward-sloping lines, as in panel (c).

Consider Figure 8.2, which characterizes optimal consumption. The key feature of point R in Figure 8.2 is that the marginal rate of substitution is just equal to the slope of the budget line, or $1+r$. To see why, suppose that Crusoe obeys his budget constraint but has a marginal rate of substitution of 1. He is willing to exchange one coconut today for one tomorrow. By lending 1 today, he gets $(1+r)$ tomorrow—a good deal for him—and can make himself better off, i.e. move towards R. If he goes too far, the marginal rate of substitution will exceed $(1+r)$. He then prefers to shift consumption back to the present, increasing his utility by doing so. Only when the marginal rate of substitution is equal to the intertemporal price of consumption has Crusoe exhausted all gains from intertemporal trade.

The endowment point now shifts from A to A', on the new budget line $B'D'$, which is parallel to the initial line BD since the real interest rate remains unchanged. It is natural to expect that Crusoe will consume more. However, the key insight is that his consumption (point R'') will rise in *both* periods. Consumption today increases less than the windfall, since part of it is saved and spread over time. A temporary increase in income is accompanied by a permanent, but smaller, increase in consumption.

Case 2: a permanent increase in income now and in the future

What if, instead, the increase in income is permanent, in the sense that both Y_1 and Y_2 rise by equal amounts? (Think of a lasting improvement in the harvest outlook, or an enduring improvement in Crusoe's coconut technology!) The new endowment point is A'' and the corresponding budget line is $B''D''$. Optimal consumption moves to point R''. As a first approximation, points A'' and R'' coincide and consumption rises in both periods.[4] Being equally better off in both periods, Crusoe sees no reason to save or borrow. A permanent increase in income is absorbed in a permanent increase in consumption of similar size.

Case 3: an expected future increase in income

Finally, consider the case when income is unchanged today, but is correctly expected to increase tomorrow. If Robinson knows that his future crop will be more plentiful, he will borrow today against his future income to afford a better standard of living right away. Borrowing, far from being reckless, makes him better off. Forward-looking consumers will try to anticipate the permanent component and save the temporary component. A good example

---

[4] This is only an approximation. Impatient consumers may bring forward some of tomorrow's windfall, whereas more patient agents would save some of today's windfall for tomorrow's consumption. The exact answer will depend on the shape and position of their indifference curves.

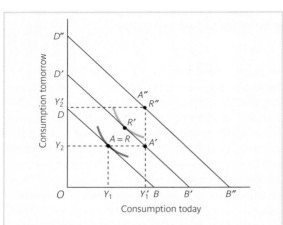

Fig. 8.3 Temporary and Permanent Income Changes

The shift from A to A' describes a temporary increase in income. Consumption rises both today and tomorrow (the household moves from R to R'). Part of today's income windfall is saved to sustain higher spending tomorrow. The shift to point A" represents a permanent increase in income. It does not require consumption smoothing through saving or borrowing. The best course of action is permanently to increase consumption (to point R").

of this idea in action is the behaviour of consumers in Ireland during its exceptional period of strong growth in the last half of the 1990s (see Box 8.5). Far from being myopic, Irish households increased their consumption only cautiously, but continued to do so later on after the high growth period had passed.

An implication of this reasoning is that only new information about the future should alter consumption behaviour. If future incomes are correctly anticipated on average, they will be incorporated into current wealth and current consumption will fully reflect this information. The only reason why consumption should change is if unexpected disturbances affect current or future income significantly enough that wealth changes. Since all that is known of the future is already taken into account in the evaluation of wealth, only true surprises can alter wealth and therefore consumption. Put differently, changes in consumption must be unpredictable. This is known as the **random walk** theory

of consumption, because changes in consumption should be random.[5]

Consumption smoothing

The common theme of the three cases is that people dislike variable consumption patterns. When faced with a temporary change in income, rational consumers save or borrow to spread the effects on consumption over time. In bad times, this may take the form of dissaving (spending from accumulated savings) or borrowing (from the bank, from relatives, or using a credit card). In good times, consumers accumulate assets or repay their debts. This phenomenon is known as **consumption smoothing**. It explains why consumption is less variable than GDP, and is in general the most stable component of aggregate demand.

This does not mean that consumption is *always* more stable than GDP. Since the evolution of actual GDP is a mixture of permanent and temporary disturbances, consumption will reflect the nature of this mixture, responding more to permanent than to temporary changes. Indeed, there are times when consumption is more unstable than GDP. A good example is the case when income is expected to fall in the future. Consumption spending declines immediately although current income remains stable. The subsequent fall in GDP is often seen as being caused by the consumption shortfall. In fact, it is simply an event which was correctly anticipated by consumers.

For Crusoe, therefore, saving and borrowing play the role of a buffer in the presence of transitory income disturbances. Moving from a particular individual to the country as a whole, the logic remains the same. Net borrowing or lending is possible only *vis-à-vis* the rest of the world. In this case, saving or borrowing takes place through the primary current account. An important consequence of aggregate consumption smoothing is that temporary imbalances in the primary current account reflect the efforts of domestic households to smooth consumption. The fundamental identity of macroeconomics tells us that the primary current account is GDP less domestic spending.

---

[5]   The random walk theory of consumption was formulated by Robert E. Hall of Stanford University. It is surprisingly difficult to reject empirically.

Box 8.2 Oil Shocks and European Current Accounts

Oil prices increased sharply five times over the past 35 years. In 1973–1974 they quadrupled. They doubled in several instalments over 1979–1980, increased by 50% in 1990 after a marked decline of about 75% over the 1980s, and then by 50% again in 2000 (Figure 8.4). In the first decade of the twenty-first century they have jumped twice: once after the September 11 attacks in 2001, and in 2007. For European countries like Denmark, which are heavily dependent on oil for their energy needs, an oil shock is equivalent to a reduction in income.[6] Even if the price increase is permanent, the short-run impact will always be larger than in the long run because, over time, conservation can reduce demand. Oil-importing countries should respond by running current account deficits, while oil and energy exporting countries would be expected to show large surpluses. Figure 8.4 shows that in the 1970s, Denmark reacted just as theory predicts, with current accounts going into deficit. In contrast, Norway, which discovered oil in the North Sea in the 1980s, was the mirror image of most oil-importing countries, moving into surplus. Later, when oil prices fell dramatically in the mid-1980s, the current account of Norway deteriorated, while that of Denmark moved into surplus.

If GDP declines while investment and public spending remain unchanged, consumption smoothing implies a worsening PCA. Similarly, a temporary increase in GDP would lead to a temporary surplus. For most countries, primary current accounts are typically small and oscillate around zero. To some extent, these may be regarded as an optimal response to temporary shifts in incomes. A specific example reviewed in Box 8.2 is the reaction of current accounts to the steep oil price increases that occurred in the 1970s.

Permanent income and the life cycle[7]

Most households do not expect a constant flow of income over their lifetimes. Typically, young people earn less than older people, as represented in Figure 8.5. The principle of optimal consumption implies that they should borrow when young and repay debts or even save when older in order to smooth the pattern of consumption over time. It is rational for young people to borrow many times their annual income to buy an apartment or house which they plan to inhabit—to consume the services of—for a long time and to pay off the loan over the course of their lives. Naturally, they must assume that they will continue to earn in the future, and no one can be sure of anything. Nevertheless, mortgage lending is a common fact of everyday life in all modern economies, usually coupled with a life insurance.

The principle of **life-cycle consumption** is illustrated in Figure 8.5. To maintain a constant flow of consumption, individuals should spend an amount corresponding to **permanent income** each year. Permanent income is that income which, if constant, would deliver the same present value of income as the actual expected income path. It is a good measure of sustainable consumption over one's lifetime. In the two-period thinking of this chapter, permanent income Y^P would therefore be defined as

$$(8.2) \qquad Y^P + \frac{Y^P}{1+r} = \Omega = Y_1 + \frac{Y_2}{1+r}.$$

The life-cycle principle can also be applied to a country as a whole. If income is expected to grow, it

---

6   At the time, it was not obvious whether these shocks were temporary or permanent. Figure 8.4 strongly suggests that the oil price increases in the 1970s were temporary, but back in the mid-1970s or early 1980s this information was not available to economic agents, and the oil price increases were generally regarded as permanent. Milton Friedman was a lone voice in the wilderness when he wrote in 1975: 'Almost regardless of our energy policy, the OPEC cartel will break down. That is assured by a world-wide reduction in crude-oil consumption and expansion in alternative supplies in response to high prices. The only question is how long it will take.' (*Newsweek*, 17 February 1975.)

7   The permanent income hypothesis was developed by Chicago economist Milton Friedman (1912–2006) and was cited as his main contribution when he was awarded the Nobel Prize in 1976. The life-cycle theory of consumption was also recognized by the Nobel Prize committee as an important contribution of MIT economist Franco Modigliani (1918–2003).

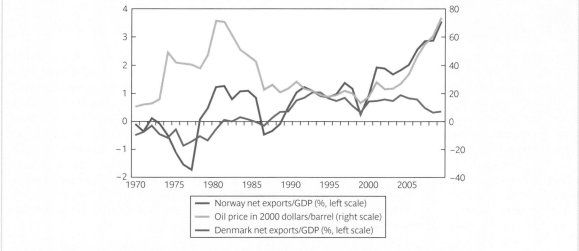

Fig. 8.4 Current Accounts in Europe and the Real Price of Crude Oil, 1970–2007

The real price of oil is computed as the ratio of the US dollar price of crude oil to the consumer price index of all industrialized countries and is plotted using the right-hand scale. In 1973–1974 and 1979–1980 the price of oil jumped by 200–300% each time. After falling sharply in the 1980s, it rose again in 1990, 2000, and steadily since 2003. In 2008 it reached the level of the late 1970s in real terms. As importers of oil, most European economies suffered large income losses when oil prices rose sharply. Denmark is typical in this regard. Consumption smoothing means temporary borrowing now (current account deficit) and repayment later (current account surplus). Norway, an oil producer and exporter, experienced a windfall which was saved abroad by means of current account surpluses. Their current accounts as a percentage of GDP are plotted on the left-hand side scale.

Sources: OECD, *Economic Outlook*; IMF.

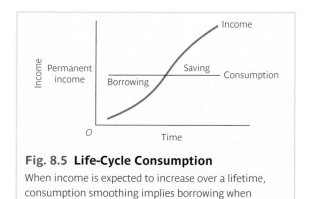

Fig. 8.5 Life-Cycle Consumption

When income is expected to increase over a lifetime, consumption smoothing implies borrowing when young and paying back when older.

is optimal for a country to borrow abroad, and thus run current account deficits for a while, and pay back later through current account surpluses. This may explain why the new EU members, who can reasonably expect to catch up with the old mem-bers, often run current account deficits. Box 8.3 tells the story of Ireland. Oil-producing countries are in the opposite situation: one day their income will decline. It is optimal therefore to run current account surpluses, invest abroad, and live off their savings when their oil reserves have become dry. The odd man out is China, see Box 8.4.

Consumption and the real interest rate

When the real interest rate rises, so do the rewards to saving. Why? Because the price of consumption tomorrow relative to consumption today declines. Will saving always increase and consumption always decline? The question is harder to answer than it first appears. Figure 8.7 shows that one de-terminant of consumption today is whether Crusoe is a net borrower (e.g. a student) or a net lender (e.g. a professional athlete). Since endowments today and tomorrow are unchanged in both panels of the figure, the budget line rotates around point *A*.

Box 8.3 The Celtic Tiger Becomes a Fat Cat: Ireland, 1995–2008

By all standards, Ireland is a leading economic miracle of the twentieth century. After decades of stagnation, slow growth, and outmigration, Ireland has literally exploded since 1990, and has now overtaken most of Europe on a per-capita GDP basis. Hundreds of thousands of Irish expatriates have returned after spending years in economic exile, and Ireland is now one of the largest recipients of immigration on a percentage basis in the EU. While there is much discussion on who should take credit for this economic success story—economic reforms, low taxes, subsidies from the European Union, very strong foreign direct investment driven by skilled English-speaking workers, or simply the luck of the Irish—the Celtic Tiger is now the focus of attention of Europe and the rest of the world.

The permanent income hypothesis can be seen at work in Ireland. The economy was already growing at a blistering pace of 9.7% in 1995, and sustained an average growth rate in the five years to 1999 of almost 10%. At this rate, GDP doubles in seven years. If consumers were myopic and spend their income mechanically,

consumption would have boomed right away. Yet as Figure 8.6 shows, consumption rose at a much more moderate pace in the early years. Moreover, as GDP growth slowed after 2000, consumption continued to grow at a steady pace until 2002, when it finally decelerated. There are two reasons for this development. First, GDP (value added on the Emerald Isle) is not the same as GNI (income to Irish residents). Because much of the growth was fuelled by foreign direct investment, much of the GDP gains were paid to USA, UK, and German investors, and not Irish residents. Yet income growth in Ireland was also significant during this period. Second, and more importantly, Irish consumers began to understand that the boom represented a permanent improvement of their standards of living and were willing, like Crusoe at point R'' in Figure 8.3, to increase consumption and enjoy the fruits of a permanent improvement in available resources. This interpretation is supported by the current account balance of Ireland. As a fraction of GDP, it moved from a surplus of 2.9% of GDP to a deficit of 0.2% in 2000, which grew to more than 4% in 2006.

Box 8.4 Why China Defies the Permanent Income Hypothesis

By the late 1980s, China was a very poor country with a GDP per capita about 7% of that of the Netherlands. By the mid-2000s, it had grown to 20% and few doubt that China will eventually close the gap. The permanent income hypothesis suggests that China should run a substantial current account deficit during this catch-up period. In fact, its current account has been steadily increasing, possibly reaching 10% of GDP.

Why this is the case is a matter of heated controversies. One view is that China is purposefully keeping its cur-

rency undervalued (the meaning of undervaluation will be explained more fully in Chapter 15) to artificially boost competitiveness. Another view is that Chinese citizens cannot borrow against future income because the banking system is rather under-developed. Yet another view is that citizens save—close to half of their incomes—because there is no social protection, so they need to provide for health expenditures and retirement income. At any rate, each of these reasons implies that China is off its optimal intertemporal consumption path.

Optimal consumption shifts from point R to point R'. Net lenders gain from higher interest rates, moving to a higher indifference curve and consuming more in both periods. The borrower who faces higher interest costs is in the opposite situation, as he must devote more resources to service the debt, and his current consumption declines. Increases in interest

rates have important redistributive effects between borrowers and lenders: an increase hurts the former and benefits the latter.

In general, the effect of the interest rate on consumption is ambiguous because it works through two channels. First, an increase in the interest rate makes the budget constraint steeper, since it

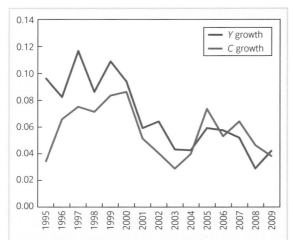

Fig. 8.6 When Irish Eyes are Smiling: GDP and Consumption Growth in Ireland, 1995–2007

Ireland's economic fortunes have been unusually good over the past two decades. Despite very strong GDP growth starting in the mid-1990s, consumption grew less rapidly at the beginning of the Irish boom. At the same time, it persisted after the years of very high growth had passed, suggesting that consumers were smoothing their consumption, just as the permanent income hypothesis would predict.

Sources: OECD, *Economic Outlook*; IMF.

determines the slope of the intertemporal budget constraint. It increases the cost of goods today relative to those tomorrow, making it more attractive to save (consume tomorrow). Second, it reduces the value of wealth W, which is the present discounted value of all income. This effect will depend on how much of our wealth stems from future, as opposed to current, income. The more wealth we have today, the more we profit from an increase in interest rates and the more likely this wealth effect will predominate.

8.2.3 Wealth or Income?

An old tradition in macroeconomics, which can be traced back to John Maynard Keynes, links consumption spending by households to current income—which we have called disposable income Y^d and defined as GDP less net taxes. Keynes argued that most people simply set aside a fraction of disposable income for saving, and consume the rest.[8] The evidence seems to support this hypothesis. Figure 8.8 shows the evidence for France, plotting consumption expenditures in each year in the period

---

[8] This assumption regarding saving and consumption is also central to the Solow growth model studied in Chapter 3.

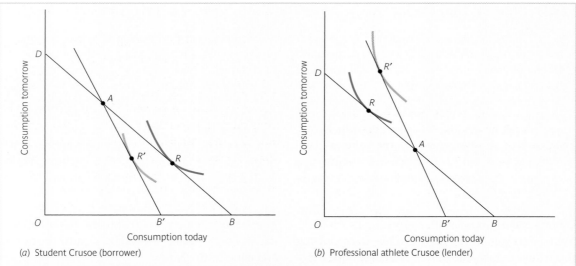

(a) Student Crusoe (borrower)   (b) Professional athlete Crusoe (lender)

Fig. 8.7 The Effect of an Increase in the Interest Rate

As the interest rate increases, the budget line becomes steeper and rotates about the endowment point A. The response of the consumer depends on whether she is a borrower or a lender. The borrower (a) will tend to consume less today because the interest rate at which resources are brought forward has increased. The lender (b) consumes more today, since the same amount of lending can increase the amount of consumption possible tomorrow without reducing today's.

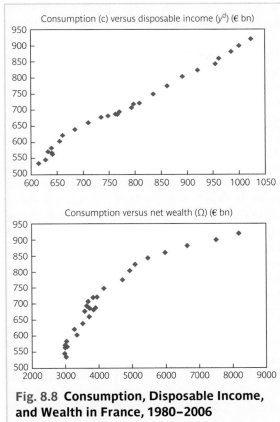

Fig. 8.8 Consumption, Disposable Income, and Wealth in France, 1980–2006

The link between real consumption and net wealth of households is strong, but appears less tight than the link between consumption and disposable income.

Source: OECD.

1980–2006 against disposable income and a measure of household wealth, which includes liquid financial assets of families as well as the value of fixed assets and real estate. The link between consumption and disposable income is strong, in fact stronger than that between consumption and wealth.

This evidence challenges a key implication of the theory developed in the previous sections: that consumption is driven by wealth, not current income, and that households strive to smooth their consumption relative to income. One possible reconciliation is that income and wealth grow in tandem, so that the observed consumption–income relationship may reflect a common dependence on wealth. Yet wealth appears more volatile than disposable income, partly because of fluctuations in share prices on stock markets. It is likely that households regard short-term stock market gains and losses as temporary and pay attention only to long-term increases in wealth. In addition, private wealth is not well known, in part because people are very reluctant to provide information about their assets, in part because expected future income—an important component of wealth—is not measurable and therefore left out.

A second explanation is related to a household's ability to borrow and lend. The Crusoe parable assumes that the representative household can borrow freely at a given interest rate. This might be the case if present and future incomes of individual households—against which borrowing is pledged—were known with certainty to lenders. In real life, banks and other lending intermediaries cannot know the repayment prospects of all individual borrowers with certainty. A common banking practice is to demand collateral—the borrower pledges tangible wealth, such as a house, in case of non-payment. This option is not available to all households. Banks charge higher interest rates to customers who appear riskier and sometimes refuse to lend at any rate, or place ceilings on the amount that can be borrowed. Consumers who cannot obtain credit in spite of future earnings potential are said to be **credit rationed**.

In the presence of credit rationing, spending is governed by current disposable income, not wealth.[9] This is shown in Figure 8.9, which uses Figure 7.11 as its point of departure. Because Robinson Crusoe is prevented from borrowing, his consumption possibilities are limited to the kinked line *CAB*. In particular, he cannot reach the segment *AD* of his intertemporal budget constraint, and his preferred consumption plan *R* is not possible. In that case, the best option for him is point *A*, where he consumes exactly his income in both periods. If

---

9   Chapter 7 provides a detailed treatment of interest rates and credit rationing. It also shows that with credit rationing, Ricardian equivalence will not hold for those who would like to borrow, so that current taxes affect current consumption as well, hence the relevance of disposable income as opposed to GDP.

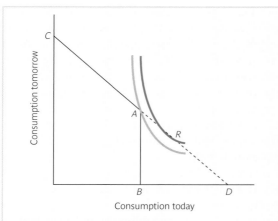

Fig. 8.9 Credit Constraints

If Crusoe cannot borrow, his budget constraint shrinks from CD to CA. He would like to be at point R, however, borrowing today and paying back tomorrow. The best outcome for him under the circumstances is to consume at point A, with consumption equal to income both today and tomorrow.

a significant proportion of households is rationed in credit markets, disposable income will also influence consumption, along with wealth, which only matters for non-rationed households. Box 8.5 illustrates the importance of national borrowing constraints in the early phase of the process of economic transformation in Eastern Europe. But even in advanced countries, credit rationing affects a substantial proportion of households. It is therefore not surprising to observe the tight link between consumption and disposable income in Figure 8.8.

8.2.4 The Consumption Function

How can we summarize all we have learned thus far? Consumption is driven primarily by wealth, and wealth is based on current and discounted future incomes of households. By this argument, current income should matter less than future expected income. At the same time, current income may be a good predictor of what is to come. In practice, however, many people cannot borrow even though their expected future income is higher. For them, disposable income is the effective determinant of consumption.

This, along with the fact that income and wealth tend to grow together, means that consumption seems to be better explained by disposable income. In fact, both matter, as can be seen from the example in Box 8.5 and as is apparent in Figure 8.10. Section 8.2.2 also noted that the real interest rate

 Box 8.5 Current Income and Spending in East Germany and Poland

The rapid conversion of East Germany (the former German Democratic Republic) and Poland to market-based economies in 1990 provides a unique example of an anticipated increase in permanent income. In both countries, the adoption of market-based institutions implied that income levels would eventually reach those of Western Europe. However, the transition to a market economy is painful, possibly leading to an initial fall in income as inefficient production capacity is shut down and workers change occupations and industries. While current observable income falls, wealth is rising because future incomes are so much higher than before. Faced with an expected windfall, optimal consumption rises, both now and in the future. Actual current consumption can increase only if people are able to borrow or receive transfers. As part of German unification, the citizens of the Eastern *Länder* had access to a well-developed domestic financial market. For the former East Germany borrowing 'abroad' meant getting loans from West German banks, or receiving credits or (deficit-financed) grants from the Government. On the other hand, Poland started out with a large external debt, which made it difficult for the Government to borrow more, and its citizens and firms certainly did not have access to credit, despite high growth. Figure 8.10 shows the dramatic difference. While GDP fell in East Germany after 1990, private consumption there rose to equal total East German GDP. Public spending and private investment also rose, bringing the current account deficit to nearly 100% of GDP. In credit-constrained Poland, spending tracked income. In fact, because of its large external debt, Poland had to run a primary surplus. In contrast, East Germany's large external debt was assumed by West Germany.

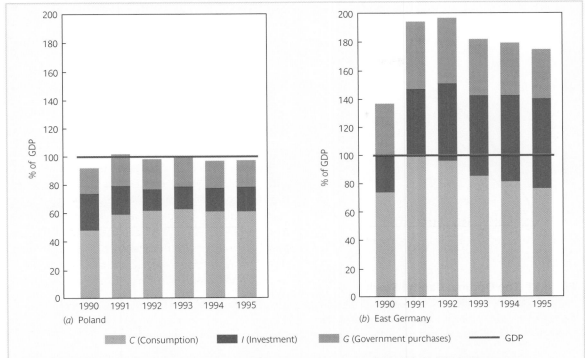

Fig. 8.10 GDP, Domestic Demand, and the Current Account: Poland and East Germany

Spending in East Germany rose after unification as firms, citizens, and authorities were able to borrow against higher expected future income. There is no link between spending and income, because 'foreign' borrowing is almost as large as income. In Poland, which has similar long-run growth prospects, spending follows income because of the impossibility of borrowing large amounts abroad.

Sources: DIW Wochenbericht; World Bank; CSO; DGII.

affects consumption, but its direct role is ambiguous. In all likelihood, a negative effect of interest rates on consumption is most likely to occur indirectly through wealth. A rise in interest rates reduces the value of wealth, and lower wealth means lower consumption. In the end, we capture these various effects by writing down the consumption function, a compact way to link consumption to its two main determinants:

(8.3)
$$C = C(\Omega, Y^d).$$
$$+ \quad +$$

The plus signs underneath the arguments of the function reminds us that consumption increases with both wealth Ω and disposable income Y^d. The consumption function is a fundamental tool that that will be used in the rest of this textbook.

8.3 Investment

The second component of aggregate demand to be explained is investment. This is frequently called gross domestic capital formation. Investment goods are not intended for consumption: machine tools, computers, office furniture, land-moving equipment, buses and lorries, and construction of new

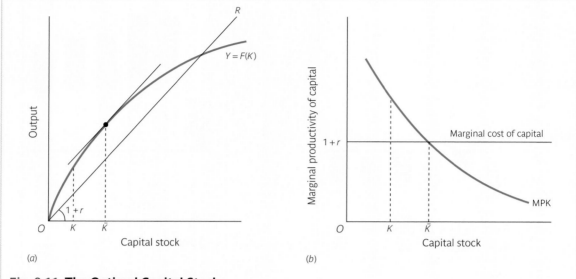

Fig. 8.11 The Optimal Capital Stock
The optimal stock of capital $\bar{K}$ is achieved when the firm's production function is furthest from the line *OR*, which represents the cost of capital. There the marginal productivity of capital is equal to its marginal cost (MPK = $1 + r$). Investment is the difference between the desired capital stock $\bar{K}$ and the previously accumulated capital stock K.

factory buildings, as well as increases in inventories of goods to be sold at a future date. They also now include software programs used in computers that are purchased by businesses. All these goods have the common trait that they make the production of goods and services possible in the future. The decision to invest is therefore an intertemporal decision.

8.3.1 The Optimal Capital Stock

As in Chapter 7, let us continue to freeze labour input $L = 1$, so we can write the production function using the shorthand $F(K)$ for $F(K,1)$. This represents the amount of output that can be produced by a representative firm, giving output Y available tomorrow when capital K is in place. The production function is depicted in panel (*a*) of Figure 8.11. A related concept, already introduced in Chapter 3, is the **marginal productivity of capital (MPK)**. This is the amount of extra output that can be obtained when an additional unit of capital is installed ($\Delta Y/\Delta K$), and is the slope of the production function at a particular input of capital.[10] Because of the principle of declining marginal productivity, the

MPK declines as more capital is put in place, as is shown in panel (*b*) in Figure 8.11.

The MPK is the return from an additional unit of capital. What about the cost? When he saves, Crusoe chooses between planting resources or lending them in the capital market. In the latter case, he can expect 'tomorrow' to receive the coconut plus interest. Alternatively, he could borrow a coconut, plant it himself, grow the tree, and pay back principal and interest tomorrow. The same is true for any firm. If the investment is funded with resources that could instead be invested in financial assets, the **opportunity cost** of the investment is $(1 + r)$. If the investment is financed by borrowing, the **marginal**

---

[10] To see why, take one point on the curve. An increase ΔK in the stock of capital is represented as a horizontal move from the initial point. How much output ΔY is available? It is measured as the vertical distance which brings us back to the production function. The ratio $\Delta Y/\Delta K$ is the slope of the line connecting the point of departure and the point of arrival back on the production function. As the initial step ΔK is made shorter, this slope becomes the slope of the curve itself (formally, the line becomes tangent to the curve).

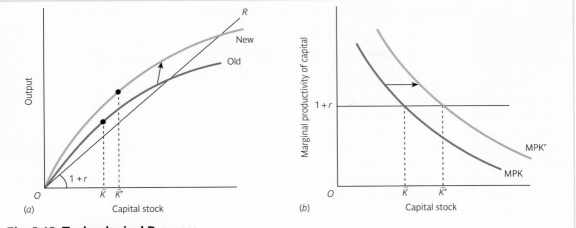

Fig. 8.12 Technological Progress
Technological progress makes more output possible with the same stock of capital. In panel (a) the production schedule shifts upward. In panel (b) the MPK schedule moves up to the right to MPK'. The optimal stock of capital is now $\bar{K}'$, which is larger than the initial value $\bar{K}$.

cost of investment is $(1 + r)$.[11] In both cases, the cost is the same: it is shown in panel (a) of Figure 8.11 as the ray OR. The ray represents the total cost, $(1 + r)K$, of capital installed today and productive tomorrow, the sum of the principal and the interest charged. (The cost of equipment here is unity because it takes one coconut to start a tree.) The marginal cost of capital, or the cost of one incremental unit of productive capacity, is simply $(1 + r)$. It is represented in panel (b) by a horizontal line.

The firm's profit in the second period is the difference between what it produces and the cost of production:

(8.4) $\text{profit} = F(K) - K(1 + r).$

In panel (a), this is measured as the vertical distance between the curve depicting the production function and the ray OR. To maximize profit, the firm chooses the **optimal capital stock** $\bar{K}$ such that the distance between the two schedules is as large as possible. This occurs where the slope of the production schedule (given by its tangent) is equal to the

slope of the cost-of-capital schedule OR. Then the marginal productivity of capital (MPK) is equal to the marginal cost, here the opportunity cost equal to $1 + r$:

(8.5) $\text{MPK} \quad = \quad 1 + r.$
          marginal   marginal cost
          productivity   of capital
          of capital

In Figure 8.11(b), the optimal capital stock $\bar{K}$ corresponds to the intersection of the MPK and marginal cost curves. Box 8.6 provides an extension of this result to the case when capital does not depreciate completely and can be resold after the second period.

If each and every firm behaves optimally, the same principles can be applied to the economy as a whole. Two conclusions follow. First, the optimal capital stock depends positively on the expected effectiveness of the available technology, captured by the marginal productivity of capital. An improvement in technology means that more output can be produced with the same capital stock. In Figure 8.12, the production function in panel (a) and the MPK schedule in panel (b) both shift upward. The optimal stock of capital increases from $\bar{K}$ to $\bar{K}'$.

Second, the optimal capital stock depends negatively on the real interest rate. If the real interest rate increases, the cost schedule OR rotates

[11] The careful reader may appreciate the following precision. Presumably, capital can be resold. Here we assume that Crusoe abandons his coconut grove upon rescue. If he could sell it, the expected resale value comes as a deduction from investment cost. Box 8.6 elaborates on this point.

Box 8.6 Optimal Capital Investment: Looking Beyond Two Periods

In the real world, capital investments typically last more than two periods—sometimes many decades. Capturing this important aspect of investment and capital is relatively easy. Suppose that Crusoe, instead of abandoning his capital stock, sells it to Friday, who chooses to stay on the island and continue his economic existence. A 'resale market' changes the investment decision in an important way. As before, the optimal decision means that MPK equals marginal cost, but now the MPK includes the resale value of capital. For simplicity, suppose first that the price of trees is equal to one (coconut). Then the optimal condition is

(8.6)   MPK   +   1   = $1 + r$

marginal product + resale value = marginal cost
   of capital   of capital   of capital.

The cost of capital is 1, the same as the value of output by assumption (1 coconut). This condition can be simplified to

(8.7) $MPK = r$.

When Crusoe can recoup the principal of his investment, the marginal product of capital is set equal to the real interest rate r, rather than $1 + r$. In practice, firms can

resell at least some of their equipment at some price, so a lower MPK will be necessary to justify an investment than if they were to abandon their investment entirely. Reality will tend to be somewhere between equations (8.7) and (8.6), depending on depreciation, or loss of value of the installed capital over time.

This loss of productive equipment can be quantified by a **rate of depreciation** δ. Tomorrow's value of a unit of today's capital is not 1, but instead $1 - \delta$. Taking this into account, (8.7) becomes

(8.8)   MPK   + $1 - \delta$ = $1 + r$,

marginal product   resale value   marginal cost

which simplifies to

(8.9) $MPK = r + \delta$.

The optimal capital stock is reached when the marginal product of capital is equal to the sum of the interest rate r and the depreciation rate δ. Because depreciation can be thought of as an additional cost of capital, the right-hand side is often called the **user cost of capital**. The original rule for the optimal capital stock (8.5) can be regarded as a special case of complete depreciation ($\delta = 1$).

counter-clockwise in Figure 8.12(*a*) and the marginal cost schedule shifts upwards in panel (*b*). The intuition behind this important result is that, for a given state of technology, higher opportunity costs of capital reduce the amount of capital that can be optimally employed and still be more profitable than simply 'lending' the resources in the financial markets.

8.3.2 Investment and the Real Interest Rate

Investment occurs for two reasons: (1) to bring the capital stock to its desired level, and (2) to make up for capital lost through physical or economic depreciation.[12] In Figure 8.13, we can find the optimal

[12] In Chapters 3 and 7 we saw that the change in the capital stock ΔK is equal to $I - \delta K$, where δ is the rate of depreciation, and therefore δK is the amount of capital that is used up each period. This relation can be rewritten as $I = \Delta K + \delta K$, which shows that I—gross investment—must cover both ΔK—the intended net investment—as well as replacing depreciated capital.

stock of capital $\bar{K}$ and the stock of capital inherited from past investment K—perhaps there were already some coconut trees around when Crusoe came to his island. Ignoring depreciation, optimal investment is simply the difference $\bar{K} - K$. Thus, given the present stock of capital and the rate of depreciation, the determinants of optimal investment are the same as those of the optimal stock of capital. An increase in the real interest rate, which lowers the optimal stock of capital, also lowers optimal investment since the capital stock brought forward from the last period and the rate of depreciation remain unchanged. Accordingly, the investment function could be expressed as

(8.10) $I = I(r)$.

8.3.3 The Accelerator Principle

In Chapter 3, the relative stability of the capital–output ratio was stressed as one of Kaldor's stylized facts about economic growth. It is reasonable to expect that, for the capital stock to reach its optimal level derived in Section 8.3.1, investment would have to move in roughly the same proportion. This idea gives rise to a simple way of thinking about investment. Suppose the optimal capital stock in the second period is proportional to the expected output level: $K = vY$ where v is a constant.[13] If firms invest to keep the capital stock at its optimal level, an increase of GDP from Y_1 to Y_2 requires a change from $K_1 = vY_1$ to $K_2 = vY_2$. Ignoring depreciation, this means an investment of

(8.11) $I_1 = K_2 - K_1 = v(Y_2 - Y_1) = v\Delta Y_2.$

This relationship captures the **accelerator principle**. It is called the accelerator because in order for investment to remain constant, output must increase. Increases in investment are therefore associated with an *acceleration* of output. In practice, the capital–output ratio is between 2 and 3 in most economies. Put differently, annual GDP represents between one-third and one-half of the installed capital stock. GDP movements therefore are associated with much larger swings in investment.[14] A second, central insight of the accelerator principle is the dependence of investment today on expected growth in output *tomorrow*. This provides a convincing reason why investment is more volatile than GDP. It is based on expectations of the future. In the following sections we will develop this idea in greater detail.

8.3.4 Investment and Tobin's q

Why do observers of the economic scene continuously monitor the evolution of the stock markets? Prices of shares often move in erratic ways which may not seem particularly related to the present economic situation, or at least in a way that is very obvious. In fact, stock prices are intimately related to macro-economics. Aggregate economic activity affects stock prices, and stock prices are important determinants of aggregate economic activity. One important linkage is household wealth. When stock prices rise, shareholders become richer and spend more. When the stock market crashes, consumption tends to slow down.

A second connection, which is our focus here, is between stock prices and investment in plant and equipment. Shares in publicly traded companies are titles of ownership. They represent claims on the present and future profits of firms. Profits are the difference between sales and costs. In the aggregate economy, these costs are primarily wages and non-wage labour costs. Share prices can be thought of as the market's best estimate of the value of those present and future profits.

This valuation may well differ from the price of the capital goods that constitute the productive assets of the economy's firms, which is sometimes called the replacement cost of a firm's capital stock. For a number of reasons, the market valuation of a firm can differ—sometimes significantly—from the replacement cost of its physical capital. One such reason is the existence of intangible assets which include such factors as the firm's know-how, its network of distributors and retailers, its reputation among customers, etc. A more important reason, from the point of view of macroeconomics, is the fact that 'Rome wasn't built in a day'. Establishing a new firm from scratch requires time and resources. These costs are greater, the more rapidly an investment project is undertaken. To summarize this, we define a ratio, called **Tobin's q**, which is defined as follows:[15]

(8.12)

$$\text{Tobin's } q = \frac{market\ value\ of\ installed\ capital}{replacement\ cost\ of\ installed\ capital}.$$

---

[13] This proposition is both empirically and theoretically tenable. The long-run stability of the capital–output ratio was one of Kaldor's stylized facts introduced in Chapter 3. Theoretically, consider a Cobb–Douglas production function with constant employment equal to 1: $Y = AK^\alpha$. Then the MPK is given by $\partial Y/\partial K = \alpha AK^\alpha = \alpha AK^{\alpha-1}/K = \alpha Y/K$. The optimal capital stock is K^* such that MPK $= 1 + r$, so $\alpha Y/K^* = 1 + r$, and $K^* = \alpha Y/(1 + r)$. Setting $v = \alpha/(1 + r)$ implies (8.11).

[14] To account for depreciation, (8.11) is simply changed to $I_1 = v\Delta Y + \delta K_1$. The same conclusions apply.

[15] It is named after US economist and Nobel laureate James Tobin (1918–2002), who pointed out in 1969 that investment should be positively related to the ratio of a firm's market valuation to the replacement value of its capital stock. In the meantime, more sophisticated analyses have shown the conditions under which this 'average q' concept—which is readily measured using stock market values and investment good prices—is equal to the marginal concept presented in the text. For our purposes, we will simply assume that these conditions are met.

The numerator of Tobin's q is the firm's value as priced by the stock market, the total value of all existing shares. The denominator is the amount that would have to be spent to replace the capital goods incorporated in existing firms.

The **q-theory of investment** relates the behaviour of aggregate investment to Tobin's q. When Tobin's q is greater than one, installed capital in the existing firm is more valuable than what it would cost to purchase it new and start a new firm from scratch. For this reason, entrepreneurs (people who start and run businesses) should take the hint and purchase new plant and equipment. Investment is then positive. For example, a Tobin's q of 1.2 would imply that a firm that spends 100 on new investment in plant and equipment increases its market value by 120. Installation and use in production adds a value of 20 to uninstalled equipment. Given the principle of declining marginal productivity, investment reduces the return on the capital over time and therefore reduces Tobin's q. Firms will continue to invest, increasing the capital stock and reducing the marginal product of capital, until Tobin's q has returned to unity.

Alternatively, when q is lower than 1, selling off equipment at replacement cost is profitable and therefore desirable from the point of view of the firm's shareholders, so net investment should be negative. In the aggregate economy, this can occur only if gross investment is exceeded by depreciation or capital is dismantled, sold, or scrapped. The dependence of investment on Tobin's q is displayed in Figure 8.13.

How is the q-theory related to the previous section, which showed that the interest rate is a key determinant of investment? The stock market values firms by discounting future earnings using the real interest rate. Any increase in the interest rate leads to heavier discounting and therefore to a decline in stock prices. Thus, the negative effect of the real interest rate on investment is actually incorporated into Tobin's q.

But Tobin's q does more than just take the interest rate into account. It also incorporates two other factors in the investment decision. First, gains in productivity of capital raise future income, and thereby increase share prices and q. An excellent

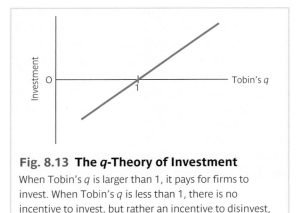

Fig. 8.13 The q-Theory of Investment
When Tobin's q is larger than 1, it pays for firms to invest. When Tobin's q is less than 1, there is no incentive to invest, but rather an incentive to disinvest, or to dismantle or abandon productive capacity.

example of how this can occur was the massive rise (and later, decline) in stock prices in the wake of the internet and new communications technologies. Second, q incorporates the role of expectations. Inevitably, investment is a bet on the future. Firms buy equipment now to produce output for several years under uncertain conditions. How they will be able to take advantage of the equipment is not known when the investment occurs. Uncertainty ranges from the general economic situation, to competition in domestic and foreign markets, to the evolution of technology and even political developments. All these aspects are continuously evaluated by the stock markets. Forward-looking share prices are volatile because the underlying factors are volatile. In the end, this explains why investment is the most volatile component of GDP. It was Keynes who linked the high variability of investment to the **animal spirits** of entrepreneurs, i.e. their fickle and volatile expectations of the future profitability of investment. It is precisely this volatility that can be seen in comparisons of investment and consumption data in any particular country.

To see how well Tobin's q predicts investment expenditures, let us consider Figure 8.14, which presents data for Germany during 1970–2002 as well from a much earlier period, the late 1920s and early 1930s, which included the Great Depression. The link is evident, with stock prices leading investment with a variable but relatively short lag. This

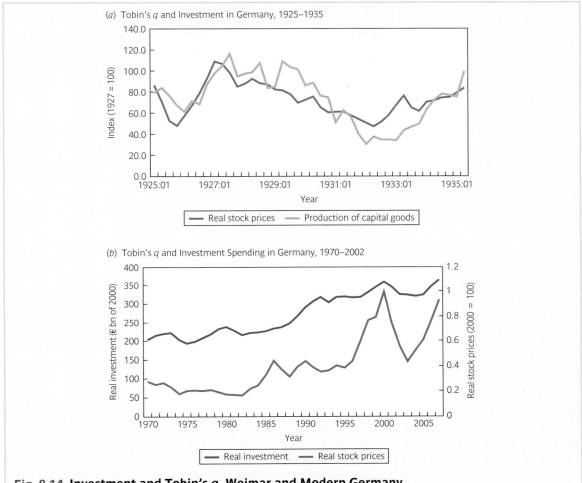

Fig. 8.14 Investment and Tobin's *q*, Weimar and Modern Germany

Both in historical and more modern contexts, investment has consistently followed movements of Tobin's *q*, as proxied by a stock price index divided by the consumer price index.

Sources: IMF; Ritschl (2004).

link is strong, despite the fact that not all companies are traded on stock markets. Frequently, firms are too small to issue shares, and many larger ones are reluctant to 'go public'. It is often cheaper for firms to draw on their own savings (retained earnings) because profits are usually taxed less when reinvested than when distributed. Some firms prefer to finance investment by borrowing rather than by issuing shares, especially in continental Europe, where bank lending plays an important, if not dominant, role. Despite these limitations, Tobin's *q* still does a pretty good job measuring the incentive to invest for these firms. It reflects both expected profitability—the numerator—and the real cost of borrowing through the discount factor and the cost of capital—the denominator.

Tobin's *q* explains the link between the stock market and the state of the economy. The economic function of stock exchanges is to evaluate the future profitability of firms and to place a value today for the whole stream of future earnings from capital ownership. For the macroeconomy as a whole, average stock prices represent the value of the capital stock in place (financial markets also assess the degree of riskiness related to unavoidable uncertainty, and this is factored into share prices— the subject of Chapter 14). Present and especially future economic conditions affect stock prices. Conversely, we should expect stock markets to affect economic conditions since stock prices influence investment through Tobin's q.

8.3.5 The Microeconomic Foundations of Tobin's q[16]

Installation costs

We now have two ways of thinking about the firm's investment decision. The first is that the firm invests to reach its optimal capital stock. The second approach sees investment as taking advantage of the difference between the market value of capital already in place (installed) and its replacement cost—the cost of new capital goods. From either perspective, one might expect firms to seize such opportunities quickly. In practice, however, they do not adjust the capital stock instantaneously to its optimal level. For this reason, q can and will differ systematically from its long-run value—unity—for some time. One reason for this is that firms face **installation costs** in addition to the direct costs considered so far.

The idea behind installation costs is simple. With adequate resources, it could have been possible to dig the Eurotunnel in just six months. Doing so, however, would have been enormously 'costly' in many ways, so it was completed over several years instead. Intuitively, the bigger the investment per unit of time, the more costly it is to install it. Examples of installation costs include the fact that each addition of new equipment in a factory disrupts existing production and that workers must be trained to operate new equipment.

Installation costs explain why Tobin's q is not always equal to unity. In the absence of installation costs, firms would always set capital input to its optimal level, equating marginal productivity and marginal cost as in equation (8.5), rewritten as

$$(8.13) \qquad \frac{\text{MPK}}{1+r} = 1.$$

MPK/(1 + r) is the present value of the return on investment. It is next period's return on the latest addition of capital discounted back to today.[17] It must be equal to the marginal cost of equipment which is unity. When installation is costly, however, the cost of investing is not just the price of equipment. It now includes an additional cost, the marginal cost of installing new equipment, φ. This installation cost can be thought of as equipment which is 'eaten up' in the installation process. Furthermore, φ is an increasing function of the investment undertaken.[18] The optimal investment decision is to invest until the present value of the MPK of new equipment is equal to the augmented marginal cost of equipment:

$$(8.14) \qquad \frac{\text{MPK}}{1+r} = 1 + \varphi.$$

Comparing (8.13) and (8.14), we see that installation costs raise the MPK required to justify the investment. This can be achieved by taking a smaller step towards the desired long-run capital stock $\bar{K}$, since marginal productivity is higher the lower is the stock of capital. Since installation costs increase with the amount of investment each period, the next round of installation is cheaper, φ is lower, so firms will engage into more investment, and so on until φ is driven down to zero and (8.13) holds. That way firms break the path towards $\bar{K}$ into small steps which entail smaller costs.

Installation costs and Tobin's q

The stock market should value the return on an additional unit of investment by the present value

---

[16] This section is a more advanced presentation of the *q*-theory of investment based on installation costs. It is similar to the reasoning used to establish the optimal stock of capital and can be skipped without any loss of continuity. The WebAppendix to this chapter presents a formal analysis.

[17] Remember, there are just two periods, so 'tomorrow' is a shorthand for the indefinite future. Otherwise we would have to discount all future MPKs.

[18] For example, the investment costs associated with a 10% increase in the capital stock could be four times the costs implied by a 5% increase.

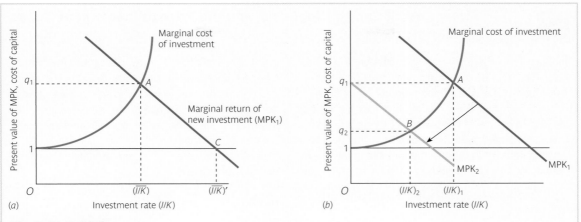

Fig. 8.15 Tobin's q

In panel (a) profits are maximized at point A, where the marginal return of investment in present-value terms is equal to its marginal cost. The marginal cost of capital is 1 (unit of forgone consumption). The optimum rate of investment is $(\overline{I/K})'$. Tobin's q corresponds to point A: it is the ratio of the marginal return on new investment to the cost of new capital. In the absence of installation costs (point C), the optimum rate of investment $(\overline{I/K})'$ brings the capital stock immediately to its optimum level. In panel (b) investment starts at point A as before. With a higher stock of capital, the MPK then declines as represented by the shift from MPK$_1$ to MPK$_2$. With Tobin's q still above unity, investment continues but at the lower rate $(I/K)_2$. The process continues until q is equal to 1, and no further investment is warranted.

of its marginal return, $\text{MPK}/(1 + r)$. In the case of Robinson Crusoe, the replacement cost of capital is simply the cost of coconuts (uninstalled equipment) which is 1. Tobin's q is therefore[19]

(8.15)
$$q = \left(\frac{\text{MPK}}{1 + r}\right)\bigg/ 1.$$

Equation (8.15) establishes the link between the two investment principles. The optimal capital stock of capital is reached when (8.13) is satisfied, that is when Tobin's q is equal to 1. When q is above 1, the MPK exceeds $1 + r$, and investment is warranted. When q is lower than 1, the MPK is low, given the replacement cost of physical capital. As new capital is put in place, the MPK declines, as does q. Investment becomes smaller and installation costs φ decline until they become negligible. At that stage $q = 1$, $\text{MPK} = 1 + r$, and the stock of capital

is at its optimal level. Installation costs cause firms to move towards the optimal capital stock incrementally. Along the way the return on investment in present value terms exceeds the replacement, or user, cost of capital.[20] Box 8.7 provides more details on both the user cost of capital and its relationship to Tobin's q.

The geometry of installation costs

Installation costs have two particular properties. First, they increase with the size of the investment. Big steps are proportionally more expensive than small ones. Second, they are transitory. Once the equipment is in place, the only relevant cost is the interest rate and depreciation—the opportunity cost of resources employed in production. Figure 8.15 modifies panel (b) of Figure 8.12 in two ways. First, investment is measured on the horizontal axis as the investment rate I/K, which gives a better indication of the intensity of disruptions which give

---

[19] We cheat a bit here. The definition of Tobin's q is based on the market value of firms, while what matters in theory is the *marginal* return on investment. The market value of firms depends on the *average* return on all capital, not just the latest addition. We overlook the difference between these two definitions of average and marginal q.

[20] A related approach, pioneered by Professors Finn Kydland of University of California, Santa Barbara and Edward Prescott of University of Arizona, stresses that it takes time to design, acquire, and put in place new equipment. The implications are similar to those of installation costs.

Box 8.7 **User Cost of Capital, Tobin's q, and the Price of Investment Goods**

In Robinson Crusoe's world, coconuts were used for both consumption and investment. In the real world, investment and consumption goods have different prices. This complicates slightly, but does not invalidate, the main line of reasoning. Let us suppose that a coconut in the ground (investment) is identical to a coconut in the mouth (consumption), but in the second period, the tree can be sold for p^K in terms of the consumption good. Now, profit in units of the consumption good is

$$(8.16) \qquad \text{profit} = \frac{F(K)}{1+r} - (1 - \delta)p^k K.$$

The optimal stock of capital will obey a modified version of (8.9) in Box 8.6:

$$(8.17) \quad \text{MPK} = (1 + r) - (1 - \delta)p^K$$
$$= [(1 + r) - (1 - \delta)(1 + \Pi^K)] \approx r + \delta - \Pi^K,$$

where $\Pi^K = p^K - 1$ is the rate of price increase for investment goods.[21] The user cost concept of Box 8.6 allows for a changing relative price of investment goods over time. An increase in the real interest rate and depreciation lowers optimal investment, all things being equal. An increase in the rate of change of investment goods

prices *increases* it. Why? By selling his investment, Crusoe reduces the effective cost of using the capital goods in production. It is easy to see that any government policy which increases the resale value of the investment, including tax breaks, will similarly reduce the user cost of capital.

Similar to equation (8.12), a reasonable approximation of Tobin's q is

$$(8.18) \qquad q = \frac{\text{MPK}/(r + \delta - \pi^K)}{1}.$$

The only difference is that the extended version of Tobin's q now compares the present discounted value of the marginal product of capital with the value of new capital goods, the price of investment goods, which is equal to 1 in the first period.

Finally, if installation costs ϕ are paid for a marginal unit of investment, optimal investment must obey

$$(8.19) \qquad q = \text{MPK}/(r + \delta - \pi^K) = (1 + \varphi).$$

At any point in time, the marginal gain from an additional unit of capital equals the marginal costs of that new capital, which includes the installation costs of investment.

rise to installation costs.[22] Second, on the vertical axis, marginal costs and returns are expressed in today's present discounted values. The marginal cost of capital in present value is equal to 1, because one unit of capital implies giving up one unit of consumption good today.

The horizontal schedule represents the cost of investment in the absence of installation costs. With installation costs, the cost of investment exceeds the cost of capital. The more equipment is put in place, the higher is the marginal cost. Hence the upward-sloping marginal cost of investment curve. The marginal return on investment is

MPK/(1 + r). It is downward sloping because of the principle of declining marginal productivity.

Firms invest until the marginal cost equals the marginal return at point A in panel (a) of Figure 8.15, where the two curves intersect. The value of an additional unit of capital installed—Tobin's q—exceeds the replacement cost of capital. Without installation costs, the firm would choose point C instead and invest more. It may be surprising that the marginal return is higher with installation costs than without them. Rather than reducing the long-term profitability of investment, installation costs simply induce firms to invest at a slower rate. In the long run, firms achieve the same desired capital stock as in the absence of adjustment costs.

Panel (b) of Figure 8.15 shows how the investment rate moves over time. With q above 1, investment first occurs at rate $(I/K)_1$ corresponding to point A. Each MPK schedule is drawn for a given stock of already

---

[21] The expression $(1 + r) - (1 - \delta)(1 + \Pi^K) = r + \delta - \Pi^K + \delta\Pi^K$ is well approximated by $r + \delta - \Pi^K$ for small values of r, δ, and Π^K.

[22] In the absence of depreciation, $I/K = \Delta K/K$. Focusing on the investment rate is justified by the idea that a given amount of investment is more disruptive in a small firm (or economy) than in a large one.

installed capital. Moving along the schedule, we find the profitability of further additions to the existing capital stock. Once the capital stock has increased as a result of investment, however, these additions become less productive—because of the principle of declining marginal productivity. So, as further investment accumulates, the MPK schedule shifts downwards in the figure, from MPK_1 to MPK_2.[23] Investment will continue as long as Tobin's q is greater than unity, but will do so at a declining rate, here at rate $(I/K)_2$ corresponding to point B. The process will continue until q is driven back down to 1 and the capital stock has reached its long-run, optimal level.

8.3.6 The Investment Function

The investment function summarizes all the macroeconomic relationships that have been developed until now in a convenient and compact way. First, investment is inversely related to the interest rate because it measures the opportunity cost of the resources invested. Higher interest rates imply lower investment spending. Second, the accelerator mechanism captures the stable long-run relationship between the capital stock and output. Since the rate of proportionality is greater than 1, increases in output lead to magnified increases in investment expenditures. Finally, Tobin's q reflects the fact that some firms finance investment expenditures by issuing shares on the stock market. High stock prices mean that the market places a high value on existing, installed capital, so firms can raise more resources per share issued, and this encourages investment. They provide a central indicator of the market's assessment of the profitability of new investment. Because a higher interest rate discounts future profits more heavily and reduces q. Tobin's q also incorporates some but not all of the effect of real interest rates on investment (for firms that raise money by issuing bonds or borrowing from banks, it is the interest rate alone that represents the cost of investment). These results can be summarized by the following investment function, which will be used in various forms throughout the book:

$$(8.20) \qquad I = I(r, \Delta Y, q).$$
$$- \quad + \quad +$$

This function states that investment depends negatively on the real interest rate r, positively on the change in GDP, and positively on Tobin's q.[24] Holding interest rates constant, an increase in Tobin's q increases investment.

❗ Summary

1 Rational consumers attempt to smooth consumption over time, borrowing in bad years, saving in good ones. Consumption is driven primarily by wealth, the present discounted value of current and future incomes, and initial net asset holdings. Over a life cycle, income typically increases. To smooth out consumption, agents typically borrow when young and pay back later.

2 Individual consumption smoothing means that, in the aggregate, temporary disturbances are met by current account imbalances (national saving or dissaving) to reduce the need to adjust

---

[23] The observant student will note that for linear marginal product and marginal cost schedules and in the absence of depreciation, the intercept of each successive MPK curve with the vertical axis is determined by the value of q in the preceding period.

[24] In theory, Tobin's q should contain all information necessary about the profitability of investment. Since many firms finance investment with retained earnings or by borrowing, the interest rate also matters directly. In addition, as with households, many firms are rationed on the credit market, so they have to rely upon current income to finance spending on productive equipment. This would rationalize a third term related to the discussion of the accelerator in Section 8.3.3.

consumption abruptly. In contrast, permanent disturbances lead to immediate consumption adjustment rather than to borrowing or lending.

3 The world is uncertain and financial markets are imperfect. Uncertainty about future incomes and the inability of banks to assess individual future prospects without error will make it difficult if not impossible for some households to borrow against future expected income. For these households, current disposable income also affects aggregate consumption.

4 The effect of changes in the real interest rate on current consumption is ambiguous. Lenders tend to increase, while borrowers decrease, consumption in response to increases in the interest rate. In the aggregate, however, higher interest rates are likely to reduce consumption by reducing wealth.

5 The consumption function relates aggregate consumption to wealth (positively) and disposable income (positively).

6 The optimal capital stock equates the marginal productivity of capital to the marginal cost of capital. The optimal capital stock increases when the real interest rate declines and when technological gains raise the marginal productivity of capital.

7 Investment over and above capital depreciation increases the capital stock. As is the case with the optimal capital stock, investment is driven by the real interest rate.

8 The accelerator mechanism links investment to changes in output. This is both a mechanical

relationship (in the long run the capital output ratio is constant) and a symptom of credit rationing.

9 The ratio of the market value of installed capital to the replacement cost of installed capital is called Tobin's q. It is an approximation of the ratio of the present discounted value of the marginal return of investment to the marginal cost of capital. This ratio is equal to unity when the capital stock has reached its optimal level. When Tobin's q is larger than unity, the capital stock is below its optimal level and firms benefit from further investment.

10 The market value of installed capital, the numerator in Tobin's q, is priced in the stock market. In setting this price, stock markets look ahead. The forward-looking nature of Tobin's q mirrors how firms take into account expected future earnings when they make investment decisions.

11 Because of various installation costs, firms do not acquire their optimal capital stock immediately. Rather, they spread investment over time, gradually bringing capital up to the optimal level.

12 The present discounted return to investment exceeds the marginal cost of capital to compensate for installation costs. Investment proceeds until the present value of its return, at the margin, equals the marginal cost of investment, the sum of borrowing and installation costs.

13 The investment function states that aggregate investment depends upon: (1) the real interest rate (negatively); (2) GDP growth (positively); (3) Tobin's q (positively).

⊙ Key Concepts

◆ **consumption function**

◆ **investment function**

◆ **indifference curves**

◆ **utility**

◆ **marginal rate of intertemporal substitution**

◆ **life-cycle consumption**

◆ **permanent income**

◆ **random walk**

- ◆ consumption smoothing
- ◆ credit rationed
- ◆ marginal productivity of capital (MPK)
- ◆ opportunity cost
- ◆ marginal cost of capital
- ◆ optimal capital stock
- ◆ rate of depreciation

- ◆ user cost of capital
- ◆ accelerator principle
- ◆ Tobin's q
- ◆ q-theory of investment
- ◆ animal spirits
- ◆ installation costs

❓ Exercises

1 A household has income of £10,000 today and £50,000 tomorrow.

 (a) If the real interest rate is 5%, what is its wealth (i) in terms of today's consumption, (ii) in terms of tomorrow's consumption? Compute the household's permanent income (see Box 8.2).

 (b) If today's income unexpectedly increases by £1000, what is the change in permanent income?

 (c) If income goes up by £1000 permanently (in both periods), what is the effect on permanent income?

 (d) Now answer the same questions with a 10% real interest rate.

 (e) Suppose the utility of the household is given by $\log(C_1) + \beta\log(C_2)$, where β is a positive constant less than 1. Derive optimal consumption today and tomorrow for (a), (b), (c), and (d).

2 Show, graphically, the effects on current and future consumption of an income windfall gain expected in the future. Now apply this reasoning to the national level. How should a consumer react to a tax cut that is announced to be temporary (in period 1 only). How would consumers react to an expected future tax cut?

3 Define the permanent income hypothesis. How does it relate to the more general theory of consumption under intertemporal utility maximization?

4 Suppose you expect to live for six decades. Your income is €15,000 in the first, €100,000 in the second, €150,000 in the third, €250,000 in the fourth, €200,000 in the fifth, and €100,000 in the last. What is your permanent income if the interest rate is 3%? 5%? If you consume your permanent income each year, what does your savings pattern look like? How does your answer change if you decide to bequeath £50,000 to your favourite charity?

5 Should a temporary increase in taxes to finance a temporary increase in public spending reduce the current account deficit? What about a permanent increase in both taxes and public spending? What is the effect on the current account in an open economy?

6 Countries which adopted the euro recently—Slovenia, Cyprus, and Malta—saw a drop in interest rates for domestic and international borrowing. Using the Fisher diagram, trace out the theoretical effect of lower world interest rates on consumption and investment in these borrowing countries. What do you expect the effect to be on the (primary) current account? State your assumptions carefully.

7 There is evidence that spending on durable goods drops faster than spending on non-durables during a recession. Can you give some economic reasons why? (Hint: think of durable goods expenditure as a form of saving.)

8 A company is considering expanding its computer equipment today by €50,000. Suppose the interest rate used in discounting future profit is 10%, and suppose that the equipment is scrapped after one period.

(a) If the new investment generates €60,000 of profit, should the company undertake the investment? How does your answer change if the firm only expects to earn €54,000?

(b) Now suppose the equipment can be sold on the resale market for €15,000. How does your answer change? Discuss how the emergence of a more efficient resale market (eBay, etc.) could increase investment.

9 Governments sometimes try to stimulate the economy by offering firms a temporary tax credit. Firms that purchase capital goods before a deadline receive a tax reduction on income made in the next year. Explain why this measure should increase expenditures on investment. Would you expect a permanent or a temporary measure to have more effect?

10 Suppose a firm produces Y_2 output in period 2 using the production function $Y_2 = A\log(K_1)$, where K_1 is the capital in place in period 1. Suppose the firm has no outlays besides K_1, the price of output is given at p_2, and that $(1 - \delta)$ of the capital can be resold for p_2^K per unit. Future outlays and revenues are discounted at rate r.

(a) Write down a mathematical expression for the profits of the firm. How do profits depend on p_2? On p_2^K? On δ? On r? On A? On K_1? Use informal arguments, a spreadsheet, or calculus to explain your answer.

(b) Use calculus to find the optimal stock of capital K_1 as function of p_2, p_2^K, δ, r, and A.

(c) Now suppose the same firm can instead *rent* capital at rate U for one period, after which the capital must be returned to the rental agency. Write down a mathematical expression for the profits of the firm. At what point should the firm be indifferent between renting and 'owning' the capital it uses?

→ Essay Questions

1 A great deal of debate has arisen in Germany on the financing of the expenditure necessary to improve the much neglected infrastructure in its new eastern states. One side favours increased taxes, which would fall largely on households. The other side favours an increased budget deficit. Which side is right? How important is it to know whether the spending increase is permanent or temporary?

2 Should wars—temporarily but abnormally high expenditures of the government—depress or raise consumption of households? In formulating your answer, think about all the budget constraints discussed in Chapter 7.

3 Over the past 20 years the price of computers and software—an essential investment good for modern companies—has dropped steadily. At the same time, the rapid rate of technical change has increased the rate of obsolescence of equipment and programs. In addition, the development of new service companies has made it easier to install and employ these new innovations. Explain, carefully, using the concepts you have learned, how these developments should affect the user cost of capital, Tobin's q, and investment.

4 In 2006, the consensus among US economists was that an additional dollar of household wealth would lead to about $0.05 of additional consumption. Between 2000 and 2006, the value of financial assets held by households fell slightly, while the value of house prices almost doubled. Can this help explain why real US consumption grew by 3% per annum during this period, although GDP only rose by 2.4% on average over the same period? What are the implications, for the recent collapse of house prices for consumption and savings of US households?

5 Booming economies frequently show negative current account balances. International organizations like the International Monetary Fund often must judge whether a current deficit is 'good' or 'bad'. Explain what this might mean or imply. Use your answer to interpret the case of Poland: in the period 2003–2007 Poland grew 5.1% per annum, as compared to 2.4% in the EU. During this period the current account deficit was 2.6% of GDP, declining from an average deficit of 4.6% of GDP in the period 1998–2002.

Money and Monetary Policy $\quad$ 9

The invention of a circulating medium, which supersedes the narrow, cumbrous process of barter, by facilitating transactions of every variety of importance among all sorts of people, is a grand type of advance in civilization.

Chambers's *Encyclopedia*, 1870

First of all let me state the simple fact that when you deposit money in a bank, the bank does not put the money into a safe deposit vault. It invests your money in many different forms of credit—bonds, commercial paper, mortgages and many other kinds of loans. In other words, the bank puts your money to work to keep the wheels of industry and of agriculture turning around. A comparatively small part of the money you put into the bank is kept in currency—an amount which in normal times is wholly sufficient to cover the cash needs of the average citizen. In other words the total amount of all the currency in the country is only a comparatively small proportion of the total deposits in all of the banks.

Franklin D. Roosevelt[1]

9.1 Overview

We have already encountered money in Chapter 6, when we established the neutrality principle, but we never really explained what it is, who makes it, how, and for what purpose. This is what the present chapter does. It seems strange to have to explain something that we use every day, yet it is surprising how little most people understand what it is. Seventy-five years ago, in the wake of a national banking panic, US President Roosevelt was forced to explain to nervous American citizens how a bank works and why they shouldn't withdraw their money all at once from their accounts. Then, as now, the system of money and banking is rather complicated, and is in a state of constant change.

Virtually every civilization has used one form of money or another, and money has been at the centre of attention in civilizations since the beginning of recorded history. Money is a form of wealth but it has a number of special qualities. Its return is typically very low—banknotes yield no interest at all—and yet it is perceived as desirable. The reason is that money uniquely facilitates commercial transactions, big and small alike. As a result, it lies at the heart of any economy.

We will start by defining money. We will then look at the supply of money and introduce an important institution with great influence over the supply of money: the central bank. The obvious next step is to study the demand for money. When this is done, we will be equipped to see how demand and supply are equilibrated in the money market, how that market works. This will take us straight to a detailed study of **monetary policy**, the way the central bank sets the interest rate or other conditions in the money market. Monetary policy affects the daily economic life of everyone in many ways. We will see that the practice of monetary policy has evolved over the years, marked sometimes by great progress, other times by adverse setbacks. In developed countries, the current conventional wisdom argues for a strategy called inflation targeting. Having thus mastered the basics of modern monetary policy, we conclude the chapter with a discussion of why banking is risky, why it crucially matters for the economy and what can be done to avert financial crises, and what to do when they occur.

---

[1] US President Franklin D. Roosevelt, in a national radio address on 12 March 1933, see <http://millercenter.org/scripps/archive/speeches/detail/3298>.

9.2 Money: What is it? Who Makes it?

9.2.1 Definitions of Money

Most of us would agree that banknotes and coins are money. But what about bank account balances? Travellers' cheques? Savings accounts? Other financial instruments? These are all various forms of money, most of which have been invented fairly recently. Once upon a time, gold, silver, and other commodities were used as money in the form of coins, sometimes bulky ingots. Slowly but surely, paper money (banknotes) have edged out these **commodity monies**. Paper money backed by commodity money became the dominant form of money by the end of the nineteenth century. In the beginning of the twentieth century, central banks began issuing paper money and coins that were not backed by any precious metal. Devoid of any intrinsic value, **fiat money**—from the Latin word '*fiat*' meaning 'let it be done'—is legal tender simply because of the government decision. Money changed again with the widespread use of sight deposits, or bank deposits which can be converted into cash on demand, or with plastic cards which give more rapid and secure access to money.

A century or so ago, there were doubts whether paper money could ever be as trustworthy as coins made from precious metals. Today, we use it to pay for whatever we want to buy without really wondering about its lack of intrinsic value. As a matter of fact, we use less and less notes and coins, relying instead on plastic cards and cheques, both of which are debited from our bank accounts, as well as on internet transfers at our home computers.

Because most of us see little difference between coins, banknotes, and bank deposits, this is a rationale for our first definition of money: currency in circulation plus sight deposits (bank accounts that are payable on demand, often called demand deposits or current accounts). This **monetary aggregate** is denominated as M1:

M1 = currency in circulation + sight bank deposits.

Sight deposits at banks have three main characteristics: (1) they may be converted into cash on demand at the issuing bank, (2) cheques can be written or bank transfers can be made against them, and (3) the interest paid is either nil or very low. They are convenient for everyday purchases, but not very attractive from the point of view of interest. This is why banks often offer other types of accounts that bear higher interest rates, but whose funds cannot be used as easily as normal money—i.e. by writing cheques or stopping at a cash dispenser. Yet such funds can often be conveniently transferred into regular sight deposits—often a phone call, a series of key-strokes on a telephone handset, or an internet connection is enough. Ease of transfer renders these assets very similar to sight deposits in the eyes of their holders. This is why they are included in a broader definition of money, M2:

M2 = M1 + time (or savings) deposits at banks
       with unrestricted access.

An even broader measure includes instruments such as large certificates of deposit, or time deposits with a longer term and possibly restricted access, foreign currency deposits, and deposits with non-bank institutions. The precise meaning of 'larger' and 'longer maturity' depends on national rules and regulations. The distinction is one of degree: these instruments are less liquid, meaning that they are more costly or difficult to convert into cash or current accounts. Thus the definition of M3:

M3 = M2 + larger, fixed-term deposits
       + accounts at non-bank institutions.

M1 is perfectly liquid, meaning that it can be used for commercial transactions, unlike the other components of M2 and M3, which must generally be converted into M1 for that purpose.

Every country has its own practices and its own definitions of monetary aggregates. While not fully comparable, the examples in Table 9.1—M0 is explained below—show that, in the UK, people

		Currency	M0	M1	M2	M3
UK	(£ bn)	32.9	41.5	874.8	1483.6	1716.4
	as % GDP	2.6	3.0	63.5	107.7	124.6
Euro area	(€ bn)	592.1	1073.3	3746.8	6811.8	8002.0
	as % GDP	6.8	12.3	43.0	78.1	91.8
USA	($ bn)	755.0	793.0	1366.8	7249.9	
	as % GDP	5.5	5.8	9.9	52.7	
Poland	(Zl bn)	57.4	73.4	295.9	506.8	521.4
	as % GDP	5.2	6.6	26.5	45.3	46.6

Table 9.1 Money in Three Countries, 2007

Notes: Currency in the UK and in Poland: 2006. The USA no longer publishes M3 figures.
Source: IMF, central banks' bulletins.

use less cash than on the continent and in the USA, but that the other monetary aggregates are proportionately larger—a sign of more sophisticated retail banking. Indeed, in Poland, the difference between M2 and M3 is small, suggesting that customers do not yet have access to higher-yield bank deposits.

The pace of technological development in banking has revolutionized the definition of money over the past century, yet more change is possibly in store. Many believe we are not far from the limit of this process, a cashless society that the Swedish economist Knut Wicksell once imagined and which is described in Box 9.1. From now on, we will refer to

Box 9.1 The Vision of Wicksell: A Cashless Society

Once upon a time, money was gold or silver, or seashells, or large stones on South Pacific islands. Such commodity money has an intrinsic value, since it is made of goods that can be used for other purposes. These goods are 'wasted' when used as money, and this is one reason why paper and cheap metal have replaced silver or gold. A century ago, the Swedish economist Knut Wicksell (1851–1926) went further. He asked: Why have money at all? He envisioned a central record keeper who would keep a tally of all credits and debits. Whenever an individual worked, his balance would be credited; whenever he spent, the balance would be debited. In principle, it would be possible to run a negative balance, i.e. to borrow from the system. In the end, instead of producing currency, the central bank would operate and guarantee this record-keeping system and determine the value of the unit of account.

At the time, Wicksell's moneyless society was dismissed as impractical science fiction. A century later, the technical problems of establishing such a 'moneyless society' have been largely solved. Large powerful computers can keep accurate, up-to-date records and investigate the creditworthiness of households and businesses. The year 2003 was a watershed. For the first time, US consumers paid more for goods and services using credit and debit cards than with cheques or cash. A number of experiments are being run to test for payment systems that could all but eliminate currency. Similar increases are expected soon in Europe, especially in France and the UK, where credit and debit cards are commonplace.

money without being specific about its definition, calling it simply M and thinking of it as:

M = currency in circulation + bank deposits.

9.2.2 The Money Makers: Central and Commercial Banks

Table 9.1 shows that currency (coins and banknotes) is but a small fraction of what we call money, regardless of the definition we use. Bank deposits make up the rest. This part of what we call money is produced by the monetary authorities—the central bank and/or the Treasury—while the bigger part, bank deposits, is created by commercial banks.

Can it be that most of what we routinely consider money is actually created by private institutions? The answer is yes. Most of modern money, often seen as a symbol of statehood, is not directly produced by the government. But then, can banks create money as they wish? Ultimately the answer is no. Banks do create money but under the control and supervision of the central bank. This is what we now examine.

Central banks

The central bank is a public or quasi-public agency with an explicit, exclusive legal mandate to control money and credit conditions.[2] It is also the 'bankers' bank'. Commercial banks—in some countries, the largest ones only—hold their own accounts at the central bank. They can use these accounts to settle payments against other commercial banks, for example, when customers transfer funds from one bank to another. Central banks generally do not take deposits from the private sector, but most serve as their respective government's bank.

Central banks produce two sorts of monies. They issue currency (sometimes, this is done on its behalf by the Treasury) and, as we will see, they also create **bank reserves**, the deposits held by commercial banks at the central bank. The sum of currency in circulation and commercial bank reserves is known as the **monetary base**, sometimes called M0.[3] Table 9.1 shows that M0 is not much larger than the amount of currency in circulation, implying that the reserves of commercial banks are relatively small. Yet, these reserves are the tool through which central banks control money creation by commercial banks.

Commercial banks

Traditionally, commercial banks collect funds from depositors and grant loans to their customers. In effect, they channel money from depositors to borrowers. This is why they are also called **financial intermediaries**. Over recent years, banks have taken on additional functions, like managing portfolios on behalf of their customers or providing insurance, but we will ignore these activities.

When you deposit money in your bank on a sight deposit, you consider that your money is there, waiting for you to withdraw or spend it whenever you fancy to do so. Reality is very different. Most likely, the money that you have deposited has promptly been lent to another customer. For the bank, your deposit is a liability of immediate or short maturity. It is due immediately if it is a sight deposit, or soon, say three months or one year. The bank may lend to customers who buy cars or houses or to firms which buy inventories, purchases, or wages, which can be paid back over several years. These loans are the bank's assets, and they tend to be of much longer maturity than its liabilities. The practice of taking on short-term liabilities and using them to acquire long-term assets is called **maturity transformation**. It is common practice among banks but is a fundamentally risky activity.

To see why, it is useful to present a snapshot of the state of a bank's financial operations, its **balance sheet**. The balance sheet is a summary statement of what the bank owns—its assets—and what it

---

[2] The Bank of England was a private institution from its founding in 1694 until its nationalization in 1946, much like the Banque de France, founded in 1800 and nationalized in 1945. The Bundesbank was established in 1949 as a successor to the Deutsche Reichsbank founded in 1876. The oldest central bank is the Swedish Riksbank, founded in 1668. Other dates of foundation are: Bank of Japan, 1882; Banca d'Italia, 1893; Austrian National Bank, 1816; Swiss National Bank, 1905. The Federal Reserve of the USA was founded in 1913 and is owned by the member banks, although profits above a statutory maximum are remitted, as in most countries, to the government (Goodhart 1988).

[3] Other expressions used are 'high-powered', 'base money', or 'central bank money'.

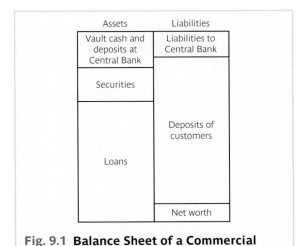

Fig. 9.1 Balance Sheet of a Commercial Bank

owes—its liabilities. Figure 9.1 gives a simplified version of the balance sheet of a typical bank. The balance sheet shows that the primary liability is the deposits of its customers. Additionally, the bank may have borrowed from the central bank. On the asset side, a commercial bank keeps some cash in its vaults or as a deposit with the central bank. It also holds various securities that can be traded on financial markets. Its main activity, however, is to make loans. These loans are assets since they are owed to the bank by its customers. The excess of assets over liabilities is the bank's net worth. It shows up as a liability since it is owed by the bank to its owners, typically shareholders.

To see why maturity transformation can be risky business, imagine that all customers of a bank wanted suddenly to withdraw all the money that they had deposited. Since most of the money has been lent out, it is no longer in the bank (recall the radio address of US President Roosevelt at the beginning of this chapter!). Yet those deposits are means of payment, and represent perfect substitutes for cash which the bank is legally obligated to convert to currency. Such a widespread conversion at short notice would be impossible. In the unlikely event that it happens, a phenomenon called a **bank run** or **bank failure** occurs: the bank is unable to meet its obligations and it must close, leaving angry customers pounding at the door.[4] Because of this risk, banks tend to be tightly regulated and supervised by governmental authorities. We will encounter some of these regulations later on in this chapter.

9.2.3 Money Creation by Commercial Banks

An even more interesting and less well-understood fact about banks is that they actually *create* money when they grant loans. To see why, consider the case of Ms A who receives €1,000 in cash from abroad and deposits in her bank, Bank No. 1.[5] Looking for a profitable use for these funds, Bank No. 1 lends this money as soon as possible to Mr B, another trustworthy customer. Mr B needs the money to buy a sofa. Soon enough, the €1,000, initially deposited by Ms A, will be handed over to the store that sold the sofa to Mr B. The store owner now owns this €1,000. Ms A too owns €1,000. As far as she is concerned, her money is in the bank. In fact, she owns a deposit in her bank which is backed by a loan in the amount of €1,000, but the €1,000 in currency is long gone. Effectively, the €1,000 now has two owners: Ms A and Mr B! And the story is not over. The sofa store owner will deposit the money in his own account at Bank No. 2, which will quickly lend it to Ms C, who will spend it to buy a laptop for her business. The computer store will rightfully think that it possesses an additional €1,000. That means we now have three owners of the same money! There is no reason to stop here, of course. The conclusion is that each loan amounts to the creation of new money, and that the process can seemingly go on and on. But it will end.

To see why the process of credit and money creation does in fact stop, imagine that Ms A wants her money back, say to take a vacation abroad. Will Bank No. 1 admit to her that the money is gone and will only be back in two years' time? Surely not!

---

4 The spectacular failure of Northern Rock bank in the autumn of 2007 in the UK is a recent example of a bank run. Bank runs are rare events in most countries—the previous one in the UK took place more than 140 years ago. They will be examined in more detail in Section 9.5.

5 The money could also come from under her mattress, or a treasure chest. The important fact is that it represents an injection of cash (currency) from outside the banking system.

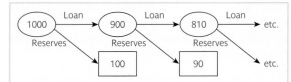

Fig. 9.2 The Money Multiplier

An initial deposit triggers a succession of loans, paid in the form of deposits. When the bank keeps 10% of any deposit as reserves (cash or deposit at the central bank), each loan is 90% of the previous one. Thus the chain of loans and deposits eventually dies out.

Bank No. 1 will have anticipated this possibility. Note first that someone down the chain is likely to be a Bank No. 1 customer, so that at least some of the initial €1,000 will come back. If Bank No. 1 were the only bank in the country and if people never held currency, the money would always come back. In practice, because there are many other banks and because people keep some money in cash, so Bank No. 1 knows that it cannot rely on returning monies to pay back Ms A. But the bank also has many other customers and it knows that they tend to keep a big part of the sums that they deposit on their accounts for a long time. On average, Ms A is not expected to withdraw all of the money that she initially deposited.

If the bank figures out that, say, only 10% of the sums deposited will be withdrawn at any point of time, all it needs to do is to keep 10% on deposits and can lend out the rest. In the case of Ms A's deposit, the bank will keep €100 in cash and lend the remaining €900. In that case, the initial amount of money created is only €900. After it is deposited in Bank No. 2, a new loan of €810 (this is €900 less 10%), will be arranged, and the process will go on as shown in Figure 9.2. At each step, the amount of newly created money declines by 10%. After a while, it will have become tiny. This is why the money creation process is not infinite. A little bit of algebra tells us that the initial €1,000 will lead to a succession of loans that add up to €9,000:[6]

$$€900 + €810 + €729 + €656.1 + \ldots = €9,000$$

There is another side to this story. Bank No. 1 received €1,000 and put aside €100. Bank No. 2 received €900 and put aside €90, Bank No. 2 received €729 and put aside €72.9, etc. Jointly, all banks put aside €1,000.[7] In the end, the initial €1,000 has led to a series of loans for a total of €9,000 and to the setting aside of €1,000. It all worked as if the €1,000 were fully set aside (more cash in the vaults) by the banking system taken together to support the creation of new money for a total of €9,000 (shown in the asset side in Figure 9.1). On the liability side, deposits increased by €10,000 as well: the initial €1,000 deposits and the €9,000 loans which have been credited to customers' accounts.

This chain of money and credit creation is known as the **money multiplier** process. It says that any time new money is injected in the economy—here we assumed that the initial €1,000 came from abroad—the result is a manifold increase in money stock. This process explains two fundamental characteristics of modern fiat money systems. First, as we just saw, money is created by private commercial banks as they grant loans to their private customers. Second, as we explain next section, central banks can still control the size of the money stock.

The new money is created 'at the stroke of a pen'—this old-fashioned expression is better described as a series of keystrokes in the bank's computerized accounting systems. Effectively, the money is 'backed' by trust in the banks—trust in the underlying value of the loans and securities on the asset side of the banks' balance sheets. Money only has value as long as those assets have adequate value.

Deposits, bank liabilities which represent the largest component of money, are guaranteed by bank assets. Cash and securities are generally considered safe. Loans in contrast are as good as the borrowing customers' willingness and ability to repay. They are not fully safe. To cushion against the risk that loans might lose value, banks' owners are required to maintain a minimum amount of

---

[6] If a proportion p is lent at each step, the sum of all loans made is $1,000p + 1,000p^2 + 1,000p^3 + \ldots = 1,000p(1 + p + p^2 + p^3 + \ldots) = 1,000p/(1 - p)$. If $p = 0.9$, we find indeed 9,000.

[7] Continuing to denote the proportion that is lent at each step by p, the amounts put aside are $1,000(1 - p) + 1,000p(1 - p) + 1,000p^2(1 - p) + \ldots = 1,000(1 - p)[1 + p + p^2 + \ldots] = 1,000(1 - p)/(1 - p) = 1,000$.

Table 9.2 Reserve Ratio Requirements in Selected Countries

Country	Deposits subject to reserve requirements	Compulsory reserve ratio requirement
Denmark	Short-term (one month) liabilities	15%
	Total liabilities	10%
Czech Republic	Deposits of less than two-year maturity	2%
Euro area	Deposits up to 2 years maturity	2%
Hungary	All deposits	5%
Poland	All deposits	3.5%
Sweden	None	
Switzerland	None	
UK	None	
USA	'Transaction accounts' in excess of $44m	10%

capital (net worth) in their balance sheets. These so-called Basel requirements impose minimal **capital adequacy**. When the value of loans declines on the asset side, the net worth can decline on the liability side without fully disappearing. If it did, the bank would effectively be bankrupt.

9.2.4 Central Bank Control of the Money Supply

In the previous example, commercial banks set aside 10% of any money deposited on their customers' accounts. Presumably, they kept it in the form of cash—which often requires an expensive and secure (theft-proof) vault. The more convenient alternative to this is to deposit these amounts with the central bank. Much like households and firms hold sight-deposit accounts with commercial banks, commercial banks also hold—usually if they are large enough—sight-deposit accounts at their central banks. They can draw on these accounts to receive cash. In effect, these are two equivalent forms of commercial bank **reserves**.

Commercial   =   cash held   + bank deposits at
bank reserves   in bank vaults   the central bank.

Together with the amount of currency in circulation, the bank reserves constitute the monetary base M0:

monetary base M0 = currency in circulation
+ commercial bank reserves.

The proportion of deposits set aside in the form of bank reserves is called the **reserve ratio**.[8] We presented it as a prudential measure taken by banks to be able to pay out requests of withdrawals by customers. In some countries, banks are free to choose their reserve ratios; in others, the reserve ratio is imposed by the central bank. Table 9.2 provides some examples.

In the previous example, the initial bank deposit by Ms A came from abroad. This happens, of course, much as some domestic currency is sent abroad (we will examine the implications of this in Chapter 11). In general, however, new money is created domestically. The story starts when Mr D requests a loan of, say, €1,000 from his bank. As the bank grants the loan, it simultaneously creates an account for Mr D and credits it with €1,000. As before, money is created by banks hand in hand with lending activities. The only hitch is that the new loan, hence the new deposit, immediately raises the amount of reserves that the bank wants or needs to hold. If the reserve ratio is 10%, the bank must find an additional amount of reserves of €100.

---

[8] In some countries, it is called the liquidity requirement.

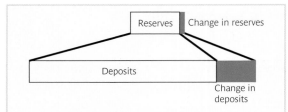

Fig. 9.3 The Reserves–Money Stock Link
When reserves are a constant proportion (*rr*) of deposits
($R = rrD$), deposits cannot grow without an increase in
reserves. Conversely, a change in reserves *DR* allows
banks to increase their deposits—by granting loans—
in much larger amounts. The reserve multiplier is the
inverse of the reserve ratio.

Most likely, the bank will not have these extra reserves at hand. But banks have an incentive to lend
as much as they can while holding as few reserves as
they must. This is where the reserve ratio kicks in.
Whether it is imposed by law or simply chosen for
prudential purposes, the reserve ratio *rr* implies
that reserves must be at least a fraction of deposits,
which can be formally stated as follows:

(9.1)   reserves $\geq rr \times$ deposits.

Since banks have an incentive to hold exactly the
amount of reserves that they need, not more, as a first
approximation, the inequality can be thought of
an equality:

(9.1′)   reserves $= rr \times$ deposits.

It is represented in Figure 9.3 as the pyramid linking reserves to existing deposits. But the figure may
also be read in reverse: the volume of deposits
cannot exceed a multiple of existing reserves. Rearranging (9.1) results in:

(9.2)   deposits $\leq (1/rr) \times$ reserves.

The factor $(1/rr)$ is often called the *reserve multiplier*.[9]
Equation (9.2) means that together, commercial
banks cannot expand their deposits, i.e. money creation beyond a multiple of existing reserves. If, as
in the previous example, $rr = 10\%$, then $1/rr = 100$,
which explains why reserves are rather small, as we

noted earlier when looking at Table 9.1. If (9.1)
holds as an equality, then (9.2) does as well, and we
now have

(9.2′)   deposits $= (1/rr) \times$ reserves,

which states that, by deciding on reserves, the central bank can control total bank deposits. Since
M = currency in circulation + bank deposits and
the central bank precisely sets currency in circulation, central banks can control the money supply.
How, central banks control reserves in practice is
our next topic.

9.2.5 Creation of Bank Reserves by the Central Bank

When you go to your bank and ask for a loan, it may
be the case that fresh loanable money in exactly the
right amount had just been deposited in cash by
some other customer. The bank is also unlikely to
tell you that you have to wait until adequate cash
deposits have been made by others before a loan is
possible (banks never do this). In fact, because it
knows you and your creditworthiness, your bank
may think it good business to lend you money that
it does not have! It will simply credit your bank
account (with that bank) by the amount that you
asked for—all assuming, of course, that you are
willing to pay back principal and interest over some
agreed-upon period. In that moment, new money is
created. In fact, this is very similar to the money
creation process described in Section 9.2.3. Box 9.2
explains why.

The next step is for the bank to set aside the corresponding amount of reserves (*rr* times your loan).
One possibility is for your bank to borrow the
required reserves from the central bank.[10] If the
central bank agrees, it will simply credit the reserve
account of your bank and thus create the reserves that
are needed. In the end, your bank created money by
depositing the amount of your loan of your account
and the central bank created reserves by depositing a proportion *rr* of your loan into your bank's
account. Easy!

---

9   Since reserves are a (small) fraction of deposits, *rr* is less than
   one. Then $1/rr$ is (much) larger than one.

10 We will see in Section 9.3.1 that the more likely step for an
   individual bank is simply to borrow those reserves from
   some other banks that neither need them nor wish to lend
   them to customers—so-called excess reserves.

Box 9.2 The Two Equivalent Money Creation Processes

In Section 9.2.3 we showed one way for commercial banks to create money. In this section we showed an apparently different way for banks to create money. It turns out that there is no difference, in fact. In Section 9.2.3, €1,000 coming from abroad was deposited in cash into the banking system and the system went on to create €9,000. All in all, the money supply increased by €10,000: €9,000 of bookkeeping money and €1,000

injected from abroad. With a reserves ratio of 10%, the corresponding bank reserves of €1,000 consisted of the initial €1,000 in cash (remember, currency is part of M0). In the present section, a loan of €10,000, increases the money stock by €10,000. The only difference is that the €1,000 of required reserves does not come from abroad, it is created anew by the central bank.

We can further understand the central bank action by looking at its own balance sheet, which is shown in Figure 9.4. The currency of circulation, money created by the central bank, is technically a liability, even though no one expects the central bank to 'reimburse' the money that it creates.[11] Its other liabilities are deposits by its 'customers', the commercial banks, and, sometimes, the government. It assets include foreign assets—called foreign exchange reserves—loans to banks and securities, often loans to the government. When a commercial bank needs cash, it asks for a central bank loan or it sells securities to the central bank, both of which appear on the asset side of the central bank balance sheet. In return, the commercial bank receives cash or has its account with the central bank credited, both of which appear on the liability side of the central bank balance sheet. Money creation by the central bank therefore 'lengthens' its balance sheet.

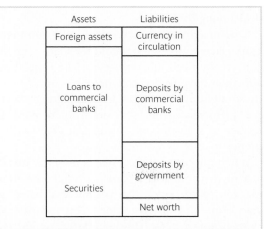

Fig. 9.4 Balance Sheet of a Central Bank

9.3 Short-run Equilibrium in the Money Market

9.3.1 The Money Market

Banks are usually quite busy places. They make loans to customers on a daily basis. At the same frequency, new deposits are taken in and many loans

are repaid. For a large bank, deposits and withdrawals are likely to more or less cancel out at the end of the day. If the day has been good, more loans were handed out than reimbursed, the loan portfolio has expanded, and the bank needs additional reserves. On a less active day, total loans outstanding have contracted and the bank holds excess reserves. Good and bad days alternate, so on some days a

[11] In the days before fiat money, banknotes promised to pay gold or silver when redeemed; now they promise nothing more than another banknote!

bank is short on reserves, sometimes it has excess reserves.

This is why, in the example of Section 9.2.5, the normal reaction of your bank will be to try to borrow from another bank which owns some excess reserves that it is willing to part with. It will go to the **money market**, also called the **interbank market** or the **open market**. This is not a physical marketplace, rather it is a network of banks which allows them to buy and sell (borrow and lend) reserves, i.e. deposits at the central bank. As long as total bank credit remains constant, some banks have excess reserves while others are short. Overall, they just deal among themselves.

Now imagine that, collectively, the commercial banks face a growing demand for loans. They will collectively need more reserves. The central bank will then have to decide whether or not to create these additional reserves (exactly like in Section 9.2.5). However, the bank does not respond face to face to a given bank. Instead, it deals with the money market as a whole.

When the central bank creates reserves, it makes a loan to commercial banks through the money market, pretty much like commercial banks provide loans to their customers. This means that it charges interest for this. Similarly, when banks lend reserves to each other, they also charge interest. Money markets vary from country to country, but they typically bring together large banks and financial institutions, such as insurance companies or mortgage lenders, which handle large amounts of cash. Since they all are highly reputable institutions that know each other well, they lend and borrow large amounts without asking for guarantees. The interest rate at which they do so is the rate at which large financial institutions can fund themselves. In effect, for them, the **interbank interest rate** is the ultimate cost of financing their needs. This rate is the basis for all interest rates. Indeed, a bank charges its customers the money market rate *plus* a premium that represents their riskiness. The interbank rate is called EONIA (European Overnight Interest Average) in the euro area, the Fed Funds in the US, the Sterling interbank rate in the UK, etc. Figure 9.5 shows that the various rates charged by commercial banks follow

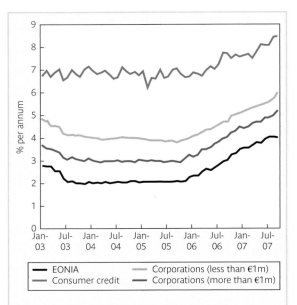

Fig. 9.5 Interest Rates in the Euro Area, 2003–2007

EONIA is the interbank interest rate in the euro area. The figure also displays the interest charged to corporations for large (more than €1 million) and smaller (less than €1 million) loans and the interest charged for consumer credits, in all cases for a one-year loan. Lenders charge a larger interest rate to borrowers that they perceive as riskier, but all rates closely follow the evolution of EONIA. *Source*: ECB, *Monthly Bulletin*, December 2007.

the same evolution as in the interbank rate in the euro area.

9.3.2 The Demand for Money

We can summarize the process as follows. The private sector—households and corporations—needs money to carry out daily transactions. This is the demand for money M. In order to satisfy this demand, commercial banks create much of what we call money when they grant loans to their customers. As they do so, they need to acquire sufficient reserves to meet their reserve ratio. Thus the public demand for money M translates into the commercial banks' **derived demand** for M0.

What determines the public's demand for money M? One simple answer is: the amount of transactions, since this is what makes money useful in the first place. We previously discussed this issue in Chapter 6 where we suggested that money demand can be represented as a constant proportion k of nominal GDP PY. This is somewhat simplistic. Suppose that you wish to hold more money (cash and 'money in the bank'). How do you get it? One way is to borrow from your bank. You will have to pay for it and the cost is the interest rate, which is high. Another way is to sell some assets. In that case, you give up something that serves you an interest for cash, which does not yield interest, or for deposit at the bank, which yields a very low interest. In both cases, the interest rate emerges as the cost of holding money. As the interest rate rises, the demand for money declines. Thus, while money demand is a proportion k of nominal GDP, this proportion is not really constant. It becomes smaller when the interest rate increases.

As we saw, different borrowers face different interest rates, depending on how risky they look in the eyes of their banks. On the other hand, Figure 9.5 shows that all these rates move together. For simplicity, therefore, we can ignore the risk premia and think of a single interest rate, that we denote i. In the end, we represent the demand for money as

(9.3) $$M^d = k(i)PY$$

where $k(i)$ declines when i rises (formally, $k(i)$ is a decreasing function of i). Now the derived demand for M0 by commercial banks is a fraction of the public demand for M, since any new bank loan, which means more bank deposits, must be accompanied by an increase in reserves as indicated by (9.2) above. It follows that the derived demand for M0 also declines with the interest rate. It is represented by the downward-sloping schedule D in Figure 9.6.

9.3.3 Market Equilibrium

Now imagine that, starting at point A, the nominal GDP increases. This means more transactions and therefore an increase in money demand M^d. Households and firms will try to borrow from banks the extra money that they need and, as banks respond by granting loans, their own need for reserves increases. This is captured in Figure 9.6 by the rightward shift of the derived demand schedule from D to D'.

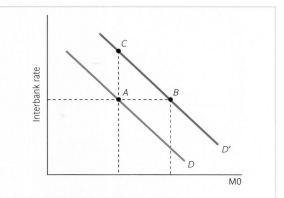

Fig. 9.6 The Money Market

The public's demand for money is negatively related to the interest rate i, which represents the cost of borrowing from commercial banks. This demand translates into a derived demand for the monetary base by commercial banks. If the public wants to hold more money, the derived demand schedule shifts to the right from D to D'. The central bank may decide to keep the interest unchanged (point B), or not to respond, in which case the interest rate rises (point C), or it can pick any combination of M0 and the interest rate as long as it lies on the demand schedule.

How can the central bank respond to the new situation? It has many options, since it is the sole producer of M0. One option is to keep the initial interest rate unchanged. This requires the central bank to provide the additional monetary base M0 needed, moving to point B. Another option is to keep M0 unchanged, which means that we move to point C and the interest rate rises accordingly. In that case, the interest rate rises enough to compensate, via a decline in $k(i)$, the impact on money demand M^d due to the increase in nominal GDP. In fact, the central bank has many options, since it can pick any point on the new derived demand schedule D'. We return to this choice below in Section 9.4.2.

9.3.4 Open Market Operations

As the sole producer of base money, the central bank exercises the dominant influence on the market. Institutional details vary from country to country, but the broad features are similar. Banks on the money market typically lend to each other over very short periods of time, from overnight to two

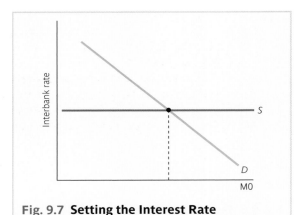

Fig. 9.7 Setting the Interest Rate

The central bank can achieve any interest rate it wishes by supplying whatever amount of money the private sector wishes to hold at that rate.

weeks. The central bank monitors the situation closely and ensures that either the interest rate or the quantity of money is in line with its intentions. Nowadays, for reasons developed in Section 9.4.1, most central banks choose to control the interest rate. This is represented in Figure 9.7 by the horizontal money supply schedule S. The schedule makes an important point: a central bank can enforce any interest rate that it wishes provided it stands ready to provide or withdraw liquidity in any amount needed to meet the derived demand corresponding to this rate.

Central banks typically announce the rate that they would like to see; the position of the supply schedule S in Figure 9.7 is public knowledge. One or two mouse clicks on a central bank's website can reveal the currently chosen interest rate. This rate is called the 'refi' in the euro area, the target rate in the USA, the Bank rate in the UK, or the 'repo' rate in Sweden.[12] In order to enforce this rate, each central bank provides its interbank market with the exact amount of reserves needed. To that effect, it carries out **open market operations**, which take various forms. For instance, the European Central Bank (ECB) conducts auctions every week, complemented with monthly ones (more details are presented in Box 9.3). The National

Bank of Hungary also conducts weekly auctions. In the USA, the Federal Reserve Bank of New York intervenes directly on the money market whenever the market rate deviates from the targeted federal funds rate. Many other central banks, such as those of the Czech Republic, Poland, Sweden, and the UK, also routinely carry out open market operations. When needed, the ECB too intervenes in the market directly (this is called 'fine-tuning operations').

In normal times, as the economy grows, demand by the public for bank credit is rising and the central banks allow bank reserves to grow. Through their liquidity-creating operations—auctions and open market operations—central banks allow bank reserves, and therefore M0, to increase. This allows commercial banks to step up lending to their customers, which increases M1 and the wider monetary aggregates. But what if a central bank wants to reduce the volume of reserves, for instance because it wants to raise the interbank interest rate? Since central bank loans are of very short duration, commercial banks are continuously repaying their

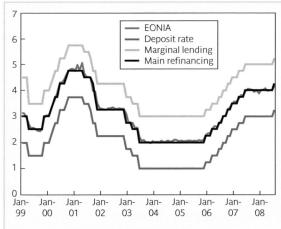

Fig. 9.8 ECB Interest Rates (January 1999–July 2008)

The ECB conducts weekly auctions at the pre-announced main refinancing interest rate. The marginal lending facility and deposit facility rates determine, respectively, a ceiling and a floor for the interbank rate EONIA (Euro OverNight Index Average) which tends to closely follow the refinancing rate.

Source: ECB.

[12] 'Refi' is ECB terminology for the Main Refinancing Rate.

Box 9.3 How the European Central Bank Does It[13]

In order to keep the interbank market rate as close as possible to its target rate, the ECB has set up a complex system for financing commercial banks.

Open market operations

The ECB carries out three kinds of open market operations.

- Main refinancing operations, which are weekly auctions for loans with a maturity of one week, is the main channel through which commercial banks obtain reserves. They submit bids and the ECB chooses how much to allocate at which interest rate.

- Longer-term refinancing operations, which take place once a month and serve as a modest complement to the main refinancing operations. The loans have a maturity of three months.

- Fine-tuning and structural operations, which are conducted from time to time to deal with special circumstances, at the ECB's discretion.

Standing facilities

The ECB also maintains two facilities open to eligible banks individually, at their request. These facilities set a ceiling and a floor for the overnight money market rate EONIA. Individual banks can either deposit their reserves at the marginal deposit rate (the floor) or borrow from the ECB at the marginal lending rate (ceiling). These facilities are always available but infrequently used under normal conditions.

To signal its intentions, the ECB publicly announces the refi rate at which it will conduct its next main refinancing operations, as well as the floor and ceiling rates. Figure 9.8 shows that the key short-term market rate EONIA moves within the tunnel set by the lending and deposit rates, closely following (sometimes even anticipating) the ECB's main rate, the refinancing rate. The ECB can thus exert tight, if not perfect control of the very short-term interest rate.

borrowings and borrowing again in a procedure which is called rolling over. When needed, the central bank can decide not to renew them, or to renew them only in part.

Since any loan is risky—you are never sure that you will be paid back—and since central banks are not expected to take risks, they take extensive precautions. First, they ask borrowing commercial banks to provide collateral—that they deposit an equivalent amount of high-quality assets, for example Treasury bonds, i.e. public debt, or bills issued by large corporations which are considered very safe. Second, they lend only for a limited period of time, usually a week or 10 days, sometimes more. When the period expires, the commercial banks must pay back the central bank in exchange for the collateral that they deposited, with no guarantee of being able to borrow again. That way, and in contrast to commercial bank lending, central banks take no risk. This is why the interest at which central banks lend is the lowest in the country, as shown in Figure 9.5—low risk means low return.

9.4 Monetary Policy in Practice

9.4.1 Objectives

The neutrality principle, presented in Chapter 6, asserts that, in the long run, the inflation rate is determined by the rate of growth of the money stock. In Chapters 12 and 13, we will show that inflation does not bring any lasting benefit, but only creates trouble. For that reason, price stability—a

low rate of inflation—is socially desirable. Bringing these two fundamental results together, it becomes quite obvious that monetary policy should, first and

[13] Full details are provided by the ECB on its website at <www.ecb.int>. Each central bank also presents in great detail its own procedures. For a list of all central banks, see <www.centralbanking.co.uk>.

Box 9.4   Hyperinflation: Historical and Current Episodes

Time and again, a country will fall into the trap of letting the money supply grow at excessive rates for long periods of time. The reason is relatively simple: the government tries to pay for its expenditures by borrowing directly from the central bank in a process that eventually gets out of control.[14] The consequence is always run-away inflation. Hyperinflation is conventionally set to describe the situation when *monthly* inflation rates exceed 50%, which means an annual rate of price increase of about 8,600%. On average, then, prices rise by some 2% every day.

Many hyperinflations occur after wars. This was the case in the 1920s in Germany, Greece, and Hungary. In

Germany, prices rose by 29,524% during the month of October 1923. This meant an average *daily* rate of 19%. The situation was so bad that factories would stop production at lunch to pay their workers and give them time to go shopping before prices had risen again and eroded the purchasing power of their wages. More recently, Serbia broke the world record when, in January 1994, prices rose by 60% *per day*. These episodes destroy the economy and put the basic fabric of society under severe strain, sometimes even leading to civil unrest and war. The most recent episode of hyperinflation can still be observed in Zimbabwe, as recounted in Box 6.2.[15]

foremost, be dedicated to achieving price stability. Indeed, with few exceptions, most central banks are delegated the ultimate responsibility of delivering price stability.

On the other hand, money is not neutral in the short run. Chapter 12 will show that, over a horizon of one to about two to three years, a lower interest rate or more abundant money supply leads to an expansion of output and employment. Conversely, a tighter monetary policy stance is followed by an output slowdown and a rise in joblessness. This implies that central banks must therefore also concern themselves with the level of economic activity. This seriously complicates their tasks. Indeed, it is much easier to have only one objective. What if, for instance, short-run considerations require that monetary policy be relaxed—that the interest rate be lowered, or the money supply expanded—at a time when inflation is already high, which calls for slowing down money growth and therefore raising the interest rate? Such conflicts of policy objectives complicate the conduct of monetary policy around the world.

Central banks are run by non-elected officials to whom the nation delegates a great deal of power.

For a long time, in many countries central banks operated under the direct control of the finance ministry. This placed an important responsibility in the hands of elected officials, as should be in a democracy. On the other hand, politicians tend to focus more on the short run, i.e. the upcoming elections, than in the long run, and inflation is the long-run consequence of monetary mismanagement. Time and again, subservient central banks have been instructed to pay more attention to the short than to the long run. The result has been uncomfortably high rates of inflation, in some cases even runaway inflation (see Box 9.4).

To deal with this problem, many countries have made their central banks formally independent from ruling governments and given precise tasks. The general thrust of these tasks is strikingly similar. For instance, monetary policy of the Norwegian central bank 'shall be oriented towards low and stable inflation', but 'shall also contribute to stabilizing

---

[14] Since the central bank *creates* money, it is an ideal place for governments to look for cheap finance. Commentators often speak of running 'printing presses'. We will explain more precisely why and how this happens in Chapters 13 and 17.

[15] Speaking in February 2006 on Government-owned television ZBC, President Mugabe not only gave advance warning for the country's hyperinflation episode, but also gave us the reason why they happen: 'Those who say printing money will cause inflation are suggesting that you just fold your hands and say "aah, let the situation continue and let the people starve." The Good Lord up there has given you a brain and the brain must function, not in a stereotyped manner but in a flexible manner . . . so I will print money today so that people can survive.'

output and employment'. The long-run objective of low inflation comes first, while the shorter-run objective of stabilizing output and employment comes next. The question is how central banks deliver.

9.4.2 Instruments and Targets

Before addressing the technicalities of monetary policy, it will be useful to summarize what we have established thus far.

Central banks affect output and inflation by making money more or less abundant, which means interest rates relatively low (when money is abundant) or high (when money supply is restrictive).

- Because it influences the growth of the money supply, monetary policy determines inflation in the long run. It takes something like two to three years for policy to affect inflation.
- Over the shorter run, monetary policy works through influencing interest rates, and thus mainly affects the level of economic activity. It takes some time for these effects to become noticeable.

Stable inflation, GDP growth, and employment are thus not directly under the control of the central bank. Its challenge is to use available instruments to affect these variables. We have already discussed three instruments under the direct control of central banks: (1) the interest rate, (2) the supply of reserves, and (3) the required reserve ratio. Figure 9.6 showed that a central bank cannot control both the money stock and the interest rate. It can only choose a position on the schedule representing the derived demand for reserves. If, as in Figure 9.7, it chooses the interest rate, it must accommodate the demand for reserves corresponding to this interest rate. It could do the opposite and choose the volume of reserves to supply, but then it would have to accept whatever interest rate the money market requires.

Monetary targeting

During much of the 1950s and 1960s, conventional wisdom was that central banks ought to maintain low and stable interest rates. This was thought to be good for investment and growth. As it turned out, with the interest rate set too low, money was allowed to grow quite rapidly. Unsurprisingly, this

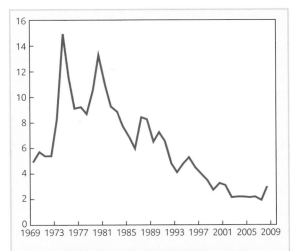

Fig. 9.9 Inflation in the OECD Countries, 1969–2008

The figure presents the average inflation rate in the OECD countries. Inflation soared in the 1970s, was reduced over the following two decades and appears to have stabilized at a low level since the late 1990s, with a worrisome uptick forecasted for 2008.

Source: OECD, *Economic Outlook*.

policy led to high inflation rates in the 1970s, as can be seen in Figure 9.9.

As an immediate reaction to the damaging inflation of the 1970s, many central banks targeted the rate of money growth. The strategy of monetary targeting rests on the link between bank reserves and deposits as stated in equation (9.2). The central bank controls the money stock by controlling directly the currency in circulation and indirectly bank deposits by choosing the size of commercial bank reserves. This allows the central bank to choose a rate of money growth consistent with the inflation rate that it hopes to deliver in the long run.[16]

Money growth targeting is widely credited for the successful disinflation of the 1980s. It was also

---

[16] This rate is simply given by equation (6.6) in Chapter 6, which indicates that in the long run inflation settles at the rate of money growth, after adjustment for the trend growth rate of GDP.

generally abandoned in the 1990s for a number of good reasons. One of them is that it was never clear which monetary stock should be targeted: M0, M1, M2, M3, or some other aggregate? This has turned into a serious difficulty once the deregulated financial sector introduced innovations that blurred the distinction between these aggregates. Another consequence has been increasing instability in the derived demand for M0. The money multiplier became highly variable and the money base M0 no longer gave central banks a precise handle on the wider aggregates.

Inflation targeting

The difficulties associated with monetary targeting paved the way for the next popular strategy, **inflation targeting**. The reasoning behind inflation targeting is relatively simple. Figure 9.6 displays the demand for M0, derived by the overall money demand as specified in (9.3). Let us look directly at the demand for money, represented by the downward-sloping schedule D in Figure 9.10. The central bank, we saw, can decide where to move the economy along this demand schedule, say point A. Under monetary targeting, the central bank determines the corresponding money supply. This is represented in Figure 9.10 by the vertical money supply schedule S^M. If it proves too difficult to control the quantity of money, the central bank can still hit point A by deciding on the interest rate. This is represented by the horizontal money supply

schedule S^i. In short, if it becomes difficult to control the *quantity* of money precisely enough, it makes sense to control its *price*, the interest rate.

This makes sense, but what is the right level of the interest rate? Under money growth targeting, point A was simply chosen according to (6.6), but this wonderfully simple rule is lost once the money supply is imperfectly controlled. The answer is inflation targeting. For reasons that will become clear in Chapters 10 and 12, inflation-targeting central banks try to determine as best as they can the future rate of inflation and move the interest rate accordingly. If, for instance, the forecasted inflation rate is too high, they raise the interest rate. This is why the strategy is better called the inflation *forecast* targeting strategy. Inflation-targeting central banks regularly publish their inflation forecasts. Figure 9.11 shows the example of Swedish central bank, the Riksbank.

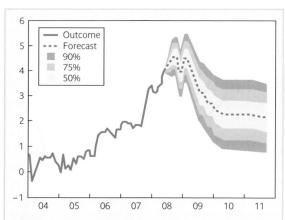

Fig. 9.11 Inflation Forecast by the Swedish Riksbank

The figure, published in June 2008, shows past inflation in Sweden and the Riksbank forecast over the following three years. In order to emphasize that any forecast is uncertain, the Riksbank reports how much trust it puts into its own forecasts. The central, lighter part of the fan indicates that the bank estimates that there is 50% probability that inflation will actually be within this area. The darker and much wider zone corresponds to a 90% probability. The further out you look, the less certain is the forecast.

Source: Riksbank (2007).

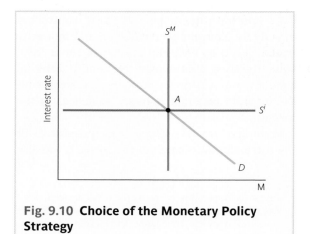

Fig. 9.10 Choice of the Monetary Policy Strategy

Box 9.5 The Governor's Letter: How the Bank of England is Made Accountable

The Bank of England adopted the inflation-targeting strategy informally in 1993 and has pursued it formally since 1997, when it received statutory independence from the Treasury. On both dimensions of inflation targeting and monetary independence, the Bank has strongly influenced the practice of central banking. The Bank of England is said to be *instrument-independent*. It is free to set the interest rate as it will, but the inflation target is set by the Chancellor of the Exchequer in an annual 'remit letter' that is made public on the Bank of England's website. The inflation target in the summer of 2008 was 2%.

Of particular interest is the sanction mechanism applied to policy mistakes. If inflation slips away by more than 1% on either side of the 2% target, the Governor must write an open letter to the Chancellor (the Minister of Finance). This happened for the first time in April 2007 when inflation reached 3.1%. The Governor dutifully obliged and wrote the letter. With inflation surging again, the Governor sent another letter in June 2008. These letters, and the Chancellor's courteous and sympathetic responses, can be read at <www.bankofengland.co.uk>.

Inflation targeting was initially implemented by the Bank of New Zealand in the late 1980s. Since then, it has been widely adopted, even though the three largest central banks, the ECB, the Fed, and the Bank of Japan, remain unconvinced, for various reasons.[17] The natural appeal of inflation targeting is that it is closest to the central bank's mandate, price stability. With a simple, verifiable target, it is easier for the central bank to explain its decisions and to reassure the public that its actions are driven by a clear and transparent commitment to price stability.

What if the central bank makes a mistake? The troubling aspect is that, when governments make mistakes, they face the consequences at the next election, and they know it. Being independent, central banks do not face any democratic sanction and may become a bit too complacent, if not downright arrogant. There is no perfect solution to this problem. Box 9.5 shows how the Bank of England is made more accountable.

Reserve requirements as a tool of monetary policy

Reserve requirements can be used to affect the money supply. For example, if the required reserve ratio is raised from 5% to 6%, with unchanged supply of reserves, deposits must contract by roughly 20% (the percent increase from 5 to 6). This is a drastic move, which not only stops commercial banks from lending, but might even cause them to call in (demand immediate repayment of) some existing loans. Because this move can be very costly and disruptive to banks and their customers, reserve ratios are normally changed only in small increments, and then only in emergency situations. Moreover, as Table 9.2 shows, the reserve ratio is purely voluntary in a number of countries.

9.4.3 The Taylor Rule

A simple way of summarizing the way central banks deal with their two tasks is the **Taylor rule**, which will be used extensively in the following chapters.[18] The Taylor rule states that the central bank will raise the interbank market interest rate, denoted by i, when the inflation rate π exceeds its target inflation rate $\bar{\pi}$, and when real GDP Y exceeds its current equilibrium or trend level $\bar{Y}$:[19]

---

[17] In practice, the major central banks seem to follow the inflation strategy but do not publicly acknowledge it. The ECB intends to be seen as a successor of the Bundesbank, whose fame was to pioneer money growth targeting. The Fed is hamstrung by its time-honoured mandate that requires that it cares about both inflation and employment. The Bank of Japan is still trying to exit from a long period of zero inflation and poor growth, which is often referred to as the 'lost decade'.

[18] This 'rule', which reflects a great deal of extensive observation of actual central bank behaviour, is named after John Taylor, a US economist at Stanford University.

[19] The trend level of output corresponds to the long-run sustainable evolution of GDP, as explained in Chapters 3 and 4.

(9.4) $$ i = \bar{i} + a(\pi - \bar{\pi}) + b\frac{Y - \bar{Y}}{\bar{Y}}. $$

The target inflation rate $\bar{\pi}$ is meant to correspond to price stability. The trend GDP level $\bar{Y}$ is defined as the GDP that would be observed if unemployment was at its equilibrium level, as defined in Chapter 5.[20] The percent difference $(Y - \bar{Y})/\bar{Y}$ between GDP and its trend is called the **output gap**.[21]

The Taylor rule anchors interest rate policy around a level $\bar{i}$ that is called the **neutral** or **natural rate**. It is the interest rate that the central bank would want if both inflation and GDP are stabilized at their desired levels. The coefficients a and b give the relative importance attributed to deviations of inflation and output from their targets; for example $a = 1.5$ and $b = 0.5$.

Figure 9.12 shows how closely the Taylor rule describes central bank decisions. For each country, the figure compares the actual interest rate and the one predicted by the rule. Given the extreme simplicity of the rule, we would not expect a close similarity and, yet, it appears that Taylor rules provide a reasonable interpretation of what central banks actually do. As a first approximation, we can think of the rule as determining where the supply schedule S is placed in Figure 9.7.

9.5 Financial Institutions and Monetary Control[22]

We have seen that money is not made out of precious metal and has no intrinsic value. It is only worth the trust that people put into it. Money is valuable only if others are willing to accept it as a means of payment, be it for something bought in a store or for one's own hard work. The fact that its value depends on widely shared trust implies that money is a public good—it must be carefully guaranteed and preserved by the government. This is why banks are tightly regulated and supervised. Despite all this precaution, confidence crises arise now and then.

9.5.1 Bank Regulation and Supervision

Money is created when commercial banks grant loans to their customers, with the hope that principal and interest will be repaid. It is a fundamental and unalterable fact that banks have less information about their customers' creditworthiness than the customers themselves. A loan customer will tend to misrepresent circumstances which would otherwise lead to a refusal of credit. This fundamental

information asymmetry has wide-ranging implications that affect virtually any financial operation.[23]

One direct implication is that banks routinely make 'bad loans', i.e. loans that are never repaid in full. A bank that makes too many bad loans can go bankrupt, and in this case the depositors—who are not investing, but simply banking—may lose their money. Depositors can thus never be perfectly certain that their money is safe and, because bank deposits are only as safe as the bank itself, the value of money itself is constantly at risk. Just as confidence in banknotes and coins rests on the quality of the central bank that issues them, the confidence in money created by the commercial banks is based on the expectation that it be freely and immediately convertible into currency at any time. The history of commercial banking is full of bank failures which turned into bank panics as worried

---

[20] In fact, most central banks do not just look at actual inflation but at forecasts. We ignore this distinction.

[21] Why do we seem to treat inflation and output differently? We don't, actually. Inflation is expressed in percent (the rate of increase of the price level), so is the output gap.

[22] This section presents non-essential material that can be skipped without loss of continuity. Its main interest is to provide background information useful to understand the banking crisis that started in 2007.

[23] Three economists, George Akerlof from Berkeley University, A. Michael Spence from Stanford University, and George Stiglitz, then at Princeton University, were awarded the Nobel Prize in 2001 for having uncovered and analysed the phenomenon of information asymmetry.

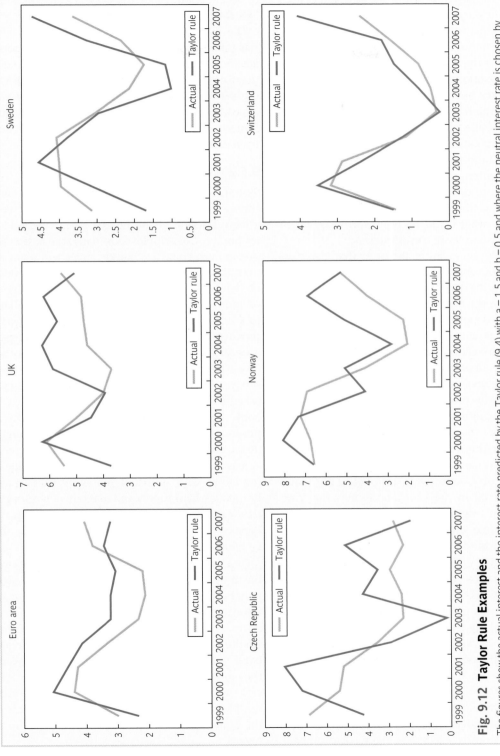

Fig. 9.12 Taylor Rule Examples

The figures show the actual interest and the interest rate predicted by the Taylor rule (9.4) with a = 1.5 and b = 0.5 and where the neutral interest rate is chosen by the authors on the basis of past experience or central bank statements.

Sources: OECD, *Economic Outlook;* IMF, *International Financial Statistics.*

depositors attempted to withdraw as much cash as possible, not only from the failing bank but from all financial institutions—just to be safe.

One bank failure is painful for its depositors, but not lethal for the economy. The greater risk is that the whole banking system could fail as a chain reaction takes hold, bringing healthy banks down along with the bad ones. **Systemic risk**, as the phenomenon is called, arises because banks (and, more generally, financial institutions) hold each other's liabilities. These so-called correspondent balances are the plumbing of the modern economy. They allow banks to deal with each other on the interbank market. Should one bank go bankrupt, its liabilities to other banks become worthless, which can easily lead to more bankruptcies.

A seriously aggravating factor is that bank depositors—households and firms—can become suspicious. Fearing that trouble in one bank could contaminate the others, they may attempt to withdraw their deposits from all banks. This panic movement is called a **bank run**. But, as already explained in Section 9.2.3, a bank can never pay back all of its deposits immediately, since they have been mostly invested or lent out. This is why bank runs can easily provoke a generalized collapse of the whole banking system. While bank runs are rare, they have occurred in Argentina and Uruguay in 2002. For the most part, they are contained to an individual bank, such as Northern Rock (2007) in the UK or Countrywide Financial (2007) and IndyMac (2008) in the USA. Sometimes the 'run' doesn't even originate with retail depositors, but with other banks which withdraw funds from suspect banks or withhold credit from them—the case of IKB Bank in Germany in 2007 is a good example.

To reduce these risks, national governments impose regulations on banks, and international agreements have been worked out to establish norms of good banking practice. Regulations include the supervision of bank accounts and operations, restrictions on asset ownership and banking activities, and the imposition of a number of prudential measures. Most important, banks are generally required to maintain a minimum net worth—the excess of assets over liabilities—in relation to their volume of deposits. As stated already, this is meant to create a buffer in case assets suffer a sudden loss of value.

The purpose of all these regulations is to limit risk-taking by banks, to give monetary authorities advance warning in case of failure, and generally to ensure prudent conduct in the provision of banking services. Bank runs are also less likely when deposits are insured, at least up to some limit. Deposit insurance is now compulsory in most developed countries.

9.5.2 Lending in Last Resort

Systemic bank failures represent one of the worst threats to modern economies. Within days or weeks, a large fraction of the money stock can suddenly evaporate. This cripples most daily transactions and precipitates countless bankruptcies and plant closures. Unemployment soon explodes and standards of living fall precipitously. GDP declined by 10% or more in the wake of systemic bank collapses in Korea in 1998 and Argentina in 2002, especially hurting the poor who lost their modest savings.

Central banks are not just in charge of price stability. They are also entrusted with the task of preserving financial stability. In normal times, they are asked to limit money growth. In bad times, when bank deposits threaten to vanish, they alone can produce unlimited quantities of money. When they do so, they act as **lenders of last resort**. In principle at least, the central bank is expected to provide failing banks with sufficient monetary base to avoid immediate bankruptcy and reassure depositors that they can continue to withdraw money from their deposits. But the lender of last resort function must be handled with great care.

On the one hand, banking systems can be unstable in the face of large, sudden withdrawals, which may be based as much on irrational fears or misinformation as real threats. Supplying liquidity in crises can spare considerable pain and suffering. On the other hand, if banks believe that the central bank will always bail them out when in trouble, they may take on excessive risks. The danger is that crisis alleviation via lending in last resort can in itself become a source of crises. Box 9.6 summarizes the policy dilemma faced by central banks in this regard.

Box 9.6 Bank Runs and Lender of Last Resort: A Double-Edged Sword

When the value of commercial bank deposits becomes suspicious, bank account holders attempt to withdraw their funds and convert them into cash. Because they only hold a small proportion of deposits in cash or cashable deposits at the central bank, commercial banks have then no other choice than to close down their offices. This does not just infuriate depositors who feel defrauded, it undermines the whole economy. Often bank runs start with one failing bank and quickly spread to the whole banking system. To prevent a financial and economic meltdown, central banks must intervene decisively to prevent contagion, at worst to bail out the whole banking system. Ideally, central banks would provide the bank(s) under pressure with enough cash to pay back all deposits and thus placate depositors' anxieties and put an end to the runs. In practice, there is just not enough paper money available—remember that currency amounts to a small fraction of bank deposits. Usually, therefore, central banks provide commercial banks with emergency cash and instruct them to pay back their customers a fraction of their deposits, in the hope that this will keep the economy going for a while.

Another limit of lending in last resort is moral hazard, another implication of information asymmetry. We have noted that banking is a risky business. One reason why banks limit the risk that they take, and the returns that come along with risk-taking, is that they want to avoid bankruptcy. But if lending in last resort systematically saves them from bankruptcy, banks have less reason to behave prudently, which undermines the banking system and the stability of the currency. The information asymmetry here comes from the fact that central banks do not know how much risk commercial banks take and that, if they expect a bail-out, banks have an interest in taking more risk than they really should.

Thus central banks are torn between two conflicting aims. On the one hand, they cannot stand by when the banking system collapses. On the other hand, they do not want to encourage risky bank behaviour, if only because excessive risk-taking is bound to result in frequent crises. One response is for central banks or supervising agencies to closely monitor commercial bank practices and, when needed, to instruct banks to take remedial actions. If the instruction is not heeded, the misbehaving bank may lose its licence. A second response is to impose prudential measures, such as increasing required bank capital (issuing shares) in proportion to the amount of risk taken. A third response is for central banks to maintain a large degree of uncertainty as to what they would do in case of bank failure. In fact, central banks routinely deny in public that they are ready to carry out lender-of-last-resort operations. This way, they hope, depositors will be encouraged to keep an eye on their banks in good times, and withhold their patronage if they find cause for concern. Finally, lending in last resort is not extended automatically. The accepted procedure is to follow the Bagehot principles (named after Walter Bagehot (1826–1877), a renowned British financial economist of the late nineteenth century).

- Lend only against marketable collateral. This forces banks to hold an adequate amount of safe assets (with low returns) alongside risky loans (with higher returns).

- Lend in large amounts at a higher rate than the market interest rate. Large amounts are meant to stop the bank run, higher rates are meant to make the operation punitively costly.

- Sell or liquidate insolvent banks, with losses to be borne by their owners. The managers and shareholders should bear the cost of imprudent lending as a way of reducing the moral hazard problem.

9.5.3 Technological Innovation in Banking and Monetary Control

Banks are constantly devising new ways of satisfying the financial needs of their customers. Many of these developments are also prompted by the banks' attempts to escape monetary policy and regulation. The central banks' objective of reining in money growth generally runs counter to individual banks' interest in increasing profitability. Similarly, banking regulation aims at protecting customers by limiting the range of banking activities, including risk-taking. Pressed by competition and prompted by continuous technological innovations—in financial instruments, computer power, and communications systems—banks constantly innovate by exploiting loopholes in existing legislation. As a result, monetary control is weakened and banks may become more fragile. This fragility is con-firmed by continuing bank failures and the collapse of prestigious institutions like Barings of Britain (one of the oldest banks) or LTCM (Long-Term Capital Management, a firm created and run by several Nobel Prize winners) in the USA. The sub-prime crisis that started in 2007, and the credit crisis that is still under way as we write, is explained in Box 9.7.

 Box 9.7 The Sub-prime Crisis of 2007 and its Aftermath

The sub-prime crisis involves many of the issues discussed in this chapter. The fact that it occurred in one of the most developed countries of the world, despite a wealth of experience accumulated over decades, illustrates the inherent instability of financial institutions as well as the unending race between innovation and regulation.

This complex situation—which we simplify greatly here—started in the US mortgage market, the market for long-term home loans. Sub-prime mortgage loans were made to low-income customers who are normally too risky to borrow the large amounts needed to buy a house ('sub-prime' refers to quality below those obtaining the prime rate). In addition, the interest rates were initially very low but that would rise steeply over the duration of the loan. This new line of business proliferated as the result of securitization, which works as follows. Soon after being granted, the loans—the right to receive payments from the borrowers—were sold to other financial institutions. This trick allowed the original mortgage lender to collect a fee for issuing the loan while escaping the associated risk of default since they no longer actually held it.

The purchasing institutions collected a large number of these risky loans and re-sold them in bulk to yet other financial institutions around the world. These 'mortgage-backed securities' changed hands frequently, going from one country to another. They ended up being held by large banks. This construction created another asymmetric information problem: the ultimate asset-holders had very limited understanding of the risk that they were taking on board.

The trigger for the crisis was weakness in the US housing market, which had been buoyed up by abundant mortgage lending for many years. House prices rose by almost 100% from 1999 to 2006. Just as the market slowed and house prices started to decline, sub-prime borrowers began to climb their adjustable interest ladders. Many of them could not afford the interest payments and defaulted. In principle, the house served as collateral and guaranteed the value of the loans. But, with declining housing prices, collateral value became insufficient. In effect, hundreds of thousands of loans had lost value. The first hitch was that no one knew how much, for house prices were still declining and the securities did not trade in transparent markets.

The second hitch was that no one knew who really was holding the sub-prime mortgages. Most financial institutions, including commercial banks, had some hidden here and there, but how much exactly? Each commercial bank started to wonder whether the others had more or less exposure to the risk. This mattered because banks lend routinely to each other on the money market. Asymmetric information was massive. No bank wanted to reveal its losses for fear of being cut out of the market. As a result, no one could be trusted, as even the highest quality institutions were involved. Soon enough, each bank stopped lending to the others, and the interbank markets dried up in many of the most developed countries, including the USA, the euro area, and the UK.

Without a malfunctioning interbank market, the whole credit system freezes up. This means an economic crisis of massive proportions. The central banks scrambled to provide liquidity to the money market, injecting hundreds of billions over days. This kept the market reasonably orderly. Ironically, the images of the 1930s, with long lines of depositors waiting in line to withdraw their funds, have been replaced by banks waiting on the sideline, refusing to lend to each other for fear of not getting their money back. At the time of this book's writing, the crisis has yet to be resolved.

ⓘ Summary

1 There are different definitions of money, all of which can be broadly summarized as the sum of currency in circulation and deposits in banks and, possibly, other financial institutions.

2 Most of what we call money and employ in everyday transactions is created by commercial banks as they grant loans to their customers. The rest of the money supply—currency, banknotes, and coins—is produced by the monetary authorities.

3 For prudential or regulatory reasons, commercial banks hold cash—currency or deposits at the central bank—in proportion to their customers' deposits. This reserve ratio forces commercial banks to acquire more reserves whenever they create more money. The banks' demand for reserves is derived from the public demand for money, i.e. for bank loans.

4 The central bank directly controls the amount of currency in circulation. It controls indirectly the other component of the money stock, bank deposits, by deciding whether to provide commercial banks with bank reserves.

5 Facing the derived demand for the monetary base, central banks can decide on which quantity to supply, or to supply whatever quantity is demanded to achieve a particular interest rate. An additional instrument available to the central bank is the required reserve ratio, when it exists.

6 The neutrality principle indicates that inflation is ultimately driven by money growth. This has led most countries to delegate to their central banks the responsibility of achieving and maintaining price stability. Central banks are usually also expected to care about output growth and employment, which are affected by monetary policy in the shorter run.

7 Combining these two objectives is not always easy, so central banks have developed monetary policy strategies, which have evolved over time. The money growth strategy proved its mettle in bringing inflation down following the faulty low-interest rate strategies of the 1960s and 1970s. With low inflation and rapid changes in banking and finances, the money growth strategy gave way to inflation targeting.

8 The Taylor rule describes monetary policy as setting the interest rate in response to deviations of inflation from its designated target and to the output gap. Despite its simplicity, the Taylor rule offers a reasonable, reliable interpretation of what central banks do.

9 Banking is inherently a risky business, largely due to the information asymmetry problem. Since banks create money and monetary stability is essential to the functioning of the economy, banks are regulated and supervised.

10 Because commercial banks supply money and credit to an economy, their failure cannot be taken lightly. An isolated bank run can increase the risk of generalized contagion. This is why central banks must be ready to act as lender of last resort, providing liquidity while sanctioning bank failure due to imprudent practices.

☺ Key Concepts

- **monetary policy**
- **commodity money, fiat money**
- **monetary aggregates (M0, M1, M2, M3)**
- **bank reserves**
- **monetary base**
- **financial intermediaries**
- **maturity transformation**
- **balance sheet**
- **reserves requirements, reserve ratio**
- **money multiplier**
- **derived demand**
- **money market, interbank market, open market**

- **interbank interest rate**
- **open market operations**
- **money growth targeting**
- **inflation targeting**
- **Taylor rule**
- **output gap**
- **neutral interest rate**
- **information asymmetry**
- **systemic risk**
- **bank runs, bank failures**
- **lender of last resort**

❓ Exercises

1 Suppose that the long-run growth rate of GDP is 3% and that the reserves ratio is 10%. What should be the money growth target if the central bank wants to achieve an inflation of 2% in the long run? How quickly, then, should it allow reserves to grow?

2 Define and explain the distinction between objectives, targets, and instruments of monetary policy. Give some examples of conflicts between different instruments, and between different targets. Do you think it is necessarily better to have many or fewer instruments and targets?

3 Table 9.1 shows that the size (relative to GDP) of the monetary aggregates varies from country to country. Explain why and how these ratios reflect the degree of financial development of the country.

4 In some countries the reserves ratio is not set by the central bank, rather it is left to the discretion of commercial banks. Does it matter for the control of the money stock? Would the same problem exist if the central bank tries to control interest rates instead?

5 Figure 9.8 shows the difference between the money growth and the inflation-targeting strategies. Consider an increase in the demand for money. How will the central bank react under the money growth strategy by keeping S^M unchanged? Under the inflation-targeting strategy if S^i is kept unchanged?

6 Explain why and how an unstable demand for money creates problems for the central bank's objective of price stability. What does it imply for the choice of a target? (Hint: consider that money demand instability means that $k(i)$ in (9.3) is changing randomly.)

7 Consider open market operations whereby central banks provide loans to commercial banks against collateral in the form of a short-term loan of the same value as the collateral. Now imagine that the value of the collateral falls unexpectedly. Explain why the central bank is unlikely to make a loss. When could it make a loss? (Hint: look at Figure 9.4.)

8 Why is deposit insurance a way of reducing the odds of a bank run? What are the limits of this scheme?

9 Consider the Taylor rule (9.4). Assume as in the text that $a = 1.5$ and $b = 0.5$ and that the neutral interest rate is 4%. What interest rate is implied by the rule when inflation is 2% above target while the output gap is zero. What is the output gap is 3%? And −2%?

10 The target inflation rate in Sweden is 2%. Looking at Figure 9.11, what do you expect the Riksbank to do over the years 2008–2009?

11 Box 9.3 describes the open market operations of the ECB. Explain carefully why the marginal lending facility establishes a ceiling on the market rate and why the marginal deposit facility establishes a floor.

➲ Essay Questions

1 The mandate of the Eurosystem sets price stability as its overriding priority. In the USA, the Federal Reserve System is legally committed to pursue both 'stability of the currency' and a 'high level of employment'. Compare and discuss these mandates.

2 One of the tasks of a central bank is to intervene as lender of last resort as described in Box 9.6. One of the trickiest parts is to determine if a bank is insolvent (it cannot recover) or just illiquid (it has no fundamental problem but is running out of cash). Explain why it matters and how this distinction might be made.

3 Why do central banks need to have targets? Discuss and evaluate the various possible targets.

4 Some countries impose a reserve ratio, not others. Does it matter for the safety of the banking system?

5 In April 2007, the Governor of the Bank of England had to write a letter to the Chancellor of the Exchequer to explain why it missed the inflation target. Read the letter <www.bankofengland.co.uk/monetarypolicy/pdf/cpiletter070417.pdf> and the Chancellor's response <www.hm-treasury.gov.uk/media/7/4/chxresponse_170407.pdf>. What are the Governor's explanations and what do you think of the Chancellor's response?

Macroeconomic Equilibrium in the Short Run

10

Long run is a misleading guide to current affairs. In the long run we are all dead.

J. M. Keynes

10.1 Overview

In this chapter we begin to provide an answer to the central question of macroeconomics posed in Chapter 1: Why do countries experience business cycles? These recurrent, irregular periods of ups and downs are presented in a stylized way in Figure 10.1. We saw in Chapters 3 and 4 that, in the long run, the GDP tends to increase secularly. This is shown by the smoother curve displaying an upward trend. In the short run, however, the GDP fluctuates around that trend, with periods of relatively fast growth followed by periods of slowdown, or even negative growth called **recessions**. This chapter shows that business cycles can be explained by disturbances that originate in goods, financial, or labour markets. These disturbances can come from home or abroad.

In order to study the short run, we will adopt the crucial **Keynesian assumption** that prices are constant. In most countries where inflation is low, it is a reasonable assumption over, say, a couple of years. This is why this chapter is about the short run. The Keynesian assumption is not only reasonable, it is also convenient. Not having to track prices will simplify the analysis a lot.

The Keynesian assumption is also surprisingly powerful. In Chapter 6, price flexibility was shown to be a reasonable assumption for the long run. Under price flexibility, the monetary neutrality principle applies, and money and prices behave independently of output. By adopting the Keynesian assumption, we will upset this **dichotomy**. Assuming that prices are constant, or just 'sticky' (i.e. moving slowly), implies that the nominal and real sides of the economy interact with each other. Macroeconomics, therefore, incorporates two fundamentally different perspectives. In the long run, prices are fully flexible and neatly separate out the nominal and real sides of the economy. In the short run, prices do not move, or move rather slowly, the dichotomy fails and everything becomes more complicated. For this reason, we will be able to explain some of the complex aspects of the business cycle.

The Keynesian model focuses on two markets: (1) the market for goods and services—which we will henceforth call the goods market, and (2) the money market, which we studied in Chapter 9. In the next chapter we will add the foreign exchange market, providing an open economy version of the Keynesian model. Our reasoning follows the **general equilibrium** method. We ask what is required

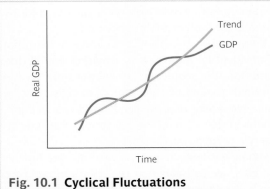

Fig. 10.1 Cyclical Fluctuations

The Keynesian assumption helps explain short-run fluctuations of real GDP around its long-run growth trend.

for all markets to be in equilibrium at the same time. This is a very powerful method of analysis, which allows us to capture in one step the many interactions that take place among the different markets. Figure 10.2 offers a preview of the full open economy analysis. Through the interest rate, the money market affects the goods market, and thus the level of output. The goods market, in turn, affects the demand for money and thereby the interest rate. Later on, we will also allow the real exchange rate to influence the demand for domestic goods. We will see how interest and exchange rates affect each other, and therefore the goods market.

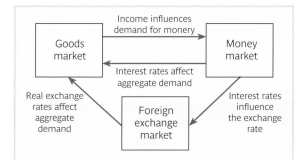

Fig. 10.2 General Macroeconomic Equilibrium

Conditions in domestic money and goods markets affect each other. Interest rates and exchange rates influence the level of aggregate demand, while income affects the demand for money and, for a given money supply, interest rates. General equilibrium occurs when equilibrium conditions in the three markets are consistent with each other.

10.2 Aggregate Demand and the Goods Market

10.2.1 The Market Equilibrium Assumption

We start with the fundamental accounting identity of Chapter 2:

(10.1) $Y = C + I + G + \text{PCA},$

where all variables are measured in real terms, i.e. in constant prices. In Chapter 2, we presented this equation as an identity which described the various categories of spending on domestic goods that make up the GDP. As a definition, this equation is verified by construction and we could leave it at that, but here we view it in a different light. We now consider that the left-hand side of (10.1) represents the **supply** by domestic producers of the goods that they produce, while the right-hand side brings together various components of world **demand** for domestically produced goods. These components are C, the demand by resident households

for consumption goods, investment spending I by firms on capital goods, the public sector's own demand for goods G, and the primary account PCA. The PCA is the difference between the world's demand for our goods, exports X, and the domestic demand for foreign goods, imports Z.

Viewed this way, (10.1) is no longer a definition or an identity. Rather, it is a market equilibrium condition. We require it to hold not only because national accountants get numbers right, but because we *assume* that the goods market is in equilibrium so that demand equals supply. But how are the two brought into balance?

When we look at a particular market (apples, oil, etc.), we consider that the good's price brings demand and supply in line. Here we look at all goods and services that enter GDP. Later on, in Chapter 12, we will follow a similar line of reasoning and look at the general price level. In this chapter, in contrast, we adopt the Keynesian assumption that prices are sticky, i.e. that they move slowly.

To see what a fundamental difference this makes, let us suppose that demand—the right-hand side of (10.1)—exceeds supply—the left-hand side. If prices were flexible, they would rise, presumably lowering demand and raising supply. If they are sticky, how can the market return to equilibrium? The Keynesian answer implies that we can now interpret (10.1) as an *explanation* of how GDP evolves. Demand responds to exogenous forces while supply is responding passively to shifts in demand.

10.2.2 Determinants of Demand

What, then, are those exogenous forces that shape demand? In order to answer this question, we need to describe the behaviour of consumers, firms, and the PCA. The public sector will be assumed to make its choice independently of economic conditions: public spending G and tax receipts T are considered, for the time being, as exogenous. To remind ourselves of this assumption, we will denote them with an upper bar: $\bar{G}$ and $\bar{T}$.

In Chapter 8 we explained the factors which drive private consumption and investment in detail. Now, all we need to do is to synthesize these results in a simple and compact way.

Let's start with consumption. We saw that consumption is driven by consumers' wealth and disposable income, all in real terms. Wealth is assumed to be exogenous and it is represented by $\bar{\Omega}$.[1] Disposable income Y^d, income after tax, is the difference between GDP Y and tax payments $\bar{T}$. This description is summarized by the following **consumption function**:

(10.2) $C = C(\bar{\Omega}, Y - \bar{T}).$ (consumption function)
$\qquad\qquad\quad + \quad +$

As before, the signs underneath the two determinants of consumption indicate the effect of each variable on demand. More wealth and a higher disposable income each raise consumption demand. Note that, while taxes are assumed to be exogenous at this stage, GDP is endogenous since it also represents total supply, which is equal to total demand, which we are getting ready to explain.

We also studied investment demand in Chapter 8. It is represented by the following form of the **investment function**:

(10.3) $I = I(q, r).$ (investment function)
$\qquad\qquad\quad + \ -$

The investment function states that investment expenditures increase when Tobin's q increases, and declines when the interest r rises. Remember from Chapter 8 that, all other things equal, investment is driven by business expectations or entrepreneurial 'animal spirits'. This is captured by Tobin's q. The interest rate matters for two reasons: (1) because a higher interest rate reduces Tobin's q; (2) because firms borrow from banks to finance investment. When borrowing costs rise, firms invest less.

The interest rate is an important variable in the analysis of this chapter, so it will be useful to make clear which interest rate we are talking about. In Chapters 7 and 8 we studied the real interest rate r, which measures the real cost of borrowing or the return to lending. Later, in Chapter 9, we examined the nominal interest rate, denoted by i, which is quoted by banks or reported in the financial press and represents the foregone interest implied by holding money. When we proceed to analyse inflation in Chapter 12, we will distinguish between the two. The Keynesian assumption that prices are sticky implies that inflation is zero or negligible. This allows us to ignore inflation and therefore the difference between these two rates. For future reference, however, we note that it is the real interest rate r that matters for spending decisions and the nominal interest rate i that is relevant when we look at monetary questions.

Then there is the last term in (10.1), the primary current account (PCA). Recall that the primary current account surplus is defined in Chapter 2 as the difference between exports (X) and imports (Z) of goods and services, measured in terms of domestic output:

---

[1] Generally, wealth changes very slowly in response to household savings, so this assumption can be justified for short-run analysis. On the other hand, when asset prices change, wealth can change suddenly. We return to this point later on.

(10.4) $PCA = X - Z.$

First consider imports. Recall that total domestic spending, or absorption A, includes spending on both domestically produced and imported goods.[2] It is logical to consider that imports are a fraction of absorption: the more we spend, the more we import. This proportion need not be constant, however. In particular, it should depend on the country's competitiveness. In Chapter 6, we saw that competitiveness can be measured with the real exchange rate σ, the relative price of domestic to foreign goods. A real depreciation—a decrease in σ—makes foreign goods relatively more expensive, and therefore discourages imports. Conversely, a real appreciation—an increase in σ—boosts imports, which are now cheaper. These observations are summarized by the **import function**, which says that imports rise with absorption and with the real exchange rate:

(10.5) $Z = Z(A, \sigma).$
                            $+\ \ +$

Turning to exports, we need only recognize that they are the imports of the rest of the world. Accordingly, they behave as our imports, from the foreign perspective. Thus our exports depend on foreign absorption A^* (and its determinants, foreign wealth Ω^*, disposable income Y^{d*}, Tobin's q^*, etc.). If our real exchange depreciates—if σ decreases—our goods become cheaper in the foreigners' eyes and stimulate our exports. Conversely, a real appreciation—an increase in σ—depresses exports, which have become more costly. We bring these observations together in the form of the **export function**:

(10.6) $X = X(A^*, \sigma).$
                            $+\ \ -$

Finally, these results can be combined in the form of the **primary current account function**, which is simply the difference between the export and import functions in (10.5) and (10.6):

(10.7) $PCA = X(A^*, \sigma) - Z(A, \sigma)$
                       $+\ \ -\quad\ \ +\ +$

                   $= PCA(A, A^*, \sigma).$
                          $-\ \ +\ \ -$

---

[2] Recall that absorption A is $A = C + I + G$.

The PCA function tells us that any factor that boosts one of the components of domestic absorption $A = C + I + G$ (increases in wealth, disposable income, Tobin's q, real growth, public spending or tax cuts, or a decline in the interest rate) will increase imports and reduce the primary current account (increase the primary account deficit). In contrast, anything that boosts foreign spending (increases in foreign wealth, disposable income, Tobin's q, real growth, public spending and tax cuts, or a decline in the foreign interest rate) will increase foreign absorption A^* and therefore our exports, which improves our primary current account. Finally, a real exchange rate appreciation (an increase in σ) leads to a deterioration of the primary account as imports rise and exports fall. Conversely, a real depreciation improves the primary account.

Macroeconomists like to take short-cuts. Because the factors that affect absorption and aggregate demand also affect output—that is the Keynesian assumption—then factors that affect absorption will ultimately affect output. The obvious short-cut is to replace the PCA function in (10.7) with the following one:[3]

(10.8) $PCA = PCA(Y, Y^*, \sigma).$ (primary current
                        $-\ +\ \ -$ account function)

In the end, we will work with this primary current account function, which states that the PCA is negatively related to domestic real income, positively to foreign income, and negatively to the real exchange rate. This completes the picture of aggregate demand in an open economy.

10.2.3 Goods Market Equilibrium

The groundwork having been laid, we can proceed to study equilibrium in the goods market. We know how much consumers want to buy, how much firms want to invest in productive equipment, and the government's spending intentions. In addition, we have characterized how much of all that should

---

[3] This is done to avoid carrying along one more variable, absorption. We could keep absorption in our formulation and, in the end, eliminate it. We would just end up where we will soon be. Exercise 11 at the end of the chapter invites you to check this assertion.

fall on domestic or foreign goods and the intentions of foreign customers. Adding up the various demand functions according to the national income identity, we obtain the planned or **desired demand function**:

(10.9) $DD = C(\bar{\Omega}, Y - \bar{T}) + I(r, q) + \bar{G} + PCA(Y, Y^*, \sigma).$
$\qquad\quad +\quad +\quad\ -\ +\qquad\quad -\ +\ -$

(desired demand function)

Why is this called 'desired' and not actual demand? In short, because a number of the factors that drive aggregate demand—real GDP, the real interest rate, Tobin's q, the real exchange rate—also depend on demand, as we shall see. For instance, real income Y affects demand, but at the same time it represents aggregate supply which, according to the Keynesian assumption, adjusts to demand. So (10.9) describes what aggregate demand would be—what the economy would desire to spend—given particular values of these endogenous variables, not necessarily what it will in fact be. Indeed, we need to ascertain that the values of these endogenous variables are compatible with each other.

While this may seem like a bad case of circular reasoning, it illustrates the fundamentally simultaneous nature of equilibrium in economics. It simply corresponds to the circular flow diagram presented in Chapter 2. This diagram shows that what is spent must be earned so that the GDP measures both total income and total output. The point of the desired demand DD function is to cut through the circularity. It tells us what demand should be *given* GDP, which is total income. At the same time, GDP also measures output, which is determined by demand under the Keynesian assumption. To express this simultaneous determination of demand and output, it is useful to turn to a graphical analysis.

We start with a description of how GDP Y affects desired demand, ignoring for the time being the other variables shown on the right-hand side of (10.9). We note that Y matters in two ways: first, it affects positively consumption. But, second, it also exerts a negative effect on the primary account since a higher income increases imports. Which effect dominates? Theory and evidence say that it is the consumption effect. The reason is that imports

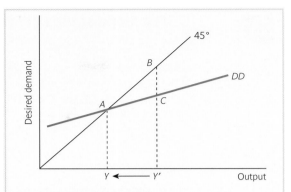

Fig. 10.3 The 45° Diagram

Desired demand *DD* increases with income (earned from output sales), but less than proportionately because part of any additional income is typically saved and part of spending is imported. Equilibrium occurs when demand equals supply, i.e. when firms deliver a level of output—measured along the horizontal axis—equal to what is being demanded—measured along the vertical axis. This happens along the 45° line. Equilibrium occurs at point *A*, where desired demand and output are equal. The corresponding output level *Y* is called equilibrium GDP. If output exceeds its equilibrium level, for example *Y'*, supply (point *B*) exceeds demand (point *C*) so firms accumulate inventories of unsold goods. Sooner or later, they will cut production and the economy will move towards equilibrium.

represent a fraction of domestic spending. When an increase in GDP causes consumption to rise, imports too rise but by a (variable, the real exhange rate matters as well) fraction of consumption. In the end, aggregate demand rises with the GDP, which is represented in Figure 10.3 by the upward-sloping *DD* schedule. But demand increases less than the GDP, which explains why the *DD* schedule is flatter than the 45° line. This is formally shown in Box 10.1.

The goods market is in equilibrium when GDP, interpreted as output, is equal to GDP interpreted as spending. Output, the left-hand side of (10.1), is represented by the horizontal axis in Figure 10.3, while desired spending, the right-hand side of (10.1) and described by (10.9), appears on the vertical axis.

Box 10.1 The Slope of the *DD* Schedule

The slope of the *DD* schedule is measured by the increase of desired demand in response to an increase in output. From equation (10.9) we see that GDP, which also measures total income, affects desired demand via consumption and via the primary current account:

$$\Delta DD = \Delta C + \Delta PCA.$$

Let's look at each channel one by one. From Chapter 8, we know that consumption increases by less than income because consumers wish to smooth changes in income:

$$\Delta C < \Delta Y.$$

A simple way of describing this result is to introduce the marginal propensity to consume *c*, which captures the response of consumption to a (marginal) change in income: $\Delta C = c\Delta Y$. If $c < 1$, then indeed $\Delta C < \Delta Y$.

Next, look at the PCA, the difference between exports *X* and imports *Z*. Exports do not demand on domestic GDP, while imports rise with spending and therefore with GDP. Overall, therefore, the primary account deteriorates when GDP rises:

$$\Delta PCA = -\Delta Z < 0.$$

Suppose, for simplicity, that imports are a constant fraction *z* of consumption, say $Z = zC$, and that all investment goods are bought from a domestic producer. Thus, we have $\Delta Z = z\Delta C$. The proportion *z* must be less than one. Since it is positive, it implies that $1 - z$ too is positive but also less than one. Putting this altogether, we have

$$\Delta DD = \Delta C - z\Delta C = (1 - z)\Delta C = (1 - z)c\Delta Y.$$

Since both *c* and $1 - z$ are both less than one, it follows that $\Delta DD < \Delta Y$, the slope of the *DD* schedule, $(1 - z)c$, is less than 1, and the *DD* schedule is flatter than the 45° line.

Market equilibrium requires that both be equal. Graphically, it means that equilibrium must occur along the 45° line. The *DD* schedule describes how much people want to spend, given their income, which they can freely choose. Point *A*, at the intersection of both schedules, represents the situation where desired aggregate demand is met, i.e. is equal to output. This state is called **goods market equilibrium** and the corresponding output level, *Y*, is **equilibrium GDP**.

To grasp the meaning of equilibrium in the goods market, consider the case where GDP is *Y'*, above its equilibrium level *Y*. Output is represented vertically by point *B*, desired demand by point *C*. The fact that *B* is above *C* means that we face a situation of excess supply. Since no one is forced to spend more than she wishes, firms can only sell the quantity represented by point *C*. In this situation, firms produce more than their customers want to buy. The excess supply, measured by *BC*, is stored aside as inventories of unsold goods. This is a situation that cannot last very long because firms will not produce goods that they cannot sell. Sooner or later, they will

reduce their production and the output level will decline. Graphically, production moves from point *B* down and to the left along the 45° line. Less production means less income and desired spending declines. Graphically, desired spending moves from point *C* down and to the left along the *DD* schedule. The process will continue until we reach point *A*. Conversely, starting below equilibrium GDP, there would be excess demand. Firms satisfy demand at first by drawing down their previously accumulated inventories but, at some point, they will raise production and the economy will move rightward until point *A* is reached.

Let's summarize what we know about the goods market. First, we have seen that GDP automatically returns to its equilibrium level because firms adjust the production level to meet the market's demand. Second, any disequilibrium in the goods market is relatively short-lived. Firms use their inventories as a buffer. They accumulate inventories when demand is weak and they run down inventories when demand exceeds production. This is why firms carefully monitor their inventory levels.

Finally, you may worry that the accounting identity does not hold out of equilibrium. The national accountants have solved that problem by treating the accumulation of inventories as final sales. Implicitly, firms sell to themselves the goods that they stock—they 'invest' in extra inventories. For instance, with output at Y', income and GDP exceed the aggregate demand forthcoming by the amount BC, while total GDP is read off point C. Conversely, inventory decumulation is treated as negative sales and subtracted from actual spending—as if firms would disinvest, or buy back from themselves the goods that they sell from existing stock.[4]

10.2.4 The Keynesian Multiplier

The DD schedule captures the effect of GDP on demand, taking as constant all the variables besides GDP. If these variables change, the DD schedule will shift and equilibrium GDP will change. Understanding these effects provides the first explanation of output fluctuations, the purpose of this and subsequent chapters.

For example, public spending on goods has been considered as exogenous thus far and constant. What would happen if it were to increase by $\Delta \bar{G}$, from $\bar{G}$ to $\bar{G}'$? We look at what happens in Figure 10.4, assuming that the economy starts from equilibrium at point A with real GDP level Y. Desired demand has now increased by $\Delta \bar{G}$, at any level of output. As a result, the desired demand schedule shifts upwards by that amount. If output remains unchanged at Y, the new situation is described by point B, where desired demand exceeds output. For a while, producers will make up the difference by drawing down their inventories but, within a few weeks, they will start raising their output to match the new demand. They will continue to do so until equilibrium output is reached at point E and output has risen to Y'.

Let us track down what happens on the way from A to E. At the initial output level Y, desired demand

first increases by $\Delta \bar{G}$. Excess demand $AB = \Delta \bar{G}$ is eliminated when firms increase production by $BA' = AB$ and the economy moves to point A'. Yet point A' is not a market equilibrium since it is not on the DD' schedule. At point A' we have neglected to account for the fact that, when output rises from A to A', income does too, raising desired demand to point B'. As firms raise output to eliminate the excess demand AB, more income is generated, which creates more excess demand in the amount $A'B'$. Firms will again raise output by $A'B'$, which takes the economy to A''. And once again, more output means more income and therefore a higher level of desired demand. The staircase process continues until the economy reaches point E, which is on both the new desired demand schedule and the 45° line.

How do we know that this apparently unending process stops at point E? Note that the first step of the staircase is of size $AB = BA' = \Delta \bar{G}$. The second one, of size $A'B' = B'A''$, is smaller. The graphical reason is that the desired demand schedule DD is flatter than the 45° line, and there are two reasons for this. First, some of the additional income created is saved and not spent. Second, some of the extra spending falls on imports, and imports create income abroad, not at home. Thus while more demand creates an equal increase in supply and therefore income, the extra spending generated by the additional income is smaller. Savings and imports operate as leakages which drain some of the newly created income away from additional spending. This is why each step in the staircase is smaller than the previous one. Eventually, the steps become minuscule. Box 10.2 gives a formal description of this process.

The other remarkable result is that the total increase of output, from Y to Y', is a *multiple* of the initial exogenous increase in demand $\Delta \bar{G} = AB = BA'$. This is why the effect is called the **Keynesian demand multiplier**. It is very general: no matter which exogenous change triggers the process, and whether the disturbance is positive or negative, equilibrium output always responds to demand by a larger amount.[5]

---

[4] More precisely, national accountants treat the accumulation of inventories as an investment: total investment is the sum of desired investment and undesired inventory accumulation: $Y = C + I^{desired} + \Delta(\text{inventories}) + \bar{G} + PCA$.

[5] The overall effect may take several months to complete.

Box 10.2 The Multiplier's Algebra

In Box 10.1, we showed that the slope of the *DD* schedule is $c(1 - z)$. So when government spending increases by $\Delta \bar{G}$, output and therefore incomes first increase by $\Delta \bar{G}$ as well. This is the size of the first step in Figure 10.4. Then desired spending increases by $c(1 - z)\Delta \bar{G}$, which is the size of the second step. The third step corresponds to an income increase of $c(1 - z)\Delta \bar{G}$, so desired spending increases by $c(1 - z)[c(1 - z)\Delta \bar{G}] = c^2(1 - z)^2\Delta \bar{G}$. Since c and $1 - z$ are smaller than 1, c^2 is smaller than c and $(1 - z)^2$ is smaller than $(1 - z)$. Continuing in the same way, the size of the next step is $c^3(1 - z)^3\Delta \bar{G}$, etc. In the end, the whole income increase is

$$\Delta Y = \Delta \bar{G} + c(1 - z)\Delta \bar{G} + c^2(1 - z)^2\Delta \bar{G} + c^3(1 - z)^3\Delta \bar{G} + \dots$$
$$+ c^n(1 - z)^n\Delta \bar{G} + \dots$$
$$= [1 + c(1 - z) + c^2(1 - z)^2 + c^3(1 - z)^3 + \dots + c^n(1 - z)^n$$
$$+ \dots]\Delta \bar{G} = \frac{1}{1 - c(1 - z)}\Delta \bar{G}.$$

The last formula is a result from standard algebra (if a is less than one, $1 + a + a^2 + \dots + a^n + \dots = \frac{1}{1 - a}$). This shows that the multiplier is $\frac{1}{1 - c(1 - z)}$, which is larger than unity. Note that, if there is no leakage to savings ($c = 1$) and to imports ($z = 0$), the multiplier would be infinite. Needless to say, this case is not of practical relevance.

The multiplier effect corresponds to the fundamental insight provided by the circular flow diagram in Chapter 2. Each individual's spending is someone else's income. By raising incomes, an exogenous increase in demand generates additional desired demand, which means more spending and income, a never-ending process, although at each stage, the effect becomes smaller, and eventually dies out. The circular flow diagram showed where these leakages occur: taxes, savings, and imports each capture a portion of any additional income.[6] These three leakages represent domestic income not *automatically* re-spent on domestic goods and services.

The word 'automatically' is important. For example, some of the additional taxes collected along the way could be used to support additional public spending but it would be an exogenous decision by the government to raise $\bar{G}$ even more than the initial boost $\Delta \bar{G}$. Similarly, higher savings are available to finance new productive equipment. However, firms must be convinced to invest more. Improved expectations of future profitability captured by Tobin's q, which we treat here as exogenous, would do this.

Finally, a rise in imports will generate higher incomes abroad, triggering there another multiplier effect which might well lead to higher foreign GDP Y^* and more exports. All of these effects are plausible but, since we consider $\bar{G}$, $\bar{q}$, $\bar{T}$, and Y^* as exogenous, at this stage we cannot logically treat them as responding automatically in the circular flow of income.

It should be clear, by now, that big leakages reduce the multiplier. We can check this a bit more formally. If a large proportion of any additional income is saved or if a large proportion of any additional spending is imported, the *DD* schedule becomes flat. Next, you can verify in Figure 10.4 that the flatter the *DD* schedule, the smaller is the multiplier effect.[7]

In practice, there is much debate about the size of the multiplier. A part of the debate, presented in Chapter 20, is associated with doubts about, or even rejection of, the Keynesian assumptions. Another part of the debate is related to more technical issues, for example what is assumed to happen to some of the variables that we have ignored in the previous reasoning (tax revenues, Tobin's q, etc.).

---

[6] Here, however, we consider taxes as exogenous and constant.

[7] This can be shown with the result in Box 10.2. A lower c or higher z increase the multiplier.

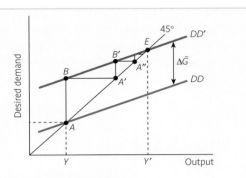

Fig. 10.4 The Multiplier

An exogenous increase in government spending shifts the demand schedule vertically by $\Delta\bar{G}$. Supply equals demand, and the economy's equilibrium output increases to point Y^*. The multiplier effect—that $Y^* - Y$ exceeds the initial impulse $\Delta\bar{G}$—can be understood by following the staircase up from point A. The direct effect, an increase in demand and output, raises GDP to point A'. However, this point is still not equilibrium, because DD lies above the 45° line. Thus, desired demand and output increases again, to point A'', and so on.

Finally, the speed at which GDP responds to fiscal policy actions varies, depending on countries and circumstances. The multipliers presented in Table 10.1 show the effect of an increase in public spending over the following two years and should be

Table 10.1 Public Spending Demand Multipliers

	Years after change	
	1	2
Euro area	1.1	1.6
UK	0.8	0.5
USA	1.9	2.2
Belgium	0.9	0.5
Germany	1.2	1.1
Italy	1.0	1.4
Portugal	1.2	1.5
Spain	1.2	1.5

Source: Henry, Hernández de Cos, and Momigliano (2004) .

regarded as very well-informed guesses. Generally, the multiplier is higher in large and relatively closed economies, like the euro area and the USA, because the import leakages are small. These estimates also tend to indicate that the multiplier is indeed larger than 1 in most cases.

10.2.5 Endogenous and Exogenous Variables

When using this framework, it is essential to be clear about the distinction between the economic variables that we take as exogenous and those which are endogenous and thus to be explained. Whether a variable is treated as endogenous or exogenous is an analytical assumption made for convenience. Indeed, by declaring a variable to be exogenous, we free ourselves from the obligation of explaining its behaviour. Naturally, if we are ambitious, we would like to explain everything! But we must be patient, first taking most variables as exogenous and, gradually, endogenizing them.

A review will be helpful at this stage. The Keynesian assumption implies that the price level P is exogenous. Fiscal policy instruments, such as government purchases $\bar{G}$ and taxes $\bar{T}$ are assumed to be under direct control of the government and thus are also treated as exogenous—hence the overbar symbol.[8] As in Chapter 8, household wealth $\bar{\Omega}$ is also assumed to be exogenous, as are foreign variables such as foreign GDP (Y^*) and the price level (P^*), since they are also not influenced by domestic changes as long as the economy under consideration is small relative to the 'rest of the world'. The nominal and real exchange rates too are also treated as exogenous, although we will change that in the next chapter. Finally, the interest rate and Tobin's q will be endogenized in the next section.

In the end, the only endogenous variable so far is output Y. Two other variables, consumption and the PCA, were also treated as endogenous in so

---

[8] We treat net taxes as exogenous for simplicity, for the time being. In the WebAppendix to this chapter, more realistically, taxes are allowed to depend positively on income Y. Indeed, in practice, governments usually set tax *rates*, which implies that tax revenues tend to rise with output and income.

far as they depend on output. This section has provided the first explanation of business cycles. It shows how output responds to changes in the exogenous variables. Figure 10.4 has treated one example, when the government increases public spending. It is good practice to consider each of the exogenous variables, ask what happens when it changes, and graphically track the effect on GDP.

10.3 The Goods Market and the *IS* Curve

In this section, we add the interest rate to the list of endogenous variables. We now aim at explaining output and the interest rate *jointly*. This will be achieved by the end of this chapter. As before, we will mainly reason graphically. The two endogenous variables will appear on the figure, output Y along the horizontal axis and the interest rate i along the vertical axis.

10.3.1 From the 45° Diagram to the *IS* Curve

In Figure 10.3, the DD schedule depicts how desired demand varies when output changes, holding everything else (the interest and exchange rates, Tobin's q, public spending and taxes, private wealth, foreign demand) constant. This is the time to remember that Tobin's q is inversely related to the real interest rate r. When r rises, future profits are more heavily discounted and Tobin's q declines. While expected future profits—animal spirits, as we called them—will be considered exogenous, Tobin's q is now endogenous to the interest rate.

We can now ask: What happens to equilibrium output when the interest rate changes? The answer is given in the first panel of Figure 10.5. The starting point A, where equilibrium is achieved, lies on the desired demand schedule drawn for an interest rate i. Now suppose that the interest rate declines from

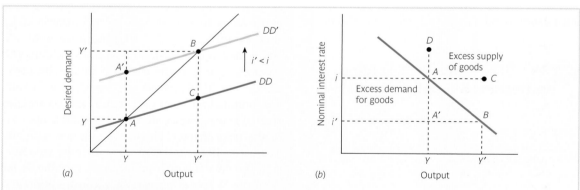

Fig. 10.5 Deriving the *IS* Curve

A reduction in the interest rate from i to i' leads to an increase in investment spending. This is met by an increase in equilibrium output, as shown in the left-hand side chart. This is summarized in the right-hand side chart by the *IS* curve. The *IS* curve is flatter the larger is the increase in equilibrium output, as measured by the horizontal distance between A' and B in both charts. The length of $A'B$ in turn depends on: (1) the sensitivity of demand to interest changes, represented by the size of the vertical shift of DD, or AA', in panel (a); and (2) the multiplier effect, measured by distance $A'B$ in the same panel. The multiplier is larger the steeper the desired demand schedule, i.e. the more sensitive is demand to changes in output.

i to i'. We know that Tobin's q will increase. Looking at the investment function (10.3), we see that investment will rise since both of its determinants, the interest rate and Tobin's q, act in the same direction. At each level of income, desired demand is now higher, which means that the DD curve shifts upwards. The new equilibrium is now achieved at point B (with a multiplier effect), which means that equilibrium output increases from Y to Y'.[9]

This result is summarized in the second panel of Figure 10.5. Points A and B correspond respectively to the initial (interest rate i and GDP Y) and final (i' and Y') situations. Of course, we can repeat the same reasoning for other interest rate levels, to obtain more points like A and B. They will trace out a negative relationship between the interest rate and equilibrium output depicted by the downward-sloping schedule known as the **IS curve**.[10] *For given values of exogenous variables, the IS curve represents the combinations of nominal interest rate i and real GDP that are consistent with goods market equilibrium.*

How do we remember that the IS curve is downward sloping? It is enough to remember two things. First, the IS curve is the response to the question previously asked: What happens to equilibrium output when the interest rate changes? Second, a higher interest rate reduces private spending on investment, which reduces demand and, *via* the multiplier, equilibrium output.

10.3.2 The Slope of the *IS* Curve and the Multiplier

What makes the IS curve more or less steep? This is not a hugely important issue. Still, we briefly

answer the question for the sake of completeness.[11] In Figure 10.5(*b*), the slope of the curve is given by the ratio of AA' to $A'B$. AA' represents the size of the assumed interest rate reduction, while $A'B$ tells us how much equilibrium GDP rises in response to this reduction. Intuitively, the more equilibrium output rises in response to a given reduction of the interest rate, the flatter is the IS curve.

In order to understand what determines the size of $A'B$, we turn to panel (*a*). The first item of interest is the upward shift of the DD schedule. The vertical distance of the shift corresponds to the initial rise in investment spending generated by the lowering of the interest rate. Obviously, the further up the DD schedule shifts, the longer will be $A'B$ and the flatter will be the IS curve. Thus, the responsiveness of investment to an interest rate reduction is the first factor that influences the slope of the IS curve.[12]

Now note that point A' in Figure 10.5(*a*) does not correspond to equilibrium in the goods market. Demand has risen, but output has not yet responded. By the arguments we have made all along, supply will rise to meet demand, which increases income and demand. This is the multiplier story all over again. So the second factor that determines the length of $A'B$ is the multiplier itself. The larger it is, the longer is $A'B$ and, therefore, the flatter is the IS curve.

Summarizing, the IS curve is flatter (1) the greater the sensitivity of demand to changes in interest rates, as measured by the vertical shift of the desired demand schedule (AA') in panel (*a*), and (2) the larger the multiplier that translates the initial exogenous change into higher total demand, as measured along $A'B$.

10.3.3 Off the *IS* Curve

More interesting is to understand what happens when the economy is *not* on the IS curve. The short

---

[9] We can add another channel. A rise in q means that stock prices are increased. Since stocks are part of wealth Ω, wealth too increases. This raises private consumption in line with the consumption function (10.2). Thus wealth can be made endogenous as well.

[10] The name of this curve comes from the identity (2.6): $I - S = T - G + PCA$, and was first derived by Nobel Prize laureate Sir John Hicks. For simplicity, he assumed government budget balance ($T = G$) and no foreign trade (PCA = 0), so the identity can be reduced to $I = S$. We draw the IS curve as a line because we do not really know, nor do we need to know, its exact shape. For a derivation of the IS curve using calculus, see the WebAppendix.

[11] The slope of the IS curve is formally derived in the WebAppendix.

[12] We noted in footnote 9 that consumption is also likely to rise. The more it does, the flatter will the IS curve be.

answer is that the *IS* curve represents the goods market equilibrium condition, so that points off the curve describe conditions of either excess demand or excess supply. But which is which?

Let us start from point *A* in Figure 10.5(*b*), on the *IS* curve, and imagine that output increases while the interest rate remains unchanged. For example, that we move to point *C* vertically above *B*. Spending has risen as well but less because of the leakages discussed in Section 10.2.4. In Figure 10.5(a) demand is represented by point *C* while supply is represented by point *B*. At point *C* in panel (*b*), therefore, there is not enough demand to absorb all of the new output. This is a situation of **excess supply** on the goods market, and inventories rise. Similarly, moving vertically up from point *A* to a point like *D* corresponds to an increase in the interest rate at unchanged output. This also leads to excess supply in the goods market because the higher interest rate reduces aggregate demand.

Thus the *IS* curve determines two regions: (1) above and to the right we observe excess supply in the goods market—inventories are being accumulated; and (2) below and to the left, we have **excess demand** in the market for goods and services, and inventories are run down. At the boundary of the two regions, the *IS* curve represents those combinations of GDP and the interest rates which are consistent with goods market equilibrium. We have seen in Section 10.2.2 that the economy can stay temporarily off the *IS* curve, while firms use their inventories as a buffer stock, but fairly soon they will adjust their output, returning the economy to goods market equilibrium on the *IS* curve. For example, from point *C* in Figure 10.5(*b*), the economy will move to point *A* as firms cut production after a period of inventory accumulation. Similarly, from point *D* the economy will move horizontally to the left until it reaches the *IS* curve. More generally, on the right of the *IS* curve where there is excess supply, goods market equilibrium requires that the economy shifts to the left so that output is brought down to a level compatible with desired demand. Conversely, starting from a situation of excess demand on the left of the *IS* curve, the economy will move to the right as firms expand output to meet

demand. This is what the Keynesian assumption implies.

10.3.4 A Key Distinction: Movements Along or Shifts of the *IS* Curve

A common pitfall is to confuse *shifts* of the *IS* curve with movements *along* it. This is directly related to the distinction between exogenous and endogenous variables examined in Section 10.2.5. The *IS* curve describes how the two endogenous variables, the real GDP (Y) and the nominal interest rate (i), are combined to achieve equilibrium in the goods market, *everything else being held constant*. What is 'everything else'? This refers to all the variables that we treat as exogenous when we draw the *IS* schedule. As long as these exogenous variables remain constant, the *IS* curve stays in place and we can only move along the curve. Any change in any exogenous variable causes the *IS* to shift.

In Figure 10.6, an example shows what happens when desired demand increases exogenously, e.g. if public spending is increased, or the real exchange rate depreciates. In both panels, we start from point *A*, with output Y and interest rate i. In panel (*a*), the desired demand schedule shifts upwards. Then the multiplier process gets under way and we eventually end up at point *B*, where output is Y'. Now remember that the interest rate is exogenous for panel (*a*). Implicitly, therefore, we have assumed that it has not changed and that is the same at points *A* and *B*. Now transcribe this into panel (*b*). Point *B* corresponds to the same interest rate i and to the new output level Y'. This point lies on the new curve *IS'*, which shows how the curve has shifted. In the end, the rule is simple: any exogenous change that raises demand shifts the *IS* curve to the right, which quite logically means more output. Conversely, when demand exogenously declines, the *IS* curve shifts to the left.

Which are the relevant exogenous variables? Fiscal policy is a premier source of shifts in the *IS* curve. The government is a large player in the macroeconomy, and changes in government purchases of goods $\bar{G}$ (e.g. military procurement or road construction) or services (e.g. the number of civil servants or their pay packets) exerts a significant

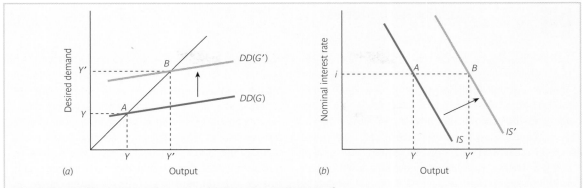

Fig. 10.6 An Exogenous Increase in Aggregate Demand
At unchanged interest rate i, an increase in any of the exogenous components of demand is represented in panel (a) by an upward shift of the aggregate demand schedule. Equilibrium occurs at point B and the new equilibrium output Y' is higher than the initial level Y. Panel (b) shows that the IS curve shifts to the right for the given interest rate.

influence on aggregate demand. Similarly, changes in taxation $\bar{T}$ alter disposable income available to households or firms, with knock-on multiplier effects on consumption.

Second, consumption depends on household wealth Ω. Wealth can take many forms, such as land, houses, financial assets, precious goods such as jewels, Persian rugs, and art, etc. Several of these components can be highly volatile and provoke sharp changes in consumption and thus the position of the IS curve. A classic example is the Great Depression of the 1930s, which followed the crash of stock prices on Wall Street. More recent episodes further illustrate this phenomenon. As we write, the world may be on the verge of a recession as overvalued house prices in the USA and global stock markets have fallen sharply. Similarly, in the early 2000s internet and technology-related share prices declined precipitously and brought about a worldwide recession, as Box 10.3 recalls. Collapsing housing prices also contributed to recessions in the UK, Sweden, and Japan in the early 1990s.

Third, changes in expectations of businesspeople represent another important factor, shifting the IS curve as they affect investment decisions. These expectations, which focus on the future profitability of investment, are driven as much by gut feelings as by rational calculus. This is why Keynes called them 'animal spirits'. These factors are captured in Tobin's q.

Finally, foreign disturbances matter for an open economy. They affect the IS curve through the primary current account. The current account is not only a source of leakage, but it also transmits foreign disturbances. Indeed, the PCA function (10.8) shows that changes in world activity Y^* can generate export-led expansions or recessions. All other things equal, an increase in Y^* will increase the PCA and cause the IS curve to shift rightwards. The same applies to the real exchange rate $\sigma = SP/P^*$, which determines the economy's competitiveness. Any change in either the nominal exchange rate S or in domestic and foreign prices P and P^* eventually shifts the IS curve, to the right when the real exchange rate depreciates and competitiveness rises, to the left in the case of an appreciation.

Box 10.3 Bubble Bath Stories

Twice in less than a decade the US economy has been badly shaken by abrupt changes in wealth brought about by unstable financial markets.[13] Over 1999–2000, fuelled by the 'information technology revolution', average share prices quoted on the NASDAQ almost tripled, as Figure 10.7 shows. Fortunes were quickly made while experts debated whether such increases were justified. Some wondered about the existence of a bubble, when stock prices lose sight of their fundamental valuations and are driven to ever-higher levels by expectations of yet more future price increases. The Chairman of the Federal Reserve, Alan Greenspan, went as far as to warn markets against 'irrational exuberance' in 1996. He later reversed his opinion and became an enthusiastic supporter of the revolution.

The ascent was fast, but the descent was even faster. Happy consumers who felt rich had kept the economy roaring during this protracted boom. Now feeling im-poverished, they cut down sharply on spending, which prompted a recession. The rest of the world could not escape as falling consumption in the USA meant less exports and weaker current accounts everywhere else.

Many observers were surprised that the recession was not even worse. One explanation was that house prices had doubled since 1995 and continued to rise even through the recession. Indeed, in a country where many citizens are home owners—the so-called American dream—rising housing prices can have just as great an effect on wealth as rising stock prices. Boosted anew by the house price bubble, the US economy quickly returned to growth. Then, in late 2006, that bubble burst too, leading to the infamous sub-prime crisis. As we write, in mid-2008, the questions are how far will house prices fall, how badly will the US economy be hurt, and what will it all mean for the rest of the world?

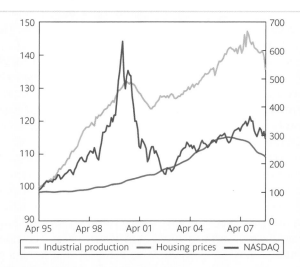

Fig. 10.7 Boom and Bust in the USA

The Case–Shiller Home Price Index measures the evolution of housing prices across the USA. The NASDAQ Stock Market specializes in high-tech industries. Both indices are normalized to take the value 100 in January 1995 and are measured against the right-hand scale. The industrial production index, also normalized to take the value 100 in January 1995, is measured against the left-hand axis. Its movements tend to track those of real GDP.

Sources: Standard & Poor/Case–Shiller, *International Financial Statistics*, IMF; authors' calculations.

---

[13] We study financial markets in Chapter 14, where the reasons for this instability are explained.

10.4 The Money Market and the *LM* Curve

10.4.1 The *LM* Curve

After studying the goods market in Section 10.3, we now ask which levels of real GDP and interest rate are compatible with equilibrium in the money market. We have already examined the money market at length in Chapter 9. We will start with the demand for money. In Chapter 6, we argued that firms and households need money to conduct their transactions and that they are interested in its purchasing power, which was denoted by M/P. Noting that holding cash rather than other assets is costly, for it means giving up interest, we concluded that the demand for real money can be written as $k(i)Y$. A more general formulation is

$$\text{real money demand} = L(Y, i),$$
$$+ \quad -$$

where the signs underneath indicate that demand rises with GDP and declines with the interest rate. Note that it is the nominal interest rate i that is the correct measure of the opportunity cost of holding money. The reason is that consistency requires that we compare nominal asset returns with the nominal return on cash, which is zero.[14]

We also discussed in Chapter 9 the strategy options open to a central bank. We noted that it was popular in the 1980s for central banks to target money growth but that, nowadays, most central banks directly set the interest rate. We will look at both cases, starting with money growth targeting.

More precisely, we assume that the central bank has decided to keep the money supply constant at $\bar{M}$. With the price level constant, this means that the central bank has decided to maintain the real money supply at $\bar{M}/P$. Put differently, we consider that both nominal and real money balances are exogenously set by the central bank. Panel (a) of Figure 10.8 reproduces the equilibrium condition established in Chapter 9. The constant-money supply rule is represented by the vertical supply schedule. The downward-sloping demand schedule captures the idea that, given the GDP level Y, money demand declines as the interest rises. **Money market equilibrium** occurs at point A where supply and demand are equal:

(10.10) $\bar{M}/P = L(Y, i).$

Now consider the effect of an increase in GDP from Y to Y', holding all else constant. The immediate consequence is that the demand for money rises because people need more money to carry out more transactions. Graphically, in panel (a) of Figure 10.8 the money demand schedule shifts out. The new equilibrium is at point B, and the interest rate rises from i to i'. As in Figure 10.5, we transpose these two equilibria in panel (b) of Figure 10.8, with corresponding equilibrium points A (Y and i) and B (Y' and i'). Money market equilibrium implies a positive relationship between GDP and the interest rate. This relationship is called the **LM curve**. *The LM curve is the combination of income and interest rates for which the money market is in equilibrium, given the price level and the exogenous variables.*[15]

10.4.2 The Slope of the *LM* Curve

The reason why the *LM* curve is upward-sloping is easy to understand. When GDP increases, money demand rises. Yet, by assumption, the central bank is keeping the supply unchanged. Clearly, something must happen to reduce demand to the level consistent with the given, exogenous supply. This is the role of the interest rate. Since a higher interest rate lowers money demand, there will be an interest rate high enough to fully offset the higher demand for money generated by a larger GDP.

---

[14] As we will see later, the real return on cash is negative in the presence of inflation. Most people are keenly aware that money loses value when prices rise.

[15] The name 'LM' originates from the fact that, along the curve, the demand for liquidity (L) equals the money supply (M) in equation (10.10). For an explicit derivation of the slope of the *LM* curve using calculus, see the WebAppendix to this chapter.

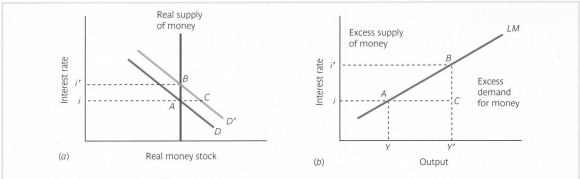

Fig. 10.8 Deriving the *LM* Curve

An exogenous increase in GDP raises the demand for money at any interest rate, hence the shift from *D* to *D'* in panel (*a*). At the initial interest rate *i*, we now have excess demand, as represented by point *C* in both panels. The return to money equilibrium is achieved through an increase in the interest rate which reduces demand. The required increase from *i* to *i'* (measured by *AB* in panel (*a*) and by *BC* in panel (*b*)) is inversely proportional to the responsiveness of money demand to the interest rate. If money demand is very interest sensitive, a small increase in the interest rate is sufficient to eliminate the excess demand.

This intuition helps us to understand the slope of the *LM* curve, shown in Figure 10.8(*b*), as the ratio of *BC* over *AC*. The segment *AC* is simply the assumed increase in GDP, so the slope of the *LM* curve is really explained by the length of *BC*. Note that *BC* represents the interest rate increase that reduces money demand by as much as it rose in response to the increase in GDP. Its length depends therefore on two characteristics. First, how sensitive is the demand for money to changes in the real GDP? If it is very sensitive (we say that the income elasticity of money demand is large), a given increase in output raises money demand by a large amount. This is segment *AC* in Figure 10.8(*a*). The return to money market equilibrium will therefore require a large compensating interest rate increase, i.e. a long segment *BC*. This means a steep *LM* schedule.

Second, how sensitive is the demand for money to interest rate changes? This aspect is captured by the slope of the money demand function *D* depicted in Figure 10.8(*a*). A steep money demand function means that a large change in the interest rate has a small effect on money demand. The demand for money is insensitive to changes in the interest rate (we say that the interest elasticity of demand is low), and the interest rate must move a lot to re-establish equilibrium for a given increase in GDP.

Hence *BC* is long and the *LM* curve is steep. If money demand is instead flat, small changes in the interest rate are sufficient to restore equilibrium and the *LM* curve will also be flat. To summarize, the *LM* curve is steeper, the more sensitive money demand is to output, and the less sensitive it is to the interest rate.

10.4.3 Off the *LM* Curve

Because the *LM* curve represents the combinations of GDP and interest rates compatible with money market equilibrium, it stands to reason that points *off* the curve correspond to disequilibrium in the money market. To see this, suppose that the economy is in equilibrium at point *A* in Figure 10.8(*b*) and that real GDP increases from *Y* to *Y'* at an unchanged interest rate, say to point *C*. The higher GDP raises the demand for real money balances. Since, by assumption, the real supply of money is unchanged, the result is an excess demand for money. As we saw, a higher interest rate is necessary to restore equilibrium.

We have just seen that the money market is in excess demand below and to the right of the *LM* curve. Conversely, the region above and to the left of the *LM* curve corresponds to an excess supply of money that calls for a decrease in the interest rate

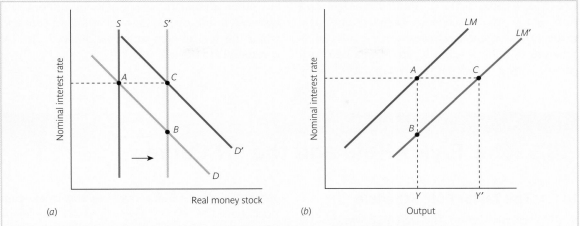

Fig. 10.9 An Increase in the Money Supply Shifts the *LM* Curve Outward

Starting from point *A*, an increase in the money supply shifts the money supply curve from *S* to *S'* in panel (*a*). At the same level of interest rates, an excess supply of money results at point *C*, which can be eliminated in two ways. First, the interest rate can fall until point *B* is reached. Second, output could rise from *Y* to *Y'*, which increases demand and shifts the demand schedule from *D* to *D'*. Equilibrium is achieved at point *C*. Summarizing this in panel (*b*), we see that points *B* and *C* identify a new curve *LM'* to the right of the initial *LM*. In fact, these are not the only two possibilities. Any combination of interest rates and output on *LM'* is compatible with equilibrium given the increased money supply.

or an increase in output to restore equilibrium. The border between these two regions, the *LM* curve, is where the money market is in equilibrium.

What happens if the economy is off the *LM* curve? Suppose that it is below the curve, with excess demand for money. This means that people (households and firms) want to hold more cash. As we know from Chapter 9, the way to get more cash is to borrow. People apply to their banks for loans. As they grant loans to their customers, commercial banks need to increase their reserves. They try to borrow on the money market but, by assumption, the central bank is unwilling to provide more reserves. The result is an increase in the interest rate on the money market. Facing a higher cost of borrowing, the banks naturally raise the interest rate at which they lend to customers, which discourages borrowing.

Conversely, if we start from a situation of excess supply above the *LM* curve, the interest rate will decline to raise money demand. In the end, starting off the curve, the economy will move vertically up or down until it reaches the *LM* curve. In practice,

this happens quite quickly, in a matter of days or weeks, so that, as a first approximation, we can consider that the economy is always on the *LM* curve.

10.4.4 Moving Along or Shifting the *LM* Curve

As with the *IS* curve, we need to distinguish movements along the *LM* curve from shifts of the curve itself. The *LM* curve remains unchanged as long as the variables assumed to be exogenous do not change. Looking at Figure 10.8(*a*), we see that a particular *LM* curve corresponds to a given real money supply ($\bar{M}/P$). As long as the real money supply remains constant, we move along the *LM* curve.[16] On the other hand, the curve shifts whenever the real money supply varies.

Figure 10.9 shows that the *LM* curve shifts rightwards when the real money supply increases— when the nominal supply increases or the price

---

[16] The curve would shift if people's preferences for holding money balances changed. Exercise 6 at the end of the chapter explores this issue.

level falls. In panel (*a*), this is captured by a rightward shift of the supply schedule. Demand must rise to meet the exogenously higher supply. This can be achieved by a lower interest rate (points *B* in both panels) or by a higher output level (points *C*), or by any other combination of output and interest rate provided it falls on the new curve *LM'*. In contrast, when the real money supply is reduced, the *LM* curve shifts to the left.

10.5 The Taylor Rule and the *TR* Curve

10.5.1 The Taylor Rule Schedule

In the previous section, the *LM* curve was derived under the central assumption that the money supply is constant. Chapter 9, however, stressed that most central banks set interest rates directly, which means that the money supply adjusts endogenously to meet demand (see Figure 9.10). In that case, the *LM* curve is ill-suited to analyse the money market. Instead, we now look at the case when the central bank behaves according to the **Taylor rule** presented in Section 9.4. There, we concluded that the interest rate setting policy of modern central banks can be represented by the following relationship:

(10.11) $i = \bar{i} + a(\pi - \bar{\pi}) + b\dfrac{Y - \bar{Y}}{\bar{Y}},$

$\underset{\text{gap}}{\text{inflation}} \quad \underset{\text{gap}}{\text{output}}$

where π is the inflation rate, $\bar{\pi}$ is the inflation target, and $\bar{Y}$ is trend GDP. Recall that $\bar{i}$ is the neutral—sometimes also called natural—interest rate, which the central bank would choose if inflation and output were both on target ($\pi = \bar{\pi}$ and $Y = \bar{Y}$). The coefficients *a* and *b* indicate how responsive the central bank is to inflation and the output gap, respectively. The Keynesian assumption that prices are sticky means that inflation is negligible. We simply assume that inflation is zero and so is its target rate ($\pi = \bar{\pi} = 0$). The Taylor rule then boils down to

(10.12) $i = \bar{i} + b\dfrac{Y - \bar{Y}}{\bar{Y}},$

which says that the central bank simply 'leans against the wind': it raises the interest rate whenever output Y increases and, conversely, cuts rates when Y declines.

In Figure 10.10, we start from point *A* where the output gap is zero, i.e. output is equal to its trend level $\bar{Y}$. We next ask what happens if output increases from $Y = \bar{Y}$ to Y'. Money demand increases and the demand schedule shifts rightwards, from *D* to *D'* in panel (*a*).

This is where we depart from the *LM* curve. Under monetary targeting, it was assumed that the central bank keeps the money supply constant along the vertical schedule S^M. The interest rate rises to preserve equilibrium in the money market at point *B*. This gives rise to the *LM* curve in panel (*b*). In Chapter 9, we also looked at the case when, no matter what, the central bank keeps the interest rate constant, as captured by the horizontal supply schedule S^i in panel (*a*).[17] Equilibrium then occurs at point *C*. In that case, money market equilibrium is represented by the horizontal line in panel (*b*), simply reflecting the fact that the central bank keeps the interest rate constant.

The general case is represented by the upward-sloping schedule TR^1 in panel (*b*) of Figure 10.10. It says that the central bank raises the interest rate above the natural rate when output Y' exceeds its trend level $\bar{Y}$. In that case the money market equilibrium occurs at point *E*.

As drawn, point *E* is between *B* and *C*. Quite obviously, the interest rate is higher under the Taylor rule than when the central bank pegs the interest rate. Less obviously, the interest rate is lower than under money targeting. The reason is

---

[17] This would be the case if $b = 0$ in (10.12).

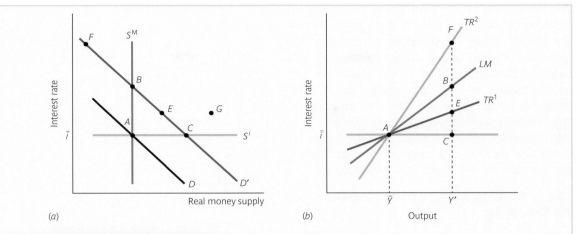

Fig. 10.10 The Taylor Rule Schedule

Starting from point *A* in both panels, we ask where will the new market equilibrium be when output increases from *Y* to *Y'*. The *LM* curve is drawn assuming that the central bank keeps the real money supply unchanged along *S^M*. In that case, money equilibrium occurs at points *B* in both panels. The opposite case is when the central bank keeps the interest rate unchanged and provides whatever amount of money is demanded. This is captured by the *S^i* schedule, leading to equilibrium at points *C*. The Taylor rule says that the central bank raises its interest rate when output increases. Points *E* provide one example. In response to the increase in output, which shifts the money demand schedule from *D* to *D'* in panel (*a*), the central bank raises the interest rate to the level that corresponds to point *E*. In so doing, the central bank allows the money supply to expand to a level that is intermediate between the constant-money case *S^M* and the interest rate-constant case *S^i*. This draws out the Taylor rule schedule *TR¹* in panel (*b*). A more reactive central bank would pick a higher interest rate, as represented by points *F*. In this case, it would contract the money supply, as seen from panel (*a*), and the *TR²* schedule in panel (*b*) would be steeper than the *LM* curve, which represents the case of constant money supply.

given in panel (*a*). When the central bank chooses point *E* on the money demand schedule *D'*, it allows for some increase in the money supply, which naturally delivers a lower interest rate. The money supply is no longer exogenous.

The **TR schedule** graphically resembles, but should not be confused with, the *LM* curve. The *LM* curve represents the money market equilibrium condition under the assumption that the central bank keeps the real money supply constant. The *TR* schedule describes how the central bank sets the interest rate in response to changes in output. Because the *TR* schedule describes the way the central bank acts, the economy is *always* on it, by construction. What about equilibrium in the money market? It is not seen in panel (*b*) but in panel (*a*). The central bank can choose whatever interest rate its Taylor rule dictates, but it must then provide the

amount of money that the market demands at that interest rate. Graphically, demand and supply are equal when the central bank chooses a point along the money demand curve. This is captured by point *E* in Figure 10.10(*a*).

10.5.2 Slope of the *TR* Schedule

The slope of the *TR¹* schedule describes how vigorously the central bank reacts to the output gap.[18] This can be illustrated in panel (*b*) with another schedule, *TR²*. This schedule is steeper than the *LM* curve, which corresponds to the situation when the central bank simply keeps the real money supply constant, as represented by schedule *S^M*. Along

---

[18] Some readers may recognize that the slope is simply the coefficient *b* of the Taylor rule.

TR^2, instead, the central bank reacts so strongly to deviations of GDP from trend that it actually lowers the money supply when output has risen to Y'. Indeed, in order to raise the interest rate to a level indicated in panel (b) by point F, it must take the money market to the corresponding point F in panel (a). In this case, the central bank actually reduces the money supply. Naturally, this means a higher interest rate than when the money supply is just kept constant and it explains why the Taylor rule schedule TR^2 is steeper than the LM curve.

10.5.3 Moving Along or Shifting the *TR* Schedule

As always, we need to be clear about whether we move along the TR schedule or whether the schedule shifts. The schedule represents the strategy of the central bank, so it only moves when the strategy changes. Equation (10.11) shows that the central bank's strategy is described by five parameters. Two of those parameters correspond to the central bank's reaction to deviations of inflation from its target (captured by coefficient a) and of output from its trend (captured by coefficient b). Another parameter is the inflation target $\bar{\pi}$, which corresponds to an exogenous definition of price stability or acceptable inflation. The parameter $\bar{Y}$ is the current level of trend GDP. Finally, $\bar{i}$ is the central bank's evaluation of the **neutral interest rate**.[19]

Unless these parameters change, we move along the TR schedule. When they do change, the TR

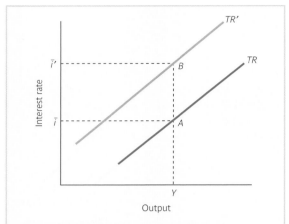

Fig. 10.11 Shifts of the *TR* Schedule

If the central bank changes its estimate of the neutral interest rate from $\bar{i}$ to $\bar{i}'$, the TR schedule shifts upwards. For instance, when output is on trend at $\bar{Y}$, the interest rate used to be $\bar{i}$. Now it is $\bar{i}'$, and we move from point A to point B.

schedule shifts. One possibility is the rotation-like shift in Figure 10.10 from TR^1 to TR^2 as the central bank becomes more 'hawkish' (anti-inflationary). Another possibility is that the central bank changes its estimate of the neutral interest rate, for instance from $\bar{i}$ to $\bar{i}'$. This implies an upward shift of the TR schedule from TR to TR' in Figure 10.11. Indeed, at any level of output, the central bank will now choose a higher interest rate, moving, for instance, from point A to point B.[20]

10.6 Macroeconomic Equilibrium

We are now ready to look at the complete equilibrium when both goods and money markets are in equilibrium. The resulting framework will provide a tool for understanding how output and the interest rate respond to exogenous disturbances. This is an important step forward. Indeed, in Section 10.2, on the basis of an analysis of the goods market, we had developed a way to understand the behaviour of

---

[19] The neutral interest rate is given, by the Fisher equation, as the sum of the equilibrium real interest rate r plus the target rate of inflation.

[20] Exactly the same would occur if the central bank were to revise upwards its inflation forecast π.

the output gap, our initial interpretation of business cycles. We now expand the analysis by adding a second market, the money market. For the time being, we ignore the exchange rate and the fact that the economy is open to financial flows. The objective of the next chapter is to show how things change when we consider these aspects.

The reasoning is deceptively simple. We have seen that the economy cannot stay for long off the IS curve and that it never wanders much from the LM or TR curves. So, for both the goods and money markets to be in equilibrium, we require that the economy lies at the intersection of the IS and LM or TR schedules.

In order to go any further, we need to decide which kind of central bank we are examining: a money targeter or an interest rate setter? We consider both cases in detail.

10.6.1 The *IS–LM* Model

Figure 10.12 shows that macroeconomic equilibrium is achieved at point A, at the intersection of the IS and LM curves. At this point there is neither excess demand nor supply for goods, nor is there excess demand or supply of money. In order to see the usefulness of the framework, we introduce some disturbance. Let us consider, for example, the effect of an exogenous increase in stock market prices, the kind of event presented in Box 10.3. As private wealth increases, consumption rises and we face an exogenous increase in the demand for goods. In addition, a higher Tobin's q raises investment spending. A higher demand for goods is captured by a rightward shift of the IS curve. The new equilibrium occurs at point B. Thus we find that an exogenous increase in demand leads to a higher output and a higher interest rate.

This is an interesting result in its own right, but it is just as important to understand what is happening in the background. First, higher demand results in higher output. After all, the Keynesian hypothesis is that output responds to demand. But there is more to the outcome than that. We know that the IS curve rightward shift is larger than the initial boost in demand because of the multiplier effect. So we know that the total increase in output results from a succession of impulses running from more

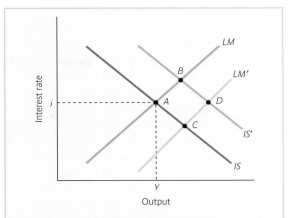

Fig. 10.12 *IS–LM* Macroeconomic Equilibrium

Macroeconomic equilibrium occurs when both the goods and money markets are in equilibrium simultaneously. This occurs at the intersection of the IS and LM curves at point A. Starting from point A, an exogenous increase in demand moves the IS curve to the right, by the full amount predicted by the Keynesian multiplier. Point B, at the intersection between IS' and LM curves, shows that output and the interest rate both increase. An exogenous increase in real money supply moves the LM curve to LM'. The new equilibrium at point C shows that, starting from point A, output increases and the interest rate declines. A combination of both events shifts IS to IS' and LM to LM', and the economy moves from point A to point D.

demand to more output, and from more output to more income and therefore yet more demand.

Second, note that the interest rate has increased. This is because the LM curve is upward sloping. By assumption, the position of the LM curve has not changed because none of the variables that determine its position—chiefly, the real money supply—has changed. Therefore, we move with the IS curve *along* the LM curve. As output rises, the demand for money increases. Since, by assumption, the central bank keeps money supply unchanged, the higher demand for money produces an increase in the interest rate (a movement along the LM curve). As the interest rate rises, however, investment spending declines. We can conclude that from A to B consumption has increased but the evolution of investment is ambiguous. It rises with Tobin's *q* but it declines due to a higher interest rate. In order to know more about investment, we would need to quantify these effects. This is what is done routinely by the models used by professional economists, but we will not pursue the matter here.

Now consider another thought experiment. The central bank increases the money supply. Graphically, the *LM* curve shifts to *LM′* in Figure 10.12, and the economy moves from point *A* to point *C*. Overall, therefore, an increase in the money supply —called an expansionary monetary policy—results in more output and a lower interest rate. This is intuitive. As the central bank provides more liquidity, banks can increase lending to their customers, and make profits along the way. Why do customers wish to borrow more? Because interest rates are lower. With a lower interest rate, investment spending rises and we move down and to the right along the *IS* curve. As we do so, the multiplier takes over and consumers start spending more because their incomes globally rise.

These are but two examples of how we can use the *IS–LM* model to decipher the impact of exogenous disturbances on output and the interest rate. We could consider more complex cases, for example a simultaneous increase in stock prices and in the money supply, i.e. a combination of the two previous disturbances called the **policy mix**. The result is that the economy moves to point *D*. In each case, we proceed as follows.

- First, we ask which schedule is affected by the disturbance. This is where the remarks presented in Sections 10.3.4 and 10.4.4 become handy.
- Second, we spot the new equilibrium at the intersection of the new *IS* and *LM* curves.
- Finally, we can go beyond the graphical analysis and interpret the results by tracking down the various channels involved in the response of the economy to the disturbance.

10.6.2 The *IS–TR* Model

Much the same analysis can be applied to the case when, instead of holding the real money supply constant, the central bank follows a Taylor rule. Because the *TR* schedule looks like the *LM* curve,

Figure 10.13 (*b*) looks like Figure 10.12 and, formally, the analysis is quite similar. The initial macroeconomic equilibrium is point *A*, at the intersection of *IS* and *TR*, where we assume that the output gap is zero so $Y = \bar{Y}$. As before, an exogenous increase in demand shifts the *IS* curve to *IS′* and the new equilibrium is at point *B*.

The key difference is the interpretation of the monetary policy, which requires looking at panel (*a*) where the shift from *D* to *D′* corresponds to the increase in output. In order to achieve its desired interest rate, the central bank must expand the money supply until point *B* on the new demand schedule is reached.

Under a constant-money supply policy, represented in panel (*a*) by the S^M schedule, the interest rate would be higher, corresponding to point *H*. Thus, in panel (*b*), the *LM* schedule (not shown) goes through points *A* and *H*.

If instead, the central bank was keeping its interest rate constant, along the S^i schedule in panel (*a*), it would have to increase the money supply and the new equilibrium would correspond to points *F* in both panels. Indeed, if the central bank is not interested in stabilizing output—this is the case of $b = 0$ in (10.12)—the *TR* schedule is horizontal and output would increase by the full amount of the multiplier. This shows how the Taylor rule operates to reduce output—and inflation, as we will see later—fluctuations. The steeper is the *TR* schedule (the larger is *b*), the more stabilizing is the chosen rule. The central bank can even prevent any fluctuation in output by raising the interest rate enough.

As with the *IS–LM* model, the *IS–TR* model can be used to study any arbitrary demand disturbance. In the chapters that follow, we will do so extensively. The same procedure applies to: (1) identify which schedule is affected by the disturbance, (2) identify the new equilibrium and (3) understand what this means for the goods and money markets, using both panels in Figure 10.13.

10.6.3 What is the Difference Between the *LM* and *TR* Schedules?

The similarity between the *IS–LM* and *IS–TR* frameworks is convenient since it allows us to use the same tools to study different monetary policy

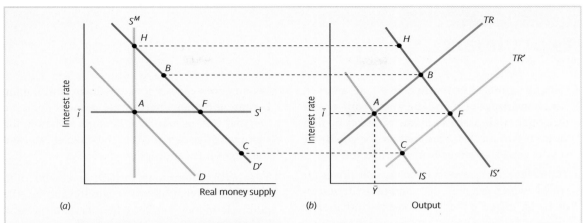

Fig. 10.13 *IS–TR* Macroeconomic Equilibrium

In panel (*b*), starting from point *A*, an exogenous increase in demand shifts the *IS* curve to *IS'*. This takes the economy to point *B* along the *TR* schedule, which shows that the central bank raises the interest rate in response to output expansion. Panel (*a*) shows that the central bank has to increase the money supply to reach point *B* on the new money demand schedule *D'*, which corresponds to the higher output level. Under a constant-money strategy, represented by S^M, the equilibrium is at point *H*. Under a constant-interest rate strategy, represented by S^i, the equilibrium is at point *F*.

A change in monetary policy occurs, for example, when a decline in the neutral interest rate induces the central bank to lower the interest rate, as dictated by its Taylor rule. This is represented by the downward shift *TR* to *TR'*. If the economy is initially at point *A*, the change takes the economy to *C*. The economy expands because the lower interest rate raises demand along the *IS* curve.

strategies. In the case of the *TR* curve, the central bank reacts to the increase in output by raising the interest rate. A central bank which targets money is seemingly passive when it keeps the money supply unchanged. In fact, in the example of the demand disturbance studied in Figures 10.12 and 10.13, the central bank lets the money market raise the interest rate. With the Taylor rule, the central bank actually controls the interest rate to achieve a chosen degree of output stabilization.

The other side of the coin is that, under the Taylor rule, the central bank does not *decide* to be expansionary or contractionary, as is the case when it sets the money supply. It merely reacts to economic conditions according to its chosen rule. For a given natural interest rate and target inflation rate, monetary policy is *automatically* expansionary when output falls below trend or inflation is expected to decline. Conversely, it is contractionary when the output gap is positive or inflation is expected to rise.

Of course, the central bank can change its rule. In that case, the *TR* curve will shift. According to (10.12), this is the case when the central bank changes its reaction to the output gap or its estimate of the neutral interest rate.[21] Let us imagine, for example, that the central bank reduces its estimate of the neutral interest rate. At each level of output, the central bank now chooses a lower interest rate. Graphically, in Figure 10.13, the *TR* schedule shifts downwards from *TR* to *TR'*. Starting from point *A*, when the *IS* curve shifts to *IS'*, the economy now moves to point *C*. Yet, as for any rule, the spirit of the Taylor rule is that it not be changed.

---

[21] It is also possible for the inflation rate target to change, even though we assumed here that it is zero.

❶ Summary

1 General equilibrium occurs when all markets simultaneously clear. In the short run, macroeconomic equilibrium is characterized by equilibrium in two markets: the market for goods and services and the domestic money market.

2 The Keynesian assumption posits that prices are sticky, which implies that output is driven by demand. When prices are constant, inflation is nil—and expected to remain nil—and the nominal and real interest rates are the same.

3 The consumption function states that private consumption spending depends on disposable income and wealth. The investment function relates investment spending by firms to the cost of obtaining funds, measured by the real interest rate and Tobin's q.

4 The primary current account improves when income and output in the rest of the world expand and the real exchange depreciates, and worsens when the domestic GDP and absorption rise at home.

5 An autonomous increase in demand for domestic goods triggers a multiplier mechanism: more demand means more output, and more output means a higher income and hence a new round of demand increases. The multiplier process is dampened by leakages in the income–demand chain: savings, taxes, and imports.

6 The *IS* curve represents the GDP levels and interest rates compatible with equilibrium in the market for goods and services. It is downward sloping because a higher interest rate reduces domestic demand and output. The *IS* curve is flatter the more sensitive demand is to the interest rate, and the larger is the multiplier.

7 The *LM* curve represents the GDP levels and interest rates compatible with equilibrium in the domestic money market when the central bank sets the real money supply. It is upward sloping because a higher GDP level raises the demand for money. The *LM* curve is steeper the more sensitive money demand is to output and the less sensitive it is to the interest rate.

8 The *TR* schedule describes how a flexible inflation-targeting central bank sets the interest rate in order to stabilize inflation around its target and output around its trend. It is upward sloping because the central bank raises the interest rate when output rises. Its position is determined by the neutral nominal interest rate and the central bank's own target inflation rate, which are exogenous in the *IS*–*TR* framework.

9 When the central bank targets the money supply, macroeconomic equilibrium is found at the intersection of the *IS* and *LM* curves. When the central bank instead follows a Taylor rule, macroeconomic equilibrium is found at the intersection of the *IS* and *TR* curves. This allows us to study how GDP and the interest rate respond to exogenous disturbances.

🔑 Key Concepts

- **Keynesian assumption**
- **general equilibrium**
- **consumption function, investment function**
- **import, export, and PCA functions**
- **desired demand function**
- **goods market equilibrium**
- **equilibrium GDP**

- **Keynesian demand multiplier**
- *IS* **curve**
- **excess supply/demand**
- *LM* **curve**
- **Taylor rule and** *TR* **schedule**
- **neutral interest rate**

❓ Exercises

1 The *IS* and *LM* curves determine four regions. Any position off a curve corresponds to market disequilibrium which can be characterized as excess demand or supply in either goods or money markets. Define each region accordingly, e.g. excess demand in the goods market and excess supply in the money market. Explain why and how the economy will return to macroeconomic equilibrium starting from any point in these four regions.

2 Why do leaks out of income into spending flatten the desired demand schedule? Show graphically that, the steeper the desired demand schedule, the larger is the Keynesian multiplier.

3 Desired demand (*DD*) is represented by the following simplified function:

$$DD = 3{,}000 + 0.8(Y - T) + G - 100i - 500\sigma.$$

Domestic and foreign price levels have been assumed constant and equal to one. Let $i = 5\%$ throughout. Initially $G = T = 3{,}000$. σ is the nominal exchange rate and is assumed fixed at one.

(a) Compute the effect on GDP of an increase in T from 3,000 to 3,500. Show your result graphically. What is the value of the lump-sum tax multiplier?

(b) Compute the effect on GDP of an increase in G from 3,000 to 3,500. Show your result graphically. What is the value of the government spending multiplier?

(c) Compute the net effect on GDP when both G and T increase by the same amount, from 3,000 to 3,500. Show your result graphically. What is the value of the balanced budget multiplier? Compare your answers and discuss.

4 When is the multiplier equal to 1? Why?

5 Suppose that the demand for real money balances has the form $L(Y, i) = 0.5Y - 300i + 500c$, where c is an exogenous scale parameter. Let $P = 1$, $M = 2{,}500$, and $c = 10$. Plot the *LM* curve in the i, Y diagram. What is the effect of an increase in c from 10 to 20 on the *LM* curve? What is the effect of an increase in the price level from $P = 1$ to $P = 2$, holding $c = 10$? Of $M = 2{,}500$ to $M = 3{,}000$?

6 The policy mix is the combination of fiscal and monetary policy actions. When the central bank targets the money supply, show graphically how these instruments can be used to increase output without changing the interest rate. To lower the interest rate without changing output. Can this be done when the central bank uses a Taylor rule? Carefully interpret your results.

7 Show how the *LM* curve shifts when demand for money exogenously increases. Explain your result.

8 Using the two-panel framework of Figure 10.9, imagine that we start from a situation of equilibrium in the money market and then the interest rate increases for some exogenous reason. Show in panel (*b*) what must happen to output to restore equilibrium and provide the corresponding analysis in panel (*a*).

9 Using Figure 10.10, explain why the TR schedule is vertical when $b = \infty$. (It may help to reason in the following way: consider the effect of a larger *b*, and then let *b* become arbitrarily large.)

10 Show the effect on the TR schedule of an increase in the sensitivity *b* of the Taylor rule. What is the effect on the interest rate? (Hint: start from a situation where output is at its trend level.)

11 Consider an increase in demand for goods in the *IS–TR* model. Using the apparatus of Figure 10.10, show graphically what happens to output, the interest rate, and money supply when the *TR* schedule is horizontal. Same question when the *TR* schedule is upward sloping. Interpret the difference.

12 This exercise confirms the argument presented in footnote 3. Ignoring foreign absorption, the PCA function is $PCA(A, \sigma)$. Note that absorption is $A = C + I + G$, so with (10.1) we have $Y = A + PCA(A, \sigma)$. Show that this implies $PCA = PCA(Y, \sigma)$. Use the simple representation of the PCA function $PCA = a - bA - c\sigma$ to compute the modified function $PCA(Y, \sigma)$.

→ Essay Questions

1 Why do the *IS–LM* and *IS–TR* models tell different stories? Take a few exogenous shocks and interpret the difference in the results that you find. In view of your results, is there any reason to prefer money targeting over a Taylor rule?

2 What, in your view, affects the choice of the slope of the Taylor rule by central banks?

3 There are many ways of conducting an expansionary fiscal policy: raising public spending, cutting income taxes, profit taxes, or VAT. What difference does it make for different groups in the country? In your discussion, as you take a general equilibrium view of the question, look at the two possible exchange rate regimes.

4 The behaviour of inventories is a closely watched indicator of the state of the economy. Discuss under which conditions it is a valid indicator of things to come. In particular, does an increase in inventories signal an economic slowdown or a boom? (Hint: a change in inventories can be either intended or unintended.)

5 'One of the advantages of high taxes is that they help stabilize the economy.' Discuss.

International Capital Flows and Macroeconomic Equilibrium

11

The immediate cause of profit-oriented capital movements is an interest-rate differential. The main point is to find out how this interest-rate differential can come about. . . . A more complete theory of capital movements is an indis-

pensable foundation for the study of the international, or more generally the interlocal, aspects of business cycles.

R. Nurkse (1961)

11.1 Overview

In Chapter 10, we studied the determination of demand and output when the Keynesian assumption holds and aggregate demand determines output in the short run. While the *IS* curve recognizes the existence of trade in goods and services, we ignored trade in financial assets. This chapter will show that repairing this omission significantly modifies the analysis. It presents the small open-economy version of the Keynesian model, the **Mundell–Fleming model**.[1] This framework is most relevant for studying the behaviour of small, open economies and is particularly relevant in a world in which financial markets are deeply integrated internationally.

This chapter also draws attention to the crucial role of the **exchange rate regime**. We will consider two possibilities. First, the exchange rate may be fixed, meaning that the central bank commits to maintaining the value of its currency in terms of other currencies. Second, and alternatively, the central

bank may let the exchange rate float freely, leaving its value to be determined by the market. The exchange rate regime turns out to be crucial to the behaviour of the economy. For this reason, the two regimes of fixed and flexible exchange rates are studied separately.

We start by looking at the implications of financial openness. In brief, we will argue that a fully financially integrated economy loses the control of its interest rate. This limits the room for manoeuvre of the central bank and explains why and in which way the exchange regime matters so much. First, we look at the fixed exchange rate regime, and then contrast the results with the case of a flexible exchange rate regime. Along the way, we develop and refine the Mundell–Fleming model. This is a powerful tool for understanding business cycles, the role of macroeconomic policies, and details of the interplay between goods markets, domestic financial markets, and international financial integration.

11.2 The Implications of Being Small

What is a small, open economy, exactly? Small means that the economy has no discernable impact on the rest of the world. Open means that it is profoundly affected by events that take place beyond its borders. Trade openness—sometimes referred to as current account openness—occurs

when goods and services can be exchanged with only limited impediments like tariffs, quotas, and various other restraints. Financial openness—sometimes referred to as financial account openness in reference to the balance of payments, see Chapter 2—describes the situation when people can lend and borrow freely. Box 11.1 further explains how openness is defined and measured. Most countries can be seen as small and open. The exceptions are the USA and the European Union. They are not that small

---

[1] It is named after the Nobel Laureate Robert Mundell (1932–) from Columbia University and the Briton J. Marcus Fleming (1911–1976), who worked at the IMF.

Box 11.1   What is Openness?

In Chapter 1, we presented a first definition of openness related to external trade in goods and services, which affects output through exports and imports.[2] Table 11.1 reminds us of how open and how closed some countries are. As in Table 1.2, we present the average of exports and imports as a percentage of GDP. As one might expect, Table 11.1 shows an inverse relationship between economic size and trade openness: the bigger the country, the less it needs foreign markets and suppliers. Even so, the two largest entities, the euro area and the USA, are far from being closed.

The second definition of openness concerns the financial markets. In Table 11.1 financial openness is measured by how much a country has lent to the rest of the world (its cross-border assets) or how much it has borrowed abroad (its cross-border liabilities), where 'country' refers to households, banks, firms, and the public sector. The table shows both assets and liabilities. In many cases, assets and liabilities are not very different (pretty much like exports and imports are usually of the same order of magnitude). Financial openness allows borrowers and lenders to scour the world to find the best financial deal. Still, some countries, such as the USA, Brazil, or Poland have more external liabilities than assets. They are called net debtor countries.[3] Conversely, Japan and Switzerland are net creditors.

Developed countries tend to be more open than developing countries, both in trade and finance. The globalization process has begun to change this relationship. Poland, Korea, Brazil, China, and India are among the growing number of so-called emerging market countries in the process of becoming fully integrated in world financial markets.

 Table 11.1   Measures of Openness and Economic Size, 2004

	Share of world GDP (%)	Trade openness (% of GDP)	Financial openness	
			Total assets (% of GDP)	Total liabilities (% of GDP)
Denmark	0.6	40.9	55.4	47.4
Poland	0.6	40.0	31.6	84.9
Sweden	0.8	42.3	213.5	223.0
Belgium	0.9	82.3	425.2	394.3
Switzerland	0.9	40.6	570.7	439.9
Netherlands	1.4	62.7	402.5	408.3
Brazil	1.5	15.7	28.3	77.6
Korea, Rep.	1.6	41.9	52.6	56.6
China	4.7	32.7	195.3	207.8
United Kingdom	5.1	26.4	357.4	370.6
Germany	6.6	35.5	167.1	159.1
Japan	11.2	11.0	89.0	51.0
European Monetary Union	23.0	10.8		
United States	28.4	11.8	84.0	106.7

Sources: The World Bank, *World Development Indicators*; Lane and Milesi-Ferretti (2006).

---

[2]   Remember the goods market equilibrium condition states that output Y is equal to $C + I + G + X - Z$.

[3]   Remember that 'liabilities' are used in the broad sense to include all inward foreign investment, including not only debt obligations and government borrowings, but also portfolio and foreign direct investments.

and their trade with the rest of the world is comparatively limited. Yet, in the financial sphere, even the EU is not large enough to have much of an impact on the world. Even the USA may be gradually losing its hegemony as new economic powers rise in Asia and South America.

11.3 International Financial Flows

11.3.1 The Interest Parity Condition

We previously encountered the exchange rate in Chapter 6. Taking the long-run view, we established the purchasing power parity principle driven by competition in trade in goods and services. At a short-run horizon, trade in financial assets is more important. An alternative parity condition will drive the determination of interest rates and nominal exchange rates. This is the **interest rate parity condition**.

Let us consider a typical international investor, for example a large bank, which routinely borrows and lends all over the world. The domestic interest rate is i while the foreign rate of return is i^*. Note that we refer to i^* as a rate of return, not an interest rate. At this stage, we simply define i^* to include the required exchange rate conversion.[4]

Imagine, to start with, that $i < i^*$. International investors will borrow at home, where the interest is low, and invest abroad, pocketing the difference. As they do so, they raise the demand for money at home and i will rise towards i^*. Simultaneously, i^* will decline towards i because of the large amounts of money that come in. This will go on as long as $i < i^*$. Obviously, if $i > i^*$, money will keep flowing from the rest of the world into our high-interest rate country, pushing i down and i^* up. The implication is that neither $i > i^*$ nor $i < i^*$ is possible. The only logical way out is $i = i^*$. This is the interest rate parity condition.

Just as the purchasing power parity condition equates price levels, the interest rate parity condition states that returns on similar assets cannot differ systematically across countries when there is free trade in financial assets—when financial capital is perfectly mobile.[5] In contrast to the purchasing power parity condition, which takes time to assert itself because good prices move slowly, the interest parity condition is a short-run property. Indeed, financial traders constantly scan the whole world. They do so minute by minute and can instantly move huge amounts of money at virtually no cost. As a result, the interest parity condition is satisfied virtually always, and any deviation is immediately corrected. Interest rate parity is simply the equilibrium condition for international financial markets.

11.3.2 The *IFM* Schedule

The interest parity condition is depicted as the horizontal **international financial markets** (*IFM*) line in Figure 11.1. Here is where the small country assumption comes in. If the economy is small relative to the rest of the world, the foreign rate of return i^* is exogenous. It changes for reasons unrelated to domestic conditions. It follows that it is the domestic interest rate i in the small economy that bears the burden of adjustment whenever the interest rate parity condition is not satisfied. In what follows, we will assume that i^* is constant, unless we explicitly consider an exogenous change.

As with our discussion of other equilibrium conditions (the *IS* or *LM* curves), it is instructive to stress

---

4 The reason is that i is measured in domestic currency, while the foreign interest rate is measured in the foreign currency. As with goods prices, a correct comparison of interest rates in different countries will require due consideration of the exchange rate. We sidestep this issue here, postponing it to Chapter 14.

5 'Similarity' refers to riskiness (e.g. short-term government bills and bonds are usually considered safe, as are those issued by large corporations) and the nature of the asset's payoffs, mainly its time to maturity.

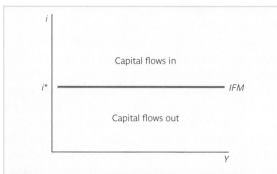

Fig. 11.1 International Financial Market Equilibrium

When capital can move freely across borders, assets of similar quality (in terms of maturity and risk) should yield the same return. Otherwise, unexploited profit opportunities would exist (borrowing where interest is low and lending where it is high). This is incompatible with the international market equilibrium. Note that i^* denotes the return on foreign assets converted in the domestic currency. For a small financially open economy, it is exogenous.

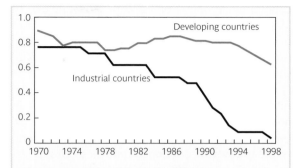

Fig. 11.2 The Evolution of Financial Account Restrictions

The figure indicates the fraction of countries that apply one form or another of restriction to capital movements. For example, by the late 1990s, the developing countries reach the level 0.6, which means that 60% of these countries are operating capital controls. This is based on official declarations by countries, which may not fully represent what occurs in practice.
Source: Kose and Prasad (2004: 51).

what happens off the *IFM* schedule. Above the line, the domestic interest rate is higher than worldwide returns. Capital inflows occur as international investors take advantage of higher returns at home. The inflows, which can be massive, promptly drive the domestic interest rate *i* down to the world level. Conversely, below the *IFM* line, capital flows out and increasing scarcity drives up the interest rate *i* back to i^*.

11.3.3 Capital Mobility and Financial Account Restrictions

So far, we have assumed that capital is freely mobile. In fact, a large number of countries impose a variety of restrictions on their financial accounts. The most extreme restriction consists of declaring the national currency inconvertible. It is then legally impossible to convert the currency into foreign ones.[6] More moderate restrictions limit or forbid some transactions, like investing abroad or the foreign acquisition of categories of domestic assets.

Capital controls, as these restrictions are generically called, used to be prevalent until the mid-1970s. As Figure 11.2 shows, the developed countries abandoned capital controls in the 1980s. The same process started a decade later among developing countries, but most continue to maintain restrictions on capital flows.

In the presence of capital controls, there is no reason for the interest rate parity to hold, because the mechanism described in the previous section cannot operate. Legal restrictions prevent traders from taking advantage of the profit opportunities. Of course, the temptation to circumvent the law is strong and indeed capital controls are systematically evaded. As long as they are not fully evaded, however, interest parity is unlikely to be systematically met.

Why do countries adopt restrictions on capital movements? We have seen how deviations from the interest parity condition can trigger massive capital flows. As we will see below, these massive movements of capital can interfere with the central bank's conduct of monetary policy, either because the central bank would like to influence monetary

---

[6] In this case, black markets usually flourish.

conditions at home, or because it would like to affect the exchange rate. Interestingly, countries more often than not give up capital controls because the forces of international financial integration are simply too powerful to resist.

As we proceed to explore the implications of the interest parity condition, it is important to keep in mind that full capital mobility is not a universal feature. The framework presented in this book is well suited to studying developed countries, but it is less helpful for developing economies. Partly because there is a wide variety of capital controls, partly because their effects vary depending on the prevalent conditions, there is no simple equivalent treatment for these countries. If the controls were watertight, we could simply overlook the interest rate parity condition and work with the macroeconomic equilibrium described in Chapter 10. As a first approximation, this is maybe the best that can be done.

11.3.4 Exchange Rate Regimes

Because it draws the attention to capital flows, the *IFM* schedule leads us to take account of the exchange rate regime. While many variants exist, we consider two polar cases: (1) fixed exchange rates, and (2) fully floating exchange rates.

The International Monetary Fund (IMF) reports that 111 of its 185 member countries have adopted one form or another of exchange rate fixity. Under a fixed exchange rate regime, the monetary authorities undertake to keep their exchange rate at a publicly announced parity. This is an official value of the national currency in terms of another currency, usually the dollar or the euro. For instance, Denmark and several countries in Central and Eastern Europe (currently, Bulgaria, Croatia, Estonia, Latvia, and Lithuania) peg their currencies to the euro. Most developing countries, including China and several African countries, have adopted fixed exchange rate regimes of various sizes and shapes. We examine this case in Box 11.3.

When the exchange rate is allowed to float freely, the central bank takes no responsibility for the value of its currency, which is set on foreign exchange markets—these markets are described in Chapter 14. This regime, which has been adopted

by the euro area, Switzerland, Norway, the UK, the USA, and Japan, is studied in Section 11.5.

In between these two polar regimes there are a number of versions of 'managed floating'. In this case, the authorities do not commit themselves to a particular parity but nevertheless attempt to prevent large fluctuations. This is currently the case for other Central and East European countries (the Czech Republic, Hungary, Poland, and Romania) and for many Latin American and East Asian countries. This regime is a 'mixed bag' that does not lend itself to a clean-cut analysis. Depending on the weight put to exchange rate stabilization, it can be approximated by either a fixed or a flexible exchange rate regime.

11.3.5 Preview of What Follows

The macroeconomic equilibrium studied in Chapter 10 included two markets: the goods market and the money market. We have now added a third market: the international financial market. For each of these three markets, we have established those combinations of real GDP and nominal interest rate which are compatible with equilibrium. The *IS* curve deals with the market for goods and services, the *LM* curve or the *TR* schedule corresponds to the money market, while the *IFM* line describes the international financial equilibrium. Each of these market equilibrium schedules are drawn 'all other things equal', meaning that they remain in place as long as the corresponding exogenous variables are unchanged.

In the following sections, we extend the Keynesian analysis of the last chapter to include a wide variety of disturbances that small open economies face. The analysis is thus inherently more realistic and relevant than in Chapter 10, yet it builds carefully on that analysis. In studying each particular scenario, it is important to ask and answer the following three questions.

(1) What is the exchange regime? The exchange rate regime is crucial for understanding how the economy reacts. As will become clear, under a fixed exchange rate regime, we ignore the *LM* or *TR* schedule and, under a flexible exchange rate regime, we ignore the *IS* schedule.

(2) Which schedule is affected by the disturbance under consideration? An exogenous disturbance affects (at least) one of the three markets and therefore leads to a shift in the corresponding schedule.

(3) Where is the new equilibrium and how should it be interpreted? How and why has the economy moved from the initial to the new general equilibrium?

11.4 Output and Interest Rate Determination under Fixed Exchange Rates

11.4.1 What is a Fixed Exchange Rate Regime?

We saw in Chapter 9 that a central bank that fixes an interest rate must be prepared to satisfy whatever reserves commercial banks want to hold. A very similar reasoning applies in the case of a fixed exchange rate. In fact, the central bank will use its assets and liabilities to perform operations in foreign exchange, just as described in Section 9.3.4. Currencies are traded on foreign exchange markets, which are described in Chapter 14. These markets resemble the interbank market. The players are much the same: large banks and financial institutions. The main difference is that, on the exchange market, domestic money is traded against foreign monies, while it is traded against high-quality domestic assets in the money market.

Imagine that, one morning, the currency appreciates above its declared parity. It is incumbent upon the central bank to weaken its own currency. The way to do so is to sell whatever quantity of the currency is necessary to bring the exchange rate back down again. This is called an **exchange market intervention**.

11.4.2 The Loss of Monetary Policy Autonomy

The similarity with open market interventions goes much further, with a crucially important implication. We have seen in Chapter 9 that a central bank cannot simultaneously choose the money supply and the interest rate. We now explain why a central bank cannot both choose the exchange rate and its monetary policy stance, either the money supply

or the interest rate. Simply put, a central bank has three possible instruments: (1) the money supply, (2) the interest rate, and (3) the exchange rate. Once it decides on any one of them, the other two are out of its reach. It follows that a central bank that adopts a fixed exchange rate cannot carry out an autonomous monetary policy. It cannot decide on the money supply, meaning that the LM curve is irrelevant. At the same time it cannot choose the interest rate, so the TR curve becomes irrelevant too. We can study the economy with the help of the two other schedules, IS and IFM.

Another way of understanding the loss of monetary autonomy under a fixed exchange rate regime is to realize that a central bank can only choose one point on the money demand schedule presented in Chapter 9 and shown again in Figure 11.3. The central bank faces two constraints: (1) the demand for money, represented by schedule D, and (2) the foreign rate of return i^* imposed by the international financial market equilibrium condition. The only possible situation is at point A. There is just no room for manoeuvre.

To make this point clear, imagine that the central bank attempted to lower the interest rate to reach point B in Figure 11.3 with interest rate i. To keep things simple, we ignore any possible impact of this action on output.[7] From Figure 11.1, we know that

---

[7] An exercise at the end of the chapter asks you to verify that the main conclusion stands when we take into account the fact that a lower interest rate should raise output. However, since monetary and financial reactions are much faster than goods market changes, so the simplified presentation is a good approximation to what happens in practice.

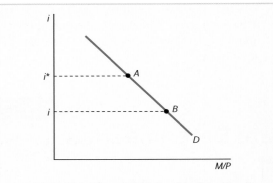

Fig. 11.3 The Money Market Under Fixed Exchange Rates

Starting from point A, the central bank decides to lower the interest rate from i^*, the foreign rate of return, to i. Money market equilibrium occurs at point B. But $i < i^*$ is incompatible with international financial market equilibrium, so capital flows out. In order to support its currency, the central bank must buy it on the foreign exchange market. As a result, the money supply declines and the interest rate rises along D. The central bank must continue its interventions as long as $i < i^*$. The only position compatible with international financial market equilibrium is point A where $i = i^*$.

capital flows out when $i < i^*$. Traders borrow at the low rate i and, in order to invest abroad and obtain the higher return i^*, they sell the domestic currency. This weakens the currency on the foreign exchange market. In order to honour its fixed exchange rate commitment, the central bank must intervene and buy back its currency.

Now remember from Chapter 9 that money is 'money in circulation'. As the central bank intervenes on the foreign exchange market and withdraws money from circulation, the money supply declines. In Figure 11.3, we move from point B up and to the left along D. How far? For capital outflows to come to an end and foreign exchange market interventions to stop, this must go on until $i = i^*$, all the way back to point A. We see that whatever money is provided on the open market must be promptly removed from the foreign exchange market. This link can be severed, as explained in Box 11.2, but only temporarily. More generally, any attempt by the central bank to change the money supply or

the domestic interest rate is undermined by its commitment to uphold the official exchange rate parity. Box 11.2 looks at sterilization, as a way to alleviate the constraint and Box 11.3 describes China's experience.

11.4.3 Demand Disturbances

We now examine how an exogenous change in the demand for goods affects the output level and the interest rate, the two endogenous variables in our framework. We already examined this question in Chapter 10, but we ignored capital mobility. With capital freely moving across borders and a fixed exchange rate, we know that we only need to consider the *IS* and *IFM* schedules. We start from point A in Figure 11.6.

To fix ideas, we look at the role of fiscal policy. An expansionary policy, e.g. an increase in public spending or a tax reduction, raises domestic demand. The same outcome would occur if firms became more optimistic and invested more, or if foreign demand for domestic goods were to rise, which would increase exports and improve the primary current account.

The increase in public spending is captured in Figure 11.6 by a rightward shift of the *IS* curve, from *IS* to *IS'*. The economy moves from point A to point B at the intersection of *IS'* and the *IFM* line. As in Chapter 10, the demand expansion results in an increase in income but now the interest rate remains unchanged, equal to the foreign rate of return i^*.

Table 11.2 Sterilized and Unsterilized Foreign Exchange Market Interventions

	Unsterilized interventions			Sterilized interventions		
	M0	R	DC	M0	R	DC
Step 1	−	−	=	−	−	=
Step 2				+	=	+
Overall	−	−	=	=	−	+

Box 11.2 **Varieties of Foreign Exchange Market Interventions**

A foreign exchange market intervention automatically affects the money supply. Can the central bank break this link? In the short run, it can, by conducting a **sterilization operation**, but this procedure only provides temporary breathing space. Sooner or later, the link cannot be avoided.

The normal procedure for a central bank to create money is through the open market. It buys assets from commercial banks and provides them with some money base M0. But the central bank can increase the money base by intervening on the foreign exchange market. It purchases foreign currency, which becomes part of foreign exchange reserves, using its own currency—a liability, high-powered money (part of M0). Thus every unit of money base has as a counterpart, either a loan to commercial banks or a sale to the foreign exchange market against foreign exchange reserves. This means that

(11.1) $M0 = R + DC,$

where DC represents domestic credit[8] and R measures the foreign exchange reserves owned by the central bank.

Unsterilized interventions correspond to the description in the text. In order to prevent its currency from weakening, the central bank buys back its monetary base. As shown in Table 11.2, this action contracts the money supply, hence the *minus* sign—and reduces the value of reserves by an equivalent amount—another *minus* sign, with no effect on domestic credit—hence the equal sign. Sterilization is achieved when the central bank offsets the foreign exchange market intervention with another operation in the domestic money market. It re-injects the previously purchased domestic currency

by purchasing other assets on the open market. As it returns to financial institutions the very liquidity it withdrew initially when it sold its foreign exchange reserves for its own money, M0 and DC increase, hence the *plus* signs in Table 11.2. Combining the two steps (see the bottom row), we see that the central bank has raised its stock of domestic assets DC and reduced its stock of foreign exchange reserves R by the same amount, leaving the money base M0 unchanged. Since the total money supply is a multiple of the base, the sterilized intervention has in fact cut the link between the money stock and the foreign exchange market intervention.

At best, sterilized interventions can only temporarily restore the ability of the central bank to carry out an autonomous monetary policy. The central bank will not be able to sustain point B in Figure 11.3. As long as i is below i^*, capital continues to leave the country, and the central bank must continue its interventions to maintain the exchange rate at its parity. This cannot go on forever, though, because the stock of foreign exchange reserves is being depleted and will be exhausted sooner or later. If the capital flows are large, and they usually are, the reserves can be depleted in a matter of days, sometimes even hours.

Can sterilized interventions support an interest rate i above i^*? In that case, the central bank accumulates reserves and there is no physical limit to how much can be accumulated. Box 11.3 tells the story of China, which has been doing just that over the recent years.

In the end, sterilized interventions allow the central bank to gain time, but it must eventually accept that the domestic interest rate cannot be moved away from the foreign rate of return.

It might seem that financial openness does not make much of a difference. This is not entirely correct. To see why, imagine the situation in the absence of capital flows, e.g. because of watertight

capital controls. In this case, we can ignore the *IFM* line, the central bank recovers its ability to carry out an effective monetary policy, and the *LM* or *TR* schedule is relevant again. The new equilibrium occurs at point C. Note that, relative to point B, income has increased less and the interest rate has risen. These two effects are related. The interest rate has increased because a monetary-targeting central bank does not allow the money supply to increase (the *LM* case). Alternatively, the Taylor rule leads the central bank to raise the interest rate to limit

---

8   Domestic credit is a general term describing any form of loan by the central bank to the non-bank sector (private or government). It could take the form of direct lending to the government, the purchase of government debt, or refinancing of commercial lending by private banks.

Box 11.3 How High is the Sky at the People's Bank of China?

In 1995, China began pegging its currency, the yuan, to the US dollar. Its successful export promotion strategy has led to large current account surpluses. Then, recognizing its increasing attractiveness, international investors have been pouring money into its economy, resulting in large financial account surpluses. As implied by the balance of payments identity, the People's Bank of China has intervened and accumulated over the years a massive stock of foreign exchange reserves totalling some $1.3 billion, a number previously unheard of anywhere in the world (Figure 11.4).

Worried about its inroads into a wide range of products, the US Congress (the parliament) accused China of unfair competition supported by an undervalued exchange rate. Under pressure, in July 2005, the central bank let its currency appreciate, albeit very, very slowly. The acceleration of its reserves stock indicates that the yuan–dollar exchange rate is still very much under direct control.

How long can this go on? With such growth in foreign exchange reserves, it is natural to expect that the Chinese money supply will grow, and grow very rapidly. Just as Table 11.2 implies, the People's Bank of China has been conducting sterilized interventions and has accumulated dollar reserves. To mop up the liquidity effects of these purchases, it has issued its own debt, i.e. reduced DC in (11.1). In fact, it has even brought DC into negative territory, meaning that the central bank is indebted to the banking sector and not the other way round, as is normally the case.[9] For a long time, the People's Bank of China was even making a profit on its sterilization activity![10] By late 2007, however, US interest rates declined as Chinese rates rose. As a result, the People's Bank of China has started to face losses. Given the huge size of its reserves, the losses are significant, probably unsustainable. This may explain why it has started to let its currency appreciate faster.

The loss of monetary policy autonomy under a fixed exchange rate regime is a consequence of free capital mobility. The only feasible way to recover some leeway is to break the link between i and i^*. This is why some countries resort to capital controls. As discussed in Section 11.3.3, however, capital controls are sometimes helpful, although in a limited fashion.

Why would a country ever adopt a fixed exchange rate at the cost of losing monetary policy autonomy? There are several reasons why the sacrifice may be worth the cost. At this stage, we can mention a straightforward one: put into the wrong hands, monetary policy can be badly misused. History is replete with misguided monetary policies. The **exchange rate anchor**, as the fixed exchange rate regime strategy is sometimes called, is one way of reducing the odds of bad monetary policy-making. Box 11.4 presents two recent examples of the use of this strategy.

Box 11.4 The Exchange Rate Anchor: Argentina and Bulgaria

The exchange rate anchor is potent medicine, but it can be tricky to administer. It can work beautifully, but it can backfire if taken for too long and with inappropriate supporting measures.

Argentina offers an example of a success story that ended very badly. Throughout its history, Argentina has been crippled by high and ever-rising inflation rates, up to 10,000% in 1990. Powerful vested interests, acting in the background, ensured that the central bank could not or would not impose the required discipline. In early 1991, the Menem Government passed the 'Convertibility Law', which tied the peso to the US dollar at the very visible rate of 1:1. Figure 11.5(a) shows that inflation quickly declined. By 1993, it was about the same as in the USA, and stayed that way for the rest of the decade.

The Argentine cure, however, was directed too much at the symptoms and not enough at the root causes of the inflation disease. By the end of the 1990s, provincial governments started to run massive budget deficits that were translated into current account deficits.[11] Mounting losses of foreign exchange reserves alarmed interntional investors. Soon capital outflows added to the loss of reserves. In late 2001, facing acute economic and political instability, the government resigned. Its successor immediately abolished the Convertibility Law. The exchange rate promptly lost two-thirds of its value, output fell by more than 10%, and inflation was on the rise again.

Plagued by acute political instability, Bulgaria found it difficult to emerge from central planning in the early 1990s. Inflation soared and the currency collapsed. By 1997, its value was less than one-hundredth of what it used to be in 1991. A year later, the exchange rate was pegged to the deutschmark—and later to the euro. Inflation promptly declined.

---

[9] In (10.3), when the value of foreign exchange reserves exceeds the money base ($R > M0$), we must have $DC < 0$.

[10] Interest rates were lower in China than in the USA, so the central bank could obtain a higher return on dollar-denominated reserves than it was paying on its yuan-denominated debt to the commercial banks.

[11] The link between fiscal and external deficits is clear from the accounting identity (2.7): $PCA = (S − I) + (T − G)$. The link between deficits and debt is shown in Chapter 5.

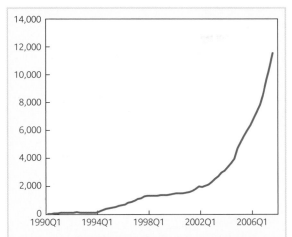

Fig. 11.4 China: Foreign Exchange Reserves (US$ million)

China has been accumulating foreign exchange reserves at extraordinary speed.

Source: IMF.

output fluctuation (the *TR* case). Relative to point *B*, output is lower at point *C* because the higher interest rate adversely affects investment spending. This crowding-out effect reflects the fact that a higher demand reduces, or crowds out, investment spending when it is met by a higher interest rate. In contrast, under full capital mobility the interest rate does not increase—there is no crowding-out effect —and the expansion is stronger.

11.4.4 International Financial Disturbances

As a further example of how to use the framework, we now look at a disturbance originating in the international financial markets. This is an important example of the interdependence of national economies. Let us consider the case when the foreign rate of return rises exogenously from i^* to $i^{*\prime}$, because, say, the monetary conditions around the world are becoming tighter. The result is the upward shift of the *IFM* line to *IFM'*, as shown in Figure 11.7. At point *A*, the initial point of intersection of the *IS* and *IFM* schedules, the interest rate is now too low. Capital flows out and the central bank must intervene on the foreign exchange market and buy back some of its own currency. The money supply declines and the economy moves to point *B*. Output declines because the higher interest rate reduces demand.

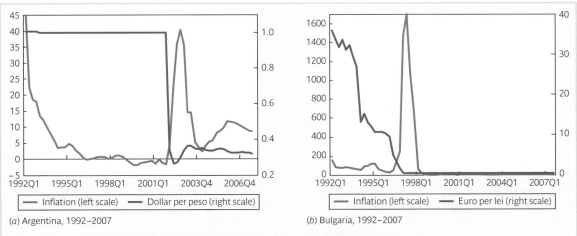

(a) Argentina, 1992–2007

(b) Bulgaria, 1992–2007

Fig. 11.5 The Exchange Rate Anchor in Argentina and Bulgaria

In Argentina, the exchange rate *vis-à-vis* the dollar was fixed at the one-for-one parity in 1991. The resulting constraint on monetary policy led to a massive decline in the inflation rate, which even turned negative for several years. When the peg was abandoned in late 2001, the exchange rate collapsed and, soon afterwards, inflation jumped. After a period of punishing inflation, Bulgaria fixed its exchange rate in 1998. As panel (b) shows, inflation promptly disappeared.

Source: IMF.

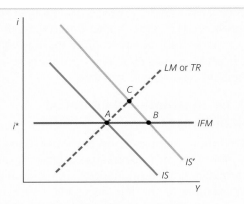

Fig. 11.6 Demand Disturbances Under Fixed Exchange Rates

The demand expansion is shown as shifting the *IS* curve from *IS* to *IS'*. The new equilibrium occurs at point *B* where the goods and international financial markets are in equilibrium. Without capital mobility, the equilibrium would occur at point *C*.

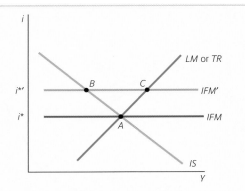

Fig. 11.7 An International Financial Disturbance

The increase in the rate of return on foreign assets is captured by the shift from *IFM* to *IFM'*. Starting from point *A*, the new general equilibrium occurs at point *B*, where output has declined. Under flexible exchange rates, starting from point *A*, the exchange rate depreciates. The resulting gain in competitiveness increases the demand for domestic goods. The *IS* curve shifts to the right (not shown) until it passes through point *C*, where the new macroeconomic equilibrium occurs.

This example shows that, under a fixed exchange rate regime, the domestic economy is exposed to international financial disturbances. If interest rates rise worldwide, they must rise at home as well, which provokes a recession (*Y* declines). The fixed exchange rate regime creates a situation of *international monetary interdependence*, which reflects the loss of monetary policy autonomy.

11.4.5 A Parity Change

Monetary policy is ineffective as long as the central bank remains committed to a specific exchange rate parity. That does not mean that monetary policy cannot be used at all. Most countries that adopt a fixed exchange *regime* allow for adjustments of the exchange rate *level*. These regimes, called fixed by adjustable exchange rates, provide some limited degree of monetary policy effectiveness.

Discrete, occasional changes in the exchange rate level are called **revaluations** or **devaluations**, depending on the direction of the change.[12] This is usually done by way of an official declaration. The cen-

tral bank announces the new parity at which it stands ready to buy and sell the domestic currency against foreign exchange. Consider the case of a nominal devaluation, a lowering of the nominal exchange rate *S*. For given price levels at home and abroad (the Keynesian assumption), the nominal devaluation translates into a decrease of the real exchange rate $\sigma = SP/P^*$. The devaluation raises the country's competitiveness, since its goods are now cheaper relative to foreign goods. Exports rise, imports decline, and the primary current account improves. Graphically, the *IS* curve shifts outwards to *IS'* in panel (*b*) of Figure 11.8. Output increases as the economy moves from point *A* to point *B* along the *IFM* line—which does not shift because the small country assumption implies that *i** is exogenous. As would be expected, a devaluation is expansionary. Conversely, a revaluation is contractionary.

What happens in the money and foreign exchange markets? A parity change may just be a declaration of intention by the central bank, but to be effective, intentions must be backed by actions.

---

[12] When the exchange rate floats, its changes are called appreciation or depreciation, see Section 11.5.

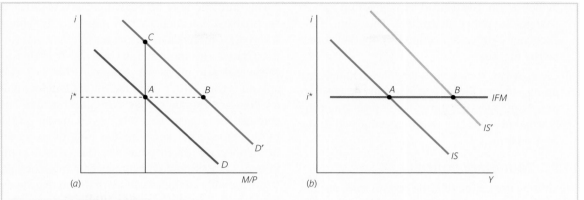

Fig. 11.8 A Devaluation

In panel (b), a devaluation shifts the *IS* curve out to *IS′*. The economy moves from point *A* to point *B* and output increases. The output expansion raises the demand for money and *D* moves to *D′* in panel (a), which shows that the central bank will let the money supply expand to keep the domestic interest rate *i* equal to the foreign rate of return *i**.

Indeed, a devaluation must be accompanied by a monetary expansion, a revaluation by a monetary contraction. This is shown in panel (a) of Figure 11.8. The increase in output found in panel (b) translates into a larger demand for money. In order to make the new parity 'stick', the central bank must supply the money additionally demanded at the going interest rate imposed by the international financial market equilibrium condition (point B). Assume that it does not. The domestic interest rate would start rising towards point C. This would trigger capital inflows, which would force the central bank to intervene on the foreign exchange market and sell the domestic currency to prevent an ap-

preciation. If the intervention is unsterilized, the domestic money supply rises and we end up at point B. Whether it is done through open market operations or foreign exchange market operations, the result is the same.

We have seen that, when capital is freely mobile, monetary policy autonomy is lost under fixed exchange rates and that monetary and exchange rate policies are just two sides of the same coin . A more accurate conclusion is that monetary policy can still be carried out, but through **realignments**— devaluations or revaluations—i.e. by changing the exchange rate level without abandoning the regime itself.

11.5 Output and Interest Rate Determination under Flexible Exchange Rates

Finally, we take up the case of a regime of freely floating exchange rates. The central bank explicitly refrains from intervening in foreign exchange markets. Three conclusions follow immediately.

(1) The central bank recovers its ability to conduct monetary policy. It can either choose the money supply (represented by the *LM* schedule) or follow a Taylor rule (represented by the *TR* schedule).

(2) By definition, the central bank gives up the exchange rate policy instrument. The value of the exchange rate is determined by market forces on the market.

(3) Given prices' stickiness, a flexible exchange rate implies that the country's external competitiveness is endogenous and so is the position of the IS schedule. This last result is established in the next section.

11.5.1 Monetary Policy

We start by imagining that the central bank decides to adopt a more expansionary monetary policy stance. It may increase the money supply or lower the interest rate at any level of output. In both cases, LM or TR shift downwards, as shown in panel (b) of Figure 11.9. There is no other exogenous change, so IS and IFM will remain where they are. Note that the three schedules now intersect each other two by two in three different positions: points A, B, and C. Which one is sustainable?

Look at point C at the intersection of the IS and LM' or TR' schedules. The interest rate has declined, reflecting the easing of monetary policy, which has led to more spending. Point C, however, is below the IFM line. With $i < i^*$, capital flows out. This time, however, the central bank will not intervene on the foreign exchange market. It lets the exchange rate depreciate freely. The resulting real depreciation, given domestic and foreign prices, in turn, means that the economy becomes more competitive. Exports rise, imports decline, the primary current account improves, and demand for domestic goods increases. Graphically, the IS curve starts shifting to the right. How far will it go? As long as $i < i^*$, capital outflows continue, the exchange rate keeps depreciating, and the IS curve keeps moving rightward. When it reaches the position IS', the three curves now go through point B and all markets are simultaneously in equilibrium. Thus point B shows the effect of the monetary policy change.

We have just seen that, under flexible exchange rates, the IS curve endogenously moves to meet the intersection of the other two schedules. This simply reflects the fact that, being left free to float, the exchange rate is endogenous and its movements affect external competitiveness and demand.

The outcome may be puzzling. Here we have a central bank that adopts a more expansionary policy stance that succeeds in raising output, and yet cannot change the interest rate because it is tied to the world rate of return. How can that be? The answer is that, with capital mobility, monetary policy does not operate through the interest rate, but through the *exchange rate*. The longer answer is told by the money market with the help of panel (a) in Figure 11.9. As in panel (b), the central bank intends to move down the money demand schedule D, presumably all the way to point C, and to provide liquidity to the open market along the way. But capital mobility implies that, as soon as the interest rate declines, money flows out. Any additional money created by the central bank immediately leaks abroad in the form of capital outflows. Is the economy stuck at points A in both panels? No, because the capital outflows depreciate the exchange rate. The depreciation, in turn, raises demand and output. With a higher volume of transactions to finance, money demand increases from D to D' in panel (a) as the economy moves from A to B in panel (b).

The central bank ends up increasing the money supply because it manages to raise real aggregate demand through an exchange rate depreciation.[13] Still, as previously noted, it does not succeed in lowering the interest rate. As under a fixed exchange regime, we see that monetary policy and the exchange rate are deeply related. Here, an expansionary monetary policy operates by bringing about an exchange rate depreciation.

11.5.2 Demand Disturbances

An exogenous increase in aggregate demand is shown as the rightward shift of the IS curve from IS to IS' in Figure 11.10. As in the previous section, the economy is not immediately in general equilibrium as the three schedules IS', LM or TR, and IFM no longer pass through a common point of intersection. Consider first point B, at the intersection of the IS and LM or TR schedules and off the IFM line. With

---

[13] In practice, given the speed of reaction of financial markets, the economy does not really go through point C.

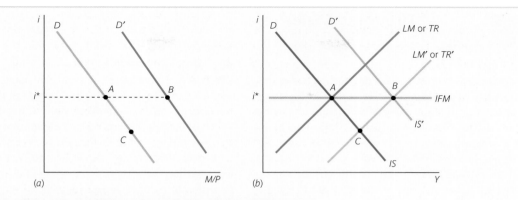

Fig. 11.9 Monetary Policy Under Flexible Exchange Rates

Starting at point A in panel (b), the central bank moves the LM or TR schedules to LM' or TR'. At point C, the lower interest rate triggers capital outflows and the exchange rate depreciates. The resulting gain in competitiveness raises demand for domestic goods and the IS curve shifts to the right. It will move all the way to IS' and full equilibrium is achieved at point B. In panel (a), we see that the central bank succeeds at increasing the money supply because money demand rises from D to D' on account of the output increase found in panel (b).

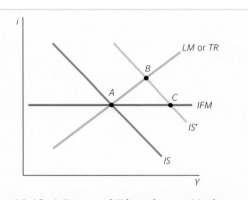

Fig. 11.10 A Demand Disturbance Under Flexible Exchange Rates

An expansionary demand disturbance shifts the IS curve to the right. At point B, however, $i > i^*$ so capital flows in, the exchange rate appreciates, external competitiveness declines, and the IS curve shifts back to its initial position. Demand disturbances are eliminated. Box 11.5 discusses some reasons why this result should be taken with a grain of salt.

the domestic interest rate exceeding the foreign rate of return, capital flows in and the exchange rate appreciates. As external competitiveness declines, the current account worsens and the IS curve

starts shifting to the left. This proceeds as long as the interest rate exceeds the foreign rate of return, and until the IS curve is back at its initial position and the economy is back at point A. The demand disturbance is simply 'crowded out' by the demand effect of the exchange rate appreciation *via* the current account.

The result applies to any of the exogenous components of real demand we encountered in Chapter 10: expansionary fiscal policies (public spending, taxes), business optimism or pessimism, or foreign demand feeding through exports. The general conclusion, under flexible exchange rates, is that an economy cannot sustainably lift itself up via higher domestic or world demand. In the end, demand impulses are eventually neutralized by exchange rate changes. Output is insulated from foreign demand disturbances.

Graphically, the position of the IS curve depends on the real exchange rate σ. With sticky domestic and foreign prices, the real exchange rate is driven by the nominal exchange rate, which is determined in the foreign exchange market. The exchange rate, therefore, is endogenous, as is the IS curve. More precisely, the exchange rate changes in such a way that the IS curve shifts to meet the two other schedules, LM or TR and IFM.

Box 11.5 Theory and Reality

You may find puzzling the result that fiscal policy—a type of demand disturbance—has no effect on output, especially when looking at the Keynesian multipliers presented in Table 10.1, some of which concern countries that let their currencies freely float. This should serve as a healthy warning that theory should never be taken literally. Theory differs from reality because it is based on assumptions that are never exactly verified. Without simplifying assumptions, theory is forced to emulate reality, which is impossible. If the assumptions are well chosen, theory can only try to reveal some important aspects that would otherwise be lost in the dense complexity of reality.

The Mundell–Fleming model makes a very large number of simplifying assumptions. For example, it is assumed that everything happens at once. In fact, it takes time for demand disturbances to work through the economy—this is why the multipliers change over time, as shown in Table 10.1. The same applies to the effects of exchange rate changes on demand. If the former operates faster than the latter, there can be some temporary—possibly extending over a few years—effects of fiscal policy on output. Another assumption is that any change in the exchange rate affects external competitiveness one for one. In fact, there is significant evidence that this is not the case. For instance, exporting firms often accept lower profit margins in order to limit the short-term impact of an exchange rate appreciation on their prices in foreign markets.

The text says that fiscal policy has zero effect on output. A more careful statement would be that the effects of fiscal policy are partly undermined by exchange rate changes. The crucial lesson is that the exchange rate will appreciate (resp. depreciate) when a fiscal expansion is enacted and that this tends to undermine the expected output effect.

Box 11.6 How to Think of a Large Economy

A large economy has two main characteristics: (1) trade represents a small share of GDP, as Table 11.1 shows, and (2) it affects but is not much affected by foreign economies. Most large economies (the USA, the EU, Japan) are well integrated financially. The key step taken in the present chapter relative to the previous one is to account for capital mobility. Yet, the better framework to think about a large economy is the one presented in Chapter 10.

Trade openness does not change the qualitative results of Chapters 10 and 11, but rather affects the size of the Keynesian multiplier. Financial integration, on the other hand, significantly modifies results because we have used the small-country assumption as we took the foreign rate of return i^* as exogenous. Since a large country affects but is not much affected by the foreign rate of return, we can ignore the IFM schedule. We are therefore left with the framework of Chapter 10, the IS and LM or TR schedules.

Think of the USA, the typical—maybe the only—large economy. When the Federal Reserve Bank changes its interest rate, asset holders reshuffle their portfolios and, in the event, all interest rates are affected, as Figure 11.11 shows. In contrast, all the other countries are financially too small to have a similar impact on the US interest rate—although the situation may be changing as the euro expands its reach.

Under flexible exchange rates, the macroeconomic equilibrium is determined by the LM or TR and IFM schedules. In the same way that the LM or TR schedule can be ignored when the exchange rate is fixed—because the money supply is endogenous—the IS schedule can be ignored when the exchange rate floats because the exchange rate is endogenous. Still, the shift of the IS curve, required to meet the two other schedules tells us what happens to the exchange rate. It appreciates when the IS curve must move to the left and it depreciates in the opposite case.

Fig. 11.11 Long-Term Interest Rates (1980M1–2008M4)

The chart displays the evolution of long-term interest rates (usually Treasury bonds of 10-year maturity) in the USA and in the other large developed countries. The levels are often quite different, for reasons that will be explained later in Chapter 14. Yet month-to-month fluctuations reveal a high degree of coherence. The chart does not say that US interest rates drive the other rates, only that all rates tend to move together. Available statistical evidence indicates that US rates are the driving force behind the common movements in interest rates over time.

Source: IMF, *International Financial Statistics*.

11.5.3 International Financial Disturbances

The effect of an increase in returns on foreign assets measured in terms of the home currency (i^*) was described in Figure 11.7 for the case of fixed exchange rates. The same diagram can be used to understand what happens under flexible exchange rates. Graphically, we know that we can ignore the *IS* curve: as the *IFM* line shifts upwards to *IFM'*, equilibrium moves from point *A* to point *C*. The interest rate must rise to meet the foreign rate of return and the economy expands.

It may come as a surprise that an interest rate increase could lead to an output expansion. Again, the reason has to do with the exchange rate. Consider point *A* immediately after the upward shift of the *IFM* line. The domestic interest rate is now below the foreign rate of return. This triggers a capital outflow. Since the central bank does not intervene in the foreign exchange market, the outflow translates into a depreciation of the exchange rate. The country's external competitiveness and current account improve and the *IS* curve shifts to the right until it goes through point *C* (the new curve is not shown).

The increase in the foreign rate of return may be the consequence of a stricter monetary policy stance in the 'rest of the world'. Think of rest of the world as a large economy that trades with us, a small open economy (Box 11.6 explains why a large, fully integrated economy can change its interest rate). As the foreign interest rate i^* rises, foreign GDP declines. At home, in contrast, the GDP rises, as we have just seen. Conversely, a monetary expansion abroad has a contractionary effect at home. This result is known as the **beggar-thy-neighbour** effect, because one country's expansionary policy comes at the expense of its neighbours. In contrast, under fixed exchange rates, the reasoning from Section 11.4 shows that foreign monetary policy has the same qualitative effect on foreign and domestic GDPs.

11.6 Fixed or Flexible Rates?

This chapter shows just how important is the exchange rate regime for the way in which a small open economy reacts to disturbances, intended (policy measures) or not. It also shows that the exchange rate regime is best understood through the prism of monetary policy. We had already seen in Chapter 10 that a central bank can control the interest rate or the money supply, but not both.

Table 11.3   The Mundell–Fleming Model: A Summary

Aspect/characterization of policy	Exchange rate regime	
	Fixed exchange rates	Flexible exchange rates
Effect on real GDP of:		
Fiscal policy expansion	Increase	No effect
Monetary policy expansion	No effect	Increase
Increase in foreign interest rate	Decrease	Increase
Exogenous monetary policy instrument	Exchange rate	Interest rate (or money supply)
Endogenous monetary policy instrument	Interest rate (or money supply)	Exchange rate

Now we find that a central bank can control the interest rate or the money supply on one hand, or the nominal exchange rate on the other hand, not both. If it chooses to peg the exchange rate, it gives up its ability to implement a domestic monetary policy, e.g. a Taylor rule or a money growth rule. It can recover some influence on the interest rate and/or the money supply only if it lets the exchange rate float. Table 11.3 summarizes most results found in this chapter. We now examine what they mean for the choice of an exchange rate regime.

A fixed exchange rate regime represents a commitment to refrain from active use of monetary policy. Graphically, the *LM* or *TR* schedules are irrelevant. The exchange rate anchor imposes a tight discipline on the monetary authorities, but it leaves the economy vulnerable to demand disturbances, both domestic and foreign. Graphically, any exogenous shift of the *IS* curve determines a new equilibrium. In addition, shifts of the *IFM* line pose a considerable risk to the sustainability of the fixed exchange rate regime. This requires a large investment in credibility—an issue we will pick up in Chapter 17. Many countries in Europe (e.g. France and Italy) in the 1980s and in Latin America (e.g. Argentina and Brazil) in the 1990s have followed the fixed exchange rate strategy. It can work as long as the currency parity is not challenged by external current or financial account deficits. When this occurs, the exchange regime comes under threat and its credibility as a disciplining device for governments is called into question. This was precisely

Argentina's problem in the 1990s, as explained in Box 11.4.

When the exchange rate floats freely, monetary independence is preserved. The *LM* or *TR* schedules describe how the central bank carries out its policy. The economy as a whole is shielded from real demand disturbances. Graphically, the *IS* curve endogenously shifts to meet the *LM* or *TR* and *IFM* schedules. Yet the exchange rate may widely fluctuate in response to international financial disturbances, upsetting external competitiveness in one direction or another and confronting firms with rapidly changing circumstances. An exchange rate appreciation, for instance, hurts exporters as much as they benefit from a depreciation.

Among the countries that operate under a freely floating exchange rate regime are those that have developed sufficient economic and political stability to entrust the central bank with the task of delivering price stability. This is the case of the USA, the euro area, the UK, Sweden, Switzerland, and a few others. Other countries have abandoned a fixed exchange rate regime, having been bruised by speculative attacks against a previous fixed regime. This is the case, among others, in Argentina, Brazil, Chile, Russia, and many other countries. Other countries let their exchange rate float because inflation is so high that any peg would quickly lead to overvaluation and crisis.[14]

---

[14] Recall that the real exchange rate is SP/P^*. With S fixed, if P rises faster than P^*, the real exchange rate appreciates. These situations will be addressed in Chapters 13 and 16.

❶ Summary

1 The Mundell–Fleming model is an extension of the *IS–LM* or *IS–TR* models to the open economy. It describes the simultaneous equilibrium of three markets: (1) the market for goods and services, (2) the domestic money market, and (3) the international financial market.

2 The Mundell–Fleming model adopts the Keynesian assumption that prices are sticky. In this case, output is driven by demand.

3 When a country's financial markets are well integrated into world markets, the domestic interest rate is tied to worldwide conditions. Under conditions of complete capital mobility, a third equilibrium condition requires that the domestic interest rate be equal to the world rate of return. This is the interest rate parity condition. This condition does not hold in the case of limited international capital mobility—e.g. because of capital controls. The *IFM* line summarizes the interest rate parity condition.

4 Bringing together the three schedules permits one to study the general macroeconomic equilibrium, when all three markets are simultaneously in equilibrium.

5 When the exchange rate is fixed, demand disturbances affect domestic GDP but, committed to uphold the declared exchange rate parity, the central bank cannot conduct an autonomous monetary policy. The *LM* or *TR* schedules become irrelevant and the equilibrium is described by the intersection of the *IS* and *IFM* schedules.

6 When the exchange rate is freely floating, the central bank recovers monetary policy autonomy, but the exchange rate is endogenous. Its movements affects the economy's competitiveness and, therefore, the position of the *IS* curve. The exchange rate movements are such that the *IS* endogenously moves to meet the *LM* or *TR* and *IFM* schedules. The fact that the *IS* curve does not determine the equilibrium outcome means that the economy is shielded from demand disturbances.

7 Monetary and exchange rate policies are just two sides of the same coin: the central bank can peg the exchange rate or it can conduct an autonomous monetary policy, but it cannot do both at the same time.

8 The choice of an exchange rate regime involves trade-offs. Different countries choose different regimes, and often adapt their regimes depending on the circumstances.

❷ Key Concepts

- **Mundell–Fleming model**
- **general equilibrium**
- **exchange rate regime**
- **interest parity condition**
- **balance of payments (BP) line**
- **exchange market intervention**
- **foreign exchange reserves**
- **sterilized and unsterilized interventions**
- **exchange rate anchor**
- **capital controls**
- **monetary policy autonomy**
- **revaluation, devaluation**
- **appreciation, depreciation**
- **realignment**
- **beggar-thy-neighbour policies**

❓ Exercises

1 Consider a central bank that targets the money supply M. The Keynesian assumption that the price level is sticky implies that the central bank controls the real money supply M/P. Show graphically what happens when the central bank decides to increase the money supply under a fixed exchange rate regime. What general conclusion can you draw?

2 Same question as (1) under a flexible exchange rate regime.

3 Show the effect of a demand disturbance under a fixed exchange rate regime: the economy moves from point A to point B. Explain why point C is not sustainable and why the economy must move to point B.

4 Show the effects of an increase of the foreign rate of return under fixed and flexible exchange rates. What happens to the money supply in each case?

5 In a situation of economic or political instability, a standard reaction of citizens is to exogenously reduce their demand for money. What happens then to the interest rate, income, and the money supply under a fixed exchange rate regime?

6 Same question as (5) but under flexible exchange rates, when the central bank applies a Taylor rule. Explain also what happens to the nominal exchange rate.

7 Same question as (6) when the central bank follows a money targeting strategy.

8 What is the effect of an exchange rate revaluation in a fixed (but adjustable) exchange rate regime?

9 What is the effect of reduction of income taxes under a fixed exchange rate regime? Under a floating exchange rate regime? Consider successively the cases when the central bank follows a Taylor rule and when it keeps the money supply constant.

10 In troubled times, it is common to observe a safe-haven phenomenon affecting currencies like the Swiss franc. Concerned international investors care less about returns than in normal times and invest in the country even if the interest rate is comparatively low. Evaluate the impact of such a phenomenon on a safe-haven small open economy with a flexible exchange rate. What can the central bank do?

11 Consider a small open economy under a fixed exchange rate regime. What happens if the price level suddenly increases and the nominal exchange rate is devalued in the same proportion? How would your answer change if the exchange rate parity remains unchanged?

12 Same question but under a flexible exchange rate regime (so there is no point in talking of devaluation). Answer the question when (1) the central bank keeps the nominal money supply constant and (2) when it follows a Taylor rule. In each case, what happens to the exchange rate?

13 Imagine that the central bank supports its depreciating exchange rate and buys, say 1 million worth of its currency on the exchange market. Use the balance sheets of the central bank and of commercial banks presented in Chapter 9 to describe this foreign exchange market operation. Use the same balance sheets to describe a sterilization operation.

→ Essay Questions

1 Integration into international financial markets means that the domestic interest rate is determined abroad. Why should a country ever abandon its exchange rate controls?

2 As their name suggests, beggar-thy-neighbour policies have a bad reputation. Discuss why this may be the case and what can be done to limit the perceived drawbacks.

3 'Adopting an exchange rate anchor is a mixed blessing.' Comment.

4 Upon joining the monetary union, many European countries have delegated their monetary policies to the European Central Bank, a huge sacrifice of national sovereignty, it seems. On the other hand, they were previously members of the European Monetary System, pegging their exchange rates to each other. Evaluate the economic loss of sovereignty of euro-area membership. (Think of both fiscal and monetary policies.)

5 Emerging market countries typically have to offer a risk premium when they borrow. This means that their domestic interest rates are higher than those abroad. What is the impact of a sudden loss of trust? Discuss the reasons why this could happen and what are, in each case, the policy options.

Output, Employment, and Inflation

12

When the demand for a commodity or service is high relative to the supply of it we expect the price to rise, the rate of rise being greater, the greater the excess demand. Conversely when the demand is low relatively to the supply we expect the price to fall, the rate of fall being greater, the greater the deficiency of demand. It seems plausible that this principle should operate as one of the factors determining the rate of change of money wage rates, which are the price of labour services.

A. W. Phillips[1]

12.1 Overview

A cup of tea in London that cost 5p in 1965 goes for £1.20 or more in 2008. The baguette in Paris which cost 40 centimes (of French franc) in 1965 fetches 13 times more (in euros) 40 years later. Prices seem to grow relentlessly. Yet inflation is not just about changes in the price of tea in Britain and bread in Paris. Inflation is about all prices. It measures the rate of increase of the price level, i.e. when virtually all prices rise. The phenomenon does not stop there. As the price level rises, so do nominal wages. Wages rise partly due to rising productivity, but they also chase prices, which in turn chase wages. And the nominal exchange rate seems to be engaged in the same kind of race. Somehow, all nominal variables seem to leapfrog each other.

Whether very low or excruciatingly high, inflation is a key feature of modern economies. It was not always so. From time immemorial to the middle of the twentieth century, prices were pretty much trendless. Continuing inflation is a relatively new event in the history of humankind, and coincides with the emergence of modern central banks and fiat money. This should not come as a surprise once we remember the monetary neutrality principle. Ultimately, the central banks and their ability to freely create money are the cause of this new phenomenon.

So far, we have studiously avoided talking about inflation. We alluded to it in Chapter 6 when we established the principle of monetary neutrality, quickly relegating it to the faraway long run. In Chapters 10 and 11, we explicitly ruled it out by adopting the Keynesian assumption that prices are sticky. These were useful steps that allow us to now to focus of this central aspect of modern economies.

In this chapter, we focus on the 'medium run'. The short run corresponds to the Keynesian view, whereby prices hardly change. The long run is described by the opposite, neoclassical assumption. When enough time has elapsed, all prices move to achieve monetary neutrality, a principle already presented in Chapter 6. In the medium run, prices move but not sufficiently to allow all markets to clear. We start by clarifying these issues.

Then we look at a very simple description of the inflation phenomenon, the **Phillips curve**. We will see that, although useful for helping us think about the short-run behaviour of inflation, the Phillips curve is in fact a somewhat unstable relationship which seems to vanish periodically. So we embark on a detective-like investigation of the puzzle of the 'disappearing Phillips curve'. This leads us to track down the various reasons why prices rise. We start by asking who sets prices (firms do) and why (mostly production costs). As we study production costs, we return to the wage bargaining process encountered in Chapter 5, and find that wage negotiators worry about prices. We end up facing the apparently circular conclusion that prices drive wages and wages drive prices, in a sort

---

[1] The son of a Kiwi dairy farmer, A. W. Phillips (1914–1975) started out as an apprentice electrician working in an Australian mine, then left for Britain via China and Russia in the late 1930s. After a tour of duty in the Second World War and time spent as a prisoner of war, he studied at the London School of Economics and became a lecturer and later professor there. Phillips is remembered not only for his curve relating unemployment to rates of wage change, but also for the *Moniac*, a complex hydraulic representation of macroeconomy, one of which is on display in the Science Museum in London.

of race between employers—who want profits to be high—and employees—who want high wages. The outcome of the analysis is an accounting of the factors that add up to a full explanation of inflation. This analysis helps us solve the Phillips curve puzzle. It also allows us to derive the **aggregate supply curve**, which will be teamed up with the aggregate demand curve developed in the next chapter to complete the system of inflation and output determination.

12.2 General Equilibrium with Flexible Prices: The Neoclassical Case

12.2.1 From the Keynesian Short Run to the Neoclassical Long Run

In Chapters 10 and 11, we made extensive use of the Keynesian assumption that prices are sticky. We justified this assumption by asserting that prices move slowly in normal times. In the short run, we said, ignoring inflation is an easy way to make things simple. When thinking about the long run, however, we need to make the diametrically opposite assumption that prices are **fully flexible**. This is the **neoclassical assumption** against which Keynes rebelled in the 1930s. He well knew the limits of his own assumption, but then famously wrote that 'in the long run, we are all dead'. This section rebels against the Keynesian assumption and presents the view espoused by neoclassical economists (neoclassicals for short) writing both before and after Keynes. While some Keynesians and neoclassicals still fight it out, most economists now agree that the Keynesian assumption is acceptable in the short run, and the neoclassical assumption is the right way to go when thinking about the long run.[2] This section, therefore, studies the long run, but we also look at how things change over time, from the short to the long run.

In the Keynesian view, the price level is exogenous and output is endogenous, fully responding to demand. In the neoclassical view, it is the price level that is endogenous and plays the equilibrating role in the goods market. It turns out that, in this case, it is demand that adjusts to supply.

We have already started to examine the neoclassical case in Chapter 6 when we established the monetary neutrality principle. From that chapter, recall the Cambridge equation:

(12.1)
$$M = kPY$$

where we treat parameter k as constant. We asked what happens when the money supply increases, say by 10%. In the short run, when prices are sticky, the only way for the money market equilibrium condition (as explained in Chapter 9) to hold is for real GDP to increase by 10%. This is the Keynesian case. If prices are flexible, however, equilibrium can be achieved with a 10% increase in the price level, without any change in real GDP. This is the neoclassical case and its underlying result is monetary neutrality.

If the Keynesian assumption is valid in the short run and the neoclassical assumption characterizes the long run, then it must be the case that an increase in the money supply is followed first by a rise in output that will be eventually dissipated into an increase in inflation. This is shown in Figure 12.1.

This fundamental division of changes in money—or more generally, nominal demand—on the one hand and prices and output on the other can be expressed in terms of rates of change. The inflation rate is the rate of change in the price level, defined as a rate: $\Delta P/P$. Equation (12.1) implies that the price level is given by

---

[2]　This intellectual debate is presented in Chapter 20.

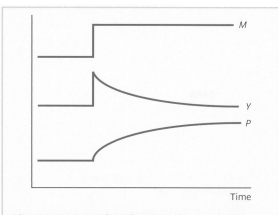

Fig. 12.1 From the Short to the Long Run

We look at the impact of a one-off increase in the money supply. The short run corresponds to the Keynesian assumption: prices are sticky and output moves to respond to demand. The neoclassical assumption describes the long run, when prices fully adjust and monetary neutrality implies that output is unaffected.

(12.1′) $P = M/(kY)$.

So for a constant k, the inflation rate, the growth of the money supply $\Delta M/M$, and the growth rate of output $\Delta Y/Y$, the following relationship must hold:

(12.1″) $\Delta P/P = \Delta M/M - \Delta Y/Y$.

This is a central 'rate of change' version of the classical quantity equation. It will help us later in thinking about the long run.

12.2.2 Supply-Determined Output in the Long Run

Why does price flexibility lead to a situation where demand adjusts to supply? Let us start with the supply side, production and the labour market previously studied in Chapter 5. Figure 12.2(a) displays the production function. Panel (b) shows the demand for labour implied by the marginal productivity of labour—as determined by the position and the slope of the production function—and the supply of labour—as shaped by labour market institutions. The resulting equilibrium at point A in panel (b) indicates how much labour is utilized. The corresponding point A in panel (a) shows how much

is produced and supplied. We can also see in panel (b) the equilibrium real wage, the ratio of nominal wages W to the price level P.

Let us first briefly examine the situation under the Keynesian assumption. Imagine a decrease in demand for goods. Chapters 10 and 11 show that supply declines, say to point B in panel (a). As they sell less, firms reduce employment. Since wages and prices are sticky, the real wage does not change and, instead of moving to point B in panel (b), firms move to point B'. At that point, involuntary unemployment is AB', which is inefficient for the labour market. Moreover, since firms are not on their labour demand curve they are unable to optimize their profits. Obviously, both firms and their employees are upset.

Given time, wage and price flexibility should allow the economy to adapt to the circumstances of reduced demand. To see that, we now adopt the neoclassical assumption: prices and wages rise when demand is strong and decline in the opposite case. In the present case, facing weak demand, firms reduce prices. Assume for a moment that nominal wages (W) remain sticky. Then real wages (W/P) rise because a lower price level (P) means a higher purchasing power of wages. This takes the labour market to point B in panel (b). This does not help, since involuntary unemployment rises from B'A to BC. Now allow for nominal wages flexibility as well. Facing involuntary employment, workers end up accepting that their wages decline and we move from B' to A. Supply is restored to its initial value. Thus, under full price and wage flexibility, we find that supply does not change in the face of changing demand. But then, goods market equilibrium requires that demand matches supply. What will bring demand back to its initial level?

The IS–LM (or IS–TR) analysis developed in Chapter 11 provides the answer. Consider first the case of a flexible exchange rate regime. In that case, we have seen that demand is endogenous, so we know the outcome: demand shocks have no effect. As demand for domestic goods declines, the exchange rate depreciates and competitiveness is improved. This process will go on until demand returns to its original level. Under fixed rates, the IS curve shifts to the left but then the fall in the price level boosts

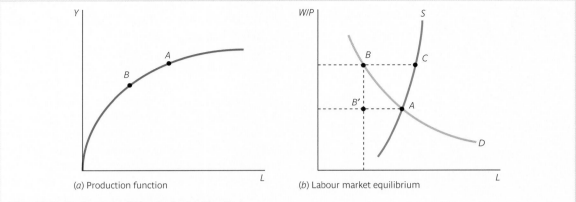

Fig. 12.2 Output and the Labour Market

An exogenous demand reduction is shown in panel (*a*) as the move from *A* to *B*. The firms' best reaction is to reduce employment along their demand schedule *D* in panel (*b*). In the Keynesian case, where wages and prices are sticky, this is impossible and the new situation is described instead by point *B'*, where real wages remain unchanged, but the labour market is not in equilibrium and there is involuntary unemployment measured, by *B'A*. In the neoclassical case, facing weak demand, firms cut prices and employees accept wage cuts, and the labour market returns to equilibrium at point *A*.

external competitiveness and the *IS* curve will shift to the right. Will it go back all the way to its initial position? Suppose that it does not. Then demand remains lower than supply, so firms must again cut prices and employees must accept further wage reductions. The process must go on until, indeed, demand matches supply. In a nutshell, either exchange rate flexibility, or price flexibility, or both will raise competitiveness enough to counteract the initial exogenous reduction in demand.

12.2.3 Implications for the Long Run

If we consider that the neoclassical assumption describes the long run, we can conclude that demand disturbances only have a temporary impact on output and employment. Thus, we start from the Keynesian short run where supply passively adjusts to demand and gradually move to the long run as prices and wages start to respond to prevailing conditions. Eventually, the economy is back to full equilibrium or, equivalently, GDP returns to its trend level and equilibrium unemployment (as defined in Chapter 5) prevails again. This description nicely fits the idea of business cycles represented in Figure 10.1 and the idea that price adjustments gradually substitute for quantity adjustments (see Figure 12.1). What remains to be done is to examine how prices and wages move in response to temporary disequilibria in the goods and/or labour markets.

Before embarking in this direction, we briefly look at supply shocks. These disturbances include changes that affect the labour market (e.g. changes in regulations, labour taxes, or labour militancy) and events that affect productivity. Supply shocks should be contrasted with demand shocks. In the short run, they have little effect in the short run, because output is demand determined, but they dominate in the long run. In fact, they determine the position and the rate of growth of equilibrium output—and comprise those factors discussed in Chapters 3 and 4. For instance, continuously occurring technological advances drive output up. This is the key reason why trend GDP rises. A one-off jump in the price of oil can shift the trend level of output downwards for many years, if not decades.

12.3 The Phillips Curve: Chimera or a Stylized Fact?

The Phillips curve has played a major role in the development of macroeconomics. For a long time, it embodied the most heated controversies. It was discovered, ditched, and transformed several times. It now enjoys widespread support and embodies the fairly wide consensus that characterizes current macroeconomic thinking. Most likely, this consensus will be shaken one day or another and chances are that the Phillips curve will be at the heart of the next controversy. Reviewing its turbulent history can shed some light on these lingering debates.

12.3.1 A. W. Phillips' Discovery

The short-run Keynesian assumption and the long-run neoclassical assumptions are fairly easy to deal with: prices either do not change at all, or they fully adjust. The medium run, as represented in Figure 12.1, is messier: prices do move, but only part of the way. The Keynesian assumption always had the major disadvantage of leaving inflation unexplained by assuming it away. Even die-hard Keynesians conceded at the high point of their influence that they had no clue on how to incorporate inflation in their model. They referred to it as the 'missing equation'. The hunt for this equation turned up the Phillips curve, a negative trade-off observed between inflation and unemployment, the twin 'bads' of macroeconomics. It is represented in Figure 12.3.

In the late 1950s, Phillips plotted the annual rate of growth of nominal wages, i.e. wage inflation, against the rate of unemployment in Britain during the period 1861–1957. He found a remarkably robust negative correlation, which was confirmed for a number of other countries.[3] Figure 12.4 plots

[3] Phillips was not the first to discover the Phillips curve. The American economist Irving Fischer published a paper in the *International Labor Review* of 1926 in which he unearthed a similar relationship in the USA.

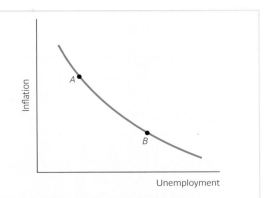

Fig. 12.3 The Stylized Phillips Curve

The Phillips curve implies a trade-off between unemployment and inflation: you can get less of one evil only by getting more of the other. It came to be seen as representing options from which governments could choose. For example, it could keep unemployment down (point *A*) at the cost of some inflation, or could limit inflation (point *B*) but only by accepting higher unemployment.

actual Phillips curves—using the rate of price inflation instead of wage inflation—for the UK and the average of sixteen advanced economies for the period 1921–1973 (excluding war years). While far less clean than the stylized version (a number of outliers correspond to exceptional events), the actual Phillips curves suggest that the relationship shown in Figure 12.3 is a general phenomenon.

The Phillips curve has been, and remains, very popular for two main reasons. First, as said already, it is the missing theoretical relationship that complements and indeed completes the Keynesian *IS–LM* or *IS–TR* apparatus. Second, even if its durability is called into question, it remains a practical tool for policy-makers. They can aim at low unemployment but they must accept substantial inflation (point *A* in Figure 12.3), or they may prefer low inflation but

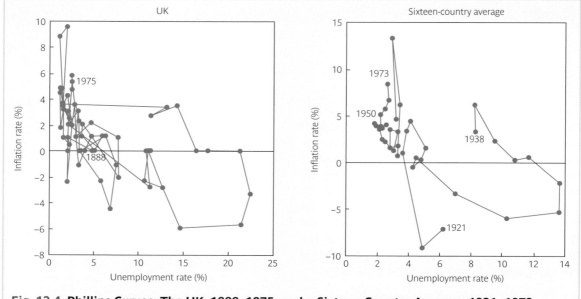

Fig. 12.4 Phillips Curves: The UK, 1888–1975, and a Sixteen-Country Average, 1921–1973, Excluding 1939–1949

Sources: Maddison (1991); Mitchell (1998). Unweighted average of observations for Australia, Austria, Belgium, Canada, Denmark, Finland, France, Germany, Italy, Japan, the Netherlands, Norway, Sweden, Switzerland, the UK, and the USA. For some years, some countries are missing.

at the cost of high unemployment (point *B*), or any intermediate situation. Once they decide, they can use their instruments (monetary and/or fiscal policy) to reach the chosen point on the Phillips curve.[4] This policy dilemma came to be known as the **Phillips trade-off**.

12.3.2 Okun's Law and a Supply Curve Interpretation

The Phillips curve relates inflation to unemployment. A closely related association, between inflation and output, will play a major role under the label of aggregate supply. The two relationships are linked through another stylized fact, known as **Okun's Law**, an inverse relationship between out-put and unemployment.[5] More precisely, Okun's Law links the **unemployment gap**, the distance between actual and equilibrium unemployment as defined in Chapter 5, to the **output gap**, the distance between real GDP and its long-run trend, as illustrated in Figure 10.1. The German unemployment and output gaps are shown in Figure 12.5. This example, which can be replicated elsewhere, makes it clear that the unemployment and output gaps systematically move in opposite directions. The logic is intuitive: when the economy grows fast and output is above trend, demand for labour is strong and unemployment falls below its equilibrium level.

Formally, Okun's Law can be represented as follows:

---

[4] This view of a trade-off was echoed by Helmut Schmidt, the ex-chancellor of West Germany, who stated in a newspaper interview in 1978 that he would prefer 5% inflation to 5% unemployment. How times have changed!

[5] The law is named after the US economist Arthur Okun (1928–1980). In his original finding about the USA, a 1% drop in the unemployment rate was associated with a 3% increase of GDP above trend. This would imply a value for *h* in (12.2) of one-third.

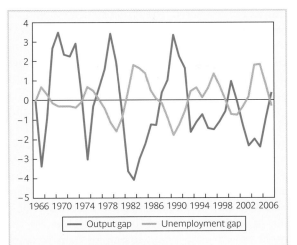

Fig. 12.5 The Output Gap and Unemployment in Germany, 1966–2007

The output gap measures the distance between real GDP and its trend and is computed in percent of trend GDP. The unemployment gap is the difference between actual and equilibrium GDP, both measured in percent of the labour force. When business conditions vary, firms adapt the supply of goods and services. To that effect, they adjust their demand for labour. For example, when the economy goes into a recession, firms employ fewer workers and the unemployment rate rises.

Notes: Trend real GDP and equilibrium unemployment are estimated as second-order polynomial functions of time.

Source: OECD, *Main Economic Indicators*.

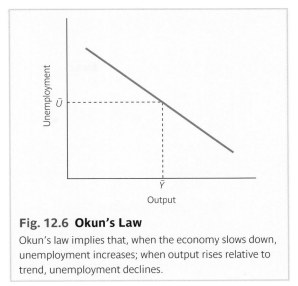

Fig. 12.6 Okun's Law

Okun's law implies that, when the economy slows down, unemployment increases; when output rises relative to trend, unemployment declines.

(12.2) $U_{\text{gap}} = -hY_{\text{gap}}, \quad \text{where} \quad U_{\text{gap}} = U - \bar{U}$

$$\text{and} \quad Y_{\text{gap}} = \frac{Y - \bar{Y}}{\bar{Y}}.$$

The unemployment gap U_{gap} is defined as the difference between the current unemployment rate U and its equilibrium level $\bar{U}$. Similarly, the output gap is the percent deviation of real GDP Y from its trend growth path $\bar{Y}$.[6] The parameter h captures the

response of unemployment to GDP fluctuations identified by the output gap. A stylized representation of Okun's Law is displayed in Figure 12.6.

We can combine the inverse relationship between inflation and the unemployment rate from the Phillips curve with the inverse relationship between the unemployment rate and the output gap from Okun's Law to obtain the positive relationship between the output gap and inflation shown in Figure 12.7. This schedule is called the aggregate supply curve. Section 12.4 provides a complete interpretation of the supply curve, but the intuitive logic that lies behind it is straightforward. The supply curve answers the following question: under which conditions will an increase in aggregate demand lead firms to supply more output and employees to work more to produce that extra output? The short answer is: inflation must increase, to boost wages and profits.

That the aggregate supply curve is upward sloping reminds us of the supply curve in microeconomics. This similarity is both intuitive and misleading. In microeconomics, the horizontal axis corresponds to the production of a particular good and the vertical represents that good's relative price. Here we deal with *aggregate* output or real GDP on the horizontal axis and the *overall* price index—or here its rate of increase, which is the inflation rate—on

---

[6] Note that the unemployment gap and the output gap are written in a different way. This is a technical detail. In Figure 12.5, both gaps are shown in percents. Since the unemployment rate is already measured in percent (of the labour force), its difference from equilibrium unemployment is also in percent. For the output gap to also be in percent, we compute the difference between GDP and its potential level—both measured in the local currency—as a proportion of potential GDP.

Fig. 12.7 The Aggregate Supply Curve

Combining the Phillips curve and Okun's Law, we obtain the aggregate supply curve. The curve says that inflation rises when output increases.

the vertical axis. This highlights the difference between micro and macroeconomics.

12.3.3 Hard Questions about the Phillips Curve

Weak foundations

Not long after its discovery, the interpretation of the Phillips curve was perceived as standing on weak theoretical legs. In the late 1960s, Milton Friedman, the Nobel laureate in 1976, and Edmund Phelps of Columbia University,[7] who received the Nobel Prize in 2006, independently attacked the Phillips curve implication of a permanent trade-off between inflation and unemployment or output. They both asked the following question: how could the rate of change of nominal variables, such as nominal wages or prices, be related to real variables, such as employment, unemployment, and output in the long run? If the monetary neutrality principle is valid in the long run, then rates of change in the price level and other nominal variables should be unrelated to the real economy.[8] In

this case, they noted, the Phillips curve should be observed temporarily. Only if workers and firms suffer from **money illusion**—i.e. if they act on increases in their own prices or wages without taking contemporaneous increases in all other prices into account—will they raise output.

To understand the critique of Friedman and Phelps, it is helpful to think about the long-run behaviour of labour markets and output as presented in Section 12.2. The principle of monetary neutrality asserts that the economy is dichotomized in the long run: the real and nominal sectors of an economy stop influencing each other. If the long run is defined as when output level is on its trend growth path $\bar{Y}$ and unemployment is at its equilibrium rate $\bar{U}$, then the rate of inflation is determined by the rate of money growth, not by the level of output or the unemployment rate. Graphically, if unemployment returns to its equilibrium level in the long run, the **long-run aggregate supply curve** and the Phillips curve must be vertical lines, as displayed in Figure 12.8. This conclusion is in agreement with the neoclassical view, developed in Section 12.2, which implies that output is determined by the supply side in the long run.

Wobbly evidence

The critique of Friedman and Phelps was largely ignored in the late 1960s, but it proved to be right on target in the 1970s when, as Figure 12.9 shows, the Phillips curve simply vanished. Quite spectacularly, in the mid-1970s and early 1980s, both inflation and unemployment started to rise. Stagflation, as the phenomenon came to be known, was incompatible with the Phillips curve and its trade-off. A number of consequences followed. Policy-makers, now grappling to beat back inflation, became sceptical of 'Keynesian activism'. They started to put greater emphasis on long-run monetary neutrality as a guiding principle for monetary policy. German Governments and the Bundesbank, never great fans of Keynesian ideas, were seen as vindicated. Nowhere was the shift of ideas more spectacular than in the UK, where Mrs Thatcher invited Milton Friedman for a cup of tea soon after her election in 1979. Elsewhere, the evolution was

---

[7] This is the same Phelps who formulated the golden rule of economic growth in Chapter 3.

[8] In his address to the American Economic Association in 1967 Friedman argued that 'there is always a temporary trade-off between inflation and unemployment, there is no permanent trade-off. The temporary trade-off comes not from inflation *per se*, but from a rising rate of inflation', Friedman (1968: 10).

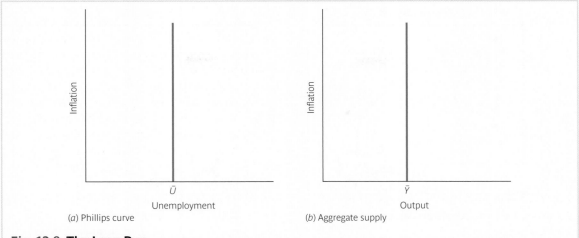

Fig. 12.8 The Long Run

In the long run, unemployment is at its equilibrium rate and output is on its trend growth path. Both the Phillips curve and the aggregate supply curve are vertical. Inflation is determined by money growth, independently of output or unemployment.

generally slower, but there is no doubt that the vanishing of the Phillips curve had a profound effect on policy-makers.

Macroeconomics also underwent a profound transformation, which can be thought of as a massive effort to rehabilitate and reconstruct the Phillips curve. It started as a puzzle. Over nearly a century, the inverse relationship between inflation and unemployment had seemed relatively robust. Why did it suddenly break down in all countries at about the same time? It can hardly be simply a case of bad luck! It turns out that the breakdown of the Phillips curve actually has helped economists better understand the true forces behind it.

The challenge is to explain both the existence of a Phillips curve and its disappearance, as well as the striking similarity between different countries' experiences. Nearly everywhere inflation and unemployment increased sharply, at first around 1973–1974, and then around 1979–1980, precisely at the time of the two **oil shocks**. Indeed, oil prices increased fourfold in 1973–1974 and then doubled again in 1979–1980. Interestingly, in between the oil shocks, and after the second oil shock, Phillips curves re-emerged, each time further above and to the right of the previous one. Two examples of these episodes are presented in Figure 12.9 and further dissected in the following section.

12.4 Accounting for Inflation: The Battle of the Mark-ups

Could the weak theoretical foundations of the Phillips curve and its successive mutations over time be two sides of the same coin? Confronted with uncompromising data, economists indeed had to go back to

the drawing board. Yet, as noted above, Friedman and Phelps had already provided the answer to the puzzle even before the puzzle emerged. This section presents an interpretation that can account for these facts.

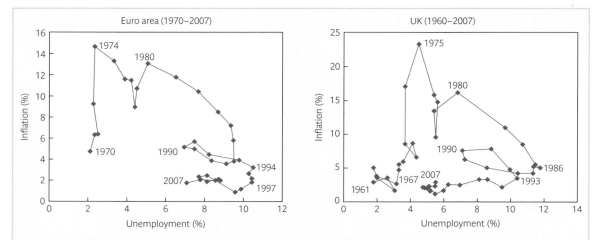

Fig. 12.9 Phillips Curves: Recent Experiences in the Euro Area and the UK

The Phillips curve broke down at the end of the 1960s. In the euro area, the sharp movements of the early and late 1970s coincide with the two oil shocks. Then the great deflation of the 1980s is compatible with the traditional Phillips curve, as are the periods 1990–1994 and, slightly below, 1997–2007. In the UK, the old Phillips curve survives over 1960–1967 until the upward jumps in 1973–1975 and 1979–1981 that coincide with sharp increases in oil prices—the so-called 'oil shocks'. As in the euro area, three different Phillips curves can be identified: during the deflation period of the 1980s, over 1986–1993 and in 1994–2007.

Source: OECD, *Economic Outlook*.

But why do we care about the fate of the Phillips curve in the first place? Recall that it deals with the medium run. In the short run, prices are sticky and we can ignore inflation. In the long run, the Phillips curve is vertical and has nothing to say about inflation. If we want to understand the inflation phenomenon, therefore, we need to understand the time in between. To that end, we will follow a pragmatic route. We will break inflation down into its most important components—an accounting exercise of sorts.

12.4.1 Prices and Costs

Price setting

The price level is the average of individual prices, but who sets the prices of goods and services and how?[9] Looking at stickers in stores and price lists in catalogues, you may correctly conclude that producers and retailers decide on the prices of their goods and services. Obviously, each producer prefers higher to lower prices, but their enthusiasm is

held in check by the need to attract enough buyers. This is the process that we now study. Box 12.1 recalls a few principles. It explains how competition limits the ability of firms to set prices, and that firms try hard to reduce these same limitations. It describes firms as setting prices as a mark-up above nominal production costs, aiming at a margin consistent with maximizing profits.

Costs

Now that we understand the price mark-up—the relationship of price to cost—it will make sense to look at those production costs, called **average** or **unit costs**.[10] Unit cost (UC) is simply the total cost of production divided by the number of units produced. It is convenient to break down unit costs into two main categories: labour and non-labour costs.

---

[9] Chapter 2 presents various ways of measuring the price level.

[10] In theory, the relevant concept is the marginal production cost, the cost of producing another unit of output. In practice, marginal costs are difficult to measure, so we approximate them by unit costs. This is an acceptable approximation under conditions of constant return to scale in all factors.

Box 12.1   When and How Firms Set Prices

When perfect competition holds in product markets, firms are unable to set prices. A good example is the fruit grower who sells his apples in the town market. With many other sellers around, the farmer cannot set his price very far from the average price for apples of the same variety. If he raises his price just a few cents, he loses all his customers; if he lowers his price, he will sell everything, but regret the forgone profits. Producers of standard products, such as agricultural products or raw materials, have relatively little choice. We say that they have no **market power**.

Yet most firms do have market power, and some firms have a lot of it. In fact, they go to extreme lengths to establish market power because this helps them achieve higher profits. This is called **product differentiation**, which means making each product special and different from the competitors'. They do so through design (similar cars always differ in many subtle ways), through advertising and marketing to win consumer loyalty (some people like Volkswagen, others Renault), or prod-

uct quality and reputation. The payoff is a higher willingness to pay of their customers, and a greater degree of market power. Firms can charge higher prices above the bare minimum that they need to survive, and still keep a large share of their customers.

Mark-up pricing is a simple way of describing how firms with market power set prices. Obviously, when setting a price, a firm wants to cover its production costs, and then it tries to do more. The margin over the cost of producing one more good, the marginal cost, is the mark-up. The mark-up depends on the sensitivity of the particular product's demand to price—its demand elasticity. If the market is highly competitive, the demand elasticity is near-infinite, as any price increase will lead customers to go elsewhere. In that case the mark-up is zero and the price is equal to marginal cost. This is the case of perfect competition. If competition is weak, because the firm has been able to differentiate its good and build a 'niche', or because other firms cannot enter the market, the demand elasticity is low and the mark-up will be large.

Unit costs in euros
= total costs in euros/number of
    units produced
= unit labour costs + unit non-labour costs.

For the economy as a whole, labour costs are the single largest component of unit production costs.

Table 12.1 shows that their share of value added ranges from 50% to 70% in developed countries, and is usually higher in labour-intensive services than in capital-intensive industries.[11] For this reason, we will focus on labour costs for the next few sections. We will consider non-labour costs later in Section 12.4.6.

---

[11] In interpreting these numbers, it is important to remember the distinction between value added and turnover or total sales, which was stressed in Chapter 1. As a percentage of total sales, wage shares are much lower because total turnover in an economy includes the costs of intermediate goods. The figures reported in Table 12.1 have netted out payments for intermediate inputs produced by other firms.

Labour costs and wages

A firm's labour costs are simply the product of the number of hours worked in the firm (L) and the average hourly labour cost (W). Gross hourly labour costs include not only direct wage and salary, but also costs such as paid vacations, direct labour taxes, social security contributions, and other benefits paid by employers on behalf of their workers. (In many European countries, these additional costs can be nearly equal to the net pay received by the worker.) A country's aggregate unit labour cost is computed in the same way. It is the ratio of total labour costs WL, also called the **wage bill**, to total real output, i.e. real GDP Y:

(12.3)

$$\text{nominal unit labour costs} = \frac{\text{wage bill}}{\text{real GDP}} = \frac{WL}{Y}.$$

Note carefully that we have defined *nominal* unit labour costs. The real unit labour costs are the ratio of real unit labour costs to real GDP or,

Table 12.1 **Wage Share of Value Added by Country and Selected Industries, 2001 (%)**

	Total economy	Manufacturing	Chemicals	Basic metal industries	Wholesale/ retail trade
Belgium	56.6	64.5	53.9	78.3	56.7
Czech Republic	50.1	54.6	46.0	60.0	43.6
Germany[a]	58.2	74.1	69.0	75.3	63.9
Denmark	60.1	64.5	40.4	54.1	67.9
Spain	53.1	67.3	59.7	73.3	44.5
Italy	43.7	54.6	51.9	61.6	32.6
Japan	52.6	56.1	36.3	60.9	60.2
The Netherlands	56.0	59.9	45.9	78.4	60.0
Poland[a]	49.8	61.0	n.a.	n.a.	26.1
United States	58.7	66.0	49.5	70.6	55.6

[a] 2000.
Source: OECD, National Accounts, Volume ii.

equivalently, the ratio of the nominal wage bill to nominal GDP:

(12.4)   real unit labour costs =

$$\frac{\text{nominal unit labour costs}}{\text{nominal GDP}} = \frac{WL}{PY} = \frac{\text{wage bill}}{\text{nominal GDP}}.$$

Another way of thinking about real labour costs is to remember from Chapter 2 that the GDP measures all earned income and ask who gets some of it. The wage-earners receive the wage bill. This is why real unit labour costs are also called the labour share of output, denoted s_L.

12.4.2 The Battle of the Mark-ups: A Simple Story

Prices as mark-up on labour costs

Mark-up pricing means that firms set the price of goods as much as they can above their nominal unit costs. We have agreed to ignore non-labour costs, so we now consider that firms will aim for a price as much above their unit labour costs as it takes to maximize its profits. This can be written as follows:

(12.5) $P = (1 + \theta)\dfrac{WL}{Y},$

where $\theta \geq 0$ is the price mark-up. A simple way of thinking of the mark-up is if $\theta = 0.3 = 30/100$, the price is set 30% above nominal labour costs.[12]

Wages as a mark-up on prices

Firms mark prices above labour costs, but what determines labour costs and nominal wages? A good starting point is Chapter 5, which notes that wages are set through negotiations between employees and employers. These negotiations deal with two different issues.

First, the employees want to secure as large an income as possible. Yet both wages and salaries as well as employment must originate in value added (GDP) of ongoing firms. Thus, while labour is likely to aim at as large a labour share of output as possible, as we saw in Chapter 5, its efforts are limited by firms' demand for labour.

Second, wage negotiators can only bargain over *nominal* wages. They do not know for sure what the evolution of the price level will be. Typically, wage agreements cover a period of one or more years,

---

[12] Formally, $\theta = \dfrac{P - WL/Y}{WL/Y}$.

and the future evolution of the price level is un-known. Naturally, employees want to protect their nominal wages from inflation. Employers normally agree to incorporate the likely evolution of the price level in wage settlements but worry about overestimating it and paying their workers 'too much'—paying workers too much means making low profits or even losses. This is why the expected evolution of the price level, which is incorporated into the wage agreement, is a central part of negoti-ations. We denote the resulting expected price level by P^e.

In the end, both sides bargain directly over the nominal wage W and indirectly over the expected labour share WL/P^eY. A simple description of the outcome of the negotiations is that the labour share is a mark-up over its 'normal' level $\bar{s}_L$, with a mark-up γ depending on the situation at the time negotiations are held:

(12.6) $$s_L = \frac{WL}{P^eY} = (1 + \gamma)\bar{s}_L.$$

Note that the mark-up γ can be positive or negative, and that it is zero on average. In some years, $\gamma > 0$, and the agreed-upon wage share is above its normal level. In other years, $\gamma < 0$ and the wage share is lower. Another, equivalent way of describing the negotiation outcome is that it is an agreement over the nominal wage expressed as a mark-up over the normal labour share multiplied by average expected labour productivity, multiplied by the expected price level. This can be shown by rewriting (12.6) as follows:

(12.7) $$W = (1 + \gamma)\bar{s}_L \frac{Y}{L} P^e.$$

This result is consistent with discussions that usu-ally surround wage bargaining, in which unions demand a 'fair share' of productivity, where the magnitude of that share generally depends on the stage of the business cycle.

Putting it all together

We have described prices as a mark-up over unit costs, agreed to ignore all non-labour costs and therefore to focus on unit labour costs, and found that the expected labour share is a mark-up over its

normal level. This in turn means that wages are a mark-up over prices. In the end, prices depend on wages and wages depend on expected prices.

Isn't this a bad case of circular reasoning? Quite to the contrary, this description captures the funda-mentally conflictual relationship between employers and employees as they divide up the GDP cake. It has earned the title '**battle of the mark-ups**'.[13] The price mark-up, equation (12.1), sets the price level as a mark-up over wages, while the wage mark-up, equation (12.7), sets wages as a mark-up over the (expected) price level. Firms increase profits by reducing labour costs relative to the prices that their products can fetch. Employees increase real wages by pushing them up relative to expected prices.

Note carefully the distinction: *actual* prices de-pend on wages which depend on *expected* prices. The apparent circularity really links actual to ex-pected prices, as can be seen by combining (12.5) and (12.7) to arrive at

(12.8) $$P = (1 + \theta)(1 + \gamma)\bar{s}_L P^e.$$

We see that the circular process has an anchor: P^e, the level of prices expected by wage negotiators to prevail over the course of the contract. We will later find that this expectation is one central determin-ant of inflation in the medium run.

12.4.3 Productivity and the Labour Share

Before we move on to the next and final step, a clarification may be helpful.[14] We know from Chapter 3 that labour productivity (Y/L) and real wages tend to grow systematically over time. Pro-ductivity does not appear at all in the final outcome of the price- and wage-setting process as repres-ented by equation (12.8). This may be surprising but a bit of reflection shows that it is not.

Equation (12.4) defines the labour share or real unit labour cost as WL/PY, the real cost of producing

[13] The battle of the mark-ups approach to understanding inflation has found empirical support in OECD countries in groundbreaking work by researchers at the London School of Economics Richard Layard, Steven Nickell, and Richard Jackman, among others.

[14] This section may be skipped without loss of continuity.

Box 12.2 Wages, Prices, and Labour Productivity

Equation (12.4) defines real nominal unit labour costs as $\frac{WL}{PY}$, which can be rewritten $\frac{W/P}{Y/L}$ or $W \cdot \frac{1}{Y/L} \cdot \frac{1}{P}$. Using the rate of change rule presented in Box 6.3, we find

$$\frac{\Delta(\text{real unit labour costs})}{\text{real unit labour costs}} =$$

$$\frac{\Delta\left(\frac{W}{P}\right)}{\frac{W}{P}} - \frac{\Delta\left(\frac{Y}{L}\right)}{\frac{Y}{L}} = \frac{\Delta W}{W} - \frac{\Delta\left(\frac{Y}{L}\right)}{\frac{Y}{L}} - \frac{\Delta P}{P}.$$

We see that the real unit costs are constant when the real wages (W/P) grow at the same rate as labour productivity (Y/L) or, equivalently, when the nominal wages W grow at the same rate as labour productivity (Y/L) plus inflation ($\Delta P/P$).

one unit of output. As formally shown in Box 12.2, real unit labour costs remain constant when the real wages grow at the same rate as labour productivity. Put differently, productivity gains allow real wages to increase without raising production costs. This is the base case, which defines the 'normal' labour share $\bar{s}_L$. The battle of the mark-ups looks at fluctuations in real unit labour costs that occur when real wages temporarily depart from this principle.

The base case is precisely what we expect to see following the principles developed in Chapter 5 and one of the stylized facts in Chapter 3. Indeed, Figure 1.2 in Chapter 1 shows that, in four countries over half a century, labour shares fluctuate from year to year, but with little discernible trend. This is just another way of saying that technical progress continuously generates higher incomes.[15]

12.4.4 Cyclical Behaviour of Mark-ups

It is now time to ask what determines the two mark-ups. The brief answer is that they tend to move over business cycles. To see which side would 'win' the battle of the mark-ups, we need to separate out the two, distinctly different mark-up decisions.

Start with the price mark-up θ. Firms naturally want it to be as large as possible, but they need to

worry about competition.[16] Competition actually increases in good times, when there is 'more money in the marketplace'. While it may be the case that firms raise their price mark-ups when demand is high, it is also possible that high volumes of business increase total profits so much that firms are willing to moderate prices to steal their competitors' customers. The effect here is uncertain.

The wage share mark-up γ is the outcome of wage bargaining. During boom periods, rising employment generally improves the bargaining position of unions and workers in general, which is reflected in a higher wage mark-up. In addition, firms may spontaneously offer higher real pay to motivate employees to work harder or longer hours, or even to encourage others to join the labour force.[17] More likely than not, the wage share mark-up is—or is likely to be—procyclical.[18]

The battle of the mark-ups, expressed by equation (12.8), shows that the expected price level drives wages via the wage mark-up, that wages drive labour costs, which drive prices via the price mark-up. Both mark-ups tend to move over the

[16] A natural tendency is for competitors to agree on large mark-ups. Such collusion is usually strictly forbidden and competition authorities uncover and prosecute anti-competition agreements.

[17] This reasoning is developed in detail in Chapter 5.

[18] It turns out that the wage share is indeed procyclical, but with a significant lag, continuing to rise past the peak of the usual cycle as summarized in a Burns–Mitchell diagram.

[15] Not only is this a fair way of distributing productivity gains, it also matches the microeconomic principles presented in Chapter 5.

business cycle, but the exact details vary from country to country. In any case, it is a well-established fact that the *product* of the two mark-ups in equation (12.8), given by $(1 + \theta)(1 + \gamma)$, is procyclical. It tends to push the actual price level above its expected level in boom times, and to pull it down in lean years.

This procyclical outcome of the battle of the mark-ups is the foundation of the Phillips curve. We now use (12.8), which describes how the price *level* P is set, to determine the inflation rate, the *rate of increase* $\Delta P/P$ of the price level. Part 1 of Box 11.3 formally shows that, when we use the symbol π to stand for the rate of inflation, we have

(12.9) $$\pi = \underbrace{\frac{\Delta\theta}{(1 + \theta)} + \frac{\Delta\gamma}{(1 + \gamma)}}_{\text{battle of mark-ups}} + \underbrace{\pi^e}_{\substack{\text{expected} \\ \text{inflation}}}.$$

We are now just two short steps away from reaching the Phillips curve. First, the change in individual mark-ups will be different for different wage bargaining situations, even at the same stage of the business cycle. For aggregate inflation—an average of many price changes—only the *average* bargaining situation in the economy is relevant. It follows that the aggregate mark-up moves with the business cycle. It rises when the real GDP Y moves above its trend $\bar{Y}$, i.e. when the output gap Y_{gap} is positive, and it declines when the gap becomes negative. Alternatively, we can use Okun's Law to describe mark-ups as rising when the unemployment rate U declines below equilibrium $\bar{U}$, i.e. the unemployment gap U_{gap} is negative, and declining in the opposite situation.

The second step recognizes that wage bargaining and price setting do not occur all at once, but are staggered over time. It is simply too costly for firms and workers to discuss wages all the time; after all, there's work to be done! Similarly, firms are not in a situation to recalculate their prices at every chance. As a result, while decisions are taken rationally, they are often based on old information. There is no single expected inflation rate π^e, but rather a complex mix of many expected rates, some relevant for the present, some coming from the past and looking to the future. For the aggregate

economy it makes more sense to write $\tilde{\pi}$, which we call the **underlying inflation rate**. As we see below, this is not only a realistic detail, it also turns out to be crucial for understanding the Phillips curve.

We have now reached our destination. The process captured by equation (12.8) is turned into a relationship between actual and expected inflation. Indeed, taking into account the cyclical behaviour of the combined mark-ups, the relationship (12.9) can be written as

(12.10) $$\pi = \tilde{\pi} + aY_{\text{gap}} = \tilde{\pi} - bU_{\text{gap}}.$$

This relationship offers a simple but very effective accounting of what drives inflation. It asserts that inflation is driven by two main forces.

(1) What people expect or have expected inflation to be, now and in the future.

(2) Cyclical conditions, with wages and prices tending to rise faster in years of rapid economic growth and slowing down in harder times.

The positive parameters a and b simply describe how the mark-ups jointly respond to cyclical fluctuations, represented alternatively by the output and unemployment gaps. They say that a high level of activity leads to higher mark-ups.

12.4.5 More on the Underlying Rate of Inflation

In the last section we introduced a new concept, the underlying rate of inflation.[19] Because this concept is so important, we will spend a little more time discussing it here.

Recall that the expected price level in equation (12.7) describes wage bargaining. It is meant to describe how wage negotiators attempt to track the likely evolution of the price level over the course of the wage contracts under discussion. In that sense, the underlying inflation rate is forward looking. In practice, it also includes a backward-looking component for the simple reason that, inevitably,

---

[19] Sometimes the underlying rate is simply called 'inflationary expectations', relying more on the interpretation that it incorporates the anticipated inflation of firms and workers. Others use the term 'core inflation'—which is sometimes also used to describe the more stable inflation rate for non-food, non-energy items.

Box 12.3 From the Battle of the Mark-ups to Inflation[20]

We show how (12.9) is a direct consequence of (12.8). We adopt two different approaches, which rely on different approximations.

(1) Using the results of Box 6.3, (12.8) can be approximated as

$$\frac{\Delta P}{P} = \frac{\Delta \theta}{1+\theta} + \frac{\Delta \gamma}{1+\gamma} + \frac{\Delta \bar{s}_L}{\bar{s}_L} + \frac{\Delta P^e}{P^e},$$

where we use the fact that $\Delta(1+\theta) = \Delta\theta$ and $\Delta(1+\gamma) = \Delta\gamma$. Further, note that $\bar{s}_L$ is the normal labour share, which is assumed to be constant. It follows that $\Delta\bar{s}_L = 0$.

(2) Another approach is to consider (12.8) in two different periods, $t-1$ and t (say, years). Then dividing year t by year $t-1$, we have

$$\frac{P_t}{P_{t-1}} = \frac{1+\theta_t}{1+\theta_{t-1}} \frac{1+\gamma_t}{1+\gamma_{t-1}} \frac{P_t^e}{P_{t-1}^e}.$$

Since the inflation rate is $\pi_t = \frac{P_t - P_{t-1}}{P_{t-1}} = \frac{P_t}{P_{t-1}} - 1$, we have $\frac{P_t}{P_{t-1}} = 1 + \pi_t$. Here we can ask whether P_{t-1}^e

correctly predicted P_{t-1}. In general, there can be forecast errors, so we can rewrite the previous equation as

$$\frac{P_t}{P_{t-1}} = \frac{1+\theta_t}{1+\theta_{t-1}} \frac{1+\gamma_t}{1+\gamma_{t-1}} \frac{P_t^e}{P_{t-1}} \frac{P_{t-1}}{P_{t-1}^e}.$$

Since the inflation rate is $\pi_t = \frac{P_t - P_{t-1}}{P_{t-1}} = \frac{P_t}{P_{t-1}} - 1$, we have $\frac{P_t}{P_{t-1}} = 1 + \pi_t$. We can similarly define expected inflation, based on the actual price level in period $t-1$, as $\pi_t^e = \frac{P_t^e - P_{t-1}}{P_{t-1}} = \frac{P_t^e}{P_{t-1}} - 1$. We also define the price prediction error in period $t-1$ as $\varepsilon_{t-1} = \frac{P_{t-1} - P_{t-1}^e}{P_{t-1}^e} = \frac{P_{t-1}}{P_{t-1}^e} - 1$. Collecting these terms, we have

$$1 + \pi_t = \frac{1+\theta_t}{1+\theta_{t-1}} \frac{1+\gamma_t}{1+\gamma_{t-1}} (1 + \pi_t^e)(1 + \varepsilon_{t-1}).$$

We can take logs and use the approximation log $(1+x) = x$ to obtain

$$\pi_t = \Delta\theta_t + \Delta\gamma_t + \pi_t^e + \varepsilon_{t-1},$$

which is another approximation.

inflation forecasts are inaccurate and stand to be found wrong *ex post*.

Indeed, imagine that future inflation has been underestimated during the previous round of negotiations. Then wage earners have lost some purchasing power—their real earnings have been less than previously agreed upon. Quite naturally, they will ask for some compensation. Conversely, future inflation may turn out to have been overestimated. Then wages went up too fast and profits were squeezed. Employers will no doubt use this observation to slow down wage increases in the future. Correcting for past forecast errors is an integral part of wage negotiations, and indeed this correction is formally shown in Part 2 of Box 12.3. This is why we have redefined the purely forward-looking price level P^e in (12.8) with a combination of forward- and

backward-looking considerations, hence the redenomination and change of notation.

Forecast errors are unavoidable. When inflation is reasonably low, the errors are small and the combination of catch-up and forward-looking forecasts encapsulated in the underlying inflation rate is acceptable. When inflation is substantial, however, this is not enough. With the inflation rate around, say, 20% per year, forecast errors can easily be of 2%, or even much more, e.g. 5%. If wages are negotiated once a year, wage-earners would be quite upset to see their purchasing power decline by 5%, much as firms would be hurt by a similar reduction in their profits. This is why various mechanisms tend to emerge during periods of high inflation. One such mechanism takes the form of explicit or implicit **indexation** clauses whereby wages are automatically linked to the evolution of the consumer price index. An alternative response to high inflation is

---

[20] This Box is for mathematically-minded readers.

to set wages for short periods, like a quarter, or a month. In periods of extremely high inflation, they may even be reset weekly or daily! Avoiding such situations is why price stability, i.e. low inflation, is so desirable.

12.4.6 Completing the Picture: Supply Shocks

It is now time to look at the non-labour costs of production, studiously ignored so far. These costs correspond to the other factors of production—e.g. capital and land—as well as to intermediate inputs such as unfinished goods, primary commodities, and energy. In general, these costs follow the general trend of final goods prices. Their effect on inflation is then adequately reflected in the underlying inflation rate, adding nothing new to the analysis.

Does it mean that we do not need to worry at all about the other production costs? Most of the time, this is indeed a reasonable way of dealing with them. Now and then, however, special circumstances arise when non-labour costs do not behave so innocuously. A leading example is sharp oil price rises, commonly referred to as an oil shock, which rose sharply in the 1970s, early 1980s, and since 2005, see Figure 12.10. During 2007, it was not just oil prices that rose, but those of virtually every primary commodity and, to top it off, many food prices. Another example is a deep depreciation because it makes all imported good prices more expensive when evaluated in the domestic currency. These events are treated as exogenous because they happen elsewhere or are special in the sense that they are not explained by the framework that we develop. Because they affect the costs of production, they are called **supply shocks**. Supply shocks may also be favourable. Oil prices, for instance, fell very fast in late 2008 after having risen considerably in 2007.

In the end, we think of non-labour costs as generally following underlying inflation $\tilde{\pi}$, but we need to remember that supply shocks can and will occur—the sharp energy price increases in 2007–2008 are a clear reminder. To that effect, we allow for an occasional additional supply shock term s, a catch-all for exogenous disturbances affecting production costs. Accordingly, we modify equation (12.10):

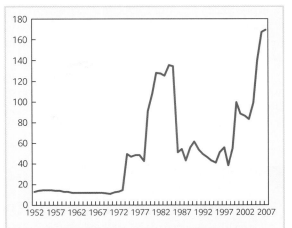

Fig. 12.10 Oil Prices in Euros, 1952–2007 (index 2000 = 100)

Oil prices are quoted in US dollars. Here we convert them into deutschmarks prior to 1999 and into euros after 1999, and we compute them as an index chosen to take the value 1000 in 2000. The first two oil shocks (1973–1974 and 1979–1981) and the two next ones (1999–2001 and 2005–2008) are clearly visible. In 1986, we had a counter-oil shock.

Source: IMF.

(12.11)

aggregate supply curve

$$\pi \quad = \quad \tilde{\pi} \quad + \quad aY_{\text{gap}} \quad + \quad s$$

or

Phillips curve

$$\pi \quad = \quad \tilde{\pi} \quad - \quad bU_{\text{gap}} \quad + \quad s.$$

| actual inflation | underlying inflation | cyclical demand pressure | supply shock |

As long as non-labour production costs are in line with the underlying rate of inflation, the supply shock term is zero. Occasionally, in unmistakable circumstances, it can be positive or negative.

Beyond changes in non-labour costs, two more types of supply shock can be important. First, we assumed that the labour share is constant. A quick glance at Figure 1.2, however, shows that it is approximately trendless, but certainly not constant. Occasionally, it rises or declines, a process that can last several years. Such changes are usually the outcome of deep socio-political events that strengthen or weaken trade unions or employers' associations. We can take care of these events by interpreting changes in the labour share as supply shocks. An exogenous increase of the labour share, for example, adds to labour costs and can be treated as $s > 0$.

Second, supply shocks may also be caused by the government. An increase in taxes or prices for regulated utilities can raise the inflation rate even though the underlying rate and labour market conditions remain constant. The variety of taxes borne by the firms relate directly to production and affect the final selling price—value added or excise taxes, profit taxes, establishment and property taxes, and so on. Other costs imposed by governments are implicit, but may have a significant impact (e.g. various labour regulations, environmental or consumer protection legislation).

12.5 Inflation, Unemployment, and Output

12.5.1 The Phillips Curve Rehabilitated

The inflation-accounting framework summarized by equation (12.11) effectively solves the puzzle of the Phillips curve. We can explain its persistence over decades, its instability over particular periods of time, and the impression that it shifts now and then. The original Phillips curve claimed that inflation depends only on the level of unemployment. The inflation account (12.11) shows that cyclical labour market conditions do indeed matter, but so do underlying inflation, equilibrium unemployment, and occasional supply shocks. For a Phillips curve to be visible, these latter factors must be stable so that changes in inflation are mostly driven by cyclical conditions. When these factors are not stable, the Phillips curve seems to vanish. This is precisely what happened during the 1970s, when price and commodity shocks became a major source of instability (see Figure 12.10). As inflation rose, underlying inflation rose as well and became more variable, reflecting rapidly changing expectations. In addition, equilibrium unemployment rose in many countries. The Phillips curve's demise reflects the emergence of underlying inflation and supply shocks. These additional explanatory factors of inflation, over and beyond cyclical fluctuations, have helped to rehabilitate the Phillips curve.

How, then, to think of the Phillips curve if it proves to be unstable? Much as with the *IS*, *LM* or *TR* curves, the answer is to keep clearly in mind which variables are endogenous and which ones are taken as exogenous. As long as the exogenous variables remain constant, the curve does not move. When they change, the curve will shift and apparently 'vanish'. This is the way the reconstructed Phillips curve explains the apparent puzzle. The modern Phillips curve is sometimes referred to as the expectations-augmented Phillips curve. This name emphasizes the central role of underlying inflation. Yet, it is more than that; it also recognizes that equilibrium unemployment $\bar{U}$ may change. It also allows for supply shocks.

The key to a proper understanding of inflation is to be careful when drawing the Phillips curve. Note that (12.11) implies that, when supply shocks are zero ($s = 0$) and when actual unemployment equals its equilibrium level ($U = \bar{U}$) and output is on trend ($Y = \bar{Y}$), the unemployment and output gaps are nil and actual inflation equals the underlying inflation rate ($\pi = \tilde{\pi}$).

This situation corresponds to point A in either chart of Figure 12.11. Point A is important for it uniquely determines the position of the Phillips or aggregate supply curves. The other points on the curves simply follow from allowing the unemployment rate to vary around its equilibrium level. This is the key intuition from the old Phillips curve that inflation varies with the business cycle. For instance, at point B unemployment is below equilibrium and output is above trend, so the demand pressure pushes inflation above its current underlying rate. Conversely, point C corresponds to the case where inflation is below its underlying rate

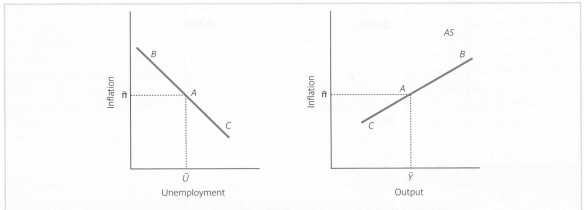

Fig. 12.11 The Expectations-Augmented Phillips and Aggregate Supply Curves
By definition, point *A* represents the case where actually observed inflation π is at its underlying rate π̄ and where unemployment *U* is at its equilibrium rate *Ū*, and output *Y* is at its trend value *Ȳ*. When unemployment is low and output high, actual inflation is above the underlying inflation rate (point *B*). When unemployment is high and output low, actual inflation is below underlying inflation (point *C*).

because the unemployment rate is above equilibrium and output is below trend. In the left-hand chart of Figure 12.11, this traces out a downward-sloping schedule that resembles the old Phillips curve shown in Figure 12.3. In fact, it is the same but with a crucial difference: its position is determined by point *A*, that is, by the underlying inflation rate and equilibrium unemployment *Ū*.[21]

12.5.2 Underlying Inflation and the Long Run

Underlying inflation, we saw, captures the rate of inflation agreed upon during wage negotiations, both now and, for some negotiating parties, at some point in the past. It has both a backward-looking (it reflects old forecasts of inflation today, as well as efforts to fix past errors of inflation forecasts used in previous contracts) and a forward-looking component (what inflation is expected to be in the future). Somehow, it must be related to the actual rate of inflation. How this is so in the short run is con-

sidered in the next chapter. In this section we deal with the long run. We already saw in Section 12.3.3 that the **long-run Phillips curve** is vertical. We now look at how this comes about.

As negotiators consider the amount of inflation to be factored into wage settlements, they strive to guess it accurately. Of course, employees have an incentive to overstate the underlying rate of inflation, but employers have precisely the opposite incentive. If there were no uncertainty and both sides always knew *ex ante* what inflation would be over the lifetime of the wage contract, underlying and actual inflation would just be equal. Uncertainty therefore means forecasting (or guessing) underlying inflation. More often than not, the guesses are wrong. Yet, the principle of rational expectations from Chapter 7 means that wage negotiators do not make systematic forecast errors. Although forecasts are almost always incorrect, the errors are largely unsystematic and average to zero: in some years inflation is overestimated, in others it is underestimated.

These observations have two important implications. First, there must be a link between actual inflation π and underlying inflation π̄. Underlying inflation must track, albeit imperfectly, actual inflation. The backward-looking component implies

[21] This is why the equilibrium rate of unemployment is sometimes called the NAIRU: the non-accelerating inflation rate of unemployment. At point *B* inflation accelerates above its underlying rate. At point *C* it decelerates. Only at point *A* does it stabilize.

that underlying inflation *lags* behind actual inflation, but the forward-looking component implies that underlying inflation *leads* actual inflation. The interplay of both components is bound to be rather murky and difficult to detect precisely. As a result, it is far from obvious how to interpret Figure 12.9. There exist statistical techniques to do so, however, and they are routinely used by economists.

The second implication relates to the long run. The rational expectations hypothesis means that actual and underlying inflation cannot remain different in any systematic way. Any discrepancy between π and $\tilde{\pi}$ must be temporary. This fits well with other views of the long run. Obviously, over the years to come, we expect booms and recessions, possibly as consequences of supply shocks, positive and negative. We cannot really guess what the situation will be five or ten years from now. The best bet is the agnostic one, that there will be no shocks and that the economy will not be far from trend, with actual unemployment equal to underlying unemployment. For this reason, it makes sense to *define* the long run as the situation where the economy is back on its trend. This means that the Phillips curve is vertical. From equation (12.11), we know that when $s = 0$ and $U = \bar{U}$, then $\pi = \tilde{\pi}$. In a way, the long run is atemporal; the backward- and forward-looking components of underlying inflation have worked themselves out.

Thus, for the third time, we conclude that the long-run Phillips curve is vertical. We first encountered this result in Section 12.2.2 when we found that long-run price flexibility implies that output is supply determined. Next, in Section 12.3.3, we argued that long-run neutrality—which really follows from long-run price flexibility—implies a vertical Phillips curve. Now, we see that a vertical Phillips curve is also a consequence of the battle of the mark-ups, once we admit that there cannot be any permanent deviation between actual and underlying inflation.

The vertical long-run Phillips curve only tells us that the actual and underlying inflation rates are equal. It leaves entirely open the question of what these rates are. We will see in the next chapter that we need to bring back the demand side of the economy to pin down long-run inflation, actual and underlying. In fact, we already know that. The neutrality principle established in Chapter 6 relates long-run inflation to money growth, i.e. to monetary policy, and nothing else. We will see that it takes time for underlying and actual inflation to catch up with each other and stabilize at whatever rate monetary policy allows for. Views vary about how quickly this happens, and herein lie some of the most fundamental controversies in macroeconomics, already encountered in Chapter 10 and to be studied further in Chapter 16.

The vertical Phillips curve carries a crucial implication: there cannot be a long-lasting trade-off between unemployment and inflation. Demand policies cannot move the actual unemployment rate permanently away from its equilibrium level. But the equilibrium level can very well shift over time, e.g. as labour markets undergo structural changes. Indeed, one of the implications of Figure 12.9 is that unemployment equilibrium must have shifted over the last decades. It has massively increased in the euro area over the 1970s and 1980s—shifting the Phillips curve to the right—and then declined in the late 1990s. In the UK, the decline of the equilibrium unemployment rate started earlier and has been more pronounced—a legacy of Mrs Thatcher's supply-side policies aimed at weakening the bargaining power of unions, lowering unemployment benefits, and reducing the equilibrium unemployment rate.

12.5.3 Aggregate Supply

All of the previous reasoning applies to the aggregate supply curve shown in the right-hand chart in Figure 12.11 since it corresponds via Okun's Law to the Phillips curve. Its position is determined by the output trend and the underlying inflation rate, and it shifts when any of the exogenous variables ($\tilde{\pi}$, $\bar{Y}$, or s) changes.

The aggregate supply curve conveys two important messages.

(1) In the short run, as GDP fluctuates about its trend growth path, the actual rate of inflation can differ from the underlying rate. In the absence of supply shocks, output and inflation move in the same direction.

Table 12.2 Equilibrium Unemployment Rates

	Austria	Belgium	Switzerland	Germany	Denmark	Spain	Finland	France	United Kingdom
1970	1.5	n.a.	n.a.	3.3	n.a.	n.a.	4.6	n.a.	2.7
1980	1.8	5.9	0.6	4.4	5.1	6.4	4.0	6.1	4.1
1990	4.3	7.3	1.7	6.9	6.8	14.5	4.8	9.4	8.0
2000	5.0	7.6	2.2	7.3	4.8	12.4	9.8	9.5	5.6
2008	4.9	7.2	2.2	7.1	4.5	8.5	8.0	8.5	5.3

	Hungary	Ireland	Italy	Japan	Netherlands	Norway	Portugal	Sweden	United States
1970	n.a.	n.a.	4.3	2.4	n.a.	1.6	n.a.	1.5	5.5
1980	n.a.	10.9	5.4	1.6	4.3	1.9	6.5	1.9	6.5
1990	n.a.	14.4	8.8	2.8	7.5	3.9	4.5	2.2	5.8
2000	7.5	6.6	9.4	3.6	4.5	3.8	4.1	4.8	5.0
2008	5.3	5.0	7.2	3.9	3.2	4.1	4.8	4.8	4.6

Source: OECD, *Economic Outlook*.

(2) In the long run, GDP must return to its growth path, regardless of what the inflation rate is. Real forces determine the growth of real activity and the growth of money supply determines inflation.

The long-run aggregate supply schedule is vertical. It will, however, shift continuously to the right since, as a consequence of long-run economic growth, trend output keeps rising.

12.5.4 Factors that Shift the Phillips and Aggregate Supply Curves

The original position of the Phillips and aggregate supply curves in Figure 12.12 is determined by point A. This point corresponds to the initial underlying inflation rate, to the equilibrium unemployment rate, and trend GDP. Thus, the underlying inflation rate and the equilibrium unemployment rate or trend GDP are taken as exogenous when we draw the curves. The fact that they determine the position of the curve, giving us the location of point A, provides two reasons why the curves can shift. The first is a change in the underlying inflation rate: an increase in underlying inflation shifts the curves up. The second reason is that equilibrium unemployment and

trend GDP may change. The supply shock s is the third exogenous variable that shifts the curve.

There is no presumption whatsoever that either underlying inflation or equilibrium unemployment are constant over time. If either changes, point A moves, and so does the whole Phillips curve. This implies that, potentially, there exists an infinity of Phillips curves, corresponding to the infinity of values that the underlying inflation rate or the equilibrium rate of unemployment can take. It just so happened that, over the hundred years surveyed by Phillips, the underlying rate of inflation and the equilibrium rate of unemployment did not change much, so there seems to have been just one Phillips curve.[22] This changed in the early 1970s when unemployment became much more stable—as the result of active Keynesian policies—while more volatile commodity prices became the dominating factor affecting inflation.

Shifts in the equilibrium unemployment rate occur occasionally. Table 12.2 presents some estimates

---

[22] There are good reasons for this. The period corresponds to the time of the gold standard and the Bretton Woods system, both of which constrained inflation from rising too much and kept underlying inflation in check.

of the equilibrium unemployment rate obtained by asking what rate would keep the Phillips curve unchanged when the actual and underlying inflation rates are equal and in the absence of a supply shock.[23] The table shows that the equilibrium rate rose in most countries in the 1970s and then declined in some countries two or three decades later, as the result of labour market reforms. This is one reason for the rightward shift of most Phillips curves in the 1970s, and for the subsequent leftward shift in those countries that managed to bring unemployment down in the 1990s or 2000s. Two examples are presented in Figure 12.9.

Trend output continuously rises as the outcome of long-run growth. To avoid dealing with a curve that constantly moves to the right, in later chapters we will draw the aggregate supply curve with the output gap $(Y - \bar{Y})$ on the horizontal axis.

Finally, the supply curve shifts in the presence of supply shocks. If these shocks raise the cost of production, the Phillips and aggregate supply curves shift upwards. If the increase is temporary, the curves will eventually return to their initial positions, unless underlying inflation rises in the meantime. Oil shocks are a prime example of sudden increases in non-labour costs. The shocks of 1973–1974 and 1980 also played a role in the shifts visible in Figure 12.9.

12.5.5 From the Short to the Long Run

We have salvaged the old Phillips curve by replacing it with two curves: (1) a short-run expectations-augmented Phillips curve, which resembles the old one but can move, and (2) a long-run Phillips curve, which is always vertical. To these two curves correspond, via Okun's Law, a short-run and a long-run aggregate supply curve. These results are brought together in Figure 12.12. In both panels, point A describes the long-run situation where actual and underlying inflation are equal ($\tilde{\pi}_1$), there is no supply shock ($s = 0$), and actual unemployment is at its equilibrium level or output is on trend. Note that point A belongs to both the short- and the long-run curves. As just noted, it represents the long-run

situation, but it also determines the position of the particular short-run curve when the underlying inflation rate is $\tilde{\pi}_1$. In other words, the only position on the short-run curve that is sustainable in the long run is point A. Any other position is temporary, as we now illustrate.

To that effect, starting from point A, imagine a demand expansion designed to reduce unemployment and shift the economy to a point like B. The short-run trade-off means less unemployment and more output, but also more inflation. This is because the new inflation π_2 exceeds the underlying rate $\tilde{\pi}_1$, which has been used in previous wage negotiations. Sooner or later, there will be another round of wage negotiations, which will recognize that inflation has increased. Let us assume that they adopt π_2 as the new underlying rate. Graphically, this means that the short-run Phillips and aggregate supply curves shift upwards, passing through point A', which corresponds to the new underlying inflation rate $\tilde{\pi}_2 = \pi_2$. (The equilibrium rate of unemployment and trend output are assumed constant throughout.) This shift worsens the unemployment–inflation trade-off, since any level of unemployment now requires a higher rate of inflation. If the authorities react by picking point C on the new curves, both unemployment and inflation will rise, while output will decline. Yet point C is not permanently sustainable either, since inflation is now even higher than the newer underlying inflation rate $\tilde{\pi}_2$. So, once again, the curves must eventually shift further up in both panels of Figure 12.12. We can imagine a succession of increasingly desperate policy reactions triggering further shifts in the short-run Phillips and aggregate supply curves, which will eventually drive unemployment and output back to their equilibrium positions at a point like Z on the long-run curve.

The fact that only one point on every Phillips curve is stable led Friedman and Phelps to predict that the historical curves would vanish if the authorities tried to exploit the short-run trade-off, for example by moving from point A to point B. In the end, the economy would end up at point Z in Figure 12.12.

This does not mean, however, that the Phillips and aggregate supply curves are useless. To the contrary, as a tool of analysis, these curves account for

---

[23] This is precisely the NAIRU as explained in footnote 21 above.

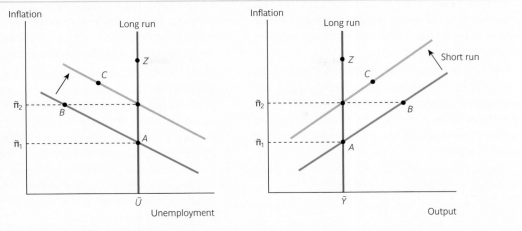

Fig. 12.12 From the Short to the Long Run

For a given underlying rate of inflation, as it moves from point A to point B, the economy can sustain lower unemployment and higher output but at the cost of higher inflation. This trade-off is not permanent, however. When underlying inflation rises to track higher actual inflation, the short-run Phillips curve shifts up. In the long run (point Z) there is no trade-off.

the cyclical behaviour of inflation. Recall from Chapter 1 that the inflation rate tended to be pro-cyclical and lag the GDP slightly. We only need to remember that, like most other curves that we have seen in the past, the Phillips and aggregate supply curves can move when the exogenous variables that determine their positions change. The additional twist is that one of these variables, the underlying inflation rate, is bound to change whenever actual inflation varies. This implies that the Phillips and aggregate supply curves are bound to shift whenever we move from the long-run point. From a policy standpoint, it means that the inflation–unemployment trade-off cannot be seen as more than a short-run relationship that may be worse than it initially appears. This last observation calls for caution when carrying out macroeconomic policies. We return to this theme in the next chapter.

❶ Summary

1 The Phillips curve was once considered to adequately describe the supply side and the inflation process. Its message was that a permanent trade-off existed between unemployment and inflation. Output could rise to meet an increase in demand but would, in the process, generate a higher rate of inflation.

2 From the late 1960s to the late 1980s, Phillips curves vanished. Contrary to the notion of an inflation–unemployment trade-off, inflation and unemployment both rose in the mid-1970s and early 1980s, a phenomenon called stagflation.

3 Okun's Law states that the output gap (the deviation of real GDP from its trend) and unemployment (as a deviation from its equilibrium level) systematically move in opposite directions. It translates the downward Phillips curve into an upward aggregate supply curve.

4 Accounting for inflation starts with the study of how firms set their prices. The result is mark-up pricing, i.e. setting prices as a mark-up over production costs.

5 Production costs are separated into two broad categories: labour and non-labour costs. Labour costs rise when wages—and related costs—increase faster than labour productivity. They often represent the most important source of cost changes.

6 Nominal wages are also set as a mark-up on the nominal price level.

7 Wages are set through negotiations that acknowledge three main factors: (1) underlying inflation, (2) productivity gains, and (3) the state of the business cycle, which largely reflects the relative bargaining strength of employees and employers. Thus nominal wages are also set as a mark-up on the nominal price level.

8 Wage contracts attempt both to catch up on past inflation and to protect wages from future inflation. Underlying inflation captures both these backward- and forward-looking aspects.

9 Inflation accounting describes the actual rate of inflation as responding to: underlying inflation, demand pressure in the goods and labour markets, and occasional supply shocks.

10 The inflation accounts explain both why a Phillips curve may have existed for a century,

and why it disappeared as the result of mounting inflation in the 1960s and early 1970s, to the two oil shocks of 1973–1974 and 1979–1980 and to deteriorating equilibrium unemployment.

11 In the long run, unemployment returns to its equilibrium rate. Equivalently, real GDP cannot permanently stray away from the productive potential of an economy. In the long run, the Phillips curve and aggregate supply schedules are vertical. The economy is dichotomized, growth and real rigidities determine the GDP and unemployment, money growth determines inflation, and there is no trade-off between inflation and unemployment.

12 The Phillips curve describes the supply side and can be transformed into an aggregate supply curve using Okun's Law. The supply curve says that, for increased output to be supplied, inflation increases because production—mainly labour—costs rise faster than anticipated, or than is reflected in underlying inflation.

13 The positions of the Phillips and aggregate supply curves are determined by the underlying rate of inflation and, respectively, equilibrium unemployment rate and trend GDP. Any change in any one of these variables leads to shifts in the short-run curves. Supply shocks, whether positive or negative, also shift the curves.

Key Concepts

- Phillips curve
- aggregate supply curve
- neoclassical assumption, price flexibility
- wage inflation
- Okun's Law
- output gap, unemployment gap
- money illusion
- long-run Phillips and aggregate supply curves
- stagflation

- oil shock
- mark-up pricing
- market power
- product differentiation
- average or unit costs
- battle of the mark-ups
- underlying inflation
- indexation
- supply shocks

❗ Exercises

1 A Phillips curve is represented by the following relationship: $\pi = \tilde{\pi} - 10(U - \bar{U}) + s$, where s is a supply shock term. Draw the curve when $\tilde{\pi} = 4\%$ and $\bar{U} = 7\%$; when underlying inflation rises to 6%. Okun's law is $U - \bar{U} = \dfrac{Y - \bar{Y}}{10{,}000}$. Draw the aggregate supply schedule when $\bar{Y} = 10{,}000$. Why is it argued that improving the performance of the supply side of the economy is good for both inflation and employment?

2 In the 1980s, when inflation reached huge rates —more than 1,000% a year—in Brazil all prices and wages were indexed week by week. Why was indexation not only popular but generally perceived as vital?

3 What could be the effect on inflation of an increase in value added taxes (VAT)? Of an increase in corporate profit taxes? Of an increase in personal income taxes? State your assumptions carefully.

4 Show the effect on the short- and long-run Phillips curves of an oil shock, i.e. a once-and-for-all increase in the price of imported energy, assuming that underlying inflation remains unchanged. Does it matter whether the country is self-sufficient, or an oil importer?

5 A reform of labour market institutions reduces equilibrium unemployment to 5%. Explain the effect on inflation and unemployment in the short term and in the long term.

6 Suppose a government underestimates the equilibrium rate of unemployment and attempts to reduce the unemployment rate below the equilibrium rate by stimulating aggregate demand. Show the likely outcome of such a policy using the short- and long-run Phillips curves.

7 Figure 12.1 describes how *real* GDP and the price level react over time to a one-off increase in the money stock. What happens to *nominal* GDP?

8 Using the *IS–TR* analysis developed in Chapter 11, consider an exogenous decline in demand, for example a reduction in public spending. Show graphically that either exchange rate flexibility or price flexibility is enough to achieve the neoclassical result that output remains constant at its trend level.

9 The supply curve is given by the following relationship: $\pi = \tilde{\pi} + 0.1(Y - \bar{Y}) + s$. Initially $\pi = \tilde{\pi} = 2\%$, $Y = \bar{Y}$, and $s = 0$. Then the authorities raise output so that $Y - \bar{Y} = 10$ and decides to keep it at this level until inflation reaches the rate of 4%, at which stage they will let the output gap return to zero. Assume that the underlying inflation rate $\tilde{\pi}$ adjusts each period by half of the difference between its previous value and the previously observed inflation rate (for example if we currently have $\pi = 6\%$ and $\tilde{\pi} = 4\%$, then next period the underlying rate will be 5%). There is no supply shock so $s = 0$ throughout. Compute period after period the actual and underlying inflation rate until the economy returns to a long-run equilibrium. What conclusion do you draw?

10 Between 2000 and 2007 the price of oil, quoted in US dollars, has increased by 92.4%. Quoted in euros, it 'only' increased by 52.8%, as shown in Figure 12.10. How can you explain the difference?

⮑ Essays Questions

1 'The most important quality of a central bank is to be credible.' This assertion refers to the ability of central banks to anchor inflationary expectations. Why does this matter, for instance in the presence of adverse supply shocks?

2 Imagine that you are back in the 1960s, when the Phillips curve was believed to be stable. How, do you believe, were politicians arguing about where it is best to be on the curve? What mistake would each side of the debate be likely to make?

3 Why do some economists plead for policy measures that increase the flexibility of wages and prices? What can the counter-arguments be?

4 'That the long-run Phillips curve is vertical means that governments should *never* attempt to reduce unemployment with expansionary policies.' Comment.

5 When does an oil shock only temporarily raise inflation?

Aggregate Demand and Aggregate Supply 13

Money influences only monetary variables and not real variables in the long run. The problem is 'how long is long?' The 'Keynesian' answer embodied in the concept of the Phillips curve was 'too long to matter!': the 'monetarist' rejoinder was 'shorter than the Keynesians think!';

extreme rationalism provides the answer 'too short for anything else to matter!'—answers that no one concerned with either the history or the practice of stabilization policy is likely to accept.

Harry G. Johnson[1]

13.1 Overview

This chapter is the watershed of the textbook. We bring together the demand side of the economy—the Mundell–Fleming model of Chapter 11—and the supply side—the analysis of the inflationary process developed in Chapter 12—into a single framework. This workhorse of macroeconomics is known as the 'AS–AD model'. Until now, aggregate demand was analysed under the assumption that prices are sticky. The task ahead is to understand how it can be adjusted to deal with inflation.[2] The result will be the downward-sloping curve AD in Figure 13.1: the higher is the inflation rate, all other things equal, the lower is aggregate demand. The upward-sloping aggregate supply curve AS has already been derived in the previous chapter. In a market economy demand equals supply, so the position of the economy is described by the intersection of the AD and AS curves.

In fact, we have identified two AS curves, one for the short run and one for the long run. This distinction is fundamental. In the short run, there is a trade-off between output (or unemployment) and inflation. In the long run, the supply curve, shown in Figure 13.1 as LAS, is vertical and the trade-off has disappeared—monetary factors have no impact on real economic variables, e.g. real GDP, unemployment, or the real exchange rate. We will see that the same conclusion applies to aggregate

demand, which is horizontal in the long run, as displayed in Figure 13.1. In the short run, inflation and demand are related; in the long run, the demand curve is horizontal and nominal variables, such as

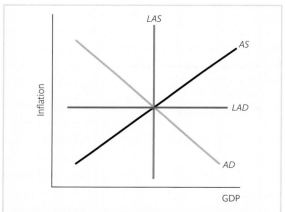

Fig. 13.1 Aggregate Demand and Aggregate Supply, Short Run and Long Run
The complete description of the macroeconomy comes in three steps. In the short run, the AD and AS schedules allow us to understand the impact of changes in the exogenous variables. In the long run, the dichotomy principle produces the LAD and LAS schedules. The medium run describes how we move from the short to the long run.

---

[1] Harry G. Johnson (1923–1979), a Canadian, was a professor of international trade and monetary economics at the University of Chicago and was known both for his dry wit and a wet whistle. Among his most important contributions is the monetary approach to the balance of payments, which lies behind our understanding of the workings of monetary policy under fixed exchange rates.

[2] The book has been concerned until now with extremes: Chapter 6 dealt with the flexible price case, while Chapters 10 and 11 assumed constant prices. The real world must be somewhere in between, with price levels and inflation moving but only gradually in response to changes in aggregate demand.

inflation and the nominal exchange rate, depend only on monetary policy. Understanding these interactions and linking the economy's short run to the long run is a key function of the *AD–AS* framework. The chapter concludes with examples of the *AS–AD* model's usefulness.

13.2 Aggregate Demand and Supply under Fixed Exchange Rates

As in Chapters 11 and 12, we distinguish between fixed and flexible exchange rate regimes. We begin with the fixed exchange rate regime. We know from Chapter 11 that, when capital is mobile, a country that fixes its exchange rate to another currency loses its ability to pursue an independent monetary policy. The central bank has no other choice but to set its own interest rate at the world level. The *LM* or *TR* schedules are irrelevant, so we will not bother to discuss them here. This simplifies matters considerably, since this means that shifts in aggregate demand will only arise because of shifts in the *IS* or *IFM* curves.

13.2.1 Aggregate Demand in the Long Run

First, we look at the long run. We showed in Chapter 6 that **purchasing power parity (PPP)**, the assumption that the real exchange rate (σ) is constant, is a good rule of thumb for thinking about the long run. With $\sigma = SP/P^*$, the fact that S is fixed and σ is constant in the long run means that the domestic inflation rate (π) must equal the foreign inflation rate (π^*):

$$\sigma = \frac{SP}{P^*} = \text{constant and } S \text{ fixed implies } \pi = \pi^*.$$

A very simple conclusion follows. *If the nominal exchange rate is constant in the long run, domestic inflation must be equal to foreign inflation.* Put differently, a fixed exchange rate regime rules out permanent differences between domestic and foreign inflation. If they could diverge permanently, the real exchange rate would appreciate or depreciate without limit. For example, if domestic inflation exceeded foreign inflation permanently despite a constant nominal exchange rate, the resulting real appreciation would make the economy increasingly uncompetitive and worsen the current account with no end in sight. This simply cannot be a long-run equilibrium.

This restriction is represented in Figure 13.3(*b*) as the horizontal long-run aggregate demand (**LAD**) **line**. It is a demand-side restriction because any permanent deviation would eventually lead to unsustainable current account deficits or surpluses.

Fixing the exchange rate means importing inflation from the country whose currency is used as a peg. The exchange rate becomes an anchor for monetary policy, pretty much like money in the case of the money growth strategy. Figure 13.2 shows how this anchor has worked for Denmark, which has fixed its exchange rate since the mid-1980s, first to the deutschmark, and then to the euro.

Chapter 6 established that long-run inflation is related to money growth. 'Related' does not mean 'caused by', however. In fact, when the exchange rate is fixed, it is imported inflation that drives the money supply. This is merely a consequence of the result, shown in Chapter 11, that monetary policy—and hence the supply of money—is endogenous under a fixed exchange rate regime. Indeed, imagine that domestic inflation exceeds the foreign inflation rate and, yet, that the central bank tries to keep the money supply constant, which is represented by the *LM* curve in panel (*a*) of Figure 13.3. The real exchange appreciation undermines the economy's international competitiveness, causing the *IS* curve to shift to the left to *IS'*. At the intersection point *B* of *IS'* and *LM*, the interest rate is below the

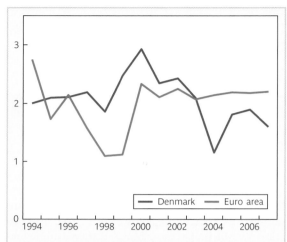

Fig. 13.2 Inflation in Denmark and the Euro Area, 1994–2007

Since the mid-1980s, the Danish central bank has pegged the value of the currency, the krone, within the European Monetary System, first to the DM and then to the euro. The figure shows that Danish inflation has remained close to inflation in the euro area. The relationship does not hold exactly every year, which reminds us that PPP is only expected to hold in the long run. Indeed, over the period 1994–2007 displayed in the figure (there is no data on earlier euro area inflation), average inflation stands at 2.02% in Denmark, slightly below the overall euro area rate of 2.25%.

Source: IMF, *International Financial Statistics*.

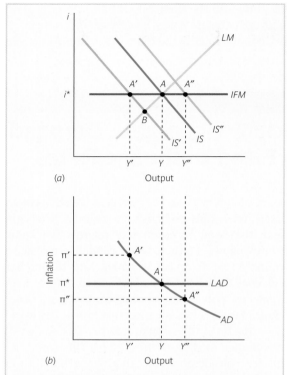

Fig. 13.3 The Aggregate Demand Curve Under Fixed Exchange Rates

Starting from inflation π* at point *A*, an increase in the rate of inflation to π′ reduces the country's external competitiveness. The *IS* curve shifts leftward in panel (*a*). The resulting decrease in demand is reported in panel (*b*). Conversely, a reduction in inflation to π″ improves competitiveness, shifts the *IS* curve rightward, and aggregate demand increases.

level dictated by the *IFM* line and capital flows out. In order to prevent the nominal exchange rate from depreciating, the central bank must intervene and buy back its currency. It cannot hold the money supply constant and must let it decline. This shows that, when the exchange rate is fixed, instead of inflation adjusting to money growth, it is money growth that adjusts to inflation. Box 13.1 formally derives the endogenous growth rate of money under fixed exchange rates.

13.2.2 The Short-Run Aggregate Demand Curve

In the short run, PPP does not hold because prices are sticky. The real exchange rate σ can fluctuate and its movements play a key role in shaping aggregate demand. Our framework for thinking about the short run is the *IS–IFM* framework. In Chapter 11, we used it assuming that the price level was constant so that there was no inflation. Now we must adapt it to allow for inflation.

To that effect, we ask what happens when the inflation rate changes, all other things being equal. In panel (*a*) of Figure 13.3, we start from general equilibrium at point *A*. We assume that this is a stable equilibrium, so that domestic inflation π is equal to foreign inflation π*. Now suppose that the rate of inflation rises from π to π′ while the foreign

Box 13.1 The Real Exchange Rate and Money Growth Under a Fixed Exchange Rate Regime

This box formally presents the long-run restrictions imposed by fixed exchange rates on the domestic inflation and monetary growth rates. Recall that the real exchange rate σ is defined as SP/P^*, where S is the nominal exchange rate, P the domestic price level, and P^* the foreign price level. Using the rule presented in Box 6.3, when the nominal exchange rate is fixed:

(13.1) $$\frac{\Delta \sigma}{\sigma} = \pi - \pi^*.$$

PPP implies that σ is constant. It follows from (13.1) that $\pi = \pi^*$. Home inflation rate is determined by the rest of the world.

To see what happens with money growth, we start from the equilibrium condition in the money market:

(13.2) $$M/P = L(Y, i).$$

In the long run, the growth rate of real output $g = \Delta Y/Y$ is given by real factors (the dichotomy assumption) and does not depend on money growth. As for the interest rate i, we know that it is also set at the world rate of return i^*, which is exogenous and assumed constant. It follows that real money demand grows at rate ηg where η is the elasticity of money demand with respect to real income—the percentage change of money demand to a one percent increase in GDP. The supply of real money grows as the

difference between the rate of growth of the nominal money supply stock, μ, *less* the inflation rate π:

(13.3) $$\frac{\Delta(M/P)}{M/P} = \mu - \pi = \mu - \pi^*.$$

The last equality recognizes that foreign and domestic inflation are equal. Market equilibrium requires that real money demand growth be equal real supply growth:

(13.4) $\eta g = \mu - \pi^*$ or, equivalently, $\mu = \eta g + \pi^*$.

The same relation applies to the rest of the world, linking inflation abroad to the rate of money growth (μ^*) abroad and to the real growth rate of the rest of the world (g^*):

(13.5) $$\mu^* = \eta g^* + \pi^*.$$

Combining (13.4) and (13.5) we find that, for the exchange rate to be held fixed, domestic money must grow at the same rate as abroad, after due adjustment has been made for relative GDP growth:

(13.6) $$\mu = \mu^* + \eta(g - g^*).$$

This shows that when the exchange rate is fixed, money growth at home is driven in the long run by the foreign money growth rate, with a correction for the difference between domestic and foreign trend GDP growth rates.

rate of inflation π^* remains unchanged. In this situation, the real exchange rate starts to appreciate and will keep appreciating as long as our prices rise faster than abroad. Our competitiveness is eroded, the primary current account worsens, and demand for domestic output declines. Graphically, the IS curve shifts to the left, say to IS'. The new equilibrium, therefore, occurs at point A' at the intersection of the new IS curve and the IFM line.[3]

If, instead, inflation were to decline to π'', below the foreign rate π^*, competitiveness would improve, the

[3] As long as domestic inflation exceeds the foreign rate, the real exchange rate continues to depreciate. Point A' is just a snapshot taken during a contractionary process that continues as long as inflation is higher at home than abroad. To keep things simple, we do not elaborate on this aspect.

real exchange rate would depreciate, and the IS curve would shift to IS''. The new equilibrium—after a period of one year, say—would be described by point A''. Connecting points like A, A', and A'' in panel (b) of Figure 13.3, we trace out the **aggregate demand curve** AD. The curve is downward-sloping because rising inflation weakens the country's external competitiveness, which reduces domestic and foreign demand for domestic goods. It represents aggregate demand because movements along the curve are induced by shifts of the IS curve, the goods market equilibrium condition under the Keynesian assumption that supply passively responds to demand. It is a short-run curve because, as long as domestic inflation differs from foreign inflation, demand continues to change (so that a year later, say, output would have moved further away from Y in Figure 13.3, further reducing demand and flattening the demand curve).

13.2.3 Movements Along versus Shifts of the *AD* Curve

As in previous chapters, it is essential to distinguish between movement along the *AD* curve and shifts of the curve itself. The rule is always the same: the curve shifts when a relevant exogenous variable changes. Since the *AD* curve is nothing more than a summary of the *IS–IFM* framework, the list of endogenous and exogenous variables is similar to those identified in Chapter 11. The difference is that the price level and the inflation rate are now endogenous. On the other hand, any exogenous variable that shifts the *IS* curve also shifts the *AD* curve. For example, starting from initial inflation rate π, an increase in government spending is represented in Figure 13.3(*a*) by a shift from *IS* to *IS″*. In panel (*b*) the corresponding point is *A″*. The new demand schedule which passes through *A″* must lie to the right of the initial schedule, as shown in Figure 13.4. The same reasoning applies to the other exogenous variables studied in Chapter 10: government purchases G, net taxes T, household wealth Ω, Tobin's q ('animal spirits'), and foreign

income Y^*. Missing in that list is the real exchange rate, which is now endogenous because it depends on the evolution of domestic prices—which are no longer fixed—relative to foreign prices.

Any change in these exogenous variables that affects aggregate demand shifts the *AD* curve, rightwards when demand rises, leftwards when it declines. Conversely, the *AD* curve stays in place when these variables remain constant. Any change in other variables implies that we move along the *AD* curve. Let us now examine how and when this happens.

13.2.4 The Complete System

In Figure 13.5 we bring together aggregate demand and supply. The demand side comes in two parts: (1) the downward-sloping short-run aggregate demand curve *AD*, and (2) the horizontal long-run *LAD* line, which reflects the endogeneity of money in fixed exchange rate regimes. The supply side, derived in Chapter 12, also comes in two parts: (1) an upward-sloping short-run supply curve *AS*, and (2) the vertical long-run schedule *LAS*. The supply side in the long run dictates that actual and trend GDP are

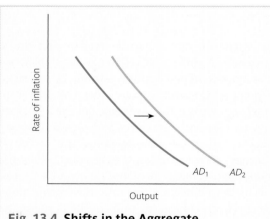

Fig. 13.4 Shifts in the Aggregate Demand Curve

Exogenous changes in demand which shift the *IS* curve also shift the short-run aggregate demand curve in the same direction.

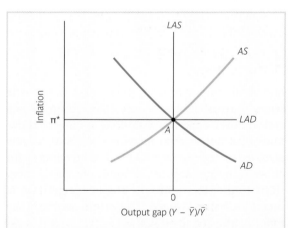

Fig. 13.5 Aggregate Demand and Supply Under Fixed Exchange Rates

In the long run, output is at its trend growth level, the output gap is zero, and inflation is equal to the foreign inflation rate. The short run is determined by the *AD* and *AS* curves. The figure depicts a situation of long-run equilibrium where all four curves intersect.

equal ($Y = \bar{Y}$), which requires that actual and underlying inflation be equal as well ($\pi = \tilde{\pi}$). On the demand side, the long-run domestic inflation rate must also be equal to the foreign rate ($\pi = \pi^*$). In other words, in the long run, the economy stabilizes when the GDP is on trend, inflation is the same as abroad, and the underlying inflation is in line with actual inflation. In Figure 13.5, the two long-run schedules intersect at point A.

Note that we have changed the horizontal axis from previous chapters. We used to track real GDP (Y) along this axis. We now represent the output gap $Y_{\text{gap}} = (Y - \bar{Y})/\bar{Y}$. This rescaling is important. We learned in Chapters 3 and 4 that trend GDP is growing continuously over time in most countries. To study the level of GDP would require a continuous rightward shift of the LAS schedule, which would be quite cumbersome and, more importantly, would divert our attention from the focus of this chapter, which is the origin and propagation of business cycles.

The situation depicted in Figure 13.5 corresponds to a **long-run equilibrium** because the two short-run schedules also pass through the long-run equilibrium point A. In the following sections, we examine several cases of **short-run equilibria** distinct from the long-run position and explain how the economy moves from the short to the long run.

13.2.5 Fiscal Policy and Demand Disturbances

Short run

We now track down the effects of an exogenous **demand disturbance**. As in Chapter 11, we can think of a fiscal policy expansion—an increase in government purchases ($\Delta \bar{G} > 0$) or a net tax reduction ($\Delta \bar{T} < 0$). Initially, at point A, the economy is in long-term equilibrium: output Y is at its trend level $\bar{Y}$, and actual (π) and underlying ($\tilde{\pi}$) inflation are both equal to the world inflation rate π^*. In the background of the demand-side analysis, the domestic interest rate is equal to the world rate of return ($i = i^*$).

The expansionary demand disturbance is depicted in Figure 13.6(a) as the rightward shift of the IS curve to IS', which moves the AD curve to AD' in the same direction in panel (b). The new curve AD' shows the short-run effect of fiscal policy, say after

one year. At point B output has increased—as with the Mundell–Fleming framework—but inflation has risen as well, which was previously ignored by assumption. The rise in inflation is an aggregate-supply effect, reflecting higher mark-ups because of improved economic conditions. The combination of a fixed nominal exchange rate $\bar{S}$ and an inflation rate higher than abroad (P is thus increasing faster than P^*) implies that the real exchange rate $\sigma = SP/P^*$ appreciates. External competitiveness is eroding and the primary current account is deteriorating. Thus rising inflation reduces the impact of the demand disturbance. This is precisely why the AD curve is downward-sloping. Indeed, imagine that inflation remained unchanged, as we used to argue in Chapter 11 when working with the IS–IFM fixed-price assumption. Then competitiveness would have remained unchanged, and the outcome would have been at point B' in both panels, along the IS' curve—constant inflation with a larger increase in output. The loss of competitiveness, however, has shifted the curve leftward to IS''. The horizontal distance between B and B' is a measure of the inflation-induced deterioration of the primary current account.

Long run

The long run is described by three observations.

◆ First, the government budget constraint rules out permanent fiscal expansions. For the initial shift in aggregate demand to be a long-run expansion, it must continue in *each period*. For fiscal policy to be sustainable and consistent with a steady state, on the other hand, the public debt must be stabilized, as explained in Chapter 7. The fiscal expansion implies that the public debt is rising, which is not sustainable. To reach a new long-run situation, the expansionary policy must eventually be reversed. When this is done, the aggregate demand curve will return to its initial position AD.[4]

---

[4] In fact, the public debt will have risen in the meantime and must be paid for by a permanently higher primary budget surplus. This requires that the AD curve shifts back beyond its original position. We overlook this additional complexity. It is acceptable to do so if the fiscal expansion does not last long enough to seriously increase the debt–GDP ratio. We return to this issue in Chapter 17.

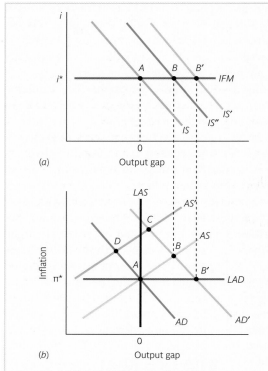

(a)

(b)

Fig. 13.6 Fiscal Policy Under Fixed Exchange Rates

A fiscal expansion shifts the *IS* and *AD* schedule to the right, to *IS'* and *AD'*, respectively. The short-run effect is shown by point *B*, an increase in real GDP accompanied by higher inflation. The increase in inflation reduces external competitiveness and shifts the *IS* curve backward from *IS'* to *IS"*. As core inflation catches up with actual inflation, the *AS* schedule shifts to *AS'*, whose position corresponds to a core inflation rate equal to the inflation rate observed at point *B*. If the government does not change its fiscal policy stance, the new equilibrium occurs at point *C*, where inflation has again increased above the core rate, leading to further shifts of the *AS* curve. If the government cancels the fiscal expansion, the aggregate demand curve moves back to *AD*, and the new short-run equilibrium is at point *D*, where actual inflation is now lower than core inflation. The *AS* curve starts shifting to the right and will do so until it returns to its initial position and the long-run equilibrium is restored at point *A*.

♦ Second, output must return to its trend and the economy will stabilize along the *LAS* line. The logic here is that any non-zero output gap implies, by construction, that underlying and actual infla-

tion differ, which is not indefinitely sustainable either.

♦ Third, inflation cannot deviate for very long from the foreign inflation rate if the exchange rate is to remain fixed. Thus, the economy must return to the *LAD* line.

The conclusion is that in the long run, the economy must return to point *A*, exactly where it started. The effect of a fiscal expansion is transitory because a fiscal expansion cannot be permanent if the government's budget constraint is to be satisfied.

The medium run

Summing up so far, in Figure 13.6 we start from point *A*, move to point *B*, and eventually move back to point *A*. The actual path taken by the economy from the immediate short run at point *B* to the long run at point *A* can be reconstructed using the observations just made. We already know that the budget constraint will force the government at some point to reverse gears and either cut spending or raise taxes. When this will happen is a political decision—it could depend on the timing of elections, for instance—and we cannot say much more about it. At any rate, the *AD* curve must eventually shift back to its initial position.

We can say more about the behaviour of the *AS* curve. Remember that its position is determined by underlying inflation $\tilde{\pi}$, which is assumed to be initially—say, at time $t = 0$—equal to foreign inflation π^*. In Chapter 12, we saw that the underlying inflation has *backward-looking* and *forward-looking* components. The backward-looking component reacts to actual inflation conditions, 'catching up' with current inflation. Now note that at time $t = 1$ when the economy has moved to point *B*, actual inflation is higher than the initial underlying inflation rate at $t = 0$. Inevitably, wage negotiators—whose appraisal determines the underlying inflation rate when they agree to raise nominal wages according to their perception of ongoing inflation conditions—will recognize that the current (time $t = 1$) inflation rate is higher than it used to be assumed. They will naturally agree to push nominal wages faster, in effect bringing up underlying inflation, say, to equal the inflation rate observed at point *B*. As they do so, the short-run AS curve shifts. We know that its position is such that actual and underlying inflation coincide when the output gap is zero. The new (time $t = 2$) short-run AS curve is AS', which cuts the LAS line at the previous (time $t = 1$) underlying inflation rate, the one that corresponds to point B, i.e. at the same horizontal level as point B.

This means that at time $t = 2$, the economy moves from point B to point C, at the intersection of the AD' and AS' schedules in panel (b). From B to C, inflation further rises. This means a faster erosion of external competitiveness and a deeper deterioration of aggregate demand, a further leftward shift of the IS curve (not shown), hence a lower GDP as we move up along AD', still unchanged. This is an instance of **stagflation**.[5] We are not yet back to the long-run equilibrium, however, if only because fiscal policy is not yet corrected. At point C, the output gap is still positive and the new current inflation rate exceeds underlying inflation (remember that along AS', underlying inflation is equal to the inflation observed when the economy was at point B). It is just a matter of time until underlying inflation rises further, pushing the AS curve further above AS'. In that case, stagflation continues as the economy moves up along the AD' schedule. Eventually, though, the government will have to reverse the fiscal expansion.

So let's now imagine that the government cancels its fiscal expansion at time $t = 2$ when the economy is at point C. The fiscal policy correction has a contractionary effect and the AD schedule moves from AD' back to AD (assuming a complete policy reversal compatible with the long run). In that case, at time $t = 3$, the economy moves from point C to point D in panel (b). Even though the AD curve is back to its initial position, output is now below trend. The reason is that the AS curve has shifted to AS' because underlying inflation has increased. The higher inflation hurts external competitiveness. In panel (a), the corresponding IS curve (not shown) is therefore to the left of the initial one (IS) since fiscal policy is back to its initial stance but external competitiveness has been degraded by inflation.

Point D is on the AS' curve, which corresponds to the underlying rate of inflation at time $t = 2$ at point C. But since point D is below point B, actual inflation is lower. In that case, the next round of wage negotiations will recognize that inflation is ebbing and will reduce underlying inflation. The AS schedule will shift down below AS' and the economy will move down along the AD curve from point D in the direction of point A. At the intersection of AD and the new AS curve (not shown), which corresponds to an underlying inflation rate equal to the actual rate observed at point D, inflation has again declined below underlying inflation. This prompts a new reappraisal of underlying inflation, a new downward shift of the AS curve, and a continuing movement along the AD curve. The process will continue until the AS curve has returned to its initial position and the long-run equilibrium is achieved at point A.[6]

To summarize, the acknowledgement of inflation requires that we reason in three steps:

(1) the immediate short run, described by the amended IS–TR–BP framework subsumed in the AD curve and by the short-run AS curve;

(2) the long run, described by the long-run AD and AS curves;

(3) the medium run—the transition from the short to the long run—a drawn-out process driven by successive shifts of the short-run AD and AS curves.

The details of the curves and their movements with reference to Figure 13.6 are summarized in Table 13.1.

The reasoning so far has emphasized the role of the backward-looking component of underlying inflation. What is the role of the forward-looking

---

[5] It might be useful to remember from Chapter 12 that the instability of inflation was considered as a proof of the non-existence of the Phillips curve—or its mirror image, the AS curve. Here we see that it still exists, but can shift around a lot!

[6] In fact, the economy will need to move temporarily below point A in panel (b), because a period when inflation is lower at home than abroad is required to bring the real exchange rate back to its initial level. Panel (a) makes it clear that inflation must be below π^* for competitiveness to be restored and for the IS curve to return to its initial position.

Table 13.1 **Tracking Down Movements in Figure 13.6**

Time	Event	Movement	Equilibrium
0	Initial situation		Point A
1	Expansionary policy	AD shifts to AD'	Point B
2	Underlying inflation catches up with inflation at point B	AS shifts to AS'	Point C
3	Expansionary fiscal policy rescinded/loses impact	Back to initial AD	Point D
4	Underlying inflation catches up with inflation at point D	AS' shifts to the right	Point E (not shown)
5	Underlying inflation catches up with inflation at point E	AS shifts to the right	Point F (not shown)
6	Underlying inflation catches up with inflation at point F, etc.	AS shifts to the right	Point G (not shown)
Long run	Underlying inflation has caught up with actual inflation	Back to initial AS	Point A

component? Anticipating the future evolution of inflation, wage negotiators will reduce the lag between underlying and actual inflation and the *AS* curve will adjust faster, which will speed up the return to departure point *A*.

The incorporation of inflation modifies some of the conclusions that we reached in Chapter 12.

◆ First, a demand disturbance does not just move output, it also changes the inflation rate as we move along the *AS* curve.

◆ Second, bringing inflation into the picture naturally leads us to think beyond the current period. This was already apparent with the Phillips or *AS* curve because we need to think about the evolution of the underlying inflation rate. On the demand side, we were led to think about the government's budget constraint, which was ignored in Chapter 12 as we strictly focused on the short run. This led us to recognize that fiscal policy is inherently temporary.

◆ Third, we found that a fiscal expansion is partly undermined by the inflation that it generates. The resulting loss of competitiveness—when the nominal exchange rate is fixed—deteriorates the current account and thus reduces world demand for our goods.

This explains why the countercyclical use of fiscal policy is much less popular than it used to be in the

heyday of Keynesianism, before the old Phillips curve was replaced by its expectations-augmented version.

13.2.6 Monetary Policy and Realignments

A key lesson from Chapter 11 is that it is impossible to carry out an autonomous monetary policy when the exchange rate is fixed. But we indicated that exchange rate parities can be changed, at least on occasion, since most fixed exchange rate regimes are considered 'adjustable'. We now show how exchange rate realignments allow for some limited role of monetary policy. A devaluation, for instance, means reducing the nominal exchange rate. How is this done in practice? Formally, the central bank simply announces the new parity and does what it takes to make it happen. This means a monetary policy expansion—achieved either on the open market or through foreign exchange market interventions.

In panel (*a*) of Figure 13.7, the initial situation at point *A* is assumed to correspond to a long-run equilibrium, with domestic observed and underlying inflation both equal to foreign inflation. Assuming, for the time being, that domestic inflation is equal to foreign inflation, the nominal depreciation translates into a gain in external competitiveness, so that $\sigma = SP/P^*$ declines when S is reduced. As a result, the *IS* curve shifts rightward to *IS'*. In the background,

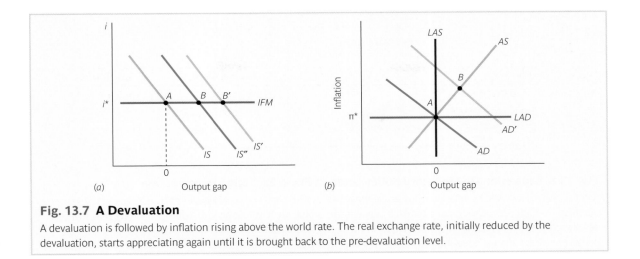

Fig. 13.7 A Devaluation

A devaluation is followed by inflation rising above the world rate. The real exchange rate, initially reduced by the devaluation, starts appreciating again until it is brought back to the pre-devaluation level.

the money supply will have expanded, as already mentioned. Recovering the monetary policy instrument is precisely the role of exchange rate depreciations or appreciations. These are fleeting moments when the central bank can do this.

The short run equilibrium is reached at point B. In panel (b), the demand expansion is shown as the shift of the aggregate demand schedule from AD to AD', and the corresponding outcome is represented by point B. As is now becoming customary, we find that an output expansion does not come for free, it is accompanied by rising inflation. This, in turn, reduces the real devaluation, which undermines partly the expansionary effect of the devaluation, which is captured by the leftward shift of the IS curve from IS' to IS'' in panel (a).

Point B does not represent a long-run equilibrium because it is neither on the LAD nor on the LAS schedules. It lies on a short-run AS curve whose position is determined by initial underlying inflation (equal to the world rate of inflation), but now at point B actual inflation has risen. As a consequence, the AS curve will shift up when underlying inflation rises. On the other hand, the rise in inflation means that the domestic price level rises faster than the foreign price level. As a result, the real exchange rate keeps appreciating, the current account deteriorates, and the IS curve further shifts leftwards in panel (a). The economy will return to point A, after

a period of inflation above the world level. During the transition back to point A, the inflation differential progressively undoes the real depreciation achieved through the initial devaluation.[7] At point A, this effect is complete: the competitiveness benefit from the initial depreciation has been entirely offset by the inflation differential with the country to whose currency the domestic currency is pegged.

This is yet another case of long-run monetary neutrality. We knew all along that the long-run equilibrium is at point A, so the question was what would take us there. In the end, if we start from long-run equilibrium, all real variables must return to their initial values, which applies to the output gap and to the real exchange rate. Inflation rate, too, must eventually return to the world level. In the end, devaluations or appreciations only have temporary effects.

Another possibility, however, is for the central bank to devalue again. If it does so, the temporary competitive advantage will again be gradually eroded by the inflation differential, leading to another devaluation, etc. In this limited sense,

---

[7] The careful reader will ask: what gets us back to point A in panel (b)? Here we would need to use the observation in footnote 4: during all the time when $\pi > \pi^*$, the curve AD becomes increasingly flatter, year after year. In the end it will coincide with LAD.

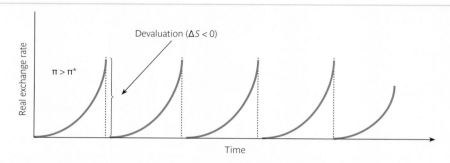

Fig. 13.8 Expansionary Monetary Policy Under a Fixed Exchange Rate Regime
A devaluation is followed by inflation rising above the world rate. The real exchange rate, initially reduced by the devaluation, starts appreciating again until it is brought back to the pre-devaluation level. The central bank may then devalue again the nominal exchange rate, which immediately depreciates the real exchange rate, triggering a new period of high inflation and real appreciation. In the end, monetary policy results in higher inflation and a succession of devaluations.

monetary policy independence is restored under a fixed but adjustable exchange rate regime. Through a succession of devaluations, the central bank can keep pushing temporarily real GDP above trend, but it will have to accept a higher inflation rate. Figure 13.8 illustrates this path of the real exchange rate over time. It will depreciate abruptly at the time of each devaluation, only to appreciate again. In the end, this strategy merely allows a country to opt for a different inflation rate from the one that prevails in the country to which the currency is pegged. Box 13.2 shows how such an arrangement existed between France and Germany for nearly two decades.

 Box 13.2 Conflict and Coexistence with Different Inflation Rates: France and Germany

France and Germany have long existed side by side with two mutually inconsistent objectives: they have very different views about inflation. Germany, still remembering the devastating hyperinflation of 1922–1923, was committed to low inflation, while France was more interested in using monetary policy to boost short-run growth. Yet as neighbours with deep trade and financial relations, France and Germany were unwilling to allow the exchange rate to fluctuate from day to day according to market forces. Their solution was to peg their exchange rates to each other, first informally in the 1970s, then formally following the launch of the European Monetary System in 1979, and then irrevocably after the adoption of the euro in January 1999. The peg was adjustable and frequent realignments did take place between the currencies, with the franc being regularly devalued *vis-à-vis* the deutschmark. Figure 13.9 shows the evolution of the real exchange rate between France and Germany during this period. It is the real-life version of Figure 13.8. Occasional depreciations of the franc *vis-à-vis* the deutschmark appear as sharp declines of the real exchange rate, which are then gradually undone by gradual appreciation, until the next devaluation. The figure also shows that, after a severe crisis in 1993, the real exchange rate stabilized. This reflects France's 'franc fort' policy. In its preparation for the monetary union, France gave up monetary policy independence, renounced boom-and-bust devaluation cycles, and gradually managed to achieve an inflation rate similar to Germany's.

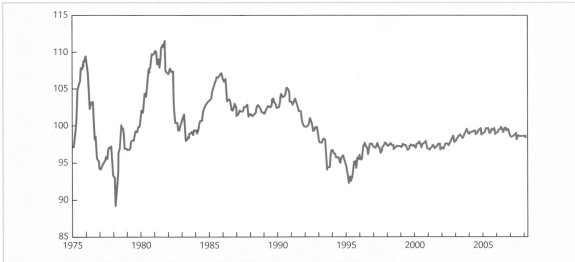

Fig. 13.9 The Real Exchange Rate Franc/Deutschmark, 1975–2007
The franc/deutschmark exchange rate was fixed but adjustable during the period 1975–1998. France's higher tolerance for inflation than Germany led to recurrent devaluations of the franc vis-à-vis the deutschmark. Each devaluation was then followed by a real appreciation, until the next one. Since monetary union in 1999, such devaluations have been ruled out—meaning that slightly lower inflation in Germany than in France since then has led to a real appreciation of the French–German real exchange rate.

13.3 Aggregate Demand and Supply under Flexible Exchange Rates

Under a flexible exchange rate regime, aggregate demand reacts to inflation, but through a different mechanism from fixed exchange rates. Effectively, monetary policy and the nominal exchange rates swap roles under flexible exchange rates. Monetary policy is exogenous and under the control of the central bank. The nominal exchange rate, in contrast, is no longer exogenously fixed, but is determined by market forces and is endogenous.

13.3.1 A Preliminary Step: The Fisher Equation

In earlier chapters, we treated nominal interest rates and real interest rates as identical. In fact they are not. With non-zero inflation, the nominal interest rate will differ from the real interest rate. But by how much? In order to answer this question, we need to define carefully the real interest rate.

Suppose we borrowed €100 for one year at a nominal rate of 5%. At the end of the year, we will have to repay the debt with interest, which will amount to €105 (€100 in principal and €5 in interest). But if inflation is positive, the value of €105 in one year in terms of goods and services will be less than €105 today; prices will be higher in a year's time. If inflation turns out to be 2%, the real value of €105 tomorrow in terms of today's euros will be about €103.[8] This means that, valued at today's price level,

---

[8] If the price index is 1 today, it will be 1.02 in one year's time and the real value of €105 tomorrow in terms of goods tomorrow will be 105/1.02 ~ 103.

the real value of our repayment in one year is €103. The real cost of borrowing €100 is therefore €3, which means a real interest rate of 3%. Note that 3% = 5% – 2%. More generally, we can state that the real interest rate (r) is defined as the difference between the nominal interest rate (i) and the expected rate of inflation (π^e):

(13.7) $$r = i - \pi^e$$
real interest rate = nominal interest rate – expected inflation.

This relationship is called the **Fisher principle** or **Fisher equation**.[9] In the presence of inflation, future repayments are made in money that will be worth less than it is today. This loss of purchasing power of money tomorrow can be seen as a gift to present-day borrowers or, more precisely, it means that the real cost of borrowing is less than the nominal cost, by an amount equal to the inflation rate between today and the future repayment.

Lenders are unlikely to agree to this 'gift' voluntarily. They will demand a higher nominal interest rate to compensate them for their expected loss of purchasing power. To see this, write the Fisher equation in a slightly different way:

(13.8) $$i = r + \pi^e.$$

Looking at (13.8), a borrower will ask for a nominal rate that includes both the forgone real opportunity cost (r) of parting with her money as well as compensation for lost purchasing power of principal as the result of inflation (π^e).

In fact, (13.7) is the way we define the real interest rate. Nominal rates are observed—they are written in loan contracts—but real rates can only be inferred from (13.7). This requires knowing what expected inflation is at the time of the loan contract but expectations are not observable. This is why real interest rates are generally not observable either. Eventually, we will know what inflation will have been during the life of a contract and compute the *ex post* real interest rate as $i - \pi$. However, whenever actual inflation differs from what it was expected to be, the *ex post* real interest rate will differ from the *ex ante* rate $i - \pi^e$. As a result, someone

will be disappointed. If inflation turns out higher than expected, the *ex post* real rate is lower than *ex ante* anticipated, which is good news for the borrower and a source of disappointment for the lender. Conversely, if actual inflation ends up lower than expected, the lender will have earned more than she was asking for.

Lenders and borrowers can reduce this uncertainty. One solution is to index nominal interest rates to inflation. In that case loan contracts include a clause that stipulates that the interest rate be adjusted for inflation over the lifetime of the loan. This is the case for a certain class of French Government bonds—Figure 13.10 shows the corresponding nominal and real interest rates. Another way of limiting the damage from inflation—prevalent in chronically high-inflation countries, is to lend only over short periods of time, sometimes not longer than a week. When these loans are rolled over at the new prevailing interest rate, they are roughly equivalent to indexed lending.

Finally, remember that in Chapter 10 we argued that it is the nominal, not the real, interest rate that matters for the money market equilibrium condition. Indeed, cash brings a zero nominal interest rate—no one gets paid for holding money. So, when comparing return on money with return on other assets, we had to use the nominal rate. The Fisher equation shows that, *ex post*, the real interest rate on money is $r = 0 - \pi = -\pi$, the negative of the inflation rate. Inflation acts as a tax on those who hold money.

13.3.2 Aggregate Demand in the Long Run

A central lesson of Chapter 9 was that central banks assert full control over monetary policy under flexible exchange rates. They do so by setting the interbank market interest rate directly. In practice, they routinely use the interest rate instrument to stabilize inflation and output. As explained in Chapter 11, they raise the interest rate when inflation or output increases, and cut the interest rate when inflation or output declines. This reaction of the central bank, we saw, is captured by the **Taylor rule**:

(13.9) $$i = \bar{i} + a\pi_{\text{gap}} + bY_{\text{gap}}.$$

---

[9]   Named after Irving Fisher, the Yale economist, already referred to in several previous chapters.

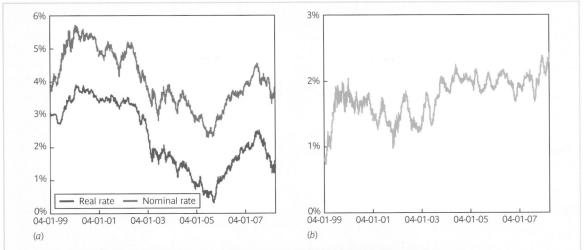

Fig. 13.10 Nominal and Real Interest Rates on French Debt, 1999–2008

Panel (*a*) shows the nominal and interest rates on a bond issued by the French Goverments. These bonds, called OATs, are indexed to inflation so that the real rate reflects the market's assessment of the real returns on financial assets, which varies in response to demand and supply. It suggests that the long-run real interest rate is around 2%. The distance between the nominal and the real interest rates reflects the expected inflation rate, which is shown in panel (*b*).

Source: Agence France-Trésor.

Recall that parameters *a* and *b*—which are both positive—express the overall monetary policy objectives or 'tastes' of the central bank. A high value of *a* relative to *b* would represent an 'inflation-fighting' central bank. In contrast, if *b* is large relative to *a*, this would signify that the central bank is more interested in reducing the output gap than keeping inflation close to its target.

The **neutral or natural interest rate** $\bar{\imath}$ was defined in Chapter 9 as the one chosen by the central bank when inflation and output are both on target— meaning that both inflation and output gaps equal zero ($\pi = \bar{\pi}$ and $Y = \bar{Y}$). But what guides the central bank's choice? The Fisher equation gives the answer: the sum of the long-run real interest rate and the target inflation rate. Let's take a careful look at each of them.

The neutrality principle tells us that, in the long run, the real interest rate $\bar{r}$ is given by the real economy. It is the return available from investments after adjusting for inflation or, according to Chapter 8, the marginal productivity of physical capital. It is driven, therefore, by technology, the availability of labour and other factors, all of which are beyond the control of the central bank.

This leaves the long-run inflation rate which is factored into the neutral interest rate $\bar{\imath}$. Since the central bank ultimately controls the inflation rate, it can logically only be the inflation target $\bar{\pi}$ that enters the Taylor rule. It follows that the natural interest rate is the nominal rate that corresponds to the economy's real rate plus the inflation target:

(13.10) $$\bar{\imath} = \bar{r} + \bar{\pi}.$$

This logic pins down the inflation rate in the long run and determines the position of the long-run aggregate demand curve. According to the Taylor rule, the central bank aims at bringing both inflation and output to their desired levels. We know from our analysis of the *AS* curve that, in the long run, the economy will ultimately return to trend, so $Y = \bar{Y}$ and $Y_{\text{gap}} = 0$. Monetary policy, therefore, will see to it that the inflation rate goes back to its desired level so that $\pi = \bar{\pi}$. Thus, a central bank characterized by the Taylor rule determines the long-run aggregate demand curve as the horizontal line *LAD* shown in Figure 13.12. It resembles the *LAD* schedule obtained in the case of a fixed exchange rate regime, but its rationale is different. When the central bank opts for a fixed exchange rate regime, long-run inflation is driven by foreign inflation; under a flexible exchange rate regime, it is set by the target inflation rate embedded in the Taylor rule.[10] The common feature is that long-run inflation and the position of the *LAD* schedule are always determined by the monetary policy strategy. This is an implication of the dichotomy principle.

13.3.3 The Short-Run Aggregate Demand Curve

The apparent similarity between the exchange rate regimes carries over to the short-run aggregate demand curve. The logic behind this curve is different as well. We now show that, under flexible exchange rates, the *AD* curve is downward-sloping because a higher inflation rate leads the central bank to raise interest rates—to pursue contractionary monetary policy. To that effect, we use the *TR–IFM* framework—remember that the position of the *IS* curve is endogenous when the exchange rate freely floats.

We need first to rethink the way we use the Taylor rule. In Chapters 10 and 11, the inflation rate was treated as exogenous and set equal to zero for simplicity, so the Taylor rule only involved a relationship between the interest rate and output. Now that we explicitly deal with inflation, we must recognize that the interest rate responds both to changes in output and in the inflation rate—that is the thrust of the Taylor rule. Remember that inflation is taken as exogenous in the *TR–IFM* diagram.[11] This means that when inflation changes, the *TR* schedule shifts. We will soon see how.

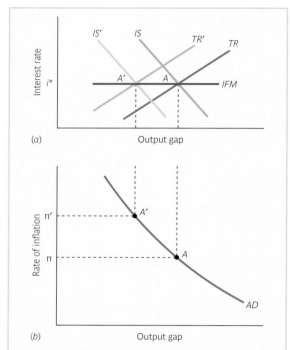

(a)   Output gap

(b)   Output gap

Fig. 13.11 The Aggregate Demand Curve Under Flexible Exchange Rates

The figure shows the effect of an increase in the rate of inflation on aggregate demand. Starting at point *A* with an inflation rate π, inflation rises to π′. The higher inflation rate at the unchanged target rate of inflation prompts the central bank to raise nominal interest rates, shifting the *TR* curve upward in panel (*a*). Demand is reduced (point *A*), hence the downward-sloping curve in panel (*b*).

[10] If the central bank chose to control the money supply instead of following a Taylor rule, the same conclusion would result. The inflation rate in the long run would be given by the chosen rate money growth minus an adjustment for trend growth in the demand for real money balances. Formally, we can use the results from Box 13.1 to describe the money market equilibrium condition (*LM*) in growth rate terms as $\mu - \pi = \eta g$, which gives the long-run inflation rate $\pi = \mu - \eta g$.

[11] Strictly speaking, it was set equal to zero. Allowing it to be positive—but sticky—in the *TR-IFM* model does not change any of the fundamental conclusions.

Let's start in Figure 13.11(*a*) from point *A*, a situation of short- and long-run equilibrium, so that inflation is, and has long been, at the level chosen by the central bank. In order to find out the shape of the short-run *AD* curve, we study the effect of changing inflation, 'all else constant', including monetary policy as summarized by the central bank's target inflation rate $\bar{\pi}$ and the neutral interest rate $\bar{\imath}$.

Suppose the rate of inflation rises exogenously from π to π′. The Taylor rule prescribes that the central bank hikes interest rates—by $a(\pi' - \pi)$—for any level of output. This means that the *TR* curve shifts upwards to *TR′* in panel (*a*). The new equilibrium point A' shows that the effect of a higher rate of inflation is a decline in output. Note, however, that this reduction is not due to a higher interest rate, since it must remain equal to the international required rate of return i^* (the IFM condition). Rather, it is brought about by a real exchange rate appreciation, which reduces the demand for goods—the implicit leftward shift of the IS curve (not shown).[12] The exchange rate appreciation is a direct effect of monetary policy tightening in the face of higher inflation. The move from A to A' when inflation rises from π to π' is reported in panel (b) to obtain a downward-sloping short-run aggregate demand curve AD.

To summarize, the short-run aggregate demand curve is downward-sloping under both fixed and flexible exchange rates, but for different reasons. When the exchange rate is fixed, a higher inflation rate reduces demand through external competitiveness. Monetary policy is a passive by-product of exchange market interventions by the central bank. Under flexible rates, higher inflation triggers an interest rate hike by the central bank via the Taylor rule.[13] Competitiveness declines too, but now because the nominal exchange rate S appreciates.

13.3.4 Movements Along versus Shifts of the AD Curve

The AD curve shifts when any of the exogenous variables in the TR–IFM model changes. Under flexible exchange rates, the IS curve is endogenously moved by the exchange rate to meet the intersection of the TR and IFM schedules. This means that neither fiscal policy, nor animal spirits, nor foreign output, nor any other exogenous change in the demand for goods, can shift the aggregate demand curve. Fiscal policy and, more generally, aggregate demand shocks fails to move the IS curve because its effects

are ultimately frustrated by the exchange rate reaction.[14]

The AD curve does shift, however, when either the TR or the IFM curves do. The TR schedule represents the monetary policy strategy. It moves when the inflation rate changes, but this is what explains the slope of the AD schedule. Changes in the inflation rate, therefore, takes the economy along the AD schedule. The remaining reasons why TR shifts would actually move the AD schedule are changes in the Taylor rule itself. This includes either changes in the central bank's target inflation rate ($\bar{\pi}$) or in the preferences of the central bank, as represented by parameters a and b in (13.9). The position of the IFM curve remains determined by the foreign rate of return i^*.

13.3.5 The Complete System

Figure 13.12 presents the complete system under flexible exchange rates. It includes the now-familiar short- and long-run aggregate supply curves as

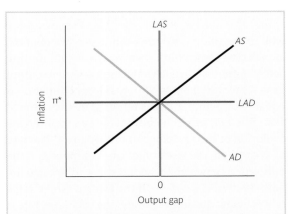

Fig. 13.12 Aggregate Demand and Supply Under Flexible Exchange Rates

In the long run, output is at its trend growth level (a zero output gap) and the central bank's target inflation rate determines the rate of inflation (the height of the LAD curve). The figure depicts long-run equilibrium when the short-run aggregate demand and supply curves pass through the same point as the long-run schedules.

---

[12] At this stage, you may need to return to Section 11.4 of Chapter 11 to remember why the exchange rate appreciates.

[13] The result is the same when the central bank sets the money growth and LM replaces TR. Graphically, this is the case because the LM and TR curves are both upward-sloping. In the case of a money growth target, the AD curve is downward-sloping because a higher inflation rate reduces the real money supply: for a given growth rate of M, M/P is smaller when P grows faster.

[14] This strong statement may be modified to acknowledge that the deterioration of the primary current account implied by the exchange rate changes (sometimes called 'external crowding out') may take several months to occur.

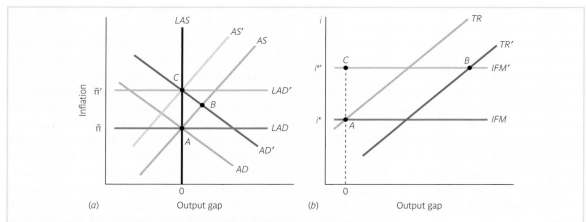

Fig. 13.13 Monetary Policy Under Flexible Exchange Rates

Starting at point A in panel (a), a monetary policy expansion—here a permanent increase in the central bank's target inflation rate—shifts the AD curve rightwards to AD'. The LAD curve also shifts to LAD', intersecting the LAS curve at point C. In the long run the economy will settle at point C, with GDP equal to trend output and the increase in inflation equal to the increase in the target inflation rate. Short-run equilibrium occurs at point B, where actual inflation exceeds underlying inflation. Thereafter underlying inflation increases to its long-run level and the economy moves from point B towards point C.

well as the short- and long-run aggregate demand curves. The figure displays a long-run equilibrium: actual output is equal to trend output—a zero output gap—as required by the supply side, and inflation is equal to target inflation as required by the demand side. The PPP principle also allows us to infer the evolution of the exchange in the long run. The rate of change in the exchange rate compensates the difference between the domestic and foreign inflation rates: $\Delta S/S = \pi^* - \pi$. If the foreign rate of inflation is below the domestic rate, the exchange rate is depreciating ($\Delta S/S < 0$); in the opposite case, it is appreciating ($\Delta S/S > 0$).

13.3.6 Monetary Policy

Central banks which follow a Taylor rule systematically change the interest either when inflation or output depart from their target levels. In that sense, the rule-based monetary policy does not change. But we now want to study a change in the rule itself. It can be the adoption of a new target rate of inflation $\bar{\pi}$, or a changing view about the natural interest rate or the equilibrium trend level of output, or a different sensitivity to the inflation or output gaps

(parameters a and b). Here we consider the case when it raises its inflation target from $\bar{\pi}$ to $\bar{\pi}'$. This means that the neutral interest rate $\bar{i}$, the real interest plus the new target inflation rate $\bar{\pi}'$, will also rise permanently.

Long run

Aiming now at a permanently higher rate of inflation, its decision implies an expansionary reduction of the interest rate, hence the rightward shift from AD to AD' depicted in Figure 13.13(a). It also implies that the long-run aggregate demand schedule shifts to LAD'. The real side of the economy is left unaffected so LAS is unchanged. In the long run, therefore, the economy will move from point A to point C. The vertical distance AC corresponds to the increase in the target inflation rate.

Short run

The initial effect of the more expansionary monetary policy is captured by the move from point A to point B. In the background, the increase in $\bar{\pi}$ shifts the TR curve to the right in panel (b) of Figure 13.13. It also shifts up the IFM schedule because PPP implies a higher rate of exchange rate depreciation (or a lower rate of exchange rate appreciation) than before for reasons that will only be explained later on, in Section 15.3.[15] This, in turn, implies that the foreign rate of return i^* increases to $i^{*\prime}$, for reasons presented in more detail in Chapter 15. The economy moves from point A to point B. Overall, output rises (and unemployment declines) and inflation increases, but by less than the change intended by the central bank.

The medium run

The transition will take the economy in steps from point B to point C in panel (a). At point B, where output is above its growth trend level, the actual rate of inflation exceeds the underlying rate. What happens during the transition—and therefore the details of the trajectory—depends on the behaviour of the underlying rate of inflation. To the extent that it is backward-looking, underlying inflation is sluggish. This is why, initially, the AS curve does not move and the economy reaches point B. Over time, as underlying inflation begins to track actual inflation, the short-run AS curve shifts upwards and the economy moves from B towards C, along the curve AD'. As in the case of a fixed exchange rate regime, along the path from B to C, actual inflation exceeds underlying inflation. As underlying inflation catches up, actual inflation rises and output declines. In panel (b), the continuously rising inflation rate prompts the central bank to tighten its stance and the TR schedule keeps moving up and to the left until it passes through point C.

Yet, underlying inflation has a forward-looking component which could anticipate that the long run is achieved at point C. If underlying inflation were purely forward-looking, it would immediately adjust to the long-term inflation rate: the short-run aggregate supply curve shifts at once to position AS', the transition bypasses point B, and the economy jumps directly from point A to point C. In that case, monetary neutrality occurs instantaneously, the dichotomy principle is verified at all times, and monetary policy loses its effectiveness. Two conditions are required for that to happen. First, underlying inflation must be entirely forward-looking. Second, price- and wage-setters must raise prices and wages to the full extent of the change in underlying inflation. The existence of either price or wage stickiness or of a backward component in underlying inflation is what makes the short run different from the long run.

In summary, an expansionary monetary policy —described here as an increase of the inflation rate target—raises output and inflation in the short run. In the long run, the effect falls entirely on higher inflation with no effect on output—this is the neutrality result under flexible exchange rates. In the short run, the backward-looking component of underlying inflation creates the non-neutrality needed for an output effect, while the forward-looking component tends to bring neutrality forwards to the shorter run. The role of underlying inflation receives closer scrutiny in Chapters 16 and 17.

13.4 How to Use the *AS–AD* Framework

This section demonstrates how the complete *AS–AD* framework is used to study real-life events and answer important macroeconomic questions. We proceed with three aims: (1) to illustrate the principles developed earlier, (2) to develop familiarity with the framework, and (3) to study and understand historical developments of general interest.

13.4.1 Lags

We start by briefly providing indications on the duration of the short, medium, and long runs, an issue already discussed in Chapter 1. Here we link this discussion with the *AS–AD* and *IS–TR–IFM* apparatus.

---

[15] Recall that PPP implies that $\Delta S/S = \pi^* - \pi$.

The short run corresponds to the Mundell–Fleming model, which is based on the Keynesian assumption of price stickiness. It lasts as long as the short-run *AS* curve remains roughly in place. It takes about one to two years for demand disturbances to affect output and about another year for inflation to fully react. When inflation triggers changes in the underlying rate of inflation, the *AS* curve starts shifting and we move to the medium run.

The long run is defined as the horizon over which the dichotomy asserts itself. This means that we look beyond the business cycle horizon. Although two business cycles are never alike, on average they last some five to six years.

It follows that the medium run lasts some three to four years. The medium run corresponds to the transition from the short to the long run. This is when the short-run *AS* curve begins to shift as the backward-looking component of underlying inflation starts catching up with actual inflation. The transition is shorter, the faster underlying inflation catches up. This depends therefore on the relative contributions of its backward- and forward-looking components. As previously noted, if the forward-looking component dominates, the short-run *AS* curve quickly reaches its final position—especially if prices and wages are not sticky. Wage and price **indexation** speeds up the transition. In countries where inflation is very high, formal or informal indexation schemes are usually in place and the long run occurs in the short run! We return to this important issue in the next section.

13.4.2 Supply Shocks

Supply shocks occur when production conditions are altered. Supply shocks come in all shapes and forms, but have the common feature that they invariably create difficulties for policy-makers who are ill-equipped to face the consequences. The reason is that the traditional demand-side policies are ineffective in this case, while supply-side policies are economically complex and often politically unappealing.

The simplest example of an adverse supply shock is the sudden loss of human or physical factors of production resulting from natural disasters or wars. This leads immediately to medium- or long-run loss

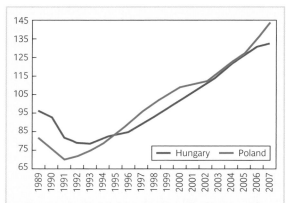

Fig. 13.14 GDP in Hungary and Poland, 1989–2007

GDP declined immediately after the collapse of central planning in 1990, but it subsequently recovered and followed a fairly dynamic growth trend.

Note: GDP indices, 100 = sample average.
Sources: Wyplosz (1999) and OECD.

of production potential. Another highly relevant example is the economic transition from central planning to a market economy in Eastern and Central Europe after 1989. As illustrated in Figure 13.14, real GDP declined for a few years and then started to rise at a fairly brisk pace. The initial decline, the supply shock, was mainly due to the disorganization that set in as markets did not yet function properly, while central planning had ceased to operate, and to the instantaneous obsolescence of the domestic production capacity once better foreign goods became available.

Supply shocks can be favourable as well, e.g. an acceleration of technological advances. The often-cited information technology revolution (described in Box 3.5) that started in the mid-1990s is a recent example. Previous major episodes include the invention of electric generation and transmission, automobiles, and plastics. The discovery of natural resources is also another instance of a favourable supply shock.

Oil shocks are the most conspicuous supply shock. Those of 1973 and 1979 represent major turning-points in the post-war economic history of Europe in the twentieth century. They marked the end of the rapid growth performance of most

Box 13.3 The Oil Shocks of the 1970s and 1980s

Major commodity prices started to rise in the early and late 1970s. While most of these increases were quickly reversed, nominal oil prices increased sixfold in two steps, with a partial reversal in 1986. The role of policy is highlighted by the choice of the exchange rate regime. At the time of the first shock, the industrial countries were trying to preserve a system of fixed exchange rates, including several European countries regrouped in the 'Snake' arrangement. Countries that were determined not to let inflation rise did not wish to maintain a fixed

exchange rate with a more complacent rest of the world. Some countries, including Austria, Germany, Switzerland, and the Netherlands, opted for the low inflation strategy. Japan, Italy, Spain, and the UK implicitly opted for the high-inflation approach. Most other European countries adopted an intermediate stance with little or no policy reaction. Along the way, the international monetary system based on fixed exchange rates could not accommodate such policy divergences and collapsed.

European countries, and were followed by markedly higher inflation and unemployment rates. Japan and the USA too were badly affected. Box 13.3 and Figure 13.15 show that, by the end of the 1980s, inflation had been rolled back, but in many countries employment and output growth have since remained significantly below the levels of the 1960s, the golden years. After a favourable counter-oil shock in the mid-1990s, oil prices started once again to rise sharply in 2000, again in 2003 in the wake of the Iraq war, and quadrupled over 2005–2008. The *AD–AS* model was developed largely in response to events of the 1970s, just as the *IS–LM* model was a response to the Great Depression.

A short-term policy dilemma

Supply shocks represent a shift of the aggregate supply curve. The increase in production costs is passed on by firms in the form of price increases at any given level of output. In Chapter 12, this was captured by the exogenous shock variable *s* in the aggregate supply equation:

(13.11) $\pi = \tilde{\pi} + a(Y - \bar{Y}) + s.$

When the shock is unfavourable, i.e. when $s > 0$, the short-run aggregate supply curve shifts upwards from *AS* to *AS'*, as shown in Figure 13.16. The move from point *A* to point *B* represents stagflation, a combination of declining real growth and rising inflation. If the relative price increase is a one-off event, the *AS* curve will shift back to its initial posi-

tion.[16] This is optimistic, however. While the economy is at point *B*, workers unexpectedly face higher prices. Quite likely, they will demand higher nominal wages and, if they succeed, the backward-looking component of underlying inflation rises. This is why, even after the commodity price increase has been absorbed (when *s* goes back to zero), the *AS* curve is unlikely to shift back quickly. The answer will depend on the behaviour of underlying inflation.

Stagflation constitutes a serious policy dilemma for governments. One approach is to soften the blow on output and unemployment by adopting an expansionary policy (monetary or fiscal, depending on the exchange rate regime). Aiming at point *C*, and shifting the aggregate demand curve to *AD'* in Figure 13.16, hastens the return to trend growth but at the cost of higher inflation. Another approach is to prevent inflation from ever rising so that underlying inflation never changes. This calls for a prompt *contractionary* policy reaction, shifting the short-run aggregate demand schedule back until it goes through a point like *D*. This reaction deepens

---

[16] A supply shock, such as a one-off increase in oil prices, directly affects the price level, not its rate of increase, unless these prices keep increasing again and again. Normally, once they have reached a new higher level, the impact is passed once into higher goods prices. While the level of these prices remains higher, inflation is no longer directly affected by the shock.

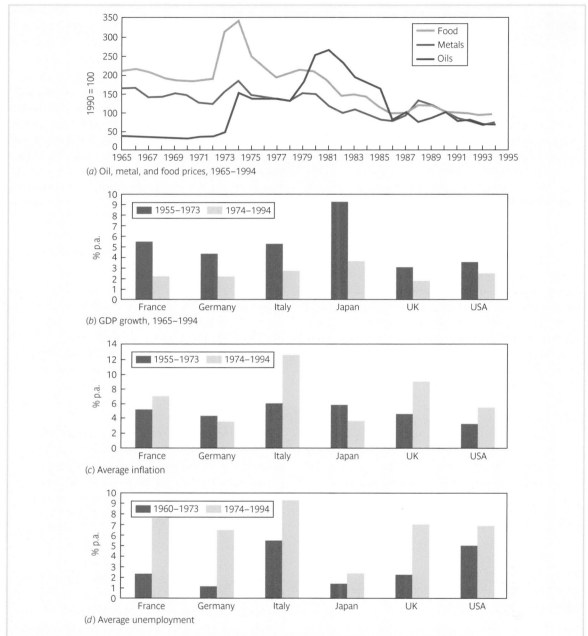

Fig. 13.15 The Oil Shocks: A Turning Point for Six Countries, pre- and post-1973

Panel (*a*) shows the prices of key commodities relative to the average consumer price index in the advanced economies. Real oil prices increased from 1973 until 1981, then declined significantly at the time of the counter-oil shock in 1986. Other commodity prices increased earlier, in 1971–1972, but were quickly reversed, and in fact declined over the following decade. Panels (*b*)–(*d*) confirm that, with few exceptions, since the first oil shock of 1973–1974 all key macroeconomic variables (growth, inflation, unemployment) have changed for the worse in OECD countries.

Sources: IMF; OECD, *Main Economic Indicators*.

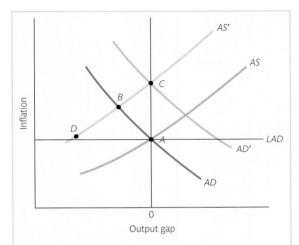

Fig. 13.16 An Adverse Supply Shock
An adverse supply shock shifts the AS curve up to AS'.
The economy will suffer stagflation as it moves from
point A to point B. If the authorities decide to avoid a
fall in output and a rise in unemployment, they can
adopt expansionary demand-side policies and move the
economy towards a long-run equilibrium at point C. This
would be achieved at the cost of a permanent increase
in the central bank's target rate of inflation. If, in
contrast, they choose to fight inflation, they can adopt
contractionary demand-side policies—a lower target
inflation rate—and aim at point D. Here the cost is a
deep recession.

ent, but what about the forward-looking component?
Much depends on which long-run equilibrium is
expected to be reached eventually. If the authorities
are known or are expected to aim at point D in
Figure 13.16, the forward-looking component is
likely to support this policy. If wage negotiators
are convinced that inflation will be kept under
control, they see the jump to point B as strictly
temporary and keep underlying inflation at the
pre-shock level. Once the shock is over, the aggregate
supply schedule promptly returns to AS and the
economy's trajectory will be from A to B and back
to A. If, instead, wage negotiators expect an accommodating policy that aims at point C, underlying
inflation will rise and shift the AS curve to AS', even
after the shock has passed. The trajectory will be
from A to B and beyond, higher and to the left of
B along the new AD' curve. However, since the output gap is negative, underlying inflation is above
actual inflation, so the AS curve will eventually start
shifting back towards AS', even though the one-off
supply shock is over. The economy winds up at
point C.

Under flexible exchange rates, it is the central
bank that determines the position of the LAD line. By
their choice of an inflation target, the monetary
authority can choose the long-run inflation rate and
decide whether point A or point C will be eventually
reached. This is not the case with a fixed exchange
rate regime where the position of the LAD line
depends on the 'foreign' inflation rate. In the presence of a severe supply shock, a fixed exchange rate
regime can be maintained only among like-minded
countries which have compatible views of how they
will react. In Europe, for instance, the oil shocks
of the 1970s and 1980s seriously strained the
European Monetary System as different countries
adopted different strategies. The adoption of a common currency, which floats freely, means that
this decision is now in the hands of the European Central Bank (ECB). While the old danger of
intra-European exchange rate turbulence is ruled
out by the euro, policy disagreements remain.
Following the rise of oil prices in 2003–2004, and
again in 2007–2008, the ECB has been criticized by
some governments as being too tight and by others
as being too lax.

the recession but, once the shock has worked itself
through (and s = 0), the aggregate supply curve
moves back to AS and the restrictive demand policy
may be lifted to return to point A. The nature of the
dilemma should be clear: the authorities can either
aim at maintaining output and employment, but at
the cost of higher inflation, or they can prevent a
sharp inflationary impact, but at the cost of a low output and high unemployment. The reason behind
this dilemma is also clear: macroeconomic management policies are demand-side policies and they are
ill-adapted to deal with supply shocks.

The exchange rate regime
The previous discussion makes it clear that a key
issue is how underlying inflation reacts after the
initial supply shock. Underlying inflation tends to
increase because of its backward-looking compon-

Lessons from supply shocks

Three general lessons can be drawn. First, a negative supply shock is bad news. It adversely affects growth, unemployment, and inflation at the same time, in contrast with the Phillips curve trade-off. Second, traditional demand management instruments are not appropriate for a supply shock. When the aggregate supply curve moves up and to the left, demand management cannot deal with both inflation and output. Demand-side policies must make the difficult choice between taking the shock as an increase in inflation or as a drop in output with higher unemployment. The appropriate response should be supply-side policies, aiming at bringing back the aggregate supply schedule as soon as possible to its initial position. This is not easy. The best hope is to shape the forward-looking component of underlying inflation and to try to 'disconnect' the backward-looking component. This requires a clear and credible signal from the authorities that they are determined not to accommodate the shock. Third, the exchange regime becomes crucial. A fixed exchange rate can be maintained only among countries that adopt the same strategy.

13.4.3 Demand Shocks

Exogenous shifts in demand are easier for policymakers to deal with. Most of these shocks are the result of macroeconomic policy actions, fiscal or monetary policy depending on the exchange rate regime. Other examples are exogenous events, like the sub-prime crisis of 2007–2008, which was followed by a worldwide slowdown. Yet another example is German reunification, the source of an unexpected demand surge during the first half of the 1990s.

In Figure 13.17, an adverse demand shock is represented by a leftward exogenous shift of the short-run aggregate demand curve from *AD* to *AD'*. The economy moves from point *A* to point *B*: inflation declines and output falls below its trend level. In principle, the government has the required instruments at its disposal—monetary or fiscal policy, depending on the exchange rate regime—that could restore the *AD* curve to its original position. In the 1960s, this was the standard policy response. Since the early 1990s, however, the reaction has been remarkably subdued in European countries.

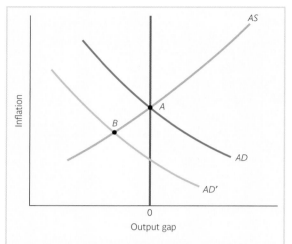

Fig. 13.17 An Adverse Demand Shock

An adverse demand shock is represented by a leftward exogenous shift of the short-run aggregate demand curve. The economy moves from point *A* to point *B*. In principle, the government has instruments at its disposal—monetary or fiscal policy, or both—which could restore the *AD* curve to its original position. This was the standard policy response of the 1960s. During the last two decades, however, European countries have relied less and less on such policy responses, choosing to sit out the temporary decline in aggregate demand and output depicted above.

There are different reasons for this reluctance. Many European economies had reacted to the initial oil shocks with accommodating policies—raising target inflation and allowing a temporary increase to become permanent. After a decade dedicated largely to erasing the scars from those oil shocks by bringing down underlying inflation, most countries were reluctant to give up those achievements again. This meant sticking to inflation targets and preventing monetary policy from becoming excessive again. Another policy achievement of the 1980s was the generally successful control over public indebtedness. Most governments felt that their budget constraint ruled out fiscal policy for offsetting a weakening of aggregate demand.[17] Finally, the

[17] Chapter 16 provides more details on governments' reluctance to use their demand management instruments. Chapter 17 studies the public debt as a limit on the government's freedom to manage aggregate demand.

Box 13.4 High-tech Bubble, 9/11, and the Sub-prime Crisis: Transatlantic Differences, 2000–2008

Stock markets all but crashed worldwide in mid-year 2000, a distant reminder of the Wall Street events that ushered in the Great Depression. Soon afterwards, growth started to stall around the world. Then came 11 September 2001 and the ensuing wars in Afghanistan and Iraq, which many feared would undermine confidence and lead households to save more and consume less and firms to cancel investment projects. The ball landed squarely in the court of policy-makers. How would they react in the face of a large negative demand shock?

The contrast between Europe and the USA is striking. Both the euro and the dollar float, so their central banks are free to use monetary policy if they choose. Figure 13.18 shows that the US Federal Reserve quickly lowered the interest rate and, when growth did not react, continued relentlessly, coming close to the lower bound of 0%. The European Central Bank moved more slowly and much less aggressively. At the same time, the US Federal Government adopted a very expansionary fiscal policy stance, bringing the budget from balance to a deficit of more than 5%. European governments, on the other hand, tried to contain their deficits. As a result, vigorous growth returned to the USA in 2003, while it remained sluggish in Europe. Much the same happened in 2007–2008 following the sub-prime crisis, which started in the USA and soon gripped financial markets in both the USA and Europe. The Federal Reserve acted decisively to reduce interest rates and increase liquidity in the money markets, while the US Government sent each US taxpayer a $600 cheque.[18] Meanwhile, seeing less immediate danger to internal demand, the ECB postponed planned increases in interest rates but did not lower them.

Why these differences? US policy-makers appear to harbour fewer qualms about macroeconomic demand management policies and feel free to move decisively. The European governments consider public debt to be too high and feel the need for restraint. What about the different reactions of the central banks, the Fed and the ECB? Recent research seems to indicate that both central banks follow similar Taylor rules. In that case, different reactions betray different economic conditions.

rational expectation hypothesis implies that policy effects are greatly reduced. While the hypothesis is not generally taken literally, many economists and policy-makers have endorsed the view that short-run macroeconomic policy is not very effective. They prefer to focus on the long run. Box 13.4 presents a striking contrast between the reactions of the European Central Bank and the Federal Reserve Board in the USA to the two great shocks of the first decade of the twenty-first century.

13.4.4 Disinflation

An important policy question faced by many developing countries is how to deal with a high rate of inflation. High and lasting inflation can only be the consequence of an excessively high rate of growth of the nominal money supply, so the cure must be to slow down money growth. How it is implemented very much depends on the exchange rate regime.

Under flexible exchange rates, the central bank can choose its inflation rate target, so the solution to high inflation is technically simple, but often very painful. Figure 13.19 shows why. We start from point A, which we take to be a long-run equilibrium. Thus we assume that the high inflation rate is indeed the central bank's target—we are on the LAD line—and that actual and underlying inflation are equal—we are on the LAS line. If the central bank exogenously reduces the target inflation rate well below the current rate of inflation, it must drastically raise nominal interest rates in the short run.[19] In the TR–IFM model (not shown), the TR curve shifts to the left, the nominal and real exchange rates appreciate, the current account worsens, and demand declines. This is captured by the leftward shift of the short-run aggregate demand curve from AD to AD′. The short-run effect of this disinflationary policy corresponds to point B: inflation declines

---

[18] Remember that the USA is not a small economy. This is one reason why fiscal policy may be effective, even though the US dollar is freely floating.

[19] To see this, consider the Taylor rule again and observe that a decrease in $\bar{\pi}$, holding all else equal, implies an *increase* in the nominal interest rate.

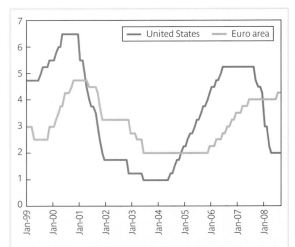

Fig. 13.18 Short-Term Interest Rates in the Euro Area and in the USA, January 1999–August 2008

When growth slowed in 2000 and again after the terrorist attacks in September 2001, the US Federal Reserve aggressively lowered its interest rates while the European Central Bank moved with considerable caution. The same development can be observed since the advent of the subprime crisis in mid-2007.

Source: IMF.

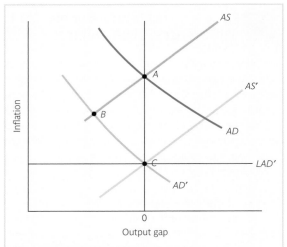

Fig. 13.19 Disinflation

Disinflation aims at bringing the economy from point *A* to point *C*. Using demand-side policies implies the use of contractionary monetary or fiscal policies which move the aggregate demand curve from *AD* to *AD′* and the *LAD* curve to *LAD′*. The short-run equilibrium at point *B* explains why disinflation is usually painful: it requires a period of low output and high unemployment. Long-run equilibrium is achieved at point *C* when the short-run aggregate supply curve has shifted to *AS′*. The speed of this shift depends on the time taken by underlying inflation to catch up with lower actual inflation.

but so does output, and unemployment rises. At point *B* actual inflation is below underlying inflation so the latter will be revised downwards and, over time, the short-run aggregate supply curve will shift downwards until it reaches the position *AS′*. At point *C*, a new long-run equilibrium is reached and the disinflation is complete. The cost has been a period of negative output gap and high unemployment, which may extend over several years as noted in Section 13.4.1.

Under a fixed and adjustable exchange rate regime, high and lasting inflation is only possible if the exchange rate is regularly depreciated, as explained in Section 13.2. Bringing inflation down requires a change in monetary policy. If the fixed exchange rate regime is to be retained, this means doing away with chronic depreciations. In that case, we know that the *LAD* line is set by the foreign inflation rate, so it is essential to peg the exchange rate to the currency of a country where inflation is suitably low. The peg becomes the anchor that will

deliver disinflation. Initially, inflation is higher at home than abroad. If inflation moves slowly, fixing the nominal exchange rate means that the real exchange rate appreciates as long as domestic exceeds foreign inflation. In the *IS–IMF* model (not shown), the *IS* curve shifts to the left. The resulting decline in aggregate demand is represented by the leftward shift of the short-run aggregate demand curve from *AD* to *AD′* in Figure 13.19. Then the logic is the same as under the flexible exchange rate regime. Underlying inflation must start declining in light of lower realized inflation rates and the economy will eventually settle at point *C* on the long-run aggregate demand *LAD′*, which corresponds to the lower foreign inflation rate. Here disinflation also requires a period of negative output gap and high unemployment.

The interesting questions are: how long does it take to move from point *B* to point *C* in Figure 13.19?

And how much output is lost along the way? The **output cost of disinflation** is lower the faster the *AS* curve comes down. That, in turn, depends on the speed at which underlying inflation adapts to a declining inflation rate. The backward component of underlying inflation slows down the speed at which the *AS* curve shifts, while the forward-looking component accelerates the adjustment. In periods of disinflation, therefore, it would be helpful to give more weight to the forward-looking component, possibly even shutting down the backward-looking component. The backward-looking component de-

pends on wage- and price-setting institutions, an issue examined in Box 13.5. The forward-looking component is often referred to as the 'psychological' nature of price- and wage-setting, but it can be influenced by policy institutions.

Wage negotiators may have opposing incentives in stating their expectations. It may be good bargaining tactics for workers to argue that inflation is high, while employers prefer to predict declines in the rate of inflation. Jointly, however, employers and employees have an incentive to be as close as possible to target, for errors may be costly in terms of

---

 Box 13.5 Wage Negotiations: The Time Dimension

In most European countries and in the USA, wage negotiations are *staggered* over a year or more. One wage negotiation takes the previous one into account, and may even anticipate the next one. Employees do not want to be out-done by their colleagues, and employers do not want the competition to undercut their labour costs. In contrast, in Japan wage negotiations are *synchronized*. They take place every year at roughly the same time, the so-called 'spring offensive' (*shunto*). Each industry opens up bargaining, but closely monitors the state of play elsewhere. When one bargain is struck, it sets the trend and all the others follow quickly. For a time, wage negotiations in Northern Europe were centralized and therefore highly synchronized. Even when they are staggered, some negotiations are *trend-setting*: they result in similar agreements later on and sometimes even trigger readjustments to previously reached ones, thus injecting a dose of synchronization. With wage staggering, aggregate nominal wages (the average of all nominal wages) move slowly, which retards the return to equilibrium unemployment. The *AS* curve will appear flatter. With full synchronization, average nominal wages are stable between negotiations, and then jump. This implies a steeper *AS* curve. The implications for the economy are profound. Either a quick return to the equilibrium unemployment rate if the real wages are set right, or a prolonged departure if they are set incorrectly.

The situation is different in economies where inflation is high and has been so for a long time. There it is common to have mandatory or mutually agreed indexa-

tion schemes for wages. Brazil was particularly advanced in this regard, indexing virtually *all* nominal prices, including house rents, corporate balance sheets, taxes, and public utilities rates. Such indexation schemes can often reduce the staggering considerably, with the same effect as an increase in synchronization of wage-setting.

Although wage indexation removes some of the costs of high inflation to households and firms, it has serious adverse side-effects. First, indexation generally perpetuates any real wage gain achieved. This gives an incentive to any group of wage-earners to be the first to bid for higher wages. The result is that all groups rush to be first, as much to protect themselves as to achieve a head start. Second, indexation reduces both public and government support for anti-inflation policies. This is why Germany, after its famous hyperinflation in the 1920s, made indexation illegal. Third, indexation makes disinflation costlier in terms of unemployment. When inflation is on the way up, nominal wages trail behind prices: real wages are reduced and labour demand is robust. When inflation is on the way down, wages indexed on past inflation trail actual inflation: real wages rise, firms' profits are squeezed, and unemployment rises. This is why most European countries with legal or simply widespread indexation clauses eliminated them in the 1980s, much against the will of trade unions. Fourth, indexation eliminates downward real wage flexibility as real wages are at least constant unless there is a sharp burst of inflation. The lack of flexibility is a source of unemployment when an adverse supply shock occurs.

competitiveness and profitability. As they aim at disinflation, the authorities have a strong interest in convincing wage negotiators that inflation will surely decline, since this will accelerate the downward movement of the *AS* curve. One solution is to credibly use the exchange rate as an anchor. To do so, the authorities must demonstrate that they will not let the exchange rate depreciate again. This is why a number of countries have adopted **hard pegs**, a variety of fixed exchange rate arrangements that makes it illegal to devalue.[20] If the exchange rate is not fixed, it is the credibility of the central bank as an inflation-fighter that becomes crucial. This is why a number of countries have given formal independence to their central banks, instructing them to aim at price stability. Many independent central banks have adopted the **inflation-targeting strategy** already described above, publicly announcing the inflation rate they intend to achieve and explicitly and publicly tying their actions to the target, and to the target only.

❗ Summary

1 The macroeconomy is analysed as the interplay of aggregate demand and aggregate supply. This framework emphasizes the distinction between the short run and the long run, when output returns to its trend growth path.

2 Under fixed exchange rates, inflation is restricted to be equal to foreign inflation in the long run. Under flexible rates, long-run inflation is determined by the target inflation rate.

3 The short-run aggregate demand curve is downward-sloping. Under fixed exchange rates, an increase in inflation above the foreign rate erodes external competitiveness and reduces demand for domestic goods. Under flexible exchange rates, an increase in the inflation rate relative to the central bank's inflation target prompts an increase in the interest rate. This in turn results in a nominal and real exchange appreciation with a contractionary effect on aggregate demand.

4 Only in the flexible rate regime can the monetary authority determine the long-run inflation rate. Under fixed exchange rates, some monetary independence is possible, but only by repeated devaluations or revaluations.

5 Under fixed exchange rates, fiscal policy can affect aggregate demand and output. The effects of a fiscal policy action are temporary, however. The change in spending or cut in taxes which leads to the shift in the *AD* curve cannot be sustained indefinitely. In the long run, the government's budget constraint prevents a permanently expansionary fiscal policy.

6 A fiscal expansion initially raises the output level at the cost of a higher rate of inflation. Over time, as underlying inflation rises and the unavoidable retrenchment of fiscal policy occurs, demand returns to trend output.

7 Under fixed exchange rates monetary policy is ineffective. This is also the case for fiscal policy under flexible exchange rates.

8 Under flexible exchange rates, a monetary policy expansion—the consequence of an increase in the central bank's target inflation—initially raises output and inflation. Over time, inflation continues to increase, ultimately sowing the seeds of the next recession, as the central bank is forced to raise interest rates and return output back to its trend growth path.

9 An adverse supply shock simultaneously lowers output and raises inflation. Demand manage-

[20] This is the strategy adopted, for example, by Argentina in 2001 and by Bulgaria in 1997. In both cases, it worked, although Argentina's arrangement collapsed in 2001. By then, however, inflation had turned negative!

ment policies are ill-equipped to deal with a supply shock. They may cushion the fall in income at the cost of more inflation, or reduce the inflationary impact at the cost of a deeper fall in output and more unemployment.

10 Disinflation requires a permanent reduction in the target inflation rate when the exchange rate is floating or sticking to the peg under a fixed exchange rate regime. It can be costly in terms of lost output and above-equilibrium unemployment.

11 The faster underlying inflation adjusts, the lower the costs of disinflation. This calls for adopting credible institutions that can convince wage negotiators that the disinflation policy is 'serious'.

🔑 Key Concepts

- ◆ purchasing power parity
- ◆ *LAD* line
- ◆ short-run versus long-run general equilibrium
- ◆ aggregate demand curve
- ◆ demand disturbance
- ◆ stagflation

- ◆ Fisher equation, Fisher principle
- ◆ output cost of disinflation
- ◆ hard pegs
- ◆ inflation-targeting strategy
- ◆ indexation

❓ Exercises

1 Use the *AD–AS* model to trace out the *short-run* effect under both fixed and flexible rate regimes of: (1) a one-off increase in government spending; (2) a permanent increase in the inflation target of the central bank.

2 Consider the *AD–AS* model where the initial situation is not a long-run equilibrium, for instance where the economy starts with a negative output gap. What happens next without any government intervention under fixed exchange rates? Under flexible exchange rates?

3 If supply shocks predominate, what can you predict about the correlation between inflation and the output gap? If demand shocks are more important? Under which conditions would you expect to observe a Phillips curve?

4 Use the *AD–AS* and *IS–TR–BP* frameworks to study the short- and long-run effects of an increase in foreign inflation under a fixed exchange rate regime.

5 Under fixed exchange rates, use the *IS–TR–BP* and *AD–AS* models to analyse the effects of a combined tight fiscal policy and expansionary monetary policy.

6 Under flexible exchange rates, use the *IS–TR–BP* and *AD–AS* models to analyse the effects of an expansionary fiscal policy and tight monetary policy.

7 What are the effects of a positive supply shock, such as a sudden decline in oil prices?

8 A government wants to use monetary policy under a flexible exchange rate to keep actual

GDP above its trend growth rate for ever. In the *AS–AD* diagram, show graphically the consequences of such a policy.

9 Assume that underlying inflation is entirely forward-looking and that expectations are rational. What are the effects of fiscal policy (under fixed exchange rates) and monetary policy (under flexible exchange rates) on output and inflation? Consider both cases of expansionary or restrictive policies.

10 Central banks that adopt the inflation-targeting strategy usually publish their expectations future inflation, thus implicitly or explicitly signalling what they plan to do in the future. It is argued that being able to convince the public of their intentions greatly enhances the effectiveness of central bank actions. Use the *AD–AS* framework to explain why?

11 Show under what condition does the Taylor rule (13.9) imply that an increase in inflation leads to a higher *ex post* real interest rate, defined as $i - \pi$. Is this a desirable feature of the rule? Why or why not?

→ Essay Questions

1 'Expansionary policies rely upon fooling people.' Comment.

2 Why does adding the supply side partly undermine the usefulness of demand management policies?

3 Why are supply-side policies more appealing than demand-side policies. What kind of policies can you imagine which might stimulate the supply side of the economy?

4 'Sluggish expectations are helpful when inflation is rising but troublesome when inflation is declining.' Evaluate this assertion and name possible policy implications.

5 Suppose you are in charge of monetary policy in a developing country and the price of primary commodities (food, oil) rises sharply, as it has in the past year. What will be the consequence of pursuing a flexible exchange rate regime with a fixed target rate of inflation? Are there disadvantages of following a fixed exchange rate regime?

Asset Markets 14

Every great crisis reveals the excessive speculations of many houses which no one before suspected, and which commonly indeed had not begun or had not carried very far those speculations, till they were tempted by the daily rise of price and the surrounding fever.

Walter Bagehot

History demonstrates that participants in financial markets are susceptible to waves of optimism. Excessive optimism sows the seeds of its own reversal in the form of imbalances that tend to grow over time.

Alan Greenspan

14.1 Overview

From Tobin's q to interest and exchange rates, we have encountered many prices which are determined in financial markets. Financial markets profoundly influence the macroeconomy. They affect wealth and spending, the cost of borrowing and investments, and the exchange rate, which lies at the heart of international trade and financial flows. Prices determined in financial markets share a number of unique features. They determine the value of **assets**—the various forms in which wealth is held. They are set in markets which are quite different from goods markets, not only because they are impersonal—transactions are almost never face to face—but also because they move around a great deal. We say that asset prices exhibit a high degree of volatility. They often appear driven by the whims of traders whose preoccupation is with very short-term gains, without much apparent concern for the impact of their actions. We often read and hear about speculators who seem to gamble in these markets, casino-style, make a lot of money and occasionally run the economy into the ground.

We will examine this possibility, although the story is much more complex.

An especially distinctive feature of assets is that they are durable. They are not consumed, but stored for later disposal. Their value is not in today's use, but in their resale price. For this reason, they are driven entirely by the future. Almost by definition, the future is uncertain, so assets are almost always risky. Another fairly general characteristic of assets is that they tend to be traded in large markets.

In this chapter, we offer a unified treatment of asset prices and markets. We start by describing asset markets and explaining some of their key features. They are big because they deal in stocks, not flows. They are fast-moving because profit opportunities are huge, but dissipate in seconds. They put a price tag on uncertainty—a special but essential economic factor. We then look at the asset prices encountered in many of the earlier chapters: **bond** prices, interest rates, stocks. We explore why markets sometimes embark on apparently senseless behaviour, producing successive phases of exuberance and bust.

14.2 How Asset Markets Work

14.2.1 Unique Characteristics of Financial Markets

There are many asset markets—money markets, stock markets, bond markets, commodity mar-

kets, foreign exchange markets, derivative markets, and more—but they share a number of unique characteristics.

First, unlike goods and services which are bought for consumption and often perishable (fruits and vegetables don't last long, cars and computers get outdated, and services are consumed while they are being produced), assets are durable. This distinguishing characteristic, plus the fact that they can be held with negligible storage costs, are two reasons why financial assets are a natural vehicle for saving for future consumption—just as Robinson Crusoe did in Chapters 7 and 8. They can be bought now and sold later, either when the time comes to use savings for consumption or when they are exchanged against other assets to cash in profit or avoid a loss.

Second, in contrast with markets which trade in *flows* of goods or services, asset markets are markets for *stocks*. Consider Table 14.1, which displays the total value of **shares** (called capitalization) listed on five large stock exchanges (New York Stock Exchange, London Stock Exchange, the Deutsche Börse, Euronext which brings together Amsterdam, Brussels and Paris, and Zurich) and the total value of trades during one month. The last column reports the average volume of daily transactions during that month as a percentage of the corresponding market capitalization. On any given day, it is usually only a tiny fraction of existing assets that are bought and sold; the rest is simply held.

Yet, at any moment, all the assets can be dumped on the market if the owners so desire. Normal days are the rule, but there can be hectic days when market participants become concerned, or indeed panic, and trading can be multiplied several times over the usual level. This explains the size and potential volatility of financial markets. Once you note that, for instance, the capitalization of the London Stock Exchange amounts to about 125% of British GDP, you can see that turmoil in financial markets is bound to affect the economy.

Third, financial markets are typically well-organized trading systems dealing in standardized assets that can be traded in large quantities with ease. In earlier times, the markets brought together market participants in a trading hall, or exchange. The action was dominated by shouting, gesticulating traders wading through seas of hastily scribbled papers. Today, most markets are computerized, and market participants are linked through telecommunication lines from terminal screens virtually anywhere in the world. The internet has created a single, global market in stocks and other financial instruments, with traders constantly in touch with each other. As Figure 14.1 shows, at any moment in time, 24 hours a day, a financial market is open somewhere in the world, and any individual in the world with access to a telephone or an internet connection may trade on it. This is perfect competition!

14.2.2 Implications: Inherent Potential Instability

These characteristics require that the usual demand and supply analysis be adapted in two ways. First, looking at the flow of transactions can be misleading. The annual supply of savings by households represents a mere flow increment to their stock of wealth. Newly created assets—from newly printed money to new shares of a company—are indistinguishable from existing ones and, at any moment, trading involves both new and old assets. At any time holders of assets can decide to sell their holdings, or buyers can emerge interested in acquiring the whole existing stock. This is why the market for assets is very different from the market for goods. In the goods market, it is demand for and supply of flows that must be balanced. In asset markets, prices move to clear the demand for and supply of the whole stock. Only a small part of the stock is traded because most owners keep what they have; their very inactivity is, in fact, a market decision.

Table 14.1 Stock Market Capitalization and Trading, January 2008 (billions of local currency)

	Total value of shares	Monthly trading	Average daily trading/total value
London	£1,765	£361	0.9%
New York	$14,611	$3,439	1.1%
Frankfurt	€1,254	€361	1.3%
Euronext	€2,515	€373	0.7%
Zurich	SFr. 1,305	SFr. 207	0.7%

Source: World Federation of Exchanges.

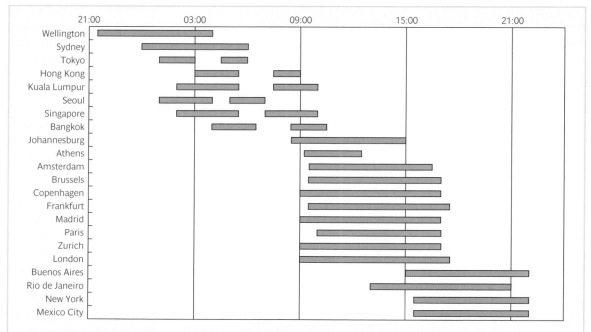

Fig. 14.1 Trading Hours of Stock Markets Around the World, Greenwich Mean Time

Stock markets are located around the world. As the world turns, some market somewhere is open, processing new information and pricing assets accordingly.

Source: Deutsche Börse.

Second, durability means that a key concern of market participants is the future value of each asset that they hold. After all, in contrast to non-durable goods that are promptly consumed, assets are acquired for keeps, not for immediate enjoyment. Two implications follow. To start with, asset markets are necessarily forward-looking. Market participant decisions are driven by their expectations of what can happen next—in five minutes or in five years. Then, since the future is unknown, financial markets and their participants constantly face considerable uncertainty. Unsurprisingly, they are jittery and sometimes tend to pay close attention to what others are doing. The reason is that no one has all the information and yet it is likely that someone does possess useful information. One of the greatest challenges of trading on the stock markets is inferring what other traders know—or think they know—and of that, what represents the truth. In a matter of minutes, changing expectations, or mere rumours, can radically alter demand and supply, swelling the volume of trade, or drying up markets. Prices, which equate demand and supply on a second-by-second basis, can therefore swing widely. This reasoning applies not just to strictly defined assets (stocks, bonds) but to any durable object that can be (relatively) easily stored and sold—artwork, commodities, or contracts for the future delivery of goods which may not yet exist (such as oil, electricity, wheat, or pork bellies). In fact, all these durable goods are traded on markets (oil in Rotterdam, wheat and pork bellies in Chicago) which closely resemble those for financial assets.

14.3 Functions of Asset Markets

The intense activity associated with asset markets, combined with the often phenomenal profits of market participants, can create the impression that financial markets are giant casinos with little economic purpose. Far from it. Asset markets are useful places for a number of reasons (which were already alluded to in Chapters 7 and 8). Markets for financial assets perform three essential economic functions. The first is to bring together borrowers and lenders. The second is to put a price on the future. The third is to create a market for risk by putting a price on uncertainty and enabling participants to control the risk they are exposed to. We now look at these functions in more detail.

14.3.1 Intermediation

Most importantly, asset markets, and more generally financial markets, are the meeting place for millions of households and firms who want to shift resources intertemporally—either saving or borrowing—or intratemporally—from one form of asset or liability to another. But most individuals do not deal directly on asset markets. This is not only because the quantities they desire to trade are small, but also because transacting in asset markets requires a great deal of expertise. To avoid these problems, they can act indirectly through **financial intermediaries**. Financial intermediaries channel resources from savers to borrowers and investors.

Like money, financial intermediaries divorce the act of saving (deferred consumption) from the act of investment (the creation of physical productive capacity). As a result, dealings in asset markets tend to resemble wholesale markets involving professional traders, who accept and execute large orders on the basis of mutual trust and charge each other relatively small fees. On foreign exchange markets, an average trade is in the order of €5 million; converting this sum from pounds sterling to euros and back again involves a transaction cost of around 0.05% or about €2,500. Similar fees are charged for large transactions involving stocks or bonds. In return for a fee, intermediaries place orders for several smaller customers at once, or may even 'make a market' by maintaining a large inventory which they can sell from or add to. In this way, intermediaries themselves become asset-holders.

14.3.2 The Price of Time

The price of the future—or the rewards for waiting—is the interest paid by borrowers, as explained in Chapter 7. By setting interest rates, financial markets price the future. Bonds, which are loan contracts, represent fixed payment streams in the future. The price of these payment streams defines the relevant interest rate. Shares, which are a partial ownership of companies, promise dividend payments over the lifetime of the companies. We will see later how share prices are related to interest rates.

As financial markets bring together borrowers and lenders, they determine the price of time by setting interest rates. Market interest rates are the result of bringing together the demand for assets by lenders with the willingness of borrowers to trade repayment later for cash now. In that sense, market rates reflect the overall impatience of borrowers and lenders.

In Chapter 9, we saw that the central bank determines the short-term nominal interest rate—usually for overnight loans, but sometimes for up to three months—by altering the supply of liquidity to the economy. At very short maturities,[1] the central bank has the monopoly of providing loans, so it can choose any interest rate that it wishes. Since it does so with macroeconomic objectives, very short maturities do not reflect the cost of time. How, then, can markets price the cost of waiting if the central bank sets the short-term rates?

---

[1] The maturity of an asset is the time left before it expires. For example, a bond that will be reimbursed in one year has a maturity of one year. A share, which will exist as long as the corresponding corporation operates, has no fixed maturity.

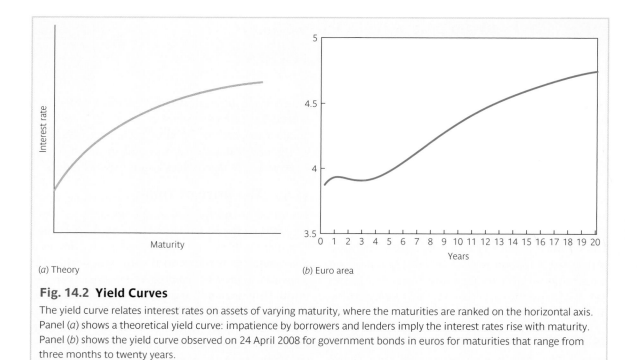

(a) Theory   (b) Euro area

Fig. 14.2 Yield Curves

The yield curve relates interest rates on assets of varying maturity, where the maturities are ranked on the horizontal axis. Panel (a) shows a theoretical yield curve: impatience by borrowers and lenders imply the interest rates rise with maturity. Panel (b) shows the yield curve observed on 24 April 2008 for government bonds in euros for maturities that range from three months to twenty years.

Source: European Central Bank.

Since the central bank stays out of the market for long-term assets, the demand and supply of assets reflect the preferences of borrowers and lenders. The link with the short term is captured by the **yield curve**, which shows how the interest rates vary according to maturity. The left-hand chart in Figure 14.2 shows a theoretical yield curve whose characteristic is that interest rates rise as the maturity increases. One reason is that uncertainty rises as the time horizon lengthens, an issue that is examined in Section 14.3.3. The other reason is impatience. For the lender, a longer maturity means that it will take more time to recover the money; it makes sense to ask for a higher interest rate. The borrower is willing to pay such a **maturity premium** because the funds will remain longer at her disposal. Quite naturally, the premium increases with the maturity, all other things being equal.

The right-hand side of Figure 14.2 shows an actual curve. It corresponds to very safe bonds, those issued by governments with good reputations as

borrowers.[2] The curve does not conform exactly to the one displayed in panel (a). The reason is interesting. We already noted that the very short-term interest rates are set by the central bank. Over the years to come, the central bank will probably be led to change these rates. Its expected decisions affect the shape of the yield curve. This is because a two-year loan can be arranged in a number of ways: one loan of two years' maturity, or two successive one-year loans 'rolled over' from one year, or a series of 24 one-month loans, etc. Because borrowers and lenders can choose any of these combinations, it stands to reason that they must be equivalent: they must impose the same cost to the borrower and the same reward to the lender. If this were not the case—let us suppose that a two-year loan carries a lower interest rate than two successive one-year

---

[2] Reputation here corresponds to the expectation that the government will indeed pay back its debt on time, or pay it back at all.

Box 14.1 The Term Structure of Interest Rates[3]

Consider a long-term interest rate of L years' maturity. Interest rates are generally quoted in annualized form, i.e. the interest rate paid each year. If the annual interest rate on the long-term loan is i^L, the total return is $(1 + i^L)^L$ because the interest is compounded over L years. If the one-year interest rate expected to prevail t years from now is i_t^e, where the superscript e denotes an expectation, the return from a succession of L annual loans is $(1 + i_1)(1 + i_2^e) \ldots (1 + i_t^e) \ldots (1 + i_L^e)$. The no-profit condition implies that these returns should be equal:

$$(1 + i^L)^L = (1 + i_1)(1 + i_2^e) \ldots (1 + i_t^e) \ldots (1 + i_L^e).$$

As a first approximation, this equality states that the long rate at time t, i_t^L, is an average of expected future short rates (possibly plus a risk premium Ψ_t^L as explained in Section 14.3.4):

$$i_t^L = \frac{1}{L} \sum_{i=1}^{L} i_{t+i}^L + \Psi_t^L,$$

which is obtained by taking logarithms and using the approximation $\log(1 + x) = x$.

loans—then no lender would be willing to lend for two years and no borrower would be willing to borrow twice for two successive years. In fact, clever financiers would borrow for two years, lend twice consecutively for one year and make a handsome profit. As many of them rush to take advantage of this opportunity, brisk demand for two-year loans drives the corresponding interest rate up as much as the rising supply of consecutive one-year loans drives the corresponding interest rates down. In the end, the two strategies will indeed imply the same lending cost and the market will be in equilibrium.

This example illustrates a basic rule of financial markets: obvious profit opportunities are quickly, if not immediately, eliminated by the market. We will encounter this **no-profit rule**, as it is called, at many places in this chapter. It implies that equivalent financial operations carry the same interest rate. The reasoning applies to all maturities. Box 14.1 formally shows that long-term interest rates can be seen as averages of the current and expected future short-term rates.

We can now see why the actual yield curve shown in Figure 14.2(b) differs from the theoretical one. We first need to realize that the theoretical curve is drawn under the assumption that the central bank will keep its current short-term rate unchanged. The slope of the curve then represents the maturity premium—later we will see that it also includes the price of risk. Then we can deal with other assump-

tions about what the central bank will decide. If, for instance, the financial markets believe that the central bank will reduce its short-term interest rate over the next two or three years, this will tend to reduce the long-term rates at the corresponding maturity. In other words, while the maturity premium implies that the yield curve is upward-sloping, expectations of declining short-term rates imply that the yield curve is downward-sloping. The outcome depends on the relative strengths of these two effects. Figure 14.2(b) shows an instance when, over a two to three year horizon, expectations of lower short-term rates more than fully offset the risk premium.

14.3.3 Allocation of Risk

Assets are inherently risky because they are held for future sale. Borrowers can default—totally or partially—on bonds, and dividends depend on firms' profitability, and firms can even go bankrupt. Asset-holders therefore look for ways to reduce their exposure to risk. They are willing to accept some risk in exchange for better returns, but to some degree only, and they wish to protect themselves from catastrophic events, such as a collapse of prices. Not all asset-holders are equally **risk averse**, and their horizons also differ. This leads us to another function of financial markets: to price risk and allocate it to those who are most willing to bear it.

Just as it is possible to protect ourselves against the costs of car accidents, fire, unemployment, and death by purchasing insurance, it is possible to use

---

[3] This box is for mathematically-minded readers.

asset markets to insure against financial uncertainty. This is done through **diversification**, the holding of a mix of several different assets. Box 14.2 explains how diversification works. In fact, many financial firms offer diversification to their customers by proposing ready-made funds, a mix of well-chosen risky assets. They can vary the riskiness of these portfolios and accommodate the different tastes of their customers. 'Funds of funds' have also been proposed to achieve further diversification.

14.3.4 The Price of Risk

Risk can be reduced, but cannot be fully eliminated. Someone must be willing to bear some risk. The way to convince people to bear risk is to compensate them for it. This compensation is called a **risk**

 Box 14.2 **Risk Diversification**

'Don't put all your eggs in one basket' is folk wisdom. The principle is remarkably simple: if you pool many risky outcomes, the result can be much less risky than any of the outcomes taken individually. Under some conditions, averaging mightily removes variability. To see how this is done, consider the following, simple example with five assets.

Assets A and B are based on independent flips of a coin. In either case, 'heads' means receiving €100, 'tails' means receiving nothing. On average, if repeated many times, both A and B yield €50. We say that each has an *expected value* of €50.

Asset C mixes assets A and B, and is simply one-half of A plus one-half of B. The expected value of C is also €50.

Asset D also combines A and B in equal fractions like C but the returns are now decided by a single coin flip: 'heads' means A pays €100 and B nothing, while 'tails' means A pays nothing and B delivers €100. Asset D pays €50 in *all* cases.

Asset E is also based on a single flip of a coin but now both A and B yield €100 if it is 'heads' and both yield nothing if it is 'tails'. Its expected value is €50, since it yields €100 half of the time and €0 in the other half.

All five assets described above have an expected return of €50, but they are very different as far as their *variability* is concerned. A and B pay €100 with a probability of 50% and nothing with the same probability. The returns from asset C are less variable. To see this, list the four possible outcomes:

A = heads/B = heads, which pays €100,
A = heads/B = tails and A = tails/B = heads, which each pays €50,
and A = tails/B = tails, which pays nothing.

Like assets A and B, asset C offers extreme returns of €100 or nothing, but each with only one chance in four; C further pays out €50 with a probability of 50% with A and B.

Asset C is less risky because it diversifies the risks attached to A and B by combining them. Since the returns from A and B are decided by different flips of a coin, they are independent events. In the language of statistics, we say that they are uncorrelated. More diversification is achieved with asset D because A and B always move in opposite directions; their payoff is determined by the same coin toss. In fact, we say they are perfectly negatively correlated since either A or B always pays €100 and the other pays nothing. In this case, diversification has completely eliminated risk. This is a special case of the general proposition that pooling assets is a way to reduce riskiness. This is what diversification is all about.

Finally, consider asset E. A single flip of a coin determines that both A and B either yield €100 or nothing. This is a case of perfectly positive correlation. The composite asset E does not reduce risk at all. It offers exactly the same yields as A and B taken separately. Perfectly positive correlation prevents risk diversification.

Financial markets are at their best when they pool assets which are negatively correlated. Diversification can reduce risk in investors' portfolios, but it cannot eliminate it (unless the risks are perfectly negatively correlated, which occurs extremely rarely). If much of the risk is macroeconomic (business cycles, policy actions), risk cannot be diversified much. Foreign assets, however, are likely to have different risk characteristics. This creates a strong incentive to pool markets across national borders, the key reason for the existence of globalized financial markets.

Box 14.3 **The Price of Risk**

Return to the first example of Box 14.2. Investments A and B have the same expected value, €50. How much would you be willing to pay to acquire either investment? Most people are risk averse, and they would rather get €50 for sure than buy a risky investment with the same expected value. (Those who don't care and would pay €50 are said to be risk neutral; risk lovers would pay even more than €50 for the thrill.) If you are willing to pay, say, €48 for A, the risk premium is €2 or 4% of the risk-free price. If total demand and supply of that asset are equated at €48, then the risk premium represents the market price of risk. Since B has the same characteristics, it should also be priced at €48.

What about investment C? It has the same expected value as A and B, but it is less risky. An investor would be willing to pay more for investment C than for either A or B. If the market price is, say, €49, the risk premium on the new asset is only €1 or 2%. Note that diversification not only reduces risk, it also reduces the market price of risk. Facing less risk for the same return, investors will prefer the new asset.[4] The issuers (sellers) of the assets A and B are also happy, as they pay a lower risk premium. This is how diversification is an efficient way of spreading the risks of individual assets in the market.

Now consider investment D of Box 14.2, when a single flip of a coin produces two opposite investments A and B. Since this composite investment is riskless, it should sell for €50, with no risk premium. This asset diversifies all the risk away, which benefits both the sellers and the buyers of investments A and B. The last investment E makes A and B perfectly positively correlated, there is no diversification at all. Composite asset E should sell for €48, with the same risk premium as for A and B.

Finally, for a more realistic example, suppose that you pay now, but the coin is flipped only in a year's time. Above and beyond the risky gamble, any investor will expect to receive interest for the time the money was tied up in the investment. Compensation for risk in this case can be expressed as a premium added to the risk-free interest rate available on, say, a government bond. Suppose that, as before, the 'investment' has an expected value of €50 and the market currently prices it at €46 *today*. Suppose, further, that the risk-free rate is 3%. Then the risk premium can be computed as 5.7% (the total expected rate of return ((€50 − 46)/€46 = 0.08696 = 8.7%) minus the risk-free rate (3%)).

premium. It means that the rate of return, or the total payouts of an asset divided by its price, increases with the riskiness of assets. Box 14.3 describes how and why.

Both borrowers and lenders benefit from the existence of financial markets. Taken in isolation, each investment is risky and would have to pay a high yield to attract wary savers. Enter the picture financial intermediaries, banks, and other specialized institutions, which pool these individual risks by offering homemade funds to savers. The borrowers pay lower risk premiums, the lenders bear less risk, and the intermediaries collect a fee. Because

diversification tends to be more complete when more assets are involved, the best services tend to be offered by the major financial centres dealing in stocks of companies from all over the world. This is precisely why asset trading tends to concentrate in few places and also why worldwide electronic trading is growing so fast. Stock market trading volume, or turnover, is often mind-boggling for the average citizen, which leads to a frequent misperception of financial markets as a sophisticated version of Las Vegas. Yet concentration and volume is the consequence of the endless search for diversification to the benefit of all, whether they are lenders or borrowers, and whether they are large or small.

The existence of a risk premium is another reason why the yield curve tends to be upward-sloping. We have seen in Section 14.3.2 that the maturity premium rises with maturity to reflect the impatience of both borrowers and lenders. We just saw that,

---

[4] The usual measure of riskiness of investments is the standard deviation. In the cases of A and B, the standard deviation of the return is 50; in the case of C, it is about 35. For risk-averse investors, C dominates A and B and the price of the latter two will decline to remain attractive to buyers.

since any lending is risky, the interest rate also includes a risk premium. It seems reasonable to consider that, at least during normal times, uncertainty grows the further we look into the future. Everything else being the same, a lender is likely to ask for a higher premium when she parts from her money for a longer time. It follows that the risk premium too rises with maturity.

14.4 Asset Prices and Yields

So far, we have looked at assets as serving interest. Being constantly bought and sold, assets have prices attached to each of them. This section explains the link between prices and yields.

14.4.1 Bond Prices

Much lending is carried out by banks for their customers. These loans, the banks' assets, are usually not traded, although Box 14.4 will show that this is increasingly the case. Other types of loan are undertaken by large borrowers—governments and large firms—that bypass banks and go directly to the financial markets. In that case, they take the form of bonds, i.e. recognition of debt by the borrower along with a schedule of payments concerning both interest and the principal. Once issued, these bonds are traded, at a price that ultimately determines their **yield**, or rate of return on an asset based on the purchase price of that asset.

Buying a bond gives the holder the right to receive all the interest payments initially promised as well as repayment of the principal—the amount initially borrowed—when the bond reaches maturity. The no-profit rule implies that, at any moment of time, a bond price must represent the value of all the payments agreed upon at the time when the bond was issued. Since these payments will be spread over time, impatience—and risk when there is some—must be taken into account. This gives rise to **discounting**, an evaluation procedure already seen in Chapter 7.

A few examples are presented in Table 14.2. We first look at how the price P depends on the yield i. Bond A is the simplest case of a bond of one-year maturity with face value of €10,000, i.e. the bondholder will received €10,000 in one year. An investor can either buy the bond at price P and receive €10,000 in one year or lend the same amount directly and receive in one year's time the principal P and interest iP (the interest rate i is applied to the total amount lent P), hence a total of $(1 + i)P$. Thus, in both cases, the investor initially spends P. In the case of acquiring the bond she will cash in €10,000, and in the case of the loan she will receive $(1 + i)P$. The no-profit rule means that both investments should be equivalent, i.e. the price P must be such that $(1 + i)P = €10,000$. The price must therefore be $P = €10,000/(1 + i)$. More generally, if V is the face value, the price of a safe

Table 14.2 **Bond Prices and Yields for a Face Value of €1**

Description of the payment stream	Price in euros given yield i	Yield given price P
A. One-year pure discount bond paying 1 euro	$1/(1 + i)$	$1/P - 1$
B. Two-year pure discount paying 1 euro in 2nd year	$1/(1 + i)^2$	$1/P^{1/2} - 1$
C. Ten-year discount bond paying 1 euro in 10th year	$1/(1 + i)^{10}$	$1/P^{1/10} - 1$
D. Consol paying 1 euro per annum, forever	$1/i$	$1/P$

one-year bond must be $P = V/(1 + i)$. This is a general expression of the principle of discounting first introduced in Chapter 7: the present value of a payment stream is simply the equivalent value which, when invested at rate i, produces that payment stream.

Table 14.2 shows a few other examples of more complicated bonds, involving periodic payments over the term of the bond (called coupons) and longer maturities. The computations are more complicated too, of course. The last example D is the 'ultimate bond' or **consol**: it exists forever—its maturity is infinite. Such a bond is also called a **perpetuity**. Each year, for infinity, the bondholder receives a coupon C, and the principal will be repaid in infinite time, which means never really. Someone who pays P for such a consol has the option of giving P to a borrower and asking indefinite payments that correspond to the prevailing interest rate i, i.e. iP each year. The no-profit rule implies that the two loans be identical so we have $C = iP$. Thus $P = C/i$ must be the price of the consol.[5] We see that the price of a bond is directly related to the interest rate. Roughly, as the consol example shows, a higher interest rate means a lower bond price.

Investors who can buy a bond with face value V at price P naturally want to know what return they will get. All they need to do is to invert the relevant formula. This is done in the last column of Table 14.2. For example, a one-year bond with face value F that sells for price P implies a rate of return $i = (F/P) - 1$. Quite sensibly, the return is larger the higher is the face value relative to the acquisition price.

14.4.2 Stock Prices

Shares in firms, or stocks as they are also called, are held by households or their intermediaries. For firms, it is an alternative way of raising money. Instead of borrowing, they 'sell a piece of themselves'. Lending to firms is already risky because firms can sometimes go bankrupt. Stocks are even riskier because, in contrast to bonds that regularly serve a predetermined interest, shareholders are paid according to profits and only after firms have covered their costs, including interest on bonds and loans.

How are stocks valued? Once again, we make use of the no-profit condition. In contrast to what precedes, we will now reason in real terms because we wish to focus on the real value of shares. A share in a company gives rise to the payment of dividends, a portion of profits (in real terms). Let us denote by d_t the dividends paid at the end of period t. The alternative to buying a share is to hold a riskless bond with a real yield r, which we assume constant. The shareholder does not just receive dividends, however. The value of the share that she holds can increase or decrease, which means capital gains when the share price rises, or losses when the share price declines. If q_t is the real share price at the beginning of period t, the rate of return on the company share is the dividend yield, d_t/q_t, plus the anticipated capital gain, $(q_{t+1} - q_t)/q_t$ (a gain if $q_{t+1} > q_t$, a loss if $q_{t+1} < q_t$), valued as a proportion of the share value. The no-profit condition implies that both assets have the same yield over period t:

$$\textbf{(14.1)} \qquad \underset{\text{yield on safe bond}}{r} \quad = \quad \underset{=\ \text{dividend yield}}{d_t/q_t} \quad \underset{+\ \text{capital gain.}}{+ (q_{t+1} - q_t)/q_t}$$

$$\underbrace{\phantom{d_t/q_t + (q_{t+1} - q_t)/q_t}}_{\text{total return on shares}}$$

This condition can be transformed into

$$\textbf{(14.2)} \qquad q_t = \frac{d_t + q_{t+1}}{1 + r}.$$

Today's stock price q_t is equal to the present discounted value of the dividend to be paid at the end of the period plus next period's price q_{t+1}. A very important aspect of this result is that today's share price depends entirely on the future: future dividends and the future share price. As already noted in Section 14.2, expectations—q_{t+1} is not known today—of the future price drive today's stock price.

---

[5] This result can be shown differently. Receiving C in one year's time is like bond A, so its value today is $C/(1 + i)$. Receiving C in two years' time is worth $C/(1 + i)^2$ today. More generally, receiving C in n years' time is worth $C/(1 + i)^n$ today. So the present discounted value of the consol is $P = C/(1 + i) + C/(1 + i)^2 + \ldots + C/(1 + i)^n + \ldots = C[1/(1 + i)][1 + 1/(1 + i) + \ldots + 1/(1 + i)^n + \ldots]$. The last term is an infinite sum which equals $(1 + i)/i$, so $P = C/i$ which gives the same result as in the main text.

Box 14.4   **The Sub-prime Debacle of 2007**

The story starts in the early 2000s in the USA. Small local banks, who specialized in granting loans for the purchase of houses, began to expand their customer base by lending to people who were considered bad risks: people with low income or even unemployed. Mortgages, as housing loans are called, are guaranteed by the value of the house. If the borrower fails to honour her commitment, the bank takes control of the house—a process called foreclosure—and sells it to recover its money. Sub-prime mortgages are simply mortgages granted to very risky borrowers, usually at higher interest rates. To the banks, they are assets—the right to receive payments from the borrowers and, if need be, to foreclose the house.

Yet the lenders which originated the mortgage loans were able to engage in this risky business only because larger financial institutions were willing to take these assets off their hands. The originating banks resold their assets to these financial intermediaries, pocketing a profit and unloading the risk. This was hardly an incentive to act prudently. Many loans were of even worse quality than the word sub-prime (below prime) implies.[6] The financial intermediaries pooled a large number of these sub-prime mortgages together into new assets, which they repackaged and sold to other investors. This process of **securitization** is based on the principle of diversification: lending to many persons or many regions should be less risky than lending to a single person, or to a single region. If these mortgage-backed securities were in fact less risky than the simple sum of the individual underlying mortgages, they could fetch a

higher value, as explained in Box 14.3. This explains why the intermediaries could buy the mortgages at a higher price from the initial lending banks and yet make a profit by immediately reselling the securities.

At the end of the day, most analysts now agree that these fancy securities were valued much too highly—simply because the value of houses that stood behind them were driven by the US real estate boom and thus much more correlated than were they based on individual default risk. By the end of 2006, after many years of rapid growth, house prices started to decline throughout the USA. In addition, many sub-prime borrowers faced higher interest rates and realized that the value of their debt—their mortgages—now exceeded the value of their homes. They defaulted on their loans. Foreclosures led to more forced sales of homes in a market in which prices were already falling. Further declines in housing prices triggered more defaults, more foreclosures, and more sales. The mortgage-backed securities were guaranteed by houses whose prices were plummeting, so the value of the securities declined. Many of the world's largest and most prestigious banks lost hundreds of billions of dollars in securities which had high ratings from the industry's most sophisticated and reputed rating agencies. Perhaps due to hubris, perhaps due to ignorance, perhaps due to the hot potato syndrome, bankers were blinded to systematic, macroeconomic risk of the simplest sort—movements in house prices—so mortgaged-backed securities were in fact hardly diversified at all.

But this is not the end of the story. If q_t depends on q_{t+1}, then q_{t+1} must depend on q_{t+2} in exactly the same way. Of course, the same will apply to q_{t+2}, q_{t+3}, etc., endlessly. In the end, substituting (14.2) for itself in an endless process of telescopic recursion, we find

(14.3) $$q_t = \sum_{i=0}^{\infty} \left(\frac{1}{1+r} \right)^{i+1} d_{t+1}.$$

This formula says that the current price (in real terms) of a share is the present discounted value of expected future dividends, forever. It shows that the market values a company on the basis of what it is expected to earn, now and in the indefinite future.[7] It also explains why stock prices can rise suddenly when market expectations of future pro-

---

[6] In banking circles these loans were often called 'NINJA' loans: no income, job, or assets.

[7] What is the relationship between this and Tobin's q used in Chapter 6? Tobin's q is the ratio of the share price (q here) to the replacement cost of installed capital.

fits rise, e.g. when new technologies are developed. It can also abruptly decline if the markets take a dimmer view of the firm's profitability in the future.

We have noted that shares are very risky. In the previous reasoning, we did not take that aspect into account, but we know how to reason. Since a share is riskier than a safe asset, its rate of return will have to carry a risk premium. Assuming that this premium is constant, we need to modify (14.1) to state that the expected return on the share is equal to the safe interest rate r plus the risk premium, denoted by ψ:

(14.4) $\qquad r + \psi = \dfrac{d_t}{q_t} + \dfrac{q_{t+1} - q_t}{q_t}.$

Following the same reasoning as before, we find

(14.5) $\qquad q_t = \sum_{i=0}^{\infty} \left(\dfrac{1}{1+r} \right)^{i+1} d_{t+1} - \dfrac{\psi}{r}.$

We see that the risk premium reduces the share price. Quite logically, the riskier the firm is perceived to be, the lower will its share price be.[8]

14.4.3 More Sophisticated Assets

Bonds, shares, and bank loans are the basic products of financial markets. As you might expect, modern finance has developed a huge number of other financial products. As time goes by, these products become considerably more complex and,

indeed, require the talents of sophisticated mathematicians, often referred to as 'rocket scientists'.

These products aim at dealing more efficiently with risk, through various means. One obvious way to go is diversification, putting together many basic assets just as shown in Box 14.2. Indeed, most investors do not buy individual assets, but **funds**, i.e. a collection of basic assets, put together by specialized financial institutions. Some funds also offer guarantees such as minimum returns, protection of invested capital, etc. **Derivatives** are complex securities which derive their value from underlying real assets or goods, and represent bets on future prices or conditions. The simplest type of derivative is a futures contract, which involves the purchase of goods—such as grain or gold—to be delivered at some future date. Derivatives might also be based on the value of a stock or a stock price index, or allow the holder to sell back certain securities before maturity, or to buy them in the future at some guaranteed price. Traders can thus take positions in the evolution of the price of some underlying good or asset without ever having to take delivery of it.

Because these financial products can become very complex, most investors do not fully understand their properties. Sometimes, even the financiers that produce them fail to understand fully the risks they are taking. The financial crisis that started in the summer of 2007 with the sub-prime debacle is a case in point. It is presented in Box 14.4.

14.5 Information and Market Efficiency

Asset prices reflect the collective judgement of market participants—borrowers and lenders alike. This judgement, in turn, is based on all the information collected by market participants. The information

concerns each single asset, its underlying value and future performance—how much it will pay under which circumstances, as in the examples of Box 14.2. It is a hallmark of properly functioning financial markets that participants are engaged in a never-ending search for profit opportunities, either for their customers or for their own accounts. Both the amount of money at stake and the speed at which information moves make it unlikely that

---

[8] The risk premium resembles the value of a consol. This is not a coincidence. The risk premium acts as a permanent drag on the value of the share just as coupons are a permanent source of value for consol holders.

opportunities not involving additional risk will be left unexploited for any significant period of time. This is the no-profit rule presented in Section 14.3.2. Markets which satisfy this condition—that publicly available information cannot earn consistently above-average returns—are said to be **efficient**. When markets are efficient, prices fully reflect all available information.[9] This observation carries a number of implications that we now examine.

14.5.1 Arbitrage

Arbitrage is an example of the no-profit rule. It concerns operations which do not involve additional risk.[10] It is customary to distinguish three types of arbitrage: (1) yield arbitrage, (2) spatial arbitrage, and (3) triangular arbitrage.

Yield arbitrage concerns two similar assets which happen to offer different returns. Strictly speaking, it applies to riskless assets, like Treasury bills, but it is sometimes applied to risky assets which bear similar risk (like assets A and B in Box 14.2). Consider the example of two riskless government bonds which offer different rates of interest. Holders of the less attractive bond will sell in favour of the one with the superior yield. In fact, the entire stock of the less attractive bond could be put up for sale. As the higher-yielding bond becomes more expensive and the lower-yielding bond becomes cheaper, the implied yields converge (the link between yields and prices is explained in Section 14.4). Arbitrage prevents such pricing misalignment from occurring: yield arbitrage imposes identical returns for identical assets.

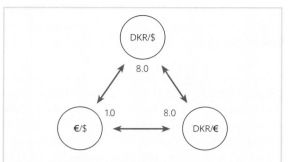

Fig. 14.3 Triangular Arbitrage

When two exchange rates among three currencies are known, the exchange rate between the remaining pair of currencies is given by triangular arbitrage. In the absence of transactions costs, any discrepancy between purchasing a currency directly and acquiring it using a third currency is eliminated.

Spatial arbitrage concerns the same assets traded in different locations. For example, large commercial banks borrow from each other at the interbank interest rate. If the interbank rate in two cities were to diverge, enterprising banks present in both cities would immediately borrow in the cheaper market and lend in the dearer one. With high capital mobility and negligible risk differences, the yields should be virtually identical. This is indeed the case.

Triangular arbitrage applies mostly to foreign exchange markets and is possible when the relative prices of three—or more—currencies are not consistent with each other. If the euro costs one US dollar and one euro costs 8 Danish krone (DKR), then the DKR/\$ rate must be $(DKR8/€)/(\$1/€) = 8$ DKR/\$. Otherwise limitless profit would be possible by buying the euro where it is cheap and selling it where it is more expensive. Figure 14.3 displays this example.

14.5.2 The Bid–Ask Spread

The risk premium takes another interesting form. To carry out the various operations described above, investors 'go to the market'. There they need to find a counterpart, someone interested in doing exactly the same operation, for the same amount, but in

---

[9] The idea of market efficiency is related to the rational expectations hypothesis introduced in Chapter 7. Rational expectations assume that agents do not make systematic forecasting errors. Market efficiency applies this concept to markets and price-setting.

[10] In financial market jargon, this distinction is not always so clear. For example, traders who search for information on corporate takeovers in order to take a position in the stock 'in play' are sometimes called risk arbitrageurs. Technically, this is a contradiction in terms: if a takeover is called off, the 'risk arbitrageur' may be left holding a great deal of stock and may suffer a large loss.

Box 14.5 The Short-Lived Market for Ostmarks

Even before the Berlin Wall fell on 9 November 1989, trade in the East German currency, the Ostmark (OM), was significant, and DM quotes for OM were published daily in major West German newspapers. After this historic date, volume increased by an order of magnitude as East Germans tried to convert their savings into harder currency. It remained unclear until March 1990 whether monetary unification would occur. This implied automatic conversion of OM currency and bank deposits into DM. The conversion rate of one DM for one OM applying to a part of East Germany's holdings and one for two for the rest—resulting in an average estimated by the Bundesbank at 1.8—was first officially suggested in March. It was then formalized as part of the state treaty of monetary and economic union between the two German states in May 1990.

Considerable uncertainty characterized this period. Furthermore, before the Berlin Wall opened, the markets were relatively thin and trade was exclusively a Western business. This is reflected in the bid–ask spread which stood at more than 30% in early 1989, as seen in Figure 14.4. As the situation became clearer, trade moved to the streets of East and West Berlin and most banks entered the game. With the decision to establish a monetary union between West and East Germany by July 1990—in effect, replacing OMs with DMs—uncertainty declined, and so did the spread.

reverse. This is extremely unlikely, so the market would be useless were it not for the presence of **market makers**. Market makers are usually big financial institutions that have an interest in keeping the market **liquid** at all times, meaning that every desired operation can be carried out instantly. They stand ready to satisfy any demand, buying or selling any amount—up to a reasonable ceiling, which can be as high as €1 million—that appears on the market. Each market maker specializes in certain trades, e.g. the euro–sterling exchange rate or bunds (the debt of the German Government). Of course, as they do so, they provide a service. They also take a risk. For example, selling forward sterling for euros represents a commitment to deliver sterling upon **maturity** of the forward contract. This means buying sterling on the spot market at a rate presently unknown. The investor who buys a forward contract gets rid of risk, passing this risk on to the market maker. Quite naturally, the market maker needs to be compensated for both the service and the risk. This takes the form of a **bid–ask spread**.

The bid–ask spread is familiar to anyone who has travelled abroad and has bought currency at an exchange booth. There, as on all foreign exchange markets, exchange rates are quoted in pairs: a lower 'bid' price for those who want to sell the foreign currency, and a higher 'ask' price for buyers. The difference is the market maker's profit. The bid–ask spread in wholesale foreign exchange trading is currently quite small—roughly 0.2% on a five-million euro transaction between euros and sterling. Yet it can be much higher for currencies which are inherently risky, or are thinly traded. Box 14.5 gives a nice example of how a bid–ask spread evolved over time for the Ostmark, the money of the German Democratic Republic, the communist German country which disappeared from the European map after German unification in 1990.

14.5.3 Implications of Market Efficiency

The efficient market hypothesis poses something of a paradox: if markets are efficient, we shouldn't have to work very hard to obtain information on assets—the market has done it for us already! The current price of bonds, stocks, foreign exchange, and other financial instruments should represent a consensus based on information available to traders in the market. If stock prices decline today, we do

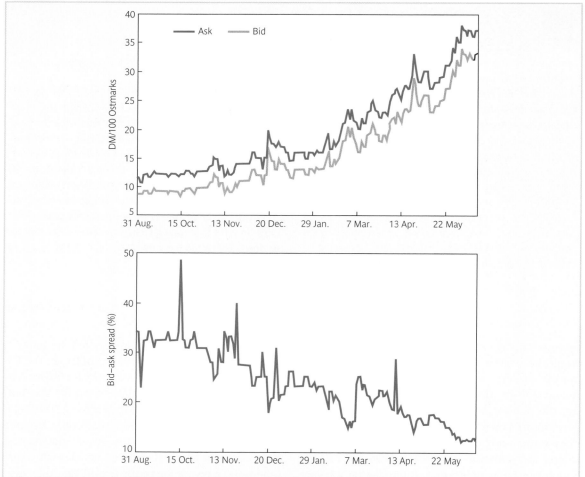

Fig. 14.4 Ostmark–DM Rate and Bid–Ask Spreads, August 1989–June 1990

As monetary union approached, the risk involved in holding Ostmarks, the currency of the vanishing German Democratic Republic, declined. This is reflected in the bid–ask spread, which fell significantly.

Source: Burda and Gerlach (1993).

not really need to find out why. The market has already processed the relevant information and drawn the correct implications. As a corollary, it is unlikely that anyone will outperform the market consistently.

Reports of investors systematically beating the markets are more likely a sign of good luck than much else. For every winner we hear about, there are as many losers, who have disappeared from the market either because they ran out of money or because they were dismissed by their bosses. Using this line of argument, Nobel laureate Milton Friedman argued that speculation cannot be destabilizing. Those traders who are responsible for pushing asset prices away from their 'fundamental' prices, e.g. such as equation (14.3), are those who buy high and sell low. If prices return to their fundamental values, these destabilizing traders should consistently lose money and ultimately exit the market.

14.6 Asset Markets and Macroeconomics

14.6.1 Financial Markets and the Transmission Channel of Monetary Policy

In Chapter 10, we saw that monetary policy works through the interest rate. Higher rates, we explained, reduces spending by discouraging consumption and investment. Unfortunately, this description is too simple. Central banks control the very short-term interest but borrowing decisions of households and firms typically depend on longer-term interest rates, from maturity ranging from, say, 1 year to 10, 20, or more years. In addition, monetary policy has wide-ranging effects, many of which affect spending and all of which operate through financial markets. This is the issue of the **channels of transmission of monetary policy**. There are four main channels of transmission: (1) the interest rate; (2) asset prices; (3) bank credit; and (4) the exchange rate. We now review the first three, leaving the fourth one for the next chapter.

The interest rate channel

We have already looked at the interest rate channel in Section 14.3.2 when we studied the yield curve. Because ordinary people and firms borrow at longer terms than the very short-term rate set by the central bank, monetary policy succeeds in affecting spending decisions to the extent that it moves the longer end of the yield curve. It does so by influencing market expectations of what the short-term interest rate will be in the future.

This is a fairly tricky exercise. Figure 14.5 provides an example. It displays the US yield curve at three points in time: January 2005, 2006, and 2007. During this period, the US central bank, the Federal Reserve Board, was steadily raising its overnight interest rate. The figure shows that the one-month rates responded—almost one for one—to the Fed's actions. For longer maturities the impact is still noticeable but quite muted.

This example illustrates an important aspect of monetary policy. The ability of a central bank to affect long-term interest rates—those that matter for monetary policy transmission—very much depends on its ability to convince the markets of its future actions. Transparency emerges as a key success factor for a central bank. This has led some central banks to first issue forecasts of inflation—to give an idea of what they might want to do—and, more recently, to even indicate what interest rates they anticipate to set. This new approach was first adopted by the Reserve Bank of New Zealand, then by the Bank of Norway, the Swedish Riksbank, and the Central Bank of Iceland.

The asset price channel

We have seen in Section 14.4 that the interest rate affects the market value of assets. For example, when the central bank raises the interest rate, stock and bond prices tend to decline, as do housing prices. This reduces private wealth. Households react by increasing their savings in order to restore their wealth to a desired level. This means less

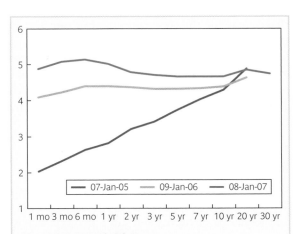

Fig. 14.5 US Yield Curve

The curve displays the interest rate on high-grade assets (Treasury bonds) at various maturities ranging from the short term (here one month) to the long term (here twenty or thirty years), depending on data availability. *Source*: Federal Reserve Board.

consumption. Similarly, declining stock prices lead firms to postpone share issues, thus depriving them from the means to carry out some of their investment projects.

The credit channel

Another possible way for monetary policy to affect the economy is via the availability of credit *independently of its cost*—since the cost of credit is the interest rate channel. As noted in Chapter 9, for regulatory and prudential reasons, commercial banks need to hold liquid assets in proportion to the credit that they grant. A tightening of monetary policy, for example, implies less liquid assets in the banking system and thus leads banks to reduce the credit that households and firms require to carry out spending. The credit channel can also be narrowed significantly by the behaviour of banks among themselves. If banks become very cautious, they may stop lending their excess reserves to each other. This leads to less lending than would otherwise be forthcoming. This mechanism has been important during the recent sub-prime crisis.

A common theme of these channels—and of the exchange rate channel as well—is that monetary policy works indirectly and that its impact is mediated by the financial markets. Importantly, because financial markets are entirely driven by expectations, changing the short-term interest rate is only the beginning of monetary policy. More important for central banks is the management of market expectations to move long-term rates and asset prices in a direction that supports their intentions. This is why central banks are very preoccupied by their communication strategy.[11]

14.6.2 Market Efficiency or Speculative Manias?

We have now seen that financial markets are crucial for two main reasons. First, they allow borrowers and lenders to achieve their aims at the best possible conditions. Since most investment spending is financed through borrowing—from banks, by issuing bonds and shares—a well-functioning financial market is crucial for economic growth. Second, and in addition, monetary policy works through the financial markets. A well-functioning financial market is essential for the conduct of monetary policy.

This is why it is important for financial markets to be efficient. The next question, then, is whether they really are. Some studies do turn up statistically measurable deviations from market efficiency. For example, if stock prices decline today, there is a tendency for them to revert over time to their previous values. This could imply that markets overreact to news, and that the markets may not be fully efficient. Yet why doesn't anyone buy these 'oversold' assets when it is profitable to do so? This would restore the price to its fundamental value immediately. The answer may lie in risk aversion, the fact that too few traders are willing to take positions and hold them long enough for this to occur. In this case, the deviation from the fundamental value may be consistent with the absence of profit opportunities, *given that the risk involved in correcting it has its own price*: the expected 'profits' are insufficient to compensate for the riskiness of betting against the irrational price. Betting against the market involves considerable risk, and deviations from fundamental values can get worse before they get better.

How and why might asset prices deviate from their fundamental values? It is always tempting to write off asset markets as irrational and prone to fads. But there are often more satisfying accounts which can be illustrated with two examples. One of them is the coexistence of professional traders and inexperienced amateurs. The other is the phenomenon of rational speculative bubbles.

Noise traders

In the first example, only a subset of traders are informed and have access to information about the true underlying value of assets. The remainder are **noise traders** who act on limited 'noisy' information. These noise traders can be either irrational or simply misinformed, and they behave accordingly.

---

[11] This was not always so. Back in the 1970s, many developed countries severely restricted the financial markets. Central banks were then able to control long-term interest rates directly and even the allocation of credit by commercial banks. This is still the case in many developing countries, in China for instance.

The result is that they systematically lose money to the informed traders. Noise traders arrive continuously on the scene, with new ones replacing those who systematically lose and quit in disgust, so that there are always some of them around. Despite perfectly efficient and rational behaviour on the part of the professionals, stock prices may again diverge from their fundamental value for long periods of time.

Bubbles

The second account of deviations from efficiency is the presence of **speculative bubbles**, persistent deviations of asset prices from their fundamental values. To see how bubbles may arise, consider the share valuation example from Section 14.4.2. Let us assume, for simplicity, that the real dividend is fixed forever at d. Ignoring the risk premium, some computation shows that the share value should be

(14.6)
$$\bar{q} = \sum_{i=0}^{\infty} \left(\frac{1}{1+r} \right)^{i+1} d = \frac{d}{r}.$$

This is called the fundamental value of the share. The puzzling observation is that an infinity of other paths of prices also satisfy the pricing relation (14.2). Consider the case where the stock price is q', higher than $\bar{q}$. This violates (14.6). The dividend is too low to justify such a price. But imagine now that, having observed $q'_t > \bar{q}$, market participants believe that the share price will increase next time to q'_{t+1}. Then, using (14.1), we can have

(14.7)
$$q'_t = \frac{d + q'_{t+1}}{1 + r},$$

satisfied for the 'right' value q'_{t+1}. Thus, it is possible for the share price to exceed its fundamental value —and violate the condition (14.6)—and yet to satisfy the pricing formula (14.2) from which the fundamental value is derived. This looks strange, and it is, but less than it seems. The fundamental value (14.6) assumes that the price remains constant forever because the dividend is assumed constant forever. But, even with a constant dividend, the share price may be expected to rise tomorrow. In fact, if it rises to $q'_{t+1} = (1+r)q'_t - d_t$, that higher price today $q'_t > \bar{q}$ becomes justified as the no-profit rule is not violated—at least for that period. The expected capital

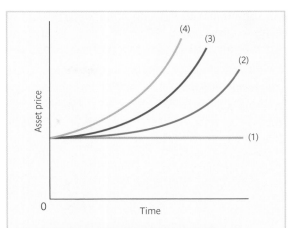

Fig. 14.6 Possible Stock Price Paths

Path (1) is the fundamental value of the asset. The price of the stock is equal to the present value of the dividend d, which is assumed constant, so it satisfies the arbitrage condition. Paths (2), (3), and (4) also satisfy the arbitrage condition, but are explosive bubbles.

gain offsets the 'too low' dividend d. Then, in period $t+1$, the story will repeat itself. With $q'_{t+1} > \bar{q}$, we need q'_{t+2} to rise again above q'_{t+1}, and so on.

Thus an overvalued share (when its price exceeds its fundamental value) can be justified by subsequent further price increases, on and on. Any price today can thus be validated by its subsequent evolution. This means that, if the price is once above its fundamental value, it becomes justified by further price increases. Figure 14.6 plots possible evolutions of the share price over time, for given r and d. Only one initial price does not 'explode', and it corresponds to the fundamental value.

The non-fundamental paths, which are exploding without any apparent fundamental justification, are self-fulfilling: prices rise because they are *expected* to, without violating any market efficiency condition. The apparently inexorable growth of the share price is called a speculative bubble. It is a bubble because it keeps growing until it bursts, and speculative because its growth is due to the expectation of future capital gains. A bubble is rational in the sense that it will continue to grow as long as traders believe that the bubble will continue to grow, validate market expectations, and offer the 'normal' return.

Box 14.6 **Tulipmania**[12]

History has given us several instances of price behaviour that looks like speculative bubbles. In Holland during the seventeenth century, the price of rare tulip bulbs rose by extraordinary rates within the space of a month, only to collapse thereafter.

The bubble involved tulip bulbs with non-negligible fundamental value because they were of exotic varieties. Yet they became exorbitantly expensive. Figure 14.7 displays the price of tulip bulbs in the first two months of 1637, when they increased by over 3,000%, and then collapsed sharply. For example, the price of the Switser variety is reported to have fallen to one-twentieth of its 2 January 1637 price. In one of the most authoritative accounts of the Tulipmania episode, Charles MacKay (1980) wrote:

The demand for tulips of a rare species increased so much in the year 1636, that regular markets for them were established on the Stock Exchange of Amsterdam, in Rotterdam, Harlem, Leyden, Alkmar, Hoorn, and other towns. Symptoms of gambling now became, for the first time, apparent. The stock-jobbers, ever on the alert for a new speculation, dealt largely in tulips, making use of all the means they so well knew how to employ, to cause fluctuations in prices. At first, as in all these gambling mania, confidence was at its height, and everybody gained. The tulip-jobbers speculated in the rise and fall of the tulip stocks, and made large profits by buying when prices fell, and selling out when they rose. Many individuals grew suddenly rich . . . nobles, citizens, farmers, mechanics, seamen, footmen, maidservants, even chimney-sweeps and old-clothes women, dabbled in tulips. People of all grades converted their property into cash, and invested it in flowers. Houses and lands were offered for sale at ruinously low prices, or assigned in payment of bargains made at the tulip mart. Foreigners became smitten with the same frenzy, and money poured into Holland from all directions. The prices of the necessaries of life rose again by degrees; houses and lands, horses and carriages, and luxuries of every sort, rose in value with them, and for some months Holland seemed the very antechamber of Pluto.[13]

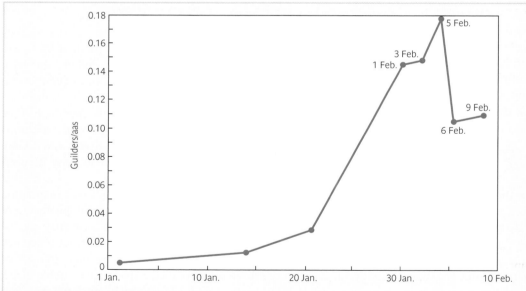

Fig. 14.7 **Tulipmania, 1637**

History has given us several instances of price behaviour that looks like speculative bubbles. In Holland during the seventeenth century, the price of rare tulip bulbs rose by extraordinary rates within the space of a month, only to collapse thereafter.
Source: Garber (1990).

[12] Part of this description is taken from Peter Garber's (1990) survey of the Tulipmania boom.

[13] Pluto was the ancient Greek god of wealth.

There is a catch, however. History shows that bubbles do eventually burst. Why? Because if an asset price were to grow indefinitely, it would eventually exceed the world's wealth, and become too expensive for anyone. And if no one can afford it, its price must decline. In the late 1980's Japanese real estate had become so expensive that the value of the Emperor's gardens were greater than the entire state of California! Sure enough, not long afterwards the bubble burst, and Tokyo, while expensive, no longer has streets paved with gold.

But the logic of a bubble is that its price must be expected to grow for a very long time with no known date T at which the price will return to its fundamental value. To see why there can be no known date, imagine the period $T - 1$ just before the price stabilizes. For the bubble to exist at $T - 1$, the price must be expected to rise. Since the price in T will be at its fundamental value, in $T - 1$ it must be below the fundamental value. This is a contradiction, however, with the earlier observation that the price of a bubble is always above its fundamental. So the period just before stabilization of the price cannot be *below* the fundamental, it can only be *at* the fundamental. Working backwards, it is easy to see that the same reasoning applies all the way to the present: there can be no bubble that is anticipated to stop growing. So a bubble can grow for a while, but rational traders know that it will eventually burst

and they stand ready to jump. Just as in a game of musical chairs, someone eventually can't move fast enough, and is left standing.[14]

Bubbles may appear bizarre because they have all the features of economic rationality and market efficiency, save for the end. Box 14.6 reviews another famous historical bubble-like episode—this time originating in the seventeenth century in Holland. One does not have to go that far back in history, however, to find suspicious episodes: the run-up of the world's stock markets before the crashes of 1929, 1987, and 1989, the explosion of property prices in the UK, Japan, and Scandinavia in the late 1980s. Much the same occurred in the US housing market in 2007, and there are indications that it may also be happening in Spain and Ireland.

In each of these instances, market participants are convinced that the boom will continue. In each case, the bursting of the bubble is followed by serious economic dislocation. Most recently, the advent of the 'new economy' ushered in by the information technology revolution was touted as the end of economics as we know it, a technological 'golden age'. For an impartial observer, however, it looks more like a confirmation of 'plus ça change...'. The breathtaking ascent of high-tech stock prices in the late 1990s, followed by an equally sharp decline which occurred in 2000–2001, is reminiscent of a bubble (see Figure 14.8).

❶ Summary

1 Asset markets are special in several ways: (1) they concern stocks and not flows, (2) they deal with uncertainty, and (3) they are purely forward-looking. These characteristics imply that financial markets are inherently volatile and, sometimes, even unstable.

2 By putting a price tag on the future and on risk, financial markets allow households and corporations to decide on saving and borrowing without having to gather the whole array of uncertain information that affects their own future. They allow those savers who are

most willing to bear risk to do so, at minimum cost.

3 Financial assets are traded with ease by professional intermediaries in large, well-organized markets. While financial intermediaries can be

---

[14] Usually the informed professionals get the seats first, which highlights an important link between noise trading and bubbles. As the great New York financier Bernard Baruch put it: 'When beggars and shoeshine boys, barbers and beauticians can tell you how to get rich it is time to remind yourself that there is no more dangerous illusion than the belief that one can get something for nothing.'

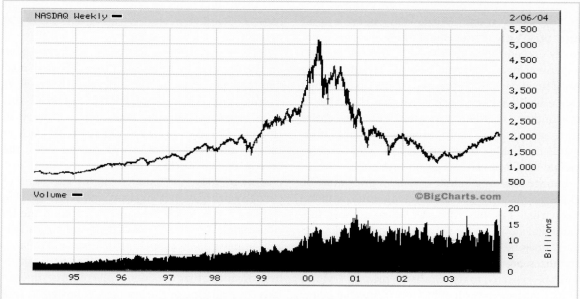

Fig. 14.8 The Rise and Fall of NASDAQ Stocks, 1996–2003

NASDAQ stands for the National Association of Securities Dealers Automated Quotation (system). It is the US stock exchange that specializes in high-technology companies, especially personal computers, telecommunication, and the internet. After more than quadrupling in value over the period 1997–2000, the NASDAQ index collapsed just as spectacularly by more than 60% from its all-time peak.

Source: <www.bigcharts.com>.

thought of as intervening on financial markets on behalf of their customers, in fact most of the transactions correspond to trade among intermediaries.

4 Bond prices are inversely related to interest rates. The same tends to apply to stock prices, which are also driven by expected dividends. Beyond bonds and shares, there exist an ever-increasing variety of derivatives.

5 The no-profit condition implies that returns among similar assets—similar in terms of risk and maturity—must be equalized.

6 The no-profit condition is a characteristic of efficient financial markets. In the absence of risk-taking, it takes the form of arbitrage.

7 In the presence of uncertainty and undiversifiable risk, the no-profit condition implies that expected returns are equalized up to a risk premium which rewards risk-averse agents for bearing risk.

8 Markets are efficient when they gather all the available information and treat it to the point where prices reflect fully what is known and the risks attached to any single asset. The evidence on market efficiency is mostly favourable, in spite of phenomena such as speculative bubbles or noise trading.

9 The asset markets play a crucial role in transmitting monetary policy actions to the economy. The three channels are: (1) the interest rate channel, (2) the asset price channel, and (3) the bank credit channel.

10 The forward-looking nature of financial markets can lead to phenomena like rational bubbles which occur when asset prices continuously rise because they are expected by enough of the market to rise further. Bubbles eventually collapse, sometimes imposing large disturbances on the overall economy.

🔑 Key Concepts

- assets
- financial intermediaries
- yield curve
- maturity premium
- risk aversion
- risk premium
- discounting
- no-profit condition
- arbitrage, no-arbitrage condition
- bonds, shares

- market maker
- market liquidity
- maturity
- bid–ask spread
- funds, derivatives
- securitization
- channels of monetary policy
- consol, perpetuity
- noise traders
- speculative bubbles

❓ Exercises

1 Explain why the bid–ask spread can be thought of as the price of risk.

2 Assets markets are considerably more volatile than goods markets. Asset markets balance stocks while goods markets balance flows. What is the link between these two observations?

3 Consider three assets *A*, *B*, and *C* with uncertain outcomes depending on three possible future states of the world.

State of the world 1: *A*: €50; *B*: €100; *C*: €0.
State of the world 2: *A*: €0; *B*: €50; *C*: €100.
State of the world 3: *A*: €100; *B*: €0; *C*: €50.

Is it possible to fully diversify risk?

4 Assume that, in the previous exercise, each state has one chance in three to happen. What is the expected return of each of the three assets *A*, *B*, and *C*? If the risk premium is 2% of the expected return, what will be the prices of these assets?

5 The yield curve is said to be inverted when it is downward-sloping. How can you explain this occasional phenomenon?

6 Suppose that the economy is expected to go into a recession that will reduce firms' profitability and will lead the central bank to reduce the interest rate. What does this imply for share prices? Why does it imply that the central bank must act more forcefully when pessimism is strong?

7 Suppose that a central bank raises its interest rate and therefore reduces the money supply. In case No. 1, the central bank promises to do so temporarily, say for three months, and then revert to the present situation. In case No. 2, it promises to maintain its action for the indefinite future. What does this mean for its impact on the economy? In your answer, examine the situation of the three channels of transmission.

8 Consider the example of a speculative bubble in the text (Section 14.6.2). Now imagine that while, as before, there are two assets, investors no longer have perfect foresight. The private asset can be purchased at variable real price q_t and pays a fixed real dividend d. Now, however, there is a probability s that in the following period $q_{t+1} = 0$ (i.e. the bubble will burst), and a probability $(1 - s)$ that it can be sold at $q_{t+1} > 0$. Investors are risk neutral and equate the rate of return on the government 'safe' asset r with the expected rate of return on the private asset.

(a) Write down the arbitrage condition.

(b) Solve for the 'non-exploding' value of current q_t.

→ Essay Questions

1 What are the conditions needed for a financial market to be efficient? Are they likely to be met in practice?

2 People have bad opinions of financial markets seen as a source of illegitimate enrichment for already wealthy people. How would you dispel this view?

3 Financial traders are often young people, who manipulate huge amounts of money and receive impressive salaries. How can you explain this?

4 'Monetary policy operates through expectations.' What does this imply for central bank communication?

5 Most central banks follow a Taylor rule and strongly resist the idea that they should also react to asset price changes. Evaluate their position.

The Exchange Rate

15

Suppose a man climbs five feet up a sea wall, then climbs down 12 feet. Whether he drowns or not depends upon how high above sea-level he was when he started. The same

problem arises in deciding whether currencies are under- or over-valued.

The Economist, 26 August 1995

15.1 **Overview**

The foreign exchange rate market is just another financial market, but it specializes in trading one currency against another one. Like other assets, currencies are durable and their value today depends on the values expected to prevail tomorrow. This market merits special attention for several reasons. First, the exchange rate is a very important variable that matters not just for financial transactions, but also for trade since it determines a country's external competitiveness (as we saw in Chapter 10). Second, the monetary authorities often decide to fix, or to stabilize, the exchange rate, and this has very important implications for the working of the economy (as explained in Chapter 11). To that effect, they intervene on the foreign exchange market. Third, the evolution of the exchange rate directly affects the interest rate, an aspect that was purposely ignored so far. It is now time to ask more carefully how the exchange rate, both nominal and real, is determined when it is endogenous and not fixed by the monetary authorities.

We start with a description of foreign exchange markets. Present virtually all over the world in the form of computer terminals, they are dominated by one currency, the US dollar, with a growing role for the euro and a handful of lesser vehicle currencies. The amounts traded are vertiginous. We then revisit the link between interest rates. The link has

been succinctly presented in Chapter 11 and plays a crucial role in later chapters. In Section 15.2, we show how to make it more precise. The results are two interest rate parity conditions that directly involve the exchange rate—current and anticipated. Section 15.4 then shows how the analysis presented in Chapter 11 can be adjusted to recognize the interest rate parity conditions.

Having thus prepared the ground, we can explain what drives the exchange rate. As in previous chapters, we separate the short and the long run. The short-run analysis, presented in Section 15.5, treats the exchange rate as an asset price, i.e. purely driven by financial considerations and market expectations. The long-run analysis developed in Section 15.6, as one might expect, focuses on the real side of the economy in the form of the national budget constraint. This leads us to develop the concept of an equilibrium real exchange rate. Thus, the long-run analysis explains the real exchange rate while the short-run analysis explains the nominal exchange. All that is left to be done is to show how the short run recognizes the long run. The result, presented in Section 15.7, offers an internally consistent treatment of the exchange rate. The last section points out some important implications of the principles developed throughout this chapter, including the regular occurrence of **currency crises**.

15.2 The Foreign Exchange Markets

15.2.1 Main Characteristics

A physical market for foreign exchange does not exist. Instead, hundreds and thousands of traders sit in front of computer terminals around the globe and round the clock and swap currencies with each other. Furthermore, they do not trade in banknotes, but rather in the liabilities of commercial banks—bank deposits. As financial intermediaries, they act on behalf of their customers, who need currencies for trade or financial transactions. Most often, they do it for their colleagues in the same financial institution, who buy and sell assets denominated in various currencies, or for their own trading accounts when they spot a fleeting deviation from the no-profit rule.

A characteristic of the exchange markets is that they are dominated by a few currencies, called **vehicle currencies**. Until recently, the US dollar was *the* vehicle currency, present in one side of nearly half of all transactions. Table 15.1 shows that its importance has receded somewhat. The euro is the second most important international currency. The other currencies play minor roles although the growing importance of emerging market economy is reflected in the shares of their currencies. In particular, the Hong Kong dollar has grown in im-portance, reflecting the expansion of the Chinese economy.

Like any other financial market, the foreign exchange market consists of wholesale trades, involving standardized transactions of large size. This feature reinforces the domination of the vehicle currency and means that most exchanges operate via the US dollar, as Table 15.2 shows. This means that, for instance, a trader who wants to change Polish zlotys into Indian rupees will first change the zlotys into dollars and then the dollars into rupees. This gives rise to triangular arbitrage, as explained in Section 15.2.3.

The volumes traded are truly astounding and have been rising very fast. Table 15.3 shows that, in 2007, on an average day, transactions amounted to 3,210 billions US dollars. This *daily* turnover represents about one-quarter of the *annual* GDP of the USA and more than four times the Dutch GDP.

Table 15.1 Shares of Currencies in Foreign Exchange Market Transactions

	2001	2004	2007
US dollar	45.2	44.4	43.2
Euro	18.8	18.5	18.5
Yen	11.4	10.1	8.3
Sterling	6.6	8.5	7.5
Swiss franc	3.1	3.0	3.4
Emerging market currencies	8.5	7.7	9.9

Source: Bank for International Settlements (2007).

Table 15.2 Shares of Currency Pairs in Foreign Exchange Market Transactions

	2001	2004	2007
US dollar/euro	20	20	27
US dollar/yen	11	11	13
US dollar/sterling	4	4	12
US dollar/Australian dollar	5	5	6
US dollar/Swiss franc	4	4	5
US dollar/Canadian dollar			4
US dollar/Swedish krona	17	17	2
US dollar/other	3	3	19
Euro/yen	2	2	2
Euro/sterling	1	1	2
Euro/Swiss franc	2	2	2
Euro/other currencies	2	2	4
Other currency pairs			4

Source: Bank for International Settlements (2007).

Table 15.3 **Average Daily Foreign Exchange Transactions (US$ billions)**

1992	1995	1998	2001	2004	2007
820	1190	1490	1200	1900	3210

Source: Bank for International Settlements (2007).

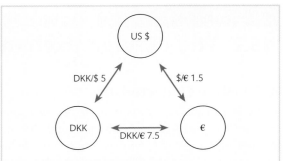

Fig. 15.1 Triangular Arbitrage
When two exchange rates among three currencies are known, the exchange rate between the remaining pair of currencies is given by triangular arbitrage. In the absence of transactions costs, any discrepancy between purchasing a currency directly and acquiring it using a third currency is eliminated.

15.2.2 Instruments

The basic deal involves immediately changing one currency for another one. The price at which this is done is called the **spot exchange rate**. An alternative is to agree now to do the transaction at some specified date in the future. The corresponding price is the **forward exchange rate**. Current forward contract maturities range from 'tomorrow' to one year. When two traders agree to a forward contract, they must guess what the spot rate will be at the corresponding horizon.

Other deals include **swaps**, i.e. an agreement by one trader to sell one currency against another one now and buy it back at the future specified date. Thus a swap combines a spot and a forward transaction, in opposite directions. In 2007, swaps represented more than half of all foreign exchange market transactions.

15.2.3 Triangular Arbitrage

Because the US dollar is used as one side of many transactions, direct exchange rates between most pairs of currencies are implicitly set by the dollar rate of each currency in the pair. The question is whether these cross rates are mutually consistent. The no-profit condition presented in Chapter 14 implies that this is indeed the case. For example, as illustrated in Figure 15.1, if the exchange rate of the Danish krone (DKK) *vis-à-vis* the euro is 7.5—it takes 7.5 krone to buy 1 euro—and if one euro is worth $1.5,

then the krone–US dollar exchange rate must be (DKK 7.5/€)/($1.5/€) = DKK 5/$.

This outcome results from triangular arbitrage. To see how triangular arbitrage works, imagine that the three exchange rates are not consistent with each other, e.g. that the DKK/$ exchange rate is 7.5, the same as the DKK/€ rate. This means that the krone is undervalued *vis-à-vis* the dollar, or overvalued *vis-à-vis* the euro. A trader would immediately take, say, DKK 10 to acquire €1.33 and then sell this to acquire $2, which she would finally use to buy DKK 15. This would yield an instant profit of DKK 5, or 50% of the amount invested. Note that this operation entails minimum risk. Indeed, the trader can execute her orders simultaneously. As a result, instead of DKK 10, she would start with DKK 10 million and earn 5 million with three clicks of her terminal keyboard! As dozens of other traders join the fray, the exchange rates would promptly move: massive purchases of the euro would lift its value while massive sales of the dollar would lead to a depreciation. Such opportunities, usually much smaller, promptly eliminate any inconsistency.

15.3 The Interest Parity Conditions

In Chapter 11, we noted that full capital mobility implies that domestic and foreign returns must be aligned. This is yet another application of the no-profit condition presented in Chapter 14. We called i the interest rate on domestic bonds and i^* the 'return' on foreign bonds, stressing that it was evaluated in the domestic currency. We now look at what this means in more detail. This will lead to two versions of the condition: (1) covered interest parity, an example of riskless yield arbitrage, and (2) uncovered interest parity, which allows for risk.

15.3.1 Covered Interest Rate Parity

The **covered interest rate parity** (CIRP) condition is the result of arbitrage between domestic and foreign currency returns in the absence of risk-taking. Consider the following example. An investor in the Netherlands can obtain an annual rate of interest i on riskless Dutch government bonds issued in euros and i^* on equally riskless British Treasury bills issued in pounds. Both investments have a maturity of one year. Although both riskless, they are not exactly equivalent because the sterling value of the euro may change over the investment period, thereby altering the total return measured in sterling for the euro-denominated investment. Let the sterling price of one euro at the beginning of the year be S_t. This is the spot exchange rate. By selling one euro at the beginning of the year, a Dutch investor obtains S_t pounds that she can invest for one year to receive $(1 + i^*)S_t$ at the end of the year. This is a completely certain return, since both the interest i^* and exchange rate S_t are known at the beginning of the year.

At the end of the year, though, she will want to convert back into euros the pounds that she earned. The hitch is that the exchange rate that will prevail then is unknown at the beginning of the year. This represents risk. Fortunately, if she so wishes, she can eliminate the risk by signing a forward contract at the beginning of the year to sell $(1 + i^*)S_t$ pounds against euros at the end of the year. The corresponding forward exchange rate, denoted by F_t, is known and agreed upon at the beginning of the year. Thus the investor can be certain that for every pound invested this way, she will receive $(1 + i^*)S_t/F_t$ euros at the end of the year. Because the forward contract eliminates all exchange risk, the foreign investment is said to be **covered** or **hedged**.

The investor could instead have invested one euro in the safe euro Dutch government bonds to receive $(1 + i)$ at the end of the year, which is equally riskless since the interest rate is known when the decision is made. Arbitrage guarantees that the two returns must be equal. The result is the covered interest parity condition, which can be formally written as

(15.1) $$(1 + i) = (1 + i^*)S_t/F_t.$$

A useful approximation of the CIRP condition can be found by arguing a bit more loosely.[1] Let the interest rate on Dutch bonds be $i = 4\%$ and that on UK Treasury bills be $i^* = 6\%$. Obviously, the UK bills look more attractive, but the investor is no fool. She knows that the 6% are earned in pounds, so she consults the financial page of the newspaper and looks up the forward exchange rate of the pound in terms of euros. Assume that it is equal to the spot rate so that $F_t = S_t$. Then pounds and euros are 'the same' and indeed the pound investment is much more attractive. In fact, it is too attractive since it violates the no-profit condition. For the condition to be satisfied, the higher interest earned on UK bills must be offset somehow.

Imagine that the forward value of the pound is less than its spot value. This means that the pounds available at the end of the year will be worth less in terms of euros. This **forward discount** implies a **capital loss** for our investor. For example, if the loss is of 3%, the return from the pound investment will

---

[1] Or by using maths, take logs on both sides of (15.1):
$\log(1 + i) = \log(1 + i^*) - \log(F_t/S_t)$ and remember two standard approximations: $\log(1 + x) \approx x$ and $\log(F/S) \approx (F - S)/S$.

be 6% in interest rate less the 3% capital loss, thus offering a total return of 3% when evaluated in euros. This is less than the 4% offered in euros by the Dutch bond. This, too, is incompatible with the no-profit condition. There might seem to be no profit here, just a loss. But, of course, a British investor will spot that investing in Dutch bonds is more profitable than investing in UK Treasury bills. Given the interest rates, the no-profit condition is satisfied when the capital loss on the UK investment due to the forward discount is exactly matching the difference in interest rates, i.e. when it is exactly 2%.

More generally, the Dutch investor compares the domestic interest rate i on one hand, and the return on the foreign investment, on the other hand. The return on the foreign investment brings an interest in pounds of i^*, but it must be converted back into euros. If the forward value of the pound in euros is less than its spot value—the pound is at a discount vis-à-vis the euro—our investor suffers a capital loss: her pounds one year ahead are worth less than today. Equivalently, the euro is at a **forward premium** vis-à-vis the pound. Measured as the interest rate in percentage terms, the forward premium of the euro is $(F_t - S_t)/S_t$. Arbitrage requires that both investment strategies yield the same return:

$$(15.2) \qquad i \quad = \quad i^* \quad - \quad \frac{F_t - S_t}{S_t}$$

interest rate   = interest rate –   forward
the Netherlands   in the UK   premium.

A positive premium means that the forward value of the euro in terms of pounds is higher than its spot value, i.e. that the euro is 'stronger' forward than spot. In that case, the euro interest rate i can be lower than the sterling interest rate i^* and, yet, the two investment strategies bring equal returns.[2]

15.3.2 Uncovered Interest Rate Parity

Instead of engaging in a forward contract, our investor can buy sterling spot at rate S_t, invest in UK bills for one year, and wait until the end of the year to buy back euros at the then prevailing

---

[2] The WebAppendix further develops the concept of the forward premium.

spot exchange rate S_{t+1}. This is risky because no one knows at the beginning of the year what the exchange rate will be by year's end. What appeared to be a good deal may turn out disappointing if the euro appreciates vis-à-vis sterling, leaving the investor with fewer pounds than expected. Of course, the euro can depreciate unexpectedly, and the deal will turn out to be terrific. Leaving her foreign investment **open**, or **uncovered**, or **unhedged**, the investor takes a risk, and this will involve a risk premium, as explained in Chapter 14.

To examine the new situation, we start by assuming that the investors are risk neutral, meaning that they do not worry about risk. Then the risk premium is zero. The strategy is the same as before, except that the pound investment will not be sold at the end of the year using the forward rate F_t agreed upon earlier, but at the then-prevailing spot exchange rate S_{t+1}. Going through the same reasoning, the expected return in euros from one euro invested in pounds is $(1 + i^*)S_t/S_{t+1}^e$, where S_{t+1}^e is the end-of-year exchange rate as expected at the beginning of the year. A one-year investment in euros still yields $(1 + i)$. The no-profit condition for a risk-neutral investor implies that both returns are expected to be equal. This gives the **uncovered interest rate parity** (UIRP) condition, which can be written formally as

$$(15.3) \qquad 1 + i \quad = \quad (1 + i^*)S_t/S_{t+1}^e$$

euro return from   = expected euro return from
investment in euros   investment in pounds,

which can be approximated conveniently by

$$(15.4) \qquad i \quad = \quad i^* \quad - \quad \frac{S_{t+1}^e - S_t}{S_t}$$

interest rate = interest rate – expected appreciation
in euros   in pounds   of euro vis-à-vis pound.

The UIRP asserts that rates of return are equalized across countries once expected exchange rate changes are taken into account. On the left-hand side of (15.4) we have the one-year euro interest rate; on the right-hand side we have the pound interest rate less the expected capital gain or loss from changes in the sterling–euro exchange rate, expressed in percentage terms, for the same one-year maturity. Expectations cannot be observed directly, but the UIRP provides an implicit measure of what the market expects. If interest rates in the euro area are lower than in the UK ($i < i^*$), then the euro must be expected to appreciate, and the expected rate appreciation of the euro is given by the difference in observed interest rates: $(S^e_{t+1} - S_t)/S_t = i^* - i > 0$.

To be willing to hold euro-denominated assets with a lower interest than pound-denominated assets, investors must expect a capital gain as compensation. If euro rates are higher, the UIRP implies that sterling is expected to appreciate *vis-à-vis* the euro.

15.3.3 Risk Premia

Empirically, the UIRP does not hold most of the time. The interest rate spread between, for example, the euro and the pound does not predict future movements in the exchange rate very well. But the interest rate spread is not only due to expectations of a depreciation or appreciation. Only if investors were risk neutral would this necessarily be the case. If investors are risk averse the UIRP need not hold at all.

The uncovered interest parity condition can be modified to accommodate risk aversion. Our Dutch saver has the choice between remaining safely invested in euro-denominated assets or assuming the risk associated with British assets, i.e. assets denominated in the UK currency.[3] The no-profit condition implies that both investment strategies must be equally desirable, but the British investment must also include a premium that makes up for the risk of choosing foreign-currency assets. If ψ_t represents the risk premium, this means that we must now have

(15.5) $$i^* - \frac{S^e_{t+1} - S_t}{S_t}i \quad = \quad i \quad + \quad \psi_t$$

euro-return from   = euro-return from + risk
investment in pounds   investment in euros   premium.

Turning things around, we can *define* the risk premium as the deviation from the uncovered interest rate parity condition, which can vary over time:

(15.6) $$\psi_t \quad = \quad (i^* - i) \quad - \frac{S^e_{t+1} - S_t}{S_t}$$

risk   = interest − expected
premium   differential appreciation.

We have looked at the situation from the point of view of a Dutch investor who seeks to be compensated for the risk of holding pound-denominated assets. At the same time, British investors are likely to hold euro-denominated assets. They face the same type of exchange risk, but the other way round. All things being equal, they too would require a premium on euro-denominated assets, i.e. a negative ψ. So, euro area-based investors want a positive risk premium, UK investors want it negative. What is the end result? As always, the answer is given by the market. In the end, the risk premium will be such that it exactly balances all these demands and supplies from the UK, euro area, and elsewhere. As these demands and supplies vary, so does the risk premium. In fact, this is known to be volatile and usually small because for any UK investor taking the action described above we are likely to find a euro area-based investor doing the same.

Clearly, the risk premium is a complicated phenomenon whose full treatment is beyond the scope of this textbook.[4] All we need to understand is that the existence of a risk premium ψ_t (which can be positive or negative) means that we should not expect the uncovered parity condition to hold exactly. It will be true up to a—generally volatile—risk premium.

15.3.4 Real Interest Rate Arbitrage in the Long Run

The UIRP conditions, with and without a risk premium, link nominal interest rates at home and abroad and embody the tight linkages implied by international financial integration. Does the

---

[3] The fact that the payoff is in pound sterling is risky because the investor lives in a region which does not use the pound as legal tender, so that every transaction involves consumption risk to the extent that exchange rate risk is equivalent to nominal price risk. This would not be true for an investor residing in the UK, but through her eyes the euro investment would be risky.

[4] Finance theory (the Capital Asset Pricing Model or CAPM) states that the risk premium is determined by the correlation between the asset's return and the return from the world portfolio.

Box 15.1 The Real Interest Rate Parity Condition

This **real interest parity** condition follows from the UIRP condition, e.g. in the form of (15.4). Rearranged, this means that the interest rate differential is equal to the expected exchange rate appreciation of the domestic currency. But in the medium to long term, relative PPP implies that the future rate of depreciation is equal to the future inflation differential:

(15.7) $$(S_{t+1} - S_t)/S_t = \pi^\star_{t+1} - \pi_{t+1}.$$

If forecasts of inflation at home π^e_{t+1} and abroad $\pi^{\star e}_{t+1}$ are consistent with PPP, the definition of the real interest

rate $r_t = i - \pi^e_{t+1}$ and $r^\star_t = i^\star - \pi^{\star e}_{t+1}$ along with (15.4) and (15.7) imply

(15.8) $$r_t = r^\star_t.$$

This relationship is called the **international Fisher equation**. As it is based on relative PPP, it is at best a medium- to long-run proposition. Nevertheless, it is a useful benchmark for evaluating long-term foreign investment strategies, as it implies that the real rate of interest should be largely the same in all countries and is independent of the evolution of exchange rates.

arbitrage argument extend to the *real* interest rate, which is decisive for intertemporal decisions? Intuitively, one might expect an arbitrage opportunity to arise if real interest rates—with similar risk characteristics—differed significantly across countries. As formally shown in Box 15.1, it turns out

that the purchasing power parity condition (PPP) does imply that real interest rates at home and abroad will be equal. While the nominal interest parity condition holds in the short run, PPP only holds in the long run and, therefore, so does the real interest parity condition.[5]

15.4 Back to Macroeconomic Equilibrium

The interest rate parity condition (IRPC) was first introduced in Chapter 11. To simplify things, we stated it as $i = i^*$, where i^* was defined as the overall return on foreign assets. Now we can see that what we earlier called i^* was really the foreign interest rate less the expected rate of exchange rate appreciation as in (15.4). The implication is that the IFM schedule should shift whenever the exchange rate is expected to change. In the case of a flexible exchange rate regime, nothing changes as long as the chosen exchange rate remains credible and is not expected to change. Indeed, with $S^e_{t+1} = S_t$ we still have $i = i^*$. When the exchange rate is floating, this simplification cannot really be defended. One example should illustrate how things change when we recognize this additional aspect.

Consider the case of a monetary expansion—the central bank raises its inflation target $\bar{\pi}$. This is shown by the rightward shift of the TR schedule in Figure 15.2 where the economy is initially at point

A. In Chapter 11, we reasoned that at point B, the economy is below the IFM line: the interest rate is now too low, capital flows out and the exchange rate depreciates. This increases the country's external competitiveness, the current account improves and the IS curve shifts to IS'. The new equilibrium was at point C. As we noted, the IS curve is endogenous; it must move to meet the TR' and IFM schedules. If we now recognize that the exchange rate depreciation is likely to be anticipated, the interest parity condition implies that the domestic interest rate must rise. As a consequence, the IFM line shifts up to IFM'. This implies that the IS curve will have to shift until it passes through point D, the intersection of TR' and IFM'.

The result is that monetary policy is more expansionary—D lies to the right of C—now that we

---

[5] We discuss purchasing power parity in Chapter 6. The relative version is employed here. The Fisher equation, which relates real and nominal interest rates explicitly, was introduced in Chapter 13.

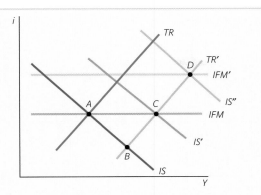

Fig. 15.2 Monetary Policy Under Floating Exchange Rates

Starting at point A, a monetary policy expansion is captured by the downward shift of the Taylor rule schedule from TR to TR'. At point B, the lower interest rate triggers capital outflows and the exchange rate depreciates. The IS curve shifts to IS' to reflect improved external competitiveness. But, if expected, the exchange rate depreciation raises the domestic interest rate according to the UIRP condition and the IFM schedule shifts up to IFM', which triggers a further depreciation and the shift from IS' to IS'' until it passes through point D.

effect, something must lead the central bank to raise its interest rate. According to the Taylor rule, this happens when output is larger. Second, why does output rise further? Since the world return—the sum of the foreign interest rate i^* and of expected depreciation—is higher, at point B capital outflows are stronger, and they still occur at point C. It follows that the exchange rate will depreciate further, which leads to even more external competitiveness and, therefore, to more demand for the domestic output.

This example shows that overlooking the expected exchange rate change, as we did in Chapter 11, does not qualitatively alter the analysis, even though it misses the fact that the domestic interest rate can diverge from the foreign *interest rate*. This divergence, though, is likely to be temporary. Indeed, once point D is reached, capital outflows stop and so does the exchange rate depreciation. As the exchange rate stabilizes, and is expected to stabilize, the UIRP condition implies that $i = i^*$ and the IFM schedule returns to its original position. But then, at point D, capital flows in and the exchange rate appreciates. The IFM schedule shifts even lower and a new equilibrium occurs at the intersection with TR'. The story will continue but the end will take place at point C, just like in Chapter 11. What precisely happens to the exchange rate is the object of the next section.

recognize the complete IRPC. This result can be understood from two related perspectives. First, the interest rate must be higher than when we ignored the effect of the expected depreciation. To that

15.5 Exchange Rate Determination in the Short Run

15.5.1 The Exchange Rate as an Asset Price

Panel (a) of Figure 15.3 presents day-to-day changes of the nominal €/£ exchange rate during 2007. Sharp changes are often followed by movements of similar magnitude in the opposite direction. The variability of nominal exchange rates is often remarkably high, with daily changes of almost ±1% per day commonplace. (A daily change of 1% corre-

sponds to an annual compounded return of more than 3,000%!) This pattern is strongly reminiscent of asset price movements, as seen in Chapter 14. It makes the point that, in the short run, exchange rates behave like asset prices. This observation suggests that they must be forward-looking, driven by market expectations of their future values.

On the other hand, longer-term fluctuations seem of a different nature. Panel (b) of Figure 15.3 shows quarter-to-quarter changes since the introduction

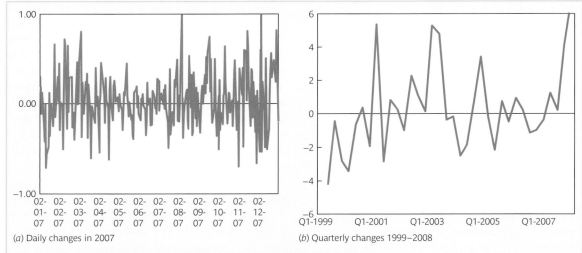

(a) Daily changes in 2007

(b) Quarterly changes 1999–2008

Fig. 15.3 Changes of the Euro/Sterling Pound Exchange Rate

Day-to-day variability of the nominal exchange rate is considerable. Sharp changes in one direction are frequently undone on the following day.

Source: European Central Bank.

of the euro in 1999. The movements are of wider amplitude but are considerably less volatile. Annual exchange rate changes are even less volatile. We already examined the exchange rate in Chapter 6. There we saw that the real exchange rate is the relative price of domestic and foreign goods and we know that prices tend to be sticky. This observation suggests that, in the long run, the exchange rate behaves as goods prices, and therefore responds to a different logic.

Thus the exchange rate is a ubiquitous economic variable. Its movements affect asset prices and returns as well as the relative prices of thousands of goods. This is why they matter so much. This is also why understanding their evolution is tricky. Fortunately, the different patterns over the short and the long run provide the key that we need to sort things out. In this section, we look at the exchange rate as a relative asset price, focusing on the short run. Later, in Section 15.6, we think about the exchange rate as the relative price of goods, focusing instead on the long run, as we did with the economy in previous chapters. As we do so, we will see how these two views are consistent with each other. In doing so, we will try to explain the set of Stylized Facts presented in Box 15.2.

15.5.2 Implications of the Interest Rate Parity Condition

The focus on the exchange rate as an asset price immediately reminds us of the interest rate parity conditions. Its volatility suggests that its movements are driven by market expectations. Indeed, exchange markets are continuously absorbing and assessing news regarding political conditions, releases of economic data, and pronouncements by government ministers, central bankers, bank analysts, prominent businessmen, gurus, etc. After the fact, much of this 'news' will be amended, made more precise, or disavowed, if not actually proved wrong. In the meantime, however, it exerts a powerful influence on the evolution of the exchange rate. This provides an explanation of the pattern shown in Figure 15.3: news—both genuine facts and rumours—move the exchange rate up one moment, and down the next. The importance of 'news' helps us to make sense of Stylized Facts 1 and 2 cited in Box 15.2.

The UIRP condition is therefore the right departure point since it involves the expected future exchange rate. Overlooking for the time being the risk premium, we start with (15.3) and note that

Box 15.2   Mussa's Stylized Facts and the Asset Behaviour of Exchange Rates

In 1979, Michael Mussa, professor at the University of Chicago at the time, assessed the first half-decade of floating exchange rates after the end of the Bretton Woods system.[6] His observations, which remain true today, can be summarized in the following Stylized Facts.

1. On a daily basis, changes in floating foreign exchange rates are largely unpredictable.

2. On a month-to-month basis, over 90% of exchange rate movements are unexpected, and less than 10% are predictable.

3. Countries with high inflation rates have depreciating currencies, and over the long run the rate of depreciation of the exchange rate between two countries is approximately equal to the difference in national inflation rates.

4. Countries with rapidly expanding money supplies tend to have depreciating exchange rates *vis-à-vis* coun-

tries with slowly expanding money supplies. Countries with rapidly expanding money demands tend to have appreciating exchange rates *vis-à-vis* countries with slowly expanding money demands.

5. In the longer run, the excess of domestic over foreign interest rates is roughly equal to the expected rate of appreciation of the foreign currency. On a day-to-day basis, however, the relationship is more tenuous.

6. Actual changes in the spot exchange rate will tend to overshoot any smoothly adjusting measure of the equilibrium exchange rate, the real exchange rate predicted by the analysis of Chapter 7.

7. The correlation between month-to-month changes in exchange rates and monthly trade balances is low. On the other hand, in the longer run, countries with persistent trade deficits tend to have depreciating currencies, whereas those with trade surpluses tend to have appreciating currencies.

---

it links the current interest rates i_t and i_t^* at home and abroad, the current exchange rate S_t, and its expected value next period S_{t+1}^e. We can reinterpret the UIRP condition as saying that the current exchange rate S_t depends on the current interest rates i_t and i_t^* and on the exchange rate S_{t+1}^e expected to prevail next period. This logical implication of the UIRP condition is shown in the first row of Figure 15.4.

This way of representing the UIRP condition is interesting because it shows that we can think of the current spot exchange rate S_t as driven by domestic and foreign interest rates and by the market's current *expectation* of next period's exchange rate S_{t+1}^e. Like all asset prices, the nominal exchange rate is *forward-looking*. What happened before is irrelevant—bygones are bygones and the exchange rate is not tied to its past. It is totally free to jump to any level warranted by current or expected future conditions. Especially important is the im-

plication that any increase in S_{t+1}^e raises S_t. In other words, an appreciation anticipated to occur in the future shows up *immediately* in the current exchange rate.

Can we say anything more about S_{t+1}^e? Next period, the situation will be the same. The UIRP condition will still be valid next period, so S_{t+1} will be explained by the interest rates i_{t+1} and i_{t+1}^* at home and abroad, and by the then expected future exchange rate S_{t+2}^e. This is shown in the second row of Figure 15.4.

Now we can imagine how the markets reason. Today's exchange rate is explained by the interest rates i_t and i_t^* and by the expected exchange rate S_{t+1}^e. As they try to guess S_{t+1}^e they are naturally led to link it with their expectations of i_{t+1}, i_{t+1}^*, and S_{t+2}^e.[7] As the third row of Figure 15.4 indicates, this means that today's exchange rate is driven by current and next period's interest rates and by the exchange rate expected to prevail two periods ahead.

---

[6] We discuss the Bretton Woods system in more detail in Chapter 19. For the moment it is sufficient to know that exchange rates during this period (1946–1971) were fixed by an international agreement and were very difficult to change.

[7] Note that i_{t+1}, i_{t+2}, i_{t+3}, etc. are actually not known as of now, so we really talk about expectations and we should add the 'e' subscript. To keep notation tidier, we dispense with this precision.

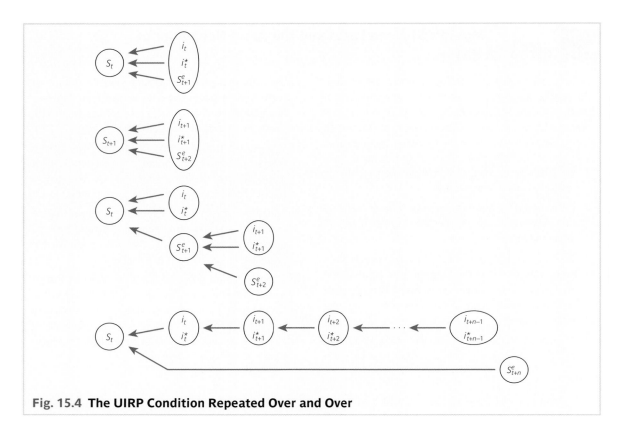

Fig. 15.4 The UIRP Condition Repeated Over and Over

Naturally, S^e_{t+2} will also be driven by the same factors, which will bring i_{t+2}, i^*_{t+2}, and S^e_{t+3} into the picture. Once we move in this direction, there is no end in sight! The last row of Figure 15.4 stops the clock n periods ahead, letting the reader imagine how far away $t + n$ may be. The reasoning is made formal in Box 15.3. It provides equation (15.10), the exact formula suggested in the last row, which will be used in what follows.

As with stock prices, the current exchange rate reflects all current and future interest rates at home and abroad, and its own long-run value. This expression shows just how important expectations of the future are for the present. Even events far into the future can have a large impact on today's exchange rate. This is why exchange markets—and asset markets in general—are so concerned with information. Even remote future events affect the present.

While not yet providing a complete theory of exchange rate determination, this analysis shows that relative conditions in national money markets

are essential for understanding how macroeconomic conditions influence nominal exchange rates. It shows how the anticipation of tight monetary policy at home in the future (i is expected to rise) can lead to an appreciation *today* (S increases).

15.5.3 An Apparent Contradiction and its Resolution

There is a subtle question, however. Suppose that the interest rate i_t at home rises unexpectedly. According to (15.9) or (15.10) or Figure 15.4, the exchange rate S_t should immediately rise, i.e. *appreciate*. Yet, looking at the UIRP condition (15.4), we see that a higher interest rate at home should be associated with an expected *depreciation* of our currency. Is this a contradiction?

It cannot be since both conclusions are based on the same UIRP condition. Using (15.4), we link the domestic interest rate i_t to the expected *rate* of appreciation $(S^e_{t+1} - S_t)/S_t$. Using (15.9), we examine the link between S_t, the *level* of the exchange rate, and

Box 15.3 **Iterating Forward the UIRP Condition**

Start with equation (15.3) and rewrite it so that it now explains the current exchange rate in the current period t:

(15.9)
$$S_t = \frac{1 + i_t}{1 + i_t^\star} S_{t+1}^e.$$

Obviously, the UIRP will also hold in the next period $t + 1$, so we will have

$$S_{t+1} = \frac{1 + i_{t+1}}{1 + i_{t+1}^\star} S_{t+2}^e.$$

This means that, as seen from today's perspective, our best guess of S_{t+1}^e is based on our best guesses of the interest rates in period $t + 1$ and of S_{t+2}:

$$S_{t+1}^e = \frac{1 + i_{t+1}^e}{1 + i_{t+1}^{\star e}} S_{t+2}^e.$$

When this is recognized, we can substitute S_{t+1}^e in (15.9) with the next period version (15.9) and, dropping the subscript 'e' for the interest rates, we find

$$S_t = \frac{(1 + i_t)}{(1 + i_t^\star)} \frac{(1 + i_{t+1})}{(1 + i_{t+1}^\star)} S_{t+2}^e,$$

and, repeating the operation n times:

(15.10)

$$S_t = \frac{(1 + i_t)}{(1 + i_t^\star)} \frac{(1 + i_{t+1})}{(1 + i_{t+1}^\star)} \frac{(1 + i_{t+2})}{(1 + i_{t+2}^\star)} \cdots \frac{(1 + i_{t+n-1})}{(1 + i_{t+n-1}^\star)} S_{t+n}^e.$$

This is the precise formulation of the symbolic link shown in the last row of Figure 15.4.

---

the interest rate i_t, given the expected future *level* of the exchange rate, S_{t+1}^e. Similarly, in (15.10) or Figure 15.4, we take as given all future domestic and foreign interest rates and S_{t+n}^e, the expected future exchange rate far off into the future. Thus, there is no real contradiction, only a confusion of future exchange rate levels and rates of appreciation.

But there is more. We have seen that a higher interest rate i_t is accompanied by an expected depreciation according to (15.4), and by a higher exchange rate S_t, according to (15.9) or (15.10). These two conclusions must both hold simultaneously. Figure 15.5 shows how it is possible. As the domestic interest rate rises i_t above the world rate $i^\star$, the current exchange rate S_t appreciates immediately, but temporarily so. Indeed, if it is expected to depreciate next period or sometimes in the future, we can now have both a current appreciation and a future expected depreciation. Put differently, the exchange rate depreciates enough now to be consistent with the expectation of depreciation in the future.

15.5.4 The Fundamental Determinants of the Nominal Exchange Rate

The 'cumulated' interest parity condition (15.10) states that the exchange rate is determined by pre-

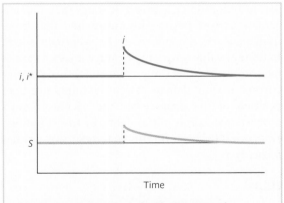

Fig. 15.5 An Increase in the Domestic Interest Rate

When the domestic interest rate (i) rises above the world interest rate, uncovered interest rate parity requires an expected exchange rate depreciation. Given an unchanged expected long-run nominal exchange rate, the exchange rate must appreciate now in order to generate that expected depreciation later.

sent and future interest rates and that is anchored by its long-run value. The exchange rate **fundamentals**, therefore, are those variables that can affect the current and future domestic and foreign interest rates as well as the long-run exchange rate. Domestic and foreign economic conditions—as captured by the *IS–TR* and *AD–AS* frameworks—drive domestic and foreign interest rates. The fundamentals thus include present and future monetary and fiscal pol-icies at home and abroad. They also include those factors that affect the exchange rate in the long run. We now examine what these are.

15.6 The Exchange Rate in the Long Run

15.6.1 The Long Run and the Primary Current Account: A Review

We now turn to the second role of the exchange rate: the relative price of domestic goods in terms of foreign goods. This notion is captured by the real exchange rate $\sigma = SP/P^*$. Given prices at home P and abroad P^*, the nominal exchange rate S determines the real exchange rate. We take these prices as given, for the time being, but we will return to this issue.

The nation's intertemporal budget constraint was introduced in Chapter 7. It states that a nation cannot borrow beyond its means and that accumulated assets can and should be eventually spent. In present-value terms, the country meets its external constraint when the current and future primary current account deficits match the initial net asset position of the country (or the surpluses must at least match the initial debt). In the simplified two-period framework, this statement was written formally as

$$(15.11) \qquad PCA_1 + \frac{PCA_2}{1+r} = -F_1,$$

where F_1 is the net external position of the country at the beginning of the period. F_1 is positive when the country was a net lender previously, and negative when the country is a net debtor.

As long as it meets its intertemporal budget constraint, the country is free to choose the pattern of its primary accounts over time. This degree of freedom evaporates in the second and 'last' period. Tomorrow's primary account must match the accumulated net external position. As in Chapter 7, 'tomorrow' is a metaphor for the long-run steady state when, on average, short-run fluctuations simply cancel out. Then the primary current account must be such that, by the end of period 2 (the proverbial 'end of time') the country repays its accumulated debt, or spends its assets, principal, and interest, inherited from period 1:

$$(15.12) \qquad PCA_2 = -(1+r)(F_1 + PCA_1) = -F_2,$$

where F_2 is the net external position of the country at the beginning of the second period. A positive asset position ($F_2 > 0$) allows a deficit in the second period, while a position of external indebtedness ($F_2 > 0$) requires a surplus.

15.6.2 The Equilibrium Real Exchange Rate and the Primary Current Account in the Long Run

The requirement that the long-run primary current account is consistent with the country's external budget constraint determines the **equilibrium**, or long-run, **real exchange rate**. The link between the primary account and the real exchange rate was studied in Chapter 10. There we described the prim-ary current account function, which relates the prim-ary current account surplus to the real exchange rate. In particular, the current account deteriorates when the real exchange appreciates. Other factors, such as current and foreign GDPs, also affect the primary current account, but they are mostly cycli-cal and therefore irrelevant for the long run. As we ignore them, we simply write the primary current account function as $PCA(\sigma, \dots)$. The dots simply remind us of these other factors. The key result is that the PCA is a negative function of the real exchange rate σ. The primary current account function is depicted in Figure 15.6 by the downward-sloping schedule. A first observation is that, everything else (the dots!) being constant, there exists a particular real exchange rate that delivers a given primary current account.

Next, we return to (15.12). The national budget constraint requires that, in the long run, the prim-

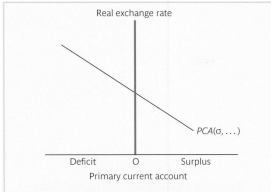

Fig. 15.6 The Primary Current Account Function

The primary current account function shows the relation between the real exchange rate and the primary account balance. It is downward-sloping because a lower real exchange rate, all other things being equal, leads to an improvement in the primary current account.

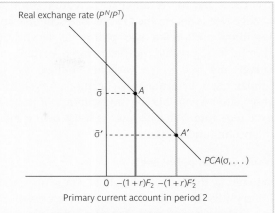

Fig. 15.7 The Equilibrium Real Exchange Rate

Long-run equilibrium requires that the future primary current account be consistent with the net asset position, F_2. To point A corresponds the equilibrium real exchange rate $\bar{\sigma}$. A less favourable net asset position $F'_2 < F_2$ implies a lower primary current account deficit (or a larger current account surplus) in the future. The vertical schedule is shifted to the right. If indebted ($F_2 < 0$), the country must have a greater future primary current account surplus to service the greater external debt and the long-run real exchange rate $\bar{\sigma}'$ must be lower to generate that surplus. If the country is already a net creditor ($F_2 > 0$), a lower level of net foreign assets today implies a smaller feasible deficit tomorrow.

ary current account be equal to the negative of the country's net foreign asset position, plus interest. It means paying off the debt (when F_2 is negative) through a surplus, or running down accumulated assets (when F_2 is positive) through a deficit. The constraint is shown as the vertical schedule $-F_2$ in Figure 15.7. This represents the obligations coming up in the future that have to be repaid. If a country is indebted, then $F_2 < 0$, so $-F_2 > 0$ and the schedule $-F_2$ will lie to the right in the figure. If, on the other hand, a country is a net creditor with $F_2 > 0$, the vertical schedule will lie to the left, since it can live beyond its means in the future. For the budget constraint to be satisfied in period 2, the economy must be at the intersection of the primary current account schedule and this vertical line. At point A, the equilibrium exchange rate can be read off the vertical axis. Quite simply, the downward-sloping primary current account schedule shows how the real exchange rate affects the primary current account, and the long-run budget constraint shows how the required primary current account determines the equilibrium real exchange rate, which we call $\bar{\sigma}$.

As it represents the long-run tendency, the equilibrium real exchange rate is unlikely to correspond to the observed real exchange rate at any point in time, if only because it varies widely. When the

real exchange rate is above its equilibrium level, it is **overvalued**. It is **undervalued** in the opposite case. In the long run, however, it must return to its equilibrium value to ensure that the budget constraint is not violated. Markets see to it and, eventually, lead the real exchange rate to its long-run equilibrium value.

15.6.3 The Fundamental Determinants of the Real Exchange Rate

The result that the net external position drives the equilibrium real exchange rate is a very powerful one. It means that, eventually, market forces will take the real exchange rate to where it should be. The time required to get there can take several years or longer. The concept of an equilibrium real exchange rate looks beyond such transitory phases to focus on the steady state. It is the beacon that shows where the real exchange rate is headed.

Graphically, the result that the equilibrium exchange rate is determined by the PCA schedule and the initial net foreign asset position is deceptively simple. It is possible, however, to go beyond the curves and ask which variables, known as the fundamental determinants, or fundamentals for short, are responsible for the evolution of the real exchange rate. What follows is a list of the most important fundamentals.

Non-price competitiveness

We start by thinking harder about competitiveness. Competitiveness is a matter of relative prices—i.e. the real exchange rate—but also of many other things. To start with, it matters a great deal how well designed and original are our goods. A bottle of champagne is unique, and can fetch a high price before consumers switch *en masse* to similar wines, which may be good or even better but do not carry the glamour of the original. Similarly, German cars have a reputation of reliability that gives them the edge, much as British bankers have built up the formidable City of London network or the Finnish manufacturer Nokia has achieved a position of leadership in the portable phone business. When something of this kind happens, the country becomes fundamentally more competitive and, for any level of the real exchange rate, its primary current account improves. Graphically, in Figure 15.8, the *PCA* schedule shifts to the right, to *PCA′*. This gain in non-price competitiveness translates into a higher equilibrium exchange rate σ̄′. This result can be explained in two ways. First, because they have become more attractive, domestic goods can be sold at a higher relative price. Second, starting at the old equilibrium rate σ̄, i.e. at unchanged relative price, more goods can now be sold, which will result in a larger primary account current than required by condition (15.12). In the long run, this surplus will have to be eliminated by a real appreciation which makes our goods more expensive and their goods cheaper.

A good example of a rapid improvement in non-price competitiveness is the transformation process in Central and Eastern Europe. As the Berlin Wall was dismantled in 1989 and the Soviet Bloc crumbled, these countries moved from central planning to the market economy. Starting with antiquated productive equipment and a dilapidated public infrastructure, they quickly started to catch up with the West. As they climbed up the export quality ladder, their non-price competitiveness quickly improved. Unsurprisingly, their real exchange rates have been continuously appreciating, as the comparison with 'Old Europe' shows in Figure 15.9.

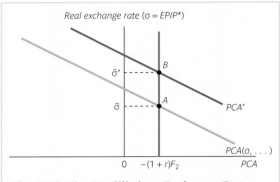

Fig. 15.8 The Equilibrium Exchange Rate and Non-Price Competitiveness
A gain in non-price competitiveness is captured by the rightward shift of the *PCA* schedule to *PCA′*. The equilibrium real exchange rate rises from σ̄ to σ̄′.

Natural resources

The Netherlands in the 1960s and the UK and Norway in the early 1980s were lucky enough to discover large reserves of gas or oil under the North Sea. In a matter of a few years, they could reduce their import bill or even become net exporters. If we break the primary current account into two components, oil and non-oil, we can write $PCA = PCA^{\text{non-oil}} + PCA^{\text{oil}}$.

Before the discovery, PCA^{oil} was substantial and negative, such as in oil-importing countries. Afterwards it became nil or even positive. If the primary current account was at its long-run level before the discovery, as PCA^{oil} improved very sizably, it became too strong. The discovery of natural resources has much the same effect as an improvement in non-price competitiveness. This is well captured by the rightward shift of the *PCA* schedule in Figure 15.8. As before, it implies that the equilibrium real exchange rate has appreciated. What happens next is told in Box 15.4.

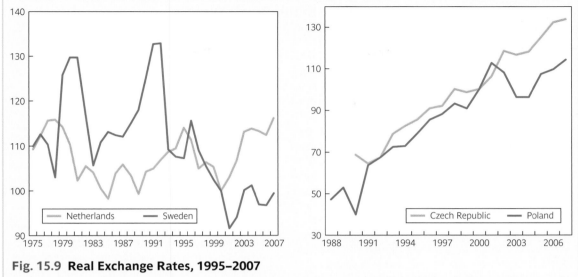

Fig. 15.9 Real Exchange Rates, 1995–2007

Countries that experience catch-up growth continuously improve their non-price competitiveness. Their equilibrium real exchange rates appreciate and, normally, so do their actual real exchange rates.

Source: IMF, *International Financial Statistics*.

Net external position

We have seen that the net external investment position is another fundamental determinant of the real exchange rate. All other things being equal, the more positive the external investment position, the more appreciated the equilibrium exchange rate will be. Similarly, indebted countries will require depreciated real equilibrium exchange rates in order to generate the resources for debt service.

To see how the net external position affects the equilibrium real exchange rate, we return to Figure 15.7. Point A describes a situation of long-run equilibrium: when the external debt position is F_2, which is actually a net debt so $-F_2 > 0$, the equilibrium real exchange rate is $\bar{\sigma}$. Now consider the same country, with the same PCA schedule, but with a net debt F'_2 that is even more negative than F_2. To this debt corresponds the new vertical schedule $-(1 + r)F'_2$, which will lie to the right of the original one, and a new equilibrium real exchange rate $\bar{\sigma}'$ that is lower than $\bar{\sigma}$. We see that the larger the net external debt, the more the real exchange rate must depreciate in the long run. Conversely, an improvement in the net external position calls for a real exchange appreciation.

The net external position of a country is a legacy of its history and evolves slowly. It may also take many years for the actual exchange rate to respond to changes in its equilibrium value. When the exchange rate is **misaligned**, meaning that it is not at its equilibrium level, its net external position must be changing. Indeed, we know that when the current account is in surplus, the country lends to the rest of the world, and it borrows when the current account is in deficit. In the long run, the real exchange rate is at its equilibrium level and we have $PCA = -(1 + r)F_2$ so that the current account is $CA = PCA + (1 + r)F_2 = 0$. Figure 15.7 shows that if the exchange rate were **overvalued**, so that $\sigma > \bar{\sigma}$, relative to point A, we would be up and to the left along the PCA schedule. This would imply $PCA < -(1 + r)F_2$ and therefore a current account deficit. A net borrower, it lives beyond its means. Conversely, if $\sigma < \bar{\sigma}$, the exchange rate is **undervalued** and the country's net asset position improves as it runs a current account surplus.

This might seem worrisome. Could debts spiral out of control? If the exchange rate is allowed to play its corrective role, the answer is no. But examples abound of countries such as Indonesia and Nigeria, which were made fabulously wealthy by

Box 15.4 **The Norwegian Cure to the Dutch Disease**

When oil was discovered in the UK's North Sea in the mid-1970s sterling's real exchange rate soon appreciated by more than 30%. Ironically, the result was a shift away from 'traditional' industry (other traded goods besides oil) towards services, with massive plant closures and unemployment as industrial workers could not be immediately absorbed by the oil industry or the service sector. This striking process of deindustrialization— needed to eliminate the non-oil current account surplus—is called the **Dutch disease**, ever since it was first diagnosed in the 1960s when gas was discovered in the Netherlands' side of the North Sea.[8] The Dutch disease explains why resource-rich countries typically find it more difficult to develop and maintain an industrial sector. The problem can be seen today in contemporary Russia. This should not be a source of long-term concern though: why produce industrial goods when Mother Nature provides easy exports? In the short run, however, the adjustment can be painful.

In order to avoid this curse, Norway established the Government Petroleum Fund in 1990 (renamed Government Pension Fund—Global in 2006). As described by the Ministry of Finance,

Central government's net cash flow from petroleum operations is transferred in its entirety to the Government Pension Fund Global via the state budget, whereas the guidelines stipulates

that only the expected real return on the Fund should be returned to the budget for general spending purposes. In this way the Fund serves as a long-term savings vehicle to let the Norwegian Government accumulate financial assets to help cope with future expenditures associated with the ageing of the population. . . . At the end of 2005 the Fund amounted to close to NOK 1400 billion or 99 percent of mainland GDP (i.e. excluding petroleum activities). Projections indicate that the Fund will grow to 180 percent of mainland GDP at the end of 2010. Given the present guidelines for fiscal policy, the Fund is expected to reach a level of around 250 percent of mainland GDP in the years after 2030, before starting to gradually decline.[9]

Importantly, all the Fund's resources must be invested abroad. This provision saves Norway from the Dutch Disease. Since much of oil income does not enter Norway, there is no pressure on the exchange rate to appreciate. As a result, the account is in perennial surplus. This would make no sense in the long run, but for Norway the long run is when oil reserves will be exhausted. In the meantime, keeping the current account in surplus prevents deindustrialization. Norway's central bank sums up the situation well: 'The Petroleum Fund makes it possible . . . to avoid abrupt shifts in the industry structure, such as we have seen in many other countries with substantial revenues from natural resources, and contributes to sustainable business and industry in the long term.'[10]

oil discoveries, but then squandered their wealth and even became highly indebted as a result. Box 15.5 looks at the case of Sweden to provide an interpretation of Figure 15.9, and at the US dollar.

15.6.4 How to Think About the Equilibrium Real Exchange Rate?

In practice, disturbances large enough to produce significant changes in the equilibrium real exchange rate are rather rare events. Thus, in many instances, the equilibrium real exchange rate is very stable or even constant. This implies PPP, which we already encountered in Chapter 6. We noted that PPP is a powerful rule of thumb. But then one must be always on the watch for the possibility

that a major change is under way. We have just seen the main fundamentals that determine the equilibrium real exchange rate, so we now know why it may change.

An important case in point is the catch-up process that poorer countries experience during a successful take-off growth phase. We already observed in Figure 15.9 that the real exchange rates of the Central and East European countries appreciated steadily since they embarked on their transformation process. This is an excellent example of a general phenomenon known as the **Balassa–Samuelson effect**. It is described in Box 15.6.

---

[8] The WebAppendix presents the phenomenon in more formal detail.

[9] 'The Norwegian Petroleum Sector and the Government Pension Fund—Global' by Secretary General Tore Eriksen, Ministry of Finance <www.regjeringen.no>.

[10] Norges Bank <www.norges-bank.no>.

Box 15.5 **Indebted and Depreciated: The Cases of Sweden and the USA**

Figure 15.9 shows that Sweden's equilibrium exchange rate depreciated in the 1990s. A plausible interpretation is the deterioration of its net external position visible in Figure 15.10. In the early 1990s, partly due to an overvalued exchange rate, Sweden suffered from a deep financial crisis. When the kronor depreciated and became undervalued, foreign liabilities, which exceeded foreign assets by some 20% of GDP, became large when evaluated in the domestic currency, hence a precipitous decline in the net external position. The exchange rate eventually recovered from its undervalued level but not to its previous value. Since then, the external position has improved, which suggests that the kronor's equilibrium real exchange rate has risen.

Figure 15.10 also shows the gradual deterioration of the US external position. In the mid-1980s, the USA switched from being a net lender to being a net debtor, and the trend has accelerated in recent years. This has prompted many observers to conclude that the equilibrium level of the dollar has fallen and to predict that the actual exchange rate would soon. For many years, the dollar defied these predictions. Since 2003, the dollar has started its much-awaited correction. Many people are surprised, or upset, with the continuing weakness of the dollar, because it boosts US competitiveness at the expense of its trading partners. The same people also lament the USA's large external debt and continuing current account deficits. But how else can the USA stabilize its net external debt without improving its current account? And what better way to do this than with a significant real depreciation of the dollar?

15.7 From the Long to the Short Run

We now reconcile the present short-run 'financial market' and the long-run or 'relative price of goods' views of the exchange rate. Each perspective is rooted in its own compelling logic, and while the situation sometimes appears schizophrenic, it is not. We first note that the short-run view encapsulated in Figure 15.4 or equation (15.10) links the current nominal exchange rate to the expected future exchange rate far into the future. Of course, no one knows what the future will be, but markets that set the exchange rate nevertheless have to make a guess. Between now and the distant future, many things will happen. There will be expansions and recessions, current account surpluses and deficits, and much more. Yet, a good bet is that, in the long run, the relative price of goods view will prevail because a country cannot forever escape its budget constraint and the real exchange rate will play a role in enforcing that budget constraint. Over- and under-valuations do occur, but not forever.

Returning to Figure 15.4 or (15.10), we can now think of the very long-run nominal exchange rate S^e_{t+n} expected far into the future with its long-run level. If n is very large, this is just the long-run nominal exchange rate $\bar{S}$. So the short- and long-run views of the exchange rate do make contact with each other. If the two are consistent, the long run must represent a stringing together of successive short runs. Yet in making this connection, we have a small problem. The long equilibrium exchange rate $\bar{\sigma}$ is in real terms, while Figure 15.4 or (15.10) relates the current to the long-nominal exchange rate in the distant future $\bar{S}$. How do we bridge that gap?

We already know about the real determinants of $\bar{\sigma}$, the long-run (or equilibrium) real exchange rate from Section 15.5. If we think of $\bar{\sigma}$ as the 'doubly-deflated' long-run nominal exchange rate, then it is also $\bar{\sigma} = \bar{S}\bar{P}/\bar{P}^*$. The price levels $\bar{P}$ and $\bar{P}^*$ are those which prevail at home and abroad, respectively, in the long run. These price levels will be the result of inflation between now and then. Chapters 6 and 12

Box 15.6 The Balassa–Samuelson Effect[11]

Experienced travellers invariably notice that wealthier countries are systematically more expensive than poorer ones. This is not merely a perception, but a hard fact (see Table 15.4). To see why, consider a poor country. Obviously most wages are much lower than in a rich country, but they will grow when and if the country catches up with the richer country. This will happen when it accumulates capital, imports advanced technology, and generally becomes more productive. As this happens, we expect standards of living, and therefore local wages, to grow. Now work backwards in time from when catch-up will have occurred and wages will have caught up with those of the most advanced economies. For this

to happen, wages must grow faster during the catching-up period. Since wages make up production costs, the same reasoning applies to price levels. To grow faster in poor rather than in rich countries and eventually converge to the same levels, prices must start from a low basis. This is documented in Table 15.4, which shows the consumer prices and GDP per capita in a sample of countries around the world, as measured in 2004. For ease of comparison, both prices and GDP are indexed relative to the USA. For example, in 2004, the Austrian GDP per capita was 78.4% of what it was in the USA, while prices were 14.2% higher. The association between income and price levels is unmistakable, although not perfect.

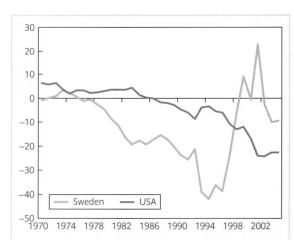

Fig. 15.10 Net External Positions of Sweden and the USA, 1970–2004 (% of GDP)

The net external position, here measured as a percentage of GDP, subtracts the liabilities to foreign residents owed by both public and private sectors from the sum of assets held by domestic against foreign residents.

Source: Lane and Milesi-Ferretti (2006).

Thus, the long equilibrium *nominal* exchange rate is driven by the long equilibrium *real* exchange rate and by the long-run price levels at home and abroad. Anything that raises the long equilibrium real exchange rate also raises the long equilibrium nominal exchange rate, holding the evolution of domestic and foreign inflation constant. Given a long equilibrium real exchange rate, the long equilibrium nominal exchange rate is higher, the higher is the foreign price level (due to higher cumulative inflation) and the lower is the domestic price level (due to lower cumulative inflation).

This helps us understand Stylized Facts 3 and 4 in Box 15.2. The higher domestic inflation is relative to foreign inflation, the higher $\bar{P}$ will be relative to $\bar{P}^*$ and the more depreciated $\bar{S}$ will be. This has direct consequences for the *current* nominal exchange rate S_t (Stylized Fact 3). Since we know that, in the long run, inflation and money growth go hand in hand, we also understand Stylized Fact 4.

The last step is to replace S_{t+n}^e with $\bar{S}$ in (15.10) and we find

inform us how to think about inflation in the long run, so we know how to think of $\bar{P}$ and $\bar{P}^*$. It only remains to use the definition of the real exchange rate to pin down the long-run nominal exchange rate, which can be rearranged as $\bar{S} = \bar{\sigma}\bar{P}/\bar{P}^*$.

[11] The Balassa–Samuelson effect is named after Bela Balassa (1928–1991), a Hungarian-born economist at Johns Hopkins University, also known as a gourmet and author of a confidential restaurant guide, and after Paul Samuelson (1915–), the 1970 Nobel laureate from MIT. A formal derivation is available in the WebAppendix.

Table 15.4 GDP per Capita and Price Levels, 2004

	(USA = 100)			(USA = 100)	
	GDP per capita	Price level		GDP per capita	Price level
Europe			**South America**		
Austria	78.4	114.2	Argentina	31.2	31.7
Belarus	34.4	11.6	Bolivia	8.2	27.4
Belgium	71.1	120.0	Brazil	19.7	33.7
Croatia	28.3	62.6	Chile	38.3	41.9
Czech Republic	43.5	60.8	Peru	11.7	48.1
Denmark	78.4	146.1	Venezuela	21.2	56.6
Finland	65.1	137.9			
France	72.7	119.2	**Asia**		
Germany	71.0	117.6	Bangladesh	5.9	16.6
Greece	46.2	99.4	China	14.6	27.5
Hungary	38.0	63.7	India	8.1	21.8
Ireland	77.4	134.2	Indonesia	10.7	22.5
Italy	64.5	109.6	Israel	57.3	85.1
Luxembourg	137.3	116.3	Japan	67.4	144.1
Norway	94.5	146.4	Korea	49.0	76.2
Poland	26.5	57.8	Pakistan	7.1	22.3
Portugal	48.7	87.6	Saudi Arabia	36.6	49.7
Russia	30.9	22.1	Singapore	80.2	80.3
Slovak Republic	30.6	61.8	Sri Lanka	12.5	19.2
Spain	59.4	101.1			
Sweden	72.4	132.1	**Africa**		
Switzerland	82.7	156.6	Central African Republic	2.4	33.7
Turkey	16.4	60.7	Chad	2.6	27.2
United Kingdom	74.5	118.7	Congo, Dem. Rep.	1.1	38.0
			Cote d'Ivoire	6.5	31.7
North America and Oceania			Egypt	12.9	17.7
Canada	79.9	95.8	Ethiopia	1.8	13.8
Mexico	22.5	68.6	Kenya	3.3	36.3
United States	100.0	99.3	Nigeria	3.3	42.9
Australia	81.4	100.9	South Africa	25.5	46.2

Source: Heston, Summers and Aten (2006).

(15.13) $S_t = \dfrac{(1+i_t)}{(1+i_t^*)} \dfrac{(1+i_{t+1})}{(1+i_{t+1}^*)} \dfrac{(1+i_{t+2})}{(1+i_{t+2}^*)}$

$$\cdots \dfrac{(1+i_{t+n})}{(1+i_{t+n}^*)} \bar{\sigma} \dfrac{\bar{P}^*}{\bar{P}}.$$

We have now fully linked the current exchange rate to its long-run value. Indeed, this expression indicates that the current nominal exchange S_t depends on three sets of fundamentals.

(1) The path of future domestic and foreign interest rates—therefore all relevant economic conditions affecting the interest rate (as captured by the *IS–TR* framework): monetary and fiscal policies, foreign demand, etc.

(2) The real exchange rate $\bar{\sigma}$ needed to meet the nation's intertemporal budget constraint—therefore the foreign debt and the country's competitive position.

(3) The level of prices $\bar{P}$ and $\bar{P}^*$ at home and abroad far into the future—therefore present and future inflation, both at home and abroad.

The list of fundamentals becomes long because of the ubiquitous role of the exchange rate in the relative price of goods and assets. In light of this, it is easy to understand why exchange markets react to a very broad range of indicators. Yet, the link between the budget constraint and the current exchange rate is long—it goes through the real equilibrium exchange rate $\bar{\sigma}$, and then the corresponding long-run spot rate $\bar{S}$—and partly clouded by the long string of domestic and foreign interest rates that appear in (15.13). This was the central point of Stylized Fact 7.

15.8 Exchange Rate Volatility and Currency Crises

15.8.1 Volatility and Predictability

Let us return to Figure 15.3. The considerable volatility of the exchange rate in the short run visible in panel (*a*) is a direct consequence of (15.13). The spot exchange rate responds to expectations of the very large number of events that may potentially affect all future interest rates and the long-run spot rate $\bar{S}$. As expectations are constantly changing, the exchange rate reacts. Much of these expectations are very noisy. Over time, much of this noise will cancel or dissipate, as panel (*b*) illustrates. As the comparison between Stylized Facts 1 and 2 indicates, gradually the long-run fundamentals that drive $\bar{S}$ come to dominate. This still leaves much room for uncertainty and correspondingly large fluctuations. Exchange rate movements largely reflect the uncertainty that we face when thinking ahead.

Stylized Fact 1 makes another point. An implication of (15.13) is that the current spot exchange rate reflects what we think we now know about the future. What makes tomorrow or next year different from now? The answer is the arrival of new information. This means that the exchange rate changes between one period and the next as a result of new information, which is unpredictable by definition—if we could predict the arrival of new information, it wouldn't be new information any more! This is why exchange rate movements are largely unpredictable.

The unpredictability of short-run fluctuations is sometimes interpreted as a proof that economists do not really understand the exchange rate. The preceding observation explains why this argument is incorrect. Quite to the contrary, it is because we understand what drives the exchange rate that we can recognize why it is unpredictable. Those who make predictions must implicitly claim that they know things that the market does not know. This may be the case now and then, but it is very unlikely that it is systematically true.[12]

---

[12] This argument holds, incidentally, for all asset prices.

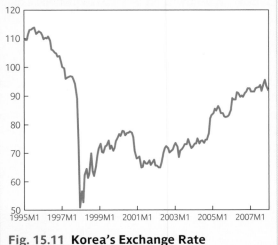

Fig. 15.11 Korea's Exchange Rate (index 100 = January 1997)

The exchange rate is measured as US$ per Korean won. In two months at the end of 1997, the won lost half of its value.

Source: IMF.

15.8.2 Currency Crises[13]

A particular form of volatility is a currency crisis. One example, among many, is the crisis that affected South East Asia in the late 1990s. Figure 15.11 shows the evolution of Korea's exchange rate. Korea was then one among several East Asian 'dragons' that had been growing at close to 10% per annum over more than a decade. It was hailed as a success story, which led to the country's admission earlier that year to the OECD, the club of developed countries. Despite this success, the Korean currency, the won, collapsed in 1997 and the economy plunged into a deep recession. It has still to recover its previous spectacular growth performance.

Currency crises occur frequently. Most often, they are the consequence of the authorities' efforts at maintaining an overvalued exchange rate. The most typical case involves a fixed exchange rate regime combined with rapid domestic inflation.

In Chapter 11, this was shown to be an untenable situation. For a given level of the equilibrium real exchange rate $\bar{\sigma}$, the corresponding equilibrium nominal exchange rate $\bar{S} = \bar{\sigma}\bar{P}^*/\bar{P}$ will decline as the price level increases. If the central bank continues to intervene heavily in the foreign exchange market to keep the actual nominal exchange rate S fixed, the currency becomes increasingly overvalued. As selling pressure mounts, foreign exchange reserves quickly decline and, eventually, the central bank must throw in the towel. A brutal adjustment follows.

The case of Korea is more interesting. Prior to the crisis, there was no serious inflation and the current account was approximately balanced, suggesting at face value that the exchange rate was not overvalued. Yet, several countries in the region had overvalued currencies. This was the case, in particular, of Thailand, which faced a currency crisis in June 1997. At that stage, the markets started to wonder whether neighbouring countries were not in a similar situation. The collapse of Korea's currency is an instance of a **self-fulfilling crisis**.

The interpretation of crises follows directly from Figure 15.4 or equation (15.10). This relationship implies that today's exchange rate S_t is driven by its expected value in the future, S_{t+n}^e. If markets expect S_{t+n}^e to fall, Figure 15.4 predicts that the current rate will fall *immediately*. When the nominal exchange rate is kept fixed at an overvalued level, it is enough for markets to expect a depreciation at some point in the future for the depreciation to occur now. This means that crises can be triggered by abrupt changes in expectations of faraway outcomes.

And this is exactly what happens when the exchange rate is overvalued. As long as the central bank continues to defend the fixed parity S_t which is overvalued relative to the long run (i.e. $S_t > \bar{S}$), the market may continue to believe that $S_{t+n}^e = S$. When the stock of reserves becomes depleted, the market knows that the central bank will not be able to uphold the fixed parity S and that the exchange rate will have to be devalued to its equilibrium level. In that instant, the expectation switches to $S_{t+n}^e = \bar{S}$. This expectation can be based on a simple extrapolation of how long the reserves will last, or even anticipate that the market may clean out the central bank sooner than that.

[13] This is a brief presentation of the currency crisis phenomenon. A more extensive analysis can be found in Chapter 19.

A crisis can even be self-fulfilling. In such a situation, the trigger is a change of view about the equilibrium exchange rate $\bar{S}$. This change of view can be brutal because it is panic-driven. Indeed, if there is a small probability that a depreciation will occur, it means that losses can be made by holding assets denominated in the currency in question. Even if most market participants do not believe that a depreciation is in the making, a rumour that it could is sufficient to convince them to sell their assets denominated in that currency as a precaution. Large sales—a capital outflow—can push the

exchange rate down and seem to confirm the expectation that the currency might be devalued. This leads to more panic sales and eventually to a full-blown crisis.

The main conclusion is that volatility and crises are part and parcel of foreign exchange markets, in fact of all financial markets. Exchange rates and asset prices are driven by expectations which can shift rapidly. Self-fulfilling crises happen when expectations, whether justified or not, are ratified *ex post* by the panic that they generate.

🛈 Summary

1 Foreign exchange markets are a worldwide network of traders who constantly swap currencies and assets denominated in different currencies. They deal in large amounts and promptly arbitrage away any potential source of profit. This ensures consistency among all bilateral cross-rates.

2 The no-profit condition, a characteristic of efficient financial markets, ensures that the covered interest parity condition is satisfied. When capital is internationally mobile, a higher domestic interest rate is matched by a forward exchange rate premium.

3 In the presence of risk, the no-profit condition leads to an uncovered interest parity condition. When capital is internationally mobile, an expected exchange rate depreciation should be compensated by a higher domestic interest rate, and conversely, up to a risk premium.

4 If both uncovered interest parity and purchasing power parity conditions hold, real interest rates are equalized worldwide. Since PPP holds at best in the long run, real interest rate equalization is only a long-run proposition.

5 Exchange rates are forward-looking variables. An implication of the uncovered interest parity condition is that today's exchange rate is driven by today's interest rates and by the expected exchange rate next period.

6 Today's exchange rate is linked to present and future interest rates at home and abroad, and to the spot exchange rate far along in the future. The link takes the form of a chain of present and future uncovered interest parity conditions. All that is currently known about the future is reflected in today's value of the exchange rate. Changes in the exchange rate occur primarily because new information arrives, including revisions of expectations about the future.

7 In the long run, the real exchange rate must ultimately be consistent with the country's budget constraint. The constraint means that past international borrowing must be repaid by eventual current account surpluses. Conversely, past international lending allows a country to eventually dissave through current account deficits. This is what defines the equilibrium real exchange rate.

8 The equilibrium real exchange rate appreciates when the net external position improves or when the economy becomes more competitive for reasons like the discovery of natural resources or gains in non-price competitiveness.

9 Purchasing power parity occurs in the long run when there is no change in the country's net external position (when the current account is balanced on average) or non-price competitive-

ness. Economies that catch up by improving their productivity see their equilibrium real exchange rates appreciate. The resulting Balassa–Samuelson effect is a key reason for PPP not to hold.

10 The long- and short-run views of the exchange rate are not inconsistent. Real factors that drive the long-run real exchange rate are present in today's nominal exchange rate via the exchange rate expected in the long run. Thus the long-run exchange rate is the *anchor* that guides the path of future expected exchange rates and relates it to the current value.

11 The fundamental determinants of the exchange rate—or fundamentals in short—include all the variables that affect the equilibrium real exchange rate and the domestic and foreign interest rates that link the current exchange rate to its long-run equilibrium level. Domestic and foreign inflation, which determine the link between the equilibrium real exchange rate and its nominal level, are also among the fundamentals.

12 The forward-looking aspect of the exchange rate explains its volatility and even the occasional occurrence of currency crises.

⊙ Key Concepts

- ◆ vehicle currencies
- ◆ spot and forward exchange rates, swaps
- ◆ covered interest rate parity (CIRP)
- ◆ uncovered interest rate parity (UIRP)
- ◆ hedging, open position
- ◆ forward premium/discount
- ◆ capital gains and losses
- ◆ international Fisher equation

- ◆ equilibrium, or long-run, real exchange rate
- ◆ fundamentals
- ◆ undervaluation, overvaluation
- ◆ misalignment
- ◆ Balassa–Samuelson effect
- ◆ currency crises
- ◆ self-fulfilling crises

❷ Exercises

1 Suppose that you could buy and sell US dollars for €1 and euros for ¥120, but that at the same time the dollar–yen rate was ¥115.

(a) What strategy would you pursue to take advantage of this 'money pump'? What would be the likely effect of the market's recognition of its existence?

(b) Question (a) ignores the existence of a bid–ask spread. How would your answer change

if the bid–ask spreads were: $0.99–1.01/€, ¥118–122/€, and ¥113–117/$?

2 The interest rate in Sweden is 5% while it is 3% in the Netherlands. What does this imply for the forward premium/discount of the krona *vis-à-vis* the euro? What is the expected exchange rate expected to do?

3 Consider the same interest rates as in the previous question. What would you do if you were

100% sure that the krona would remain constant *vis-à-vis* the euro. How much would you expect to gain if you were to invest €1 million in the operation?

4 Same question in the case you would expect that the krona will appreciate by 5% *vis-à-vis* the euro.

5 For decades, interest rates in Switzerland have been lower (by 1–2%) than in Germany while the exchange rate between the Swiss franc and the deutschmark first and now the euro has changed little. What does this mean for the interest rate parity condition? How could you explain this phenomenon?

6 Within the euro area, interest rates on Treasury bonds are similar but not identical. For instance, at end April 2008, interest rates on similar government bonds were: 4.00% in the Netherlands, 4.04% in Austria, 4.13% in Portugal, and 4.17% in Italy. Interpret these numbers.

7 Since 1970, Australia's current account has almost always been in deficit, sometimes large ones. The real exchange rate has lost very little, some 10%. Is it surprising? How can this be explained?

8 Figure 15.11 shows that Korea's nominal exchange rate has considerably appreciated since the 1997–1998 crisis described in Section 15.8.2. What are the possible explanations?

9 'The equilibrium real exchange rate remains constant when the actual real exchange rate remains durably close to its equilibrium level.' What is the logic of such an assertion? Is this always true?

10 Facing a depreciation pressure, central banks sometimes raise their interest rate. Why?

◆ Essay Questions

1 'The advantage of a fixed exchange rate regime is to greatly reduce exchange rate uncertainty.' Comment.

2 Why can exchange rate volatility create difficulties for trade in goods and services?

3 'The fact that currency crises can be self-fulfilling is greatly disturbing because it suggests that any country can see its money hugely devalued, for no good reason.' In commenting on this statement, carefully draw the difference between self-fulfilling and other types of crises.

4 Equations like (15.10) suggest that the market must look at horizons so far out that they seem to make little sense. Use the logic of the yield curve presented and explained in Chapter 14, explain the similarity between the two logics and provide an interpretation of how the markets think about the very long run.

5 Given what you know, explain and justify Stylized Fact 7.

PART IV

Macroeconomic Policy in a Global Economy

What can a government, or several governments acting together, do to influence macroeconomic outcomes? Having worked through two-thirds of this book, the answer to that question might seem obvious to many readers, but the right answers are in fact never always clear. While governments are in fact always 'bigger' than individual economic agents and can affect their economic conditions in a number of important ways, it is important to ask: Can they? Should they? Will they?

The following four chapters deal with different aspects of these questions. Chapter 16 is concerned with the potential for aggregate demand management policies, i.e. government actions which steer the economy's path by moving the *AD* curve. In Chapter 17, particular aspects and issues of fiscal and monetary policies are taken up in detail, regarding the stability, credibility, and political and economic sustainability of such policies. Since moving only one of the two curves may not be appropriate in all situations faced by policy-makers, it is important to discuss supply-side policy as well. In Chapter 18, we confront the issues already raised in Chapter 4. How can countries improve their standards of living and possibly their rates of growth in a sustainable way? Finally, Chapter 19 examines the scope of policy and policy coordination in the international financial arena. This has achieved enormous importance through the globalization of capital markets but, more urgently, in light of the recent banking and credit crises.

Demand Management Policies

16

Policymakers are unable to predict with great confidence even how (or how quickly) their own actions are likely to affect the economy. In short, if making monetary policy is like driving a car, then the car is one that has an unreliable speedometer, a foggy windshield, and a tendency to respond unpredictably and with a delay to the accelerator or the brake.

Federal Reserve Governor Ben Bernanke

16.1 Overview

Writing in 1930, John Maynard Keynes yearned for the day when economists 'could manage to get themselves thought of as humble, competent people on a level with dentists'. Since Keynes and the Great Depression, policy-makers have hoped that macroeconomic management of the business cycle would be no more complicated than getting a tooth filled. In this chapter, we explore the theoretical possibility of demand management policy, and at the same time address a number of factors that limit what macroeconomic policy can achieve. In the 1970s, attempts to manage the macroeconomy ended with high levels of inflation, unemployment, and public indebtedness. The painful medicine administered in the early 1980s to combat those problems left a bitter taste and little stomach for experimentation with policy activism. Yet while confidence in governments' ability to smooth out aggregate fluctuations systematically has been on the wane for several decades, it is hard to deny that governments can affect demand, and sometimes significantly so. Often, well-timed aggregate demand policy can put an economy back on track.

The age-old controversy between **neoclassical** and **Keynesian** economists has evolved a lot since 1936, when Keynes launched his celebrated attack on the economic orthodoxy of his time. Over the decades, waves of new arguments have been brought forward by each side of the debate, only to be undermined by new counter-arguments from the other side. Yet despite ever-increasing sophistication, the same familiar themes continue to dominate the discussion. First, how quickly do goods and labour markets adjust to shocks? Second, how do agents form expectations and how quickly are these embedded in their decisions? Third, given that inflation is usually a short-run by-product of demand policy, what are its costs to households, businesses, and society as a whole? These questions comprise the first section of this chapter.

The next section deals with the fundamentally random nature of the business cycle and the feasibility of demand management policy. Even if the thorny issues of scope and credibility of managing demand are resolved, economists must admit that they are not gods. Even if they are asked to make pronouncements on television and advise governments, they aren't oracles either. Even if they knew the correct model, random influences in the economic system prevents them from predicting with perfect precision. This fundamental uncertainty—shocks as we call them—cannot be forecast by definition. Few anticipated the oil shocks in the 1970s, and no one foretold the fall of communism and the Iron Curtain in the late 1980s, the terrorists attacks on the World Trade Center and the Pentagon in 2001, or the current banking and credit crises. These events have all proven to be portentous in the economic sense, heralding large adjustments of the economy, but were wholly unanticipated by economic actors.

Finally, the chapter concludes by asking about the nature of the business cycle. Are the shocks which set an economy in motion primarily real, or do they come from the monetary or financial economy? Do they originate in demand or supply? While it is not easy to settle this, it is possible to assess particular episodes, much like a doctor diagnoses a patient with many contradictory symptoms. Economic policy, like medicine, is often as much an art as it is a science.

16.2 Demand Management: What are the Issues?

16.2.1 Equilibrium or Disequilibrium: That is the Question

Since the publication of *The General Theory* in 1936, a fierce debate has raged between the Keynesians, who had embraced the Keynes' way of thinking about the macroeconomic short run, and those who tend to defend the classical framework of flexible prices and rely on the inherent self-corrective nature of the economic system. The latter group, known as the neoclassicals, initially put much emphasis on the role of money and monetary developments while de-emphasizing the usefulness of fiscal policy. Many older disagreements were focused on arcane issues. The debate now revolves to a large extent around the question of nominal price rigidity. While there is near-universal consensus that prices and wages are sticky, disagreement persists about the extent of that stickiness and its relevance for shaping the evolution of output.

The debate is neatly illustrated in Figure 16.1. Starting from point *A*, an expansionary demand policy (monetary policy under flexible exchange rates, fiscal policy under fixed exchange rates) takes the economy first to point *B*, and then to point *C*. There the effect is entirely absorbed by a permanently higher rate of inflation, which is ratified by a proportional exchange rate depreciation. The path taken from *B* to *C* depends on the speed at which the short-run *AS* curve shifts. This in turn depends on how the underlying inflation rate reacts to actual inflation. As discussed at length in Chapters 12 and 13, the underlying rate of inflation reflects the forward-looking anticipations of wage- and price-setters, who are free to set prices at the present, the anticipation of future inflation embedded in wages and prices set in earlier periods but not free to change, and elements of contracts which are simply based on past inflation, such as wage and price indexation. Quick adjustment means a fast move from *A* to *C*, in which case policy only creates inflation, at best with a temporary

boost to GDP. And if the economy always remains on its long-run aggregate supply schedule *LAS* anyway, a superior solution is simply to aim at point *D*, where inflation is low. In this view, the move from *A* to *D* is very rapid and low inflation can be achieved at little or no output cost. This is the neoclassical perspective.

Keynesians do not think that the economy is always on its *LAS* schedule, and tend to endorse **activist demand policies** aimed at returning it to its long-run potential. They are interested in situations like the one corresponding to point *A* in Figure 16.2, where output is below its trend level, and unemployment is above its equilibrium level. By construction, at point *A*, actual inflation is below its underlying rate. Over time, the underlying inflation will decline and the short-run *AS* curve will shift downwards until point *C* is reached. In the Keynesian view, this adjustment may take a very

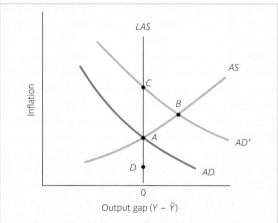

Fig. 16.1 The Neoclassical Case

A monetary expansion moves the economy from point *A* to point *B* in the short run and to point *C* in the long run. If deviations from trend *T* are short-lived, the move is actually from point *A* to point *C*, which is not really helpful. It is more desirable to aim at point *D*, where inflation is low.

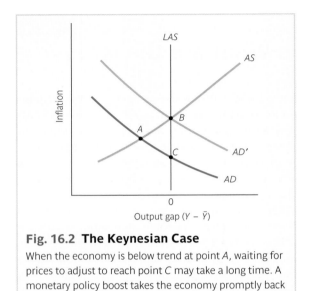

Fig. 16.2 The Keynesian Case

When the economy is below trend at point *A*, waiting for prices to adjust to reach point *C* may take a long time. A monetary policy boost takes the economy promptly back to full employment at point *B*.

long time, during which unemployment is high and output is forgone. This means frustration among the unemployed, and inefficiency as productive resources remain under-utilized. The preferred solution for Keynesians is to pursue an expansionary policy, shifting the aggregate demand schedule out to *AD'* and bringing the economy quickly to point *B*.

Thus, the disagreement boils down to a simple question: Can the economy stay away from the vertical aggregate supply schedule for a long time? Put differently, how quickly does the short-run *AS* shift to bring the economy to rest on the vertical *LAS*? Neoclassicals argue that these shifts occur too fast for policy to make much difference and, anyway, policy is not needed if GDP is never far from its growth trend. They assert that the forward-looking component of underlying inflation dominates the backward-looking component. Keynesians disagree. It is remarkable that so sharp a divergence about the desirability of policy actions arises from an apparently narrow dispute concerning what seems to be a point of detail. Indeed, it is possible to agree completely about the analysis of demand and supply—as presented in Chapter 13 and recalled here—and yet disagree on every aspect of economic

policy simply because there is some doubt about the speed at which the *AS* curve shifts.

16.2.2 Persistence of Expectations and Underlying Inflation

The speed at which the *AS* curve shifts depends on the relative importance of the forward-looking component of underlying inflation. This raises the question of whether this component correctly anticipates developments that will determine the future inflation rate. For some time, Keynesians argued that people learn slowly about events and therefore adjust their expectations very gradually. Put differently, the forward-looking component of underlying inflation was thought to be driven by the past and not to contain information that fundamentally differs from the backward-looking component.

Neoclassical economists achieved a great victory when they argued that the only consistent way of thinking about expectations is to treat them as rational. The **rational expectations** hypothesis discussed in Chapter 7 posits that people do not make systematic errors. They may occasionally underestimate future inflation, and then overestimate it, but on average they get it right. If they do, and if the forward-looking component of underlying inflation dominates, then the *AS* curve will move fast. Two implications follow. First, on average, the economy will always be close to, if not exactly spot on, the *LAS* schedule. Second, the only departures from the *LAS* schedule will be the result of random expectation errors, which does not provide much room for policy to play a useful role. Indeed, in that case policy must rely entirely on surprises and errors. If surprises can be engineered now and then, they cannot be systematic, simply because there is no such thing as a systematic surprise. As for expectation errors, they can only be exploited by policy-makers if they know better than the public at large, but then the solution is for the government to share that knowledge, which is what democracy would call for.

The intellectual force of the rational expectation hypothesis is that any alternative description of the formation of expectations implies that people make systematic mistakes, for instance that they always underestimate inflation when it is rising.

This is a hard case to argue. In any country, banks and economic consultants produce and sell economic forecasts to firms, trade unions, the media, and even the government. Their services are valued if they are right, or at least not systematically wrong. And, as they all compete for the same customers, it is reasonable to expect that those that are systematically wrong would eventually go out of business.

Modern Keynesians are usually willing to concede this point, but they have two answers. First, they note that underlying inflation consists not only of expected inflation. Even if all agents perfectly anticipate the future, they may have signed nominal contracts in the past that lock them into prices and nominal wage increases based on rationally expected inflation at that earlier point in time. Thus, when inflation deviates from these older expectations, there will be some interval of time when agents can do little or nothing about their errors. During that interval, which can be long-lasting, the economy deviates from trend output. Second, the speed at which the short-run *AS* curve moves depends on the speed at which actual inflation—i.e. prices—reacts to expected inflation. Once again, therefore, price stickiness is at the heart of the debate.

16.2.3 The Costs of Inflation

There is an important drawback to the Keynesian policy response of demand management depicted in Figure 16.2. It is accompanied by higher inflation. Unless contractionary policy is pursued with the same vigour as expansionary policy, demand management policies can easily display an inflation bias. Some politicians argue that this is an acceptable price to pay. Couldn't lower joblessness and higher output outweigh the inconvenience of permanently higher inflation? The cost of inflation is another source of disagreement between Keynesians and neoclassicals. Inflation is certainly undesirable, yet it is surprisingly difficult to identify and quantify those costs. Below is a list of potential reasons why inflation bothers economists.

Income and wealth redistribution

Inflation has important redistributive effects. To start with, inflation often distorts relative prices.

When prices rise rapidly, even small differences in rates of increase of particular goods or of wages can lead to dramatic relative price changes. If unions are powerful, real wages will tend to stay ahead, which hurts firms' profitability, eventually deterring investment and harming growth. Those on fixed incomes and with limited political clout, such as pensioners or dole recipients, do not keep up. Real exchange rates tend to swing widely in high inflation environments. This shifts income between local and foreign producers, and between the local producers of traded and non-traded goods since exchange rates exert strong influence on traded good prices but leave non-traded good prices relatively unaffected.

In addition, inflation redistributes wealth. In contrast to real assets—such as housing and land, durable goods, foreign exchange, and precious metals—the value of nominal non-indexed assets is eroded if inflation comes as a surprise. Nominal assets factor a certain rate of inflation into the agreed nominal rate of return. When inflation lies significantly above the underlying expected level, real interest rates can become negative, and wealth is redistributed from lenders to borrowers. Hyperinflations, in particular, can leave a legacy that survives many generations: 85 years after the terrible hyperinflation of the early 1920s, Germans still consider inflation as an absolute evil.

Uncertainty and the value of price signals

In a market economy, prices play a central role as signals. They tell producers what and how to produce, consumers what and how to consume, whether to save, etc. In all cases, what matters is not absolute but relative prices, i.e. the price of one particular good measured in terms of another. A correct interpretation of (relative) price signals is crucial to the efficiency of a market economy. It turns out that high inflation usually means more variable inflation. The more variable inflation is, the less confidence firms and households have that price changes they observe correspond to real changes in economic opportunities. Firms and households under-react to true relative price signals, confusing movements in the price level with changes in relative prices. Evidence for such distortionary effects of inflation is presented in Figure 16.3. Panel (*a*)

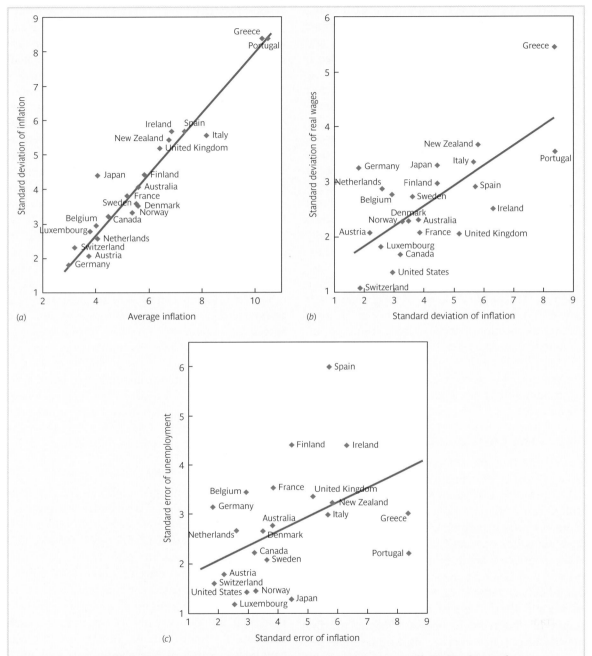

Fig. 16.3 Variability of Inflation, Real Wages, and Unemployment: All OECD Countries, 1960–2003

Comparing across all OECD countries over forty years, it appears that higher inflation is accompanied by more volatile prices (partial correlation = 0.84). The other associations are less strong but still significant: more volatile inflation is accompanied by more volatile real wages (partial correlation = 0.35) and more volatile inflation is accompanied by more volatile unemployment rates (partial correlation = 0.24).

Sources: IMF; OECD, *Economic Outlook*; Bureau of Labor Statistics.

documents the positive link between inflation level and variability. Panels (b) and (c) show that more variable inflation is positively associated with more variable real wages and unemployment. This is a clear indication that nominal fluctuations have real effects. When the efficient functioning of the price mechanism is attenuated, overall productivity declines, eventually resulting in lower growth and higher unemployment. Indexation—the contractual linking of individual prices or wages to the overall rate of inflation—can worsen matters because it tends to freeze the hierarchy of all relative prices and to lock in real rigidities. This further dulls the reaction of economic agents to relative price signals.

The value of money

While indexation may hurt the efficiency of the price system, it is often touted as the way to prevent income and wealth redistribution. If all nominal values—all prices and wages, but also nominal interest rates, asset prices and the exchange rate—are indexed, the losers are simply those who hold money, which, by definition, is not indexed. The losses suffered when the value of money declines steadily—more frequent trips to the bank—may seem trivial. Yet examples of hyperinflation in history show that the consequences can be highly disruptive. Box 16.1 describes these costs and explains the concept of an ideal or 'optimal' rate of inflation.

16.3 Feasible Demand Management Policy

16.3.1 Frisch, Slutsky, and the Modern View of the Business Cycle

An important aspect of demand management policy is that it be *feasible*—that the central bank or the finance ministry can actually execute it, and do a good job at it. An important controversy between Keynesians and neoclassicals concerns the ability of governments to conduct policy effectively. The most important reason for scepticism is the nature of the cycle itself.

Economists' initial optimism about demand management policy was driven by a belief that understanding business cycles was a matter of understanding a more or less **deterministic** system, meaning that the present depends mechanically on the economic history of the past. Business cycles do in fact exhibit important regularities and seem to follow an internal logic. Throughout the history of economic thought, economists have sought the mechanism by which each cycle sows the seeds of its successor, so that cycles go on reproducing themselves, just like the rising and falling of the tides. This would be the case if the economic system constantly generated forces that successively speeded it up and then slowed it down. It turns out that it is quite possible to imagine

how this can come about. And it would be easy to imagine how a good dose of demand policy could correct it, interfering perfectly with the wave to produce a flat growth path.

This optimistic view was badly shaken by the discovery that cycles can be generated from purely random, or stochastic, factors. This **stochastic view of business cycles** can be traced to the work in the late 1920s and early 1930s by the Russian Eugen Slutsky (1880–1948) and the Norwegian Ragnar Frisch (1895–1973).[1] To understand this important discovery, consider an economy which starts away from its stationary-state equilibrium but returns to it over time—for example, the growth model of Chapter 3. How did it get off the path in the first place? Slutsky and Frisch reasoned that economies are constantly subject to random disturbances, or shocks. These might come from demand (e.g. alternating optimistic and pessimistic entrepreneurial

---

[1] Ragnar Frisch received the first Nobel Prize in Economics in 1969. Eugen Slutsky, who perhaps deserves more credit than he received, was a researcher at the Conjuncture Institute in Moscow during Stalin's dictatorship and was unable to publish this discovery until eight years later, when his work was finally translated into English.

Box 16.1 **Optimal Inflation**

The late Milton Friedman argued that the optimal rate of inflation should be negative—a **deflation**, a period in which the price level falls steadily. More precisely, Friedman argued that the optimal inflation rate should equal the negative of the real interest rate and thus the nominal interest rate should be set to zero.[2] Friedman's radical argument rests on a principle that production of a good should be expanded as long as the marginal benefit, i.e. what consumers and firms are willing to pay for it, exceeds the marginal cost. This principle can be readily applied to money produced by a central bank. For the public, the price of money is the opportunity cost of holding it, and in Chapter 9 that was shown to be the nominal interest rate. The cost of producing money turns out to be virtually nil (even an additional €100 banknote costs the central bank or minting company a few cents). In theory, the state can make its citizens better off by providing them with the public good of money, which costs virtually nothing to make, at no cost. Naturally, if it did so, interest rates would have to be very low. As the argument goes, they should be zero.[3]

In principle, Friedman was right. Money is expensive to hold, especially if you own a lot of it. Its cost is most evident when inflation and nominal interest rates are very high. In such episodes, the demand for money all but vanishes, and people spend a lot of energy to avoid using it. Yet for a number of good reasons, Friedman's pre-

scription has never been taken up in practice. To start with, deflation means that goods and services will be cheaper tomorrow than today—why buy anything now when prices will be much lower next year? This pattern has been visible in Japan recently, as it suffered a prolonged slump for the decade of the 1990s. More importantly, a fact of life is that almost all goods and services are taxed, so why should money be treated any differently? Inflation is a tax on money holdings, and has a role to play alongside all other taxes. In fact, in many countries where tax collection is weak, because of the costs of setting up a non-corrupt administration, inflation is one of the very best sources of tax revenues that can be tapped. For these countries, it may be efficient to have significant inflation. In the developed countries, tax collection is not a problem so money should simply be taxed like all other goods, following the principles of optimal taxation.[4]

As already noted in Chapter 9, many central banks around the world have adopted **inflation targeting**, meaning that they publicly state and commit to some inflation rate as an objective of policy. The underlying presumption is that inflation is acceptable when people stop worrying about it. Table 16.1 presents their targets for 2003. Typically, these central banks aim at inflation rates around 2%. This is also the rate identified by the European Central Bank as the limit of price stability.

animal spirits or the consumer mood, or policy actions) or supply (e.g. exceptionally bad or good crops and natural disasters; important inventions or discoveries like the steel furnace, railways, elec-

tricity, or computers, as well as minor ones; social unrest). The list of potential shocks is endless. Like drops of rain generating ripples on a lake, these shocks constantly buffet the economy, moving it away from its previous position.

These shocks, often referred to as **impulses**, change the demand or supply conditions in the

[2] From standard microeconomic theory, the real interest rate should equal the marginal product of capital plus depreciation, as was presented in Box 8.6 in Chapter 8. The real interest rate r is the nominal interest rate i less the inflation rate π, i.e. $r = i - \pi$. When $i = 0$, it follows that $r = -\pi$.

[3] It is important to stress that Friedman did *not* advocate handing out money on every street corner! To the contrary, he argued that as monopoly provider of money, the central bank should strive to hold down the opportunity costs of holding money—and the way to do this is to reduce inflation *below* zero, and drive the nominal interest rate to 0. In the end, this actually means being quite stingy with monetary growth!

[4] The principle of optimal taxation, which we take up in detail in Chapter 18, is that taxes should be spread across all goods and services and that the tax rates should be inversely related to the sensitivity of demand to the price of that good (the price elasticity). For example, the optimal tax rate on petrol is high because its demand reacts less to increases in petrol prices. The optimal taxation principle often runs into resistance due to equity considerations. By the same argument, food should be heavily taxed.

Table 16.1 Inflation Targets Set by Inflation-Targeting Central Banks in 2003

	Australia	Brazil	Canada	Chile	Colombia	Czech Republic	Hungary
Inflation target	2–3% 'central tendency'	8.5%	1–3%	2–4%	6%	2–4%	3.5 ± 1%

	Iceland	Israel	Rep. of Korea	Mexico	New Zealand	Norway	Peru
Inflation target	2.5 ± 1.5%	1–3 %	3 ± 1%	3%	1–3%	2.5%	2.5 ± 1%

	Phillippines	Poland	South Africa	Sweden	Switzerland	Thailand	United Kingdom
Inflation target	4.5–5.5%	less than 4%	3–6%	2 ± 1%	less than 2%	0–3.5%	2.5 ± 1%

Source: Fracasso, Genberg, and Wyplosz (2003).

economy. Once randomly disturbed, the economy embarks on a deterministic adjustment described in the previous section, until the occurrence of the next shock. The **propagation mechanism** transforms, or cumulates, random impulses into irregular cyclical oscillations. The fact that individual reactions are damped does not weaken this result, since old oscillations are constantly being supplemented by new ones corresponding to more recent shocks. In this vision of the business cycle shown in Figure 16.4, it is sufficient to accept the view that an economy is regularly buffeted by endless series of shocks, and never really settles down to its stationary state. The rest of this chapter follows on this lead, which is the cornerstone of modern business cycle theory.

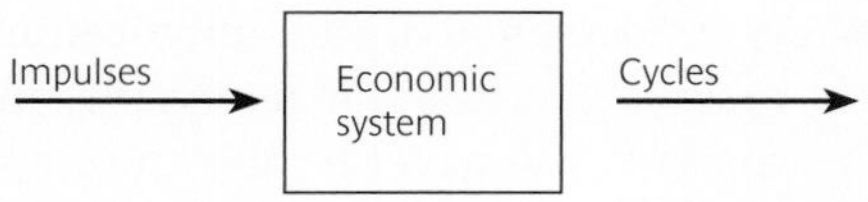

How likely is it that purely random impulses working their way through the economy actually generate the kind of behaviour corresponding to our earlier stylized facts? Can shocks which continuously move the economy away from its steady state and followed by its internal dynamic actually explain business cycles? Box 16.2 recalls how this question received an affirmative answer at the dawn of the computer era. Random shocks can even transform the rather boring multiplier-accelerator model into realistic cycles. In panel (*a*) of Figure 16.5, 200 purely random shocks drawn over time are plotted.[5] Such observations—truly random impulses—could represent a succession of unforeseeable events, large or small. Panel (*b*) shows what happens when these shocks are 'filtered' by a propagation mechanism. In this case, we use the *AS–AD* model we have used in previous chapters and described more precisely below in Box 16.3. The result is a succession of artificial business cycles which resemble those of, say, the UK data presented in Figure 1.5. Although the impulses themselves are not cyclical at all, the transformed variable exhibits

Fig. 16.4 The Impulse-Propagation Mechanism

Random shocks hit the economic system, which reacts by generating business cycles. The cycles result from the averaging or accumulation of these random disturbances over time.

[5] Such a random variable which is identically and independently distributed is often called white noise. White noise has the property that current and past values contain no information helpful in forecasting future values.

Box 16.2 **Computers, Scientists, and Business Cycles**

While Slutsky and Frisch discovered that purely random events can be responsible for cycles in the 1930s, hard evidence that random influences can generate cyclical behaviour resembling actual economies was not forthcoming until the late 1950s, when computers became widely available to researchers. Frank Adelman, a nuclear physicist, and his wife Irma, an economist, studied an economic model developed by Lawrence Klein, the 1980 Nobel laureate from the University of Pennsylvania, and Arthur Goldberger of the University of Wisconsin. (This model consisted of 25 equations summarizing the most important macroeconomic relationships in the US economy.) First, the Adelmans found that the Klein–Goldberger model could not generate a deterministic cycle on its own because the fluctuations died down after a few years. Yet, when perturbed by random shocks, it produced data that had the same statistical properties as actual US business cycles. They concluded that:

Ever since the path breaking article of Frisch on the propagation of business cycles, the possibility that the cyclical movements observed in a capitalistic society are actually due to random shocks has been seriously considered by business cycle theories. The results we have found in this study tend to support this possibility . . . The agreement between the data obtained by imposing uncorrelated perturbation upon a model which is

otherwise non-oscillatory in character is certainly consistent with the hypothesis that the economic fluctuations experienced in modern, highly developed societies are indeed due to random impulses. (Adelman and Adelman, 1959: 620.)

The Adelmans simulated, or solved, their model 100 years into the future on an IBM 650 and were proud that 'computations for one year could be made during an operating time of about one minute'. Now that simulations take seconds or less on a laptop, this approach has become routine. Much effort has gone into improving and enlarging models and the algorithms used for simulations. More recently, Robert E. Lucas of the University of Chicago and 1995 Nobel Prize laureate in economic sciences, made this research strategy explicit:

Our task as I see it . . . is to write a FORTRAN [a programming language] program that will accept specific economic policy rules as 'input' and will generate as 'output' statistics describing the operating characteristics of time series we care about, which are predicted to result from these policies. (Lucas, 1980: 709–10.)

In the last decade, the economics profession has taken Lucas's challenge to heart. Rather than isolated policy interventions, central banks and finance ministries are more likely to evaluate the macroeconomic effects of policy *rules*—Taylor rules for monetary policy, and tax and stabilization rules for fiscal policy, for example.

irregular, periodic movements which resemble real business cycles.

The impulse-propagation mechanism is now the dominant way of thinking about business cycles, because it accords well with the stylized facts. Box 16.3 explains in detail how the *AS–AD* model provides a natural framework for thinking about how cycles arise. Since they are random, the shocks typically generate cycles of different sizes and magnitudes. If many of these impulses are related to permanent technological innovations, not only will they trigger cycles, but in the long run they will also cumulate into a process of long-run growth. This is consistent with the observation that in the long run, the growth process (the accumulation of posit-

ive shocks) dwarfs business cycles (the reaction to individual productivity and other shocks).

16.3.2 Uncertainty, Policy Lags, and the Friedman Critique of Demand Policy

For policy, fundamental uncertainty behind the business cycle is bad news. It necessarily implies that governments will never be able to completely iron out the cycle. The mere fact that markets fail to adjust due to nominal rigidities does not imply that governments can offset. The same uncertainty or incomplete information that prevents markets from making the best possible use of available resources may also plague government actions. Why should policy-makers have a better ability than

Box 16.3 Impulse-Propagation Mechanisms in the *AS–AD* Model

Chapter 13 showed how the *AS–AD* model can help us understand the determinants of output and inflation in the short and long run. It can also be used to study business cycles. The point of departure is to identify the shocks as factors that shift either the *AS* or *AD* curves. **Demand shocks** shift the *AD* schedule, while **supply shocks** affect the position of the *AS* curve. Both demand and supply shocks can be positive or negative. Positive shocks, for example, move the relevant schedule rightwards. Lags in economic relationships are the central source of dynamics in the *AS – AD* framework. Lags exist for various reasons: slow responses of demand to income and of supply to demand imply that the *AD* schedule reacts gradually to demand disturbances. The supply side may also be a source of **persistence**, if underlying inflation catches up only gradually with past inflation.

As an example, consider a permanent increase in the target inflation rate of the central bank operating in a system of flexible exchange rates.[6] Assume that underlying inflation is equal to last period's inflation and start with an economy already in a stationary state at point *A*. (This assumption simplifies matters considerably, because there are no other cycles under way that would interfere with the one under study.) The cycle triggered by this disturbance is tracked in Figure 16.6. The reduc-

tion in the target inflation rate leads to a reduction in the nominal interest rate and an increase in aggregate demand. This takes the economy to point *B* in panel (*a*), with an increase in both output and inflation. Owing to demand lags, the initial shift of the *AD* curve to *AD'* represents only an initial, partial, response. For a time, the *AD* schedule will continue to move rightwards towards *AD"*. Indeed, the lagged response of output means that the longer-run shift of the *AD* curve always exceeds that of the short run and that, as output rises, the *AD* keeps moving to the right.

The *AS* curve will also shift upwards, as underlying inflation gradually catches up with the actual inflation rate. Over time, the economy moves towards point *C*. With actual output in excess of its trend level, inflation catches up and eventually overtakes the target inflation rate.[7] This implies that the real money stock declines and with it output. Declining output means that the *AD* curve begins to move leftwards. Actual inflation then starts to decline, followed by underlying inflation and a downward shift of the *AS* schedule (not shown). Pursuing this reasoning, it appears that the adjustment will be characterized by the 'loops' shown in panel (*b*), with alternating periods of output above and below equilibrium level—i.e. business cycles.[8]

markets to deal with uncertainty? And what if governments too make mistakes? When they set prices wrong, private agents—firms, wage negotiators—have a strong incentive to discover their mistakes promptly and take remedial action. It is not obvious that governments face the same incentives or, even if they do, that they can react as fast.

Indeed, macroeconomic economic policy is plagued by a number of lags. First, a **recognition lag** plagues policy-makers' ability to intervene effectively. This is simply the time needed to discover

that some policy intervention is required. As the previous section suggests, there is good reason to believe that fundamental uncertainty will always be present, and governments will be just as surprised as private agents. Then governments need time to formulate policy, the **decision lag**. Depending on

---

[6] A formal analysis is provided in the WebAppendix to this chapter. While such a shock is not commonplace, it is useful to help focus ideas. A similar shock worth discussing is a permanent increase in the *foreign* inflation rate under fixed exchange rates.

[7] How do we know this? We know that, as long as money growth exceeds inflation, the real money stock *M/P* rises. In the long run, the economy returns to trend GDP and the demand for money roughly returns to its initial value (since $M/P = L(Y, i)$ and both *Y* and *i* approximately return to their initial levels). For *M/P* to return to its initial level, inflation must exceed money growth at some point.

[8] The example was chosen because a single impulse induces a cyclical reaction which resembles a cycle. More generally, this property is not a necessary condition for stochastic shocks to generate cyclical behaviour.

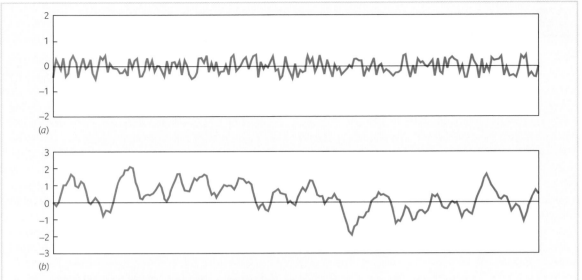

Fig. 16.5 **Impulses and Propagations: An Example**

Panel (a) depicts 200 observations of a random variable, ε_t. Panel (b) displays data from panel (a) after they were transformed, or 'filtered', by the formula $Y_t = 1.3\,Y_{t-1} - 0.4\,Y_{t-2} + \varepsilon_t$, starting from a given Y_0 and Y_{-1}. This 'filter' has the ability to mimic a true data series, working only with purely stochastic influences.

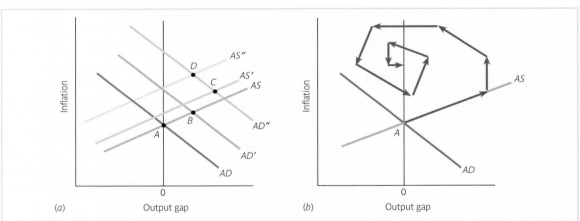

Fig. 16.6 **The Propagation Framework in the _AS–AD_ Model**

In this example, the initial impulse is a permanent increase in target inflation by the central bank. In panel (a), from its initial stationary equilibrium at point A, the economy first moves to point B, as the AD curve begins to respond to the monetary impulse. Gradually, underlying inflation increases in response to actual inflation, and the AS curve, whose position depends on underlying inflation, slides to AS'. Further lagged responses of demand to money growth result in gradual shifts of the AD curve towards AD", bringing the economy to point C. Further movement in underlying inflation towards actual inflation moves the AS schedule towards AS" (point D). Because output has begun to decline, the AD curve begins a descent. As inflation declines, underlying inflation follows and the AS curve also moves downwards. The economy follows a loop of the kind exhibited in panel (b).

the government structure, this can be coupled with an **implementation lag**, as ministries must originate, and parliaments must pass, legislation. Even if implemented quickly, policies need time to produce their effects. This is especially true of monetary policy. It can take several quarters before the easing of money market conditions and depreciating exchange rates have an impact on real activity. To make matters even worse, the duration of this **effectiveness lag** is quite variable, ranging from a few months up to two or three years.

This is why Milton Friedman argued in the 1950s that the best policy is to do nothing at all! According to the **Friedman critique**, ill-timed policy interventions may actually worsen the cycle. Under the best of circumstances, there is no guarantee that policies will be implemented in time, or achieve the stated objectives. If the government has no information advantage over the private sector, it might even do more harm than good. The best policy that governments can pursue is a steady hand, rather than making matters worse by adding uncertainty.

Figure 16.7 illustrates the point. The blue line represents the path of output subjected to business cycle fluctuations that would arise if the economy were just left to itself. A perfectly thought-out and

implemented policy would begin to stimulate the economy just when it is nearing a peak so that, given the various lags described, its effects come into play just at the time it is needed. Similarly, it would turn restrictive just when the trough is passed, so as to moderate the strength of the upturn. Ideally, the outcome would be curve *A*. Now add uncertainty about the recognition, decision, implementation, and effectiveness lags. In the worst case, we face the risk of achieving curve *B*. The stimulus planned for the downturn affects the economy exactly when it is coming out of the recession, while restraint comes into play just when the economy has peaked. Here, policy makes things worse!

At the same time, the problem may not always be as severe as Friedman's critique makes it out to be. Returning to Keynes' metaphor, we might say that if the dentist is called early enough and allowed to act decisively, he may prevent the most serious of toothaches. He might also be able to prescribe some medicine which may act automatically and take some of the pain and swelling the next time a molar must be pulled. For example, ministries can prepare tax cuts or increases in advance, in order to cut down on the implementation and effectiveness lags. Governments can be given greater budgetary authority to reduce the time associated with the decision lag. The adoption of **automatic stabilizers** is an effective way for legislators and policy-makers to get around the machinations of politics. Automatic stabilizers, which are discussed in more detail in Chapter 17, slow an economy down in a boom phase and stimulate it in recessions. The most important aspect is the automatic part. They need little or no political decisions and can thus evade the eternal wrangling that may impart a decision lag on an otherwise well-informed government.

With respect to monetary policy, central banks have entered the forecasting business, either generating their own 'in-house' predictions or employing outside consultants to help. In practice, national policy-makers use the many indicators of business conditions discussed in Box 16.4. For example, real stock prices and real money balances are relatively reliable leading indicators, and anticipate downturns by roughly four to six quarters. Another

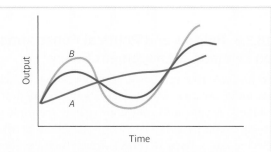

Fig. 16.7 Lags and Demand Management Policy

The blue line shows the business cycle arising from fluctuations in aggregate demand in the private sector. A demand management policy correctly implemented would smooth out the fluctuations (curve *A*). If there are significant effectiveness lags, the government may need to enact these measures well in advance of the turning points in the cycle. If instead the government reacts passively, it may simply reinforce the cycle (curve *B*).

Box 16.4 Leading and Lagging Indicators

Central banks and ministries are in the business of forecasting GDP. Not only do they need to get ahead of the curve when making policy, they also need to communicate overall economic trends to the public. In Chapter 1 we learned that many variables move together over the cycle, or are coincident (e.g. consumption, investment, and interest rates). Yet if one variable systematically leads or lags another, contemporaneous correlation may be small or nil, an important link may exist. These links can help policy-makers anticipate turning points in the cycle and reduce the bite of the Friedman critique. The Burns–Mitchell diagrams in Figure 16.8 display the cyclical behaviour of a number of frequently tracked macroeconomic variables, averaged over eight OECD economies.[9] Recall that the horizontal axis of the Burns–Mitchell diagram indicates the number of quarters before (–) or after (+) the peak of the reference cycle for GDP. The vertical axis generally displays the value of an index which takes a value of 1.0 on average over the reference cycle (in some cases we display percentage deviation from an average value). The diagrams show average tendencies, and by no means perfect regularities. Evidently, some variables tend systematically to peak ahead of, and others systematically to trail behind, out-

put. For example, share prices in stock markets, real money balances, the primary current account, the real exchange rate, vacancies, and inventory investment are all examples of **leading indicators**. They tend to predict the emergence of recessions and expansions. Other variables, such as unemployment and inflation, tend to be **lagging indicators**. Employment, investment, short-term interest rates, and capacity utilization are examples of **coincident indicators**.

Our knowledge of the macroeconomy can account for these regularities, and you are asked to do so in the exercises at the end of this chapter. Financial variables are extremely useful leading indicators because they are forward-looking. Share prices start declining three to four quarters in advance of a downturn. Since real stock prices are a measure of Tobin's q, financial markets anticipate the next phase of the cycle and, for example, expect poorer profitability during the downturn phase. The real money supply starts to decline six months to a year in advance of the onset of a recession. The real exchange rate appears to depreciate sharply five to six quarters before the onset of a recession. It even appears to overshoot, and starts to appreciate, just before the business cycle peak is reached.

leading indicator is the differential, or spread, between interest rates on debt of private corporations and 'safe' government bonds. When the spread increases sharply, a recession tends to be in the making. Capacity utilization, changes in inventory stocks, investment spending plans, and real exchange rates can sometimes prove useful in the forecasting game, offering somewhat less lead time. The very fact that the lead time of these indicators is frequently less than a year suggests that keeping ahead of the cycle is difficult.

---

[9] Burns–Mitchell diagrams are used as a descriptive device to summarize the average behaviour of variables over a 'representative cycle'. They are described in detail in Chapter 1. The eight economies considered are the UK, Spain, Canada, France, Germany, Italy, Japan, and the USA.

16.3.3 Politics and Political Constraints on Demand Management Policy

So far, governments have been described as well-meaning entities which care about the nation's welfare. A very different approach is to think of them as run by politicians who care about getting elected and staying in power. Policy then becomes endogenous to both economic and political circumstances, and, reciprocally, economic circumstances are partly shaped by policy actions. The loop is closed and provides interesting, if not always encouraging, insights into the role and function of demand management policies. Demand management policies may not be employed to stabilize the economy, even if they are effective. What's more, their abuse by politically motivated governments can even be a *source* of business cycles.

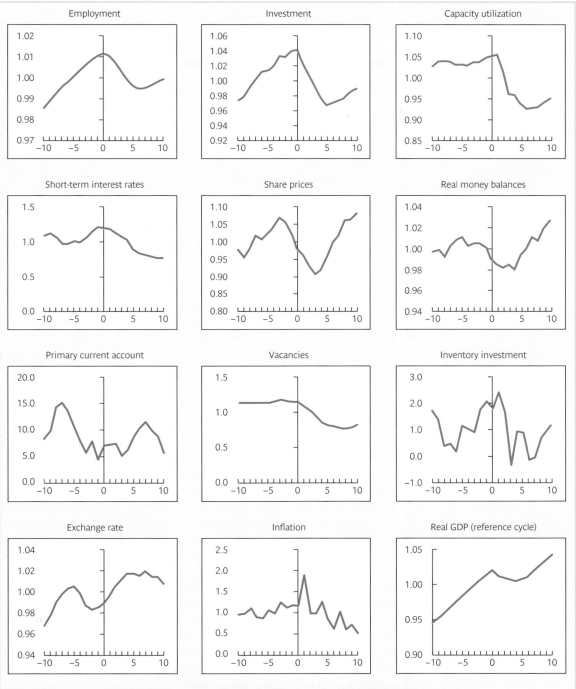

Fig. 16.8 Burns–Mitchell Diagrams, Eight OECD Economies, 1970–2006

Note: For detailed explanations see Figure 1.6

Sources: OECD; IMF; authors' calculations.

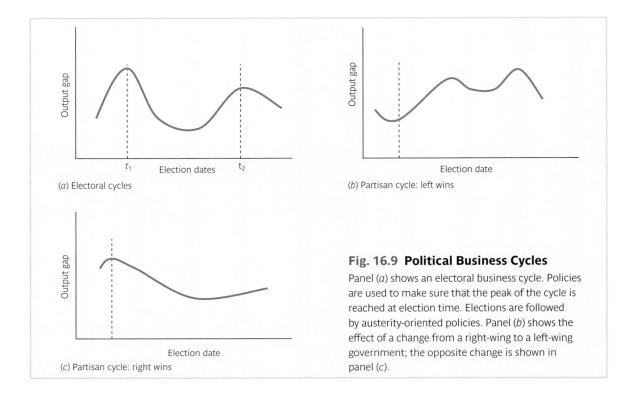

Fig. 16.9 Political Business Cycles
Panel (*a*) shows an electoral business cycle. Policies are used to make sure that the peak of the cycle is reached at election time. Elections are followed by austerity-oriented policies. Panel (*b*) shows the effect of a change from a right-wing to a left-wing government; the opposite change is shown in panel (*c*).

If governments care about their own re-election chances, they will use macroeconomic policies to boost their re-election prospects. The outgoing governments will make sure that the economy is booming and employment is high on election day. Naturally, this might soon be followed by inflation so, in the aftermath of its election, the government will proceed to tighten its policies. Panel (*a*) of Figure 16.9 shows the prediction from this view of **electoral business cycles**.

A different view is that, when in power, a political party pursues a partisan agenda. This agenda can be motivated by ideology or by the coalition of interests that back the party. The **partisan business cycle** view predicts that changes of party in power result in policy changes that generate their own cycles. It is customary to describe left-leaning governments as being Keynesian and right-leaning governments as being neoclassical. Then, if a left-leaning government replaces a right-leaning government, we should expect to see GDP growth

initially increase and unemployment decrease, at the expense of rising inflation and deficits, which will require a contractionary correction, followed by yet another expansion, etc. This pattern is shown in panel (*b*) of Figure 16.9. The opposite political shift, from left to right, is expected to generate policies that focus more on price stability and are less activist, as shown in panel (*c*). The interesting innovation of the partisan business cycle hypothesis is that by the very nature of the election process, the economy is in for a surprise or shock after every election. Agents, if they are rational, will prepare for an election by expecting some 'average' of the parties contending for public office. By construction, they will be wrong *ex-post*. This shock, combined with the propagation mechanism already discussed, can give rise to business cycles.

The existence of **political business cycles** is not firmly established. The evidence in favour of electoral cycles is stronger than the evidence in favour of partisan cycles. There are good theoretical and empirical reasons to be sceptical. The general view that governments can manipulate their macroeconomic instruments to achieve political gain on election day runs sharply against the forward-looking view of rational expectations adopted in this book. Citizens who care about the future should see through government attempts to manipulate voters' sympathies. They should understand, for instance, that a boom designed to blossom on election day will be followed by restrictive policies soon afterwards. Not only should they not be impressed, but also they could be expected to vote against a government that actually destabilizes the macroeconomy.

Similarly, the idea that partisan governments use macroeconomic policy to favour interest groups is not as straightforward as it may seem. Presumably, voters span the whole spectrum of opinions, as shown symbolically in Figure 16.10. To be elected, a party must gather support from all the voters who share most of its views *plus* the '**median voter**' in the centre. This median voter, who holds the key to electoral success, does not hold right- or left-wing views, so why should there be a shift in policies? The only reason is that the median voter is first seduced, only to be cheated upon later. This would explain both partisan policy swings and the rejection of governments which have served the interests of its constituencies at the cost of incurring the

Fig. 16.10 Partisan Politics

Voters' views are spread over the range of ideologies and political preferences. To be elected, a party needs to collect a majority, its own supporters *plus* the median voter.

median voter's wrath. The other possibility is to form coalitions of left- and right-wing parties that shun the centrist electorate. In that case, the equilibrium of the extremes could still deliver policy stability.

In practice, it is probably an oversimplification to presume that left-leaning governments are always Keynesian while right-leaning governments are neoclassical. As noted above, in times of dominating supply-side shocks, the pendulum shifts towards the neoclassical view, with the opposite shift in times of dominating demand-side shocks. The late 1990s, a period of rising popularity of the neoclassical views, witnessed the emergence of the 'third way' among left-leaning parties in a number of countries (New Labour in the UK, Schröder in Germany, Clinton in the USA, etc.), while right-leaning parties have adopted the 'compassionate Conservative' image championed by Bush and Chirac.

16.4 Demand Management and the Sources of Business Cycle Fluctuations

16.4.1 Demand or Supply Shocks?

The analysis of Section 16.3 and the example in Box 16.3 showed how the *AS–AD* framework can account for business cycles. The next step is to isolate the nature of those cycles, as predicted by the *AS–AD* framework, and to identify the component that demand management policy might be used to counteract. Only when the policy-makers are convinced

that they face a demand shock can it make sense to pursue activist demand policy.

It is natural to start with the distinction between demand and supply shocks. The case studied in the previous section—a permanent increase in the central bank's target inflation under flexible exchange rates—is an example of a long-run demand shock. Using similar reasoning, one can see that a cut in taxes, an increase in government spending, or an attack of 'animal spirits' or exuberant consumers would cause a short-run surge in demand. Is the theory's prediction, that demand shocks lead to loops of the type depicted in Figure 16.6, borne out by the facts?

The case of German unification, as seen from the perspective of West Germany, represents a readily identified demand shock.[10] While output in the East was collapsing, consumption, investment, and government spending by East German residents was rising rapidly. Consumers who had been repressed for several decades and anticipated an increase in their future incomes met West German banks eager to attract new customers, especially as none of them was indebted. This also applied to local governments, which loaded up on new infrastructure and equipment. Most of this spending went to West German firms, which were poised to satisfy this extra demand.

Figure 16.11 shows that the outcome was indeed a counterclockwise loop. The initial demand was accommodated without significant inflationary pressure. After two years of expansion, the signs of overheating became more and more evident: increasing nominal wage demands by unions, high-capacity utilization rates, etc. In the end, the Bundesbank (the German central bank at the time) refused to tolerate further inflation and money growth, and sharply raised interest rates. Inflation declined, but at the cost of a recession.

The second example traces an economy's reaction to a supply shock, the first oil price increase in 1973–1974. Panel (a) of Figure 16.12 shows the theory. The AS curve shifts up to AS' because the cost of a major input, energy, abruptly rises. Without any policy reaction, the shock moves the economy from point A to point B. Thereafter, once the initial burst of cost increases is absorbed, the AS curve moves back to its initial position—but only gradually so, since underlying inflation is on the rise, trailing actual inflation. Similarly, with a reduced GDP, the AD curve also moves down, so that the return is shown as the curved trajectory from B to A. If, instead, the authorities decide to fight the inflation-

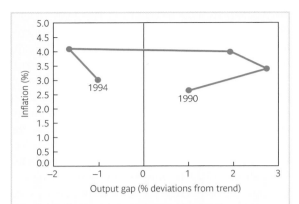

Fig. 16.11 A Demand Shock: The Effect of German Unification on West Germany, 1990–1994

German economic and monetary unification occurred in 1990. Spending by former East German households, firms, and governmental authorities increased dramatically, and most of this demand fell on West German producers. The figure traces out the effect on West German GDP—measured as a deviation from its trend—and rate of inflation.

Sources: OECD, *National Accounts*; OECD, *Main Economic Indicators*.

ary implication of the oil shock and tighten up demand, the AD curve shifts leftwards to AD' and the economy moves from B to C and will return to point A via point D, for example.

Panels (b) and (c) give two examples of reactions to the oil shock. Panel (b) shows that the Swiss National Bank adopted an explicitly anti-inflationary strategy. After the shock, inflation increased and output continued to grow as it completed the expansion phase started a few years before. But then, restrictive demand policies, brought about by a reduction of the target inflation rate, provoked a sharp recession followed by a gradual decline in inflation—the overall cycle matching trajectory ABCD in panel (a). In contrast, authorities in the UK did not fight inflation, which was already high at the time: panel (b) depicts a loop similar to the ABA trajectory in panel (a).

To think about cycles using AS–AD analysis—and how to deal with them—it is crucial to know which types of shock predominate. When supply shocks

---

[10] For East Germany, it was more likely a mixture of negative demand and supply shocks.

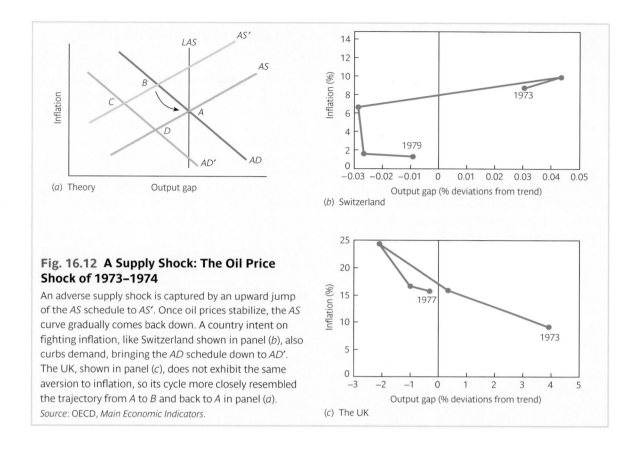

(a) Theory

(b) Switzerland

(c) The UK

Fig. 16.12 A Supply Shock: The Oil Price Shock of 1973–1974

An adverse supply shock is captured by an upward jump of the AS schedule to AS'. Once oil prices stabilize, the AS curve gradually comes back down. A country intent on fighting inflation, like Switzerland shown in panel (b), also curbs demand, bringing the AD schedule down to AD'. The UK, shown in panel (c), does not exhibit the same aversion to inflation, so its cycle more closely resembled the trajectory from A to B and back to A in panel (a).

Source: OECD, *Main Economic Indicators*.

are prevalent, demand policy will not be particularly useful since restoring output will be at the cost of much higher inflation. In the face of a large demand shock, a missed chance to employ demand policy may be costly. Identification of shocks is a tricky business, and economists employ both sophisticated statistical methods as well as historical comparisons to help pin down the facts. An example of the latter type of analysis is provided in Box 16.5, which compares the experiences of Germany and the UK over a longer historical perspective.

16.4.2 The Real Business Cycle Challenge

Many, if not most, of the shocks that hit modern economies are real in nature. This would seem logical, since the job of central banks is not to subject the economy to arbitrary shocks but rather to create stable, predictable monetary conditions. A number

of researchers have used this as an argument to ignore the monetary and financial dimension of the economy when explaining the business cycle. While this **real business cycle (RBC)** theory represents a minority of macroeconomists, it is a group which has nevertheless contributed in important ways to the way that macroeconomists think.[11]

In the AS–AD framework, business cycles are propagated in part because prices are sticky. Prices adjust slowly to shocks, and during that time, shifts in nominal demand have real effects, as shown in Chapters 10 and 11. Does this mean that business cycles are impossible when prices are perfectly flexible? Real business cycle theory argues that

[11] In 2004, the Norwegian Finn Kydland (1943–), a Norwegian, and the American Edward Prescott (1940–) were awarded the Nobel Prize in economics for their work in this and related areas.

Box 16.5   Demand and Supply Shocks: An Anglo–German Comparison

Fundamentally, a Keynesian thinks of unemployment and recession as periods when resources are underutilized, or when output and employment are below their equilibrium levels. In Chapters 5 and 12, unemployment at a point in time was decomposed into a structural or equilibrium component, and a part due to cyclical fluctuation around equilibrium. The first panel of Figure 16.13 shows that the UK unemployment rate has fluctuated very widely over a century, ranging from under 3% at times in the early 1900s, the 1950s, and 1960s, to almost 25% of the labour force in the early 1930s. Do these joint fluctuations mostly reflect changes in equilibrium or are they deviations from a reasonably stable equilibrium rate? Put differently, do the periods of high unemployment correspond to severe supply shocks, or are they the effects of demand shocks that call for demand management?

A comparison with other countries reveals a strikingly similar evolution. For example, the second panel of Figure 16.13 shows that Germany too underwent high unemployment in the 1920s and 1930s, the result of a difficult recovery from the First World War, followed by the Great Depression, both symptoms of insufficient demand. Unemployment was low in the last decades of the nineteenth century, when the industrial revolution ushered in rapid technological progress, an obvious supply shock. Unemployment was also low during the post-war boom of the 1960s and early 1970s, when both

demand and supply were buoyant. The late 1970s and the 1980s were characterized in both countries by a sharp increase in unemployment, the result of the oil shocks—supply-side shocks—followed by restrictive demand policies designed to bring inflation down. In the 1990s and early 2000s, the two countries parted ways: unemployment in the UK has fallen to below 5%, while it remains stubbornly high in Germany. This reflects a different evolution of equilibrium unemployment. It remains high in Germany where labour markets remain highly rigid, while the UK has enjoyed the long-run effect of reforms enacted by Thatcher in the 1980s and maintained by all successor governments. In recent years, German labour market performance has begun to improve, due to reforms implemented since 2004 as well as wage moderation and a recovery of aggregate demand.

This broad overview illustrates that both supply and demand shocks can and do occur. Most of the time these are just reasonably small shocks, as can be seen from Figure 16.13. The larger, widespread, and long-lasting shocks described above are events that strike contemporaries and deeply affect economic thinking. When demand-side shocks prevail, as in the 1920s and 1930s, and possibly the 2000s, Keynesian ideas gain currency. Conversely, neoclassical views prevail at times of supply-side shocks, as in the 1980s. And yet, both are right or, more precisely, each view is true at least some of the time.

fluctuations can be seen, to a first approximation, as a market-clearing, equilibrium phenomenon. The approach is provocative. In an economy with completely flexible prices, the only shocks that affect the real economy are supply shocks which shift the *LAS* schedule right and left. To the extent that monetary and fiscal policies do not affect the *LAS* line, they are irrelevant. At the same time, if the economy is always on its long-run supply schedule, the propagation mechanism of the *AS–AD* model is shut down. Real GDP simply moves randomly in response to random supply shocks. So it would seem that such an economy would be free from cyclical tendencies.

The hallmark of RBC theory is its emphasis on propagation mechanisms other than price stickiness and dynamics of underlying inflation. It starts by focusing on supply shocks related to the production technology. The main source of impulses is new discoveries, inventions, product innovations, or process improvements. These shocks alter the productivity of factors of production, change the environment of economic agents, and cause them to change their behaviour. In the RBC framework, shifts in the aggregate production function—which correspond to shifts in total factor productivity—are called technological shocks. They are the sole exogenous impulses that disturb the

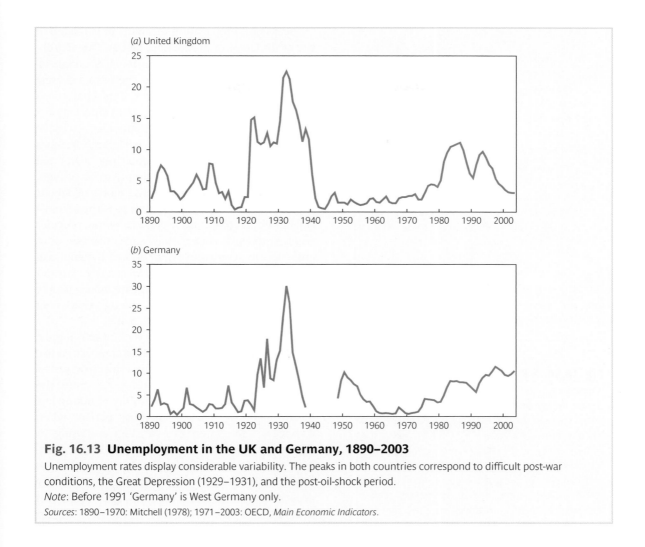

Fig. 16.13 Unemployment in the UK and Germany, 1890–2003

Unemployment rates display considerable variability. The peaks in both countries correspond to difficult post-war conditions, the Great Depression (1929–1931), and the post-oil-shock period.

Note: Before 1991 'Germany' is West Germany only.

Sources: 1890–1970: Mitchell (1978); 1971–2003: OECD, *Main Economic Indicators*.

economy.[12] The propagation mechanism assumed in the RBC theory can be linked to the paradigm of Robinson Crusoe developed in Chapters 7 and 8: the accumulation and decumulation of capital. In fact, the RBC approach is frequently associated with more advanced versions of the growth theory presented in Chapter 3.

The RBC theory asserts that the *LAS* curve is the only one of interest. But how does the RBC approach translate the shock to technology into a cycle? RBC

stresses two main channels. The first involves physical capital. The increase in marginal productivity of capital provides an incentive to invest. The build-up of capital takes time, and contributes to a higher output level along the way. Since the technology shock is temporary, its passing will mark a decline in the productivity of capital, triggering a process of disinvestment and a fall in productive capacity back to the initial level. The second propagation mechanism involves the response of labour supply in the short run to what is a temporary opportunity. The result is a flexible-price business cycle.

Figure 16.14 illustrates the initial impact of a favourable temporary productivity shock. In the

---

[12] In the sticky price interpretation of the business cycle, fluctuations in the Solow residual—which is highly correlated with real GDP—are endogenous and are one of several manifestations of a normal business cycle.

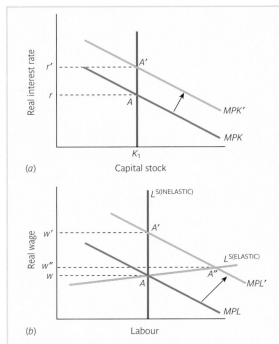

Fig. 16.14 A Productivity Shock

A productivity shock raises the marginal productivity of capital and labour. In the short run, the stock of capital is unchanged and the real interest rises. When aggregate labour supply is inelastic ($L^{S(INELASTIC)}$), the labour supply curve is vertical so the effect on productivity gain is to raise the real wage rate without any change in employment. When aggregate labour supply is elastic ($L^{S(ELASTIC)}$), the response is a small changes in wages with larger fluctuations in employment.

first instance, it raises the marginal productivity of both capital and labour. Holding the stock of capital constant, the rate of return on capital must rise.[13] In panel (a), labour supply is inelastic—the labour supply schedule is vertical—so the real wage rises. Output goes up since the same amounts of capital and labour are now more productive. On the demand side, wealth rises because both wage and profits are higher, so consumption also increases.

The second propagation mechanism is related to the other factor of production, labour. One feature of the second panel of Figure 16.14 is unappealing: if labour supply is inelastic, there is no change in employment over the cycle. This contradicts the aggregate evidence (Figure 16.8) that employment and unemployment fluctuate a lot. To make productivity shocks consistent with large changes in labour supply, we need a good reason for the aggregate elasticity of labour supply to be so high. The primary determinant of the slope of labour supply, as emphasized in Chapter 5, is the leisure–consumption choice: each period a worker decides whether to work, earn money, and consume—or to enjoy leisure. Our conclusion, backed by empirical evidence, was that the supply of labour is inelastic at the household level. A flat aggregate labour supply curve would only result from the aggregation of different households (see Figure 5.4).[14]

To explain the high elasticity of labour supply, the RBC approach relies on intertemporal choice between leisure today and leisure tomorrow. Just as Crusoe chooses when to consume over time, the RBC approach stresses the possibility of taking less leisure—working harder—in those periods when its price is high—when wages are high and rising. To the extent that the shock in Figure 16.13 is a short-lived event, Crusoe will work harder if he is ready to substitute leisure for work. A favourable temporary productivity shock raises today's wage and the real interest rate. This has two effects. First, a higher wage and a higher real interest rate today make work effort worth more today relative to tomorrow. The substitution effect means that Crusoe works harder today. Second, and in contrast, the income effect implies that Crusoe works less today and tomorrow, since more leisure can be afforded in both periods at the same work effort. If the substitution effect dominates the income effect, the labour supply schedule in Figure 16.14 is elastic and significantly more labour is supplied. GDP rises

---

[13] If the same shock affects the whole world, the world real interest rate is likely to rise. If it affects only one country, the real interest rate can still rise temporarily even if the nominal interest rate cannot change when the exchange rate is fixed. Expected inflation absorbs the difference.

[14] In principle, a flat collective bargaining curve would achieve the same result, but the RBC approach has generally avoided considering these forms of market imperfections. Instead, they have preferred to focus on the fixed costs of going to work and the lumpiness of individuals' decisions to take a job.

over and above the direct productivity effect of the productivity shock. In later periods, after the boom subsides, workers 'cash in' and work less. As labour supply is reduced, GDP decreases. All of that occurs without invoking any wage or price rigidity.

Bluntly put, the RBC view represents an extreme version of the *AS–AD* model which admits no role for nominal variables nor the evolution of aggregate demand. For many economists, the advent of the RBC theory was an exciting development because it forced researchers to explain business cycle facts without appealing to wage and price stickiness, which themselves are hard to explain. Yet in the end, the RBC agenda has failed to convince the majority of the profession. Box 16.6 offers a quick summary of some of the debating points in this regard. At the same time, the RBC movement provided researchers with a number of new ideas and methods for understanding how shocks are transmitted, and the newest macro models at central banks have incorporated many of them into orthodox thinking.

Box 16.6 Why the RBC Challenge Failed

While the *AS–AD*, or sticky price, account of business cycles relies on disequilibrium in markets—prices do not adjust immediately to changing demand and supply conditions—the RBC theory views rising and falling tides of economic conditions as an equilibrium response to productivity shocks. It studiously avoids the terms 'demand' and 'supply' since technology shocks affect both, and economic agents are fully aware of this. One important conclusion of the RBC approach—and one that is disturbing for many economists—is that it is impossible to use demand management policies to improve matters in the macroeconomy. A striking implication of the RBC theory is that it is not even desirable to smooth out the business cycle. This is because households and firms are doing the best they can, given changing constraints, so there is nothing to lament. Deep recessions, for example, are seen as the economy's best response to severe adverse productivity shocks.

There are a number of problems with the RBC approach that led to its decline. Productivity shocks are usually measured as the Solow residual of Chapter 3, i.e. growth in total factor productivity (TFP). An example of TFP growth calculated for the UK in the past half-century is plotted in Figure 16.15. The extreme volatility and cyclical behaviour of TFP growth is suspect. It is known that neither labour nor capital hired by firms is always fully employed. With sizeable dismissal costs and human capital often firm-specific, firms avoid firing employees immediately in downturns. While production is reduced, workers perform tasks unrelated to production, such as maintenance, building improvements, painting, and cleaning. Later, during an expansion

phase, a reserve of labour is available which can be tapped. The same argument applies to the utilization of the capital stock, which is not constant over the cycle (see Figure 16.8). The stylized fact of procyclical total factor productivity is likely due to a faulty measure of inputs: in recessions labour is employed but not in directly productive activities—we say it is hoarded—and it is gradually put back to more directly productive use in the upturn that follows. Similarly, capital is used less intensively in downturns, leading to underestimation of its productivity in these periods. It is hard to rule out that the procyclical behaviour of the Solow residual largely reflects similar behaviour of the utilization of hoarded production factors.

One particular difficulty with RBC theory is its denial of any role for monetary policy in the business cycle. This view calls into question the existence of central banks and monetary policy because the *AS* curve is always vertical and money is neutral—even in the short run. We saw in Figure 16.8, however, that the *real* money stock is procyclical, and in fact is a leading indicator. The RBC view isn't disturbed by this. It sees money and credit demand as passive, expanding with the economy but without any causal effect on real variables. They support their argument with the coincident and strongly procyclical behaviour of interest rates in Figure 16.8. In the sticky price business cycle (*AS–AD*) model, this is consistent with expansive money policy leading and causing booms. It is less consistent with the fact that interest rates are procyclical and coincident. Indeed, in the *IS–TR* framework, a money supply impulse is expected to work on output via declining interest

Box 16.6 (*continued*)

rates. *Only* if shifts to the underlying *IS* curve predominate—if most impulses come from the real demand side (spending, fiscal policy, the current account)—and if monetary policy works with a lag, is it possible to reconcile procyclical money and interest rates in the sticky price world. In that case, an increase in real aggregate demand is accompanied—or even led—by an increase in demand for money that is passively supplied by the central bank. In recent years, new generations of models stressing the instability of the real demand side—some using techniques pioneered by RBC theorists—have had some successes in reconciling the *AS–AD* model with these facts.

Ultimately, the crux of the debate is about the relevance of wage and price rigidity in the macroeconomic system. Ignoring it or pretending that it is absent is hardly a substitute for proving that it is irrelevant. Evidence indicates that prices—measured as aggregate indices—do appear to be rigid in the short run. It is this element of realism that is lacking in the RBC theory of macroeconomic fluctuations, despite its intellectual rigour. It limits its acceptance by a wide spectrum of the economics profession. While realism is not essential for a good macroeconomic model, this particular detail has such wide-reaching implications that it would appear essential to include it, or at least to explain why it is unimportant.

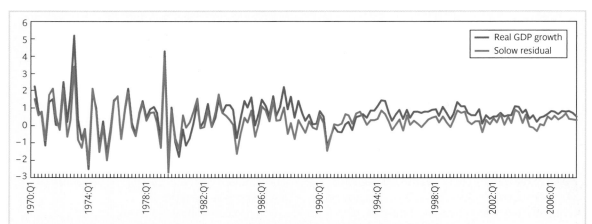

Fig. 16.15 The Solow Residual and GDP, UK 1961–2007 (% growth per annum)

Growth in total factor productivity, as measured by the Solow residual, is strongly correlated with output. To some extent, the movements in total factor productivity growth appear random.

Sources: OECD; authors' calculations.

16.4.3 Taking Stock: Is Demand Management Worth the Trouble?

The message of this chapter may seem pessimistic at first glance—that aggregate demand management is inherently problematic and can backfire. Yet in practice policy-makers are frequently called to decisive action in the light of large exogenous shocks. After the terrorist attacks on 11 September 2001, much of the world faced an immediate crisis:

fear of the unknown, a meltdown of financial markets, a collapse of confidence and animal spirits. The consequences for aggregate demand were foreseeable and dire. The reaction of the USA was swift. A massive increase in government spending on security and military gave a boost to demand. Most importantly, the Governor of the Federal Reserve System, Alan Greenspan, ordered the Fed to intervene massively and to provide liquidity to the banking system; the Federal Funds Rate was reduced several times in succession. Despite considerable scepticism, there is little doubt that the surge in military and national security expenditures in 2002 helped engineer the recovery of the US economy in 2003.

Similarly, the international reaction to the subprime crisis has been cooperation between central banks across the globe to provide liquidity to banks, to maintain orderly trading conditions, and even to help one major investment bank buy another which had suffered large losses on securitized mortgage investments. The US Government has hastily—but decisively and in a remarkably non-partisan manner—organized a tax rebate to be paid out in 2008. This is designed to stimulate demand. At the same time, the aggressive relaxation of monetary

policy pursued by the Fed will have its own price later on, as inflation continues to rise.

In Europe, aggregate demand management faces more fundamental limitations. While the ECB has come under increasing pressure to follow the Fed's lead, it is committed to fighting inflation. More importantly, the representative European country —to the extent it uses the euro—has no access at all to monetary policy, and even if it could set it, would have to use it on the entire euro area. Second, even though fiscal policy is effective under fixed exchange rates, most European countries are too small and too open to have a fiscal policy that has any sort of meaningful multiplier.

❶ Summary

1 While it is theoretically possible for demand management policies to smooth out business cycle fluctuations, recent experience and economic principles suggest a more modest approach.

2 A justification for demand management arises when markets do not clear rapidly, leading to low levels of output and employment over a longer period of time. Neoclassicals and Keynesians mostly disagree on the *degree* to which prices and markets achieve continuously efficient allocation of resources and optimal satisfaction of individual needs.

3 Neoclassicals argue that market-clearing is a good first-order approximation, and that markets are closer to perfection than governments. Keynesians generally believe that markets suffer from a host of imperfections and that economies can suffer from persistent underutilization of resources.

4 One reason that output may remain below equilibrium output for some time is the speed at which inflationary expectations can be validated and adjusted. Even if economic agents have rational expectations, they may have taken

decisions at an earlier date and locked in outdated expectations. This will affect macroeconomic variables today.

5 Uncertainty plays an important role in the debate. For Keynesians, private decisions are taken with imperfect knowledge of future conditions. This results in wrong pricing and resource allocation decisions. For neoclassicals, uncertainty means that policy mistakes are more likely to make matters worse than to improve them.

6 The modern conception of the business cycle is the culmination of many small and large random influences. These shocks are difficult, if not impossible, to forecast. It is thus hard to imagine a government that would be able to offset all these shocks, especially given the recognition, decision, implementation, and effectiveness lags associated with policy.

7 One way to get around this problem is to make judicious use of leading indicators. Another is to make extensive use of automatic stabilizers which reduce recognition and decision lags.

8 Real-life policy-makers do not always have the best intentions, caring more about being

re-elected instead. This may lead some governments to employ demand management policies in a politically opportunistic way.

9 Political business cycles may take the form of expansionary policies being introduced just before elections, to be followed by corrective, contractionary policies after elections. Partisan business cycles may result from the alternation of governments that defend the interests of their constituencies.

10 The real business cycle is an attempt to understand the business cycle as a purely real phenomenon without reference to the financial or monetary sector. While this approach has the attraction of being a self-contained and logical construct, the fact that it fails to address the real or apparent rigidity of wages and prices has limited its acceptance.

11 Demand management policies are no longer as attractive as they were in earlier times. This is partly because economies are more open today, both real and financially. Yet in times of acute crisis, demand management policy can have effects and should be considered.

🔑 Key Concepts

- **neoclassicals, neoclassical economists**
- **Keynesians, Keynesian economists**
- **activist demand policies**
- **rational expectations**
- **deflation**
- **inflation-targeting strategy**
- **deterministic, stochastic view of business cycles**
- **impulses**
- **propagation mechanisms**
- **demand shocks, supply shocks**

- **persistence**
- **recognition, decision, implementation, and effectiveness lags**
- **Friedman critique**
- **automatic stabilizers**
- **electoral business cycles**
- **partisan business cycles**
- **political business cycles**
- **median voter**
- **real business cycle theory**

❓ Exercises

1 Explain the motivation for Keynesian activist demand policy using a diagram. Explain the neoclassical rejection of that type of policy.

2 Why is the behaviour of underlying inflation so critical to evaluating the effectiveness of policy? What determines this behaviour?

3 How important is the slope of the *AS* curve for evaluating the effectiveness of demand policy?

What underlying characteristics of the economy might contribute to a steeper *AS* curve?

4 What are the costs of inflation? Are there any benefits of inflation? If so, what are they?

5 Flip a coin 50 times, writing down +1 for heads, −1 for tails (you may use a spreadsheet program if you like). Call this variable ε_t. Now create a new variable, defined as $y_t = \frac{1}{4}\varepsilon_{t-1} + \frac{1}{2}\varepsilon_t + \frac{1}{4}\varepsilon_{t+1}$, so

the new variable is a weighted average of present, past, and future lagged values. (You will not be able to compute the first and the last values of y). Plot both time series and comment on them. How do your results change if you use $y_t = \frac{3}{4}\varepsilon_t + \frac{1}{4}\varepsilon_{t-1}$ instead?

6 Now repeat your experiment, using a normally distributed random variable for ε_t instead of the coin flip (you will definitely need a spreadsheet for this). Plot your results. How do they compare to those of the previous problem?

7 Define the Friedman critique. What is an essential element for it to be true? What could be done by governments to avoid it?

8 Describe the lags that affect economic policy-making and their consequences for the effectiveness of: (a) fiscal policy and (b) monetary policy. How does your answer depend on the exchange rate regime?

9 Name some leading, some lagging, and some coincident indicators. Explain the behaviour of these variables, using the *IS–TR–BP* and *AS–AD* framework.

10 Suppose there is a sharp rise in oil prices, much like in the 1970s under a regime of flexible exchange rates. Suppose that in the first instance, central bank policy does not adjust the inflation target. Explain the consequences, using the *AS–AD* model. Given this outcome, is there an argument for demand management policy, and if so, what kind of policy? What would be the argument against it?

→ Essay Questions

1 'Aggregate demand policy is based on exploiting misperceptions of the private sector in order to increase GDP.' Discuss.

2 Can activist demand management policies affect equilibrium unemployment?

3 Discuss the advantages and disadvantages of inflation targeting versus fixed exchange rates from the perspective of the Friedman critique of active demand management.

4 China's economy has been growing at more than 10% per annum for more than a decade. In recent years inflation has begun to creep steadily upward. Is there a role for demand policy in this case? If you were advising the Chinese Government, what policies would you recommend?

5 Discuss the strengths and weaknesses of the RBC approach from the following perspective. Consider how a positive shock to total factor productivity is propagated in that framework and compare your answer to the same shock in the *AS–AD* model under a regime of flexible exchange rates. Now use the Burns–Mitchell diagrams of Figure 16.8 to discuss the strengths and weaknesses of the two approaches. How would your answer change for discussing a financial or monetary shock—e.g. an increase in the demand for money?

Fiscal Policy, Debt, and Seigniorage

17

Chancellor: In my old age I have been freed from pain.
Listen and look at this portentous bill
Which has made welfare out of all our ill:
'Be it known to all men who may so require;
This note is worth a thousand crowns entire.
Which has its guarantee and counterfoil
In untold wealth beneath imperial soil.
And this is hereby a substitute approved
Until such time as the treasure can be moved.'
Emperor: And do my people think it negotiable?
Do army and court take it for pay in full?
Strange though I think it, I must ratify it.

Steward: To collect those fluttering notes, one couldn't try it;
Once issued, they are scattered in a flash.
The Exchanges stand wide open for the queue
Where every bill is honoured and changed for cash—
Silver and gold—at a discount it is true.
And then to butcher, baker, pub it goes,
Half the world only seems to think of stuffing;
While the other half in brand new clothes goes puffing.
The clothier cuts the cloth, the tailor sews.
Long live the Emperor! Makes the cellars gush
In a cooking, roasting, platter-clattering crush.

Goethe

17.1 Overview

Governments play an important role in our economic lives. Especially in Europe, they are big, and have been growing bigger for most of the post-war period. Table 17.1 shows that governments in the European Union spend close to half of GDP, leaving the other half to the private sector. What do they spend their money on? A large part, about one-third of GDP, consists of transfers and subsidies to individuals (health and unemployment insurance, poverty alleviation). Transfers represent income redistribution from the haves to the have-nots,

from the lucky ones to the needy ones, expressing a sense of solidarity among citizens and a rejection of excessive inequalities. Governments are also big consumers, constructing roads, purchasing buildings and the services of public employees, and much more. Of course, to pay for all that, they raise taxes, capturing close to half of GDP. Governments are not known to be particularly strict in managing their budgets. Deficits are frequent, and most governments are heavily indebted to the private sector and foreigners. While European countries have consolidated their budgets in recent years, on average public debt still represents nearly three-quarters of a year's GDP, and in some countries, such as Belgium and Italy, the gross stock of public debt still exceeds a full year of national output.

This chapter looks at the economic functions of governments and how they fulfil their tasks. Do governments have an economic role to play at all? This question has been debated since time immemorial between right, left, and centre, between partisans of laissez-faire and interventionists. In this chapter we focus on two economic functions of governments: the microeconomic function, which includes the provision of **public goods** and services and income redistribution, and the macroeconomic function, which aims at stabilizing aggregate activity.

Table 17.1 General Government Spending and Finances: Euro Area, USA, and Japan, 2007

	EU	USA	Japan
Total spending (% of GDP)	40.4	37.4	35.9
Public consumption			
as % of GDP	20.2	16.0	17.9
as % of private consumption	36.0	21.9	32.3
Budget surplus (% of GDP)	−0.7	−2.8	−3.4
Gross debt (% of GDP)	72.4	62.2	180.3

Source: OECD.

Governments frequently run budget deficits. Like households, if they spend more than they earn, they must then borrow and accumulate debt. This process is inherently explosive, since more debt means more debt service, hence the need to borrow even more. To get this process under control, governments must run a primary surplus in the future, just as we learned from Crusoe in Chapter 7. But governments also have a unique feature: they can borrow from their central banks, which in turn create money to finance public spending, just as Mephistopheles did in Goethe's *Faust*. This unique privilege, based on their monopoly right to create legal tender, is called **seigniorage**. It provides relief to the government when in need to borrow, but it eventually means fast money growth and inflation. Another temptation that some hard-pressed governments find hard to resist is to default, partially or totally, on the public debt. Unlike private agents, which generally face drastic consequences, governments frequently default with impunity, in effect legally confiscating the wealth of its creditors. Fortunately, this most radical solution is only resorted to in times of national emergency.

17.2 **Fiscal Policy and Economic Welfare**

17.2.1 **Provision of Public Goods and Services**[1]

Governments 'produce' goods and services, mostly for collective consumption. Why are they involved in such an activity? The two main reasons are that some goods are fundamentally public goods while others are produced under increasing returns.

The particularity of public goods is that they cannot be appropriated for individual consumption. Once they are available for one, they are available for all. This applies, for example, to law and order, defence, public gardens, or foreign affairs. In addition, some public goods exhibit a special characteristic: their use by one person benefits others. This is called an **externality**. A good example is education. All of society benefits from mass literacy. For example literate workers, who are on short supply in some poor countries, interact more effectively, which raises their productivity. Indeed, there is considerable evidence that economic growth is powerfully enhanced by the population's education level, which we called **human capital** in Chapter 4. The generic feature of collective goods is that they cannot be appropriated by anyone—think of law and order, for instance—and therefore cannot be sold. For this reason, private producers would not produce them, and if they are needed, governments must step in.

Futhermore, the existence of externalities implies that individuals would only buy what they need personally, overlooking the benefits to others. In general, they would buy less than is desirable for society as a whole. For example, if no one else knows how to write and read, my own incentive to learn is close to nil. This is why basic education is not only public and free, but also compulsory. Police protection is another example. Security could be privately organized, but safe streets are good for everyone, whether they pay for them or not. In practice, only better-off, homogeneous neighbourhoods could afford to set up public safety on their own. Society has an incentive to combat lawlessness on a wider scale than do individuals interested only in protecting their own safety.

A similar reasoning applies to the case of goods produced under increasing returns. One example is the usage of streets: the cost of paving and maintaining a road is roughly the same whether there are few or many users. Streets could be private and their use charged to users. This would undoubtedly relieve traffic congestion in cities, but perhaps too

---

[1]   Chapters 4 and 18 discuss the characteristics of public goods and their role in economic growth.

much. Each of us could react to street tolls by reducing our movements to the point where the cost
per remaining user would lead to the curtailment of
street provision in some areas, in the end hurting
everyone.

While there is a strong justification for *some* government consumption, there is no clear-cut border
between goods and services that can be provided
only publicly and those that could be provided privately. One key role of democracy is to choose
that border, and adapt it from time to time as economic and social factors dictate. The absence
of unequivocal criteria for deciding what should
be publicly provided explains why there is much
national soul-searching on the issue. In many countries, debates resurface constantly concerning such
cases as education (private schools and universities
exist alongside public education), social security
(health and retirement insurance are increasingly provided privately), and utilities (highways
are built and run by private companies; electricity
and telephone networks are privately owned and
operated).

17.2.2 Redistributive Goals: Equity versus Efficiency

A fundamental result from microeconomics is that
productive efficiency—the optimal use of available
productive resources—is achieved when each factor of production is paid its marginal productivity.
This may result in a very unequal distribution
of income and wealth. Indeed, we observe the coexistence of much individual wealth alongside grind-
ing poverty. While this outcome may be efficient
from a productive point of view, an altogether
different logic emphasizes that human beings have
similar basic needs that should be met under all
circumstances. Equity or fairness is often seen as
a requirement for society to be cohesive and stable.
Yet equity and efficiency often work against each
other. There is a fundamental **equity–efficiency
trade-off**.

Governments can and do reduce inequalities.
Progressive income taxes reduce the differences in
post-tax incomes. Taxes levied on the better-off pay
for transfers to the worse-off. In fact, a significant part
of public spending is dedicated to income redis-

Table 17.2 Government Transfers, Various Countries, 1960 and 2007

	Transfers as as % of GDP		Transfers as % of government outlays	
	1960	2007	1960	2007
Austria	14.8	30.4	51.8	63.1
Belgium	12.7	26.2	44.8	54.2
Denmark	7.6	25.0	35.1	49.4
Finland	9.0	26.5	41.6	55.2
France	16.3	29.6	53.5	55.8
Germany	14.1	26.3	50.2	59.4
Greece	5.3	27.6	30.6	63.8
Ireland	9.6	18.5	38.7	53.2
Italy	11.2	28.4	45.4	58.6
Japan	4.5	18.6	34.5	51.0
Netherlands	8.6	20.5	n.a.	44.7
Portugal	3.7	24.4	24.5	54.9
Spain	2.9	20.4	23.1	52.6
Sweden	8.6	27.3	32.2	50.7
UK	9.0	22.9	30.7	51.4
USA	6.0	21.4	24.4	57.1

Sources: European Economy; OECD, *Economic Outlook*.

tribution. Table 17.2 shows the size of transfers,
both as a share of GDP and as a proportion of total
government outlays. In some countries, this is the
single largest item in the government budget. Not
surprisingly, different countries deal differently
with the equity–efficiency trade-off. Austria and
Sweden seem to place more weight on equity than
Japan or the USA, for example.

There is a trade-off, however. Income redistribution for the sake of equity has disincentive effects.
Highly paid—and presumably highly productive—
people may reduce their work effort in response to
heavy taxation, or may even move abroad. On the
other hand, those who receive transfers from the
state may find it pointless to work hard for little net
reward.

Table 17.3 **Budget Balances, Various Countries, 1975–2007 (% of GDP)**

	1975	1980	1985	1990	1995	2000	2007	Average 1970–2007
Austria	−2.4	−2.0	−3.0	−2.5	−5.7	−1.6	−0.8	−2.1
Belgium	−6.4	−10.2	−9.9	−6.7	−4.4	0.1	−0.2	−5.2
Denmark	−2.4	−3.5	−2.1	−1.3	−2.9	2.3	4.8	−0.3*
Finland	5.1	3.8	3.5	5.4	−6.2	6.9	4.0	2.6
France	−1.9	−0.1	−3.0	−2.4	−5.5	−1.5	−2.5	−2.3
Germany	−5.6	−2.9	−1.1	−1.9	−3.2	1.3	0.0	−2.0
Greece	−2.6	−2.3	−10.4	−14.0	−9.1	−3.7	−2.9	−5.4
Ireland	−11.2	−11.2	−10.8	−2.8	−2.1	4.7	2.2	−3.9
Italy	−10.3	−7.0	−12.4	−11.4	−7.4	−0.9	−2.2	−7.0
Japan	−2.0	−3.2	−0.6	2.1	−5.1	−7.6	−3.4	−2.7
Netherlands	−3.4	−4.2	−3.7	−5.3	−4.3	2.0	−0.1	−2.5
Norway	3.0	5.4	9.7	2.2	3.2	15.4	17.1	6.2
Spain	−0.2	−3.0	−7.3	−4.1	−6.5	−1.0	1.9	−2.4
Sweden	5.1	−5.8	−3.7	3.4	−7.4	3.8	2.9	−0.2
UK	−5.2	−3.7	−3.3	−1.8	−5.8	4.0	−2.9	−2.8
USA	−5.2	−2.6	−5.0	−4.2	−3.1	1.6	−2.8	−2.9

* 1971–2007
Surplus (+) or deficit (−)
Source: OECD, *Economic Outlook*.

17.3 **Macroeconomic Stabilization**

Providing public services and redistributing income does not imply that total government spending systematically exceeds revenues. The government could perform its microeconomic functions without running budget imbalances, it only needs to raise enough tax revenue. As Table 17.3 shows, however, significant surpluses and deficits are the rule rather than the exception. Why do governments go through such gyrations in their accounts? This section shows that there are good reasons for this. In short, the second function of public budgets is to stabilize aggregate income and spending, which also results in stabilizing employment.[2] To

achieve these goals, governments dissave in bad years and save in good years, just as many people do. Public imbalances cannot always be justified on this basis, however, as we will see.

17.3.1 **Consumption and Tax Smoothing**

A general fact of life is that people dislike fluctuations in their consumption levels. As a result, in bad years they borrow to sustain the previously reached level, and during good years they pay back and, if possible, save for the rainy day. The citizens' desire for **consumption smoothing** applies to their consumption of public goods and services as well, and it is the responsibility of governments—and a determinant of their electoral success—to provide a steady flow

[2] The link between output and unemployment is given by Okun's Law, which is presented in Chapter 12.

Box 17.1 Tax Smoothing after German Reunification

When he endorsed swift reunification early in 1990, Chancellor Helmut Kohl promised that there would be no new taxes for West Germans. Yet the former East Germany entered the Federal Republic with precious little dowry, a hugely inefficient productive sector, a large external debt (mostly to West Germany), poor infrastructure, and considerable environmental liabilities. In the eastern states, output fell by about 50%, unemployment—official and unofficial—rose to about 30%, and state-owned enterprises needed cash to stay afloat until they could be sold. From a budgetary viewpoint, the new eastern states required massive public spending but could not contribute much to financing. The pressure on the federal budget is apparent in Table 17.4 and continued well into the next decade. At the same time, and for many years, Germany's current account surplus of

5% of GDP melted to a deficit of 2%, showing that the world also helped finance German unification. Yet this evolution is best regarded as temporary. Within a decade or two the eastern provinces will have very good prospects of catching up with the West, and Germany's current account has already moved into surplus again.

In the face of a temporary shock, tax smoothing calls for accumulating public debt and limiting tax increases, possibly borrowing abroad as well through current account deficits. Yet as the full costs of reunification are still being tallied, many have begun to question how much of the obligations of the eastern states are temporary. Kohl's successors, Schröder and Merkel, have come under increasing public pressure to stem the rise of the national debt and close the current account deficit, even if there are good economic reasons to put up with it.

Table 17.4 Fiscal Implication of German Reunification (% of GDP)

	1989	1990	1991	1992	1993	1994	1995	2000	2005	2008
Government expenditures	43.11	43.55	46.05	47.28	48.27	47.88	48.27	45.10	46.97	43.66
Budget balance	0.08	−1.89	−3.07	−2.47	−3.01	−2.30	−3.20	1.31	−3.37	0.09
Gross public debt	39.83	40.38	41.10	40.93	46.25	46.58	55.73	60.37	71.05	64.55
Current account	4.57	3.02	−1.31	−1.08	−0.97	−1.42	−1.16	−1.79	4.61	6.02

Source: OECD, *Economic Outlook*.

of public goods and services. To do so, like individuals, governments have to borrow and save, depending on the economic situation. This is more important because government income is very sensitive to cyclical fluctuations. Tax revenues fall when peoples' incomes decline, simply because taxes are usually set as a percentage of income. There is even more to it than that. Taxes reduce individuals' incomes and, therefore, their private consumption possibilities. Changing the tax pressure—taxing less in bad years and more in good years—cushions private net incomes. **Tax smoothing** is the natural fiscal companion to consumption smoothing.

This principle has a central implication for the conduct of fiscal policy. If a series of bad years reduces the country's income, which is also the tax base, the government's best course of action is not to maintain the budget in balance. Rather, in order

to enhance its citizens' welfare, it should maintain a steady flow of public goods and services, and finance the revenue shortfalls by borrowing.[3] Conversely, a few particularly good years, during which taxable income rises, should not be used to raise government consumption temporarily, but to increase its own savings. Acting on behalf of the public at large, a government should behave like any economic agent, meeting temporary income disturbances by saving or borrowing, within the limits of its budget constraint. Box 17.1 applies

---

[3] Section 15.3.4 returns to this issue from an international perspective. Public sector borrowing can be done domestically or abroad. Globally, a country with a temporary fall in income must borrow. As a first approximation, it does not matter whether it is the private or the public sector that borrows abroad.

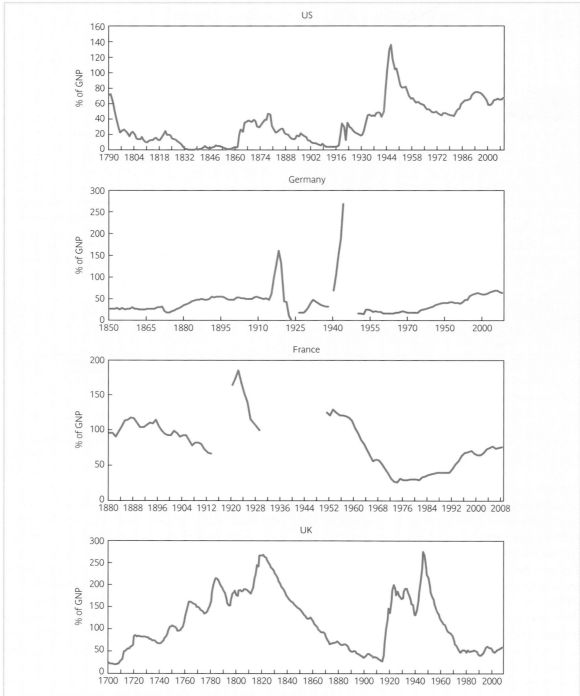

Fig. 17.1 Public Debt in Four Countries (% of GDP)

The UK had a debt-to-GDP ratio of over 100% in 1855, a legacy of the Napoleonic wars. During the First World War the British debt rose to about 200%, and during the Second World War to 300%. The war efforts are also visible for the USA (including the Civil War).

Sources: OECD, *Economic Outlook*; IMF, <http://pages.stern.nyu.edu/~rsylla/>.

the principle of tax smoothing to the controversial case of Germany's unification.

Budget deficits met by public borrowing increase the public debt. Figure 17.1 shows how public debt (as a percentage of output) has evolved in selected countries. Debt rises, sometimes spectacularly, during wars and declines afterwards. Wars are periods of unusually high public expenditure, yet they are rarely expected to last very long. The tax-smoothing principle seems to have been applied here (even if some countries eventually defaulted on part of their debt). Similarly, the oil shocks of the 1970s were met in many countries by debt accumulation.

17.3.2 Output and Employment Stabilization

A cyclical downturn means that personal incomes decline temporarily. The laissez-faire view is that, facing a temporary income fluctuation, individuals should borrow and/or save to smooth their consumption pattern, with government playing no particular role. This prescription would be correct if all individuals could indeed borrow during a recession. Credit rationing, however, changes the situation.[4] Individuals who cannot borrow, or cannot borrow as much as they need, are unable to smooth out their consumption. Not only are they hurt, but their declining demand deepens the slowdown through the demand multiplier effect. This effect is illustrated in Figure 17.2 where, starting from long-run equilibrium at point A, a recession occurs, which is captured by the leftward shift of the aggregate demand curve from AD to AD'. Under fixed exchange rates, the government can use fiscal policy to stop this process. To keep the curve in its AD position and prevent the move from point A to point B, it either increases its own spending or provides tax relief. In effect, the government borrows on behalf of its credit-constrained citizens. Conversely, a demand boom provides the government with the opportunity to run a budget surplus and pay back the debt accumulated during previous downturns. These are

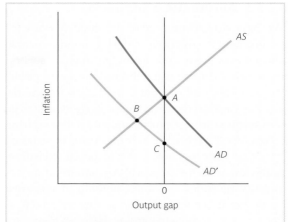

Fig. 17.2 Stabilization Policies

When demand exogenously falls, the economy moves from point A to point B. In the absence of stabilization policy, the economy will eventually move to point C. Fiscal policy can be used to speed up a return to trend output at point A, or even to prevent the AD schedule from shifting.

examples when the government leans against the wind and conducts **countercyclical fiscal policies**.

The fact that unemployment rises during recessions provides another rationale for countercyclical fiscal policies. The mere increase in unemployment is not a justification for active fiscal policies. If unemployment rises because its equilibrium level has permanently increased, the economy will eventually settle along its long-run aggregate supply schedule and demand management is bound to fail. Attempts to keep unemployment below equilibrium through fiscal expansions will only lead to more public debt. However, short-run fluctuations in unemployment around its equilibrium rate occur because price and wage rigidities prevent an optimal utilization of available resources. Countercyclical fiscal policy may be a corrective device to keep unemployment close to its equilibrium level, and output near its trend growth path. Sustaining aggregate demand with public spending when private demand weakens, or directly boosting private demand with tax relief, has the potential to limit the size of business cycles.

---

[4] We explain the mechanism and importance of credit rationing in Chapter 6.

17.3.3 Automatic Stabilizers

We have argued that there are good reasons for governments to use their budget to smooth income and consumption. Interestingly, when a government refrains from using discretion to vary public spending and tax revenues, its budget automatically leans against the wind. Public budgets tend to go into surplus during upturns and into deficits during recessions. To see why, it is necessary to separate spending from revenues. While public consumption is less sensitive to cyclical fluctuations, transfers and tax revenues are fundamentally determined by economic conditions. Many transfers, such as unemployment benefits and welfare payment, are tightly linked to the state of the economy. Similarly, when incomes and spending rise, tax collection automatically increases. Conversely, during economic slowdowns tax collection decreases. The reason is that nearly all taxes are set as *rates* applied to incomes or spending. In the end, given the budgetary process described in Box 17.2, public spending is little—if at all—affected by business cycles. This means that the budget balance is therefore automatically procyclical, as Figure 17.3 readily confirms.[5] Cyclical budget fluctuations can be avoided only if the government takes explicit avoidance measures.

To summarize, we have seen that, when an economy slows down, the budget deficit will normally increase, or its surplus will shrink or even shift into deficit. This automatic lowering of taxes amounts to an implicit fiscal expansion. Conversely, a better-than-expected economic performance reduces the budget deficit or increases the surplus because of enhanced tax income for the government, a contractionary fiscal policy of sorts. In the end, we see that exogenous shifts in private demand are automatically cushioned—but not completely offset —by budgetary shifts. These are the so-called **automatic stabilizers**. They work in the absence of any

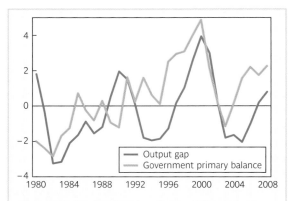

Fig. 17.3 Cyclical Behaviour of the Primary Budget in the Netherlands, 1980–2008
When the economy enters a slowdown (the rate of capacity utilization declines), tax receipts fall and transfers rise usually with a lag of a year or two. The primary budget—excluding service of the public debt—moves in the same direction as the output gap. It is procyclical.
Source: OECD, *Economic Outlook*.

policy action. Simply by enacting the budget, as approved by the parliament, the government finds itself conducting a countercyclical fiscal policy, dampening both recessions and expansions.

17.3.4 How to Interpret Budget Figures

With automatic stabilizers in place, the budget is partly endogenous. Policy choices plan a surplus or a deficit, but economic conditions determine the outcome. This is why raw budget figures do not always fully reveal the government's intentions and can be misleading. Table 17.3 shows that most countries underwent budget deficits in 1975 and 1980. Did this reflect a collective enthusiasm for expansionary policies? Quite to the contrary, these years coincided with the post-oil-shock recessions and the associated deterioration of public finances. Norway, an oil-exporting country, provides a neat counter-example: it underwent a boom and tax revenues were further boosted by oil taxes.

The endogeneity of government budgets means that it is not straightforward to determine whether the stance of fiscal policy is tight or easy. A growing

---

[5] The budget balance is $T - G - TR$, where G is public spending on goods and services, TR are transfers, and T are tax revenues. G is not cyclical, TR is procyclical, and T is countercyclical. Net taxes are $T - TR$, and are countercyclical (note that if T is countercyclical, $-T$ is procyclical).

Box 17.2 The Budgetary Process

All democracies follow roughly the same budgetary process. Once a year, the government presents a budget to its parliament, which then debates on—and sometimes amends—each item before voting on it. One part of the budget concerns spending by the various ministries or departments; the other part concerns tax revenue. The parliament approves tax rates, literally hundreds of them, from VAT to income, from petrol to corporate profits or property. While spending authorizations are set in amounts (say, euros) and are therefore immune to changes unless the law is amended, tax receipts in euros are uncertain, depending upon how much is to be taxed at the set rates. This is why parliament cannot decide exactly what the deficit or surplus will be. Instead, it is presented with a forecast of GDP, which underlies a forecast of tax receipts and the associated deficit or surplus. It is well understood that economic conditions will settle the matter as the fiscal year goes on. In general, most governments have a tendency to forecast high growth, large tax receipts, and small deficits, since such forecasts are not binding and make the authorities look good, at least for a while. It takes an unusually good year to have a better budgetary outcome than announced, while a moderate slowdown may easily result in large 'unexpected' slippages.

In 2006 things turned out better than expected. Table 17.5 presents the forecasts produced twice a year by the OECD. Initially, its estimates of budget outcomes were rather pessimistic. With the exception of Italy, all countries in the table did much better than expected. In the case of the Netherlands and Spain, the overestimate of the deficit was of the order of 2% of GDP, a rather significant amount. The general interpretation of this pleasant error was an underestimate of the recovery of the euro area economy in 2006, which has been robust for European standards.

Table 17.5 Expected and Realized Budgets in 2006 (% of GDP)

Forecast time	December 2004	June 2005	December 2005	June 2006	December 2006	Actual
France	−2.9	−3.0	−3.2	−2.9	−2.7	−2.6
Germany	−2.7	−3.2	−3.6	−3.1	−2.3	−1.6
Italy	−3.6	−5.0	−4.2	−4.2	−4.8	−4.5
The Netherlands	−1.9	−1.7	−1.8	−0.5	−0.4	0.5
Spain	−0.1	0.6	0.3	1.1	1.4	1.8

Source: OECD, Economic Outlook.

deficit may signal an explicit government decision to respond to a cyclical downturn, but it may also reflect the automatic worsening of the budget as the economy slows down. This is bothersome, not just for observers and analysts, but for the government as well. How can it know that its response is appropriate if it does not even know what its effect on the budget is?

Any budget law—which authorizes a given level of spending and sets all tax rates—includes an estimate of the expected balance, explicitly based on a forecast of GDP for the corresponding year. In Figure 17.4 the schedule FP (for fiscal policy) corresponds to such a budget law, i.e. spending and tax rates are taken as exogenous. The positive slope represents the working of the automatic stabilizer. Given the amount of spending and the tax rates approved by the parliament in the budget law, an increase in the output gap—a rate of growth of GDP in excess of its trend growth rate—improves

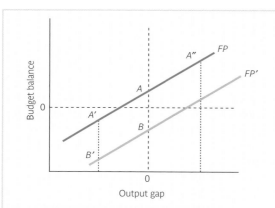

Fig. 17.4 Endogenous and Exogenous Components of Budgets

The line *FP* describes how the actual budget responds to cyclical fluctuations of output about its trend for a given fiscal policy stance. The move from line *FP* to line *FP'* describes a more expansionary policy stance. The cyclically adjusted budget is measured assuming a zero output gap. For fiscal policy stance *FP* it is given by point *A*, and for *FP'* by point *B*.

the budget balance because tax revenues grow. Conversely, the budget balance deteriorates when the output gap declines. For instance, if the budget law assumes that the economy will be on trend during the corresponding fiscal year, it predicts the budget surplus indicated by point *A*. If the actual growth outcome is not as good as expected, point *A'* shows that the budget will end up in deficit.

What if the government decides to react to the budget deterioration by increasing spending or cutting taxes? This discretionary action is captured by a shift of the budget schedule, which moves to *FP'*. This schedule lies everywhere below *FP*, simply because the higher spending level or lower tax rates imply that, for any output gap, the new budget surplus will be lower than the previous one. What, then, does this fiscal expansion mean for the budget balance? If the economy does not respond to the fiscal boost during the fiscal year and the output gap remains the same as the one corresponding to point *A'*, the budget deficit will widen, as shown at point *B'*. If, on the contrary, the fiscal expansion

manages to limit the slowdown, the budget will be described by a point on the *FP'* schedule, somewhere up and to the right of point *B'*. For example, if the fiscal expansion succeeds in keeping GDP on trend, the new situation is described by point *B*.

The figure reveals why it is difficult to interpret budget figures. Suppose, for instance, that last year's situation is described by point *A* and that, in the present year, the outcome corresponds to point *B'*. We observe a sizeable worsening of the budget balance. Is it due to a fiscal expansion or to an economic slowdown? Both, in fact, but how do we know the role of each contributing factor? This is the question that we need to deal with.

The procedure is to ask what the budget balance would be if real GDP were on its trend path. The corresponding budget balance, which is constructed to be free of cyclical effects, is called the **cyclically-adjusted** (or sometimes **structural**) **budget**. Figure 17.4 considers two budget laws, represented by the schedules *FP* and *FP'*. The corresponding cyclically adjusted budgets are represented by points *A* and *B*, respectively. The distance *AB* is a measure of the fiscal relaxation corresponding to the shift from *FP* to *FP'*. In general, actual budget outcomes are not equal to the cyclically adjusted budget because the GDP is not at its trend level. Looking at the budget law represented by *FP*, it is easy to see that a positive output gap implies an actual budget surplus larger than the cyclically adjusted surplus: compare points *A* and *A''*.

Cyclically-adjusted budgets are routinely calculated and discussed. For example, the European Stability and Growth Pact, designed to impose fiscal discipline within the monetary union, initially considered only actual budget outcomes. But the emphasis is increasingly shifting to structurally-adjusted balances. The difference between the two budget measures is illustrated in Figure 17.5, which displays changes between 2000 and 2005. All countries that appear to the left of the vertical line have seen their budgets deteriorate. All those that appear above the horizontal line have actually tightened their fiscal policies. Very few of them have managed to reduce the actual deficit, or improve the surplus, because of the marked cyclical downturn that has been felt nearly everywhere.

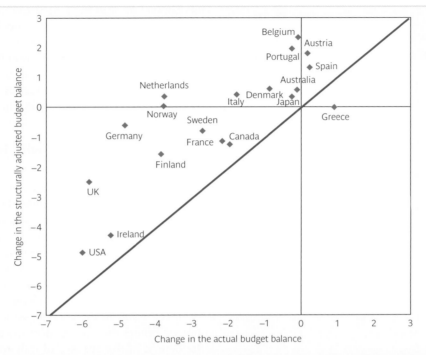

Fig. 17.5 Changes in Actual and Cyclically Adjusted Budget Balances from 2000 to 2003 (% of GDP)

The horizontal axis shows the change of the actual budget balance, the vertical axis displays the change in the cyclically adjusted budget balance, comparing 2000, a year of generally high activity level, and 2003, a slowdown year in many countries. In the north-east quadrant, for example, the actual budget deteriorates while the structural budget surplus increases (or the deficit is reduced): fiscal policy is contractionary and yet the actual budget surplus declines (or the deficit increases); the reason is that the output gap has fallen, dragging down the actual budget in spite of the government's effort to contain the deficit. More generally, all points above the diagonal correspond to cases where the slowdown contributes to a worsening of the actual budget, over and above the actual stance of fiscal policy. The case of the USA is quite striking: fiscal policy has been massively relaxed as the increase in the structural deficit indicates, and this has been accompanied by an even larger worsening of the actual deficit.

Source: OECD, *Economic Outlook*.

17.4 Deficit Financing: Public Debt and Seigniorage

According to Table 17.6, public indebtedness in almost every OECD country is large and growing.[6]

6   The table presents gross debt. In contrast, net debt takes into account the state's assets. Net debt figures exist but are considered unreliable because of the diffculty in determining the value of state assets.

Government debt grew especially during the 1970s, with this growth slowing down for some during the 1980s but accelerating for others. Yet there is good news. The intertemporal budget constraint does prevent the permanent accumulation of public debt, just as Chapter 7 foresaw. At some point,

Table 17.6 Gross Public Debt, Various Countries, 1970–2007 (% of GDP)

	1970	1980	1990	2000	2007
Austria	18.5	35.8	57.2	69.4	64.2
Belgium	61.9	74.5	125.8	113.4	87.3
Denmark	n.a.	43.7	66.4	57.1	31.3
Finland	n.a.	13.6	16.3	52.3	42.4
France	40.0	29.7	38.6	65.2	71.9
Germany	17.5	30.2	40.4	60.4	66.2
Greece	18.8	22.8	79.6	114.9	103.8
Ireland	n.a.	69.5	93.3	37.8	29.2
Italy	55.1	86.6	97.3	121.6	116.9
Japan	12.0	55.0	68.6	136.7	180.3
Netherlands	65.5	59.1	87.8	63.9	53.4
Norway	41.7	39.7	29.4	34.1	76.0
Spain	n.a.	19.9	47.7	66.5	42.8
Sweden	29.1	47.2	46.7	65.7	46.5
UK	80.9	55.9	32.9	45.6	47.2
USA	46.3	41.7	63.0	55.2	62.2

Source: OECD, *Economic Outlook*.

budget deficits must be closed and turned into primary surpluses. Figure 7.9 showed how this rule had worked for several 'problem cases'. Yet public debt continued to rise in the 1990s in several countries. Not surprisingly, **debt stabilization** has emerged as a central concern, and has come up in discussions regarding European Monetary Union as well as annual reports by the OECD on its member states.

Table 17.6 shows that considerable progress has been achieved in many countries, yet not everywhere. Most spectacular successes—in the sense of stopping exploding debt paths and sometimes even reversing them—have been observed in Belgium, Denmark, Ireland, the Netherlands, and Spain. Greece and Italy also made marginal progress, most of which was a requirement for these countries to adopt the euro.[7] It is striking that fiscal responsib-

ility slipped most in the largest economies: France, Germany, the UK, and the USA seemed unable or unwilling to get their debt under control. This section examines the debt stabilization issue. It allows us to understand the forces that lie behind the debt accumulation process, the challenge of stopping this unsustainable evolution, and what happens if it is not done.

17.4.1 The Public Debt with No Growth and No Inflation

Let us start with the easiest case, where the central bank does not finance the public deficits. We can therefore ignore the role of seigniorage. It also makes things easier if we assume that inflation is nil because then we do not need to worry about the distinction between nominal and real variables. The government budget deficit is the sum of the primary deficit—the excess of purchases G over net tax receipts T—and of debt service—the (real) rate of interest r times the existing debt stock B. To finance the deficit, in the absence of monetary financing, the government must borrow and issue new debt ΔB. This observation can be formalized as

(17.1)
$$\underbrace{\Delta B}_{\substack{\text{debt} \\ \text{accumulation}}} = \underbrace{\underbrace{G - T}_{\substack{\text{primary balance} \\ \text{deficit}}} + \underbrace{rB.}_{\substack{\text{debt} \\ \text{service}}}}_{\substack{\text{total budget} \\ \text{deficit}}}$$

If the overall budget is in deficit—technically, 'the public sector borrowing requirement' is positive—the government must borrow, which means an increase ($\Delta B > 0$) in the public debt B. If it is in surplus, the government can retire some of its existing debt or accumulates assets ($\Delta B < 0$).[8]

Looking at public budgets in this way highlights that the debt accumulation process can easily become explosive. The reason is that the debt feeds and grows on itself; the higher the current stock of

---

7   Chapter 19 provides more details on the requirements imposed by the EU and the European Central bank for those countries adopting the euro, of which the most important involve fiscal policy.

8   Note that B represents the net public debt, which is the government's gross debt less its assets. The reason is that the government should normally receive interest or income from its asset holdings, which tends to reduce the overall budget deficit, exactly in the way debt service tends to increase the deficit.

Table 17.7 **Net Government Indebtedness and Primary Budget Balances, 2008[a] (% of GDP)**

| | Net debt in 2008 | Actual primary budget surplus in 2008 | Primary surplus[b] | |
			Required to stabilize the size of debt	Required to stabilize the debt/GDP ratio
Belgium	69.1	3.1	3.5	1.7
Germany	45.0	2.5	2.3	1.1
Ireland	−1.6	0.9	−0.1	0.0
Italy	89.8	2.0	4.5	2.2
Netherlands	28.8	2.3	1.4	0.7

[a] Forecasts produced in 2007 by the OECD.
[b] Required surplus assuming a 5% real interest rate and a 2.5% real GDP growth rate.
Source: OECD, *Economic Outlook*.

debt B, the higher is debt service rB, and therefore the larger the deficit and the need to accumulate more debt. Even when the primary budget is balanced $(G - T = 0)$, the overall budget is in deficit and the debt continues to grow. In this case, the government keeps borrowing to pay interest on the existing debt, which means more indebtedness. Without any further effort to control it, debt will accumulate at rate r.[9] This feature of indebtedness is general and applies to any debt, be it public or private, domestic (i.e. held by domestic residents) or external.

To halt the accumulation of its debt, the government must run a permanent primary surplus large enough to service the existing debt without having to rely on borrowing. Formally, we ask what must happen to have $\Delta B = 0$ in (17.1). It is easy to verify that this implies

(17.2) $$T - G = rB$$
primary budget surplus = debt service.

Stabilizing the absolute level of debt can be a formidable task. The longer the government puts off the day of reckoning, the larger the debt becomes, and the larger is the surplus ultimately required to stabilize it. This observation is illustrated in Table 17.7, which presents net debt levels and primary

budget balances (as a ratio to GDP, more on that later) for a sample of countries. The third column gives the primary surplus needed to stabilize the net debt at its 2008 level, assuming a real interest rate of 5%. Of the countries shown, Germany, Ireland, and the Netherlands fulfilled this requirement in 2008, but Italy still had a long way to go. Fortunately, the following sections show that this debt stabilization criterion is excessively stringent because it ignores both growth in GDP and the possibility of monetary finance.

17.4.2 The Public Debt with Growth and No Inflation

It would seem wrong to compare the absolute government indebtedness of the USA with that of France and Sweden. This is because the absolute size of the USA is much larger than France or Sweden. A country's ability to service debt (to repay it with interest) is fundamentally related to its economic magnitude. This is precisely why all the data presented so far have been in terms of ratios to GDP, and why the stabilization of the ratio of debt to GDP is a more sensible objective than the stabilization of the debt level itself.

This distinction matters crucially because GDPs grow secularly over time. Box 17.3 shows formally how the debt accounts change when we look at debt–GDP ratios. Beyond the arithmetic details, the logic is easy to understand. When we look at the

---

[9] The tendency for the debt to grow at the rate r can be seen by looking at (17.1) when the primary budget is balanced: then, $\Delta B = rB$ or $\Delta B/B = r$, which is the growth rate of the public debt.

Box 17.3 **Debt–Deficit Arithmetic**

Growth, no inflation

In order to study the evolution of the debt–GDP ratio, it is helpful to apply the rule for rate of change in a ratio; (B/Y) grows at a rate equal to the difference in the growth rates of numerator and denominator. Using the annual budget account (17.1), we see that the numerator grows at rate $(G - T)/B + r$, while the denominator grows at rate g of GDP (here we use the trend GDP growth rate, since we are considering longer periods of time). Subtract the latter from the former, multiplying by (B/Y) and rearranging yields

(17.3) $$\Delta\left(\frac{B}{Y}\right) = \frac{G - T}{Y} + (r - g)\frac{B}{Y}.$$

In absolute terms, the debt–GDP ratio increases with the budget deficit (as a share of GDP) and debt service on the debt–GDP ratio adjusted for GDP growth rate (g). As long as the real interest rate exceeds the growth rate, the debt process is explosive. Note, however, that it tends to grow at the rate $r - g$, lower than r as implied by (15.1). For a given ratio of the primary deficit to GDP, more debt means more deficit and greater borrowing requirements. The primary budget surplus required to stabilize the debt–GDP ratio is the one which sets the left-hand side of (17.3) to zero:

(17.4) $$\Delta\left(\frac{B}{Y}\right) = 0 \text{ when } \frac{T - G}{Y} = (r - g)\frac{B}{Y}.$$

If the rate of interest r is below the GDP growth rate g, the debt–GDP ratio can be stabilized while running a budget deficit. In theory, fast-growing countries can outgrow their deficits.

Growth and inflation

When inflation is positive, the role of money and money creation in government finance has to be accounted for. The WebAppendix shows how budgetary accounts are modified to recognize that the deficit can be financed by both new debt issue and seigniorage finance—loans by the central bank to cover the deficit. These loans are equivalent to the creation of additional monetary base, M0:

(17.5) $$\Delta\left(\frac{B}{Y}\right) = \frac{\Delta(M0/P)}{Y} = \frac{G - T}{Y} + (r - g)\frac{B}{Y}.$$

Stabilizing the debt–GDP ratio now requires an even smaller primary budget surplus, or can even be achieved with a primary deficit if enough monetary base is created:

(17.6) $$\Delta\left(\frac{B}{Y}\right) = 0 \text{ when } \frac{T - G}{Y} = (r - g)\frac{B}{Y} - \frac{\Delta(M0/P)}{Y}.$$

Finally, in Chapter 12 we derived the long-run relationship between inflation, monetary growth, and output: $\pi = \mu - g$. But $\Delta(M0/P)$ is equal to $(\mu - \pi)M0$. The stabilization condition for debt then becomes

(17.7) $$\Delta\left(\frac{B}{Y}\right) = 0 \text{ when } \frac{T - G}{Y} = (r - g)\frac{B}{Y} - g\frac{M0}{Y}.$$

In the long run, the relaxation of the government budget constraint is only possibly if the economy (and the demand for real money) is growing.

---

evolution of the debt–GDP ratio, we can think of a 'race' between the numerator—the real debt level—and the denominator—real GDP. The faster the real GDP grows, the less the ratio increases. The debt itself may well increase in level and yet decline as a ratio to GDP; all it takes is for the GDP to rise faster than the debt level.[10] By the same token, in a growing economy, were the absolute stock of the debt to remain stable, as in the case studied in the previous section (see (17.2)), the debt-to-GDP ratio would vanish over time. Since the real debt tends to grow at the rate r and the GDP grows at the rate g, the debt-to-GDP ratio tends to rise at the rate $(r - g)$. When the GDP growth rate exceeds the real interest rate, a balanced primary budget is sufficient for the debt–GDP ratio to shrink. When the real interest rate exceeds the economy's growth rate, the debt process is explosive. Yet, the primary surplus required to stabilize the *ratio* of the debt to GDP is significantly smaller than the primary surplus

---

[10] The rate of growth of the debt-to-GDP ratio B/Y is
$\frac{\Delta(B/Y)}{B/Y} = \frac{\Delta B}{B} - \frac{\Delta Y}{Y}$ a formula that we have encountered in many contexts, for the first time in Chapter 6. The debt–GDP ratio declines when the real debt grows at a lower rate than the real GDP.

required to stabilize the *level* of the debt. This is precisely because GDP growth helps contain the increase in the debt–GDP ratio. This is illustrated by the last column in Table 17.7, assuming a 5% real interest rate and a 2.5% real GDP growth rate. We see that in 2008 all countries listed in the table managed to stabilize their debt–GDP ratios, the only exception being Italy.

These results help us understand why debt increased so much in the 1970s and 1980s. Over the 1960s and early 1970s, real GDP growth exceeded the real interest rate in most countries. For example, real interest rates in the UK during the period 1960–1980 averaged 0.9% while real growth was 2.4%. Under such conditions, budget deficits need not imply a growing debt–GDP ratio. The debt accumulation process was not explosive, at least relative to GDP, a fact that probably encouraged complacency about deficits and debt. In contrast, over the period 1980–1995, UK real growth hardly changed (2.4%), while real interest rates averaged 4.7%! The debt process became explosive and required prompt and vigorous action. Several countries failed to adjust quickly enough.

17.4.3 The Public Debt with Growth and Inflationary Finance

Inflationary finance represents an alternative way of relaxing the budgetary stringency required for debt stabilization. Simply put, the government exploits its monopoly right to create money in the narrow sense (monetary base) and uses that money to pay its bills. Technically, the government borrows directly from the central bank, or prevails upon it to purchase existing debt and to hold that debt on its balance sheet (see Chapter 9). When the money is spent, it becomes an addition to monetary base, the foundation for money creation by the banking system.

Producing monetary base is virtually costless: a stroke of a pen—more precisely keying in a few zeros in the computer—or activating the printing press. Since the national government uses the money it creates at face value to acquire real resources, it (or the central bank, which is owned by the government) makes a comfortable profit. The revenue from this lucrative activity is called seigniorage.[11] Seigniorage remains the main source of profit for central banks. As public institutions, central banks are usually required to turn over most of their profits to their governments. Although seigniorage can represent substantial source of government revenue in times of high inflation, it has rarely done so in recent years.

Naturally, the greater use of seigniorage results in faster money growth (via the money multiplier effect) and, eventually, higher inflation. Formally, the role of seigniorage can be seen when the budget account (17.1) is modified to recognize that any increase in the nominal monetary base $\Delta M0$ provides real resources to the government. Since the real value of seigniorage is $\Delta M0/P$, the account is rewritten as

$$(17.8) \quad \underset{\substack{\text{new} \\ \text{debt}}}{\Delta B} + \underset{\text{seigniorage}}{\Delta(M0/P)} = G - T + \underset{\substack{\text{interest} \\ \text{payments}}}{rB}.$$

Seigniorage is a cheap source of financing for the government. It severs the link that makes the debt process explosive because little or no interest is paid on the monetary base. But the explosiveness is simply transferred elsewhere—into inflation. All hyperinflationary episodes can be linked to a government's attempt to break away from its budget constraint. For the same reason, hyperinflations ultimately end when governments close their deficits, or when central banks stop financing them.

Yet inflation, especially when it is unanticipated, can *help* the government solve its financing problems, via the second mechanism of inflationary finance, the **inflation tax**. The inflation tax simply means that inflation which arises from monetary growth erodes the real value of obligations the

---

[11] This expression can be traced back to the Middle Ages, when local lords had the monopoly over coinage. Often, they abused this power to reduce—debase—the gold content of coins minted in their lands. In a similar fashion, governments exploit the monopoly power of the central bank in creating the medium of exchange to acquire valuable resources from the private sector. Modern seigniorage is just another form of taxation. The authorities exchange money, which is costless to produce, against goods and services. It is as if these goods and services were simply confiscated.

government has issued in its own currency. Most important in this regard is the public debt, which primarily takes the form of non-indexed, nominal bonds, but also includes money issued by the central bank. Because the nominal face value of the debt remains unchanged, its real value is eroded, and debt-holders suffer a real capital loss. The inflation tax is just the mirror image of this loss: the reduction of the real value of the debt is a gain for the government.

Seigniorage and the inflation tax go hand in hand. Seigniorage leads to money growth and therefore to inflation and debt relief via the inflation tax. Naturally, the inflation tax applies only to debt issued in local currencies. In addition, the inflation tax works only if inflation is unexpected. The reason is that, when debt-holders anticipate inflation, they demand a nominal interest rate which compensates them for the expected erosion of the principal. This is the Fisher principle of Chapter 13. The nominal interest rate rises in line with expected inflation, leaving the real interest rate unchanged. In that case, the bondholders do not lose, nor do governments gain from inflation—except for the inflation tax on money balances, which do not bear interest.

17.5 **Three Ways to Stabilize the Public Debt**

What are the options open to a government that wants to stabilize an exploding debt–GDP ratio? There are three, and only three, known ways of achieving that objective: (1) fiscal stringency—reducing the deficit and achieving the required primary surplus by reducing public spending, raising taxes, or both; (2) inflationary finance—the monetization of deficits and use of the inflation tax; and (3) outright default on some or all of the existing debt. All three amount to different forms of taxation: standard taxation in the first case, taxing those who happen to hold nominal assets (money, and nominal bonds) in the second case, and taxing those who own Treasury debt in the last case.

17.5.1 **Cutting the Deficit**

Deficit reduction is the virtuous road to debt stabilization. Politically, though, it is also the hardest to implement. Public spending cuts elicit significant resistance from those directly affected, e.g. government employees who will fight for their jobs, or public construction contractors that want to keep their business going. Raising taxes is notoriously unpopular with everyone. And yet, deficit reduction has been successfully implemented in a number of European countries. As can be seen from Table 17.3, countries with some of the most serious debt problems—Belgium, Denmark, Ireland, and Italy—have turned their primary budgets around. The recent European consolidation can be attributed largely to the adoption of the monetary union, as explained in Box 17.4.

17.5.2 **Recourse to Seigniorage and the Inflation Tax**

In the end, monetary finance of fiscal deficits is just another form of taxation, like excise, income, or consumption taxes. It operates by reducing the value of the money base (the central bank's liability) and of the public debt (the Treasury's liability). Inflationary finance is simply a tax on money and bondholders.[12]

This result can be seen in a different way. In the budget accounts, (17.1) for example, it is the real interest rate that matters. For the inflation tax to work, the real interest rate must fall, otherwise the real cost of servicing the debt remains unchanged. When inflation rises unexpectedly and quickly enough, nominal interest rates on long-maturity assets cannot be modified as they are contractually

---

[12] More generally, unanticipated inflation redistributes wealth from borrowers to lenders when the assets are nominal, i.e. set in money terms and not indexed to a price level.

Box 17.4 Euro Area and the Stability and Growth Pact

When a country has its own currency, it can use seigniorage to finance at least part of its deficits. Once it has fixed its exchange rate or joined a monetary union, this source of financing is lost, as is its ability to determine the domestic inflation rate.[13] The consequences for national fiscal policies are profound. First, the debt stabilization requirement becomes more stringent, as a comparison of (17.1) and (17.7) shows. Second, default is the only option for a government unwilling to face the facts of the intertemporal budget constraint and run primary surpluses. The spectre of default was a great concern for the founding fathers of the European monetary union. Europe continues to consist of sovereign countries with their own individual histories and traditions. Sanctions for bad fiscal behaviour available to that other large monetary union, the USA, are non-existent.

For this reason, admission to the monetary union is restricted to countries that fulfil strict criteria of good budgetary behaviour. Also, once a member, each country is subjected to the Excessive Deficit Procedure. This procedure is defined by the Stability and Growth Pact. In brief, the pact sets upper limits on annual consolidated budget deficits of 3% of GDP. Should a country exceed this limit, it is given an initial 'early warning' and must then take prompt corrective action. Failure to correct the situation exposes the country to a fine. For the reasons presented in Section 17.3.3, during the 2000–2003 slowdown many countries exceeded the 3% limit. In late 2003, the fine procedure should have been triggered against France and Germany, but real politics took over and the pact was 'suspended', a decision that has subsequently been found to be illegal by the European Court of Justice. While the Stability and Growth Pact has not been adhered to, it has still restrained most governments, as can be seen from Figure 17.5. Whether it will continue to do so in times of economic stress remains to be seen.

---

fixed for the whole life of the asset. This explains why *ex post* real interest rates are just the mirror image of inflation.

To a fiscally undisciplined government, the inflation tax may seem like an easy way to escape its debt obligations. It is not as painless as it looks, though. When inflation rises, buyers of new bond issues will demand higher nominal interest rates to avoid getting 'burned'. In addition, suspicious lenders will be less and less willing to agree to long-term loans. As the maturity of the debt shortens, the government must constantly issue new bonds to pay back its maturing debt, and it must then pay the new higher nominal interest rate. If the debt accumulation process remains unstable, the government will be forced to create more money, leading to more inflation, which will soon lead to higher nominal interest rates, calling for yet another increase in inflation, and so on.

This is precisely how many hyperinflations get started. A surprise inflation tax wipes out the value of nominal assets and eliminates the real public debt, but leaves a hyperinflation it its wake. As the recent episodes of Bolivia, Serbia, or Zimbabwe show, hyperinflations take a terrible toll on the economic and social structure of a country, and stopping a hyperinflation can be very costly too. This is why it is an option only used under extreme political situations. It is no surprise that most hyperinflation episodes occur during wars (Congo and Serbia in the 1990s) or in their aftermath (Germany, Greece, Hungary after the First World War), or in troubled times (several Eastern European countries at the time of the collapse of the communist regimes) when the government is too weak to enforce fiscal discipline.

---

[13] Seigniorage still takes place at the level of the European monetary union. Indeed, the ECB is required to turn over its profits to participating countries. But the decision on how fast to let the money base grow, and how much seigniorage to collect, no longer lies with national governments, but solely with the ECB. By virtue of its founding statutes, the ECB is formally independent and required to aim at price stability. It is legally prohibited from financing the government budgets. For a detailed account of the fiscal policy restraints facing countries wishing to join the European monetary union, see Baldwin and Wyplosz (2005).

Box 17.5 Mussolini and the Public Debt[14]

Italy emerged from the First World War with a large debt and a sizeable budget deficit. Between 1923 and 1926, having eliminated all political opposition, Mussolini re-established near budget balance and brought the debt–GDP ratio down by reducing spending and raising taxes (Table 17.8). Yet, concerned that the debt was too short in maturity, and therefore vulnerable to market conditions, in November 1926 the government imposed a mandatory conversion of debt of less than seven-year maturity into fixed-rate (5%) longer-term bonds. In 1934, these bonds were again forcibly converted into 25-year loans bearing a 3.5% interest. The first conversion is estimated to have resulted in a partial default of 20%, the second one in a loss of 30%. After these moves, the government found it very hard to undertake new borrowing. It was forced to cease issuing short-term debt in 1927 and paid a premium estimated at 2–3% on borrowing from banks.

17.5.3 Default

The most brutal way for a government to stabilize the debt is simply to default, i.e. to repudiate it. Except for post-war or post-revolution periods—when the blame can be put on exceptional circumstances or previous regimes—governments rarely resort to this approach, and do so only under severe stress. Outright default is always perceived as a major breach of confidence and leaves long-lasting scars on the reputation of governments. Box 17.5 describes major Italian defaults in the Fascist era. Defaults can also be seen as a form of specific taxation that affects bondholders, much as inflation does. Indeed, partial default is exactly equivalent to a tax on bond income. If, for example, a government reduces the value of its debt by half, this is the same as imposing a 50% tax on interest and repayment of the principal.

The issue of default has different implications when the debt is owned by foreigners. Thus far, it was implicitly assumed that the public debt was held by residents. In that case, debt accumulation or stabilization amounts to a redistribution of income across generations, between those who are taxed now and those who will be taxed in the future. When debt is owned by foreigners, the situation is different. As Chapters 7 and 15 have shown, honouring external debt implies transferring resources to the rest of the world. This requires running a current account surplus, i.e. spending less than is earned. On the other hand, once it has defaulted on its external debt, a country cannot borrow abroad for a few years. During that period of 'international pariah status', the country will find it difficult to run a current account deficit. Comparing the two situations, honouring the debt requires a current account surplus, possibly for decades, while defaulting only requires a balanced current account, usually for a few years. This explains why sovereign nations are often more willing to default on the external than on the domestic debt when the going gets rough.

Table 17.8 Public Finances in Italy, 1918–1928

	1918	1922	1924	1926	1928
Tax revenues as % of public spending	23	46	90	100	90
Debt–GNP (%)	70.3	74.8	65.1	49.7	53.8

Source: Alesina (1988).

---

[14] This box draws on Alesina (1988).

❶ Summary

1. One fundamental purpose of fiscal policy is to provide public goods and services. The boundary between what has to be produced publicly and what can be produced privately is not clear-cut.

2. A second function of fiscal policy is the redistribution of income and the alleviation of inequities that may be generated by the market mechanism. Doing so, however, may lead to inefficiencies.

3. A third function is to use the budget to offset temporary or cyclical fluctuations. This is done by running deficits in bad years (financed by borrowing) and surpluses in good years (to repay previous borrowing).

4. Countercyclical fiscal policy has three main benefits: (1) tax smoothing, (2) private consumption smoothing, and (3) private income maintenance.

5. The fact that some households sometimes cannot borrow provides a justification for fiscal policy to step in and support private consumption smoothing.

6. If prices and wages are not fully flexible, fiscal policy can be used to stabilize demand, either directly through government spending, or indirectly through taxation by reducing fluctuations in private sector incomes.

7. When they vote on the budgets, parliaments set public spending levels and tax rates. During a recession (respectively, an expansion) tax receipts decline (respectively, an increase), leading to a deficit (respectively, a surplus). As a result, the budget acts as an automatic stabilizer.

8. The operation of automatic stabilizers makes it difficult to interpret changes in the budget. The cyclically adjusted budget balance provides a way of disentangling the endogenous response to cyclical fluctuations from exogenous discretionary government actions.

9. Indebtedness is an inherently explosive process. When the primary budget is balanced and the debt is positive, borrowing is necessary just to service existing debt. The real debt accumulates at a rate given by the real interest rate.

10. To stabilize the level of the real debt, in the absence of real economic growth or monetary finance, the government must run a primary budget surplus equal to the interest charge. The longer it waits, the larger will be the debt and the interest burden that it faces, and the larger the required primary budget surplus.

11. In a growing economy, stabilizing the ratio of debt to GDP is a less stringent condition than stabilizing the absolute debt level. The required primary surplus is proportional to the difference between the real interest rate and the real GDP growth rate. Not only is this smaller than the real interest rate, it may well be negative, thus allowing permanent primary deficits.

12. Inflationary finance reduces the debt burden for two reasons. First, seigniorage provides resources directly to the government, virtually free of charge. As money growth eventually leads to inflation, the real value of nominal debt declines. Second, the inflation tax reduces the real value of nominal government debt which is not indexed. The inflation tax can be collected, however, only if inflation is unexpected. Otherwise the nominal interest rate rises, which protects lenders.

13. In addition to lowering the deficit—through spending cuts or tax increases—or resorting to money finance, debt can be stabilized by default. This drastic form of taxation has severe consequences for a government's reputation.

14. As long as the public debt is held by residents, debt stabilization or reduction implies income redistribution within the country. When part of the public debt is held by non-residents, stabilization requires a net transfer by residents to the rest of the world. A default redistributes wealth in the opposite direction.

🔘 Key Concepts

- public goods
- seigniorage
- externalities
- human capital
- productive efficiency
- equity–efficiency trade-off
- consumption smoothing

- tax smoothing
- countercyclical fiscal policy
- automatic stabilizers
- cyclically adjusted budgets
- debt stabilization
- inflation tax

❓ Exercises

1 Are bank notes and coins part of the public debt? Should they be? Why or why not?

2 The budget law sets public spending at €11,000 million and the tax rate that applies to all incomes is 25%. Last year's GDP was €40,000 million and the forecast is that it will grow by 3%. What is the budget balance set by the law? What will happen to the balance if the economy does not grow at all?

3 A country growing at a rate of 3.5% has a debt–GDP ratio of 40%. What is the primary budget surplus that keeps this ratio constant when the real interest rate is 2%? When it is 6%?

4 Suppose the debt–GDP ratio is 100%, growth is 3% per annum, and the real interest rate is 5%.

(a) What is the primary government budget surplus (as a percentage of GDP) that can stabilize the debt–GDP ratio?

(b) How does your answer change if interest rates fall to 2%? If growth falls to 1%?

5 The demand for (real) central bank money, the source of seigniorage, declines with the rate of inflation. Suppose, as an example, that this demand (in billions of euros) is given as follows:

Π	0%	1%	2%	5%	10%	20%	25%	50%
$M0/P$	1,000	905	819	607	368	135	82	7

Seigniorage is a tax applied to this demand, whose rate is just the rate of inflation. Compute seigniorage as a function of the inflation rate. (Hint: an inflation rate of 5% corresponds to a tax rate equal to 0.05.) Which inflation rate maximizes seigniorage?

6 Figure 17.5 determines four quadrants (ignoring the diagonal). Characterize and comment on the situation in each quadrant.

7 The budget balance is −300 and GDP is 20,000. Potential GDP, however, is 20,600. Compute the structurally adjusted budget using the following information:

- public consumption is not cyclical;
- transfers operate as follows: $TR = 13,000 - 0.5*Y$;
- taxes are: $T = 2,000 + 0.3*Y$.

8 Consider a country where the public debt stands at 60% of GDP. The real interest rate is 3% and the trend growth rate is 2%. In the absence of seigniorage, what is the primary budget required to stabilize the debt level? The debt–GDP ratio?

9 Why does a primary surplus in excess of what is found in (17.2) imply that the public debt will eventually disappear? Why does a primary surplus in excess of what is found in (17.4) imply that the public debt will eventually disappear as a fraction of GDP?

→ Essay Questions

1 Make a list of all public services that you can think of. In each case, examine whether they can be privately provided.

2 'The national debt is a great scam, because it will never be repaid.' 'The national debt is irrelevant because we owe it to ourselves.' Comment on these two popular characterizations of government indebtedness.

3 Critics of the Stability and Growth Pact argue that it prevents the operation of automatic stabilizers during cyclical downturns. The proponents respond that the way to deal with the pact is to run structurally adjusted surpluses. Explain and comment.

4 Between 1990 and 2004 the Irish public gross debt fell from 94% to 31% of GDP. Collect data on Irish budgets and growth during this period to explain this remarkable evolution (possible sources: OECD *Economic Outlook* database, Ireland's Finance Ministry's website: <www.finance.gov.ie>).

5 Debt stabilization is controversial. One view is that it requires running balanced budgets, irrespective of the possible cyclical implications. Another view is that it is far better to use fiscal policy to support rapid growth. Evaluate these arguments.

Policies for the Long Run 18

For almost twenty years now, European unemployment has been a major social problem and the sign of under-utilized resources at a time of unfilled needs . . . Faced with such a prospect, European economists cannot remain silent.

Jacques Drèze and Edmond Malinvaud

18.1 Overview

In Chapter 16, we explored the role of demand management in macroeconomic policy-making, and Chapter 17 highlighted the potential role as well as limitations of fiscal policy in the management of demand. Recessions are costly in terms of unemployment and lost output; recovery from these recessions can be accelerated by well-chosen activist policies. Yet some have concluded that no policy is better than a misguided activist one. Since the economy returns to its long-run path anyway, they claim, demand policy can do more harm than good. All the same, most governments do make use of demand policy, and some rather frequently at that.

An alternative or even a complementary policy to demand-side management is to increase the productive potential of an economy, irrespective of the state of aggregate demand. Policy measures which raise the long-run or potential GDP ($\bar{Y}$) are known as **supply-side policies**. This is shown in Figure 18.1, which plots on the horizontal axis output Y itself, rather than its deviation from potential output ($Y - \bar{Y}$). Successful supply-side policies raise potential GDP from $\bar{Y}$ to $\bar{Y}'$ faster than if it were left to the normal process of economic growth. The attractiveness of such policies is that they bypass the uncomfortable trade-off between output and inflation. In the short run, more output and lower inflation are possible as the economy moves from A to A'.[1] Similarly, adverse supply-sided policies reduce $\bar{Y}$, causing higher inflation in the short run and higher unemployment in the long run.

In this chapter, we survey supply-side policies and assess their effectiveness. These policies may be directed at the labour, product, or financial markets. They may also involve fine-tuning existing, harmful government interventions such as taxation or subsidies. One general conclusion is that, regardless of their effectiveness, supply-side policies do not produce immediate miracles. They can improve incentives to save, work, and produce. They can

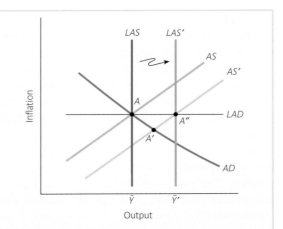

Fig. 18.1 The Macroeconomics of Supply-Side Policies

Supply-side policies aim at mobilizing productive resources to increase equilibrium output. Shifting the aggregate supply curve yields both more output and less inflation in the short run (point A'). In the longer run, inflation returns to its previous level (as indicated by the long-run aggregate demand schedule) but output is permanently higher.

---

[1] Note that the short-run effect of the shift is a reduction in the rate of inflation, as the new short-run and long-run AS curves shift rightwards. After the adjustment is complete, inflation will return to its previous level, the target inflation rate set by the central bank (point A'') (see Chapter 13).

increase general efficiency, possibly by requiring industries to shrink, freeing resources for other, more valuable uses. All these measures take time to work, five to ten years, or even longer.

We examine three broad approaches to increasing the economy's long-run potential. First, good supply-side policy should aim to make markets as efficient as possible; and when markets fail that test, government intervention can improve matters. This was also the message of Chapters 4 and 17. Second, given that governments are already interfering in the market place for both good and bad reasons, they should strive to minimize the negative impact of their intervention. One example is regulation; another is taxation; yet another is subsidy policy. Third, unemployment remains a deep concern in much of Europe where roughly 10% of the labour force is out of work. Yet, in the last 15 years, the UK, the Netherlands, Denmark, Ireland, Finland, and Sweden have proved that unemployment need not be a curse. Even if the political resistance is strong, all of Europe can share in these successes.

18.2 Market Efficiency and the Theory of Supply-Side Policy

18.2.1 The Benchmark of Efficiency: Perfect Competition

Adam Smith (1723–1790), perhaps the most famous economist of all time, claimed in his book *The Wealth of Nations* that efficient resource allocation was best left to the market system. One of the greatest achievements of modern economics has been to confirm that, under ideal conditions, market economies achieve optimal employment of resources.[2] What are those ideal conditions? Most importantly, markets must 'work', prices must be free to adjust. There must be sufficient competition so that new firms can offer similar or identical products and eliminate excessive profits due to their monopoly position. The externalities identified in Chapter 4 and 17 must be absent. Not surprisingly, these ideal conditions are unlikely to be met in practice. If this is the case, governments can intervene to improve the use of resources and achieve a larger level of output in the economy.

An important example is the labour market, studied in Chapter 5. Consider Figure 5.7. Firms' demand for labour is given by the downward-sloping marginal product of labour curve (MPL). Firms hire labour to the point at which its marginal productivity equals the real wage. Similarly, workers supply hours of work until their opportunity cost—leisure—outweighs the real wage. The market-clearing equilibrium point A can be seen as an ideal state. Increasing employment beyond point A in Figure 5.7 reduces the MPL below what workers are willing to work for. Reducing employment below A would raise the MPL above the real wage necessary to motivate labourers to give up their free time. Put differently, if wages are above the market-clearing level, firms would restrict employment and workers would increase their supply, resulting in involuntary unemployment. If real wages are too low, firms demand more man-hours than workers are willing to supply.

What pushes the real wage towards its equilibrium, **market-clearing** level $\bar{W}$ at point A? The answer is: competition. Just for the sake of the argument, let us imagine that workers' labour is traded in a perfectly flexible market. If a firm offers a wage lower than $\bar{W}$, it will not attract as many workers as

---

[2] In the 1950s, Nobel laureates Kenneth Arrow of Stanford and Gerard Debreu of Berkeley showed how Adam Smith's intuition could be rigorously established. They identified the conditions under which a market economy delivers the socially optimal allocation of resources.

it seeks. Competition among firms will lead some to improve their wage offer. As they succeed in luring workers from their previous jobs, other firms will have to respond with yet a higher offer. Competition will bid up wages until they reach the market-clearing level. Conversely, imagine that the wage exceeds $\bar{W}$. Some will not find a job, or will not be able to work as many hours as they wish. Forces of competition will trigger a decline in the wage as unemployed workers underbid those who have jobs, eventually driving wages to point A.

That point A represents an ideal state is a general principle: for an economy to achieve the optimum allocation of resources, all markets must clear. Either all prices are right and all productive resources are fully employed, or none of them is, and underutilization and inefficiency spread throughout the economy. Economists tend to be split into two camps on this issue. Some are convinced that markets are naturally efficient, so there is no need for governments to interfere. This is the **laissez-faire** view. Others believe that few markets meet the high standards set forth by Adam Smith. The existence of **market failures**, when and where they can be identified, provides a justification for government intervention. Note, however, how cautiously this statement is worded. Interventions are only justified if two conditions are met. First, they should be limited to clearly identified market failures. Second, they should be targeted directly at the market failure to avoid creating additional distortions of their own. We next identify several generic market failures and the associated range of interventions.

18.2.2 Imperfect Competition and Economic Rents

When several firms compete with each other in the same market, they are under constant pressure to adapt the price and design of their product to the desires of the consumer—otherwise they will disappear from the screen. They will try to operate as efficiently as possible, and in doing so perform the function society wants them to: allocate available resources to their most efficient uses. And that is exactly what Adam Smith predicted.

Competition, however, can be painful. Every economic agent wants protection from competition. Firms strive to acquire a premier position in the market at the expense of their rivals, thereby earning substantial profits aptly called **economic rents**. How do they do this? Firms normally strive to establish market power, or even market dominance or monopoly status, by exploiting increasing returns to scale or by differentiating their products. When production exhibits increasing returns to scale, larger firms can squeeze out smaller firms by producing more and thus reducing their costs. Eventually a few of them survive and dominate the market (think of the market for automobiles). Firms sometimes restrict competition by preventing others from entering their markets. Most means of maintaining dominance in a market are prohibited; threats against competitors and extortion are illegal. Yet it is standard practice for producers to spend significant amounts of money creating brand names and convincing consumers that their products are fundamentally different or unique. Customers who enjoy consuming products that are different—or merely believe that they are—will be willing to pay more for them. Firms use clever marketing as a means of obtaining and defending this monopoly power, and the amounts spent on product differentiation are evidently justified by the resulting profits. Product differentiation thrives on individuals' desire for variety in the market place. It is indisputable that the consumer would prefer variety to monotony, and the quest by firms to innovate and produce variety is spurred by competition.

Measures which increase competition and thereby economic output are generally referred to as **competition policy**. Competition policy can take a number of forms. In many countries, monopolies are regulated or supervised closely. Firms are seldom allowed to acquire excessive shares of their markets. Collusion in the form of cartels and price-fixing schemes are illegal. More recently, governments have also limited the ability of firms to dominate their input and output markets. The famous Microsoft court case is an attempt to limit the power of this firm. Similarly, the UK Government

Box 18.1   EU Competition Policy and National Preferences

Economists have a particular affinity for competition because it leads to greater efficiency. This enthusiasm is rarely shared by producers in non-competitive markets, where large profits may be at stake. Yet policy-makers and consumers may be sceptical as well. Especially in the European Union, where cultures and traditions are defined by national boundaries, there may be reservations that unbridled competition might destroy or weaken national identities. It may be difficult indeed to discern the difference between respect for consumer preferences and restraint of trade. The latter means less competition, less efficiency, lower output, and fewer jobs without any real gain to consumers.

Examples of this dilemma facing the EU abound. In a highly publicized case involving beer quality in the late 1980s, Germany was taken to the European Court of Justice, which has the final say in matters of EU competition policy. Since 1516, German brewers had produced the golden beverage according to the *Reinheitsgebot* ('beer purity law'), which restricted the content of beer to four ingredients (water, yeast, malted barley, and hops). Such strict regulation of beer quality did not exist elsewhere in Europe. This law was used to exclude 'impure'

foreign beer which did not meet the exacting standards of the *Reinheitsgebot*. The European Court of Justice found that beer brewed using rice and other ingredients should be permitted, while allowing German brewers to market their beer as conforming to the previous regime. Many years later and despite the new import rules, national tastes prevail; most German beer drinkers continue to drink German beer. Similarly, Italians now must have a choice between *grano duro* pasta and those made with other wheat varieties. French cheese consumers can try Danish *blø* if they wish. In theory, the consumer is better off.

Still, the *Reinheitsgebot* case raises a number of interesting questions. Should the EU forbid the import of beef from the USA, which may be treated with hormones or antibiotics? Should genetically modified plants be allowed? Should imports of foreign 'culture'—in particular, audio and video recordings—be limited? Should a minimum price of books in bookstores be guaranteed, as in France, Germany, or Austria? Such regulations are usually justified using non-economic arguments. The question remains whether these truly outweigh their economic costs.

---

has separated electricity generation from electricity distribution and the EU Commission has moved in this direction at the Community level with respect to both electricity and gas transmission. More generally, as European integration proceeds, anti-monopoly powers are being transferred to Brussels, which now monitors market shares at the EU level. Some interesting cases of EU competition policy are discussed in Box 18.1.

Firms are not the only economic agents which try to avoid competition. Labour markets are frequently characterized by non-competitive behaviour. First, labour supply is intimately linked with the human condition, and competition among workers for jobs is often considered inappropriate, in bad taste, or even unethical. Second, wages are often set in bilateral negotiations, and trade unions

are seen as protecting interests of employed workers in a vulnerable situation. An alternative perspective sees trade unions as monopolists with high real wages in mind.[3] With high real wages, labour demand is low and equilibrium unemployment high. If a majority of trade union members accept this trade-off, they will press for an outcome that is not efficient. In a similar way, firms like to control or even reduce competition on labour costs, and are frequently organized in employers' associations. In Europe, these associations frequently take decisions that are also binding for members, and may be followed by non-members (usually smaller firms). If

---

[3]   The analysis of trade unions is developed in Chapter 5.

Box 18.2 The Supply-Side Economics of Immigration

Because labour is so abundant relative to capital in developing countries, many, many people there are very, very poor. In India, for example, GDP amounts to roughly €2 per day. Yet many Indians are highly educated and would readily migrate to Europe where the hourly wage might average €20–25 per *hour* or even more. Even those without exceptional skills but who are able-bodied and willing to work could compete with the less skilled. Almost on a weekly basis, we hear of Kurds, Chinese, Vietnamese, and Indians who are caught trying to cross EU borders. Most of these people are not seeking political asylum as much as economic betterment. One can hardly blame them for wanting to move. Is it economically efficient to keep these people out?

The analysis of Chapter 5 suggests that it is not, and Figure 18.2 shows why. Two labour supply curves are drawn, one corresponding to that of the natives only, without the immigrants. The second curve to the right is the sum of the natives *plus* the newly arrived migrants. For the moment, the labour demand curve is assumed unchanged by migration. It represents the marginal product of labour. For a given wage level, the area under the curve and above that wage represents total profits earned by firms in the economy. In Figure 18.2, profits are thus *AWB* before the migrants arrive. When they do, the aggregate labour supply curve shifts outwards, wages decline from *W* to *W'* and employment rises from *L* to *L'*. Total GDP rises by the amount *BLL'D*, the sum of the additional marginal products of the newly employed. Without migration, this increase in GDP would not have occurred.

So if immigration is economically efficient, why all the fuss? First, the distribution of the increase in GDP is not shared by all: profits rise by *WBDW'* and the migrants earn *CDL'L"*, but wages of native workers have in fact declined from *WBLO* to *W'CL"O*. Only if the demand for labour shifts out—which may occur if there is new investment by natives, or if the immigrants themselves bring capital with them—is this situation likely to be remedied. Second, immigrants may place undue demands on infrastructure and the social safety net which they have not helped to pay for. Finally, although economists like to emphasize the efficiency of immigration, other sociological aspects may be more important: humankind's complex tribal, if sometimes crude and primordial, instincts.

labour and management set wages in collective bargaining without considering the interest of non-member workers, typically the unemployed, and of non-member firms, the level of competition is reduced, and the economy is less efficient. This subject is picked up again in Section 18.4.

Competition in labour markets is not limited to labour unions and management. A number of practices by professional associations—of lawyers, doctors, and architects, for example—also restrict the supply of labour and raise wages. Limitations on international immigration can be interpreted as the ultimate restriction of competition for labour. Because so many political and sociological issues are associated with immigration, it would be premature to advocate open borders for everyone on purely economic grounds. Yet it remains true that immigration is efficient, usually increasing GDP enough to compensate any losers in the receiving country. Box 18.2 gives more details.

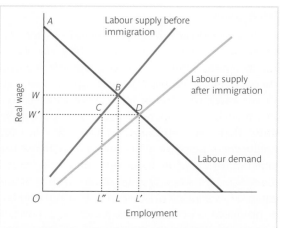

Fig. 18.2 The Supply-Side Economics of Immigration

The consequence of immigration is to shift total labour supply outward. In the new equilibrium, wages decline from *W* to *W'* and employment increases from *L* to *L'*. While GDP rises unambiguously by *BLL'D*, this gain is not evenly spread: the income of capital increases from *AWB* to *AW'D*, migrants now earn *CDL'L"*, while the income of natives declines from *WBLO* to *W'CL"O*.

18.2.3 Market Failures and Overall Market Efficiency

The goal of supply-side policy is to improve the functioning of markets and thereby create efficiency gains. Greater efficiency is like a free lunch—in theory, it can be redistributed to other members of society without making anyone worse off, as discussed in the context of immigration in Box 18.2. In general, this means intervening in markets which do not function properly. While Chapters 16 and 17 dealt with temporary interventions to speed up the elimination of demand shortfalls, here we look at structural failures which call for more or less permanent policies which help raise the equilibrium level of output. But many of these failures simply cannot be eliminated; they are in the nature of things. Supply-side policies may help by reducing the extent and the impact of these failures. We start by looking at the origins of 'natural' market failures, which we group in four general categories:

- externalities;
- public goods;
- increasing returns;
- information asymmetries.

Externalities

As discussed already in Chapters 4 and 17, an externality occurs when someone's action inevitably affects others. Pollution is a good example of a **negative externality**: when a firm dumps its waste in a river, those who live or work downstream suffer and may have to spend resources to purify the water that they drink. Market incentives are for producers of negative externalities to generate too much of these for the social optimum. In contrast, **positive externalities** provide others with a better outcome. A general conclusion is that not enough is produced when activities generate a positive externality. Putting flowers in your windows costs money, while passers-by enjoy looking at them at no cost. Since you bear the costs of putting flowers on your balcony, you balance the price and the benefits (your pleasure). Putting out even more flowers might actually raise society's pleasure, but you have no incentive to do so.

The market alone apparently cannot redress the externality problem. If, however, **property rights** are well-defined, and it is not too costly to enforce these rights, it can.[4] If, for example, the law specifies that everyone has a right to clean water, it is the polluting firm that will have to spend resources to clean up the water. In facing this situation, the firm will adopt cleaner production processes. Alternatively, it will offer to indemnify those who live downstream to prevent them from taking the case to court (where it would probably lose anyway). Conversely, the law could specify a right to pollute. Then the costs would be borne by the people who live downstream, who would pay for cleaning the water, or offer money to the firm for it to reduce its disposal or adopt other production processes. The second solution may seem unfair, and it probably is. The point here is that, once property rights have been established, the market is more likely to deliver the best possible outcome, given the presumption that nature makes it impossible to produce without creating waste.

Externalities that are transmitted by market prices are called **pecuniary externalities**. Assigning property rights and creating a market is often enough to solve the problem. But other, inherently **non-pecuniary externalities** are more challenging. An example is training and education. Better trained people share their knowledge with co-workers and their own children. Thus their knowledge has a value for society at large and, if they are not compensated, they will not accumulate as much human capital as is optimal from the standpoint of the economy. For this reason, society has an interest in stepping in, and subsidizing education. In Chapter 4 we saw how externalities involving education, law and order, and health can influence long-run growth. We look at the policy implications in Section 18.5 below.

Public goods

Public goods, such as parks, clean air, or information, are special. They are non-rival, meaning that

---

4 This result is known as Coase Theorem, named after Ronald Coase, a US economist who received the Nobel Prize for his work on the importance of property rights in a market economy.

consumption by one does not make them less available to others, and they are non-excludable, meaning that, when they are available, everyone can use them freely. As a consequence, no one can be charged for using them, and they must be provided by the state. Law and order is an externality, but it is also a public good that can and must be provided by a functioning government. In societies which have become 'failed states', law and order are insufficiently provided, private justice and local warlords take over, economic activity collapses, and poverty spreads. This has been the case in countries torn by civil wars, such as Liberia, the Ivory Coast, or Somalia.

Increasing returns

Some industries are characterized by increasing returns to scale. We have excluded that possibility in earlier chapters because it creates new problems. A good example is railways. A railway that just serves two cities will only be used by people living in or going to these two cities. If it includes a vast network, the link between the same two cities will be used by many more people, many of whom will only pass through these two cities. The larger the network, the more valuable is each of its sections, and the larger the profits to be earned from each section. Left to the market, competition can easily lead to a **natural monopoly**, with just one company owning the entire network. But we know that, once it has established itself, a monopoly will tend to charge monopoly prices, resulting in the socially inefficient under-use of its product. There is a need for the state to intervene, in this case by granting monopoly rights to a company—which can be public—in exchange for a regulation which will prevent monopolistic pricing. Recent discussions concerning the divestiture of European power transmission networks and the privatization of the German railways reflect these concerns.

Information asymmetries

It is a simple observation that we know more about ourselves than others. This information asymmetry plays a pervasive role in all sorts of markets. Traders often hide information that may reduce the price they can get for their products. Two examples: used car salesmen and traders in financial markets. Both

have little incentive to tell the truth in their businesses. In the first case, the market can easily dry up, even if the salesmen really do tell all they know about the cars they sell. In the second, traders make profit by reacting faster to new information, so they will naturally tend to hide they what they know and what they are up to. Moreover, one trader's move, if badly interpreted by the others, can trigger a stampede. Such herd behaviour seems to lie at the root of financial crises. In both cases, information is a fact of nature, with serious economic implications for the functioning of markets. The state can play a constructive role by prescribing what information must be provided by sellers of used cars or by forcing financial firms to disclose much information that they would prefer to keep for themselves.

Even die-hard free market advocates recognize that markets are subject to failures, that these failures may have serious implications for economic performance, and that only the state can solve most of the associated difficulties. Should the state intervene and solve all market failures? Here economists often disagree. Some, e.g. the public choice school led by Nobel Prize winners Friedrich Hayek and James Buchanan, maintain that, when it intervenes, the state does more harm than good. Others view state intervention as unavoidable, especially in modern societies where economic interactions can be quite complex and thus potential conduits for the diffusion of adverse effects of market failures. It is fair to say that in no country does the state completely refrain from intervening, for the right or wrong reasons. We look at supply-side policies directed at labour markets in Section 18.4, and at goods markets in Section 18.5. Many market failures not only affect the level of output, but also growth rate. In Chapter 4 we considered the potential for those policies mainly directed at enhancing growth. Similarly, Chapter 14 dealt with policies that deal with financial market failures.

In the following sections, policies are discussed which have the objective of rooting out market failures, improving the functioning of markets by increasing competition or the availability of useful information to market participants, or simply making government intervention less costly for the economy. All are examples of good supply-side policy.

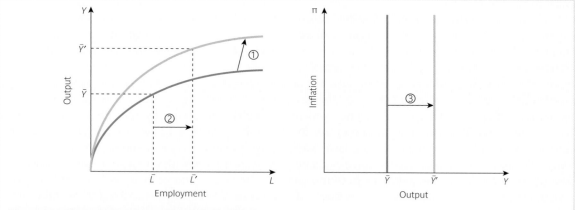

Fig. 18.3 The Impact of Supply-Side Policies
Beneficial supply-side policies are depicted in panel (*a*), either as a shift in the production ① resulting from an increase in total factor productivity or an increase in equilibrium inputs of other production factors holding labour input constant, or as an increase in labour input, holding the production function constant ②. All three possibilities lead to an increase in the long-run equilibrium level of output ③ shown in panel (*b*).

They have the common feature of shifting out the *AS* curve by either working to shift out the aggregate production function, holding productive inputs constant, or shifting out the production function, as in the case of total factor productivity improvements. Figure 18.3 shows that the ultimate outcome is to shift the vertical *LAS* curve to the right from $\bar{Y}$ to $\bar{Y}'$.

18.3 Taxation as the Price of Intervention

18.3.1 The Necessity of Taxation

Public goods are special because they are naturally non-rival and non-excludable. Being non-excludable, public goods cannot be charged to their users. A toll booth can be installed at a bridge's entrance, but what price should its owner charge? Non-rivalry means that the marginal cost of their use is very small; thus the price ought to be low. But fixed costs can be large (a bridge is very expensive to build!), so how can the producer be compensated? In addition, a bridge is a natural monopoly if it is the only one in the vicinity. If the owner charges a high price and

makes large profits, market competition will lead to the multiplication of bridges next to each other, an inefficient outcome. Markets are hard-pressed to cope with such failures. Most often, public goods are provided collectively (free bridges), or their provision is regulated (privately built bridges are generally subject to strict regulations, including pricing and quality of service).

Public goods are pervasive: transportation and amenities, but also justice and police, passports, national defence and security, and diplomacy, etc. In each case, there is a market solution, but it is inefficient as not enough—sometimes none at all—

Box 18.3 **The Deadweight Loss from Taxation**

Why are taxes a source of market distortion? Figure 18.4 shows the general case of an *ad valorem* tax paid as a percentage rate of the value of the activity. Under perfect competition, the demand curve summarizes the marginal willingness of the market to pay for the good in euros, while the supply curve describes the marginal cost of producing it. At point *E*, where the two curves intersect, the consumer at the margin is willing to pay exactly what the producer requires. Perfect competition achieves the social best. Taxes alter the situation. The price paid by the buyer must differ from the after-tax price received by the seller. The new supply curve *S'* shows that the producer receives only a fraction of the market (relative) price. At the new market equilibrium point *D*, the price is higher and the amount consumed and produced is lower. Both consumers and producers are worse off.

What are the losses to an economy from **distortionary taxation**? Figure 18.4 gives us the answer. The loss to consumers of not enjoying the price *OG* is given by *ADEG*. This can be thought of as consumers' willingness to pay above the market-clearing price, or **consumer surplus**. At the same time, the lower price (net of tax) to producing firms means that firms will lose profits on goods they would have sold at cost lower than the no-tax price. The existence of these profits is due to the fact that the supply curve is upward-sloping. This second area *BCEG* is known as **producer surplus**. This consumer and producer surplus are not lost entirely. Despite the price rise, purchases of *AD* will still occur. The tax income from an *ad valorem* tax is given by the rectangle *ABCD*. This leaves the two triangles, *DEF* and *CFE*, which represent lost consumer and producer surplus, or deadweight loss to society. These losses can therefore be quantified. Economic consultants frequently estimate these deadweight losses as the cost of taxation when considering different policy options.

would be privately provided. And in each case, the insufficient provision of the public goods would greatly impair economic activity, possibly leading to the breakdown of other, well-functioning markets. This is why the provision of public goods is a fundamental supply-side policy. The more efficient the provision, the more productive the economy will be. Efficiency means that public goods are produced at the lowest possible cost—which also involves issues of corruption. We discuss this further in Section 18.5. Efficiency also requires that resources be collected to finance the production of public services, an issue to which we now turn.

18.3.2 The Effect of Taxation on Efficiency

Once a society has agreed to let government perform certain public functions, public resources need to be raised in order to pay for them. This is done through taxation of final goods and services, factors of production, and other activities. Taxation gener-

ally distorts markets by driving a wedge between the cost of producing goods and services and the price paid by the consumers. This violates a fundamental principle of economic efficiency, which states that the marginal benefit of the good or service involved should be set equal to the marginal cost of supplying it. When this principle is violated, there is a loss of welfare to both consumers and producers, which can be quantified. This **deadweight loss of taxation** is described in more detail in Box 18.3.

In order to provide public goods, the government must thus raise taxes and accept the associated distortions. Still, it should do so in the least inefficient way. The **Ramsey principle of public finance** states that this is best achieved, first, by spreading taxes as widely as possible over different goods and services and, second, by taxing most heavily those goods with the most inelastic (i.e. steepest) demands and supplies. Implementing this principle is politically contentious. Each producer stands to be hurt when

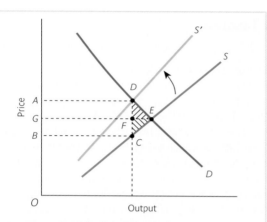

Fig. 18.4 The Effect of Taxation

Taxes drive a wedge between the price faced by the buyer and the price charged by the seller. Here a sales tax (e.g. VAT) shifts the supply curve upward. The new equilibrium occurs at point *D*, with less output, a higher buying price (distance *OA*), and a lower selling price (*OB*) than at the tax-free equilibrium point *E*. Tax revenue for the government is measured by area *ABCD*, the quantity sold times the tax rate (the difference between the two prices). Consumers, who could buy quantity *GE* at price *OG*, suffer a 'welfare loss' measured by the area *ADEG*. Similarly, producers suffer a loss represented by the area *GECB*. Of these two losses—area *ADECB*—the government receives *ABCD*. What is left, the triangles *DEF* and *EFC*, represent, respectively, lost consumer and producer surpluses—deadweight losses—arising from the tax.

a tax is applied to its production—because the producer surplus is reduced, as Box 18.3 shows—and therefore lobbies hard to obtain as low taxes as possible. Consumers, on the other hand, tend to be spread out and difficult to organize politically. As a result, tax reforms bring a diverse coalition of private interests that often succeed as the silent majority that stands to benefit from them remains inactive.

18.3.3 Adverse Effects of Taxation on the Tax Base

By definition, non-distortionary taxes do not affect economic behaviour, either because supply or de-

mand is inelastic, or because the tax is independent of economic decisions. An example would be lump-sum taxes levied on individuals without any reference to incomes, wealth, or spending, or taxes levied unexpectedly on past incomes and wealth so that it is too late to react. For this reason, non-distortionary taxes are appealing to governments. In practice, retroactive taxation is considered unfair precisely because it takes people by surprise. Lump-sum taxes are also unpopular, as UK Prime Minister Thatcher's fateful experience with the poll tax in 1990 showed. She tried to implement it and was promptly voted out of office. As a result, nearly all taxes are distortionary.

Because distortionary taxes move the economy away from its first-best equilibrium, it is entirely conceivable that raising tax rates actually results in lower tax revenues. This is because the tax *base* shrinks faster than the tax rate itself increases. This effect is sometimes called the **Laffer curve** and is depicted in Figure 18.5.[5] This curve describes a theoretical relationship between *total* government tax revenues on the vertical axis and the *average* tax rate (the ratio of tax receipts to GDP) on the horizontal axis. The tax rate ranges from 0 to 100%. At a 0% rate, tax revenue is nil (point *A*). When the tax rate reaches 100%, no one is likely to work or produce at all so tax receipts are also nil (point *B*). At intermediate tax rates, tax receipts are positive, as at point *C*. The hump-shape of the curve indicates that the tax rate distorts the economy so much that beyond some tax rate, taxable income falls faster than the tax rate increases. The threshold point *D* corresponds to the average tax rate for which tax receipts are at a maximum. Any rate of taxation to the right of point *D* is inefficient because the same tax income can be raised with a lower tax rate, i.e. less distortion.

The Laffer curve was not taken too seriously for policy purposes when it was first proposed. This is because its most important detail is unknown: the location of point *D*. In the early 1980s, Laffer

---

5 Economist Arthur Laffer, then from Chicago, is reported to have been influential in persuading US President Ronald Reagan to cut taxes in the early 1980s.

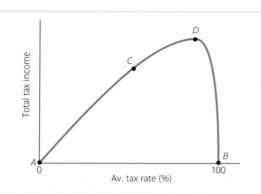

Fig. 18.5 The Laffer Curve

When the average tax rate is 0% there is no tax income (point A). When it is 100%, tax income is also likely to be zero (point B). At intermediate tax rates, there is some tax income, e.g. at point C. By continuity, the Laffer curve assumes a hump-shaped relationship between tax income and average tax rates. The maximum tax intake occurs at point D.

claimed that the USA had passed this point. When the USA did cut tax rates, tax revenue actually declined. In recent years, however, economists have begun to pay more attention to the Laffer curve. One reason is that the incentives to work and pay

taxes at very high tax rates are very low. As a result, many well-paid individuals in high tax countries expend significant resources to avoid or evade tax, or take lots of vacation and otherwise restrict their labour supply. In countries where the underground economy is pervasive (see Box 2.4), the tax base may be especially sensitive to tax rates.

Professor Martin Feldstein of Harvard University has estimated the effects of declared taxable income in response to a US tax reform in 1986. He found that those taxpayers whose tax rates were the highest before the tax cuts experienced the sharpest rise in their contribution to total tax revenues afterwards. Obviously, the sensitivity of these taxpayers' declared income was the highest—and would indicate a high elasticity of supply and a high deadweight loss as a result of taxation. Combined with the Ramsey principle, these findings raise disturbing questions. Should tax rates for the most productive individuals be the lowest? While this may be efficient, it would seem to be distasteful for most—it certainly flies in the face of any ethic of 'from each according to his ability, to each according to his need'. Yet the logic of efficiency must be addressed, and will continue to pose a major puzzle for social policy.

18.4 Labour Market Policy

Section 18.2 established that markets can fail and require government action. This is doubly true for labour markets. Besides the obvious human dimension—that individuals and their well-being are associated with labour supply, wages, and unemployment—it turns out that a number of aspects of labour markets make them fundamentally different from markets for fish, steel, or tomatoes, even under ideal conditions. In this section, we will explore a number of these differences. To the extent that policy-makers recognize the special aspects of labour markets, they can design policies

which keep the equilibrium rate of unemployment low and the level of output high.

18.4.1 Heterogeneity and Imperfect Information

One of the most striking facts about labour markets is the degree of turnover, or the rate of flow between the states of the labour force shown in Figure 5.14. Chapter 5 noted that annual inflow into and outflows out of unemployment are frequently larger than the stocks of unemployment at any given point in time. The high rate of in- and outflow points to two important aspects of labour markets: (1) heterogeneity of labour, and (2) incomplete information about its quality.

First, neither workers and the labour hours they supply nor the jobs at which they work are identical. Workers and jobs are heterogeneous. A trivial example of heterogeneity lies behind the turnover noted in Table 5.7, which is concentrated among young, female, and unskilled workers. Even in high labour turnover countries like the UK or USA, it turns out that most workers stay at a given job for a very long time. High turnover is frequently a transient phenomenon in the life cycle. It is more characteristic of newcomers to the labour market, and reflects a complicated process of 'picking and choosing'.

Second, because workers and jobs can be so different, or heterogeneous, information is likely to be incomplete. Even with the help of modern technology, such as the internet, it is still impossible to know about all jobs on offer at any point in time. It may be necessary to search harder to find the most attractive jobs. Some employers do not actively advertise job openings and may open a position only after meeting an acceptable candidate. Workers must decide on accepting a job or searching further without knowing what may lie ahead. Most likely, they will have had some employment experience in the past, which guides their expectations concerning pay and work conditions. The offers they can expect in the future may not always correspond to patterns in the past. For example, it is a fact that computer operators—workers who once programmed and serviced large mainframe computers—were highly trained and well-paid professionals in the 1970s and 1980s. As personal computer and local networking technologies became dominant, the demand for computer operators shrank dramatically. Those who lost their jobs may have had difficulties finding new ones at a similar pay level to that in the past. Similarly, a job and the employer who is deciding how to fill it have particular needs and expectations which may not be met by every applicant. In times of tight labour markets it may not be very easy for employers to find the dream candidate.

It is for this reason that unemployment must be interpreted carefully. To the extent that the unemployed are really 'unemployed resources', they represent a lost opportunity and a reason that trend GDP is lower than it could be. Indeed, Chapter 5 gave a number of reasons why workers ready to work at current wages are unable to do so. Yet unemployment also contains some elements of efficiency. Those who have lost their jobs involuntarily through layoff or plant closure frequently possess industry- or firm-specific human capital which would be wasted or underutilized were the worker forced to accept the first new job opportunity that came along. A crude indicator of the 'efficiency' of **job matching** in a given labour market is the extent to which jobs openings—called vacancies—and job-seeking, unemployed workers coexist at the same time in a labour market. Because job descriptions and worker qualifications are often specific, one can speak of a job-matching process. Forcing jobs and workers together indiscriminately would certainly not be efficient.

The extent of mismatch in the labour market is summarized by the **Beveridge curves** of Figure 18.6. Named to honour the work of British economist William Beveridge in the 1940s, Beveridge curves relate unemployment and vacancy rates in an economy over time. Movements in the north-west and south-east directions are associated with the business cycle: firms offer fewer jobs and unemployment is higher in recessions, while the vacancy rate rises and the unemployment rate declines in economic expansions. The *position* of the Beveridge curve, on the other hand, indicates the longer-run efficiency of job-matching in labour markets. The coincidence of a large number of vacancies with high unemployment—a Beveridge curve far away from the origin—indicates either that workers are badly informed, unable to take up the offers for lack of mobility or adequate skills, or unwilling to change and adapt. The Beveridge curve seemed to shift away from the origin in the mid-1970s, suggesting increasingly inefficient or mismatched labour markets—in fact, a rise in the equilibrium rate of unemployment. In the USA, this shift was of temporary duration. It has been much longer-lasting in the UK, while in Germany, the return to the earlier position has been very slow, if at all.

Shifting the Beveridge curve towards the origin— put differently, reducing the unemployment rate at

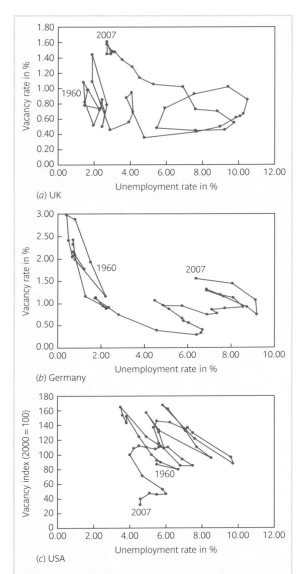

Fig. 18.6 Beveridge Curves in the UK, Germany, and the USA, 1960–2007

The Beveridge curve is the empirical inverse relationship between vacancies and unemployment. In a recession vacancies tend to decline and unemployment increases. The more efficient is the job-matching process—the way unemployed workers and unfilled job vacancies are matched—the closer to the origin the Beveridge curve is. Over the past 30 years, the Beveridge curve seems to have shifted outward in several European economies, although not in the USA. In the UK, the curve is now shifting back, the result of numerous labour market reforms.

Sources: OECD, *Economic Outlook*; Eurostat.

any level of vacancies—can be good supply-side policy. For policy-makers, it means implementing measures which improve the job-matching process. One is to improve information on job openings by increasing the number and effectiveness of job agencies. Advances in networking technology have made it possible for the unemployed seeking work to know about job offers all over a country—as long as they are posted. Recently, Germany embarked on a comprehensive reform of its national employment agency, making data on jobs and training positions available nationwide. Second, the adaptability of workers' skills may be enhanced via job retraining programmes. This means giving workers whose skills are unwanted or obsolete new ones which are in demand. Another possibility is to increase workers' and firms' geographical mobility, e.g. by making the housing market more efficient or providing subsidies to firms in search of new locations. In recent years, countries have begun to make more use of **active labour market policies**. This is nothing but the creative and flexible use of all of the measures already mentioned and more—as opposed to the passive policy of simply paying out unemployment benefits. Box 18.4 gives some details on the Nordic approach to labour market policy.

18.4.2 Imperfect Contracts and Labour Market Regulations

Because of their social and political aspects, labour markets are often heavily regulated. Regulations cover a wide range of aspects: paid holidays, the length of working days and weeks, safety standards, works councils, union representation, and other facets of the employment relationship. These regulations often have efficiency costs and sometimes seem only marginally motivated by good economic arguments. The columns of Table 18.2 report the relative severity of the most common types of labour market regulation in OECD Europe.

Besides the problem of imperfect information noted in the last section and that of imperfect competition discussed in Section 18.2, a number of economic factors have led governments to implement such regulations. Again, most of them have to do with the special nature of the labour relationship. For one, they are a response to the impossibility of writing and enforcing labour contracts which

Box 18.4 Active versus Passive Labour Market Policies

Despite a number of adverse shocks in the past decade, the Nordic countries continue to boast the world's lowest unemployment rates, proving that generous but strictly administered unemployment benefit programmes are consistent with 'European' solidarity with the unemployed. In Sweden, unemployed workers may claim benefits for roughly 300 days of unemployment. Unlike most countries, however, at the end of this period benefits are not renewed, but a position is offered in a job training programme. Employment offices may even require that an unemployed person move to another city. Refusal can, and sometimes does, result in benefit cuts. As a result, the Scandinavian countries spend less on unemployment benefits and more on active labour market policies, i.e. programmes involving direct job creation, targeted job subsidies, retraining, relocation of families away from distressed regions, and special programmes to get young people started. In general, the unemployed are supervised more closely and kept in touch with the labour market. Table 18.1 gives details. In relative terms, Nordic countries spend more on active labour market policies than other Western European countries, while maintaining much lower long-term unemployment rates.

Table 18.1 Labour Market Programme Expenditure, 2005 (% of GDP)

	Denmark	Finland	Norway	Sweden	France	Germany	UK
Active measures							
Training	0.51	0.37	0.37	0.34	0.29	0.25	0.09
Employment incentives	0.45	0.16	0.03	0.5	0.13	0.05	0.01
Supported employment and rehabilitation	0.48	0.1	0.15	0.22	0.07	0.13	0.01
Direct job creation	0	0.07	0.07	0	0.18	0.1	0
Start-up incentives	0	0.02	0	0.03	0	0.09	0
Total active programmes	1.44	0.72	0.62	1.09	0.67	0.62	0.11
Passive measures							
Out-of-work income maintenance and support	1.83	1.47	0.87	1.2	1.57	2.3	0.19
Early retirement	0.68	0.44	0	0	0.06	0.05	0
Total passive programmes	2.51	1.91	0.87	1.2	1.63	2.35	0.19
Administration	0.31	0.18	0.12	0.23	0.24	0.35	0.38
Total	4.26	2.81	1.61	2.52	2.54	3.32	0.68
Long-term unemployment rate[a]	2.10	3.51	1.16	2.14	5.94	6.74	1.83

[a] Six months and over

Source: OECD, *Employment Outlook*.

specify all possible events which could occur, and all responses to those events (nor is it particularly efficient, given what lawyers would charge to write such contracts!). The enormous complexity of the world of affairs and the inability or unwillingness of workers to deal with it may lead to exploitation. Leaving the rest to the market may disadvantage workers in particular situations. For that reason,

Table 18.2 Measures of the Strictness of Labour Market Regulation (2 = most strict, 0 = least strict)

	Working time regulations	Regulation of limited-time contracts	Job protection regulation	Minimum wage legislation	Aggregate index
Euro area					
Austria	1	1	1	0	3
Belgium	0	1	1	1	3
Finland	1	1	1	1	4
France	1	1	1	2	5
Germany	1	1	1	1	4
Greece	2	1	2	2	7
Ireland	2	0	2	0	4
Italy	1	2	2	2	7
The Netherlands	1	0	1	1	3
Portugal	1	1	1	1	4
Spain	2	1	2	2	7
Memo: Arithmetic Average	1.1	0.9	1.3	1.1	4.4
Other EU					
Denmark	0	0	0	0	0
Sweden	1	2	1	1	5
United Kingdom	0	0	0	0	0
Other OECD					
Norway	1	2	1	0	4
Switzerland	1	1	1	0	3
United States	0	0	0	0	0

Source: OECD, *Employment Outlook* (Paris, 1994) Table 4.8.

governments have often stepped in—although not always in the most appropriate way.

Imperfect mobility and regulation

One situation of possible exploitation relates to worker mobility. Mobility of demanders and suppliers is a central mechanism for correcting imbalances in a perfectly competitive market. If they feel they are getting a bad deal, they simply move elsewhere. In labour markets, things may not be so simple. The suppliers of labour are human beings. Mobility means changing jobs, an industry, occupation, or residential location, and people by their very nature tend to be immobile. Furthermore, they may even

value their 'immobility', preferring to take a pay cut or even risk unemployment to stay put rather than to move to a faraway place or accept a radically new occupation. This is one reason that, even in the UK with its highly dynamic labour markets, differences in unemployment rates between North and South, between Scotland and the Midlands, and between London and the entire country have persisted for decades.

Under certain circumstances, an employer might try to exploit this immobility. For example, after the employment relationship has begun, employers may try to take advantage of the employed by cutting their wages. In perfect market situations, the worker would simply leave the firm, and look else-where. In doing so, mobility costs must be incurred. In advanced economies these costs may be rather significant, and this may not be a desirable mechanism. Minimum wages can be seen as a response to such local market power by employers. Another response is to extend union contracts to uncovered workers and firms in the sector.[6] Similar arguments are often invoked to justify work-week and work-time regulations, job protection, and rules concerning job safety. Naturally, minimum wages have a number of disadvantages as well, mostly related to the closing down of labour markets for young workers and those with little skill or training.

Regulation of dismissal

A related argument has been invoked for regulations of dismissal 'without cause' or for 'economic reasons', i.e. not due to malfeasance or misbehaviour on the part of the worker. Lay-offs for reasons related to the business cycle are associated with uncertainty and economic dislocation. In many European countries, prior notice of termination of employment must be given to workers—during which time the employee remains on the payroll and represents a cost to the firm. 'Social plans' are often required for large-scale redundancies, in which the exact list of employees is decided using criteria like age, family status, and re-employability. Severance payments are often legally mandated for workers dismissed for economic reasons. While common in EU countries, job protection is by no means the norm in the OECD. The USA and the UK are examples of countries where 'employment at will' contracts prevail.

While severance regulations make it difficult for firms to reduce employment in the short run, they also increase the effective cost of labour to firms. They make firms more reluctant to hire in good times, precisely because they worry about consequences in bad times. Firms will tend to use the 'intensive' margin more often (overtime, conversion of part-time into full-time) before hiring new workers. The third column of Table 18.2 reports a ranking of the degree of 'job security' provisions offered in a number of industrial countries. It is noteworthy that countries in which youth unemployment rates are high tend to have the most restrictive dismissal laws. Surveys consistently reveal that workers in those countries in which dismissal laws are the most liberal—the USA, the UK, and Denmark—feel the *least* insecure about their job. This perception, which is hardly intuitive, must be to do with the perception workers have about the ease of finding a new job, should their firm go out of business or move abroad.

As the economy becomes increasingly subject to global influences and technological advances, the nature of employment relationships has changed fundamentally. Employment is less likely to involve a lifetime relationship, and is increasingly likely at some point to be 'restructured' or reoriented towards fully new areas of activity. Severance rules of the type described are likely to inhibit the growth of new firms as well as the expansion of existing ones. As the pressures for more flexible employment grow, firms have become increasingly creative in finding ways to undo the intended effects of the legislation. For example, they may chain several short-term contracts together for the same employee, or hire workers from temporary help agencies, shifting the burden to others. In the end, it may be worth considering market solutions in which workers accept to work under 'employment at will' for a wage premium. This would allow firms to pay for additional flexibility while preserving employment protection.

18.4.3 Social Policies Incentives and Taxation

The social safety net

The social safety net refers to the system of transfers and benefits designed to help the disadvantaged and vulnerable in society. These include unemployment benefits, social welfare, old-age pensions, early retirement, health insurance, and disability payments. A large gap divides European countries, which transfer between 20% and 30% of their national income to individuals or firms, from the USA, Japan, and Switzerland, which transfer only

---

[6] Minimum wages are also justified with arguments related to equity and income distribution. For example, if the elasticity of labour demand is thought to be low at low wages, then raising the minimum wage does little harm while increasing the income of the lowest-income working families.

10–15%. This might lead a casual observer to conclude that high European unemployment is a product of the 'social welfare state', which puts weight on solidarity but at the cost of productivity and economic efficiency. Yet it is hasty to claim that Europeans have erred too far in the direction of social protection, in comparison to the rest of the OECD. The high level of transfers observed in Europe is to some extent a *response* to high unemployment, which may have other underlying causes. At the same time, these transfers—in the form of unemployment benefits, welfare, and premature retirement and disability pensions—take the pressure off workers and firms to adjust to a changing world economy. The greatest danger is that the safety net becomes a trap, leading to long-term unemployment.

It is useful to use the tools developed in Chapter 5 to help think about the adverse effects of the safety net on incentives. The social systems of most countries share two institutional features. First, poor or unemployed people receive transfers—income maintenance programmes or unemployment benefits—from the state. Second, income taxes are progressive: the rate of taxation increases as income rises. Taking up a job not only means receiving a salary, but also paying taxes if the salary is high enough, and thereby losing eligibility for income maintenance programmes. It is conceivable, then, that people can be financially worse off by taking a job, not to mention incurring a loss of leisure, and possibly some activity in the underground economy. Implicitly, these people face an effective marginal tax rate—considering the overall effect of work on their income—in excess of 100%. Box 18.5 shows how safety net programmes may lead to a **welfare trap**, inducing people to remain unemployed or stay out of the labour force, thereby reducing the productive potential of the economy. Recent experience of 'work-to-welfare' in the UK and the USA indicates that the incentive aspect is important for bringing workers on social assistance back to work.

Labour taxation

Because labour is so essential in any economy, it is natural to expect governments to tax it. Perhaps because the Ramsey principle of public finance (Section 18.3.2) is so compelling, labour is one of

---

 Box 18.5 Crusoe Caught in the Safety Net

In Figure 18.7, Crusoe is faced with a budget constraint which is no longer strictly linear. This is because, when not working at all in the market ($l = \ell$), he receives a transfer of T from the government—unemployment benefits, welfare, or other payments associated with the social safety net. Moreover, if Crusoe works a little bit, he loses benefits by exactly the amount of his additional income —an effective marginal tax rate of 100%. This is representative of the current situation in many European countries. Since Crusoe loses a euro of benefit for every euro he earns in work, the budget line is flat up to the point at which Crusoe receives T, whether he works or not. Crusoe values leisure, so it is hard to see why he would accept part-time work in this regime. Unless the after-tax wage is high enough, Crusoe is unlikely to work.

Figure 18.7 also shows the impact of reducing the effective marginal tax rate from 100% to some lower rate which is nevertheless higher than that for someone already in work and not receiving welfare payments, holding T constant. As the tax rate declines, the budget line for the household becomes steeper. At some point Crusoe can make himself even better off than he was at A, by choosing point B. In doing so his income is added to the tax base and contributes to higher GDP. The effect can be intensified if the carrot (the lower effective marginal tax rate) is combined with a stick (lowering T), although this type of reform is politically difficult to implement.

In Germany, the Hartz labour market reforms (adopted after 2004) can be seen as reflecting some of these principles. One measure reduced the effective marginal tax rate on work by exempting some earnings from counting against social benefit. Effectively, this becomes a top-up provision (the so-called *Zuverdienstmöglichkeiten*). Another measure implemented benefit cuts ('sanctions') for those who consistently turn down job offers.

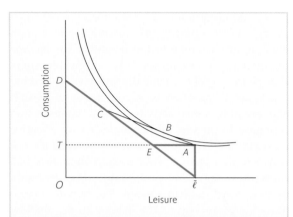

Fig. 18.7 Incentives and the Social Safety Net

In a social welfare system with benefit *T* when out of work but with 100% marginal tax rate, the individual depicted in this figure chooses not to work (point *A*), because no net additional income results from modest increases in labour supply, starting at zero. The budget constraint is $\bar{\ell}\, AED$. If the individual is allowed to keep some additional income (changing the budget constraint to $\bar{\ell}\, ACD$) the individual can improve her well-being by working (point *B*). The most important problem with lowering the effective marginal tax rate to unemployment benefit and welfare recipients is the cost to the state, which can be considerable.

the most highly taxed 'commodities'. As Box 18.6 explains, labour is subject not only to income taxes paid by households, but also to a number of social security contributions by both employees and employers. It is also natural to expect that labour taxation might influence the demand for labour. Higher taxes raise the real cost of labour faced by firms, leading to lower employment in the sector that pays the tax.[7] Table 18.3 shows the rate of taxation on labour in various countries in its various guises. Despite high unemployment, efforts have been rather slow in Europe to reduce the tax burden placed on the labour market. France, for example, has begun to exempt low wage workers from contributions to social security or at least to reduce them.

Yet, the net effect of high taxes on employment depends on the elasticity of labour demand and supply. If collective labour supply is relatively inelastic—perhaps reflecting the inelastic labour supply of households—the burden of the tax will fall primarily on wages, and employment will be relatively unaffected. In Europe, however, wages are set in collective bargaining, leading, in all likelihood, to a flatter collective labour supply curve. Under these conditions, high labour taxes might reduce employment significantly, and be associated with a large loss of consumer and producer surplus.[8] In the very long run the elasticity of labour demand is likely to be high, since firms may simply move to other locations where labour costs are lower. It is for this reason that the integration of European economies is leading to a harmonization of taxation across national boundaries, with or without explicit government coordination.

18.4.4 The Political Economy of Labour Market Reform

Unemployment is generally regarded as a curse of modern market economies, and remains the subject of intense political discussion. In Europe, joblessness levels have been high for almost three decades. In addition, it was seen in Figure 1.1 that, in contrast to the USA, European unemployment has risen steadily over successive business cycles. Unemployment represents underutilized labour resources. If this underutilization is not the conscious choice of households, it is involuntary and represents a supply-side problem. As the leading quote at the beginning of this chapter indicated, an important challenge for the nations of Europe is to address this issue, perhaps using the ideas and concepts developed here.

Suppose there is agreement—among policymakers, at least—that labour markets should be reformed. How should a country go about it? Several problems arise with simply 'deregulating'. Consider the example of abolishing job protection. First, many companies that had wanted to reduce

---

[7] This qualification is important. If some type of labour is untaxed, demand, employment, and wages may rise when labour taxes rise elsewhere. The obvious example is the underground economy, which always thrives when taxes are high.

[8] Chapter 5 provides more details on the collective labour supply curve. Producer and consumer surplus are defined and discussed in Box 18.3.

Box 18.6 Taxes and the Labour Market in Europe

Labour taxes can be grouped into three classes: (1) income taxes, (2) social insurance charges paid by employers, and (3) social security contributions paid by the employees. All three can be added up, as they either reduce the workers' net receipts and thus affect the supply of labour, or increase the cost of labour and reduce demand (governments prefer to call the last two 'contributions'—to funds for unemployment benefits, national health insurance, retirement and pension benefits, disability insurance, solidarity with various causes, including low-cost housing and special retraining programmes, etc). Let τ_P be the employer's wage tax rate, let W be the wage of the employee before his own income taxes and employee social security contributions, let τ_W be the tax rate of contribution of the employee, and let τ_P be the personal income tax rate. The take-home pay for the worker after taxes will be $W_{\text{take-home}} = (1 - \tau_W)(1 - \tau_P)W$, while the cost of labour to the firm is given by $W_{\text{labour costs}} = (1 + \tau_F)W$. As a result, the effective labour cost is equal to the take-home pay multiplied by the factor $\dfrac{1 + \tau_F}{(1 - \tau_W)(1 - \tau_P)}$ which is often called the

labour tax wedge. Holding $W_{\text{take-home}}$ constant, increases in the tax wedge increase labour costs and reduce the demand for labour. In addition to all this, workers also pay income tax on their take-home salary, which may be progressive, meaning that it increases at the margin as taxable income itself rises.

Does high labour taxation necessarily lead to high unemployment? Not at all. It depends on how the supply of labour or the collective bargaining system reacts. Equilibrium unemployment rate will remain unchanged only if after taxes wages fall by exactly the amount of tax—i.e. if workers shoulder the entire burden. But the collective labour supply curve will not be vertical in general. Households may find it attractive at high taxes to work less, work in the underground economy, or take overtime pay in the form of a holiday (leisure), as is often done in Scandinavia. It is thus likely that such high taxes make hiring labour unattractive, and that a reduction of such taxes could increase employment. The problem for governments is how to replace the revenue that is lost.

---

employment under the old regime will certainly take advantage of deregulation, and lay-offs are likely to increase in the short run. In most European countries, the political consequences of such a move are severe enough to make reform unthinkable. Second, an issue of *time consistency* arises.[9] Suppose a firm that would like to hire more employees

---

[9] The time consistency problem was first identified by Nobel Prize Laureates Finn Kydland and Edward Prescott, and is concerned with the incentives of those who announce a policy to actually follow through with that policy after others have reacted to the announcement. Time inconsistency is a very general phenomenon, which applies to many fields besides economics. A son will promise to drive carefully if lent his parents' car; a person in prison always pledges not to engage in unlawful activity if released early; politicians promise the moon if elected. All of these promises are time-inconsistent. The risk is that only time-consistent solutions, which are less desirable for all involved, are adopted: no son is lent a car; no inmate is released early; and politicians are never trusted.

expands its employment in response to deregulation. At this point, a government that is fishing for political support might re-impose the dismissal regulations, 'trapping' the firms at higher employment levels. Firms will anticipate this, with the sad result that no new workers will be hired, despite deregulation! Governments will need to pre-commit themselves to a 'no-reregulate' regime before employers are convinced.

It is also true that an overwhelming majority (90–95%) of workers are employed, so that their domination over the unemployed might even be regarded as democratic, and is generally mitigated by unemployment benefits. Governments often cannot reform labour market institutions because their interventions are often regarded as interference in the collective bargaining process. One noteworthy approach is that followed by Spain, which had a serious structural unemployment problem. Since the mid-1980s, temporary contracts for workers

Table 18.3 Labour Taxation in 2003 (% of GDP)

Country	Total tax receipts	Fraction of total tax receipts due to:			Highest rate of personnal income tax
		Income tax	Social security contributions		
			Employee	Employer	
Euro area					
Austria	45	8	14	23	50
Belgium	55	21	11	24	52
Finland	45	20	5	20	53
France	48	9	9	29	58
Germany	51	17	17	17	51
Greece	35	0	12	22	40
Ireland	24	10	4	10	42
Italy	46	14	7	25	46
Luxembourg	32	7	12	12	39
The Netherlands	36	6	19	10	52
Portugal	32	4	9	19	40
Spain	38	10	5	23	45
Other EU					
Denmark	43	32	11	1	59
Sweden	48	18	5	25	57
United Kingdom	30	14	7	8	40
Switzerland	30	9	10	10	39
Czech Republic	43	8	9	26	
Hungary	46	13	9	24	40
Poland	43	5	21	17	40
Other OECD					
Australia	24	24	0	0	
Canada	31	18	6	7	46
Japan	24	6	9	10	50
New Zealand	20	20	0	0	
Norway	37	19	7	11	
United States	30	15	7	7	42

Source: CESIfo.

have been permitted, with some restrictions.[10] Such contracts allow firms to hire workers without

[10] For example, firms were not allowed to 'roll over' the same worker in a series of short-term contracts. Naturally, employers have devised numerous loopholes to deal with this restriction.

restrictions on a limited-time, contractual basis. As a result, roughly four-fifths of all new employment in Spain since the late 1980s has been under such limited-time contracts. This response suggests that firms are willing to hire more workers when job security obligations are absent. Second, young people

Box 18.7 Trade Unions and Reform in the UK and the Netherlands

At the end of the 1970s, both the UK and the Netherlands faced similarly distressing economic conditions. Both had high rates of unemployment and low growth in economic output. The root of the unemployment problem in both countries seemed to be that real wages were out of control, exceeding wage growth warranted by growth in total factor productivity. In the UK, a Tory government led by Prime Minister Margaret Thatcher took the position that the system needed to be changed. Her programme, which was passed by Parliament with much resistance, was a radical overhaul of the UK collective bargaining system. In a series of open confrontations, she limited trade unions' ability to disrupt the workings of the economy. New legislation limited the wide immunity enjoyed by unions from civil suits to those directly involving industrial action, and forced unions to elect their officials in secret balloting. In the decade 1980–89, union membership in the UK declined by 21% and union density declined from 50.7% to 41.5%. Over the same period, unemployment declined considerably, as seen in Figure 18.8. Although condemned at the time by many academic economists, Thatcher's reforms evidently did reduce equilibrium unemployment significantly in the UK in the years which followed.

In the Netherlands, a radically different course was taken. In a widely publicized 'Wassenaar agreement' reached by labour and management in 1982, unions consented to moderate real wage growth in both private and public sectors and management agreed to expand part-time employment. While not officially part of the agreement, the government followed with tax breaks for part-time jobs as well as cuts in public sector employment and wages. Most importantly, tax rates on labour were reduced, blunting the net impact of real wage moderation on households' incomes. In the years that followed, real wages in the Netherlands grew much more slowly than in neighbouring EU economies, as Figure 18.8 indicates. In fact, Dutch real wage behaviour in the 1990s more closely resembles that of the USA than neighbouring Germany! The employment growth and decline in unemployment which later followed in the Netherlands confirm that wage moderation is one important element of a successful labour market reform package, but need not include 'union busting', the radical dismantling of collective bargaining mechanisms that was pursued in the UK.

were the primary beneficiary of such reforms, which has helped relieve an acute youth unemployment problem. Finally, increasing the relative number of workers who have jobs with less protection increased the consensus for broader reforms which followed. By increasing the power of the outsiders, labour market reform became more acceptable.

In general, the political economy of labour markets may be the most important element determining the success or failure of reforms. Efforts to increase the attractiveness of part-time work have often been blocked by unions, which see their bargaining power diluted by new employees who are unlikely to be members. Work-sharing proposals which increase the cost of labour are resisted fiercely by employer associations. Recent successful reforms in France have shown that management and labour often put many different elements on the negotiating table, trading reduced working time and relief on labour charges for flexibility, wage moderation, and reform of the unemployment benefits system.

Box 18.7 provides more detail on the extremes of labour market reform strategies. In rare cases, such as Britain under Margaret Thatcher, unions have been reformed against their will by democratically elected governments, with much social tension. The other extreme, in the Netherlands, was engineered in a consensual fashion, with the active involvement of unions, management, and the government. While both approaches involve radically different levels of social consensus and cohesion, they have one important aspect in common: they both required about a decade to bear fruit and the patience of the electorate to stay the course until the benefits were realized.

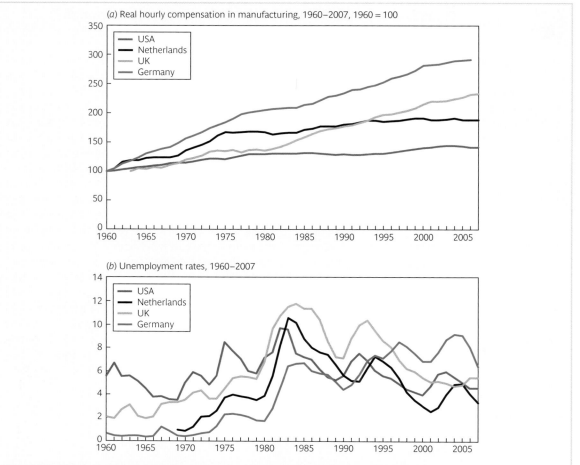

Fig. 18.8 Real Wages and Unemployment in the UK, Netherlands, Germany, and USA, 1960–2007

The recent experience of the UK and the Netherlands suggests that equilibrium unemployment declined in the late 1980 and early 1990s, in contrast to Germany. Much of this improvement can be linked to real wage moderation since the early 1980s. In the UK, this moderation was accomplished by a significant reduction in union power. In the Netherlands, it was the outcome of a broad agreement between labour unions and employer associations, with the tacit and sometimes active support of government. It appears that the recent Hartz reforms in Germany have moved equilibrium unemployment downwards, for the first time in many decades.

Sources: Eurostat; OECD; US Department of Labor.

18.5 Product Market Policies

18.5.1 Dealing with Externalities

The basic principle is to internalize externalities. This means making those that create an externality bear its costs or the benefits. In the pollution example above, this is achieved by making clean water a right. We have illustrated this principle with a few important examples which have recently received prominent attention.

Human capital accumulation

The first example, also mentioned in Section 18.2.3, is investment in **human capital**. It is one of the most crucial factors of economic development. Human capital is acquired at school, of course, but also at work. In addition school years may well be spread over a lifetime to allow people to update their depreciating capital and learn about newly acquired knowledge. The knowledge of an individual person benefits society in a myriad of ways. It helps co-workers, of course, but better-educated people can make better decisions in everyday life—including taking better care of themselves and their children, or voting as informed citizens. An individual's return from human capital is believed to be significantly smaller for the individual than for society. If she invests with only her individual return in mind, she will underinvest regarding what is justified by the broader social return. For this reason, societies have an interest in encouraging people to invest in more human capital than they would on their own. Free and compulsory education was the first response to this externality. Subsidizing traineeships in firms or continuing education further the same goal. In addition, unemployed people tend to see their human capital depreciate. This provides an additional justification for measures that reduce the duration of unemployment spells and for the active labour market policies described in Box 18.8.

Law and order

Law and order has all the characteristics of a market failure: it is an externality, it is subject to increasing returns to scale, and it is a public good. It is an externality since everyone benefits from others being honest. Investment in physical and human capital is threatened when crime robs people and firms of their assets, and will be less attractive in the absence of law and order. It is subject to increasing returns to scale, since commonly accepted and enforced law works better than when everyone sets their rules and practises self-enforcement. Private protection, the spontaneous market response to the absence of law and order, is inefficient. It also accentuates the effect of inequality, as rich people can better defend themselves than poor people. Law and order is also a public good since it is non-excludable and non-rival. Thus, on all three grounds, leaving law and order to the market results in a massive failure. Indeed, from time immemorial, one of the key attributes of any political power has always been the provision of law and order.

Health

Health is obviously a private 'good'. Everyone enjoys good health. It is also a source of externality. People with poor health do not work well and are often absent, so their productivity is reduced. If they are not paid while sick, they can become destitute, relying on society's generosity, or resorting to criminal activity to survive. Sicknesses can also be contagious, a vivid example of externality. Health can be provided privately, as it is in many countries. Private health programmes generate inequalities, and most people think that it is unacceptable that the rich receive better treatment than the poor. But, in addition, because of the externalities that it generates, privately provided health is inefficient, as everyone will only spend up to the point where their (marginal) benefit equals marginal cost. This is why most countries have established systems of social security and enforce compulsory medical examinations and vaccination. A healthy society is a rich society. Causality undoubtedly runs from wealth to health, but it also runs in the opposite direction.

18.5.2 Dealing with Malfunctioning Markets

The solution to market failures is not always to produce public goods and services. In fact, it is increasingly being recognized that private producers tend to be more cost-efficient than publicly owned ones, provided that they are adequately regulated. In this section, we look at monopolies and review some prominent examples of the **privatization** process and of how regulation operates.

Monopolies

Markets characterized by increasing returns tend to evolve to a situation where a very few firms buy out or eliminate the others. When only one firm survives, it is a monopoly. Once it has achieved that position, its incentive is to charge high prices, and possibly to stop innovating, and let the quality of its goods decline. When just two or three dominate, they have incentives to agree among themselves to raise prices and lower competition in terms of quality and innovation. This is called collusion. Thus, in the presence of increasing returns, markets evolve spontaneously to a situation where competition is insufficient to match the principles of market efficiency. Examples of industries prone to increasing returns include automobile and aeroplane production, transport, and telecommunications.

One response is to regulate these industries. Governments step in and either break down the monopolies (e.g. the ongoing deregulation in the electricity, telecommunication, and airline industries), or prevent mergers, and actively fight against collusion. Because competition increasingly takes place at the world level, such anti-trust and anti-collusion policies are often conducted at the supranational level. In Europe, the European Commission has been granted wide authority in that area. For instance, it has blocked several mergers between international giants and imposed pro-competition conditions on others.

Privatization

In many countries, the other response to market failures, especially the existence of natural monopolies, has been to set up state-owned companies that would not seek to exploit their monopolistic power. This has been the case of railways, electricity generation and distribution, water distribution, telecommunications, etc. Starting in the early 1980s in Europe, the performance of these state monopolies has been found wanting. The prices that they charged were regulated, and based on their costs, but who controlled the costs? Suspicion grew that, in the absence of competition, these firms were not particularly interested in producing at the lowest possible cost. The infamous monopolistic rent was not captured in the form of private profits, but in the form of slackness in production, poor quality of service, technological backwardness, and sometimes comfortable salaries, and other advantages. The contrast between Europe and the USA, which relied to a much lesser extent on publicly owned companies, had become glaring.

The response has been a wave of privatization, which is still underway. Once a company had become private, it was interested in expanding across borders. The presence of state-owned monopolies in some countries prevented the entry of foreign competitors, while allowing the national company to expand abroad. Clearly, this was an unfair situation. This is why the Single Act of 1992 has given the European Commission the right to force national governments to privatize most of their state-owned monopolies and to open their markets to foreign competition. Ten years down the road, the process is still far from complete, a testimony of how entrenched the interests are. Box 18.8 recalls the successful privatization process in the telecommunications industry. This process has freed a dynamic force for economic growth and job creation.

Regulation

Regulation is often the best response when markets are not well behaved. Financial markets are essential for economic growth, since banks and financial intermediaries collect savings to finance investment by firms and public deficits. Yet financial markets are often considered with suspicion, partly because of markets' tendencies to undergo violent crises, a manifestation of the asymmetric information problem. In response, they are regulated. Banks are forbidden to take excessive risk. This is because depositors cannot effectively monitor their banks

Box 18.8 **Privatization, Deregulation, and European Telecommunications**

In the early 1990s a number of European countries, led by the UK and later by Germany, began to privatize and deregulate their telecommunications industries. These had been the domain of the national postal systems, which had moved slowly to introduce new technologies and continued to charge high prices for services which cost little at the margin to produce. In effect, the Europeans were doing little more than recognizing the successes of the USA in the early 1980s after the break-up of the monopoly ATT (American Telephone and Telegraph) and the resulting deregulation of long-distance telephone services. The Europeans went farther than the Americans, however. By agreeing on a pan-European standard for wireless technologies and wireless application protocols, they created a common market for an activity which obviously involves massive external effects. They also intensified direct competition with local telecom service provision—which remains a local monopoly in most countries.

The deregulation of telecoms in Europe has led to visible positive supply-side economic effects. The telecom industry has not only been a source of value added and income growth for Europeans, but has also generated hundreds of thousands of new jobs. Most importantly, consumers have benefited. Table 18.4 shows the extent to which prices for telecommunications services have fallen in Germany. While prices were dropping all around Europe, the relative price declines in long-distance service and portable telephone services is closely associated with deregulation in this country in the late 1990s. More recently, the public auction of third-generation mobile communication radio frequencies heralds the combination of these technologies with the internet, and promises the introduction of new products and services that the old national postal services could never have offered.

Table 18.4 **Telecommunications Prices in Germany, 1995–2007 (2000 = 100)**

	1995	1996	1997	1998	1999	2003	2007
All telephone services	127.1	128.9	124.0	122.4	108.4	96.2	92.5
All trunk line systems	117.1	120.9	118.2	117.4	104.6	98.6	100.2
by service:							
Fixed fees	90.5	99.5	99.2	99.8	100.0	109.4	118.5
Call-by-call fees	137.8	137.6	133.0	131.0	108.3	92.1	89.1
Local	80.3	93.1	93.1	93.6	99.4	95.3	93.0
National long distance	216.4	201.0	185.7	187.6	110.4	94.8	90.5
International long distance	236.3	212.8	212.2	188.8	159.4	85.5	85.0
Cell phone systems	236.0	201.3	157.9	144.0	114.4	105.0	87.7

Source: German Federal Statistical Office.

and stand to lose part of their savings if the bank collapses. Financial operators also face legal restraints on the risk that they can take, in an effort to limit the occurrence of financial crises.

That regulation affects nearly every aspect of economic life does not only show how widespread market failures are, but also highlights the tendency of the state to do too much. Asymmetric information explains why food labels, airline services, or driving licences are regulated. Yet the regulation of store closing times in much of Europe, tree-felling in Germany, or chimney-sweeping in Switzerland might

Table 18.5 Subsidies in Various Countries (% of GDP)

	1975	1990	2007
Belgium	0.03	1.71	1.79
France	2.02	1.76	1.45
Germany	1.72	1.71	1.08
Italy	2.55	1.83	1.01
Netherlands	1.43	2.25	1.23
Spain	0.60	0.97	0.98
Sweden	2.37	3.58	1.57
USA	0.28	0.46	0.34

Source: OECD, *Economic Outlook*.

be a step too far, possibly protecting private interests at the expense of the public good.

Subsidies and industrial policy

For a variety of non-economic reasons, many countries operate elaborate systems of subsidies which shield certain firms and industries from the discipline of the market. Table 18.5 displays the evidence for some OECD countries. Subsidized firms can sustain losses and avoid adjusting to changing economic conditions. In doing so, they keep resources (e.g. labour) employed, but inefficiently so. They do not face the full cost of their operations (part of the costs are charged to taxpayers), or else the factors of production are paid more than their true marginal productivity.[11] In fact, they may even keep factor prices artificially high and hurt productive activities that are not subsidized.

Public ownership of firms is another form of subsidization. Unlike private firms, state-owned enterprises (SOEs) rarely face demanding shareholders and are almost never shut down. When they lose money, they generally receive public resources.

This may come either as an explicit subsidy from the government to cover the loss, or as a loan to the company at interest rates unavailable to other firms. SOEs operate in virtually every major industry in Western Europe.

Most countries regard certain economic activities as indispensable for strategic or political reasons. These include defence-related industries, such as steel, energy, high technology, aircraft, and shipbuilding. As many of these activities exhibit increasing returns to scale, governments often try to guarantee that the firms are large enough. This is often the underlying logic behind **industrial policies**. Industrial policies amount to official backing of national corporations or whole industries. This takes the form of subsidies, public orders, and trade policies. **Trade policies** include tariffs on foreign goods, quotas on imports, export credits financed at concessionary rates, and procurement policies whereby domestically produced goods are chosen over cheaper foreign ones, not to mention 'buy domestic goods' campaigns.

The ultimate effect of these policies is to raise prices above competitive levels. Consumers or taxpayers make up the difference. Once again, the principle that prices reflect efficient production costs is violated. Supply-side considerations have led to a reassessment of strategic requirements. The European Single Act (1992) bans most trade policies mentioned above for intra-European trade. Yet industrial and trade policies survive, often conducted at the EU rather than national level, with such celebrated examples as Airbus and Ariane. More recently, private European banks have complained that state savings banks and their parent entities enjoy hidden subsidies in the form of government guarantees. EU competition authorities have demanded that these be privatized or at least set on an equal footing, singling out the German *Sparkassen* and the *Landesbanken*. These institutions respond that they represent the only means of achieving blanket availability of banking services in remote, rural areas, and provide financing for projects that private banks generally shun. As the issue of state aids becomes increasingly political, it assumes the aspects of national preferences discussed in Box 18.1.

---

[11] For example, after the oil shocks, a reduced world demand for tankers and the emergence of competitors in Asia (Japan, Korea) combined to create major difficulties for European shipyards. The UK, Germany, France, and many other countries reacted by subsidizing their shipbuilding companies. In the end, the costs became too large and the situation too hopeless for the subsidies to be maintained. While the subsidies did save jobs for a few years, they did so in a very ineffcient way.

❗ Summary

1 Supply-side policies are appealing because, in contrast to demand-side policies, they do not imply a short-run trade-off between unemployment and inflation. They increase output permanently at any given level of inflation and economic growth, and may even increase the rate of growth itself. They do take some time to take effect, however, and require a longer-term perspective.

2 One principle underlying supply-side policies is that markets do not function perfectly. By removing market imperfections, the economy's overall output and productivity can be enhanced.

3 There are three main sources of market failures: (1) externalities, (2) increasing returns to scale, and (3) asymmetric information.

4 Externalities occur when someone's economic activity has an effect, positive or negative, on others. Positive externalities imply that one does not recognize the benefits to society of one's actions, and will undertake less than is socially desirable. Negative externalities imply that one does not recognize the costs to society of one's economic actions, and will undertake too much of them. Pecuniary externalities are solved once property rights are ascertained. Non-pecuniary externalities require government interventions.

5 Increasing returns lead to monopolies. Some monopolies are natural, inherent to the task itself. The solution used to be state ownership. Increasingly, state monopolies are privatized and government interventions take the form of regulations.

6 Asymmetric information occurs when one's actions are not known to others. It may lead to inefficient outcomes. Regulation can be designed to alleviate this problem.

7 Public goods that are non-rival and non-excludable tend not be privately provided. Governments can and should step in, and provide these goods which can be highly productive.

8 Taxation is necessary to pay for the operation of government. It is also a source of inefficiency because it drives a wedge between the price paid by the consumer and the price received by the producer, reducing demand and supply.

9 Because the operation of governments requires resources with alternative uses in the private sector, supply-side considerations call for limiting public spending to the production of goods and services that cannot be produced by the private sector. There is much debate on the correct size of government.

10 High structural unemployment is a supply-side problem. It arises as a result of labour market distortions, some of which are due to private agents and others to interventions of government.

11 Eliminating structural unemployment is possible by better management of labour taxation, severance regulations, labour relations, and the social safety net. Active labour market policies can help prevent the emergence of long-term unemployment.

12 Labour market reforms are highly politicized and controversial. Because the beneficiaries of reform are usually in the minority, their interests may be difficult to protect. Broad-based reforms almost always require give and take of the involved parties. Whether conflictual or consensual, reforms require time—as long as a decade—to have a measurable effect.

13 Governments often subsidize firms and industries. Although the objective of subsidies is to protect firms, they remove the incentive to compete, and ultimately cost jobs. State ownership has similar effects. The supply-side response is to cut down on subsidies and to privatize.

🔑 Key Concepts

- supply-side policies
- market-clearing
- laissez-faire
- market failures
- economic rents
- competition policy
- property rights
- pecuniary and non-pecuniary, positive and negative externalities
- natural monopoly
- human capital
- Ramsey principle of public finance

- distortionary taxation
- consumer and producer surplus
- Laffer curve
- job matching
- Beveridge curve
- active labour market policies
- welfare trap
- labour tax wedge
- privatization
- industrial policies
- trade policies

❓ Exercises

1 Why are supply-side policies both more promising and more difficult to implement than demand-side policies?

2 Why does immigration policy represent a supply-side policy? Why is it so controversial?

3 According to the Ramsey principle of public finance (see Box 18.3), on which would you levy higher taxes, jewellery or petrol? Labour income or capital income?

4 It is often alleged that the Laffer curve is more likely to be relevant in countries with a large underground economy. Explain. How might the underground economy contribute to the 'unemployment trap' described in Box 18.5?

5 Chapter 15 discussed the 'Dutch disease', the reaction of the real exchange rate to an increase in domestic wealth associated with a resource discovery. In the case of Britain and Norway,

both countries enjoyed the benefits of the North Sea oil discoveries of the 1970s. Norway subsidized its exporting industries as a response, while Britain used the resources to help balance the budget and therefore pay for transfers and government spending. Why might a subsidy be good supply-side economics in this case?

6 It is sometimes claimed that overtime working contributes to the unemployment problem. In particular, hiring and firing costs make it more attractive to pay current workers to work more (the intensive margin) than to hire more workers (the extensive margin). Furthermore, tax provisions may shield overtime income from normal labour taxation. How might reform of overtime working be difficult under these conditions? Can you think of reform measures that might encourage fewer overtime hours?

7 What is an unemployment trap? How does it work?

8 Show diagramatically how a leftward shift of the collective labour supply curve can lead to a long-run decline in output.

9 What is the difference between active and passive labour market policies?

10 Trace through the macroeconomic effects, in the short and long run, of a policy that reduces equilibrium output (for example, an increase in labour taxation). Under what conditions could this lead to a permanent increase in the rate of inflation? (Hint: use the *AD–AS* framework developed in Chapter 13).

→ Essay Questions

1 'A cut in income taxes in Europe would have significant supply-side effects.' Comment.

2 Why do some countries find it easier to carry out reforms than others?

3 How would you try to convince workers that they would globally benefit from lower employment protection?

4 Taxes are distortionary but they are used to finance public goods. How would you appraise a proposal for severely cutting public services in order to reduce tax distortions?

5 Define economic rent. Identify an economic rent that you find particularly objectionable and propose ways to eliminate it.

The Architecture of the International Monetary System

19

When we understand that Lombard Street is subject to severe alternations of opposite causes, we should cease to be surprised at its seeming cycles. We should cease too, to be surprised at the sudden panics. During the period of reaction and adversity, just even at the last instant of prosperity, the whole structure is delicate. The peculiar essence of our banking system is an unprecedented trust between man and man: and when that trust is much weakened by hidden causes, a small accident may greatly hurt it, and a great accident for a moment may almost destroy it.

Walter Bagehot (1873)

19.1 Overview

Currency and banking crises keep occurring all the time and everywhere. As we write, the world is gripped with a crisis of historical proportions, which started in the USA and spread to Europe. Its effects are now felt worldwide. Although it is much worse than most others, the current crisis is in many ways all too familiar. Going back to the early 1990s, the Exchange Rate Mechanism of the European Monetary System fell victim to a speculative attack in the late summer of 1992, and all but collapsed in 1993. Action then moved on to Mexico in late 1994. It reappeared in Thailand in mid-1997 and spread to all South-East Asia over the next six months, ravaging the area's banking systems. It hit Russia and Brazil in 1998 and Argentina in 2001.

When large crises occur, the international community does not stand idly by. The **International Monetary Fund** (IMF), in particular, has been set up to provide emergency funds to lessen the burden of hard-hit countries and to try and prevent contagion. Yet, its actions, and those of other international institutions, are often criticized. Could not the crisis have been prevented? Was the international response adequate? Over the last decade, there have been frequent calls to overhaul the international financial system, but very little has happened.

It may well be that financial crises are inherent to financial markets. If so, the international monetary world is clearly a dangerous place. It is also constantly changing. Emerging economies that were once dirt-poor are catching up with the developed world. They have joined the bandwagon of globalization, a process both hailed and feared. Many of the questions on the table are age-old: What exchange rate regime to adopt? Should capital movements be restrained? How to balance the relationship between the developed North and the poor South? What role for international financial institutions like the IMF and the World Bank? In this chapter, we revisit these old questions, and some new ones as well, with a fresh look. We have learned a great deal over the last decade, both about the theory of exchange rate crises and about the practice of exchange rate regimes.

Section 19.2 provides a brief overview of the history of the international monetary system that will help us to understand the current situation. Section 19.3 describes the role and structure of the IMF, the linchpin of the present system, in some detail. The crises of the 1990s are presented and interpreted in Section 19.4, paving the way for the perennial question of the appropriate exchange rate regime.

19.2 History of Monetary Arrangements

19.2.1 The Gold Standard and How It Worked

For centuries, both domestic and international trade was carried out with gold and silver. Metallic monies were used for thousands of years because, as explained in Chapter 9, they were easily recognizable and acceptable by others. Because they were scarce, precious metals were a reasonably stable store of value: they were not easily subject to manipulation, and were a reliable medium of exchange. National currencies as we know them did not exist. Progressively throughout the nineteenth century, banknotes began circulating alongside gold and silver. These notes were a promise to pay the bearer in precious metal. They were as good as the name of the issuer, mostly his honesty in not issuing more notes than he had precious metal. Initially at least, the notes were issued by private bankers, who often failed to exercise adequate self-discipline. Even if they did, banknotes were not always fully backed by metallic reserves, which led to occasional banking crises. This is one reason why central banks were created, and why they displaced private banks as issuers of paper money. Central banks were formally required to hold close to 100% gold or silver to back their issues of banknotes. These notes were convertible into gold, coins, or bullion at the holder's request, and conversion was indeed routine. With close to 100% backing, banknotes simply represented another, more convenient way of holding gold or silver.

The resulting arrangement, known as the **gold standard**, lasted from 1879 to 1914, less than 40 years (see Box 19.1), and collapsed one month before the outbreak of the First World War. The gold standard era is sometimes nostalgically associated with the fast growth and rapid industrialization of the time, and is regarded as a great economic success story. This 'success', in turn, is often attributed to the gold standard's automatic adjustment mechanism. In fact, the gold standard had many problems, and adjustment mechanisms were by no means as automatic as is often believed. But it remains a benchmark and, in many respects, new developments, such as monetary unions and currency boards (studied in Section 19.5.3), attempt to re-create some of its most desirable features. So it is well worth a long, hard look.

Domestic operation of the gold standard

In principle, the gold standard was a simple affair. Money was gold, or paper 'backed' by gold—redeemable on demand. Demand was stable, driven by the need to carry out everyday transactions. Supply too was quite stable. Even large discoveries amounted to small monetary shocks, for the flows of newly coined gold or silver were small in comparison to existing stocks. The role of the monetary authorities was merely to establish and guarantee the gold content of their own currencies, the gold exchange rate.

International operation of the gold standard
Fixed exchange rates

Pegging a currency's value to gold fully determined all exchange rates *vis-à-vis* other gold currencies. For instance, if the Dutch guilder was set at the price of 50 per ounce of pure gold (the usual weight reference) and sterling was set at £25 per ounce, the guilder was worth £0.5. If the exchange rate were to decline to £0.4 (a depreciation of the guilder relative to sterling), it would make sense to purchase gold in the Netherlands with guilders, ship it to the UK, tender it to the Bank of England in exchange for sterling, and, finally, convert sterling into guilders. For every 100 guilders tendered in the Netherlands for gold, the transaction would yield 2 ounces of gold, sold in the UK to acquire £50. Selling these sterling balances against guilders at the 0.4 exchange rate would yield 125 guilders, a 25% profit! Such a prospect was sure to trigger large sales of sterling and large purchases of guilders in the exchange markets,

Box 19.1   Bimetallism and Gresham's Law

It was only at the end of the nineteenth century that gold became the premier international medium of exchange. For centuries, silver and gold had competed against each other. **Bimetallism**, as the system was called, established a fixed parity between gold and silver, and coins in both metals were usually accepted for all transactions, both nationally and internationally. The relative value of gold and silver was set by international agreements, which were occasionally called into question as new discoveries of either metal threatened to upset the parity. Troubled times then followed with the operation of **Gresham's law**. This principle states that the currency (metal) that is more valuable (in non-monetary markets) than its official rate stops circulating: 'bad money chases out good'.[1]

Partly because silver became more plentiful, bimetallism ceased to exist in Europe in the 1870s. The last major countries to defend bimetallism formed the Latin Monetary Union in 1865, setting a parity of 15.5 ounces of silver for 1 ounce of gold. This union consisted of Belgium, France, Italy, and Switzerland (for this reason all, save Italy, adopted the 'franc' as the name of their national money). In the USA, where a central monetary authority was absent, bimetallism survived for a longer time. The final blow occurred when the newly created German state switched to gold and unloaded large amounts of silver on the free market. The risk of complete gold loss in a world under a gold standard forced the remaining countries to abandon bimetallism entirely.

promptly appreciating the guilder's value back to its only sustainable sterling value, £0.5. To be sure, the example ignores transaction costs, especially the cost of transporting the gold across the sea. Once these are accounted for, the exchange rate can move a little bit from the gold-implied parity, leaving a **band of fluctuation** within which it is not worth undertaking the buying, selling, and shipping. These bands were known as 'gold points', and are similar to exchange rate intervention bands employed in modern fixed exchange rate systems. They implied margins of fluctuation of about 1%.

Endogenous money supply

Being the way to settle exchanges, nationally and internationally, gold was freely flowing as the counterpart of payment imbalances. A country running a trade deficit would lose gold to its trading partners. The metal was often physically shipped abroad to pay for the excess of imports over ex-

ports.[2] The exported gold coins were then minted and coined in the currency of the surplus country. Thus, a trade deficit implied a shrinking money supply, a surplus meant an expanding money supply. This had two consequences. First, the reduction of the money supply in the deficit country led to higher interest rates and to a capital inflow. Capital account surpluses financed trade deficits. Second, higher interest rates tended to slow down economic activity and to depress prices, which improved the country's competitiveness and restored the trade balance. In the surplus country, the process went in the opposite direction: balance of payment surpluses led to gold inflows, which raised the money supply and depressed interest rates. In the medium run, higher inflation would tend to reduce the surplus, as competitiveness is eroded (the real exchange rate appreciates). This symmetric process is the

---

[1] Living in the sixteenth century, Sir Thomas Gresham had been in charge of royal finances, then became a foreign exchange trader in Antwerp until he created the Royal Exchange, better known today as the London Stock Exchange. It is sometimes argued that the gold standard in the UK was an artefact of Isaac Newton's decision in 1717 to undervalue silver in terms of gold. Within little time, Sir Isaac had only gold on his hands.

[2] Considering the high shipping, insurance, and security costs involved, this was a very costly way of settling international payments. To save on these costs, some central banks, such as the Federal Reserve Bank of New York, offered (and still offer) custodial services for gold owned by other central banks. In the late 1990s, the New York Fed was the guardian of about 270 million troy ounces of monetary gold, or about one-third the holdings of all central banks. At market price this gold is worth about a quarter of a trillion dollars!

Table 19.1 **Inflation Rates in Five Countries, 1900–1913 (annual average rate of increase in GDP deflator, %)**

France	Japan	USA	Germany	UK
0.9	2.8	1.3	1.3	0.9

Source: Maddison (1995).

Hume mechanism, named after the Scottish economist and philosopher David Hume who first described it.

The main benefits of the gold standard

The world has never seen, and probably never will see, a true pure gold standard. Still, some observers regret the passing of the gold standard. Why? First, the Hume mechanism had the virtue of credibility. Under a gold standard, monetary policy is entirely determined by the stock of gold. In principle, it is out of the politicians' hands. Second, with the money supply naturally constrained by the availability of a rare resource, inflation is not likely to emerge on any significant scale, and it didn't. This is documented in Table 19.1. Third, there is no need for a particular country to be at the centre of the world monetary system, avoiding competition and conflict regarding which country that should be.

The gold standard certainly produced a stable price level. People were able to base their expectations on a fairly predictable stable evolution of the value of goods in terms of money—in Chapter 16 we learned about the advantages of low inflation rates. In the theory of economic policy, the Hume mechanism and the gold standard illustrate the advantages of **rules** over **discretion**. When expectations are being formed, private agents try hard to guess the intentions of policy-makers. For example, we saw in Chapter 12 that workers and firms want to estimate the path of inflation. They also need to estimate the path of central bank policy. Often they base their expectations on past behaviour. If the central bank has misbehaved in the past, these expectations will be pessimistic. Thus even if the central bank has good intentions, a bad outcome is possible: agents

expect high inflation which the central bank may then feel compelled to validate with an expansionary monetary policy, usually to avoid a recession. The gold standard, by implementing automatic rules, made it easy for economic agents to reckon with the economic policy. By removing policy-makers' discretion to adjust policy, rules can lead to a more credible environment for economic agents.

Limits of automatism

Despite these appealing aspects, the gold standard had several limitations. Sterling was the main currency, backed by the most developed financial centre, London. Britain had been on the gold standard longer than other countries, since 1819 when the Bank of England received its key statutes (Peel's Act). Furthermore, as the largest creditor country, Britain provided the rest of the world with sterling balances which often ended up as reserve currency held by other central banks.[3] Three consequences followed from Britain's hegemonic position. First, the Bank of England was able to set the interest rate for the rest of the world, but with its eye on British economic conditions. Second, the demand for sterling as a reserve currency allowed Britain to finance long-running balance of payments deficits, paid with sterling-denominated debt issued by the Bank of England. Britain was able to escape the automaticity of the Hume mechanism: its money supply did not decline because gold was not shipped to cover its deficits. Third, the widespread acceptability of sterling balances allowed the Bank of England to maintain a ratio of reserves to deposits—known as 'the Proportion'—well below 100%. At the height of the gold standard late in the nineteenth century, the Proportion fluctuated between 30% and 50%. To the extent that its gold stock was shielded from the vagaries of the balance of payments and since the Proportion could vary, the Bank of England possessed considerable freedom to set its interest rate.

Britain was not the only country that tinkered with Hume's mechanism. Some countries actually imposed limits on gold exports and imports, as well as on minting and coinage. Many central banks accumulated sizeable reserves of foreign curren-

---

3 During the 40 years preceding the First World War, some 20% of British savings were invested abroad.

cies, first and foremost in pounds sterling. Thus, the assumed link between metal and money supply was less than fully automatic. Furthermore, the gold reserves of the Bank of England eventually fell below the value of the Bank's liabilities towards other central banks, leading to an 'overhang' of unbacked British debt. Many scholars consider it a miracle that the overhang never threatened the credibility of external sterling liabilities.

The limits of a metallic standard

The automatic mechanism that is often considered as the main advantage of the gold standard does not come for free. It has a cost in terms of economic instability. And indeed the gold standard years typically display low inflation but greater output variability. As described above, there is a trade-off between rules and discretion. If respected, the rules of the gold standard are very strict: the money supply is determined solely by the balance of payments, so macroeconomic adjustments must entirely be dealt with through wage and price changes. If wages and prices adjust slowly in a recession—that is a central message of Chapters 12 and 13—this adjustment process may take a long time. In the meantime, the economy 'goes through the wringer' of unemployment and recession. Despite the credibility of the mechanism, it has severe costs in some situations.

Another problem is that the overall supply of gold depends on natural discoveries. Economic growth, on the other side, implies a continuously expanding demand for real balances. If gold discoveries do not match the demand needs, increases in the real money supply can occur only if the price level declines—i.e. the price of gold must rise. Figure 19.1 shows that the gold supply has flowed regularly, with periods of scarcity coming on the footsteps of great discoveries in California, Alaska, and South Africa, as well as technological advances in mining and mineral processing. As these shocks were largely random, the money supply and the price level were hardly stable.

19.2.2 The Inter-War Period

Inter-war monetary arrangements can be conveniently arranged around three subperiods. The first ranges from the end of the First World War to the return to the gold standard in 1926. The gold standard was then maintained until 1931, and was followed by a period of managed float marked by competitive devaluations and a collapse of world trade as a consequence of the Great Depression.

The free float period (1919–1926)

In 1919 two countries, the UK and the USA, dominated the world monetary scene. During the First World War, USA remained on the gold standard, but the UK had suspended the mechanism and allowed the pound to depreciate by some 30%. Under the leadership of a young Chancellor of the Exchequer, Winston Churchill, Britain made the fateful decision to return to the gold standard at the pre-war parity. With strongly deflationary policies in place, the pound was brought back to its pre-war parity in 1925, but remained still greatly overvalued because of the persistent inflation since 1914. Germany and a number of other Central European countries returned to the gold standard only after experiencing and vanquishing their celebrated hyperinflations. France devalued the franc immediately after the war but underwent rapid inflation in the years 1922–1926. Its return to the gold standard in 1926 after the Poincaré stabilization marked the return to the pre-war situation, albeit at a devalued parity. In doing so, France was able to avoid much of the macroeconomic distress suffered by the UK, just as the Mundell–Fleming framework would predict.

Ephemeral gold standard (1927–1931)

The newly restored gold standard was a poor shadow of its predecessor. It had two competing centres, London and New York. Many currencies were badly misaligned: some were overvalued, like sterling; others were undervalued, like the French franc. Gold holdings became an ever smaller part of foreign exchange reserves as most central banks were accumulating dollar and pound balances. Free convertibility between banknotes and gold was suspended, and most central banks actively discouraged or prohibited the circulation of gold coins.[4]

---

4 In some cases, e.g. Britain, convertibility was possible only for large denominations, since the Bank of England restricted its conversion to bullion (as opposed to coins). The system is sometimes referred to as the 'gold bullion standard'.

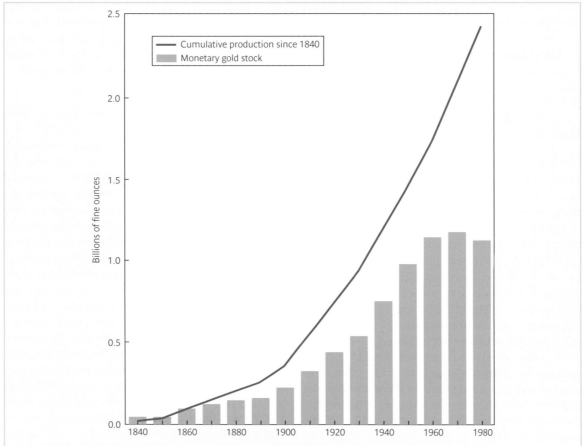

Fig. 19.1 Monetary Gold Stock and Cumulative Gold Production, 1840–1980
Although gold production has continued over time, its rate of increase has tapered off. At the same time, the demand for gold for industrial purposes has increased over the past 100 years. Perhaps not coincidentally, gold stocks held by central banks have remained flat for several decades.
Source: Cooper (1982).

The Hume mechanism was circumvented by sterilization operations. The vestiges of the system were the principle of currency convertibility[5] and fixed exchange rates.

When the Great Depression hit after 1929, the gold standard was already weak. With its overvalued currency, Britain was particularly vulnerable.

Its gold reserves shrank quickly while France, with an undervalued currency, was accumulating gold and selling off its sterling balances. Soon Britain's official liabilities exceeded its gold reserves and it had to suspend convertibility in September 1931 and let sterling float. The gold standard was over.

The managed float (1931–1939)

Britain allowed the pound to depreciate sharply to about $3.3/£, and a number of countries holding large sterling balances followed suit (Table 19.2). Formerly overvalued currencies became undervalued. At a time when all countries were struggling

---

[5] A currency is convertible when holders, both private and official, may exchange it without restriction. Convertibility does not necessarily imply a fixed exchange rate, since a floating rate system also allows participants to freely purchase and sell foreign exchange.

Table 19.2 Beggar-thy-Neighbour Depreciations, Various Countries, 1931–1938 (value of currencies as a % of their 1929 gold parity)

	1931	1932	1933	1934	1935	1936	1937	1938
Belgium	100.1	100.2	100.1	99.9	78.6	72.0	71.7	71.8
Denmark	93.5	70.3	55.8	50.0	48.5	49.0	48.6	48.1
France	100.1	100.3	100.0	100.0	100.0	92.4	61.0	43.4
Germany	99.2	99.7	99.6	98.6	100.3	100.1	99.7	99.6
Italy	98.9	97.4	99.0	97.0	93.0	82.0	59.0	59.0
Norway	93.5	67.2	62.7	56.3	54.5	55.2	54.7	54.1
The Netherlands	100.1	100.3	100.1	100.0	100.0	94.9	80.9	88.8
Switzerland	100.6	100.6	100.2	100.1	100.0	92.6	70.2	70.0
UK	93.2	72.0	68.1	61.8	59.8	60.5	60.0	59.3
USA	100.0	100.0	80.7	59.6	59.4	59.2	59.1	59.1

Source: League of Nations, Statistical Bulletins.

against the Great Depression, these devaluations were a tempting means of exporting the recession to other countries by achieving a competitive trade advantage. A gold bloc, including France, Belgium, the Netherlands, Italy, Switzerland, and Poland, was established to resist the temptation of retaliatory depreciations. The situation worsened seriously in 1933 when the USA, the remaining centre of the gold standard, imposed an embargo on gold exports, introduced exchange controls, and depreciated the dollar from \$20.67 to \$35 per ounce of pure gold. The *coup de grâce* was the dissolution of the gold bloc following the devaluation of the Belgian franc in 1935. 'Beggar-thy-neighbour' policies (competitive devaluations) followed, but were self-defeating since each country attempted to devalue *vis-à-vis* all the others. The next step was a 'tariff war': each country raised its tariffs to restrict imports, thus encouraging the substitution of domestically produced products. Imports declined but so did exports, as other nations followed suit. While the aim of boosting output failed, international trade collapsed, as shown in Figure 19.2.[6]

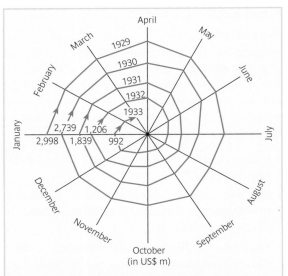

Fig. 19.2 The Decline of World Trade During the Great Depression

During the period 1929–1933, the enormous increases in world trade that had been accomplished in the previous three decades were wiped out by a spiral of protectionist measures. This famous illustration by Professor Charles Kindleberger of MIT, taken from a 1934 publication of the League of Nations, shows just how quickly trade wars can get out of hand.

Source: Kindleberger (1973).

---

[6] Remember: $Y = C + I + G + X - Z$: *ceteris paribus*, reducing Z raises Y, but if X falls by the same amount, there is no net gain.

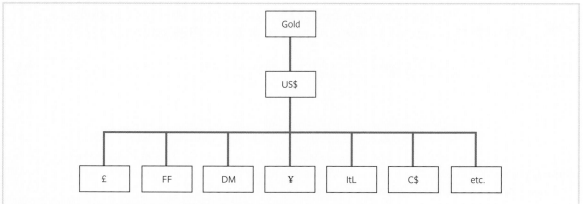

Fig. 19.3 The Three Layers of Bretton Woods
The three layers of the Bretton Woods system consisted of gold, the US dollar, and the other participating currencies. The USA declared a gold parity for the dollar, thereby pegging to gold. Intervention took place mostly in dollars, but implicit was the understanding that gold stood behind the dollars.

19.2.3 The Bretton Woods System of Fixed Exchange Rates

The principles

Preparations for the **Bretton Woods conference** of July 1944 started long before the end of the Second World War.[7] The conference led to the creation of the International Monetary Fund (IMF). The new world monetary order was conceived as the antidote to the inter-war situation.

- Exchange rates were to be fixed; realignments required prior IMF approval.

- The IMF could provide loans as an alternative to devaluation for countries facing balance of payments difficulties.

- The dollar was the centre of the system. All countries officially declared a fixed parity, called a par or central value, *vis-à-vis* the US dollar, which itself pegged to gold directly. Currencies were allowed to deviate by no more than 1% from the par value.

- Exchange controls and tariffs were allowed only as temporary measures for the immediate post-war period.[8] In the event, full currency convertibility was only achieved in Europe in 1958, and a number of developing countries still have non-convertible currencies and capital controls.

Gold and the dollar

Officially, all currencies were defined in terms of gold. Yet, at the end of the Second World War, the USA held about 70% of all gold reserves and was the only country credible enough to set a gold parity. With the US Marshall Plan providing them with dollar balances, the most obvious approach for the other countries was to declare a parity *vis-à-vis* the US currency.[9] The outcome was a *de facto* three-tier system, represented in Figure 19.3. Gold remained the fundamental standard of value, but for all currencies this was mediated by the dollar, hence the name **gold exchange standard** given to the Bretton Woods system. The system thus relied on the ability of the USA to maintain the declared parity of $35 per ounce of gold.

---

[7] Named after a small ski resort in the US state of New Hampshire. The conference considered two plans published in 1943, prepared for the USA by Treasury Secretary Harry White, and for the UK by John Maynard Keynes. The White plan eventually prevailed.

[8] Keynes was in favour of controls on short-term capital flows. The rolling back of tariffs was later entrusted to the GATT (General Agreement on Tariffs and Trade).

[9] The Marshall Plan was a massive aid programme for post-war Western Europe and Japan funded by the USA.

The International Monetary Fund

For a long while, the Bretton Woods system worked rather well. After a rash of post-war parity adjustments—including an unauthorized devaluation of the French franc in 1948—exchange rate stability prevailed. Trade expanded quickly and was easily financed by dollar balances, provided initially by the Marshall Plan, then by US trade deficits and the resulting capital flows. The IMF became the respected watchdog of the fixed exchange rate system. It developed an elaborate system of loans to countries suffering balance of payments difficulties. Its resources were provided by member-country deposits, 25% in gold or US dollars—depending on the country's gold stock—and 75% in the country's own currency. The size of a country's deposit, based on its size in international trade, determines its **quota**. Quotas determine each member country's voting weight and its borrowing rights, and are set anew every five years.

Devaluations were in principle restricted to cases of 'fundamental disequilibria', i.e. balance of payments deficits not of a temporary (cyclical) nature. In order to help member nations avoid devaluation, the IMF made, and still makes, resources available for immediate lending—called 'purchase agreements' when effected and 'repurchase' when reimbursed. Each member country is eligible for immediate lending up to its quota. Beyond that, lending becomes conditional. The IMF requests a formal agreement on specific policy steps and results designed to solve the 'non-fundamental' part of external disequilibria. This **conditionality** has become the central source of power of the IMF, and has survived the collapse of the Bretton Woods system.

The Triffin paradox and the collapse of the Bretton Woods system

As economies grew and international trade developed, more 'international money' was needed. Since the US dollar was the international money, more dollars would have to be made available to the world economy. For internationally held dollar balances to grow, the USA must run balance of payments deficits, just as Britain did during the days of the gold standard. Inevitably, US official liabilities abroad must outgrow the country's gold reserves.

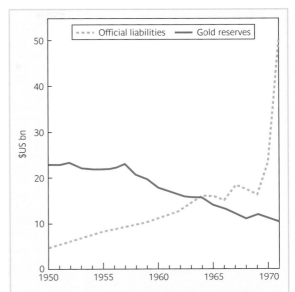

Fig. 19.4 US Official Liabilities and Gold Reserves, 1950–1970

As long as foreigners were willing to hold dollars, the USA could finance its large balance of payments deficits by increases in foreign holdings of official assets (dollars held by central banks). Yet the gold reserve of the USA declined over the entire period shown, as foreign central banks occasionally tendered their dollars for gold. Sometime in 1964, the stock of external official claims against the US gold exceeded the dollar's gold backing. At that moment, the credibility of the gold exchange standard was called into question.

Sources: Dam (1982); IMF.

Figure 19.4 shows that this happened in 1964. Yet at this point, the USA can no longer guarantee the gold value of the US dollar. This is the **Triffin paradox**,[10] a fatal weakness of the gold exchange standard.

A conjunction of economic and political events brought the situation to a climax. The Vietnam War and ambitious domestic social programmes (President Johnson's 'Great Society') led to increased public spending in the USA, which accelerated growth and inflation, and deepened the current account deficit. At the same time, countries critical

---

[10] It is named after the late Belgian economist Robert Triffin who identified the 'fundamental flaw' of the Bretton Woods system.

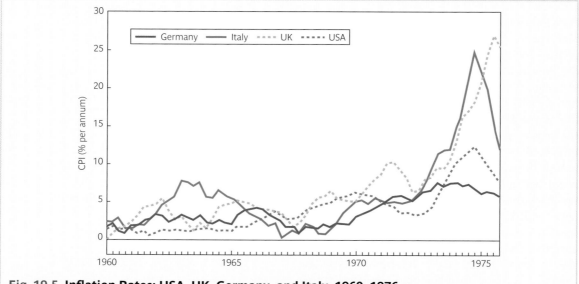

Fig. 19.5 Inflation Rates: USA, UK, Germany, and Italy, 1960–1976

Inflation rates during the Bretton Woods era moved closely together, which is characteristic of a fixed exchange rate regime. As soon as the system collapsed in 1971, inflation rates diverged sharply.

Source: IMF.

of the Bretton Woods arrangement began to protest loudly. French President de Gaulle publicly complained about the 'privilège exorbitant', which allowed the USA to use seigniorage to finance its political activities (the Vietnam War) and economic power (the acquisition of European corporations by US companies at the time). In a dramatic gesture, France began to swap dollars for gold in the mid-1960s, increasing its precious metal stock from $3.7 to $5.2 billion between 1964 and 1966.

The markets took notice. Anticipating an increase in the price of gold, they sought to buy it while it was still cheap. The response of the monetary authorities was to form the Gold Pool (Belgium, Italy, the Netherlands, Switzerland, West Germany, the UK, and the USA, with France inactive after 1967), an agreement to sell gold to maintain the $35/ounce parity. As the drain on official gold holdings accelerated, the Pool pulled out of the gold market and declared that they would henceforth trade gold only among themselves—they would neither sell to nor buy from private parties—at the official price. The market price of gold rose substantially higher

than the official parities. Tensions within the Gold Pool grew until President Nixon's historic decision to suspend the gold parity of the US dollar on 15 August 1971.

From the Smithsonian Agreement to Jamaica

The severing of the gold–dollar link destroyed a key component of the Bretton Woods arrangement, but the gold crisis was not the sole factor in its demise. Inflation had been rising in most countries in the late 1960s, but at increasingly different rates (Figure 19.5). This challenged the exchange rate parities that had remained unchanged since the late 1940s.[11] Speculative capital movements followed. Britain and Italy came under IMF conditionality in 1969. The pound was devalued in 1967, followed by the French franc in 1969, while the Deutschmark was revalued. The delinking of the dollar from gold opened the Pandora's box for further realignments. The credibility of the exchange rate system was severely damaged.

[11] The French franc was devalued in 1958; the deutschmark and Dutch guilder were revalued in 1961.

The last major effort to save the sinking ship was an agreement reached in December 1971 during a conference at the Smithsonian Institution in Washington, DC. The dollar was devalued *vis-à-vis* gold to $38 per ounce, yet remained inconvertible into gold, even among central banks. Some currencies were revalued, others devalued. The margins of fluctuations were enlarged from 1% to 2.25% around par value, while the European countries maintained a reduced (half) margin. This was the 'Snake' arrangement. By the end of 1972, the pound was floating, soon to be followed by the Swiss franc, the Italian lira, and the Japanese yen. In March 1973, the remaining 'Snake' members decided to float jointly *vis-à-vis* all other currencies, including the dollar, within a wider 2.25% margin. France left, then re-entered, as did Italy; then both left again. Sweden and Norway joined informally. By 1975 the principle of fixed exchange rates was more or less dead, at least for the convertible currencies of the industrialized countries. In January 1976, the Jamaica agreement made official the new role of the IMF. From then on, it would be in charge of overseeing a world monetary system of increasingly flexible exchange rates.

19.2.4 The European Monetary System and the Monetary Union

For Europe, the Bretton Woods system had offered a convenient, if indirect, way of pegging their currencies to each other. This arrangement had deepened economic ties within the Common Market, consisting of the member countries of the European Community (EC).[12] The demise of the gold exchange standard posed a problem with both economic and political implications. The response was the establishment of the European Monetary System (EMS), which began operation in March 1979. All nine European Community (EC) members at the time formally joined the EMS, but the UK deferred participating in the **Exchange Rate Mechanism** (ERM), the system of fixed exchange rates, until October 1990. With the exception of

Sweden, all newer EC (henceforth EU) members (Greece, Spain, Portugal, Austria, and Finland) subsequently joined the ERM. After violent **speculative attacks** on the ERM parities in September 1992, Italy and the UK left the ERM; Italy rejoined in 1997. The ERM disappeared formally with the launch in 1999 of the **European Monetary Union** (EMU) (we discuss this further in Section 19.5.4). A new EMS-II was established. The modified ERM serves as a gateway to EMU for new EU members and a possible arrangement for EU member countries, such as Denmark, that do not wish to adopt the euro but nevertheless want to fix their exchange rates to the euro. As of January 2009, 16 of the 25 EU member countries had adopted the euro.

Key features of the EMS

Three original features characterized the first version of the ERM.

Bilateral parities

Exchange rates were fixed but adjustable. In theory at least, there was no specialstatus currency, like the US dollar under Bretton Woods. Fixity was defined as an official central **parity** between any pair of member currencies: a central rate, and a band of fluctuation initially set at ±2.25%, which was expanded to ±15% in August 1993, following a major exchange rate crisis.[13]

Consensus decisions

A country could not alter its parity within the system unilaterally. Realignments had to be agreed upon by every member. Despite the apparent restrictiveness of this rule, realignments are not infrequent.

Mutual support

In order to defend the parities, member central banks were allowed to borrow virtually unlimited amounts from each other at very short notice. Prompt repayment was required—normally within 45 days—but revolving credits were possible.

---

[12] The European Community is the predecessor of the European Union. The name change was officially decided in Maastricht in 1991.

[13] Technically, the ERM parities were defined *vis-à-vis* the ECU, the forerunner to the euro, which was simply a basket of currencies of all EMS members. Bilateral parities were derived as cross rates implied by the central ECU parities. A special ±6% band was employed temporarily by Italy, the UK, Portugal, Spain, and Greece.

In practice, the German mark emerged as the central currency. The Bundesbank intervened mostly in US dollars, whereas the other members used EMS currencies more frequently. Germany appeared to manage its exchange rate *vis-à-vis* the US dollar, leaving it to the other central banks to manage theirs *vis-à-vis* the deutschmark.

The four phases of the EMS

During the first phase, from its establishment until the mid-1980s, the ERM operated as a fairly loose system which tolerated member countries' diverse tastes for inflation. Realignments were frequent and undramatic, aimed at correcting deviations from purchasing power parity (PPP) resulting from persistent differences in inflation rates between participating countries.

The second phase, from the mid-1980s to 1992, was marked by the gradual emergence of the deutschmark as the system's anchor currency. Realignments were successfully avoided from January 1987 to September 1992. All countries tried to emulate the mark's strong currency status and identified low inflation as the main objective of monetary policy. During this period, the EMS came to be perceived as a major success: the absence of any realignment for nearly six years was attributed to adroit policy co-ordination. Emboldened by success, the authorities proceeded to prepare a shift to a single currency. The result was the Maastricht Treaty adopted by EU heads of state late in 1991.

This period of tranquillity and optimism came to an abrupt end in the summer of 1992. During the subsequent third phase of crisis and turbulence, continuous upheaval rocked the ERM ship, and it nearly sank. Not only did several realignments occur in quick succession, but two currencies actually left the ERM to float on their own. Roughly a year later, in August 1993, the margins of fluctuation were widened to ±15%, and the fixed exchange rate system hardly differed from free floating.

The fourth and last phase of the EMS, which represented two decades of European monetary history, an 'ERM without teeth', was hastily designed in the wake of speculative attacks. With 15% wide bands, the situation was stabilized, allowing an orderly transition to EMU.

The impossible trilogy

With hindsight it is easy to understand why the ERM was under duress. The globalization of international financial markets brought near-perfect capital mobility with it, allowing investors and speculators to swap billions of short-term assets at the push of a button. A central bank which commits to fixing an exchange rate in effect becomes the ultimate market maker in the money market, and is obliged to accommodate at the set parity all transactions that the market does not. This commitment, as was made clear in Chapter 9, is inconsistent with an independent monetary policy.

The coexistence of fixed exchange regimes and capital controls is thus more than coincidental. Capital controls enable countries participating in fixed exchange rate arrangements to preserve some monetary autonomy. The countries that use capital controls tend to have higher inflation. Indeed, controls may be essential to organize orderly realignments in the face of market attacks.

These policy conflicts and dilemmas are summarized neatly as the **impossible trilogy**. This principle states that the following three aspects of a monetary system are jointly incompatible:

(1) full capital mobility;

(2) fixed exchange rates;

(3) monetary policy independence.

They are, however, taken in pairs, feasible and have been observed throughout monetary history, and even today. The impossible trilogy is a direct implication of the Mundell–Fleming (*IS–LM*) framework: if capital is fully mobile, the interest rate is given exogenously by the foreign rate i^*, and the *LM* curve is given by cumulated net capital inflow.

This principle offers a powerful framework for reviewing the EMS experience. The early EMS was able to survive because of the presence of capital controls. During the first phase, it allowed for the coexistence of fixed exchange rates and some degree of monetary independence in the form of different inflation rates compensated for by periodic realignments. The second phase was an attempt to adopt the same monetary policy everywhere under German leadership. As long as economic conditions did not call for different policies, this was a relatively costless way to cope with the impossible trilogy. It is during that period that capital controls were dismantled. However, the shock of German unification and a worldwide recession in the early 1990s, which raised the costs of the loss of monetary policy independence, changed all that. The crises that followed correspond to the travails that go with ignoring the impossible trilogy. The solutions adopted—free floating in Italy and the UK, wide bands elsewhere—correspond to the abandonment of the fixed exchange rate.

Once capital controls are removed, the choice boils down to either a single monetary authority or a free float. The experience of 1992–1993 shows that the temptation of monetary independence plays havoc with a fixed exchange rate arrangement. Politically, it was probably unavoidable that countries relinquishing monetary independence in a system of fixed exchange rates would challenge the Bundesbank's leadership, just as France challenged the American *privilège exorbitant* three decades previous. It is not surprising that the countries that pledged to abandon capital controls in the mid-1980s—Belgium, France, Italy, and Spain —soon thereafter proposed the creation of a European Monetary Union. Nor is it surprising that the Bundesbank initially expressed doubts about the urgency of taking a step which amounted to sharing its undisputed control over European monetary policy.

19.3 **The International Monetary Fund**

The influence of the IMF is probably stronger today than in the heyday of the Bretton Woods system, if only because it is now in charge of a system that is less internally inconsistent than before. In the post-Bretton Woods 'system', each country is free to choose its own exchange rate regime, and there is no agreed-upon international currency. Gold has long been 'demonetized', meaning that it is no longer a reference, and many countries have since sold large parts of their gold stocks.

19.3.1 **IMF Assistance and Conditionality**

Countries continue occasionally to face balance of payment problems, although they are somewhat different from those of the Bretton Woods era. In principle, countries are now free to depreciate their currencies in response to adverse shocks, and over the longer haul such policies can bring the current account back to levels consistent with an intertemporal budget constraint. Frequently, though, the authorities prevent their exchange rate from adjusting to shocks by intervening in the foreign exchange markets, sometimes with borrowed foreign exchange. Eventually they may exhaust their foreign exchange reserves. What can they do then? An obvious answer is to treat the causes, and not the symptoms of the crisis. Taking remedial action, usually moving away from undisciplined monetary and fiscal policies, requires time, however, and the house is burning. The solution is to call the IMF, the international firefighter.

When called upon in an emergency, the IMF proceeds in three steps.

(1) It assesses the situation and makes recommendations to the authorities.

(2) Conditionality follows: an emergency loan is extended to the troubled country, which in return commits to a number of policy actions.

(3) As the loan is disbursed, typically in several instalments, the IMF monitors the implementation of the agreement and may suspend further disbursements if the country in question is violating its commitments.

In an average year, some 10–20 standby loans are arranged.[14] The average volume of loans outstanding represents about 12% of world exports. In 2008, 185 countries were members of the Fund.

It is important to stress that the Fund's assistance is not a gift, but a loan, generally with a maturity of 1–4 years. The interest rate charged is slightly above the market rate to discourage using the Fund as a cheap source of money. Most private financial institutions deal only with sovereign borrowers in good standing with the IMF, so the Fund usually has a great deal of leverage over borrowing countries, which are generally excluded from the private capital market. This explains, of course, why countries in trouble turn to the IMF and are also willing to accept the conditions that it requests. Despite popular beliefs to the contrary, most countries actually pay back their loans. The reason is that the IMF has priority over all other creditors, and not repaying the IMF means being excluded from all other sources of international financing. Only a handful of 'pariah' countries have defaulted on IMF loans. They will have to pay back when and if they want to re-enter the international financial arena. Most eventually do.

19.3.2 Special Drawing Rights

Despite having lost the official status it enjoyed in the Bretton Woods system, the US dollar remains the *de facto* means of payment for international trade and the foreign exchange reserve of choice at central banks. Although it is sometimes asked whether the euro might challenge or replace the US dollar, the more interesting question is: Why should the international means of payment be any particular country's currency? In the late 1960s, many countries lobbied for the creation of a new world currency, reviving an old idea which had been defeated at the Bretton Woods conference in 1946.[15] If the IMF could be transformed into the world central bank, it was thought, it could issue its own currency for all

central banks to settle their payments, borrow from each other, and intervene on exchange markets. Unsurprisingly, the USA, the Fund's largest shareholder—with a veto right—objected.

With the objective of increasing and stabilizing the supply of international liquidity, it was decided at the Rio Conference in 1967 to create the **special drawing right** (SDR). SDRs can be seen as a line of credit allocated by the IMF to each country in proportion to its quota (defined above). Each member country can draw on its line of credit to obtain convertible currencies from the Fund. At the time of its conception, the SDR was valued at the rate of SDR 35 per ounce of gold, thus making it worth exactly US$1. The SDRs were not, however, backed by gold or dollars. Just like money created by banks, SDRs are valued simply because they are accepted.[16]

After gold convertibility was suspended, the SDR's value was redefined as a basket of four currencies.[17] SDRs yield an interest rate—the weighted average of interest available on the four underlying currencies. Symbolically, the SDR is the IMF's unit of account. As a basket, it is less volatile than any of its components, which has made it convenient for other purposes. Some countries peg their exchange rate to the SDR. Private debt issues have been denominated in SDRs, although technically they are just a basket of the constituent currencies. Some 9 billion SDRs were initially created in 1970, and more were subsequently added, the last time in 1981, to a cumulative total of 21.4 billion. A new allocation was decided in 1997.

19.3.3 Surveillance

The IMF is not just a firefighter. It is also a safety inspector. It continuously monitors the macroeconomic scene in each member country in order to

---

[14] Standby loans are made in emergency cases. The IMF offers a large menu of lending facilities tailored after particular needs. They can be seen at the IMF website: <ww.imf.org>.

[15] The 'Keynes Plan' envisioned the creation of an international reserve currency, the bancor, which would play the role gold did in the old gold standard era, but which would be supplied by an international agency, i.e. not the USA.

[16] Hence the following quote by the economist Fritz Machlup: 'Now the forward-looking experts of the Fund and the negotiating governments have proved that their reputation for backwardness in economic thinking had been undeserved. All that matters for the acceptability of anything as a medium of exchange is the expectation that others will accept it. . . . Money needs takers, not backers.' (Quoted by Dam, 1989: 152.)

[17] The four currencies, and their weights in the basket, are the US dollar (44%), the euro (34%), the yen (11%), and the pound (11%), reflecting their international use. The weights are revised every five years.

Box 19.2 How the IMF is Managed

The ultimate authority is exercised by the IMF's Board of Governors which meets, in principle, once a year. The governors are the finance ministers or central bank governors of all member countries. Quotas are distributed according to a formula that involves GDP, current account transactions, foreign exchange reserves, and a measure of volatility of international transactions. Voting rights are proportional to quotas plus a fixed number of 'basic votes' designed to increase the rights of the smaller countries. Table 19.3 displays the quotas and voting rights of the top twenty countries. The most important decisions require 85% of the votes, which gives the USA *de facto* veto power.

In practice, the Board of Governors delegates managing authority to the Executive Board, which consists of 24 Executive Directors. They reside at the IMF's headquarters in Washington and meet nearly every day. The largest-quota countries (the USA, the UK, Germany, France, Japan, China, Russia, and Saudi Arabia) have one executive director each, while the other executive directors represent several countries, grouped along regional lines. The Executive Directors select the Managing Director to run the professional staff.[18] All decisions are taken by the Board of Executive Directors, which cast votes in the name of each country according to its quota. In this way the Executive Directors represent the interests of their countries, while the staff and the Managing Director represent the institution.

Table 19.3 IMF Quotas and Votes in 2008

	Quotas		Votes
	SDR mns	% total	% total
1 United States	37,149	17.09	16.77
2 Japan	13,313	6.13	6.02
3 Germany	13,008	5.99	5.88
4 France	10,739	4.94	4.86
5 United Kingdom	10,739	4.94	4.86
6 China	8,090	3.72	3.66
7 Italy	7,056	3.25	3.19
8 Saudi Arabia	6,986	3.21	3.16
9 Canada	6,369	2.93	2.89
10 Russia	5,945	2.74	2.69
11 Netherlands	5,162	2.38	2.34
12 Belgium	4,605	2.12	2.09
13 India	4,158	1.91	1.89
14 Switzerland	3,459	1.59	1.57
15 Australia	3,236	1.49	1.47
16 Mexico	3,153	1.45	1.43
17 Spain	3,049	1.4	1.39
18 Brazil	3,036	1.4	1.38
19 Korea	2,927	1.35	1.33
20 Venezuela	2,659	1.22	1.21

Source: IMF.

detect possible risks to its currency and to keep abreast of the local situation, should an emergency arise. Surveillance takes several forms.

♦ Annual visits and evaluations (called Article IV consultations). The IMF's economic assessments and recommendations, once highly confidential, are now posted on the Fund's website (each country has the right to refuse the release of this information, but that is considered a bad signal).

♦ Twice a year, the IMF publishes the *World Economic Outlook*, which outlines its views of the situation in member countries.

♦ For countries in difficult situations, the IMF conducts 'enhanced surveillance', which means more frequent evaluations and recommendations.

♦ For countries that have borrowed from the Fund, the so-called programme countries, the monitoring is more or less permanent, based on agreed-upon targets for policies and outcomes.

♦ Each government knows that its policies are monitored and that the conclusions are presented to the Executive Board of the Fund. Box 19.2 explains

[18] A long-standing gentlemen's agreement that the IMF's Managing Director is from Europe while the President of the World Bank is from the USA is increasingly being challenged by the developing countries.

how decisions are made. Surveillance is justified as a preventive means of avoiding disruptive policies that wrecked the world economy during the inter-war period. When countries pursue economic policies that are criticized by the IMF, this disapproval is noticed by the outside world and usually results in internal and external political and financial pressure, which can go far in correcting aberrant policies.

19.4 **Currency Crises**

In Chapter 15 we briefly explained the reason for recurrent currency crises. This section expands on this presentation and describes the role played by the IMF in dealing with crises.

19.4.1 **Crises, crises**

Over the 1990s, the world has become globalized, meaning, among other things, that trade and financial integration has accelerated. Long-standing trade barriers were brought down as many countries (especially in Latin America and Asia), which had long protected themselves from international competition, shifted gears and have become fierce competitors themselves. They also opened up their financial accounts, establishing full currency convertibility and allowing almost complete capital mobility. These liberalization moves were first met by successes. Growth picked up, often led by exports and fed by very sizeable capital inflows. Figure 19.6 shows the case of Thailand, one of the East Asian Tigers.

Then something very ugly happened in many emerging market economies. Capital flows reversed themselves, first slowly, then in a panic rush for the exit. The authorities scrambled to defend their currencies, quickly exhausted initially plentiful reserves, and then threw in the towel. The result was a string of massive depreciations (some of the order of 50%). Indebted local firms and banks which had borrowed in foreign currency, mostly dollars, saw their debts double overnight, making them effectively bankrupt. Domestic and foreign speculators sold the shares of indebted companies on the local stock markets and parked the proceeds in foreign exchange, doubling the pressure

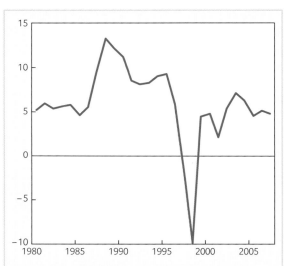

Fig. 19.6 GDP Growth Rate in Thailand

Growth picked up speed, and momentum was carried by massive capital inflows in the 1990s. When these flows reversed direction in 1997, the currency collapsed and the economy went into a tailspin.

Sources: World Bank and Bank of Thailand.

on the beleaguered countries. Many economies simply folded, plunging millions of bewildered people into unemployment and poverty.

Such **boom-and-bust cycles** are nothing terribly new. They have been observed in Chile in 1982, in Mexico in 1986 and again in 1995, in Thailand in 1997, from where it spread to Korea, Indonesia, and the Philippines, then on to Russia and Brazil in 1998. It had also happened, in a milder way, in the UK in 1991, in Finland and Sweden in 1992–1993, and in the US, Spain, and the UK in 2007.

Boom-and-bust cycles share a number of common features. The boom starts with liberalization. It attracts foreign investment which feeds growth. Growth becomes too rapid to be sustainable, and soon inflationary pressures arise. The authorities, on the other hand, are so pleased that they overlook the growing overvaluation of the exchange rate— who wants to spoil the party with a devaluation? These easy years are usually characterized by unbounded optimism and laxity, and considerable risk-taking. Domestic banks have little trouble obtaining funds from abroad in foreign currencies and lend them on freely in domestic currency. Governments too often borrow abroad in foreign currency, getting better interest rates and betting on the continuation of the miracle. The IMF is either as optimistic as the local authorities, or is a voice in the wilderness as its danger warnings go unheeded. International investors marvel at their successes, but keep a critical eye on the situation.

Then something happens. The current account deficit deepens too much, or some miracle country elsewhere in the world stumbles. Then the investors move out faster than they came, accompanied, if not preceded, by local investors. The crisis erupts and output falls, often deeply. As Figure 19.6 illustrates, growth eventually returns, and often surprisingly fast. Yet the confidence of citizens in free markets has been badly shaken, governments have fallen, things may never be the same again. What is remarkable is that things can get so bad after having been so good.

Why do crises occur, then? Crises are like automobile accidents: they seem to happen randomly and unexpectedly, but this is generally not the case. A first class of explanations maintains that dangerous drivers are more likely to have more accidents. Not only can we see the accidents coming, but we can do something to prevent them, either by sending bad drivers to school or by increasing the penalties for hazardous practices. This is the first-generation theory of crises. Further theories are more subtle. They hold that crises can occur even among the (almost) perfect, merely because they are *expected* to occur. While impeccable drivers may be reasonably immune to such accidents, most of the average ones may not be.

19.4.2 First-Generation Crises

The first-generation theory sees crises as the outcome of policies that are inconsistent with a fixed exchange rate regime. We already know from Chapter 11 that, with perfect capital mobility, monetary policy must be fully dedicated to the fixed exchange rate if that is the chosen regime. Not all governments recognize this point, however. They let the domestic money supply grow too fast, often because this looks like an easy way to finance a budget deficit. We know what happens next: interest rates decline and capital flows out. If the flow is not too large, because of limitations to capital mobility or because real-life markets are a bit more hesitant than theory claims, the authorities believe that they can have the cake and eat it too. They expand money domestically, buy it back on the foreign exchange markets to keep up the peg, and sterilize to keep things going.

Figure 19.7 tells the story. Recall from Chapter 9 that the asset side of the monetary base is the sum of the central bank's foreign exchange reserves and domestic credit ($M = R + D$). The policy mistake is for the central bank to intervene on the open market to increase the amount of domestic credit that it offers to commercial banks. This is the upward-sloping trajectory of D. While supply rises, what happens to demand? It is driven by the public's preferences, and leads to the familiar LM equilibrium condition:[19]

(19.1)
$$M = R + D = L(i)$$

where we ignore the evolution of output because it moves little over the weeks or days that lead up to a crisis. For the same reason, we have assumed that the price level is constant and indexed it as $P = 1$. In this short horizon, therefore, money demand is only driven by the interest rate. What then drives the interest rate? We know that, if capital is freely mobile, it must satisfy the interest parity condition presented in Chapter 15. This condition states that the domestic interest rate is equal to the foreign

---

[19] For simplicity, we treat money and monetary base as the same, or equivalently, look at the derived demand for the monetary base M0.

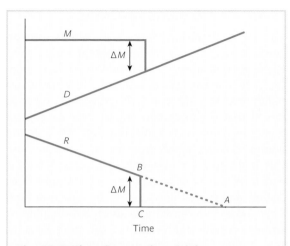

Fig. 19.7 First-Generation Crisis

The central bank follows a policy of continuous expansion of the domestic component D of the money supply M. To keep the exchange rate constant it must intervene on the foreign exchange market and keep the money supply constant in face of a constant demand. Foreign exchange reserves R steadily decline towards ultimate exhaustion. The attack occurs at point B, when reserves are just sufficient to absorb the sales of domestic money $\Delta M = BC$ induced by the expectation that, after the crisis, the exchange rate will float and depreciate continuously, raising the domestic interest rate and reduce money demand by ΔM.

rate less the expected rate of currency appreciation. Formally, it is written as

(19.2) $i = i^* - \Delta S/S.$

As long as markets believe that the fixed exchange rate will be upheld, if only for just another day, the expected change in the exchange rate ($\Delta S/S$) is nil, and the domestic interest rate i is equal to the foreign rate i^*. This implies that the demand for money stays constant. But how can the money supply stay constant when the monetary authority is increasing domestic credit at the same time?

The formal, short answer is easily seen in (19.1). To keep the money supply M equal to the constant money demand $L(i)$, the central bank has to spend its reserves R at the same time as it expands domestic credit D. The more detailed explanation is as follows. The central bank attempts to expand the money supply by providing commercial banks with

more money base M against more domestic credit D. But the public is not interested in acquiring more money ($L(i)$ is contant as long as i is constant), so the extra money is invested abroad. As money flows out, it puts pressure on the exchange rate, forcing the central bank to intervene, in effect reabsorbing the money base that it has created in the first place. This looks silly, and it is. It is the policy mistake that will lead to a crisis.

Figure 19.7 tracks the opposite evolution of domestic credit D and foreign exchange reserves R over time. For a while, foreign exchange reserves can be run down gradually. Yet this process cannot continue forever: one day the reserve stock is bound to be depleted. A reasonable central bank would stop its attempt at monetary expansion before it is too late, but here we study what happens if the central bank carries on its misguided policies. It is crucial to realize that when reserves are exhausted, the fixed exchange rate system must be abandoned for lack of ammunition. A naive extrapolation of this trend would point to A as the 'day of reckoning'. After that day, one might reason, inflation will rise, as will nominal interest rates and the exchange will plummet, as will the demand for money, as investors stampede out the door.

This reasoning is flawed, however! Market traders will not wait idly by until the exchange rate collapses. Indeed, the message of Chapter 15 is that they will anticipate this event. They understand that once the fixed exchange regime is abandoned—a certainty given the central bank's assumed determination to let D expand—the exchange rate will be floating, and depreciating, so ΔS will be negative. In this case, the interest rate parity condition predicts that the interest rate i must increase (see (19.2)). If the interest rate increases, the demand for money falls. Equation (19.1) even tells us by how much, say ΔM.[20] This reduction occurs as agents—called speculators in this capacity—sell their own

---

[20] Precisely, the money base will contract by $\Delta M = L(i^*) - L(i^* - \Delta S/S)$, since $L(i^*)$ is money demand before the crisis (when $i = i^*$) and $L(i^* - \Delta S/S)$ is money demand after the crisis when the domestic interest rate has risen to take into account the rate of depreciation once the exchange rate is floating after the crisis (remember that $\Delta S/S < 0$).

money for foreign currency, in effect signalling the onset of the crisis. Who buys the domestic currency? Only the central bank does, to honour its standing commitment to defend the parity under attack. To do so, it draws on its remaining stock of foreign exchange reserves. The fall in money demand ΔM is exactly matched by the loss of foreign exchange reserves ΔR.

We now see why the crisis is unavoidable and how it takes the form of a sudden sale of domestic currency. The only remaining question is: When will the crisis occur? The decision is in the hands of the public. The would-be speculators know that a crisis will occur and must guess when to start running on the currency. Buy foreign exchange too late, after the exchange rate has already depreciated, and you suffer a capital loss. Buy foreign exchange too early, when the central bank can still defend its parity, and you gain nothing, only incurring the conversion costs. There is one good time to attack: it is represented by point B in Figure 19.7. This is when reserves reach the level ΔM, the correctly anticipated decline in the money supply post-attack. This is the last moment when everyone will be able to swap domestic for foreign money at the still fixed exchange rate. The crisis takes the form of a sudden sale of domestic money—a speculative attack—which provokes a dramatic fall in central bank reserves from point B to point C, where the reserves have been exhausted. With no reserves left, $R = 0$, the parity must be abandoned. Thereafter, by (19.1) $M = D$ will continue to grow while the exchange rate, now floating, continues to depreciate.

This simple story captures the essence of an exchange crisis. Two aspects are quite striking. First, while it might appear that it is the attack that causes the collapse of the exchange rate regime, nothing could be further from the truth. The exchange rate regime was doomed long before the crisis, its day of reckoning only being delayed by the existence of a large enough stock of foreign exchange rate reserves. The attack merely determines the timing of the collapse. Second, no one is surprised. All was quiet before the storm, but it was deceiving. Everyone saw it coming and was just waiting for the right time to act. The crisis was fully

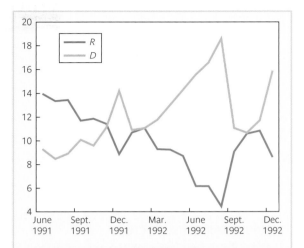

Fig. 19.8 British Foreign Exchange Reserves and Domestic Credit: The 1992 Crisis (£ billion)

The evolution of domestic credit and reserves in the months preceding the September 1992 crisis conforms well with the first-generation theory of crises. Easy money (a rising volume of credit) made a crisis almost inevitable. As the Bank of England was maintaining its ERM peg, foreign exchange reserves were declining. What the monthly data do not show is the precipitous fall on 12 September, estimated by some at £20 billion. *Source*: IMF.

anticipated. In real life, of course, there is some uncertainty and things are not quite so clean—Figure 19.8 shows the evolution of British foreign exchange reserves and domestic credit in the run-up to the September 1992 exchange crisis—but the two conclusions remain valid.[21]

19.4.3 Further Generation Crises

First-generation crises are the outcome of policies that are incompatible with a fixed exchange rate regime. Some might even say they are well deserved.

---

[21] This highly stylized model neglects—intentionally—a number of aspects which are possibly more realistic, but don't help us to understand the underlying mechanism. Economic growth, asymmetric information among traders, and uncertainty about central bank policy could all, in principle, be introduced. That we don't means that the underlying intuition survives these modifications. That is what makes a good model!

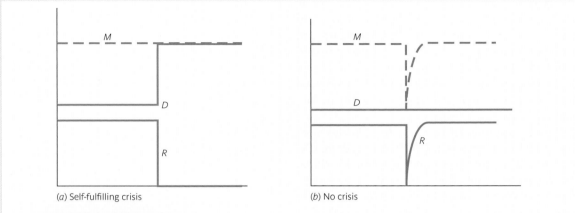

(a) Self-fulfilling crisis　　　　　　　　　　　　(b) No crisis

Fig. 19.9 Self-Fulfilling Crises

The central bank has a policy fully compatible with the maintenance of a fixed exchange rate: domestic credit is kept constant. If a crisis suddenly occurs, it can behave roughly in two ways. In panel (a), the market believes the central bank will attempt to offset losses of reserves in foreign exchange market interventions to keep the money supply, and the interest rate, unchanged. The attack and its consequences vindicate the markets' view that the central bank will cave in to pressure. In panel (b), instead, the market believes that the central bank is much less likely to increase domestic credit, so the money supply falls by the full amount of foreign exchange market interventions. The interest rate increases, which attracts capital from abroad and replenishes the stock of reserves. The central bank proves its mettle, reserves are not exhausted, and the crisis does not occur. The aftermath for the real economy may, however, be quite painful.

In contrast, there exist other descriptions of currency crises of a very different nature. Second- and third-generation crises share a common feature: they are **self-fulfilling**. They do not have to occur, but they do so, once it is expected that they will. The reasoning may sound circular, and it is. A simple variant of the previous example illustrates starkly how crises can be self-fulfilling. The central bank is now assumed to keep domestic credit D constant. The exchange rate peg is credible, as it should be—no one expects the exchange rate to change and the interest rate parity conditions indicate that the interest rate is constant. The demand for money is therefore also constant, as is the stock of foreign exchange reserves. The situation appears perfectly stable and could have gone on forever, were it not for a sudden loss of confidence in the domestic currency, for reasons that are soon to be discussed. If such an exogenous loss of confidence occurs, domestic money is sold and the central bank is forced to spend its foreign exchange reserves to uphold the exchange rate peg. In the two panels of Figure 19.9

we assume that the resulting attacks exhaust the remainder of the central bank's reserves.

The crucial link in the chain of events is the market's expectation of the central bank reaction to the exogenous attack. If market participants anticipate that the central bank will maintain the money supply at its previous level by creating sufficient domestic credit, then the crisis will be vindicated *ex post*. This outcome is shown in panel (a). The money supply remains constant, but the central bank has lost its reserves and is unable to maintain a fixed exchange rate. There is, however, an alternative outcome. If the central bank does not increase domestic credit, the money supply contracts by the full amount of the attack, as seen in panel (b). In that case, the interest rate increases sharply. This makes domestic assets attractive to international investors, capital promptly flows back in and reserves are quickly replenished. The attack fails. If market participants are convinced that this is the case, an attack is pointless, and will not occur. Both outcomes are equally possible, both are in equilibrium.

To summarize, if the market expects the central bank not to 'give in' to an attack by relaxing monetary conditions, it will expect the interest rate to rise after the attack, and there can be no attack.[22] If, on the other side, the market correctly anticipates that the central bank will not let the interest rate rise, or at least not enough to attract a sufficient capital inflow, then any attack will be justified *ex post* by central bank behaviour. The attack is entirely self-fulfilling: it occurs because it is expected to succeed, even though pre-attack monetary policy was fully compatible with the fixed exchange rate regime. Reserves were not declining and the regime could have been maintained forever. The weakness does not lie in *observed* policies but in the *expected* central bank reaction.

Central to this story is the behaviour of the central bank when the attack takes place. Why should it ever behave as in panel (*a*), a clearly less desirable reaction than the one depicted in panel (*b*)? Herein lies the true explanation of self-fulfilling attacks: the central bank must fear the consequences of a sudden increase in the interest rate. Raising the interest rate is never free but, given the catastrophic consequences of a crisis, the cost of doing so must be even more forbidding. For that to be the case, there must pre-exist some **vulnerability** that makes the interest rate defence unappealing. Two broad categories of vulnerabilities have been identified.

Second-generation of crises: Macroeconomic vulnerabilities

A good example of second-generation crises is the presence of high unemployment. A restrictive monetary policy is bound to worsen an already bad situation, to the point where the markets calculate that the central bank will prefer to let the exchange rate go. Another example may be a stock market that is perceived to be too high and at risk of crashing. A sharp increase in the interest rate lowers stock prices (see Chapter 14) and could tip the whole market into an uncontrolled free-fall. Examples of second-generation crises include Sweden in 1992, Mexico in 1995, and Argentina in 2001.

Third-generation of crises: Balance-sheet vulnerabilities

A good example is the case of a highly indebted government, with a debt that is indexed to the interest rate. With debt service already high, a sharp increase in the interest rate raises debt service, increases the overall budget deficit, and sends the debt even higher, possibly to levels deemed unsustainable. More generally, when the government, banks, or firms have on their balance sheets liabilities which are indexed or in foreign currency, they are extremely vulnerable, and this is bound to sap the central bank's resolve. Much the same applies. The East Asian crises of 1997–1998, described in Box 19.3, provide examples of third-generation crises.

The upshot is that self-fulfilling attacks can occur, but only if some underlying vulnerabilities exist already. The vulnerability is not lethal, as in first-generation crises, but when combined with an attack, it makes the cost of a defence of the exchange regime unacceptably high. The existence of a vulnerability is not a guarantee that an attack will occur; it may or it may not, and if it does, it will succeed.

Self-fulfilling crises underline the importance of central bank credibility, a concept studied in Chapter 16. Even in the pre-existence of a vulnerability, a central bank may decide to resist any challenge to the existing regime, as in panel (*b*) of Figure 19.9. If its determination is known, then there will be no attack. On the other side, a decline in central bank credibility may trigger an attack. The attack may succeed if the central bank's resolve has indeed declined, but it may fail if the perception was erroneous.[23] What is not clear is what triggers

---

[22] This is especially true when one considers that many 'one-way speculators' often operate with near zero capital. The speculator borrows domestic money at the domestic rate and purchases foreign exchange at the rate believed to be overvalued, and then invests it at the foreign interest rate. When the attack comes, the debt is paid off using part of the capital gain. Nothing scares such a speculator more than a sudden rise in domestic interest rates because that means painfully higher refinancing costs and often financial ruin. *Sic semper mercatoribus!*

[23] Note that the reasoning assumes that markets are behaving rationally. This stands in contrast with frequent explanations that appeal to unspecified 'psychological factors', hinting that markets behave irrationally. While not ruling this out, as economists, we prefer to avoid explanations which lie outside our purview, even if this has its costs.

Box 19.3 The South-East Asian Crisis of 1997–1998

In June 1997, pressure started to build on the baht, the Thai currency. On 2 July, the Bank of Thailand abandoned its peg, which was followed by an immediate 20% depreciation. Speculation immediately turned to the Philippines peso and to the Malaysian ringitt. The peso was allowed to float (within bands) on 11 July, the ringitt on 14 July. Next in the eye of the storm, the Indonesian rupiah too was left to float on 14 August. By mid-October, bowing to months of pressure, Vietnam widened the band of fluctuation of the dong, and the Taiwan dollar was devalued. Brazil and Argentina started to feel the pressure at the end of October, while the Bank of Korea started to intervene heavily in defence of the won. When it had to give up on 17 November, the won promptly fell by 10%, which triggered a new wave of attacks against the other currencies in the region (Figure 19.10). Stability finally returned when, following the other crisis countries, Korea reached an agreement with the IMF on 3 December, involving the largest ever loan. A conspicuous exception was Indonesia, where a political crisis was under way. The ringitt continued to collapse until President Suharto resigned in late May 1998. By then the ringitt had shed 75% of its initial value.

the attack, and why it occurs in some vulnerable countries and not in others. All that is needed, it seems, is for some smouldering embers to fall on the powder keg.

19.4.4 Contagion

The striking spread of exchange crises in 1997–1998 has rekindled interest in the **contagion** phenomenon. A number of observers have rushed to the conclusion that markets are too erratic to be left on their own and ought to be regulated.[24] The principles developed above provide three reasons for contagion. A good illustration is offered by the Asian crisis of 1997–1998, which is described in more detail in Box 19.3.

First-generation contagion: Competitiveness

The Asian Tigers trade among themselves and export broadly similar goods to the developed countries. So, when the baht, the currency of Thailand, fell by 20%, the neighbouring Tigers lost a few teeth and claws. To recover the earlier competitiveness, they would need a painful decline of local currency prices and compressed profits, or an exchange rate depreciation. Thus trade competition works as a natural channel for contagion. This story is remarkably similar to the inter-war period described in Section 19.2.3.

[24] The issue of capital controls, and of the Tobin tax, is taken up in Section 19.5.2 below.

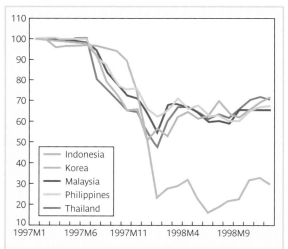

Fig. 19.10 Currency in Crisis (index 100 = January 1997)

The Thai currency was the first to fall in June 1997. The other Asian currencies soon followed, a spectacular case of contagion. When the dust settled, most currencies had lost one-third of their initial value, the Indonesia ringitt being down by 70%.

Source: IMF.

Second- and third-generation contagion: Learning to know central banks and vulnerabilities

Self-fulfilling crises can occur if doubts persist about a central bank's resolve in the event of a crisis. The collapse of the baht and of the fixed exchange regime in Thailand made two points. First, it was readily apparent that banks and firms had borrowed huge sums of dollars, and that the banking system was weak. This made the country vulnerable to a depreciation, since many banks and firms would become bankrupt as dollar liabilities would sharply increase in local currency terms. Furthermore, the central bank was prevented from vigorously defending the baht, as high interest rates would induce loan defaults and similarly damage the banking system. Early reports indicated that the situation was similar elsewhere in the region.

Second, the Bank of Thailand was not in a position to resist the pressure. Having liberalized its financial account, it faced a massive exit of capital that had flowed in during the years of fast growth. Other countries in East Asia were in similar, if not identical, positions. Thus a self-fulfilling crisis, long ruled out on the basis of the remarkable growth performance of the Asian Tigers, became distinctly possible. The Thai crisis provided the trigger.

Three features of this process are remarkable.

* 'Cheap talk' and 'life as usual' before the crisis. Local and international investors who know the situation are aware of both the vulnerability and limited resolve of the central bank. They are concerned, but no one moves, since moving alone would achieve nothing.

* Herd behaviour when the crisis hits. When the first spark flies, previously concerned investors see their worst fears confirmed. They do not wait to see how events unfold, they make the event by withdrawing their funds in a state of panic.

* 'I told you so', after the crisis. Once the crisis has occurred, the vulnerability that seemed, and was, benign *ex ante* becomes conventional wisdom.

International investors' duress

Many international investors were clearly surprised by the Thai crisis, and suffered losses as they engaged in fire sales, selling their local assets at any price. For a number of reasons, their best next reaction is to move out of other similar countries, thus spreading the virus.

Many financial institutions, like pension funds and insurance companies, are limited in their holdings of risky assets in their portfolios. When Thailand fell, Asian assets previously considered safe were suddenly considered riskier by rating agencies, and dumped *en masse* by institutional investors.[25]

Individual asset managers are rewarded for doing better than the market. Most lost heavily in Thailand. Elementary prudence encouraged them to avoid the risk of future losses by promptly moving out of the region.

The other investors, observing their colleagues' behaviour, come to suspect that they do not know the full story and that things are far worse than they thought. They too rush for the exit door.

19.4.5 Supervision

One conclusion from our post-mortem of the Asian crisis is that where there is smoke there is fire, but that fire may range from an innocuous cigarette in an ashtray to the stove burning out of control. Do you call the fire department (the IMF) in every case? To extend this metaphor: in the former case, there is no 'fundamental' reason for a speculative attack, but under certain conditions, speculative attacks can still occur, and are a surprise (unlike crises of the first generation, which are bound to occur). Could more supervision have helped? One noteworthy and surprising aspect of the Asian crisis was the extent to which sovereign governments were *not* direct contributors to the crisis. A cursory examination of the Tiger economies confirms that fiscal policy was prudent if not tight, monetary policy was under control, and the IMF evidently shared this view.

The big mistake Asian governments and central banks seem to have made was to guarantee dollar loans made by foreign banks to local private sector entities. By doing this, governments reduced the true level of foreign exchange reserves available for intervention, and wrote a blank cheque for bad lending by international banks. This also rendered their pristine fiscal positions a poor indicator of their true financial strength in a crisis. In any case,

---

[25] The major rating agencies have been blamed for not foretelling the Asian crisis and hurriedly downgrading regional assets.

the world financial system was sailing in un-charted waters, and it was not clear what kind of supervision, if any, could avoid similar problems in the future.

Lacking an international bank supervisory agency, it seems that the best stop-gap solution to pro-blems of financial architecture is to open the door a little bit wider, publish even more information—and do it on the internet—making it a bit more difficult for situations such as East Asia in the 1990s to arise. In any case, it is unreasonable to expect the private sector to help much in this regard. One characteristic of asset traders is their strategic dis-incentive to disclose bad news, especially if its truth is not 100% guaranteed. Better to sit on negative information and wait and see. Disclosing it can make one the laughing stock of the market. In con-trast, disclosing good news can never hurt—after one has taken the positive position in the asset, of course.

19.5 The Choice of an Exchange Rate Regime

Ever since the end of the gold standard, policy-makers and economists have debated the choice of an exchange rate regime. The choice was perceived to be between fixed-but-adjustable exchange rates Bretton Woods style, or more or less freely floating rates. Fashions have come and gone, from Bretton Woods to Jamaica. Nowadays the pendulum seems to have swung back to a revival of pseudo-gold standard arrangements (monetary unions, currency boards, dollarization) which rely largely on the Hume mechanism. Prompted by the globalization phenomenon and recent crises, the debate has also raised the old question of the desirability of capital liberalization. In this section we review the old debate and move on to the more recent ideas.

19.5.1 The Old Debate: Fixed versus Flexible Exchange Rates

The case for flexible exchange rates

Two arguments favour flexible rates, and two crit-icize the case for fixed rates. They boil down to the view that it is better to leave the exchange rate to the markets than to the authorities.

Exchange rate changes are needed to compensate for inflation differentials (the PPP principle). Fixed exchange rates can only be adjusted sporadically, which leaves long periods when they are mis-aligned. In addition, such realignments are easily predictable and lead to speculative attacks.

Exchange rate changes are also needed to cope with shocks which alter external competitiveness, e.g. changing energy prices, the emergence of new competitors, etc. With a fixed exchange rate re-gime, either all prices have to adjust, or the exchange rate must be changed. With wage and price rigidity as a fact of life, the first solution can be protracted and painful, possibly requiring pressure on wages and prices to be brought about by the Phillips curve mechanism, i.e. unemployment.[26]

The case against fixed exchange rates is essen-tially as follows.

(1) We do not know with much precision what the equilibrium value of the exchange rate should be. Policy mistakes are likely to arise from ignor-ance, or from misguided political motivations.

(2) Fixed exchange rates are vulnerable to crises. As noted in Section 19.4.4, only those countries with impeccable credentials (no vulnerability, a highly credible central bank) may consider

---

[26] In a famous metaphor, a key proponent of flexible rates, Chicago economist and Nobel Prize winner Milton Friedman noted that the shift to summer time can be achieved by having everyone adapt behaviour and do the same things an hour earlier, or by moving the clock ahead by one hour. The latter is much easier, he argued, than changing the habits of millions of people. Changing the exchange rate is easier than changing millions of prices.

themselves immune to speculative attacks. All the others may be subject to a crisis, first, second, or third generation, with devastating consequences.

The list of cases of exchange rate mismanagement is impressive. It starts with Britain's painful return to an obviously overvalued pre-First World War gold parity in 1925, to the dollar overvaluation that preceded the collapse of the Bretton Woods system, to numerous cases where thriving black markets indicate that the official parity is off the mark. More recent cases include the decisions of Italy and the UK to leave the European fixed exchange rate mechanism, the Asian crisis, and several crises in Latin America.

The case for fixed exchange rates

This is really a case against flexible rates, and against the view that markets do a better job than the authorities. The case is built on the observation that flexible exchange rates tend to fluctuate widely, too widely to be explained by inflation differentials or real disturbances. Two explanations are usually offered, which are not mutually exclusive.

(1) Overshooting implies that the exchange rate tends to move away from its equilibrium level.

(2) Exchange markets deal with considerable uncertainty with large payoffs when betting right, and large losses when wrong. This leads markets to move in fits and starts, imparting additional uncertainty and instability to the economy.

For good or bad reasons, most European countries have demonstrated a keen attachment to exchange rate stability since 1945. The fear has always been that exchange rate volatility would hurt intra-European trade and threaten the Common Market. The decision to create a monetary union may be seen as the last step in continuous efforts at keeping intra-European exchange rates stable.

19.5.2 The New Debate: Financial Liberalization

Capital controls: The pros and the cons

The process of financial integration, which began in the 1980s and accelerated in the 1990s, has become controversial, if only because it has been linked to the wave of currency crises in the emerging markets. One after another, developed and then developing countries have dismantled capital controls which were put in place at the end of the Second World War, and sometimes long before. The restrictions can take a variety of forms: (1) outright prohibitions of export or import of money and other financial instruments, (2) limits on such transfers, (3) dual exchange markets (one fixed, for commercial transactions, one flexible for financial transactions), and, more recently, (4) the Tobin tax which is described in Box 19.4. While capital controls are highly controversial, the principles involved are quite straightforward.

Critics of capital controls argue that restrictions to the free movement of capital prevent savers from getting the best available returns, and prevent firms from borrowing on the best possible terms. Saving and investment both suffer, with adverse effects on long-term growth. They further observe that, by isolating its domestic financial markets, a government can 'milk' them to finance its own budget deficits at costs lower than the international capital market would offer. Furthermore, when capital controls are effective, national interest rates cease to reflect the local economic situation. Since high and rising interest rates signal a worsening situation, they tend to discipline imprudent governments. Shutting down the signal offers relief to governments, but at the cost of a worsening situation in the future, possibly leading to a crisis on the way.

Those in favour of capital controls present three main arguments. First, following on an argument initially spelled out by Keynes, they claim that financial markets are unstable, prone to fads and panics. The result is volatility that is unjustified by underlying economic fundamentals, and is costly to firms and households.

Second, following on the Mundell–Fleming result that full capital mobility prevents the use of monetary policy under fixed exchange rates, and makes fiscal policy impotent under flexible rates, they argue that restricting capital mobility restores the option of using demand management instruments. When applied to monetary policy, this principle is

Box 19.4 The Tobin Tax

Back in 1972, James Tobin, a Yale economist and Nobel Prize laureate, proposed to 'throw sand in the wheels of international finance'. He identified two main objectives, reducing exchange rate volatility and preserving the autonomy of macroeconomic policy (see the main text for the argument), and concluded that restraining capital movements was a worthy effort. The proposal was not well received. As Tobin recalls, 'It did not make much of a ripple. In fact, one might say that it sank . . . I realize that I am opposed by a powerful tide. A widespread orthodoxy holds that financial markets know best, that the discipline they exert on central banks and governments is salubrious.' (Tobin 1996.)

Tobin claimed that capital movements ought to be slowed down. He was not in favour of the market-unfriendly, administrative restrictions in use at the time. He observed that the vast majority of foreign transactions involve round trips of seven days or less, speculative money which serves no investment or saving purpose. He argued that a single flat tax on every foreign exchange market transaction of very small size would deter the unproductive short-term trips without much affecting long-term capital movements which underlie productive foreign investment. Why? Investors compare the returns from any deal to the returns from holding safe

assets, such as government bonds. To do so, they compute profits and losses from any transaction in annualized terms. For example, a small tax of 0.1% per transaction implies a total cost of 0.2% for a round trip (invest, earn your profit, and bring it back). If the trip takes a year, it means an annualized cost of 0.2%. If the trip lasts less, say half a year, the annualized value of the tax about doubles (the law of compounding applies, so it is a bit more but negligibly so). As the horizon shortens, the annualized tax becomes very high, e.g. 10.9% on a week-long trip (see Table 19.4). Conversely, on very long-term investments, the tax becomes negligible.

Recently, the tax has undergone a revival among both serious economists and anti-globalization demonstrators. One of the new motivations is the tax revenue that its proponents expect, e.g. $300 billion annually with a 0.1% tax. Being an international tax, it could be used for international purposes: the UN and its agencies, NGOs, etc. It is felt, however, that should a Tobin tax be imposed, its yield would be many times smaller because the markets will organize themselves to minimize the volume of transactions, and also because they would migrate to safe havens—most likely a computer-laden ship in international waters.

Table 19.4 The Impact of a 0.1% Tobin Tax and the Holding Period of Investments

Holding period of investment	1 day	2 days	1 week	1 month	6 months	1 year	5 years
Implicit tax (annualized basis)	55.2%	24.6%	10.9%	2.4%	0.4%	0.2%	0.04%

the impossible trilogy already discussed in Section 19.2.4.

Third, saving is a source of growth if it is invested in productive uses such as plants, machinery, schooling and training, etc. The proponents of capital controls note that the bulk of international capital movements are of a very short-term nature, even aimed at intraday trading opportunities, rather than long-term investment in human or physical capital.

The link with exchange rate regimes

The macroeconomic policy independence argument has a direct bearing on the debate on the choice of an exchange rate regime. The main weakness of fixed exchange rate regimes under full capital mobility is that in most cases they require the abandonment of an independent monetary policy. It requires some discipline for central bankers to give up any hope of influencing local monetary conditions, and few central banks have lived up to the requirement.[27] As a result, fixed exchange rate regimes are prone to speculative crises and have shown rather limited survival ability.

The argument can be turned on its head, however. A direct implication of the impossible trilogy principle is that fixed exchange rate regimes are more likely to survive when capital controls are in place. A good example is Europe's EMS. It operated reasonably well in the 1980s until capital controls were removed by 1990. The system was badly shaken shortly thereafter in 1992. Thus the choice is not just between fixed and flexible exchange rates, but also involves the capital mobility regime. Countries which value exchange rate stability should not rule out restrictions on capital movements altogether. Similarly, countries which favour full capital mobility should not stick to a fixed exchange rate regime for too long. The question of fixed versus flexible exchange rates has become central to the accession process of transition countries, and it is reviewed in Box 19.5.

However, if full capital mobility is considered an inexorable evolution of economic relations, the fixed exchange rate option may be going the way of the hula hoop and bell-bottomed pants. The impossible trilogy means that monetary policy autonomy must be sacrificed, but few countries are prepared for such a step that may be difficult to defend on the domestic political front. Furthermore, the phenomenon of second-generation crises suggests that it may take years, possibly decades, before the central bank has achieved a level of credibility which eliminates vulnerabilities. In the meantime, the threat of currency crises looms large. The **hollowing-out hypothesis** maintains that the choice of exchange rate regimes is no longer between floating rates and soft pegs—the traditional fixed-and-adjustable exchange rates—but between floating rates and hard pegs (regimes described in the next section). Critics of the hollowing-out hypothesis argue that soft pegs are still feasible, provided bands of fluctuations are large enough or the peg is allowed to vary (e.g. crawling pegs) to account for changing economic conditions.

Optimal sequencing

Back in the early 1950s, nearly all countries operated in strictly controlled environments. Many prices were fixed, some goods were even rationed, commercial banks were heavily regulated, and financial markets were limited or non-existent. External controls regulated exports and imports, tariffs were heavy, and capital flows were essentially forbidden. What a difference half a century can make! Liberalization seems an inescapable trend, and basic economic principles support this trend. On the other hand, liberalization has not always been an easy journey. The Asian crisis once more showed that there can be serious setbacks on the way. Is there a better way of liberalizing? The response is to adopt a proper **sequencing** of liberalization. McKinnon[28] has proposed an optimal order of sequencing. It is based on two main ideas. First, liberalization should start with the restrictions that are costliest in terms of economic efficiency. Second, some steps need to be taken before others to avoid inconsistencies.

The first step should be the creation of well-functioning domestic goods markets: free prices and abolish rationing. It makes little sense to have free external trade if domestic trade is heavily constrained.

The second step should be the gradual liberalization of international trade, starting with administrative measures (quotas on exports and imports), moving on to eliminating export tariffs, and then finally reducing import tariffs to avoid shocks to domestic producers.

Soon after the first step, the domestic financial sector should be liberalized, under competitive conditions. Banks should be allowed to set interest rates freely on deposits and loans, to open branches as they see fit, and to choose the range of services that they offer their customers. Bank regulation and supervision should be developed in parallel to ensure the soundness of the banking system.

---

[27] One excellent example is the central bank of the Netherlands after the mid–1980s, which almost dogmatically tracked German monetary policy until monetary union was implemented.

[28] Ronald McKinnon, a Stanford economist, has also contributed to the theory of optimum currency areas.

Box 19.5 Exchange Rate Regimes in the New EU Member Countries

The ten countries that joined the European Union (EU) in 2004 and the two countries that joined in 2007 are committed to adopt the euro as their own currencies as soon as possible. Meanwhile, they are pledged to join the ERM (see Section 19.2.4), i.e. to peg their currencies to the euro. As Table 19.5 shows, seven of them promptly joined the ERM, and four of them have adopted the euro. The three remaining countries are the Baltic states, which have expressed their desire to join the euro area. Lithuania actually applied in 2007 but entry was refused because it did not fulfil all the required conditions. Yet, Lithunia and Estonia have rigidly fixed their exchange rate to the DM first, and the euro next, for more than a decade. Their currency board arrangements (described below) make them *de facto* members of the euro area. Bulgaria is also trying to hitch its monetary fate to the euro, adopting a similar currency board regime.

The three larger new EU members, the Czech Republic, Hungary, and Poland, have not yet joined the ERM, and allow their exchange rates to float more or less. With current inflation rates often much higher than in the euro area and occasional budgetary problems, their chances of being admitted to the monetary union are rather slim in the near term.

Some older EU members have not adopted the euro. Two of them, Denmark and the UK, have been given an 'opt-out' clause, which gives them their right to do so. Denmark decided to join the ERM when the euro was launched in 1999, even though it is not pledged to it either. While Sweden does not have an opt-out clause, it behaves as if it does. Sweden and the UK, therefore, operate a fully floating exchange rate regime and have no plan to change policy. There are occasional discussions in Denmark regarding euro area membership, which would have to be approved by a referendum.

 Table 19.5 Situation of Recent EU Members and Non-Euro Area Members

	EU membership	ERM membership	Euro adoption
Bulgaria	2007	No	No
Cyprus	2004	2005	2008
Czech Republic	2004	No	No
Denmark	1973	1999	Opt-out
Estonia	2004	2004	No
Hungary	2004	No	No
Latvia	2004	2005	No
Lithuania	2004	2004	No
Malta	2004	2005	2008
Poland	2004	No	No
Romania	2007	No	No
Slovakia	2004	2005	2009
Slovenia	2004	2004	2008
Sweden	1995	No	No
UK	1973	Opt-out	Opt-out

Domestic financial markets come next. Bonds and stock markets are allowed to compete with the banking system to both collect savings and finance borrowing by firms and public entities. Here again, regulation and supervision must proceed in parallel to guarantee a proper functioning of naturally unstable markets.

External financial liberalization comes next. The Asian crisis well illustrates the risks of full capital mobility when the domestic financial sector is not functioning properly. Furthermore, the exchange regime must be appropriately adapted to changing circumstances, as rigidly fixed exchange rates are unlikely to survive capital mobility when full capital mobility is established.

19.5.3 Monetary Unions, Currency Boards, and Dollarization

The menu of exchange rate regimes has recently been enlarged. A number of countries have adopted new arrangements which were once regarded as curiosities. These 'hard pegs' differ from the soft pegs by the fact that they do not allow margins of fluctuations and that they rule out realignments

Box 19.6 The *N* – 1 Problem

Take *N* countries with *N* currencies. There are *N* – 1 independent bilateral exchange rates, as Figure 19.11 illustrates. All the other bilateral rates can be retrieved from these *N* – 1 rates via triangular arbitrage. Now link these currencies together, either in a monetary union or just a system of fixed exchange rates. As *N* – 1 independent bilateral exchange rates are frozen, *N* – 1 central banks lose their independence, and the *N*th remains free of policy constraints. In the Bretton Woods system, all central banks were pegged to the US dollar, leaving the Fed with the task of pegging the dollar to gold. In the EMS, no *N*th country was designated, but the Bundesbank captured the *N*th degree of freedom. In a monetary union, such as EMU, all *N* central banks lose their policy-making autonomy and a new central bank is created to manage the new currency.

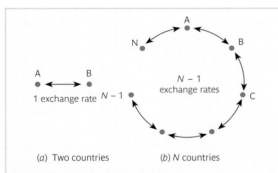

(a) Two countries   (b) N countries

Fig. 19.11 The *N* – 1 Problem

Two countries which decide to fix their exchange rate lose one degree of freedom. When *N* countries form a fixed exchange rate system, they commit *N* – 1 exchange rates, or *N* – 1 degrees of freedom (all the bilateral exchange rates can be calculated from just the *N* – 1 rates shown in panel (b): all the missing arrows can be drawn).

(devaluations or revaluations). Hume's mechanism has made a comeback by eliminating discretionary monetary policy entirely and reducing central banks to the role of passive *bureaux de change*. Three varieties of hard pegs have been observed which are worth noting: (1) monetary unions, (2) dollarization and euroization, and (3) currency boards.

Monetary unions

A monetary union involves the irrevocable fixing of exchange rates and the abandonment of margins of fluctuation among a number of countries. In fact,

it means that individual currencies are no longer distinguishable; a common currency may be substituted. The immediate implication is that individual central banks lose any remaining autonomy, although one central bank is needed to manage the common currency. This is a special case of the ***N*–1 problem** spelled out in Box 19.6. The union's central bank manages the overall money supply. Interest rates are the same across the union since money can flow freely. National money supplies are then determined entirely through the Hume mechanism.[29] If a country runs a balance of payments surplus, money is flowing in and the national money supply rises. A deficit results in a loss of money supply.

It might seem strange for independent countries to give up their currencies. In fact, it is the logical consequence of the impossible trinity: with full capital mobility, fixed exchange rates imply the loss of monetary policy autonomy. Yet, the threat of currency crises remains. The only way to eliminate that threat is to eliminate the currencies themselves. Since there is no real policy autonomy to lose, the system can only be strengthened. At the same time, however, there are costs of a monetary

---

[29] It should be noted that the mechanism described here is somewhat more general than Hume's in the following sense: an expansion of the money supply need not require a trade surplus, but could also be achieved with a capital account surplus (an excess of private capital flows).

Box 19.7 **Optimum Currency Area Theory**

A region constitutes an optimum currency area when its use of a common currency implies no loss of welfare.[30] The best way of thinking about it is to ask what is lost when the exchange rate instrument is abandoned. This becomes problematic when the union is buffeted by asymmetric shocks, i.e. shocks which hurt some members but not the others, for this is when the exchange rate is useful. Adjustment to asymmetric shocks must now take place through prices, which can be very painful. The theory looks for criteria which makes this adjustment unnecessary. Two main criteria have been suggested.

Factor mobility. Consider the case when an adverse shock, e.g. a loss of competitiveness, hits a country. The country soon goes into a recession, and laments the loss of its exchange rate, which could have been handy to restore its external competitiveness. If, however, its factors of production could move out to more fortunate members of the monetary union, the pain would be spread out, and the common central bank could use the common external exchange rate to adjust optimally. If capital or labour, or both, are mobile, there would be little cost in unemployment of factors, and the loss of internal (within the union) exchange rates would be trivial.

Absence of asymmetric shocks. Most of the shocks concern the world demand for and supply (competitiveness) of locally produced goods. If the members of the union produce a similar menu of goods, then the likelihood of asymmetric shocks diminishes. The same applies if the member countries produce a very diversified menu of goods. In that case a particular shock is likely to be of little import.

union. Giving up monetary or exchange rate policy has its own consequences. In the end, it depends on the company a country chooses. The theory of **optimum currency areas** spells out criteria for creating a monetary union and is presented in Box 19.7.

The wave of capital account liberalization, when combined with the attachment of some countries to exchange rate stability, makes it attractive to move from a soft peg to a hard peg, hence the renewed appeal of monetary unions. Europe has adopted this scheme, which is described in the WebAppendix. Previously, monetary unions had been established in French-speaking Africa and in the Caribbean Islands. Some think that this is the world's future.

Dollarization and euroization

Dollarization is the unilateral adoption by a country of the US dollar as sole legal tender, which can be thought of as a one-sided monetary union with the USA. It can involve the link to another currency, e.g. the euro. It is as close to the gold standard as a monetary system can be, without having gold itself circulate. It functions in the same way, including Hume's mechanism. It is another variety of hard pegs.

A number of countries never had their own currency. Panama and Liberia have been dollarized since their independence. Ecuador and El Salvador adopted the dollar in 2000 and 2001, respectively. Argentina flirted with the idea in 1999. Kosovo has euroized. One reason for dollarizing is the perception that a foreign central bank will do a better job at enforcing price stability than an indigenous one. Another reason is a proven inability to come to grips with inflation, as in the case of Ecuador. If trade links with the country whose currency is adopted are intensive, it seems like a good idea. It remains, however, that the interest rate is driven by foreign economic conditions, which may be awkward.

Currency boards

Currency boards used to be the arrangement of choice in the British Empire. They have made a comeback, starting with Hong Kong in 1983, followed by Argentina in 1991, Estonia in 1992, Lithuania in 1994, and Bulgaria and Bosnia-Herzegovina in

[30] The seminal work on optimum currency areas is by Robert Mundell, the same economist who shaped the Mundell–Fleming framework presented in Chapter 11.

1997. Currency boards resemble dollarization, except that the local currency is maintained. There are three key features of a currency board.

(1) A fixed exchange rate is established *vis-à-vis* an anchor currency. The local currency is fully convertible into the anchor currency at that rate, with no limit.

(2) The local currency is fully backed by reserves. This is required to ensure full and unlimited convertibility.

(3) Currency boards often hold reserves of 105% or 110% of their liabilities, a precaution since most money is produced by commercial banks which are not restricted to 100% backing. In practice, it means that the high-powered money supply is entirely driven by the balance of payments via Hume's mechanism. Monetary authorities are completely passive.

With the exception of Hong Kong, currency boards have usually been adopted by countries that have long suffered high inflation and felt that there was no political will to establish a full-blown independent central bank dedicated to price stability. One transition country, Estonia, started off with a currency board, and its success at avoiding inflation has inspired Lithuania and Bulgaria.

 Box 19.8 Charlemagne's European Monetary Union

One of the most interesting attempts to use monetary union as an instrument of political union was by the first Carolingian king, Charlemagne. In his quest to unify Europe, Charlemagne was not loathe to employ the sword, but understood the importance of a single, harmonized currency for the promotion of commerce and trade. At the Council of Frankfurt in 794—which was ostensibly about religious matters—a supposed minor detail was also on the table. Charlemagne, who was fascinated by economic affairs, saw the advantage of a common *standard* for coinage in the conquered territories of Spain and Southern and Central Europe. Even if the conversion of precious metal into coins was decentralized, it would be advantageous to use a single definition and metal content for those coins. Apparently, Charlemagne also understood that sticking to the gold standard could have deflationary consequences; gold was so rare at the time that trade using gold was impractical for all but the most valuable transactions.

So the gold *sou* was replaced by the silver *livre carolinienne* (which eventually became the pound!). It was worth 240 of the denarius (penny), which might have been inspired by the contemporaneous success of the Islamic dinar. Common currency, with common standards, enlarged the trading area and reduced transactions costs. Furthermore, the new currency was legal tender:

Everywhere, in every city and every trading place, the new denarii are also to be legal tender and to be accepted by everybody. And if they bear the monogram of our name and are of pure silver and full weight, should anyone reject, in any place, in any transaction of purchase or sale, he is to pay 15 soldi [roughly the price of a cart load of wheat]. (Article 5 of the protocol of the Council of Frankfurt.)

After Charlemagne died, his realm was partitioned among his sons and the political union of Europe soon dissolved into the Middle Ages. Obviously, monetary union was not a sufficient condition for the political unification of Europe, but it did sustain the economy of the Carolingian empire for a number of centuries. Later, the Edict of Pitres in 864 (during the reign of Charles the Bald) would tighten the grip on seigniorage rights, significantly restricting the number of authorized coinage sites. Perhaps the wisdom of Charlemagne was undermined by the greed of his grandson?

A coin of Charlemagne.

Charlemagne (left) and Pippin the Hunchback.

19.5.4 The European Monetary Union

We conclude this chapter with the European Monetary Union. This unique arrangement has existed since 1999, and euro coins and banknotes have circulated in the 'euro area' since 2002. The European Monetary Union is an important and growing component of the global financial architecture. Starting with 11 countries, by 2009 16 countries with a population of more than 300 million—the human equivalent of the USA—share the same currency. More and more European nations have chosen to use the euro, or peg their currencies to the euro. The waiting list continues to grow as the new EU members want to get on board. The role of the euro in international payments is well established and will probably grow over time.

Many economists were, and still are, sceptical that a common money will indeed further the cause of European integration. This is because, at the outset, Europe didn't seem to meet the requirements put forth by Mundell and described in Box 19.6.[31] By most accounts, Europe is still far from achieving the status of an integrated single economic region such as the states of the USA, or the provinces of Canada, or Mexico, or Brazil. Yet ever since the founding of the Economic Community in 1957, Europeans have been fascinated by the notion that increasing integration was the secret to securing a lasting peace and preventing future armed conflict. Ironically, Europe has a chronic history of armed conflicts over the past two millennia, many of which coincided with or were followed by monetary unions. In particular, monetary union frequently coincided with the rise of new nation-states. Box 19.8 gives one example of an early attempt to institute a monetary union in Europe. It failed, yet it shared many of the motives of the euro—to create the fundamental conditions for greater peace and prosperity. It highlights how economic, political, and social progress in Europe was rough sailing at the outset. In times of growing globalization and international turbulence, the 'European project' may finally reach smoother waters as the continent comes to political and social terms with itself.

ⓘ Summary

1 International monetary arrangements initially arose from the need to provide international trade with an easy means of settling transborder payments. For centuries, both domestic and international trade was carried out using gold and silver. On the other hand, the famed gold standard lasted less than 40 years, from 1879 to 1914.

2 Taken literally, the gold standard implied a rigid monetary rule and a fixed exchange rate regime. By the Hume mechanism, a trade deficit caused a shrinking money supply, while a surplus meant an expanding money supply. Both processes act to equilibrate trade imbalances.

3 The evolution of the monetary system after the First World War can be seen as a series of *ad hoc* responses to international crises and system inadequacies. In particular, the Bretton Woods system was designed to avoid the competitive devaluations of the inter-war period by establishing a system of fixed exchange rates based on the US dollar's link to gold. Nevertheless, this 'gold exchange standard' was not a gold standard in the strict sense.

4 The collapse of the Bretton Woods system was due to the internal inconsistencies of a system that required increasing amounts of international reserves to be provided by the USA, which were, in theory, convertible into gold. Large US balance of payment deficits in the late 1960s created a dollar overhang of official external

---

[31] The influential economist Martin Feldstein stated in a widely-publicized article in 1997 that European Monetary Union could lead to civil war.

liabilities which far exceeded the USA's gold assets.

5 The IMF fulfils two main roles: (1) it exercises surveillance over member countries on a routine basis, and (2) it provides emergency assistance to countries which face balance of payments difficulties. Its loans are conditional on the adoption and implementation of programmes designed to cope with the source of payment imbalances.

6 Currency crises can be divided into two types. (1) First-generation crises occur when domestic policies are incompatible with the exchange rate peg. They are usually anticipated. (2) Second-generation crises are self-fulfilling. They afflict central banks which appear vulnerable or uncommitted to an exchange rate target, or which have not acquired sufficient credibility. They may occur under these conditions, but do not have to.

7 Currency crises seem to be contagious for three reasons: (1) first-generation contagion through loss of competitiveness; (2) second-generation contagion when markets discover similar vulnerabilities or lack of central bank commitment; and (3) investors' contagion when losses in one country prompt international players to withdraw from other countries which suddenly appear risky.

8 Capital liberalization brings about long-term benefits. But financial markets are prone to bouts of instability which may result in currency crises. In addition, full capital mobility severely restricts the ability to carry out macroeconomic policies (Mundell–Fleming).

9 The choice of an exchange rate regime involves various trade-offs. In the end, small, open economies may favour some degree of exchange rate stability, while larger countries may prefer to integrate themselves in the world economy at fluctuating real exchange rates.

10 The widespread shift to capital account liberalization has had the effect of sharpening the choice between floating and fixed exchange rates. Soft pegs are increasingly seen as dangerous, hence the fashion for hard pegs: monetary unions, currency boards, and dollarization.

🔑 Key Concepts

- **International Monetary Fund (IMF)**
- **gold standard**
- **bimetallism**
- **Gresham's law**
- **band of fluctuation**
- **Hume mechanism**
- **Bretton Woods conference**
- **gold exchange standard**
- **quota**
- **conditionality**
- **Triffin paradox**
- **Exchange Rate Mechanism (ERM)**
- **speculative attacks**
- **central parity; parity**

- **European Monetary Union (EMU)**
- **impossible trilogy**
- **special drawing rights (SDRs)**
- **boom-and-bust cycles**
- **first-, second-, and third-generation theories of speculative attacks**
- **self-fulfilling attacks**
- **vulnerabilities**
- **contagion**
- **hollowing-out hypothesis**
- **sequencing**
- $N - 1$ **problem**
- **optimum currency area**

❓ Exercises

1 Why can't beggar-thy-neighbour policies work? What is the difference with tariff wars?

2 Does the Hume mechanism work within a monetary union?

3 'Currency crises cannot be foreseen, markets attack as soon they expected a crisis.' Comment. In your answer, you may distinguish between first-generation and self-fulfilling crises.

4 Draw the implications of the $N - 1$ problem for the international monetary system and for regional exchange rate arrangements like the EMS.

5 Can self-fulfilling crises also affect the banking system?

6 'The developing countries cannot borrow in their own currencies. This puts them at permanent risk of a currency crisis.' Explain and comment.

➲ Essay Questions

1 The poorer countries regularly propose that the IMF issue more SDRs and that they be distributed mostly to the poorer countries to support their development. The richer countries refuse, contending that this would be inflationary. What is your view?

2 It has been said that the Bretton Woods system was doomed from its start. Explain why. Could its demise have been avoided? How?

3 Is a return to the gold standard feasible? Desirable?

4 The choice of an exchange rate regime is difficult. The European Monetary Union combines fixed exchange rates among its members with a floating exchange rate *vis-à-vis* the rest of the world. Does it square the circle?

5 Quotas and voting rights at the IMF have been changed in April 2008. The decision is presented in <www.imf.org>. How would you evaluate this change?

Epilogue 20

The ideas of economists and political philosophers, both when they are right and when they are wrong, are more powerful than is commonly understood. Indeed the world is ruled by little else. Practical men, who believe themselves to be quite exempt from any intellectual influences, are usually the slaves of some defunct economist.

J. M. Keynes

Throughout this book, we have emphasized the usefulness of macroeconomics as a tool for understanding and improving the way the world works. To this aim, we have presented a unified treatment of the field, and have downplayed the historical evolution of ideas over the years as well as important controversies, past and present, which have accompanied these ideas. Focusing on controversies can be fascinating, but it can also cloud the extent of agreement and common understanding, leaving the unsatisfactory impression that macroeconomics is too conflict-ridden to be of any practical use. Once the basic framework is well understood, it is both interesting and illuminating to track the field's intellectual history. In this concluding chapter we present a highly compressed survey of the major steps of the field's development, the key players, and the policy debates. Its emphasis is on the European scene.[1]

20.1 The Keynesian Revolution

John Maynard Keynes, 1883–1946

The birth of macroeconomics is conventionally associated with the publication in 1936 of Keynes' *General Theory of Employment, Interest and Money*. Its influence has been phenomenal. Some even claim that it changed more lives in the twentieth century than any other single work. Many factors explain this success.

The book came out towards the end of the Great Depression and can be seen as the response of economic research to challenges of the time. To contemporaries who had witnessed the rapid rise of mass unemployment, the classical laissez-faire view looked factually wrong and almost immoral. Others had already moved in the same direction, but Keynes brought together many apparently disparate themes. The idea that prices do not necessarily clear at full employment had been put forward by the British economist Robert Malthus (1766–1834).

Knut Wicksell (1851–1926) and his successors, who came to be known as the 'Stockholm School', had gone quite a long way towards what was to become the *IS* curve. Other economists—including Hjalmar Schacht, who single-handedly vanquished the German hyperinflation in 1923 and later went on to become Hitler's Finance Minister—had long advocated deficit spending on public works during the Great Depression. But Keynes' attack was unique in many ways. The *General Theory* proposed a wholly new concept of equilibrium, even though it took decades to fully decipher what it really meant. It was a combination of scholarly analysis, strident criticism, and practical policy recommendations that appealed to both theoreticians and policy-makers. Keynes did not just aim at fellow researchers. He frequently descended the ivory tower of academia to promote his ideas in the media, where his reputation as a brilliant and provocative polemicist was well established.

The truth is that Keynes was a man of many talents and, by 1936, of great experience as well. As a

---

[1] In preparing this chapter, we have benefited from very useful comments and suggestions from Charles Bean, Irwin Collier, Barry Eichengreen, Hans Genberg, Francesco Giavazzi, Guido Tabellini, and Jürgen von Hagen.

young economist during the First World War, he had worked in the UK Treasury, which he represented at the Versailles Peace Conference, until he resigned in a rather undiplomatic fashion. In *The Economic Consequences of the Peace*, he criticized the harsh reparations imposed on Germany, maintaining that it would be destabilized by the economic burden of the Treaty. His analysis turned out to be prophetic, and established his reputation among policy-makers. The book also strained Keynes' relations with British government circles until the Second World War. His strident criticism of Chancellor Winston Churchill's decision to return the pound to its pre-war parity did not help in this regard. Maynard, as his friends called him, was also a charismatic intellectual leader. He assembled a group of brilliant economists at Cambridge University who went on to dominate the profession in Britain and beyond.

One important message of the Keynesian revolution was that fiscal policy can be used to fight recessions, in particular when monetary policy is ineffective—either because expansionary monetary policy no longer lowers the nominal interest rate or when investment spending is depressed by bad 'animal spirits'. Deficit spending, as it was then called, was taken on board in many countries after the war, in effect becoming conventional wisdom. German-speaking countries too have been influenced by Keynesian ideas, but scepticism there has been present and, to this day, a large segment of the policy-making and academic establishments see them as dangerous. German reluctance towards Keynesianism is linked to the role that deficit finance had in the hyperinflation of 1922–1923. This mistrust of Keynesian policies has found its way, in a subdued form, in the monetary union's Stability and Growth Pact and in the statements of the European Central Bank (ECB), in which fiscal deficits tend to be seen as a source of concern rather than as a potential means of output stabilization. In most of Europe, though, Keynesian ideas are still alive, although their limits—described in Chapters 16 and 17—are generally well recognized.

Keynes' theory was not fully worked out. The *General Theory* is difficult to read, frequently lacks precision and can sometimes be downright confusing. It fell upon Keynes' disciples to dot the i's. Most of the effort was conducted in his native Britain and in the USA, with some important contributions from other countries, including that of the Polish economist Michal Kalecki (1899–1970), who had anticipated many of Keynes' ideas and went on to try to merge Keynesian and Marxist schools of thought.

Beyond clarifying Keynes' views, one task that his disciples had to grapple with was to reconcile the Keynesian construction with generally accepted theories. It soon emerged, indeed, that the attack on the 'classics', as Keynes labelled established neoclassical economics, was not at all general and rested on the assumption that the price level is constant. This assumption was acceptable in situations of low employment, like the Great Depression, but was seriously at odds with post-war economic conditions, characterized by full employment and, later on, rising inflation. The necessary reconciliation effort, the neoclassical synthesis introduced in Chapter 12, was carried out mostly in the USA, with Nobel Prize laureate Paul Samuelson (1915–) and his MIT colleagues at the forefront, but also by Keynes' colleague in Cambridge, John Hicks (1904–1989), and by Don Patinkin from Hebrew University in Jerusalem (1922–1995).

European macroeconomists were not particularly productive during this period, with a few notable exceptions. Some Swedish economists, under the leadership of Assar Lindbeck (1930–), and their Norwegian colleagues developed a small open economy version of the Keynesian model. Nobel laureates Jan Tinbergen, from the Netherlands, and James Meade (1907–1995), a student of Keynes' in Cambridge, also made major contributions in extending Keynes' framework to the small open economy case. The most innovative construction in the Keynesian tradition was the Mundell–Fleming model presented in Chapter 11. Its architects were Marcus Fleming (1911–1976), a British economist working in the International Monetary Fund, and Nobel laureate Robert Mundell (1932–), who was undoubtedly inspired by the smallness and openness of his native Canada and of Switzerland, where he lived for a time.

An important implication of Keynesian economics was that countries as a whole could be a research subject. Today, it is hard to believe that pre-Keynesian economics was mostly preoccupied with sectors and firms, and had little to say about questions such as growth or employment.[2] In fact, aggregate data, like GDP, the unemployment rate, or the consumer price index, were sporadically collected and seldom the subject of great research interest. The rise of Keynesian economics prompted a vigorous effort at developing the relevant concepts and assembling the data. This effort started in the late 1930s at a time when most of the leading economists were either in the USA or in Great Britain. Unsurprisingly, therefore, the main contributions were developed in these two countries, with early pioneers such as Simon Kuznets (1901–1985) from Columbia University and Richard Stone (1913–1991), a Keynes student from Cambridge, both of whom were eventually awarded the Nobel Prize for their work. Once data was available, and with the advent of the first computers, economists have undertaken to build large-scale models that were meant to mimic the economy. Following early work by Italian-born Nobel Prize laureate Franco Modigliani, these large models have become standard fares in most finance ministries, international organizations, and economic forecasting companies, where they are routinely used to produce forecasts and simulate the effects of policy decisions. Despite the subsequent decline of Keynesian economics, these models continue to exert great influence on day-to-day decisions made by governments, banks, and businesses.

The neoclassical synthesis shows that the Keynesian equilibrium is a special case, which applies when prices are sticky. Obviously, the next task was to explain how prices move, when they eventually do. This led to a search for what was known as the 'missing equation'. This equation was discovered as an empirical regularity by A. W. Phillips (1914–1975) at the London School of Economics, whose work is extensively discussed in Chapter 12. This discovery prompted the next question: What is the theory behind the Phillips curve? Work on this question, mostly in the USA, was well under way just when the curve started to vanish. The disappearance of the Phillips curve, correctly anticipated by Friedman in the late 1960s, paved the way for the rise of the monetarists, a rival school of thought committed to exposing what was seen as fundamental flaws in Keynesian economics.

20.2 The Monetarist Revolution

Milton Friedman, 1912–2006

Source: Copyright Hulton-Deutsch Collection/Corbis.

By the late 1940s, the Keynesian school had established a strong foothold in the USA, where most of macroeconomic research was conducted, but it

---

[2] An important exception was the work of Gottfried Haberler (1900–1995), who in 1937 published an important compendium of contemporary business cycle theories—with the important exception of Keynes', which Haberler later strongly criticized.

never enjoyed total supremacy. The University of Chicago, in particular, remained the bastion of the classical economics that Keynes had sought to upend. Keynesian ideas certainly attracted attention at Chicago. In the 1940s, Chicago economist Lloyd Metzler published an influential attempt to characterize Keynes' ideas formally. But the Chicago academic tradition must have seen a fundamental threat in Keynesian macroeconomics. It is thus not surprising that the 'Chicago School' led an intellectual attack against the Keynesians. Eventually, it was as successful as Keynes' own attack against the classics. Part of the success of the Chicago School is due to Milton Friedman, whose many talents matched those of Keynes himself.

Friedman combined extraordinary intellectual vigour, leadership, charisma, government experience, and communication skills. Like Keynes, he spent the war years at the Treasury, the US Treasury in his case, where he contributed to the war effort. Like Keynes, he assembled a group of young economists, who regularly met in the 'Workshop in Money and Banking' and went on to rewrite macroeconomics. Like Keynes, he devoted much time and effort to popularize his ideas, writing a regular column in the US magazine *Newsweek* and becoming a popular guest on television shows. And, like Keynes, he did not shy from contacts with politicians, providing advice to unsuccessful presidential candidate Barry Goldwater, as well as to the considerably more successful President Ronald Reagan and to Prime Minister Margaret Thatcher. Many of his Chicago associates became known as the 'Chicago boys'. They achieved considerable—and still controversial—influence in South America and elsewhere.

Friedman pursued several ideas, all of which undermined the key building blocks of Keynesian economics. First, he was an unabashed defender of free markets, which Keynes saw as chronically prone to failures. This led him to actively promote the view, long-advocated by the Austrian-born economist Friedrich von Hayek (1899–1992), that governments are a threat to freedom, and not just in economic matters.[3] Friedman and his colleagues resuscitated the influence of the laissez-faire school, which had been shattered after the Great Depression.

Second, Friedman confronted Keynes' view that fiscal policy is a useful tool for macroeconomic stabilization and that monetary policy is useless. The label 'monetarist', widely applied to the Chicago School, comes from this aspect of Friedman's work.[4] His *A Monetary History of the United States,*

1867–1960, written in 1963 jointly with Anna J. Schwartz (1915–), is generally regarded as a masterpiece that fundamentally changed the way we look at monetary policy. At the empirical level, this book attributes the Great Depression to bad monetary policy, in contrast with Keynes, who tended to blame procyclical fiscal policies. At the theoretical level, the book re-established the classic 'quantity equation' $MV = PY$, where V is the velocity of money. This equation, which was dismissed by the LM equation, brings home the neutrality of money: if velocity V and Y are taken as exogenous, the price level P is directly driven by money. In the classical view, Y is at full employment and V is constant, whereas in the Keynesian view Y is highly variable, P is constant, and V depends on the interest rate.[5] Monetary neutrality, an old wisdom of classical economics discarded during the Keynesian heydays, returned and has not left us ever since. Its implications are profound and lie at the core of the theory and practice of central banking, as explained in Chapter 9.

Third, in a careful study of consumption patterns in the USA, *A Theory of the Consumption Function*, a book published in 1956, Friedman argued that the Keynesian function $C = C(Y)$ had little theoretical foundation and questionable empirical validity. Instead, he put forward the permanent income hypothesis, which relates consumption to permanent income, or wealth. This effectively reinvented the intertemporal analysis presented in Chapters 7 and 8, and previously explored by US economist Irving Fisher (1867–1947) of Yale University. The important consequence of this work was to weaken the significance of the Keynesian multiplier and the view that fiscal policy can be a tool for output

---

[3] Friedrich von Hayek (1899–1992), another Nobel Prize winner, was a prominent product of the Austrian School, which was disbanded in the late 1930s when the Nazis took over. Hayek moved first to the London School of Economics and in 1950 to Chicago, where he was a colleague of Milton Friedman.

[4] In a true gesture of modesty, Friedman is known to have given credit to Henry Simons (1889–1946) for founding the Chicago School.

[5] The debate was really about which assumption one is willing to make. There is no incompatibility between the quantity and LM equations: the LM equation $M/P = L(Y, i)$ can be rewritten as $M/P = l(i)Y$ if one assumes that output elasticity of money demand is 1, which means then that $V = 1/l(i)$. But the LM equation must be considered along with the IS equation to explain the interest rate, and with the AS curve to explain inflation, while the quantity equation is meant to be the only equation that is needed to understand prices. The quantity equation is also known as the 'Cambridge equation', in deference to pre-Keynes Cambridge.

stabilization. Later on, the Keynesians restored some of the clout of the old consumption function by arguing that many consumers are credit rationed, as explained in Chapter 8.

Finally, in what may have been his greatest triumph, Friedman explained why the Phillips curve, then still considered as the missing equation linking the short and long run, would vanish as soon as the authorities attempted to exploit the output–inflation trade-off. Not only did he restore the importance of expectations—and thus established the expectations-augmented Phillips curve—but he restated the long-run neutrality proposition—and thus invented the long-run vertical aggregate supply schedule. His work was published in 1968, and the Phillips curve went awry thereafter, in the early 1970s. Not only were the Keynesians proven wrong, they were once more 'missing an equation'. Monetarism became the new accepted wisdom, in academic circles first, and then among policy-makers. It is important to note, however, that Nobel laureate Edmund Phelps (1933–), from New York's Columbia University, who had reached the same result as Friedman and at roughly the same time, regarded himself as a Keynesian. Phelps essentially foreshadows the eclectic future of modern macroeconomics, as presented in this book, which accepts the expectations-augmented Phillips curve as the missing equation, even if it means that there is no lasting trade-off between output and inflation.

In general, Europe was slow to recognize the power of the monetarists' attack, and did not contribute much to the research effort. In the UK, the academic establishment was dominated by Keynesians, most of whom refused to acknowledge that a major battle had been lost. The election of Mrs Thatcher changed all that. She brought in Milton Friedman as an adviser, proclaiming that her government would follow the master's precepts, including rolling back government, pushing for wage stability by destroying the trade unions' grip on labour markets and, of course, a strict application of the monetary neutrality principle. She had been converted to monetarism by two close advisers working in a think tank that she had created, the Centre for Policy Studies: Alan Walters

(1926–), a British economist then working at Johns Hopkins University in the USA, and Patrick Minford (1943–), who had resisted Keynesian influence in his bastion at Liverpool University. When, early on during her first term, the scope of Thatcher's policy intentions became clear, 364 academic economists signed a manifesto that promised disaster if these policies were implemented. Two decades later, most of the signatories agree that 'we all are Thatcherites now'.

Elsewhere in Europe, the evolution was gradual, mostly the result of generation changes, as freshly graduated macroeconomists started to popularize either monetarist ideas or less orthodox versions of Keynesian economics. Still, in some countries, such as France, Keynesian ideas remain to this day the dominant reference in policy-making circles. In the 1970s, two French economists, Edmond Malinvaud (1923–), who served for two decades as Head of the national statistical institute, and Jean-Pascal Benassy (1948–) of the Centre National de la Recherche Scientifique, had already developed a disequilibrium interpretation of the Keynesian model. The particular feature of this interpretation, which has now been abandoned, is that it assumes that there can be lasting excess demand or supply in goods and labour markets.

In German-speaking countries, as mentioned above, Keynesian ideas never quite displaced the classical view, so there was little need for a monetarist counter-revolution. Economists and policy-makers saw the movement as a vindication of their own views, even though monetarism is considerably more subtle than classical economics. During the years of Keynesian domination, the flame of classical economics was carefully maintained at the annual Konstanz seminar, which was initially created by two early monetarists, the Swiss economist Karl Brunner (1916–1989), who worked at Rochester University, and Alan Meltzer (1928–) from Carnegie Mellon University in Pittsburgh.[6] The Konstanz Seminar still meets every year.

---

[6] The tradition at Konstanz is to display a flag that bears '$MV = PY$'.

The Chicago school also contributed much to our understanding of the open economies. Much of Mundell's work was produced when he was in Chicago, where he also trained a generation of international macroeconomists who developed the 'monetary approach to the exchange rate'. This approach shapes much of Chapter 15, including the stylized facts proposed by Michael Mussa (1944–) and the overshooting hypothesis of German-born Rudiger Dornbusch (1942–2002), both students of Mundell. Many other Chicago economists—including Mundell himself—worked at the IMF, where they forged the Fund's doctrine and produced important work under the leadership of Dutch economist Jacques J. Polak (1914–).

Yet, Friedman's ideas have not always been widely accepted. One of his other major contributions is the intellectual defence of freely flexible exchange rates, as noted in Chapter 19. He gathered ammunition for this position when he was in Paris in 1950, working at the US governmental agency which administered the Marshall Plan. At the time, he concluded that the European Common Market could not work with fixed exchange rates and he considered the European Monetary Union as a mistake. This view receives much support in the UK.

20.3 The Rational Expectations Revolution

**Robert Lucas Jr,
1937–**

Source: The Nobel Foundation.

**Thomas Sargent,
1943–**

Source: New York University.

account of what Chapter 12 defines as the backward-looking component of underlying inflation. Although Phelps had made some headway in introducing the forward-looking component, the next major step was achieved in Chicago again where Nobel Prize laureate Robert E. Lucas Jr, a student of Friedman, spearheaded the rational expectations revolution.[7] Rational expectations are presented in Chapter 7 and this idea permeates much of this textbook. Lucas and his colleagues[8] argued that if the forward-looking component dominates and if expectations are not systematically biased, the Phillips curve is always vertical, in the short as well as in the long run. As a result, they asserted, systematic policy cannot work. In particular, monetary

The attack on Keynesian economics was by no means over yet. Another blow came with the rational expectations revolution. The expectations-augmented Phillips curve of Friedman and Phelps had left an important question unanswered: What drives expectations? Most economists thought that inflation expectations gradually caught up with actually observed inflation, i.e. they were only taking

---

[7] Lucas was not the first to formulate this view. It was first advanced by a number of American economists from Carnegie Mellon University—they inspired Lucas, who spent several years there before taking up a chair in Chicago—John Muth (1930–), Ed Prescott (1944–), and Finn Kydland (1943–).

[8] In particular Thomas Sargent (1943–) and Neil Wallace (1939–).

policy affects output and employment only to the extent that it creates inflationary surprises. Since creating short-lived surprises is hardly a basis for macroeconomic policy, the circle was closed. Friedman's contribution meant that fiscal policy is not helpful but that monetary policy is a powerful instrument, although one whose effects are eventually dissipated in inflation. The rational expectations revolution's message was that macroeconomic policies should not be used on and off with complete discretion. Instead, policy should obey rules and aim at establishing credibility for adhering to the rules.[9] This was not a complete vindication of the classic laissez-faire approach, but an indictment of Keynesian policy activism.

The view that 'only unanticipated money matters' was never very popular with policy-makers. One could say that it is hardly surprising that central banks explicitly reject the view that their role is limited to creating surprises. Yet, empirical evidence failed to support this view, paving the way for the New Keynesian macroeconomics.

20.4 The Microfoundations of Macroeconomics

Finn Kydland, 1943–

Source: Carnegie Mellon University.

Edward Prescott, 1940–

Source: Federal Reserve Bank of Minneapolis.

Because of its compelling logic, the rational expectations hypothesis attracted immense interest and opened the way for further innovations in other directions. Clearly, if it is appropriate to assume that expectations are rational, then why shouldn't all other economic decisions be rational as well? Researchers at 'freshwater universities' in the USA—Chicago, Minnesota, Rochester, Carnegie-Mellon, and University of Pennsylvania—have established the microeconomic foundations of the consumption, investment, and primary account functions studied in Part II of this book. European economists from all countries—many after a sojourn in those US universities—are deeply involved in this research programme.

Insisting on the rigorous discipline of microeconomic foundations may be intellectually attractive, yet business cycles remain a fact of life that must be explained. This led neoclassical economists to the Real Business Cycles (RBC) research programme discussed in Chapter 16. The aim of this effort is to show that models with flexible prices and fully rational agents—in brief, the Robinson Crusoe parable developed in Part II—can reproduce the key features of actual business cycles. The 'RBC school', inspired by the American Ed Prescott from Arizona University and Norwegian-born Finn Kydland from Carnegie Mellon University, has a significant following in Europe. These researchers received the Nobel Prize for their work in 2004.

---

[9]   The preference of rules over discretion was first expressed by Milton Friedman in an essay written in the 1950s.

20.5 New Keynesian Macroeconomics: The Latest Synthesis

Michael Woodford, 1955–

Source: Photo courtesy of Michael Woodford.

John Taylor, 1946–

Source: <www.stanford.edu>.

Despite its intellectual attractiveness, the RBC approach was not a great empirical success. Many of the most important stylized facts of the business cycle remain unaccounted for. Price stickiness simply appears to be a fact.[10] This opened up an opportunity for the New Keynesians, who were already at work on their own response to the rational expectations revolution. Their main aim has been to show that price stickiness is not incompatible with microeconomic foundations and full rationality. New Keynesians have thus been able to produce a new synthesis, which fully rests on rational behaviour but delivers the traditional Keynesian results. Much of this work has been carried out at traditionally Keynesian 'saltwater universities' in the USA (Harvard, MIT, Yale, Princeton, Berkeley),[11] with some important contributions from Michael Woodford, now at Columbia University in New York. In Europe, Jordi Gali, from Pompeu Fabra University in Barcelona, has investigated the microfoundations of the expectations-augmented Phillips curve.

The synthesis starts with RBC microeconomic foundations—complete with rational expectations—and adds price stickiness. The result turns out to be very similar to the *AS–AD* presented in Chapter 13. It contains an *IS* curve, which incorporates the aspect that next period's demand affects that of the current period—and reflects the idea that households strive to smooth their consumption. Second, it also includes a Phillips curve that is almost identical to the one initially proposed by Friedman and Phelps. It allows both for rational expectations of price setters, but admits that some agents do not change prices very often, or do not have the information or the wherewithal to do so. Most importantly, the new Keynesian Phillips curve implies that 'anticipated money matters', so that monetary policy can systematically affect output. Third, it also includes the Taylor rule, named after John Taylor from Stanford University, which is seen as the deliberate and systematic response of monetary policy to fluctuations in inflation and output.

The New Keynesian framework has been wholeheartedly embraced by policy-makers who now read the same books as economists. Importantly, the new *IS* curve and the old-new Phillips curve attract attention to the crucial role of expectations, which has led central banks around the world to become more transparent about their own forecasts and intentions. From the policy perspective, the view that fiscal and monetary policies can play a role as tools for output and employment stabilization is now generally accepted. So too is the recognition that the role of expectations requires much more prudence and care than the traditional Keynesians dared to admit, as explained in Chapters 16 and 17.

[10] This is hardly news! Milton Friedman and Anna Schwarz wrote extensively on long and variable lags with which monetary changes affect the price level. Even the old Scot David Hume (1711–1776) was fascinated by the fact that gold inflows in seventeenth-century Spain had so little short-run influence on the price level.

[11] Saltwater universities are located on the East and West coasts of the USA, while freshwater universities are inland, often close to the Great Lakes.

20.6 **Institutional and Political Economics**

Friedrich August von Hayek, 1889–1992

Source: Copyright Bettmann/Corbis.

James Buchanan, 1919–

Source: Photo courtesy of James Buchanan.

Since the rational expectations revolution in the early 1970s, macroeconomics has managed to avoid further paradigmatic earthquakes. A number of innovations have occurred at the frontier between economics and political science. This ongoing research programme starts from the obvious observation that policy actions are not taken in a vacuum, but by policy-makers, who are real-life politicians and keenly sensitive to public opinion as they seek re-election and power. In doing so, they need to calculate what will be the effects of their actions on the economy—the traditional macroeconomic question—and their voter's reactions.

Once these questions are asked, it becomes clear that political systems matter a lot. We need to look at the respective influences of government and parliament, at the degree of independence of the central bank, and at the electoral rules. Here, the variety of institutions across Europe offers a unique source of observation. It comes as no surprise that European economists—some of whom are based in the USA—have often played a leading role in this area of research.

The roots of this new approach are both old and interesting as it has brought together some very different traditions. German-language economists in the tradition of the Historical and Austrian schools have long explored these issues and their *Ordnungspolitik* (this term is hard to translate but formally means 'policy of establishing or maintaining order' or, more precisely, the institutional framework for economic activity) remains very influential in this part of Europe. However, with few exceptions,[12] these approaches have not exerted much international influence, partly for language reasons, and partly because they rejected the formalization of their ideas. The same questions were explored independently by US-based economists of the 'Public Choice School', including Nobel Prize laureates James Buchanan (1919–) and Douglass North (1920–). Most economists associated with the public choice research programme consider themselves more aligned with the laissez-faire view.[13] Coming from a radically different perspective, New-Keynesian economists began to study why governments make policy mistakes, rather than simply criticizing them, as do laissez-faire economists. They stress that sometimes policy-makers pursue bad policies because they have distorted incentives. Since incentives are determined by institutions, to improve policy-makers' incentives, institutional reforms may be needed. Important contributions have been made by Alberto Alesina, an Italian economist at Harvard University, Torsten Persson (1954–) from Stockholm University, and Guido Tabellini (1956–) from Bocconi University, among others. Finally, a few French microeconomists—brought together at Toulouse University by Jean Tirole (1953–) and Jean-Jacques Laffont (1947–2004)—have explored the question of incentives and decision-making under uncertainty. Their results are gradually percolating into macroeconomics, where they

---

[12] Prominent examples are Bruno Frey (1941–) of Zurich and Roland Vaubel (1948–) of Mannheim University.

[13] Many members of the Public Choice School are part of the Mont-Pélerin Society, a group created by Friedrich von Hayek in Mont-Pélerin near Lausanne, Switzerland.

allow the study of the interaction between policy-makers and the private sector.

This work indicates that the kinds of differences that oppose laissez-faire advocates and interventionists are too blunt when stated as 'the government should stay out of economics' versus 'governments must take responsibility for economic welfare'. There are some tasks that some governments can usefully perform and others cannot, and tasks of general interest that are better left to the markets. For example, fiscal policy may play a stabilizing role, but governments tend to suffer from a deficit bias, especially in political regimes where decisions are made by divided parliaments. Equally important is the realization that some economic policies cannot be improved unless the political institutions are first reformed. A good example is that central bank independence is generally a precondition for good monetary policy. Employment and growth are two further examples of the important innovations brought by this fundamental intuition.

20.7 Labour Markets

Richard Layard, 1934–

Source: British Academy.

Stephen Nickell, 1944–

Source: Bank of England.

One of Europe's sad distinguishing features is the high rate of unemployment which prevailed since the mid-1970s. In a number of reassuring cases, however, some—mostly smaller—European countries have been able to roll back unemployment. As Chapters 5 and 18 emphasize, the problem lies in labour market structures, institutions, and policies. Here again, comparison and analysis of the diversity of situations in Europe has offered a wealth of lessons about the nature of unemployment and the ways to deal with it. European economists have made significant progress, if only to develop a genuine understanding of their own labour markets, which differ profoundly from those in the USA.

Much of the pioneering effort has been conducted at the London School of Economics' Centre for Labour Economics, led by Richard Layard (1934–) and Steve Nickell (1944–). Other important early contributors are Edmond Malinvaud (1923–) from France, Jacques Drèze (1929–) from the University Louvain-la-Neuve in Belgium, Herbert Giersch (1921–) from the University of Kiel in Germany, and Assar Lindbeck (mentioned above), who, together with Dennis Snower (1950–) from the University of London, developed the insider–outsider theory. According to this theory, labour representatives defend the interests of the employed workers—the insiders—at the expense of those who are not employed—the outsiders. The overwhelming evidence is that labour market rigidities lie at the root of Europe's unemployment problem. This assessment is not much disputed today but was initially rejected by Keynesian economists, who blamed instead restrictive demand management policies. One way of simplifying the debate is whether the problem lies with a high equilibrium unemployment rate (the case of rigidities) or whether actual unemployment is kept above its equilibrium rate. Interestingly, monetarists always took the view that the equilibrium unemployment rate had risen. The diagnosis that structural problems are at the root of the unemployment problem in Europe is hardly disputed, except by a handful of die-hard Keynesians. In fact, it has been accepted by many governments.

This conclusion has triggered a search for appropriate solutions. Structural problems call for structural reforms, and reforms are always controversial. In the area of labour markets, the controversies are laden with emotional political and social undertones; in some countries deep ideological battles have resurfaced. The reason is simple, and is reminiscent of the problem of dynamic efficiency discussed in Chapter 3. To get to where we want to go, up-front sacrifices are necessary. Real wage moderation, cuts in unemployment benefits, reform of job protection, and the deregulation of product markets may well hurt many individuals today, even if later ultimately leading to future increases in employment and GDP. Finding out how to convince and compensate the losers in reforms is the magic formula which smaller European economies seemed to have found. Several European economists are actively investigating conditions under which politically difficult economic reforms can be adopted. What has to be done is now subject to much agreement, with important detailed work carried out by the economic staff of the OECD and IMF. Some countries have implemented many of these measures, and unemployment has indeed declined, sometimes significantly. In other countries, governments have been too sensitive to even acknowledge the need for action.

20.8 **Growth and Development**

Robert Solow, 1924–

Source: The Nobel Foundation.

Paul Romer, 1955–

Source: Hoover Institution.

Robert Barro, 1944–

Source: Hoover Institution.

Much as our understanding of labour markets has greatly benefited from institutional economics, one of the most important—and more vexing—issues involving the wealth and poverty of nations has also been profoundly rethought. As explained in Chapters 3 and 4, research on the neoclassical growth model[14] conducted at MIT by Nobel Prize laureate Robert Solow, had two key implications: (1) capital is more productive where it is scarce, and (2) the key source of sustained growth is unexplained—or exogenous—technological progress. Both implications were deeply unsatisfactory, and both have motivated important innovations to conventional growth theory.

As noted in Chapter 4, Robert E. Lucas Jr challenged economists to explain why capital doesn't flow from rich to poor countries. Poor countries are characterized by low capital intensity and, in

---

[14] This theory is called neoclassical because it relies on standard microeconomic principles, much like neoclassical macroeconomics. But Bob Solow, as he is generally called, has been a leading and enthusiastic proponent of Keynesian economics.

theory, must have a much higher marginal productivity of capital than rich countries. One important solution to his puzzle is that high productivity may be high in theory, but in fact is significantly reduced by the prevalence of poor institutions that allow corruption, instability, and war to discourage investment.

However, if technological change is exogenous, however, it is not possible to explain why institutions matter. In the mid-1980s, Paul Romer (1955–) from Stanford University showed how technological progress could be treated as endogenous. As explained in Chapter 4, the crucial step was to recognize that knowledge does not suffer from decreasing returns. This established a link with Lucas' question: education is an investment in human capital, and it is deterred by poor institutions exactly as investment in physical capital. This discovery allowed many others to explore the process of growth and economic development. Much empirical evidence has since been produced by Robert Barro (1944–) at Harvard University, in collaboration with Spanish-born Xavier Sala-i-Martin (1963–) from Columbia University, with important contributions by many others, including French-born Philippe Aghion (1956–) from Harvard University.

The result of this research has been a thorough reappraisal of underdevelopment and of policies that try to deal with extreme poverty in many parts of the world. The emphasis has shifted from earlier recommendations by the rich countries to 'do as we do' to try to encourage the establishment of better institutions that would provide political leaders in the poor countries with the incentives to adopt pro-growth policies. This literature has also profoundly affected the international financial institutions, in particular the World Bank and the regional development banks. The results are slow in coming but some important successes have been achieved. The same message also concerns the rich countries, especially Europe, which stopped catching up with the USA in the mid-1980s. The message is that reforms are needed to make the political system interested in supporting agents of change rather than established economic interests.

20.9 Conclusions

Because economists are not free from their own prejudices, it is crucial that they focus as much as possible on developing rigorous theories and conduct dispassionate evaluations of their policy implications. By and large, this is what they have done. Controversies abound, but over time intellectual exchange and the search for unifying truths have brought economists closer together in an ever-increasing degree of agreement. For example, Patrick Minford was harshly criticized in the 1980s when he argued that high unemployment benefits discouraged unemployed workers from looking for new jobs. His former Keynesian critics have now accepted the view that unemployment benefits need to be structured in a way that reduces the potentially adverse effects on work incentives. In contrast to much of the public debate, professional macroeconomists see their field as an intellectual challenge to solve pressing problems, and not as an ideological exercise.

Macroeconomics was born in Europe as a revolt against classical economists in the wake of the Great Depression. Much of the ensuing research was carried out in the USA. These developments clarified the limits of Keynesian economics and eventually allowed a field to emerge. It is not yet fully unified but controversies are now well understood and circumscribed. Prompted by problems of low growth and high unemployment, European economists have made important contributions that make macroeconomics a lively field with its own flavour. Although there is no such thing as European macroeconomics, a number of macroeconomic issues in Europe merit more attention than they receive in the USA. These range from the role of regulations, taxes, and transfers in labour markets to the functioning of monetary unions. More than anything else, Europe consists of 'small and open' independent countries, and this fact sets it apart from the highly integrated states of the USA. If the last fifteen years of our textbook is any evidence, it is these differences which make macroeconomics in Europe so special.

→ Essay Question

1 Make your list of future Nobel Prize winners, and explain why you chose them.

📖 References

Adelman, I. and Adelman, F. (1959), 'The Dynamic Properties of the Klein–Goldberger Model', *Econometrica*, 27.

Alesina, A. (1988), 'The End of Large Public Debts', in F. Giavazzi and L. Spaventa (eds), *High Public Debt: The Italian Experience*, Cambridge University Press.

Baldwin, R. and Wyplosz, C. (2005), *The Economics of European Integration*, McGraw Hill.

Bank for International Settlements (2007), 'Foreign Exchange and Derivatives Market Activity in 2007', *Triennial Central Bank Survey*, December.

Barro, R. J. and Sala-i-Martin, X. (1991), 'Convergence across States and Regions', *Brookings Papers on Economic Activity*, 1.

—— —— (2004), *Economic Growth*, 2nd edn, MIT Press.

Bloom, D., Canning, D., Graham, B., and Sevilla, J. (2000), 'Out of Poverty: On the Feasibility of Halving Global Poverty by 2015', CAERE Discussion Paper No. 52, Harvard Institute for International Development.

Bruyn-Hundt, M. (1996), *The Economics of Unpaid Work*, Thesis Publishers.

Burda, M. and Gerlach, S. (1993), 'Exchange Rate Dynamics and Currency Unification: The Ostmark–DM Rate', *Empirical Economics*, 18.

Burns, A. and Mitchell, W. (1946), *Measuring Business Cycles*. New York: National Bureau of Economic Research.

Collier, P. and Gunning, J. W. (1999), 'Why Has Africa Grown Slowly?', *Journal of Economic Perspectives*, 13(3).

Cooper, R. (1982), 'The Gold Standard: Historical Facts and Future Prospects', *Brookings Papers on Economic Activity*, 1.

Dam, K. W. (1982), *The Rules of the Game*, University of Chicago Press.

— (1989), *The Rules of the Game*, University of Chicago Press.

DeLong, J. B. (1997), 'What Do We Really Know about Economic Growth?', <www.j-bradford-delong.net>.

Easterly, W. (1999), 'On Good Politicians and Bad Policies: Social Cohesion, Institutions and Growth', The World Bank.

Fisher, I. (1930), *Theory of Interest*, Pickering Masters Series.

Fracasso, A., Genberg, H., and Wyplosz, C. (2003), 'How Do Central Banks Write?', *Geneva Report on the World Economy*, Special Report 2, CEPR, London.

Friedman, M. (1968), 'The Role of Monetary Policy', *American Economic Review*, 58.

Garber, P. (1990), 'Famous First Bubbles', *Journal of Economic Perspectives*, 4(2).

Goodhart, C. (1988), *The Evolution of Central Banks*, MIT Press.

Gordon, R. (2000), 'Does the "New Economy" Measure up to the Great Inventions of the Past?', NBER Working Paper 7833, August.

Hall, R. and Jones, C. (1999), 'Why do some Countries Produce so Much More Output per Worker than Others?', *The Quarterly Journal of Economics*, 114.

Harding, D. and Pagan, A. (2001), 'Dissecting the Cycle: A Methodological Investigation', *Journal of Monetary Economics*, 49(2).

Henry, J., Hernández de Cos, P., and Momigliano, S. (2004), 'The Short-Term Impact of Government Budgets on Prices: Evidence from Macroeconometric Models', Working Paper No. 396, ECB.

Heston, A., Summers, R., and Aten, B. (2006), *Penn World Table Version 6.2*, Center for International Comparisons of Production, Income and Prices at the University of Pennsylvania, September.

Hume, D. (1752), *Of Money*.

Kindleberger, C. (1973), *The World in Depression*, University of California Press.

Kose, A. and Prasad, E. (2004), 'Liberalizing Capital', *Finance & Development*, September, p. 51.

Kuhn, T. S. (1982), *The Structure of Scientific Revolutions*, University of Chicago Press.

Lane, P. and Milesi-Ferretti, G. M. (2006), 'The External Wealth of Nations Mark II: Revised and Extended Estimates of Foreign Assets and Laibilities, 1970–2004', IMF Working Paper.

Lucas, R. E., Jr (1980), 'Methods and Problems in Business Cycle Theory', *Journal of Money, Credit and Banking*, 12.

— (1990), 'Why Doesn't Capital Flow from Rich to Poor Countries?', *American Economic Review*, 80(2).

Maddison, A. (1991), *Dynamic Forces in Capitalist Development*, Oxford University Press.

— (1995), *Monitoring the World Economy 1820–1992*, OECD Development Centre.

— (2006), *The World Economy: Volume 1: A Millennial Perspective*, OECD Development Centre Studies, Paris.

— (2007), 'Historical Statistics for the World Economy: 1–2003 AD' in *Contours of the World Economy 1–2030 AD: Essays in Macro-Economic History*, Oxford University Press.

Mackay, C. (1980), *Extraordinary Popular Delusions and the Madness of Crowds*, New York: Harmony Books. With a foreword by Andrew Tobias. First published 1841.

Marx, K. (1867), *Capital*, Foreword to Volume I.

Mitchell, B. (1978), *European Historical Statistics*, Columbia University Press.

— (1983), *International Historical Statistics*, Macmillan.

— (1998), *International Historical Statistics*, Macmillan.

Mitchell, W. (1951), *What Happens During Business Cycles*, New York: National Bureau of Economic Research.

Ndulu, B. and O'Connell, S. (1999), 'Governance and Growth in Sub-Saharan Africa', *Journal of Economic Perspectives*, 13(3).

Nurkse, R. (1961), *Equilibrium and Growth in the World Economy*, Harvard University Press.

Riksbank, *Monetary Policy Update*, December 2007.

Ritschl, A. (2004), 'News from Tobin's *q*: Capital Markets were Efficient in 1929', Working Paper, HU.

Schneider, F. and Enste, D. (2000), 'Shadow Economies: Size, Causes, and Consequences', *Journal of Economic Literature*, 38.

Tobin, J. (1996), 'Prologue', in M. ul Haq, I. Kaul, and I. Grunberg (eds), *The Tobin Tax*, Oxford University Press.

Wyplosz, C. (1999), 'Macroeconomic Lessons from Ten Years of Transition', in B. Pleskovic and J. E. Stiglitz (eds), *Annual World Bank Conference on Development Economics*, The World Bank.

🔑 Glossary

This glossary presents brief definitions of the key concepts listed at the end of each chapter. Numbers refer to the corresponding chapter(s).

absolute purchasing power parity (**6**): theory asserting that price levels are equalized across countries once they are converted into a common currency

absorption (**2**): total national (private and public) spending on goods and services

accelerator (**8**): the positive effect of an increase in GDP on the rate of investment

accounting identities (**2**): relationships linking macroeconomic magnitudes to each other by definition

active labour market policies (**18**): programmes involving direct job creation, job security, retraining, relocation of families from distressed regions, or special programmes to get young people started in the job market

activist policies (**16**): government policies which try to improve market outcomes by correcting market dysfunctions

aggregate demand (**1**): the sum of planned consumption, investment, government purchases of goods and services, plus net export of goods and services (the primary current account)

aggregate demand curve (**13**): downward-sloping curve relating aggregate demand negatively to the rate of inflation

aggregate production function (**3**): a relationship linking total output to employed resources such as capital, labour, and other factors of production

aggregate supply (**12**): total volume of goods and services brought to market by producers at a given price level

aggregate supply curve (**12**): upward-sloping curve linking inflation to aggregate output supplied by firms

animal spirits (**8**): term referring to entrepreneurs' optimism and willingness to undertake risky investment projects

appreciation (exchange rate) (**6, 11**): a market-determined increase in the value of a currency (less of that currency must be relinquished to buy one unit of foreign currency); *see*: **depreciation; revaluation**

arbitrage (**6, 14**): the simultaneous purchase and sale of assets of identical characteristics to earn a profit without risk-taking: spatial arbitrage responds to diverging asset prices across different market locations, yield arbitrage responds to differing asset returns, and triangular arbitrage to three asset prices that are not mutually consistent

assets (**14**): forms in which households, firms, or governments are able to hold wealth, such as stocks and bonds, bank deposits, cash, or real estate

autarky (**7**): the state in which a country operates when it does not trade with the rest of the world

automatic stabilizer (**16, 17**): the economic mechanism that automatically cushions the impact of exogenous changes in aggregate demand, via the effect of income on saving decisions

average or unit costs (**12**): production costs per unit of output

balance of current transfers (**2**): payments which are not associated with commercial or financial transactions. An example is the remittance of guest workers to their home countries. When a Polish plumber living in London sends money to relatives living in Warsaw, this counts as a surplus to the Polish balance of transfers and as a deficit to the UK's. Another example is development or emergency aid offered by one country to another one

balance of goods and services (**2**): includes merchandise trade as well as trade in intermediate inputs, goods repair, goods held in ports, and non-monetary gold. The balance of trade in services incorporates a wide and growing variety of invisibles such as transport and travel, communication, insurance, financial and other services. It also includes royalties and license fees

balance of international income (**2**): the net income of a nation which originates abroad: wages and salaries paid for work by individuals in countries different from their place of residence and profits or interest income received by residents *less* profits and interest served to foreign residents

balance of payments (**2, 11**): a summary of all real and financial transactions of a country with the rest of the world

balance sheet (**9**): a statement of the financial position of a firm or other entity at a particular point in time, indicating its assets, liabilities, and net worth

Balassa–Samuelson effect (**15**): the observation that price levels in richer nations are systematically higher than in poor ones; attributed to higher non-traded goods price inflation in fast growing countries

bank reserves (**9**): the central bank liabilities (cash or central bank deposits) that commercial banks choose or are required to hold to meet demands of depositors and/or the requirements of regulators

bank run/bank failure (**9**): a situation in which a large number of bank customers attempt to withdraw their deposits at the same time, leading to difficulties paying those depositors

in conversion of other, less liquid assets, sometimes even inducing bankruptcy

battle of the mark-ups (**12**): the interpretation of the wage and price setting mechanism whereby firms set prices as high as possible over costs, including wages, while employees try to have wages grow faster than the inflation rate

beggar-thy-neighbour policies (**11**): policies, especially exchange rate policies, designed to divert domestic demand away from foreign goods and towards domestically produced goods

Beveridge curve (**18**): downward-sloping curve relating the unemployment rate to the vacancy rate; the position of this curve measures the efficiency of the job-matching process

bid–ask spread (**14**): in the foreign exchange market, the bid is the price at which one can sell foreign exchange; the ask is the price at which one can buy it on the market. The spread is the difference—usually quoted as a percentage—between the two prices

bimetallism (**19**): the use of both gold and silver as a commodity money standard

bond (**14**): a standardized borrowing instrument issued by large firms or governments with clearly stipulated conditions of payment of principal and interest by the borrower, with prices set in financial markets

boom-and-bust cycles (**19**): period of expanding/contracting aggregate economic activity

Bretton Woods Conference (**19**): meeting held in 1944 and attended by officials from 45 nations to shape a new international money order after the Second World War

British terms (**6**): one of two ways of quoting the exchange rate, here in units of the foreign currency per one unit of domestic currency (e.g. US$1.52 for $1 for UK residents); *see also* **European terms**

budget line (**7**): the line expressing the resource constraint of households in consuming today and tomorrow, the slope is the negative of the gross interest rate.

Burns–Mitchell diagram (**1**): a diagram displaying the behaviour of macroeconomic variables over the typical business cycle as a deviation from their values at the cyclical peak

business cycles (**1**): succession of periods of rapid growth and slowdown or decline in which output fluctuates around its long-run trend

Cambridge equation (**6**): the simplest formulation of the demand for money, expressing it as a constant (k) times nominal GDP (PY): $M = kPY$

capacity utilization (rate) (**1**): the proportion of installed equipment currently employed; higher rates occur during booms, lower rates correspond to recessions

capital (**1**): one of the factors of production; usually refers to plant, equipment, inventories, and structures

capital account (**2**): component of the balance of payments accounts that records financial transactions with the rest of the world

capital accumulation (**3**): the increase of the stock of capital, sometimes called net investment or net formation of capital. It differs from gross investment, which also includes the capital put in place to replace depreciated equipment

capital controls (**11**): restrictions on the movement of assets into and out of a country

capital gain/loss (**15**): refers to the gain or loss that is realized upon sale of an asset relative to its acquisition price

capital–labour ratio (**3**): the ratio of the stock of capital to the use of labour

capital-widening line (**3**): the straight line in the diagram of the Solow-model with population growth, which shows the investment per capita needed to maintain a constant per capita capital stock per unit per capita (in efficiency units)

circular flow (**2**): the fact that each final sale of a good or service represents income to factors of production employed to produce it; similarly, income to factors of production is either spent or saved, while savings are used to finance final purchases of goods by others

classical dichotomy (**6, 10**): the situation pertaining when equilibrium values of nominal variables can be determined independently of real variables; the real side of economic activity (growth, unemployment, etc.) is affected only by technology and tastes

collective labour supply curve (**5**): the link between the amount of man-hours that workers supply collectively (via wage negotiations or through their unions) and the real wage

commodity money (**9**): forms of money that have intrinsic value in other uses, or derive their value from the commodity out of which they are made, chiefly gold or silver

competition policy (**18**): policies aimed at decreasing monopoly power and increasing rivalry among sellers in markets

conditional convergence (**4**): the notion that economies converge to well-defined levels of economic prosperity (steady states) which are not identical, but depend on individual attributes of the nation or region concerned

conditionality (**19**): requirements imposed by the IMF on member-countries' macroeconomic policies for obtaining certain types of loans

constant returns to scale (**3**): term describing a production function in which simultaneous equiproportional increases in the factors of production result in an equiproportional increase in output

consumer price index (**2**): an index of prices of a basket of goods representative of the consumption pattern of the 'average consumer', using fixed quantity weights in some base year

consumer surplus (**18**): the difference between the maximum amount that a consumer would be willing to pay for a specified quantity of good and what she must actually pay for it

consumption (**2**): goods and services produced and sold to households for the satisfaction of wants

consumption function (**8, 10**): a symbolic way of stating that the aggregate consumption is positively related to aggregate wealth and, if a significant proportion of households is constrained in credit markets, to disposable income

consumption–leisure trade-off (**5**): the fundamental determinant of the labour supply decision: in order to consume, we need income and therefore we need to work, which means giving up leisure time

consumption smoothing (**8, 17**): optimal choice by households to smooth out the impact of temporary disturbances to income on consumption plans by either borrowing (in the case of a negative shock) or saving (in the case of a positive shock)

contagion (**19**): situation arising when one country devalues in a fixed exchange rate system, causing others to lose competitiveness and become candidates for devaluation, even if this was not initially justified

convergence clubs (**4**): groups of countries that experience convergence to similar levels of GDP or GNI per capita

convergence hypothesis (**4**): the hypothesis of a negative association between per capita growth and initial per capita GDP

coordination failure (**1**): situation occuring when agents (households, firms) fail to realize that their actions are interdependent, and that acting jointly might benefit all

copyrights (**4**): a legal right that prevents commercial usage by others of works like books, music, etc.

core or underlying inflation rate (**12**): the inflation rate taken into account during wage bargaining to anticipate future inflation or to recuperate losses from past inflation

countercyclical (**1**): term used to describe an economic variable when it is negatively correlated with the state of the economy; that is, it moves in the opposite direction to aggregate output over the business cycle

countercyclical fiscal policy (**17**): corrective device intended to keep the economy near its equilibrium level by increasing or decreasing aggregate demand via public spending or tax policies

covered interest rate parity (CIRP) (**15**): a no-arbitrage condition equating the difference between domestic and foreign interest rates to the forward exchange discount

credit rationing (**8**): a condition in loan markets in which there is excess demand for loans at the market interest rate

currency crises (**15**): episodes of sudden capital outflows from countries—most often which have fixed their exchange rates—leading to sharp losses of foreign exchange reserves held by the central bank and ultimately to a devaluation of the currency

current account (**2**): the sum of a country's trade in goods, services, and unilateral transfers with the rest of the world

cyclically adjusted budgets (**17**): budgets adjusted for the effect of the business cycle on tax revenues

debt stabilization (**17**): the process of arresting explosive growth in the debt–GDP ratio, usually achieved by cutting government expenditures and raising taxes

decision lag (**16**): time lag in policy effectiveness needed by government to formulate policy

decreasing returns to scale (**3**): describes a production function for which an equiproportional increase in the factors of production results in a less than equiproportional increase in output; *see also* **constant returns to scale**

deflation (**16**): a period of sustained decrease in the general price level, or more generally a sustained decline in the inflation rate demand determined output: when suppliers produce whatever is demanded at a given price level

demand disturbance (**13**): an exogenous shift in the level of aggregate demand at given levels of inflation, underlying inflation, and nominal interest rates

demand for money (**6**): the level of money, either narrow or broad, which households firms and governments choose to hold, given the level of economic activity, nominal interest rates, and the cost of moving between money and other assets

demand shock (**16**): sudden increase or decrease in aggregate demand

demand side (**1**): the analysis of spending decisions by economic agents

depreciation (capital) (**2, 3, 11**): the loss of original value of a physical asset owing to use, age, and economic obsolescence

depreciation (exchange rate) (**11**): a market-determined decrease in the value of a currency; *see*: **appreciation, revaluation**

depreciation line (**3**): the straight line in the diagram of the Solow-model without technical progress and population growth, which shows the investment per capita needed to maintain a constant capital stock per capita

derivatives (14): securities that derive their value from the behaviour of other underlying securities

derived demand (9): a demand for something which arises as a product of a demand for something else

desired demand function (10): total planned spending given the interest rate and real GDP

devaluation (11): decision by the monetary authority to reduce the value of the currency; *see*: **revaluation, appreciation, depreciation**

diffusion (4): the process through which discoveries are progressively adopted by various industries

diminishing marginal productivity (3, 7): the tendency that, as the inputs into production are increased, the increments of output will decline

discounting (7, 14): valuing future goods or money in terms of goods or money today; *see also* **intertemporal price**

distortionary taxation (18): *see*: **tax distortions**

dynamic inefficiency/efficiency (3): an economy is dynamically inefficient when a reduction of current savings can make all generations better off; it is dynamically efficient when future generations can be made better off only by reducing consumption (i.e. increasing savings) today

economic agents (1): term used to denote individual decision-makers, households, and firms

economic growth (1, 3): secular increases in the output of an economy, usually measured by the annual growth in GDP per capita

economic rents (18): returns to factors of production that exceed the minimum amount necessary to keep those factors of production in operation

effective exchange rate (6): an index consisting of a weighted average of a country's exchange rates *vis-à-vis* its main trading partners

effective labour (3): a measure of labour input which accounts for not only the number of hours worked but also for the effect of technical progress on the productivity of those hours

effectiveness lag (16): time lag resulting from a slow or delayed impact of economic policies on real activity

efficiency wages (5): wages paid in excess of the marginal productivity of labour in order to induce sufficient effort on the part of the workers

elastic (5): generally, the sensitivity which the demand for something reacts to the price, in particular, when the demand for labour is sensitive to its price, the real wage, holding everything else constant

electoral business cycles (16): business cycles which result from governments' use of macroeconomic policies to boost their re-election prospects, implying that the economy should be booming and employment is high on election day and that in the aftermath of its election, the government tightens its policies

employers' associations (5): organizations of employers which represent their interests, especially in collective bargaining

endogenous and exogenous variables (1): endogenous variables are explained by economic principles; exogenous variables, in contrast, are determined outside the system under study

endogenous growth theory (4): in contrast with the theory of exogenous growth, which explains sustainable growth by exogenous technological advances, endogenous growth theory tracks down the sources of growth to the accumulation of factors of production, with particular emphasis on knowledge

endowment (5, 7): the exogenous resources that economic agents expect to have in the present and in the future

equilibrium GDP (10): the GDP level at which the desired demand for goods and services is equal to the supply

equilibrium rate of unemployment (5): the unemployment rate that occurs when employment and unemployment stabilize, i.e. when aggregate demand for labour is met by aggregate supply. Because labour supply may not perfectly reflect individuals' preferences, this unemployment may in part be involuntary (structural unemployment), but it may also reflect the efficiency of the labour market (frictional unemployment)

equilibrium real exchange rate (**15**): the theoretical level of the real exchange rate (the nominal exchange rate doubly deflated by price indexes at home and abroad) necessary to enforce the national budget constraint with the rest of the world

equity–efficiency trade-off (**17**): the fact that improving equity among society's members often has a negative impact on the economy's efficiency

European Monetary Union (EMU) (**19**): the group of countries that share the same currency, the euro

European terms (**6**): one of two ways of quoting the exchange rate, here in units of domestic currency per one unit of the foreign currency (e.g. 7.8 Swedish kronor or 1.1 Swiss franc for $1); *see also* **British terms**

excess demand (**10**): a market situation in which demand exceeds supply at prevailing prices

excess supply (**10**): a market situation in which the quantity supplied exceeds desired demand at prevailing prices

exchange market intervention (**11**): the central bank buys or sells its own currency against foreign currencies on the foreign exchange market in order to prevent unwanted exchange rate movements

exchange rate (**1**): the rate at which foreign money is traded for domestic money

exchange rate anchor (**11**): a strategy for pursuing monetary policy which fixes the nominal exchange rate to another currency in order to lower expectations of future inflation

Exchange Rate Mechanism (ERM) (**19**): the fixed exchange rate arrangement of the European Monetary System

exchange rate regime (**11**): description of the exchange rate system adopted by a country: the exchange rate may be fixed, so that the central bank maintains the value of the domestic money in terms of another currency or group of currencies or it may be freely floating

export function (**10**): function representing part of a country's foreign spending and therefore following its fluctuations—the greater the foreign spending, the greater will be exports

external competitiveness (**6**): the ability of countries to export goods to others at given levels of nominal wages, nominal prices, and nominal exchange rates

externalities (**17**): activities that affect the welfare of economic agents not undertaking them directly

factors of production (**1**): inputs in the production process, such as labour, capital, or land, which create value added (in contrast to intermediary inputs)

fiat money (**9**): money which the state declares to be legal tender although its intrinsic value may be little or nothing

final and intermediate sales (**2**): final sales refer to sales of goods and services to the consumer or firm that will ultimately use them; intermediate sales refer to producers who use and transform these goods or services as part of their own production of goods and services

financial account (**2**): net sales of foreign assets by private domestic residents (a purchase by domestic residents worsens the financial account balance, a sale improves it)

financial intermediaries (**9, 14**): economic entities that collect funds from depositors and lend them to borrowers

financial intermediation (**2**): the channelling of savings of households by banks and other financial institutions to those willing to undertake physical investment

finding rate (**5**): the rate at which unemployed workers find a job, calculated as a ratio of job finds (per month or per year) to total unemployment

fiscal policy (**1**): the use of the government budget to affect the volume of national spending, or more generally to provide public goods and services, as well as to redistribute income

Fisher principle (**13**): the decomposition of the nominal interest rate (i) into the sum of the real interest rate (r) and the expected rate of inflation (π^e)

fixed capital formation (**7**): *see* **investment**

flows and stocks (**2**): a flow is an economic variable measured between two periods of time; a stock is a magnitude measured at a given time

foreign exchange interventions (**2**): purchases and sales of foreign money in exchange for domestic money undertaken by monetary authorities

foreign exchange reserves (**2, 11**): foreign currencies held by the monetary authority for the purpose of intervening in the exchange markets

forward exchange rate (**15**): an exchange rate agreed upon today for a currency exchange that will occur at a future date

forward premium or discount (**15**): price of a forward contract with respect to the spot price

frictional unemployment (**5**): unemployment resulting from individuals' changing jobs or entering the labour force

Friedman critique (**16**): the view that inherent lags in decision, design, implementation, and effectiveness of activist monetary and fiscal policies may negate its influence on the business cycle or even increase its magnitude

fundamentals (**15**): factors driving the exchange rate; the net external position, and determinants of the primary current account as well as monetary conditions and the degree of price rigidity: in general, the underlying real factors that determine the value of an asset

GDP deflator (**2**): a (Paasche) price index for total value added of an economy, given by the nominal GDP divided by the real GDP (GDP valued at price of some base year)

general equilibrium (**10, 11, 13**): condition of equilibrium applying simultaneously to several markets at the same time, recognizing the interdependencies between markets

gold exchange standard (**19**): the system established at the Bretton Woods conference in 1944 whereby gold was the fundamental standard of value, but for all currencies the gold parity was mediated by the dollar

gold standard (**19**): a system whereby a country defines its monetary unit in terms of gold

golden rule (**3**): proposition that per capita consumption is maximized in a growing

economy at the point at which the marginal product of capital is equal to the growth rate

goods market equilibrium (**10**): the situation in which the desired demand equals supply

Gresham's Law (**19**): the proposition that money which is more valuable than its official exchange rate will disappear from circulation: 'bad money chases out the good'

gross domestic product (GDP) (**1, 2**): a location-based measure of a country's productive activity, corresponding to the value added generated by factors of production, both local and foreign-owned, within a country

gross investment (**3**): an economy's total expenditure on capital goods—equipment and machines, the construction of housing, and inventory changes—including those which are intended to replace losses due to wear, loss of value, or obsolescence

growth traps (**4**): phases of economic development when low growth leads to low investment in physical, human and infrastructural capital, which in turn reduces growth prospects

hard pegs (**13**): a fixed exchange arrangement which intentionally makes it costly or even illegal to devalue, thereby increasing the regime's credibility

hedging (**15**): techniques used to protect oneself against foreign exchange fluctuations; more generally, any trading techniques used to eliminate risk

hollowing-out hypothesis (**19**): the hypothesis that the menu of exchange rate regimes has been narrowed to either fully floating rates or hard peg, implying that fixed-but-adjustable exchange rates are no longer feasible

household labour supply curve (**5**): the number of hours a household is willing to work as a function of the wage per hour

human capital (**4, 17, 18**): the education, training, and work experience acquired by individuals

human rights (**4**): the rights of individuals in a society to express views or religious beliefs, to associate with others, to engage in economic activity, and to be free from political persecution

Hume mechanism (**19**): the process by which trade imbalances were equilibrated under the gold standard system: a trade deficit (surplus) implies a reduction (increase) in gold and money supply, which leads to higher (lower) interest rates, to capital inflows (outflows), and to falling (rising) prices improving (worsening) the country's competitiveness

hyperinflation (**1**): term used to describe periods of extremely high inflation, usually when the monthly rate exceeds 50%

imitation (**4**): process whereby technical discoveries are copied

implementation lag (**16**): time lag in policy effectiveness as a result of the time taken by parliaments and ministries to pass and originate legislation

import function (**10**): function representing part of domestic spending and therefore following its fluctuations: the greater domestic spending, the greater will be imports

impossible trilogy (**19**): the result that it is impossible to simultaneously operate a fixed exchange rate regime, allow full capital mobility, and conduct an independent monetary policy

impulse-propagation mechanism (**16**): mechanism that transforms shocks (impulses) into irregular oscillations like the business cycle

income effect (**5**): the portion of change in quantity demanded which is attributed to the change in real income that results from the price change

increasing returns to scale (**3**): a characteristic of the production function which occurs when a simultaneous equiproportional increase in the factors of production results in a more than equiproportional increase in output.

index (**1**): a number that has no dimension (i.e. is not expressed in units such as DM, tons, hours, etc.); it is usually set to take a simple value like 1 or 100 at a specific date

indexation (**12, 13**): a provision in wage or other contracts by which nominal values are adjusted frequently to reflect changes in some price index and to maintain the real value of the contract's provisions

indifference curves (**5, 8**): a graphic representation of all possible combinations of two items that will yield equivalent utility (satisfaction)

industrial policies (**18**): these amount to official backing of national corporations or whole industries, taking on the form of subsidies, public orders, or trade policies

inelastic (**5**): insensitivity of demand to price, all other things equal

inflation (**1**): the sustained increase in prices over longer periods of time, as measured by the rate of change in a price index (an average of many or all prices in an economy)

inflation differential (**6**): the difference between the domestic and foreign inflation rates

inflation targeting (**9**): a policy approach taken by some central banks in which an inflation rate or band of inflation rates is explicitly and publicly announced

inflation-targeting strategy (**13, 16**): the central bank announces a target for the inflation rate that it aims to reach within 2–3 years, publishes its inflation forecast, and adjusts its policy in reaction to the difference between the target and the forecast

inflation tax (**17**): real revenue that the government obtains by inflation. Inflation erodes the real value of nominal assets and therefore may improve the financial condition of the government, reducing the value of its nominal liabilities

information asymmetry (**9**): a situation in which one party has better information than the other/s about the probability of an outcome, and all parties know it

insiders and outsiders (**5**): a distinction applied to workers who are already employed in long-term employment relationships

installation costs (**8**): the costs of installing new productive equipment

intellectual property rights (**4**): the rights of artists, authors, designers, inventors, or scientists to some of the economic profits their innovative or inventive activities may generate

interbank interest rate (**9**): the interest rate at which banks lend high-powered money (reserves) to one another

interbank market (**9**): a wholesale market for money, which brings commercial banks together

interest rate parity (**11**): the condition that interest rates are equalized across countries taking account of expected exchange rate changes

international Fisher equation (**15**): uncovered interest parity and purchasing power parity imply that the real interest rates are equal across countries *ex ante*

International Monetary Fund (IMF) (**19**): an institution set up at the Bretton Woods conference in 1944 to promote international monetary co-operation and exchange rate stability, to establish a multilateral system of payments for current transactions, and to assist members facing balance of payments difficulties

intertemporal budget constraint (**7**): the relationship summarizing resources and opportunities available in the present and the future to a household for consumption; the present value of spending must be less than, or equal to, wealth

intertemporal price (**7**): the price of goods tomorrow in terms of goods today; how much we would be willing to pay for—or sell for—the good today for delivery at some future date

intertemporal trade (**7**): trade conducted by households and firms across time

interventionism (**1**): policy whereby a government supports, co-ordinates, and even controls certain aspects of private activity; *see*: **laissez-faire**

investment (**2, 7**): the acquisition of productive equipment for later use in production; also called fixed capital formation

investment function (**8, 10**): relationship between investment and its fundamental determinants: aggregate investment depends positively upon Tobin's q and GDP growth, and negatively upon the real interest rate

***IS* curve** (**10**): for given values of exogenous variables, the combinations of nominal interest rate i and real output (GDP) that are consistent with goods market equilibrium

job-finding rate (**5**): the average proportion of unemployed people who find a job during a given period, e.g. during a year

job matching (**18**): the matching of job offers of firms' and unemployed workers

Keynesian assumption (**10**): the assumption that the evolution of the price level is insensitive to aggregate demand in the short run

(Keynesian) demand multiplier (**10**): a ratio indicating the effect of increases in exogenous components of aggregate demand on total aggregate demand

Keynesian revolution (**1**): the development of ideas and policies to deal with situations where price and/or wage rigidities lead to recessions; these ideas stand in opposition to (neo)classical economics, which holds that markets are able to take care of themselves

Keynesianism (**16**): the view that government demand management policy should play a key role in macroeconomic policy: Keynesians hold that markets suffer from imperfections—for example slow clearing of labour and product markets—which are responsible for the occasional underutilization of resources

labour (**1**): factor of production, usually measured in man-hours, i.e. the total number of hours worked in a firm, an industry, or a country

labour demand (**5**): the relationship linking the number of man-hours that firms wish to hire and the cost of labour

labour force (**1, 5**): the total number of individuals who are either working or actively looking for a job

labour force participation (**5**): the proportion of working-age people who are in the labour force

labour market institutions (**5**): formal and informal arrangements that regulate wage negotiations, working hours, health safety regulation, workers' influence, etc.

labour share (**1**): the fraction of national income or aggregate value added paid to labour as wages or other forms of compensation, including payments of firms to social insurance schemes on behalf of their employees

labour tax wedge (**18**): the difference between labour's cost to firms and wages actually received by workers

***LAD* line** (**13**): The long-run aggregate demand curve, which states that inflation is ultimately set by demand, more precisely monetary policy

Laffer curve (**18**): the relationship between government tax revenues and the average tax rate: beyond some point, increases in tax rates are associated with decreases in tax revenues, because the distortionary effects outweigh the revenue gained

laissez-faire (**1, 18**): term used to describe the view that properly functioning markets will deliver the best possible social outcome, and that intervention by the government in economic affairs should be rejected; *see*: **interventionism**

learning-by-doing (**4**): the on-the-job adoption of new technologies

leisure (**5**): time spent not working

lender of last resort (**9**): the central bank, in its implicit commitment to protect bank customers by providing failing banks with sufficient monetary base to prevent collapse

life-cycle consumption (**8**): theory that consumption choices are made with a planning horizon equal to the individual's expected remaining lifetime; that an individual will build up savings during working years and exhaust them during retirement years

LM **curve** (**10**): for given values of the exogenous variables and the price level, the combinations of real output (GDP) and interest rates for which the money market is in equilibrium

logarithmic scale (**1**): on a normal scale, one moves up by the same distance when going through 1, 2, 3, etc. On a logarithmic scale, the same distance takes us to the squared value of the previous step; for example 10, 100, 10,000 are equally spaced up. A variable growing exponentially is plotted as a line

long run (**13**) The long run is what economists mean when they talk about the behaviour of an economy over a period of decades, rather than over short time spans of quarters or a few years

macroeconomics (**1**): the study of the aggregate or average behaviour of the economy, as opposed to microeconomics, the behaviour of individual households, firms, and markets

marginal cost of capital (**8**): the cost of an additional increment to productive capacity

marginal productivity of capital (MPK) (**8**): additional output produced by employing an additional unit of capital in the production process

marginal productivity of labour (**5**): additional output produced by employing an additional unit of labour in the production process

marginal rate of substitution (**5, 8**): the rate at which one commodity can be substituted for another without changing the level of utility

market-clearing (**18**): term describing a market that works perfectly by equalling demand and supply at every instant

market failures (**18**): when markets are not functioning as in theory, for example because competition is imperfect with dominant players or when all the relevant information is available to all market participants

market liquidity (**14**): a financial market is liquid when it is easy at all times to find counterparts when selling or buying assets. The opposite case is that of shallow markets

market maker (**14**): traders or institutions that stand ready to deal in a particular asset

market power (**12**): the ability for producers to set a price that differs from those of close competitors. This is trivially the case of monopolists but can also occur when producers are able to differentiate their products (often using brand names), thus creating some limited monopoly power. The limit is that excessive prices may lead consumers to choose another brand. In this case, we talk of monopolistic competition

mark-up pricing (**12**): the percentage by which a firm increases the selling price of goods above the average or unit costs of production

Marshallian externality (**4**): an externality for which there is no market price.

maturity (**9, 14**): the length of time before an agreed-upon financial transaction will take place

median voter theorem (**16**): if voters' preferences are evenly spread along some dimension, then a political party's maximizing election strategy is to advocate policies that are most favoured by the median ('middle') voter

minimum wages (**5**): the lower bound set on wage rates that may be paid to workers, usually but not always by law

misalignment (**15**): a persistent deviation of the real exchange rate from its equilibrium value

Modigliani–Miller Theorem (**7**): the proposition that the way a firm finances its activities—either by issuing debt or equity shares (stock)—is irrelevant for the valuation of the firm

monetary aggregates (**9**): various definitions of the money stock, differing largely by their degree of liquidity

monetary base (**9**): the sum of currency in the hands of the public and bank reserves

monetary economy (**1**): the part of the economy dealing with monetary and financial, nominal phenomena

monetary policy (**1, 9, 14**): actions taken by central banks to affect monetary and financial conditions in an economy

monetary policy autonomy (**11**): the ability of a central bank to decide and implement the interest rate that it wishes

money growth targeting (**9**): a central bank strategy that sets the rate of growth of a chosen money stock aggregate (e.g. M1, M2, M3)

money illusion (**12**): term used to describe the failure to distinguish monetary from real magnitudes

money market (**9**): this is where banks and other financial institutions borrow from each other, usually for very short periods. Central banks may intervene on the money markets. Alternative names: interbank market, open market

money market equilibrium (**10**): equality of the exogenous and the central-bank-controlled money supply and the money demand that corresponds to a particular output level and exogenous transaction costs

money multiplier (**9**): the link between the monetary base and wider monetary aggregates

Mundell–Fleming model (**11**): the open economy version of the *IS–LM* model

N – 1 problem (**19**): in a fixed exchange rate system with *N* countries, the fact that *N* – 1 bilateral rates can be sufficient to determine all, leaving one degree of (monetary) independence

natural monopoly (**18**): occurs in industries exhibiting increasing returns (telecommunications, transport, etc.)

NDP (net domestic product) (**2**): in the national income accounts, GDP less depreciation

neoclassical (**15**): model claiming that flexible prices clear all markets even in the short run

neoclassical assumptions (**12**): the view that prices adjust even in the short run, so that the economy is always dichotomized

net taxes (**2**): the government's tax income from households and firms after transfers have been subtracted

neutral interest rate (**9, 10**): the interest rate at which monetary policy is neither expansionary nor contractionary

neutrality of money/monetary neutrality (**6**): the principle that the money supply does not affect real variables such as real output or unemployment, but rather the price level

no-profit condition (**14**): the requirement that it is not possible to make an obvious profit without taking associated risks on financial markets

noise traders (**14**): irrational or misinformed traders who cause deviations of stock prices from their fundamental value for a long time

nominal exchange rate (**6**): the value of foreign currency in terms of domestic money

non-excludable goods (**4**): a good is non-excludable when making it available to one person makes it available to all. An example is knowledge (e.g. understanding gravity or why Newton got hit on the head by a falling apple)

non-rival goods (**4**): a good is non-rival when its usage by one person does not detract from others' usage. Examples are clean air or knowledge

normative economics (**1**): economics that passes judgement or provides advice on policy actions; *see*: positive economics

official account (**2**): net transactions performed by the monetary authority on the foreign exchange market (net sales of foreign exchange)

Okun's law (**12**): the observed inverse relationship between fluctuations of real GDP around its trend growth path and fluctuations of the unemployment rate around its equilibrium level

oil shock (**12**): a sharp increase in oil prices

open market operations (**9**): transactions undertaken by a central bank which exchanges securities for its own liabilities; these operations have the effect of supplying reserves to, or draining them from, the banking system

open position (**15**): a trader has an open position in a given asset when she stands to gain or lose if the asset price changes. The opposite, a cover position, can be arranged by committing to buy or sell the asset at a pre-arranged price

openness (**1**): the ratio of exports or imports—or the average of exports and exports—to GDP, which is a measure of the extent to which a country trades with the rest of the world

opportunity cost (**7, 8**): the value of a resource in its best alternative use

optimal capital stock (**8**): the stock of physical capital that maximizes the value of the firm, for which the marginal productivity of capital is equal to the marginal cost of investment

optimal currency area (**19**): a region for which no welfare loss is implied by the use of a common currency

output cost of disinflation (**13**): the sacrifice ratio, which compares the cumulated increase in the rate of unemployment with the reduction in inflation achieved over some period of time

output gap (**9, 12**): temporary deviations of GDP from its trend or equilibrium level

output–labour ratio (**3**): the ratio of output to the labour used to produce that output

overall balance (**2**): sum of the current and financial accounts (including errors and omissions), which by double-bookkeeping is the mirror image of interventions by the monetary authorities

parity/central parity (**19**): when the exchange rate is fixed *vis-à-vis* another currency, the monetary authorities declare the official value of the currency; this is called the parity. Usually, the exchange rate is allowed to vary around a value called the central parity

partisan business cycles (**16**): business cycles resulting from the succession in power of parties with different economic priorities and preferred policies; *see*: **political business cycles**

patents (**4**): a legal right granted to exclusive commercial use of an invention, normally for a limited period of time

PCA function (**10**): an expression describing how the difference between exports and imports is related to domestic spending, foreign spending, and the real exchange rate

pecuniary/non-pecuniary externalities (**18**): externalities that are/are not transmitted by the market's price mechanism

permanent income (**8**): the flow of income which, if constant, would deliver the same present value as the actual expected income path

perpetuity (**14**): a loan agreement with an infinite maturity

persistence (**16**): long-lasting effect of a shock hitting the economy

personal disposable income (**2**): household net income from all sources after taxes have been paid and transfers received

person-hours (**5**): a measure of labour input which is equal to the number of people employed times the average number of hours spent working

Phillips curve (**12**): an empirical relationship linking the inflation rate negatively to the unemployment rate

physical capital (**2**): a factor of production consisting of durable inputs such as machines, buildings, computer hardware and software, and physical inventories

policy mix (**10**): the joint use of monetary and fiscal policies

political business cycles (**16**): business cycles resulting from the use of macroeconomic policies to improve the state of the economy just before elections; *see*: **partisan business cycles**

positive economics (**1**): the description and explanation of economic phenomena; *see*: **normative economics**

positive/negative externalities (**18**): an externality occurs when one's action has an impact on others. It is positive when the effect on others goes in the same direction as on the agent at the source of the externality (e.g. reducing pollution). It is negative in the opposite case (e.g. using a seat in a public park)

PPP (purchasing power parity) line (13): a horizontal line corresponding to the foreign inflation rate, because at fixed exchange rates purchasing power parity rules out permanent differences between domestic and foreign inflation

present discounted value (7): the value of a stream of income or spending spread over time and valued at today's price; *see also* **intertemporal price**

price flexibility (12): prices are flexible when they respond immediately and completely to any market disequilibrium

price level (1): the average level of prices in an economy

primary budget deficit (7): the budget deficit net of debt service (i.e. net of the payment of interest on the public debt)

primary current account (7): the current account less net interest payments (net investment income); alternatively, the difference between gross domestic product output and aggregate domestic spending when unilateral transfers are equal to zero

private income (2): income to the private sector which remains after taxes have been removed from, and transfers have been added to national income (more precisely, GDP plus net factor income earned abroad)

privatization (18): the sale or transfer of part or all of state-owned enterprises to the private sector

procyclical (1): an economic variable that is positively correlated with the state of the economy; that is, it moves in the same direction as aggregate output

producer surplus (18): difference between the price that a producer actually receives for a given quantity of goods and the amount corresponding to the minimum price at which he would be willing to supply the same quantity

product differentiation (12): a strategy used by firms to make consumers perceive their products as different from those of their competitors. A good example are cola drinks

production function (7): theoretical relationship linking aggregate output to inputs of factors of production

productive efficiency (17): the optimal use of available productive resources

property rights (4, 18): rights to private ownership. The absence of effective enforcement of property rights stunts economic growth

public goods (4, 17): goods and services that are provided free of charge and the consumption of which by one person does not prevent the consumption by another person (characterized by non-excludability and non-rivalry)

public infrastructure (4): physical means collectively provided that raise a country's productive capacity. Some means are freely available (e.g. streets or public schools), others can be purchased (e.g. electric lines or trains)

q-theory of investment (8): theory linking investment to Tobin's q, the ratio of firms' market value to the replacement cost of installed capital

quota (IMF) (19): a country's voting and borrowing rights in the IMF, based on its initial deposit upon joining

Ramsey principle of public finance (18): principle that, for a given amount of revenue to be raised, goods with the most inelastic demands and supplies should be taxed most heavily in order to minimize overall loss of consumer and producer surplus in an economy

random walk (8): a variable that changes randomly from period to period, where the only change between its value today and its value tomorrow will be white noise and can be positive or negative

rate of depreciation (3, 8): the rate at which the capital stock loses economic value, either by becoming obsolete or by wear and tear, usually expressed as percent per annum

rational expectations hypothesis (7, 16): hypothesis asserting that agents evaluate future events using all available information efficiently so that they do not make systematic forecasting errors

real business cycle theory (16): theory of the business cycle which explains economic fluctuations primarily as a consequence of technology shocks assuming price flexibility

real consumption wage (5): the ratio of nominal wages to the consumer price index; a measure of the price of leisure (or the return to work) in terms of consumption goods

real economy (1): term referring to the production and consumption of goods and services, and the incomes associated with productive activities; *see*: **monetary economy**

real exchange rate (6, 15): the cost of foreign goods in terms of domestic goods, defined as the nominal exchange rate adjusted by prices at home and abroad

real interest rate (7): the difference between the nominal interest rate and the expected rate of inflation

real wage rigidity (5): rigidity arising when unemployment fails to cause real wages to decline

realignment (11): a change in the official exchange rate parity

recognition lag (16): time lag in discovering that policy intervention is called for

relative price (5): the price of one good in terms of another, usually computed as the ratio of two nominal prices

relative purchasing power parity (6): situation occurring when the cost of the same basket of goods in different countries increases at the same rate once converted into a common currency

reserves ratio (9): the ratio of a commercial bank's reserves (vault cash or deposits at the central bank) to the total demand deposits it has issued

residual claimants (7): those who receive income from an enterprise after all other claimants have been paid

returns to scale (3): the impact on output of an increase in all inputs by the same proportion: if output increases equiproportionally, the production function is said to exhibit constant returns to scale; if output increases more or less than proportionally, we have respectively increasing or decreasing returns to scale

revaluation (11): decision by the monetary authority to increase the value of the currency; *see*: **devaluation, appreciation, depreciation**

Ricardian equivalence (7): hypothesis that the time profile of taxes needed to finance a given stream of government purchases has no effect on agents' intertemporal budget constraint and therefore on real spending and saving decisions; then public debt is not considered as private wealth

risk averse (14): behaviour characterized by a preference to avoid risk

risk premium (14): compensation above and beyond the expected rate of return on an asset required by agents to hold it

saving (2): postponement of consumption using some part of disposable personal income

saving schedule (3): the schedule shows how much a nation saves when the capital stock increases

Schumpeterian theory of innovation (4): the view that growth occurs because enterprising entrepreneurs constantly innovate

securitization (14): a financial procedure whereby an asset that is not traded (e.g. a housing loan) is transformed into a tradeable asset, essentially through standardization

seigniorage (17): exploitation by the government of the monopoly power of the central bank to create money as a means of raising real resources

self-fulfilling attacks (19): exchange rate attacks that are not justified by the exchange rate fundamentals, but occur because, if they succeed, the authorities will relax monetary policy, proving the attack to be rational *ex post*

self-fulfilling crises (15): a crisis that occurs simply because it is expected to occur

separation rate (5): the rate at which employed workers become unemployed per unit of time; *see*: job-finding rate

sequencing (19): principles that indicate in which order a country that has long prevented the normal operation of markets and has at least partially isolated its economy can remove existing restraints and integrate itself in the world economy

share (14): a claim on a part of the profits or earnings of a firm after operating costs and interest have been paid

Solow decomposition (**3**): the three-way decomposition of the sources of economic growth into capital accumulation, increase in labour utilization, and the Solow residual capturing technological progress

Solow growth model (**3**): a theory that analyses growth as being driven by exogenous technological change and the accumulation of factors of production

Solow residual (**3**): the part of GDP growth unexplained by the increase in factors of production and conventionally ascribed to technological progress

sovereign borrowing (**7**): borrowing undertaken by national governments *vis-à-vis* foreigners, usually in the form of bond issues or loans by international banks

special drawing rights (SDRs) (**19**): a reserve money created by the IMF in 1967 and allocated on the basis of quotas; used among central banks as an additional source of liquidity

speculative attacks (**19**): sudden loss of foreign exchange reserves of central banks, arising when exchange market participants anticipate an imminent devaluation

speculative bubbles (**14**): persistent deviations of market prices from their fundamental values

spot exchange rate (**15**): the exchange rate that applies to an immediate currency exchange

stagflation (**12, 13**): periods when both inflation and unemployment increase

steady state (**3**): a hypothetical state in which all variables have responded fully to exogenous changes in the environment

sterilized intervention/unsterilized intervention (**11**): actions undertaken by central banks to offset the impact of a foreign exchange intervention on the domestic money supply, usually a money market purchase or sale of securities in the same amount as the foreign exchange market intervention

stochastic view of business cycles (**16**): the view that business cycles do not respond to systematic inherent causes but to events that happen randomly

structural unemployment (**5**): unemployment arising as the result of a mismatch of demand and supply of labour

stylized facts (**3**): regularities in macroeconomic data which guide economists in their search for models to account for economic phenomena

substitution effect (**5**): the component of the total change in quantity demanded that is attributable to the change in relative prices

supply shocks (**12, 16**): exogenous increases in non-labour production costs

supply side (**1, 18**): the productive potential of an economy and the factors that determine its overall efficiency

swap transactions (**15**): exchange of sums of money of the same currency but on different terms, for instance selling francs for delivery now while simultaneously buying them back for delivery in three months' time

systemic risk (**9**): the risk of a generalized collapse of the banking system, arising because banks and financial institutions hold large amounts of each other's liabilities

tax distortions (**18**): effects on real behaviour arising from the wedge that taxes introduce between the price received by the provider of a good or service and the price paid by its consumer

tax smoothing (**17**): the proposition that a government should not change tax rates in response to temporary causes of budget deficits, but should borrow instead

Taylor rule (**9, 10**): a simple description of how central banks set the interest rate in response to output fluctuations and to deviations of inflation from its desired rate

technological progress (**3**): the contribution to economic growth of technological change, usually captured by the rate of increase of total factor productivity

Tobin's *q* (**8**): the ratio of the present value of the return from new investment to the cost of installed capital; often approximated as the ratio of share prices to the replacement price of equipment

total factor productivity (**3**): productivity in the production process that is attributable not to any particular factor of production, but to all; growth in total factor productivity is often measured as a weighted average of growth in average productivities of all factors of production

TR schedule (**10**): a graphical representation of the Taylor rule, which states that central banks adjust the interest rate to reduce fluctuations in output and inflation

trade policies (**18**): policies designed to support a domestic product's sales through tariffs on foreign goods, or quotas on imports

trade union voluntary/involuntary unemployment (**5**): unemployment resulting from the fact that trade unions ask for higher real wages than if the market were perfectly competitive, which may be involuntary from the perspective of individuals

trade unions (**5**): organizations of workers formed for the purpose of taking collective action against their employers to obtain improvements of pay and other working conditions

trademark (**4**): the protected use of a name (brand) or graphic device (logo)

trend (**1**): long-term tendency in a time series

Triffin paradox (**19**): the inconsistency of the US dollar (a national currency) as a world reserve currency with its gold backing: in order for internationally held dollar balances to grow with the world economy, the USA had to run balance of payment deficits over time which eventually outstripped its gold reserves

uncovered interest rate parity (UIRP) (**15**): the condition that rates of return on assets of comparable risk are equalized across countries once expected exchange rate changes are taken into account

underground economy (**2**): economic activities from which income earned is not reported and therefore is untaxed

undervaluation/overvaluation (**15**): a currency is undervalued/overvalued when its exchange is

below/above its long-run equilibrium value, or the level consistent with its long-run fundamentals

unemployment (**5**): individuals without a job who are actively seeking work

unemployment benefit (**5**): financial assistance to those seeking a job but unable to find suitable employment

unemployment gap (**12**): the difference between the actual and equilibrium unemployment rate

unemployment rate (**1**): the ratio of the number of unemployed workers to total labour force

user cost of capital (**8**): the effective cost to a firm of using the production factor physical capital, including the opportunity cost of resources tied up in the capital, depreciation, changes in the value of capital, as well as tax treatment of these factors

utility (**5, 8**): the satisfaction that a consumer derives from the consumption of goods and services

value added (**2**): increase in the market value of a product at a particular stage of production; calculated by subtracting the value of all inputs bought from other firms from the value of the firm's output

vehicle currencies (**15**): currencies that are widely used to trade or save outside of the country that issued them

vulnerabilities (**19**): economic or financial conditions that make a self-fulfilling crisis possible

wage inflation (**12**): the annual rate of growth of nominal wages

welfare traps (**18**): situations where public subsidies—part of the welfare state—discourage private activities and keep recipients dependent on welfare payments

yield curve (**14**): a curve which represents how the interest rate changes according to the maturity of assets

Index